Transition of Power

*Britain's Loss of Global Pre-eminence
to the United States, 1930–1945*

This book addresses one of the least understood issues in modern international history: how, between 1930 and 1945, Britain lost its global pre-eminence to the United States.

The crucial years are 1930 to 1940, for which until now no comprehensive examination of Anglo-American relations exists. *Transition of Power* analyses these relations in the pivotal decade, with an epilogue dealing with the Second World War after 1941. Britain and the United States, and their intertwined fates, were fundamental to the course of international history in these years. Professor McKercher's book dissects the various strands of the two Powers' relationship in the fifteen years after 1930 from a British perspective – economic, diplomatic, naval, and strategic: security and disarmament in Europe; economic diplomacy during the Great Depression, especially the introduction of the Ottawa system of tariffs and the Roosevelt Administration's determination to get freer trade after 1933; threats to the Far Eastern balance of power between 1931 and 1941 and the British and American responses; growing American interests in the British Empire and their impact upon Imperial unity; and strategic thinking and planning at London and Washington revolving around naval power and armed strength in the wider world, from the London naval conference through such events as the 1935 Anglo-German naval agreement to the response to Axis and Japanese aggression after September 1939.

BRIAN MCKERCHER is Professor of History, Royal Military College of Canada. His previous publications include *The Second Baldwin Government and the United States, 1924–1929: Attitudes and Diplomacy* (1984) and *Esme Howard: A Diplomatic Biography* (1989).

Transition of Power

Britain's Loss of Global Pre-eminence
to the United States, 1930–1945

B. J. C. McKercher

CAMBRIDGE
UNIVERSITY PRESS

E
183.8
.G7
M4
1999

PUBLISHED BY THE PRESS SYNDICATE OF THE UNIVERSITY OF CAMBRIDGE
The Pitt Building, Trumpington Street, Cambridge CB2 1RP, United Kingdom

CAMBRIDGE UNIVERSITY PRESS
The Edinburgh Building, Cambridge, CB2 2RU, UK
  http://www.cup.cam.ac.uk
40 West 20th Street, New York, NY 10011–4211, USA   http://www.cup.org
10 Stamford Road, Oakleigh, Melbourne 3166, Australia

First published 1999

Printed in the United Kingdom at the University Press, Cambridge

Typeset in Plantin 10/12pt [CE]

A catalogue record for this book is available from the British Library

Library of Congress Cataloguing in Publication data

McKercher, B. J. C., 1950–
Transition of power: Britain's loss of global pre-eminence to the United States,
1930–1945 / B. J. C. McKercher.
      p.   cm.
Includes bibliographical references.
ISBN 0 521 44090 4 (hardback)
1. United States – Relations – Great Britain. 2. Great Britain – Relations –
United States. 3. United States – Foreign relations – 1929–1933.
4. United States – Foreign relations – 1933–1945. 5. Great Britain – Foreign
relations – 1910–1936. 6. Great Britain – Foreign relations – 1936–1945.
I. Title.
E183.8.G7M4   1998
303.48′273041 – dc21   98-13369 CIP

ISBN 0 521 44090 4 hardback

For my son, Asa

Contents

Acknowledgments

The research for this book would not have been possible without the generous support of both the Social Sciences and Humanities Research Council of Canada and the Department of National Defence Academic Research Programme.

I would like to thank the following for permission to quote and make reference to the private or public manuscripts under their control: Sir Colville Barclay; the British Library of Economic and Political Science, London; the Master and Fellows of Churchill College, Cambridge; the Hoover Institute of War and Revolution, Stanford University, Palo Alto, California; the Herbert Hoover Presidential Library, West Branch, Iowa; the Houghton Library, Harvard University, Cambridge, Massachusetts; Lord Howard of Penrith; Professor A. K. Lambton; the National Archives, Washington, DC; the National Maritime Museum, Greenwich; the Public Record Office, Kew; the United Nations Library, Palais des Nations, Geneva; the Library of Congress, Washington, DC; the United States Army Historical Center, Carlisle Barracks, Pennsylvania; the University Library, the University of Birmingham; and the Syndics of the University Library, Cambridge.

I would like to thank the following for their help at various stages of the research: Angela Raspin and her staff at the British Library of Economic and Political Science, London; Corelli Barnett at the Churchill Archive Centre, Churchill College, Cambridge; the staff of the Hoover Institute of War and Revolution, Stanford University, Palo Alto, California; Dwight Miller and Shirley Sondergard of the Herbert Hoover Presidential Library, West Branch, Iowa; the staff of the Houghton Library, Harvard University, Cambridge, Massachusetts; the staff of the Institute of Historical Research, London; the staff of the Manuscripts Reading Room, the British Library, London; the staff of the Library of Congress, Washington, DC; the staff of the National Maritime Museum, Greenwich; the staff of the Public Record Office, Kew; the staff of the Franklin Delano Roosevelt Presidential Library, Hyde Park, New York; Samuel Alexander, Benoit Cameron, and their staff at the Massey Library, the Royal Military College of Canada; Dr U.-M. Rüser and Antonio Figuiero of the League of Nations Archives, the United Nations Library, Palais des Nations, Geneva; the staff of the United States Army Historical Center, Carlisle Barracks, Pennsylvania; the staff of the Government Publications Reading Room, Cameron Library, University of Alberta; Dr B. Benedicx and the staff of the Heslop Reading Room, the University Library, the University of Birmingham; and the staff of the Manuscripts Reading Room, the University Library, Cambridge.

A number of scholars were kind enough to share their expertise, ideas, and criticisms with me. I would like to mention Kathy Burk, Sebastian Cox, John Alan English, Erik Goldstein, David Ian Hall, Michael Hennessy, the late Barry Hunt, Greg Kennedy, Charles Morrisey, Keith Neilson, Michael Ramsay, Scot Robertson, Donald Schurman, and David Woolner. Diane Kunz was particularly helpful concerning Anglo-American economic relations; David Reynolds provided some valuable insights on looking more broadly at issues. The audiences to whom I presented some preliminary observations on this topic were helpful: the 1992 Canadian Historical Association; the 1994 Winston Churchill Conference at Churchill College, Cambridge; the 1994 Society of Military History Conference; 1995 SHAFR Conference; and the 1995 International History Seminar at the London School of Economics. I even include here the lunchtime seminar series of the Department of Strategy at the US Naval War College. The late Barry Hunt, Ronald Haycock, and Jane Errington have done everything as department heads to smooth my path.

I must also mention some special contributions. William Davies, my editor at Cambridge University Press, has been kind and more than patient; Chris Doubleday, who sub-edited my manuscript, saved me many embarrassments. My friends Paul and Lynn Hurst and their children, Kati, Danny, and Sally, offered me the hospitality of their London home whenever I needed it during research trips. Glen Berg knows how much I owe him. Michael Roi and Amy Castle often gave me a safe haven in an apartment filled with good books and better conversation; I am forever in their debt. And to Michael, with his special knowledge of Vansittart and the interwar Foreign Office, I am particularly indebted. Three scholars and friends were never too busy to find time for me in their busy schedules when I needed to consult them whilst on research trips to England or in correspondence. To Michael Dockrill, Zara Steiner, and Donald Watt, I give special thanks for their every kindness and support.

Lastly, my son, Asa, has learnt to put up with me being away or, worse, isolated in the next room whilst I was pounding away on my word processor. He has been understanding and more than willing to put up with all manner of inconveniences when he was with me. I will never be able to repay him for the genuine support and affection he has given to me in the past few years. A large part of the reason this book is finished is due to him. The other part is because of Cathie. The central part she has taken in my life in the past few years has been incalculable. Swans and roses will never be the same again.

Abbreviations

ADM	Admiralty
AHR	*American Historical Review*
AJPH	*Australian Journal of Politics and History*
BDFA	*British Documents on Foreign Affairs*
BIS	Bank for International Settlements
BJIS	*British Journal of International Studies*
C-in-C	Commander-in-Chief
CAB	Cabinet
CC	Cabinet Conclusion
CCS	Combined Chiefs of Staff
CEH	*Central European History*
CID	Committee of Imperial Defence
CJH	*Canadian Journal of History*
CNO	Chief of Naval Operations
COS	Chiefs of Staff Committee
CP	Cabinet Paper
CR	*Contemporary Review*
DBFP	*Documents on British Foreign Policy*
DBPO	*Documents on British Policy Overseas*
DCNS	Deputy Chief of the Naval Staff
DH	*Diplomatic History*
DOT	Department of Overseas Trade
DPR	Defence Policy and Requirements Sub-Committee
DPR(DR)	Defence Policy and Requirements (Defence Requirements) Sub-Committee
DRC	Defence Requirements Sub-Committee
DS	*Diplomacy and Statecraft*
EcoHR	*Economic History Review*
EHR	*English Historical Review*
FA	*Foreign Affairs*
FDRFA	*Franklin D. Roosevelt and Foreign Affairs*
FO	Foreign Office

FRUS	*Papers Relating to the Foreign Relations of the United States*
GB	Great Britain
GDP	Gross Domestic Product
HJ	*Historical Journal*
HZ	*Historische Zeitschrift*
IA	*Journal of the Royal Institute of International Affairs*
IHR	*International History Review*
IJ	*International Journal*
IJN	Imperial Japanese Navy
INS	*Intelligence and National Security*
JAH	*Journal of American History*
JBS	*Journal of British Studies*
JCH	*Journal of Contemporary History*
JICH	*Journal of Imperial and Commonwealth History*
JEEH	*Journal of European Economic History*
JEH	*Journal of Economic History*
JRUSI	*Journal of the Royal United Services Institution*
JSS	*Journal of Strategic Studies*
LND	League of Nations Published Document
LNU	League of Nations Union
LNP	League of Nations Private Papers
LNR	League of Nations Registered Files
LNS	League of Nations Section Files
NCM	Naval Conference Ministerial Committee
PCIJ	Permanent Court of International Justice
PRO	Public Record Office
PSF	Private Secretaries File
RAF	Royal Air Force
Reparation	Official Documents of the Allied Reparations Commission
RIIA	Royal Institute of International Affairs
RN	Royal Navy
RP	*Review of Politics*
SAQ	*South Atlantic Quarterly*
SDDF	State Department Decimal Files
SWC	Supreme War Council
T	Treasury
UDC	Union of Democratic Control
USN	United States Navy
USNGB	United States Navy General Board
VfZ	*Vierteljahrshefte für Zeitgeschichte*
WCP	War Cabinet Paper

Prologue
Power and purpose in Anglo-American relations, 1919–1929

The Americans seem to me to have made the great mistake of taking
for granted that what suited them & seemed just to them must at once
appear equally suitable & just to all the world.
Austen Chamberlain, August 1927[1]

This is a study of power. More particularly, it is a study of how power
has been lost and won in international politics, of how Great Britain, the
greatest of the great Powers in 1930, came to surrender its pre-eminence
to the United States by the end of the Second World War. In this
context, it shows how British leaders responded to the American
question in their diplomacy; and why the British side of this relationship
evolved as it did. What constitutes 'power' is a vexed question. Political
scientists have devised theoretical models to find an answer; but in the
recent words of one of them: 'Even if they were substantially correct,
these statements would not be very satisfying, if only because all forms
of guessing are not equally imprecise.'[2] For thirty years, international
historians have embarked on the same crusade, particularly American
'revisionists', whose explanations for their country's advent as the
world's leading Power have touched its logical corollary – Britain's
enfeeblement.[3] Concentrating on the crude connexion between wealth
and national potency, they have been joined lately by Paul Kennedy,
who provides the apotheosis of economic determinism respecting
Britain and the United States. 'Austria-Hungary was gone, Russia in
revolution, Germany defeated,' he observes about the situation after the

---

[1] Chamberlain to Mary Carnegie [his stepmother], 7 Aug. 1927, AC 4/1/1278.
[2] A. L. Friedberg, *The Weary Titan. Britain and the Experience of Relative Decline,
1895–1905* (Princeton, 1988), 11. His introductory chapter discusses the theoretical
literature.
[3] The seminal work is W. A. Williams, *The Tragedy of American Diplomacy* (Cleveland,
1959), esp. 108–201. Cf. L. C. Gardner, *Economic Aspects of New Deal Diplomacy*
(Madison, 1964); G. Kolko, 'American Business and Germany, 1930–1941', *Western
Political Quarterly*, 15(1962), 713–28; C. P. Parrini, *Heir to Empire: United States
Economic Diplomacy, 1916–1923* (Pittsburgh, 1969).

First World War; 'yet France, Italy, and even Britain itself had also suffered heavily in their victory. The only exceptions were Japan, which further augmented its position in the Pacific; and, of course, the United States, which, by 1918 was indisputably the strongest Power in the world.'[4]

But this is disputable, the reason hinging on the one-dimensional nature of 'power' sketched by economic determinists. Lately a subtler, yet more satisfying definition of this difficult concept and its relation to foreign policy has emerged amongst British international historians.[5] As economic determinists argue convincingly, 'power' is measurable in quantifiable statistics like gross national product, volume of trade, and industrial capacity. Just as tangibly, a point ignored by American revisionists and glossed over in *The Rise and Fall of the Great Powers*, it can be computed in the numbers of troops, ships, aeroplanes, and other implements of war, *and* their strategic dispositions, available to support diplomatic initiatives.[6] As Kennedy rightly shows, national strength can be shown by the ultimate test – going to war. *But* it can also be shown by threatening war. And along similar lines, it can be determined by the strength of allies thrown into the balance in either war *or* peace. Less palpably, 'power' also entails the willingness and ability of leaders to use these resources, and the prestige of their state, to scare off potential opponents. Put coarsely, 'power' is also a matter of will, tied to perceptions of potential threat entertained by those same opponents.[7]

The more subtle definition asserts that 'power' is each of these things and all of them. In peacetime, the essence of power is 'influence', using a state's corporeal resources with abstract ones tied to prestige, perception, and will. In simplest terms, as Gordon Martel argues, power

[4] P. M. Kennedy, *The Rise and Fall of the Great Powers. Economic Change and Military Conflict from 1500 to 2000* (New York, 1987), xix, 274–343. Along similar lines is C. Barnett, *The Audit of War. The Illusion and Reality of Britain as a Great Nation* (1986). For a more subtle view, see A. Orde, *The Eclipse of Great Britain. The United States and British Imperial Decline, 1895–1956* (NY, 1996), 99–159.

[5] D. French, *The British Way in Warfare, 1688–2000* (1990), esp. 175–201; B. J. C. McKercher, 'Wealth, Power, and the New International Order: Britain and the American Challenge in the 1920s', *DH*, 12(1988), 411–41; D. Reynolds, *Britannia Overruled. British Policy and World Power in the Twentieth Century* (1991), 5–37. Also see the special issue of the *IHR*, 13(1991) on 'The Decline of Great Britain': G. Martel, 'The Meaning of Power: Rethinking the Decline and Fall of Great Britain', 662–94; K. E. Neilson, ' "Greatly Exaggerated": The Myth of the Decline of Great Britain before 1914', 695–725; J. R. Ferris, ' "The Greatest Power on Earth": Great Britain in the 1920s', 726–50; B. J. C. McKercher, ' "Our Most Dangerous Enemy": Great Britain Pre-eminent in the 1930s', 751–83.

[6] Kennedy provides tables on 'Military and Naval Personnel of the Powers, 1880–1914', 'Warship Tonnage of the Powers, 1880–1914', 'War Expenditure and Total Mobilized Forces, 1914–1919', and more: Kennedy, *Great Powers*, 203, 274, 324, 332.

[7] Orde, *Eclipse, passim* does not dismiss 'will'.

determines who gets what, when, where, and how. But power is not absolute. Great Powers, including interwar Britain and the United States, no matter what their real or perceived strength is, never obtain everything they seek, when they seek it, or in the manner they seek it. Power is relative, something economic determinists admit in inter-state relationships. But power is also relative according to circumstance, to the way particular situations mould it, and by it not transcending time and space unaltered. Using tables and charts to evaluate the tangibles is counter-productive. Doing so only freezes the tangibles in a time and space continuum that is fluid and varying, saying nothing about the realities of international politics shaped as much by prestige, perception, will, and human agency.

This is why Anglo-American relations in the decade and a half after 1930 is arresting. A pervading idea in twentieth-century international history, particularly amongst economic determinists, is that the United States had eclipsed Britain by 1918. The argument is that Britain was rapidly declining as a world Power because of its supposedly weakening economy. This argument has several strands. First, within the anti-German coalition between 1914 and 1918, the British loaned vast sums of money to their allies to prosecute the war. To do this, some British overseas investments were sold and loans floated abroad, chiefly in the United States. By 1918, Britain had become a net debtor and the United States a net creditor, the opposite of 1914. Second, when the war ended, British industrial demand prompted by the fighting abated, putting large numbers of workers on the dole just when two million soldiers were being demobilised; this produced chronic unemployment that bedevilled interwar governments wedded to free trade and fiscal orthodoxy. Finally, given the structure of Britain's manufacturing base and the conservatism of British investors, Britain's legacy as the first industrial nation, British industry fell behind that of other Powers. Conversely the American economy, tied to innovative technologies and investors more willing to take risks, produced an accumulation of vast wealth. This accumulation compounded the gains that the war had provided for American industry and agriculture.

This pervasive idea is misconceived. No doubt exists that by 1918–19, Britain had lost economic and financial ground to newer industrial Powers compared to the mid-Victorian period. In 1860, Britain produced 19.9 per cent of the world's manufactures, the United States only 7.2 per cent.[8] By 1928, the figures were, respectively, 9.9 and 39.3 per cent, and a similar trend occurred in the production of

---

[8] Table 2 in P. Bairoch, 'International Industrialization Levels from 1750 to 1980', *JEEH*, 11(1982), 275.

basic industrial commodities like coal, pig iron, steel, and more.[9] The case of Britain's change relative to the United States mirrored that of Britain relative to the other great Powers.[10] This is not surprising. As the nineteenth century progressed, other states saw in British industrial and financial innovation the way of the future. What is surprising is that 'declinologists' should argue that Britain declined because its edge as the first industrial nation eroded in relative terms. As the most recent work shows, British economic strength since the seventeenth century had been based more on its financial resources and expertise than industrial output. In this sense, Britain entered the First World War as the world's leading Power.[11] And when peace returned in 1918, Britain was much stronger economically than it had been in the mid-nineteenth century. In 1855, British gross domestic product amounted to £620 million.[12] By 1918, it had reached £5,266 million. In every major industrial commodity, British production by the early 1920s vastly exceeded that of the third quarter of the nineteenth century.[13] In the field of trade, the life-blood of the British economy, the Americans only drew even by the 1920s; and the arrival of the Great Depression

---

[9] For instance:

Coal production (in millions of tons)

	Britain	United States
1854	64.7	7.4
1920	229.5	568.7

Pig iron production (in thousand of tons)

	Britain	United States
1860	3,827	2,873
1920	8,035	67,604

Steel production (in thousands of tons by all processes)

	Britain	United States
1876	828	597
1920	9,067	46,183

The above reflect the earliest dates for both countries with available figures. B. R. Mitchell, *British Historical Statistics* (Cambridge, 1990), 247, 249, 281, 283, 288–9; Department of Commerce, *Historical Statistics of the United States. Colonial Times to 1970* (Washington, DC, 1975), 589–90, 599–600, 693–4.

[10] See coal, crude petroleum, natural gas, non-ferrous metal ore, non-metallic mineral production, and more in B. R. Mitchell, *European Historical Statistics 1750–1970* (1975), 353–483. Cf. P. Bairoch, 'Europe's Gross National Product: 1800–1975', *JEEH*, 5(1976), 273–340, esp. tables 4 and 5, 280–81.

[11] P. J. Cain and A. G. Hopkins, *British Imperialism, vol. I: Innovation and Expansion 1688–1914* (1993).

[12] Mitchell, *British Historical Statistics*, 828–29. '1920' does not include southern Ireland's GDP.

[13] See note 8, above.

prevented them from overtaking the British in this important indicator of economic strength.[14] Although its financial dominance had been eroded by 1918, the London money market still competed effectively with New York.[15] Consequently, the argument that pre-eminence is pinned to a state being economically hegemonic is ill-conceived. Relative decline in manufacturing, accumulating capital, and investment does not necessarily produce a concurrent political and strategic decline. Granted, Britain's economy was smaller than its American counterpart as the Great War ended; but it remained powerful, stronger than fifty years before. Thus, the term 'decline' is inappropriate when discussing Anglo-American relations in the interwar period. It is a loaded word, evoking the image of Britain irrevocably moving down the slippery slope to second-rank status, with the United States rising inevitably to become a superpower.

In the interwar period, as throughout the twentieth century, British diplomacy remained the preserve of an elite. In its broadest definition, this group included those responsible for making and implementing foreign policy in the Cabinet and Civil Service, MPs and peers on the government and opposition benches, and journalists, writers, and private organisations with an interest in external affairs.[16] Admittedly, the circle of those in government that determined Britain's external policies had widened considerably compared to that at the turn of the century. This included not only the Foreign Office, but the Treasury, the service ministries, and, depending on the question, other departments of state.[17] In addition, the Great War had spawned non-governmental groups concerned with foreign policy, from the Royal Institute of International Affairs (RIIA) to the League of Nations

[14] About 25 per cent of British national wealth by the end of the 1920s came from external sources – including exports, re-exports, and sales of gold and silver bullion – approximately $6.5 billion; the American total was in the order of 5 per cent to 6 per cent, roughly $6.4 billion. McKercher, 'Wealth, Power', 433, and the relevant notes.
[15] P. J. Cain and A. G. Hopkins, *British Imperialism, vol. II: Crisis and Deconstruction 1914–1990* (London, New York, 1993), 49–75.
[16] D. C. Watt, 'The Nature of the Foreign-Policy-Making Elite in Britain', in Watt, *Personalities and Policies. Studies in the Formulation of British Foreign Policy in the Twentieth Century* (1965), 1–15. Cf. M. G. Fry, *Illusions of Security. North Atlantic Diplomacy 1918–22* (Toronto, 1972); B. J. C. McKercher, *The Second Baldwin Government and the United States, 1924–1929: Attitudes and Diplomacy* (Cambridge, 1984); K. E. Neilson, *Strategy and Supply. Anglo-Russian Relations, 1914–1917* (1985).
[17] F. T. A. Ashton-Gwatkin, 'Thoughts on the Foreign Office, 1918–1939', *CR*, 188(1955), 374–8; D. Dilks, 'The British Foreign Office Between the Wars', in B. J. C. McKercher and D. J. Moss, eds., *Shadow and Substance in British Foreign Policy, 1895–1939. Memorial Essays Honouring C. J. Lowe* (Edmonton, 1984), 181–202; Lord Strang, 'The Formulation and Control of Foreign Policy', *Durham University Journal*, 49(1957), 98–108.

Union (LNU).[18] Increased public awareness of international politics, it was surmised, would help prevent another 'July crisis' and other Sommes. Still, the interwar elite remained small. Domestic affairs preoccupied most ministers, their bureaucratic advisers, the political parties, and the wider public. In peacetime, general interest in foreign policy might suddenly develop in moments of crisis but, just as quickly, recede as other issues came to the fore. Moreover, after September 1939, as the war crisis required speedy policy decisions, the circle constricted.

In this way, British foreign policy in the quarter-century after 1919 evolved via a massive series of individual transactions carried out within an array of closely linked groups of individuals. Collectively, these groups formed the 'foreign-policy-making elite'. It had several distinguishing features: the continuity of its membership over time; the comparatively free debate within its ranks; and the fixed, though not necessarily inviolable, barrier controlling the flow of information about these debates to the public or, rather, the various publics in whose names its members acted, whose interests they believed they served, and from whom, through the political process, they derived their authority. Because of its special nature, British foreign policy in these years also differed from its domestic cousin. Whereas politicians, civil servants, parliamentarians, journalists, and others could experience first-hand the daily swirl of the country's economic, political, and social climate, the same did not hold true for international affairs. For those who advised, decided on, and implemented foreign policy, who criticised in Parliament, or commented in the press, books, and articles, a mass of second-hand information conditioned much of what they thought. This arrived by despatch and telegram to Whitehall, by conversation with British and other diplomats temporarily in London, from British and other travellers, writers, and journalists who had been abroad, and from the importation of books and magazines. Of course, some knowledge came from personal experience but, usually, this was limited. Politicians, Foreign Office officials, and other civil servants attended conferences or held discussions in foreign capitals. Journalists and writers toured occasionally to gather material for their jottings. And in peacetime, these people, along with others who could afford to do so, sometimes took holidays in Europe, the Empire, and other places. Consequently,

[18] D. Birn, *The League of Nations Union, 1918–1945* (1981); J. A. Thompson, 'The League of Nations Union and the Promotion of the League Idea in Great Britain', *AJPH*, 18(1972), 52–61; C. Thorne, 'Chatham House, Whitehall, and Far Eastern Issues, 1941–1945', in Thorne, *Border Crossings. Studies in International History* (New York, 1988), 163–92, esp. 164–5.

both inside and outside of government, foreign policy existed as a sphere where images formed the basis of knowledge about what was happening in the wider world.[19]

Interwar British foreign policy derived from and was shaped by the attitudes of those in government who created it and those outside who sought to influence its direction. What held true for foreign policy in general was particularly so for policy concerning the United States. By the end of the Great War, the foreign-policy-making elite contained three broad lines of thought.[20] On one end of the spectrum, based on pan-Anglo-Saxonism, 'atlanticism' entailed attitudes about Britain and the United States being natural allies through a supposed shared history and the common ties of culture, language, and politics. After 1918, 'atlanticist' thinking held that joint Anglo-American economic, diplomatic, and naval efforts could safeguard international peace and security, despite American failure to join the League of Nations and the discord created by war debts and the naval question.[21] When a Labour government took office in June 1929, James Ramsay MacDonald, the strongly 'atlanticist' prime minister, emphasised the need for creating strong Anglo-American bonds. 'I do not believe real peace will come', he wrote to an American friend, Senator William Borah, 'until you and we stand together and proclaim from the house tops together that in that respect we have the same mission and inspiration.'[22]

At the other end of the spectrum stood 'Imperial isolationism'. Thinking here held the Empire to be the cornerstone of Britain's global pre-eminence; thus the Imperial edifice had to be preserved at all costs and, if possible, its economic and political strength enhanced. To maintain a strong and cohesive Empire, Britain had to keep

---

[19] B. J. C. McKercher, 'The British Diplomatic Service in the United States and the Chamberlain Foreign Office's Perceptions of Domestic America, 1924–1927: Images, Reality, and Diplomacy', in McKercher and Moss, eds., *Shadow and Substance*, 221–47. More generally, P. Conrad, *Imagining America* (New York, 1980); R. L. Rapson, *Britons View America: Travel Commentary, 1860–1935* (Seattle, 1971).

[20] D. C. Watt, 'United States Documentary Sources for the Study of British Foreign Policy, 1919–39', in Watt, *Personalities and Policies*, 211–22. This paragraph is based on their fruitful use in Fry, *Illusions of Security*; McKercher, *Baldwin Government*; B. J. C. McKercher '"The Deep and Latent Distrust": The British Official Mind and the United States, 1919–1929', in B. J. C. McKercher, ed., *Anglo-American Relations in the 1920s: The Struggle for Supremacy* (1991); D. C. Watt, *Succeeding John Bull. America in Britain's Place, 1900–1975* (Cambridge, 1984).

[21] Cf. W. V. Griffin, *Sir Evelyn Wrench and His Continuing Vision of International Relations During 40 Years* (New York, 1950); P. Kerr and C. P. Howland, 'Navies and Peace: Two Views', *FA*, 8(1929), 20–40; W. T. Layton, 'The Forthcoming Economic Conference of the League of Nations and Its Possibilities', *JRIIA*, 6(1927), 2–24; A. Salter, 'The Economic Conference: Prospects of Practical Results', *JRIIA*, 6(1927), 350–67.

[22] MacDonald to Borah, 26 Aug. 1929, MacDonald PRO 30/69/673/1.

extra-Imperial commitments to a minimum. Sir Maurice Hankey, the secretary to both the Cabinet and Committee of Imperial Defence (CID) from 1916 to 1937, embodied such sentiments. Richard Casey, an Australian diplomat in London, reported in early 1928: '[Hankey] said that he sometimes had periods of wondering whether we were well advised in these islands to adopt the policy of involving ourselves in Europe's troubles to the extent we do, rather than an isolationist policy.'[23] By 1918, 'Imperial isolationism' saw the United States as the principal threat to the Empire because of Washington's demand for naval parity together with American economic penetration of important parts of the Empire like Canada. Just as they turned against foreign pressures threatening Imperial strength, 'Imperial isolationists' directed their ire against those within the Empire who were perceived to be undermining Imperial unity, whether dominion politicians, like William Lyon Mackenzie King, the Canadian sovereigntist premier, or colonial nationalists, like Mahatma Gandhi.[24]

The third line of reasoning – 'world leadership' – reckoned that Britain could never distance itself from great Power politics. The war demonstrated that continental problems could not be ignored; after 1918, to ensure peace and security, British diplomatists had to maintain and exert influence on continental affairs. Sir Austen Chamberlain, the foreign secretary from November 1924 to June 1929, arrogated for Britain a leading European role through active participation in the League and commitments to regional security arrangements like the 1925 Locarno treaty. After leaving office, he argued the 'world leadership' case before the RIIA: given Europe's geographic proximity to Britain, the Continent stood first in Britain's diplomatic priorities.[25] But because Britain was a global Power, 'world leadership' could not neglect other parts of the earth, particularly the Far East, where Britain and other imperial Powers like Japan had sizable interests.[26] To protect and sustain Britain's pre-eminence, British foreign policy had to be outward looking. There could be no retreat into the Empire, nor a reliance on friendly relations with a single Power, like the United States. To a large

---

[23] Casey to Bruce [Australian premier], 29 Mar. 1928, in W. J. Hudson and J. North, eds., *My Dear P. M. R. G. Casey's Letters to S. M. Bruce 1924–1929* (Canberra, 1980), 322–3.

[24] For example: 'The Canadian election was rather a disappointment, except for the fact that MacKenzie King is eclipsed temporarily.'; in Casey to Bruce, 5 Nov. 1925, *ibid.*, 103.

[25] A. Chamberlain, 'Britain as a European Power', *JRIIA*, 9(1930), 180–8. Cf. A. Chamberlain, *The League* (1926).

[26] R. A. Dayer, *Finance and Empire: Sir Charles Addis, 1861–1945* (New York, 1988); J. R. Ferris, 'A British "Unofficial" Aviation Mission and Japanese Naval Developments, 1919–1929', *JSS*, 5(1982), 416–39.

degree, 'world leaders' were the disciples of Lord Palmerston, who once said that 'Britain has no eternal friends or enemies, only eternal interests.'

In the interwar period, 'world leadership' dominated the foreign-policy-making elite. This came as much from the cold realism, and pragmatism, that marked its reasoning as it did from inherent weaknesses in 'atlanticism' and 'Imperial isolationism'. For men like Chamberlain, foreign policy entailed ascertaining what precisely British interests were and, when other Powers had to be considered, what were theirs. If interests differed, they had to be weighed and a compromise found. If a compromise proved impossible, then British policy had to remain firm. This is how Chamberlain succeeded over the difficult diplomacy surrounding Locarno.[27] He was a francophile. But as little would be achieved by supporting Paris over Berlin, he endeavoured to be the 'honest broker' in the Locarno negotiations because favouring one side would destroy the chances for a settlement.[28] Afterwards, he continued showing an even hand to make the 'Locarno system' work. This does not mean that 'world leaders' were neutral in their personal beliefs – Chamberlain never was; but it does mean that when pursuing policy, they tried not to let sentiment interfere with their reasoning.[29] Whilst not always repressing sentiment, 'world leaders' tended to have a clearer perception of the world and the problems confronting Britain.

Interwar advocates of 'world leadership' were not a homogeneous group. There were those whose ideas about foreign policy had been shaped before 1914 and had not changed as a result of the war; and there were others, on the whole but not exclusively, a younger group affected by the war, who saw danger in adhering to some pre-1914 methods of conducting foreign policy. In positions of influence until the rise of Neville Chamberlain to the premiership in May 1937, the older group clung to what has been labelled 'Edwardian' precepts of foreign policy.[30] During the reign of Edward VII (1901 to 1910), thanks to Britain's isolation caused by the Boer War, the 'Victorian' notion of eschewing foreign commitments was superseded by another arguing that Britain could best maintain the balances of power in Europe and

---

[27] J. Jacobson, *Locarno Diplomacy. Germany and the West, 1925–1929* (Princeton, 1972), 3–67.

[28] Selby [Chamberlain's private secretary] to Phipps [*chargé*, British Embassy, Paris], 10 Mar. 1925, Chamberlain FO 800/257; Chamberlain to his wife, 3 Feb. 1926, AC 6/1/636.

[29] B. J. C. McKercher, 'Austen Chamberlain's Control of British Foreign Policy, 1924–1929', *IHR*, 6(1984), 570–91. For balanced criticism of 'Locarno diplomacy', see J. Jacobson, 'The Conduct of Locarno Diplomacy', *RP*, 34(1972), 62–81.

[30] For the seminal discussion of 'Edwardianism', see K. E. Neilson, *Britain and the Last Tsar: Anglo-Russian Relations, 1894–1917* (Oxford, 1996), ch. 1.

elsewhere by combining with Powers that shared British interests and concerns in opposing potential adversaries.[31] Accordingly, in the 1920s, the Washington and Locarno treaties mirrored the pre-1914 Anglo-Japanese alliance and the *ententes* with France and Russia. After 1919, however, the 'Edwardians' were gradually opposed by those who felt that British differences with potential adversaries in Europe and other places could better be settled by bilateral arrangements. Thus, the difference between the two divisions of 'world leaders' was not over diplomatic ends but, rather, over means. Although this difference did not affect British foreign policy in the decade and a half after 1918, it began to do so by the latter half of the 1930s.

The thinking of the other two wings of the foreign-policy-making elite lacked such clarity. 'Atlanticism' contained a glaring defect: that Americans would join with Britain to maintain the post-1918 international status quo, an integral part of which was the British Empire. Despite their own empire in Latin America and the Philippines, Americans claimed to be anti-colonial. For instance, at the Washington conference in 1921–2, Senator Oscar Underwood, an American delegate, criticised proposals for foreign dictation in Chinese local affairs: Americans 'would be very much opposed to the [Washington] treaty if they felt that the government of the United States had in any way coerced China into an obligation that is not clearly satisfactory to China'.[32] In addition, some ethnic groups in the United States like German Americans were virulently anglophobic, whilst others gave financial succour to Irish republicans and Indian nationalists.[33] The assumption that Washington would always support Britain and its Empire in moments of crisis was folly. The flaw in 'Imperial isolationist' reasoning came from blindness to the fact that not all parts of the Empire wanted to continue either being under British domination or having close ties with London;[34] retreating into the Empire would not necessarily augment Britain's strength.

It follows that some elite members did not hold one line of thought to the exclusion of the others. In some cases, for instance, during a crisis,

[31] C. Howard, *Splendid Isolation* (1967); G. Monger, *The End of Isolation: British Foreign Policy, 1900–1907* (1963); Z. S. Steiner, *The Foreign Office and Policy, 1898–1914* (Cambridge, 1969).

[32] Meeting 31, Committee on Pacific and Far Eastern Questions, 3 Feb. 1922, FO 412/117.

[33] See Washington embassy reports on the activities of 'Indian seditionists' in the United States in 1928: FO 371/12814/41/41 to FO 371/12815/8951/41.

[34] Cf. J. M. Brown, *Gandhi's Rise to Power. Indian Politics, 1915–1922* (Cambridge, 1972); D. Harkness, *The Restless Dominion: The Irish Free State and the British Commonwealth of Nations, 1921–31* (London, Dublin, 1969); P. Wigley, *Canada and the Transition to Commonwealth: British–Canadian Relations, 1917–1926* (Cambridge, 1977).

the borderline in individual cases could become indistinct, with these people possessing two or even all three attitudes in varying degrees. But the essential points remain: after 1918, a small group of individuals participated in making and carrying out British foreign policy; this group was an elite; it was divided both over how best to preserve Britain's position in international politics and about the British role in them; and through a process of debate amongst the differing viewpoints, this elite controlled British foreign policy.

In the 1920s, British leaders confronted a series of external problems with the potential to undermine Britain's position as a Power of the first rank. Broadly speaking, these problems centred on helping to reconstruct Europe, thereby ensuring peace and security, and defending the Empire. More narrowly, they involved grappling with Franco-German animosity so that the emerging continental balance was not upset to Britain's disadvantage; settling the nettled issues of reparations and war debts; guarding the paramountcy of the Royal Navy (RN); and helping to protect and extend British Imperial and commercial interests around the globe, particularly in Latin America and the Far East. Despite its return to isolationism from international politics after March 1920, following final Senate rejection of the Treaty of Versailles and the League Covenant, the United States had an interest in all these matters. Yet, for the British during the 1920s, the American question generally remained at the second level of diplomatic problems, especially since French doggedness to keep Germany weakened endangered the peace settlement. Hence, the United States remained just one of several Powers that had to be considered in British foreign policy calculations. This did not mean that London could treat the Americans lightly. Successive American governments pursued United States' interests aggressively, two of which touched Britain directly: the payment of war debts and the desire for equality between the United States Navy (USN) and the RN. With the added dimension of increased commercial competition over access to raw materials, air routes, and cable networks, Anglo-American relations were at times uneasy. There is no doubt that in the 1920s the Americans challenged Britain's pre-eminence in the pursuit of their interests, and that they sought to influence British policy to enhance the United States' global position. But, equally, there is no doubt that the British successfully resisted this challenge so that, as the 1920s ended, Britain remained the greatest of the great Powers.

As the war ended, the British government, a coalition led by David Lloyd George, believed that the chances for Anglo-American co-operation were good. Between 1914 and early 1917, Anglo-American relations had been strained by British blockade policies, which restricted

American trade with the Central Powers and pro-German neutrals, and London's reluctance to support President Woodrow Wilson's mediation to produce a negotiated peace settlement.[35] However, United States entry into the war on the Allied side in April 1917 brought the two English-speaking Powers closer together. The USN joined the RN in applying the blockade, and contact increased at the highest political levels to co-ordinate strategy, supply, and peace-planning. Admittedly, Anglo-American relations within the context of 'coalition diplomacy' were sometimes difficult given different strategic ideas, Wilson's desire to encase 'the freedom of the seas' in the peace settlement, and Irish nationalist efforts to wrest Ireland's independence from Britain by armed force.[36] Still, by 1918, Lloyd George and Arthur Balfour, the foreign secretary, looked forward to working with Wilson to ensure a lasting peace. Although some of the president's announced war aims, particularly support for 'national self-determination', created discomfort within the Cabinet because of their implications for the Empire, a range of opinion outside of the government supported Wilsonian ideals of open diplomacy and the preservation of democracy.[37] On the other hand, to protect Britain's interests, British officials had worked hard during the latter stages of the war to give shape to Wilson's chief obsession, the creation of the League.[38] Consequently, for Lloyd George, if not for most of his ministers, Anglo-American co-operation at the Paris peace conference would have to develop from compromise over war aims.

But co-operation proved to be a mirage because of, first, growing discord between British and American policies and, second, Wilson's failure to secure ratification of Versailles. Anglo-American disharmony emerged early on over the naval question. In 1916 and 1918, the

---

[35] C. M. Mason, 'Anglo-American Relations: Mediation and "Permanent Peace"', A. Marsden, 'The Blockade', both in F. H. Hinsley, ed., *British Foreign Policy Under Sir Edward Grey* (Cambridge, 1977), 466–87, 488–515.

[36] D. C. Allard, 'Anglo-American Naval Differences During World War I', *Military Affairs*, 44(1980), 75–81; J. P. Buckley, *The New York Irish: Their Views of American Foreign Policy, 1914–1921* (New York, 1976); M. G. Fry, 'The Imperial War Cabinet, the United States and the Freedom of the Seas', *JRUSI*, 110(1965), 353–62; E. B. Parsons, 'Why the British Reduced the Flow of American Troops to Europe in August–October 1918', *CJH*, 12(1977), 173–91.

[37] On co-operation, M. L. Dockrill and J. D. Goold, *Peace Without Promise. Britain and the Peace Conferences 1919–23* (1981), 23. On Cabinet concern, Jones' [Lloyd George's private secretary] diary, 15 Oct. 1918, in K. Middlemas, ed., *Thomas Jones. Whitehall Diary*, vol. I (1969), 67–70. On support for Wilson by key segments of British opinion, L. W. Martin, *Peace Without Victory: Woodrow Wilson and the British Liberals* (Port Washington, NY, 1958); G. C. Osborn, *Woodrow Wilson in British Opinion and Thought* (Gainesville, FL, 1980).

[38] G. W. Egerton, *Great Britain and the Creation of the League of Nations: Strategy, Politics and International Organization, 1914–1919* (Chapel Hill, 1978).

American Congress approved massive battleship building programmes, in part to deter future RN blockades against American merchantmen. At the peace conference, the British resisted American pressures to reduce the RN to the level of the USN, and to accept the freedom of the seas.[39] Saying that they were not building against the United States, the British asserted that RN strength reflected concern for other naval threats. Over the freedom of the seas, Lloyd George's government proved more intransigent. Blockade remained crucial to Britain's survival; the Cabinet would not guarantee the neutral right to trade. In early April 1919, Lloyd George finally demanded that unless the Americans acknowledged Britain's special naval concerns, he would withdraw his support for the League, as well as recognition of the Monroe Doctrine. Lord Robert Cecil, the chief League advocate on the British delegation, and Colonel Edward House, Wilson's anglophile foreign policy adviser, scrambled to find a compromise: in return for the Americans cancelling the 1918 programme and deferring new construction for 1919–20, the British would support the League and accept the Monroe Doctrine. Notwithstanding, the 'naval battle of Paris' created ill-feelings on both sides as the intense diplomacy surrounding the German settlement progressed.

Although Anglo-American efforts concerning Germany and ancillary issues like handling Bolshevik Russia saw a substantial amount of cooperation – for instance, in disarming Germany and in preventing French annexation of the Saar – the two Powers divided over major questions like the borders of reborn Poland, reparations, and disposing of German colonies.[40] And Wilson's actions produced growing disfavour towards him in Britain in the government and amongst public opinion.[41] For instance, he adopted a high moral tone in his arguments, chiefly about secret wartime treaties concluded by Britain and its allies for Middle Eastern spheres of interest, whilst hypocritically reversing himself over 'national self-determination' in the Balkans. Still, compromise seemed possible. Lloyd George ultimately endorsed the League, and Wilson, willing to involve the United States in European affairs, supported an Anglo-American guarantee of French

[39] M. Klatchko and D. F. Trask, *Admiral William Shepherd Benson. First Chief of Naval Operations* (Annapolis, 1987), 127–53; A. J. Marder, *From Dreadnought to Scapa Flow: The Royal Navy in the Fisher Era 1904–1918*, vol. V (1970), 224–36.
[40] Dockrill and Goold, *Without Promise*, 31–129. Cf. A. Lenton, *Lloyd George, Woodrow Wilson, and the Guilt of Germany: An Essay in the Prehistory of Appeasement* (Baton Rouge, 1985); K. Schwabe, *Woodrow Wilson, Revolutionary Germany, and Peacemaking, 1918–1919: Missionary Diplomacy and the Realities of Power* (Chapel Hill, 1985).
[41] A. S. Link, *President Wilson and His English Critics* (Oxford, 1959) argues that Wilson was misunderstood.

security.[42] Thus, by the time Versailles was signed on 28 June 1919, the British and Americans had come together, albeit with difficulty, to ensure a basis for peace and security in the postwar world. This collapsed with the Senate's refusal to ratify Versailles.[43] Wilson had blundered politically by failing to include senior Republicans on the American delegation, essential to winning bipartisan Congressional support for treaty ratification. Later, he opposed a series of reservations in the Senate, the locus of isolationist opposition, limiting American support for the sanctions provisions of the League Covenant. Crippled with illness brought on by a stroke and touched by a personal dispute involving his wife and a member of the British Embassy, the president refused to see Lord Grey, the former foreign secretary, sent to Washington to smooth over the rough spots in Anglo-American relations.[44] A sense of betrayal permeated the British government, feelings reflected by the British public. When, promising isolation in foreign policy, the Republican Party under Warren Harding took the White House and both houses of Congress in elections in November 1920, the possibility of Anglo-American co-operation evaporated.

As the 1920s unfolded, therefore, the British faced their external problems believing not only that the United States would probably remain aloof from political entanglements, but that its foreign policy was by nature unreliable. This is why 'atlanticist' arguments had little influence within the elite after 1920. Furthermore, notions of retreating within the Empire could not be countenanced because of the peace treaties, earlier commitments like that concerning the Bosporus, and new responsibilities assumed by joining the League. Both the Foreign Office and the Admiralty emphasised this to the CID in the summer of 1920.[45] As the 1920s progressed and additional obligations like Locarno were undertaken,[46] 'Imperial isolation' increasingly lacked credibility in policy discussions. It is not surprising, therefore, that 'world leaders' dominated foreign policy. Austen Chamberlain best

[42] L. S. Jaffe, *The Decision to Disarm Germany. British Policy towards Postwar German Disarmament, 1914–1919* (Boston, 1985), 193–203.
[43] L. E. Ambrosius, *Woodrow Wilson and the American Diplomatic Tradition. The Treaty Fight in Perspective* (New York, 1987).
[44] G. W. Egerton, 'Britain and the "Great Betrayal": Anglo-American Relations and the Struggle for the United States Ratification of the Treaty of Versailles, 1919–1920', *HJ*, 21(1978), 885–911; G. W. Egerton, 'Diplomacy, Scandal, and Military Intelligence: The Craufurd-Stuart Affair and Anglo-American Relations, 1918–1920', *INS*, 2(1987), 110–34.
[45] FO memorandum, 'British Commitments Abroad', 10 Jul. 1920, Admiralty memorandum, 'Naval Commitments', 19 Jul. 1920, both CAB 4/7.
[46] FO 'Memorandum on the Foreign Policy of His Majesty's Government, with a List of British Commitments in their Relative Order of Importance', 10 Apr. 1926, *DBFP*, series IA, vol. I [hereafter in the style *DBFP IA*, I], 846–81.

embodied this line of thought during the decade, and Lloyd George, Balfour, and others, like Lord Curzon, the foreign secretary from 1919 to 1924, and Sir Stanley Baldwin, prime minister twice between 1923 and 1929, shared his general sentiments. Certainly, Lloyd George continued to entertain 'atlanticist' sentiments over naval issues, whilst Curzon's attitudes suggested an over-weaning need for Imperial unity that harkened to his service as the Indian viceroy from 1899 to 1905. But in the 1920s, these men were responsible for British foreign policy with its myriad concerns in Europe, the Mediterranean, the Far East, and the places in between. They had to ensure Britain's voice in the councils of the world and the strength to give that voice weight. They wielded British power, using it to protect British global pre-eminence in the ten years after the Paris peace conference.

The narrow concerns of British foreign policy after 1920 – Franco-German animosity; reparations and war debts; sustaining the supremacy of the RN; and safeguarding British Imperial and commercial interests – were interconnected. Not surprisingly, the Senate's rejection of Versailles put paid to the Anglo-American guarantee to France, and, because Lloyd George's government refused to supplant this with a unilateral pledge, this resulted in Paris adopting the hardest line possible against Germany. This translated into successive French governments, apprehensive about German resurgence, working to keep Germany in perpetual weakness. Fashioning a series of treaties in eastern Europe with Poland and the 'Little *Entente*' of Romania, Czechoslovakia, and Yugoslavia, Paris demanded that Germany honour the letter of Versailles, particularly its reparations provisions. Surrounded by states that had either suffered from German aggression between 1914 and 1918 or profited territorially at German expense at the peace conference, or both, Berlin had little room for manoeuvre. Lloyd George and Curzon sought vainly to moderate French excesses in a series of meetings at Cannes, Genoa, and other places in the sunny south; all that developed was intense Franco-German animosity and Germany's apparent impoverishment.[47] In January 1923, after economic crisis in Germany produced a default in reparations deliveries, the French and Belgians occupied the industrial Ruhr Valley to siphon off its wealth in lieu of what they claimed was owed them. Unstable after November 1918, the continental balance of power wobbled dangerously.

Whilst these European problems engaged Lloyd George and Curzon – and, after Lloyd George fell from power in October 1922, the new

[47] Cf. C. Fink, *The Genoa Conference: European Diplomacy, 1921–1922* (1984); S. White, *The Origins of Detente: The Genoa Conference and Soviet Western Relations, 1921–1922* (1985).

Conservative premier, Andrew Bonar Law – the question of Britain's war debt to the United States required an answer.[48] During the war, the British lent the Allies almost £4,000 million and, in turn, borrowed almost £1,000 million from the United States. Thus, although a debtor to the United States, Britain was a creditor respecting France, Italy, and other Powers. But there were problems with collecting. The Bolshevik Russians refused to honour tsarist debts; and the French claimed that whilst the Anglo-American contribution to German defeat had been primarily pecuniary, France paid far more in blood. In February 1922, the Republican Congress established the World War Foreign Debt Commission to collect all debts by 1947 at a minimum $4\frac{1}{2}$ per cent interest. The British had long pressed for all-round cancellation, ostensibly to allow for easier European reconstruction but, just as much, to pressure the Americans into cancelling. Finally, in August 1922, when it became clear that Washington would not budge, Britain issued a note stating that they would collect from their allies only what they owed the United States. Signed by Balfour, this note indicated that Britain still supported rescinding all inter-Allied debts, plus a similar amount of German reparations.[49] But the Harding Administration refused to link war debts and reparations, or to accept payments in kind, and the French contended that debt payments had to wait until German reparations were fully paid.

Baldwin, Bonar Law's chancellor of the Exchequer, and Sir Montagu Norman, the governor of the Bank of England, led a mission to the United States in January 1923 to settle the debt issue. Although some in Britain, including Bonar Law, found the terms distasteful – $4,600 million (about £980 million at par) to be paid off by 1985 at 3.3 per cent interest – the Cabinet accepted the agreement. Other problems like the Ruhr pressed on them, and the City opposed cancellation because it wanted to get back its inter-Allied loans. Although the settlement seemed amicable on the surface, underneath resentment existed. In 1920, the Americans had imposed customs duties to protect their domestic markets, which limited tariffless Britain's access to American dollars through trade. As Baldwin said in Washington:

We intend to pay – but how can international credits be made liquid when the creditor nation is unwilling to permit liquidation through the direct delivery of goods, and is also unwilling to see the current sale of her products to the debtor

---

[48] Except where noted, the next two paragraphs are based on M. J. Hogan, *Informal Entente. The Private Structure of Cooperation in Anglo-American Economy Diplomacy, 1918–1928* (Columbia, 1977), 50–5; W. N. Medlicott, *British Foreign Policy Since Versailles 1919–1963* (1968); K. Middlemas and J. Barnes, *Baldwin. A Biography* (1969), 136–49.

[49] Cmd. 1737.

nation interrupted, and when the debtor nation is unwilling to be put in the position of being unable to buy the products of the creditor nation?

The answer lay in conceding to American demands and, then, expanding British trade elsewhere. German economic revival – before 1914, Germany was Britain's best European customer – would mean a revitalised European economy with concomitant trade.[50] It follows that by 1923, Britain had not been bankrupted; instead, it faced a cash flow problem. It settled with the United States and 'eliminated, temporarily at least, a source of irritation and tension between the British and American governments'.[51]

Over the next two years, the British used the debt agreement as the basis for steadying the German economy and, from this, giving stability to Europe.[52] The fruit of this emerged with the Dawes Committee, a group of international bankers first suggested by Charles Evans Hughes, Harding's secretary of state, in December 1922. A year earlier, the Reparations Commission, the legacy of the peace conference, fixed German reparations at $131 billion. Hughes' suggestion came just as Germany's crumbling economy prevented Berlin from meeting its scheduled payments; the Ruhr occupation acted as a catalyst giving it form. Charles Dawes, a Chicago banker, and his colleagues were charged with stabilising the mark and balancing the German budget. Once the committee began meeting in 1923, Dawes and the senior British delegate, Sir Josiah Stamp, despite initial differences over Germany's capacity to pay, expanded its mandate to readjust the entire reparations issue. In these deliberations, the British tended to be lenient and the French, Belgians, and Italians severe, whilst the Americans occupied the middle ground. Still, fostered to a degree by the debt settlement and the franc's dependency on the American and British central banks,[53] Anglo-American views converged about quickly getting Germany back on its economic feet. They had different reasons for joining together – the British looked to improve trade; American loans were unlikely to be paid until Germany's economy stabilised; still, Anglo-American unity of purpose overcame French obstructionism by

[50] B. Dohrmann, *Die englische Europapolitik in der Wirtschaftskrise, 1921–1923: Zur Interdependence von Wirtschaftsinteressen und Aussenpolitik* (Munich, 1980).
[51] Hogan, *Informal Entente*, 55–6.
[52] The next paragraph, except where noted, is based on M. P. Leffler, *The Elusive Quest. America's Pursuit of European Stability and French Security, 1919–1933* (Chapel Hill, 1979), 40–157; W. A. McDougall, *France's Rhineland Diplomacy, 1914–1924: The Last Bid for a Balance of Power in Europe* (Princeton, 1978), 250–359; A. Orde, *British Policy and European Reconstruction After the First World War* (1990), 227–65; S. A. Schuker, *The End of French Predominance in Europe. The Financial Crisis of 1924 and the Adoption of the Dawes Plan* (Chapel Hill, 1976).
[53] Schuker, *French Predominance*, 98–108.

the time the committee reported in April 1924. The Dawes report proposed annual reparations on a fixed scale, political control of the German economy through a series of commissions, and a reorganised German central bank, supported by a foreign loan, to stabilise the mark. By the end of 1924, the Reparations Commission had endorsed the Dawes Plan, and American banks were prepared to loan Germany money. Five years after the Senate's rejection of Versailles, Anglo-American co-operation brought economic stability to Europe.

But economic stability constituted only half the equation. There also had to be political security, the crux of French concern. French severity towards Germany after 1920 occurred largely because the demise of the Anglo-American guarantee had created feelings of insecurity in Paris.[54] In 1923, following the Ruhr occupation, the British government, now led by Baldwin, sponsored an initiative called the Draft Treaty of Mutual Assistance to foster French security. It obliged all League members to assist any of their number in resisting wars of aggression, permitted the Council of the League to allocate national responsibilities, encouraged regional security agreements, and, respecting the latter, limited military obligations to those against aggressors on the same continent.[55] The short-lived Labour ministry under MacDonald, in power from January to October 1924, killed the Draft Treaty. The new Cabinet reckoned that a heavy burden would be placed on the RN in the wider world, and any regional agreement concerning Europe not only echoed the pre-1914 alliances, but could also weaken Britain because of dominion diffidence to honour British commitments. British League activists countered with the 'Geneva Protocol', a three-part undertaking by which League members would accept arbitration in international disputes, disarm by agreement, and undertake mutual support in the event of unprovoked aggression anywhere in the world.[56] Although removing regional commitments, bringing arbitration to the fore, and tying security to disarmament, the Protocol disappeared with Labour losing office.

Judging that Britain lacked the resources to enforce universal peace and security, the new ministry, Baldwin's second government, jettisoned the Protocol early in 1925. The CID, where the debate occurred, reflected 'world leadership' ideas by arguing that Britain should assume

---

[54] Except where noted, the next two paragraphs are based on J. R. Ferris, *Men, Money, and Diplomacy: The Evolution of British Strategic Policy, 1919–1926* (Ithaca, NY, 1989), 1–14, 142–57; Jacobson, *Locarno Diplomacy*, 3–67; A. Orde, *Great Britain and International Security, 1920–1926* (1977), 37–154.

[55] Cmd. 2200; R. Cecil, 'The Draft Treaty of Mutual Assistance', *JRIIA*, 4(1924), 45–82.

[56] A. Henderson, *Labour and the Geneva Protocol* (1925); P. J. Noel-Baker, *The Geneva Protocol for the Pacific Settlement of International Disputes* (1925).

obligations only in areas of the world vital to British interests. American disquiet with the Protocol also played in CID deliberations. Wary of League involvement in the Western Hemisphere, Hughes told Sir Esme Howard, the British ambassador at Washington, that he hoped the proposal would 'die a natural death'.[57] With the Dawes Plan underwriting European economic recovery, Austen Chamberlain searched for a way to bring political stability to the continent. The result was his conversion to a guarantee of the Franco-German border, the heart of Locarno. By October 1925, with Britain and Italy guaranteeing the Franco-German border, and eastern European frontier disputes to be handled by a series of arbitration treaties amongst Germany and its eastern neighbours, the French were presented with a system of political and military security to balance Dawes. Given the Baldwin government's support for German admission to the League, including a permanent Council seat, the recognition of great Power status, Franco-German reconciliation seemed possible. The French began withdrawing from the Ruhr, and Chamberlain played the 'honest broker' with Aristide Briand and Gustav Stresemann, the French and German foreign ministers, respectively, to reconcile differences between Paris and Berlin; the sense of European crisis receded.

Locarno also inaugurated a crucial decision by the Baldwin government concerning the League that added immensely to the political strength of British foreign policy.[58] Until this time, although British leaders since Lloyd George had praised the organisation, actual political support had been minimal. However, when Chamberlain became foreign secretary, he kept League affairs under his personal control. He did so for two reasons. The first involved Britain having a single foreign policy voice. Until then, British policy on the League had largely been determined not by the foreign secretaries but by other ministers. This created difficulty when the Foreign Office took one line and British representatives at the League in Geneva another. In November 1924, Chamberlain used his leading position in the Cabinet to bring League policy under his authority. The practical expression of this came with his regular attendance at the quarterly meetings of the League Council and his heading the British delegation to the annual Assembly each autumn. The second reason involved Locarno. Just as Chamberlain travelled to Geneva every three months, so, too, did Briand and Stresemann. The three men worked together within the League; the net result for British

[57] Howard to Chamberlain, 9 Jan. 1925, Chamberlain FO 800/257. Cf. D. D. Burks, 'The United States and the Geneva Protocol of 1924', *AHR*, 64(1959), 891–905.
[58] A. Cassels, 'Repairing the *Entente Cordiale* and the New Diplomacy', *HJ*, 23(1980), 133–53; McKercher, 'Chamberlain's Control'.

diplomacy, which other diplomatists saw as balancing between France and Germany, came with great and small Powers seeking British support over a range of issues. With Chamberlain seeing the League as another tool in the arsenal of British diplomacy and not an end in itself, he arrogated for Britain a leading position within the organisation. The political influence of British foreign policy increased markedly.[59]

Once Locarno appeared a certainty in the autumn of 1925 and in line with its promotion of the League, Baldwin's government supported a League-sponsored general arms limitation agreement. This course devolved from British domestic concerns and, externally, it stood as an issue in which the United States and the other great Powers were interested. More specifically, League-sponsored disarmament would not only contribute to the system of security then arising in Europe, it would conform to a naval arms limitation agreement made in 1922 to which Britain and the United States were partners and which had laid the basis for a system of security in the Far East. In the autumn of 1925, the League established a Preparatory Commission to furnish a draft treaty for a world disarmament conference. With non-League Powers like the United States and Bolshevik Russia sending delegations, the Commission began deliberating in March 1926. In this realm the other two narrow concerns of the foreign-policy-making elite came to the fore: conserving RN supremacy and protecting and extending British Imperial and commercial interests.

Postwar British domestic pressures over disarmament were twofold. The first arose out of public reaction to the terrible human and material cost of fighting the war. Within six months of the 1914 'July crisis', radical critics of British foreign policy began producing tracts under the aegis of a group called the Union for Democratic Control (UDC).[60] They argued in part that secret diplomacy, augmented by the Powers' reliance on armaments, bore heavy responsibility for the outbreak of general European war; and, though other pressure groups like the LNU proved more effective than the UDC in holding public attention after 1919, its contention about the possession of arms nurturing the seeds of war permeated postwar public attitudes about military spending.[61]

[59] Chamberlain to Baldwin, 16 Sep. 1927, Chamberlain FO 800/261.
[60] UDC Pamphlet no. 1, *The Morrow of the War* (n.d.); no. 4, *The Origins of the Great War* (n.d.); no. 14, *The Balance of Power* (n.d.). Cf. M. Swartz, *The Union for Democratic Control in British Politics During the First World War* (Oxford, 1971).
[61] P. J. [Noel-]Baker, 'Menace of Armaments', *Nation*, 35(1924), 613–14; J. E. Grant, *The Problem of War and Its Solution* (1922); K. Page, *War: Its Causes, Consequence and Cure* (1924). Cf. M. Ceadel, *Pacifism in Britain, 1914–1945: The Defining of a Faith* (1980); K. Robbins, *The Abolition of War. The 'Peace Movement' in Britain, 1914–1919* (Cardiff, 1976), 176–217.

Ypres, the Somme, and Passchendaele provided persuasive confirmation. After 1918, as 'the war to end all wars' had just been fought, popular sentiment to curtail arms spending could not be ignored by politicians and civil servants. This was tied to a second domestic concern: bringing about prosperity by getting the economy quickly onto a peacetime footing.[62] Declining industrial demand, an increasing number of unemployed being joined by demobilised servicemen, and rising taxation to meet public expectations for Lloyd George's promise of 'a land fit for heroes' prompted cries inside and outside government for retrenchment in arms spending. Not coincidentally, public monies saved could be shifted to social programmes. Using 1920 as a base, because figures for 1918–19 are difficult to assess, British defence spending was reduced by two-thirds (almost £320 million annually) by 1922.[63] With further cutbacks over the next two years, bringing the total defence budget to £106 million by 1924, after which it levelled off, British defence spending fell below that of 1914 given inflation over ten years.[64]

But there were limits beyond which the British could not reduce their national armoury.[65] As a global Power with interests on every continent and the seas in between, Britain required armed force to support its

[62] D. H. Aldcroft, *From Versailles to Wall Street, 1919–1929* (Berkeley, Los Angeles, 1977), 11–77; D. H. Aldcroft, *The British Economy*, vol. I: *The Years of Turmoil 1920–1951* (Brighton, 1986), 1–14; P. B. Johnson, *Land Fit for Heroes. The Planning of British Reconstruction 1916–1919* (Chicago, 1968); S. Pollard, *The Development of the British Economy 1914–1950* (1962), 87–91.

[63] The figures (in £millions) are:

	Army and ordinance	Navy	Air force
1920	395.0	156.5	52.5
1921	52.5	88.4	22.3
1922	95.1	80.8	13.6

Mitchell, *British Historical Statistics*, 121, 591.

[64] The figures (in £millions) are:

	Army and ordinance	Navy	Air force
1914	28.3	48.8	–
1923	45.4	56.2	9.4
1924	43.6	52.6	9.6

From *ibid.* With July 1914 as 100, the cost by 1924 of food had increased to 170 and of all other items to 175; *ibid.*, 739.

[65] On the Army, B. Bond, *British Military Policy between the Two World Wars* (Oxford, 1980); K. Jeffery, *The British Army and the Crisis of Empire, 1918–1922* (Manchester, 1984); on the RAF, D. E. Omissi, *Air Power and Colonial Control. The Royal Air Force, 1919–1939* (Manchester, 1990), 2–82; M. S. Smith, *British Air Strategy Between the Wars* (Oxford, 1984); on the RN, J. K. McDonald, 'Lloyd George and the Search for a Postwar Naval Policy, 1919', in A. J. P. Taylor, ed., *Lloyd George: Twelve Essays* (1971), 191–222; S. W. Roskill, *Naval Policy Between the Wars*, vol. I (1968), 71–130.

foreign policy and defend Imperial and commercial interests. With the maritime nature of the Empire and British trade, this meant that the RN had to be kept at the greatest strength possible. It got the lion's share of funds. On the other hand, after the politicians ensured that Imperial outposts could be garrisoned and London's fiat imposed in Ireland, the Army bore the brunt of the defence cuts; with the creation of the Irish Free State in 1921, the Army suffered further. The junior service, the Royal Air Force (RAF), whose principal function in the 1920s also centred on Imperial defence, fared only slightly better. By 1921, Britain's position as a global Power and the effectiveness of its foreign and Imperial policies depended on a strong RN.

By 1918–19, the prewar threats to the RN had disappeared: Germany's fleet lay at the bottom of Scapa Flow; those of France and Russia had withered away. But in their place stood the USN and the Imperial Japanese Navy (IJN). British unease stemmed from the intentions of the Americans and Japanese, both with the wealth and technological ingenuity to challenge the primacy of the RN. The Naval Defence Act of 1889 compelled British governments to maintain a two-Power standard, that the RN equal the strength of the next two naval Powers combined. Although this standard was later modified, the RN was always kept at a strength greater than that of the next greatest naval Power. Nevertheless, in 1920, because of costs, the British adopted a one-Power standard. Lloyd George's ministry now confronted a dilemma: how to effect naval spending cuts, yet protect the superiority of the RN? The CID calcu-lated that the 1916 and 1918 American building programmes would give the USN first place in the battlefleet tables by 1923.[66] Moreover, both Washington and Ottawa were pressuring London to abrogate the Anglo-Japanese alliance when it came up for renewal in 1922.[67] To do this might antagonise Japan unnecessarily, with the possibility of dire consequences for Britain's Far Eastern interests. Lloyd George's govern-ment was wrestling with these questions when, in August 1921, the Harding Administration suddenly invited Britain and other interested Powers to a conference at Washington to deal with naval and Far Eastern questions.

The outcome of the Washington conference, which sat from November 1921 to February 1922, is well known.[68] In place of the Anglo-Japanese alliance, three new agreements emerged: a ten-year

[66] CID Note, 'Naval Shipbuilding Policy', 13 Dec. 1920, Beatty [first sea lord] memorandum, 'Naval Construction', 10 Dec. 1920, Admiralty memorandum, 'Naval Commitments', 26 May 1921, all CAB 4/7.
[67] Fry, *Illusions of Security*, 121–53; I. H. Nish, *Alliance in Decline. A Study in Anglo-Japanese Relations, 1908–23* (1972), 305–53.
[68] W. E. Braisted, *The United States Navy in the Pacific, 1909–1922* (Austin, 1971);

treaty establishing building ratios for capital ships and aircraft carriers over 10,000 tons; a nine-Power guarantee of Chinese sovereignty and existing foreign trade concessions in China; and a four-Power pledge confirming the post-1919 status quo in the Pacific. Although Harding's Administration won accolades by calling the conference, especially since Hughes' opening speech contained startling proposals making the naval treaty possible, the British emerged with several gains. First, with British, American, and Japanese capital ships fixed in a ratio of 5:5:3, respectively, the threat of an Anglo-American race in the most expensive warships abated at a crucial moment in Britain's postwar reconstruction. This had extra profit since such a race would have prompted Japan to keep pace with the two English-speaking Powers. Second, despite forfeiting the Anglo-Japanese alliance, a system of security, no matter how tenuous it might be, emerged in the Far East. In keeping IJN strength at 40 per cent less than either the RN or USN, Japan received regional naval supremacy: Britain could fortify no bases east of Singapore; the United States none west of Pearl Harbor. Here lay the supposed value of the nine- and four-Power treaties. Lastly, by resolving Anglo-American differences without estranging the Japanese, the British could turn to other pressing diplomatic issues. In practical terms, this saw a concentration on European affairs that led to the Dawes Plan and Locarno.

The Washington conference left unsettled the limitation of warships displacing less than 10,000 tons: auxiliary craft like minesweepers, submarines, destroyers, and, critically, cruisers, the main weapon for attacking and defending maritime lines of communication. Although accepting capital ship equality with the Americans at Washington, the British refused to do so respecting cruisers. All that could be agreed were displacement and gun calibre maxima – 10,000 tons with eight-inch weapons. At Washington, by not yielding over cruisers – and having a global network of bases with which to project naval power – Britain had not surrendered its naval supremacy on the altar of good Anglo-American relations; the symbol rather than the substance of naval strength had been abandoned.[69] By 1927, this had precipitated an Anglo-American crisis because of differences in strategic doctrine.[70] British naval planning before and after the war adhered to ideas

---

T. Buckley, *The United States and the Washington Conference, 1921–1922* (Knoxville, 1970); Fry, *Illusions of Security*, 154–86; Roskill, *Naval Policy*, I, 300–30.

[69] J. R. Ferris, 'The Symbol and Substance of Seapower: Great Britain, the United States, and the One-Power Standard, 1919–1921', in McKercher, ed., *Struggle for Supremacy*, 55–80.

[70] The next two paragraphs are based on K. J. Hagan, *This People's Navy. The Making of American Sea Power* (New York, 1991), 275–6; Roskill, *Naval Policy*, I, 433–66. Cf.

popularised by the naval thinker, Sir Julian Corbett, who argued that command of the sea derived from keeping open one's sea lanes whilst disrupting those of adversaries. This involved a blend of concentration of forces – the battlefleet – and dispersal – the cruiser squadrons. The RN's successful blockade after 1914, or, at least, its perceived success, came from disrupting Central Power maritime lifelines. Such ideas shaped British naval thinking after 1918, playing heavily in a determination to avoid cruiser parity with the USN. American doctrine differed significantly. Devolving from the teachings of Admiral Alfred Thayer Mahan, it necessitated destroying the enemy fleet in a decisive Trafalgar-type battle to achieve unfettered command of the sea.

In the 1920s, contrasting doctrine produced different cruiser requirements. The RN sought a large number of light cruisers, from 3,500 to 7,500 tons, but averaging 6,000 tons, carrying six-inch guns; numbers were necessary because of the quantity and length of sea routes to guard, and the importance of overseas trade to Britain's economic survival – one-quarter of British GNP.[71] Furthermore, British bases around the world gave RN light cruisers strategic advantages. The USN, conversely, wanted a smaller fleet comprised chiefly of heavy Washington-treaty vessels to augment the main battlefleet. Although American navalists argued that their lack of bases required larger vessels with greater cruising *radii*, the range of eight-inch guns would give the USN an edge over six-inch ones in ship-to-ship combat. As it evolved, the cruiser question was fraught with difficulty, and it arose in 1927 to usher in a crisis that marked Anglo-American relations at the end of the 1920s.

This crisis developed out of deadlock in the Preparatory Commission.[72] By early 1927, after a year's fruitless discussion, the Commission had become bogged down. Two competing draft treaties, British and French, were under consideration. Difficulty came with the dissimilar security requirements of the major maritime Powers – Britain, the United States, and Japan – and terrene ones led by France and its eastern European allies. German annoyance at French refusal to count trained reserves in the number of ground effectives – Versailles denied reserves to the Reichswehr – and Franco-Italian rivalry in the Mediterra-

J. S. Corbett, *Some Principles of Maritime Strategy* (1911); A. T. Mahan, *The Influence of Sea Power Upon the French Revolution and Empire, 1793–1812*, vol. II (1892).
[71] See note 8, above.
[72] B. J. C. McKercher, 'Of Horns and Teeth: The Preparatory Commission and the World Disarmament Conference, 1926–1934', in B. J. C. McKercher, ed., *Arms Limitation and Disarmament, 1899–1939: Restraints on War* (New York, 1992), esp. 177–8.

nean complicated the situation. Wanting to win domestic support for the Republican Party and upstage the League, Calvin Coolidge, Harding's successor, invited Britain, Japan, France, and Italy to hold separate naval talks at Geneva. Coolidge aspired to extend the Washington-treaty capital ship building ratio to lesser craft, the idea being that any agreement by the naval Powers could be foisted on the Preparatory Commission.

Meeting at Geneva from June to August 1927, the Coolidge conference failed.[73] First, the French and Italians did not participate. France demanded a higher ratio than Italy, which Rome rebuffed. Second, and more important, although the other three Powers agreed on limiting submarines, destroyers, and other auxiliaries, Anglo-American division occurred over cruisers. The British sought seventy vessels – fifteen heavy and fifty-five light – the Americans just forty-five – twenty-five heavy and twenty light. Not opposing the Americans building to the British level, Baldwin's government made clear that the RN had an 'absolute need' for Imperial and trade defence. The Americans asserted that their needs were 'relative', that the USN could be smaller or larger depending on RN and IJN requirements. When the American delegation resisted endorsing a cruiser fleet of more than forty-five vessels, the conference broke up with frayed feelings on both sides of the Atlantic over whether limitation should be at a figure convenient to Britain or to the United States.

The cruiser question was symptomatic of a deeper problem: the incompatibility of the British doctrine of maritime belligerent rights with the American theory of the freedom of the seas. Through Howard's reports, the Chamberlain Foreign Office correctly surmised that blockade lay at the bottom of Anglo-American differences.[74] By November 1927, Chamberlain won Baldwin's support to have the CID investigate whether Britain could compromise with the Americans by modifying its established blockade policies. The Belligerent Rights Subcommittee began deliberating in January 1928 and had yet to reach a decision when, in the summer, problems in the Preparatory Commission brought Anglo-American relations to a new low. In March 1928, as British and French differences threatened to destroy the Preparatory Commission, its chairman implored London and Paris to find a compromise. Secret discussion resulted in an Anglo-French com-

---

[73] D. Carlton, 'Great Britain and the Coolidge Naval Conference of 1927', *PSQ*, 83(1968), 573–98; C. Hall, *Britain, America, and Arms Control, 1921–37* (1987), 36–58; McKercher, *Baldwin Government*, 65–76; D. Richardson, *The Evolution of British Disarmament Policy in the 1920s* (1989), 119–39.

[74] McKercher, *Baldwin Government*, 92–103; B. J. C. McKercher, *Esme Howard. A Diplomatic Biography* (Cambridge, 1989), 309–18.

promise in July; it was communicated to the leading Powers on the Commission.[75] Its essential point was that the British would withdraw their opposition to counting reserves in land effectives and the French would support a proposal to limit heavy, but not light, cruisers. Whilst constituting a basis for renewed Preparatory Commission discussions, and not being hewn in stone, only the Japanese supported it. To get discussion going, the French concession was not mentioned at that stage. But rumours that Britain had backed down over trained reserves soon emerged, along with wild stories about a secret Anglo-French alliance. Coolidge became incensed. Angered with the compromise's cruiser provisions and convinced of European obstructionism over limiting arms, he chastised the European Powers on Armistice Day, 11 November, and called for American naval supremacy over Britain.[76] Although a new Republican president, Herbert Hoover, had been elected five days earlier, which meant Coolidge would leave office in March 1929, the departing president endorsed a bill before Congress calling for fifteen new cruisers. Baldwin's government confronted the possibility of an Anglo-American naval race.

Under Chamberlain's sure hand, the Belligerent Rights Sub-committee reported in February and March 1929.[77] It advised the Cabinet that belligerent rights should remain as high as possible, that they not be mentioned in a new Anglo-American arbitration treaty then being examined at the Foreign Office, and that should a conference to codify international law be called, there be a secret approach to the White House to find common Anglo-American ground concerning blockade. The latter point became urgent in early 1929 when Borah, chairman of the Senate Foreign Relations Committee, promoted the convening of such a conference. Indeed, he succeeded in February 1929 in having a resolution to this effect appended to the fifteen cruiser bill. After Hoover's inauguration, therefore, Howard impressed British concerns on the new president.[78] Desirous of improving Anglo-American relations, Hoover responded that nothing would be done for some time. His secretary of state-designate, Henry Stimson, the governor of the

---

[75] Cf. D. Carlton, 'The Anglo-French Compromise on Arms Limitation, 1928', *JBS*, 8(1969), 141–62; McKercher, *Baldwin Government*, 140–57; Roskill, *Naval Policy*, I, 544–9.

[76] United States Office of the President, *Address of President Coolidge at the Observance of the 10th Anniversary of the Armistice, Under the Auspices of the American Legion* (Washington, 1928).

[77] The reports are in CAB 16/79. See B. J. C. McKercher, 'Belligerent Rights in 1927–1929: Foreign Policy Versus Naval Policy in the Second Baldwin Government', *HJ*, 29(1986), 963–74.

[78] Howard telegram (143) to FO, 17 Mar. 1929, FO 371/13541/1932/279.

Philippines, who would not arrive in Washington till April, had to be consulted.

Hoover's anodyne words were actually part of a process of improving Anglo-American relations that had begun at the time of Coolidge's Armistice Day speech.[79] In early November, Baldwin had suggested to William Castle, a leading State Department official visiting London, that he would be willing to travel to Washington in 1929 to settle the naval question. Almost immediately Howard and Castle in Washington, and the Foreign Office and Downing Street in London, began preparing for a prime ministerial visit. However, it could not occur until preliminary discussions had taken place over the naval question, and after an impending British General Election had been held. With the British amenable to a naval settlement, Hoover had the American delegate at the April 1929 Preparatory Commission, Hugh Gibson, the American ambassador in Brussels, announce that Washington was considering a 'naval yardstick' to equate heavy and light cruisers. Adding to his willingness to compromise, Hoover appointed the anglophile Charles Dawes as the new American ambassador to London. By late April, armed with the Belligerent Rights Sub-committee's blueprint for settling the American question, Baldwin's Cabinet endorsed the idea of the prime minister travelling to Washington. By mid-1929, the settlement of Anglo-American naval differences seemed at hand.

Of course, commercial competition suffused all of these political, naval, and strategic questions during the 1920s. In Europe, South America, the Middle East, and East Asia, British and American entrepreneurs strove for advantage over cables, air routes, access to raw materials, and investment. The record does not show either unbridled American success or Britain's inevitable debilitation. Rather, it is mixed, reinforcing the assertion that during the decade, 'informal *entente*' marked this element of the transatlantic relationship.[80] There are two reasons. First, whilst intense and occasionally vituperative, the quest for commercial advantage lacked the sustained emotive quality that marked the other issues. So, unlike the naval dispute, which touched the most visible element of national potency, commercial competition remained obscured from public view.[81] Second, and more important, co-operation rather than confrontation offered substantial commercial and financial

---

[79] The rest of this paragraph is based on B. J. C. McKercher, 'From Enmity to Cooperation: The Second Baldwin Government and the Improvement of Anglo-American Relations, November 1928–June 1929', *Albion*, 24(1992), 64–87.

[80] Hogan, *Informal Entente*.

[81] Politicians and civil servants were a different matter; see Steel-Maitland [minister of labour] to Tyrrell [FO permanent under-secretary], 22 Jan. 1926, with minutes, FO 371/11167/489/10.

gains for both countries. The Federal Reserve Bank of New York (FRBNY), in essence the United States' central bank, saw the wisdom of this in the aftermath of the Dawes Committee, embarking on a co-operative policy with the Bank of England and other European central banks.[82] And, when states like Venezuela encouraged foreign development of their oil after 1919, British petroleum interests responded first and American ones followed; this laid the basis for subsequent Anglo-American competition in oil development both there and in the Middle East over the next ten years.[83]

This does not downplay the notion of rivalry.[84] Rivalry existed, but the British withstood American pressures. In China, for instance, despite concerted efforts by the State Department and United States business interests, American influence had not displaced that of Britain by the time of the 1931 Manchurian crisis. This resulted less from the endeavours of the government in London and more from those of private British concerns, like the Hong Kong and Shanghai Bank headed by Sir Charles Addis, which used their experience and capital to dominate initiatives like a loan consortium set up in 1919–20.[85] Moreover, when violence that accompanied Chinese nationalism endangered British holdings, as occurred at Hankow and other places on the Yangtze River in early 1927, London despatched troops and ships to maintain order – something Washington would not do.[86] Similarly, in 1926, when Hoover, then Coolidge's secretary of commerce, attacked Britain's monopoly of world rubber production – 75 per cent of the total – Baldwin's government refused to increase production and lower prices; the economy of Malaya, strategically important to the eastern Empire, had been savaged by a rubber glut after 1919, and only a Colonial Office imposition of quotas and set prices salvaged it.[87] This

[82] S. V. O. Clarke, *Central Bank Cooperation, 1924–1931* (New York, 1967); R. H. Meyer, *Bankers' Diplomacy: Monetary Stabilization in the Twenties* (New York, 1970). Cf. K. M. Burk, 'The House of Morgan in Financial Diplomacy, 1920–1930', in McKercher, ed., *Anglo-American Relations*, 125–57.
[83] Cf. J. C. Brown, 'Why Foreign Oil Companies Shifted Their Production from Mexico to Venezuela during the 1920s', *AHR*, 90(1985), 362–85; S. G. Rabe, 'Anglo-American Rivalry for Venezuelan Oil, 1919–1929', *Mid-America*, 58(1976), 97–110; W. Stivers, *Supremacy and Oil. Iraq, Turkey, and the Anglo-American World Order, 1918–1930* (Ithaca, NY, 1982).
[84] F. C. Costigliola, 'Anglo-American Financial Rivalry in the 1920s', *JEH*, 27(1977), 911–34; M. D. Goldberg, 'Anglo-American Economic Competition 1920–1930', *Economy and History*, 16(1973), 15–36.
[85] Dayer, *Finance and Empire*, 109–230.
[86] W. R. Louis, *British Strategy in the Far East, 1919–1939* (Oxford, 1971), 131–3.
[87] J. Brandes, *Herbert Hoover and Economic Diplomacy: Department of Commerce Policy, 1921–1928* (Pittsburgh, 1962), 84–105; McKercher, *Baldwin Government*, 44–6. Cf. Colonial Office memorandum, 'Short History of the Rubber Restriction Scheme', Feb. 1928, FO 371/12831/1867/507.

issue subsided quickly when American rubber manufacturers like
Harvey Firestone accepted that the British would not acquiesce and
looked to establish their own plantations in other parts of the world –
which were not successful.

To be sure, the Americans expanded their commercial interests at
British expense in some areas of the globe, particularly in Latin
America. Through economic advisers being despatched from the
United States, Washington seeking to influence nationalist regimes like
that in Mexico, and some corporations eschewing co-operation with
Britain in places like Colombia,[88] the United States stole a march on the
British. Much of this stemmed from successful American actions during
the war and the encouragement of the pan-American movement by
American political and business leaders in the 1920s.[89] It also came
from Washington using diplomatic coercion and armed strength to
enforce the Monroe Doctrine.[90] But in a number of places besides
China – the Baltic states, the Middle East, and Africa – the British more
than held their own.[91] Thus, the suggestion that the United States had
emerged as the 'heir to the British Empire' by the early 1920s is
inaccurate.[92] American commercial and financial gains made during the
war were not necessarily permanent, and they might not withstand the
efforts of British commercial interests to regain what had been either
lost or eroded. During the American intervention in Nicaragua in 1927,
for instance, Sir Robert Vansittart, the head of the Foreign Office
American Department, proposed despatching a British warship to
adjacent waters: 'there was a distinct United States tendency to stretch
the Monroe doctrine so illegitimately that we should have been –
according to the latest theory – debarred from looking after our own

[88] S. J. Randall, 'The International Corporation and American Foreign Policy: The
United States and Colombian Petroleum, 1920–1940', *CJH*, 9(1974), 179–96; R. F.
Smith, *The United States and Revolutionary Nationalism in Mexico, 1916–1932* (Chicago,
1972); R. N. Seidel, 'American Reformers Abroad: The Kemmerer Missions in South
America, 1921–1931', *JEH*, 32(1972), 520–45.

[89] B. I. Kaufman, 'United States Trade and Latin America: The Wilson Years', *JAH*,
58(1971), 342–63; E. S. Rosenberg, 'Economic Pressures in Anglo-American
Diplomacy in Mexico, 1917–1918', *Journal of Inter-American Studies and World Affairs*,
17(1975), 123–52.

[90] W. Kamman, *A Search for Stability: United States Diplomacy toward Nicaragua,
1925–1933* (Southbend, 1968); R. V. Salisbury, 'United States Intervention in
Nicaragua: The Costa Rican Role', *Prologue*, 9(1977), 209–17.

[91] S. F. Evans, *The Slow Rapprochement: Britain and Turkey in the Age of Kemal Atatürk,
1919–1938* (Beverley, Humberside, 1982); M.-L. Hinkkanen-Lievonen, *British Trade
and Enterprise in the Baltic States, 1919–1925* (Helsinki, 1985); H. Sabahi, *British Policy
in Persia, 1918–1925* (1990)

[92] Parrini, *Heir to Empire*.

interests in a far more important eventuality, i.e. if the United States provoke a revolution in Mexico'.[93] The British understood that in some areas of the globe, like Latin America, the American commercial position was improving at their expense.[94] But this did not mean that Britain meekly succumbed, as Addis' successful policies over the China loan consortium showed. Even after Britain returned to the gold standard in 1925, sterling remained an indispensable currency for international trade; and, despite some structural weaknesses, the London money market had not been surpassed by New York.[95] Consequently, during the 1920s, the British used their capital and expertise to protect their commercial and financial position vis-à-vis the United States. In fact, the British also competed favourably with other commercial and financial rivals. As the decade ended, Britain retained significant commercial and financial strength and had yet to be surpassed in the wider world by the United States.

At the time of the May 1929 General Election, Britain remained pre-eminent in the world because, for ten years, its leaders inside and outside of government had resisted the American challenge. United States economic strength undoubtedly increased at British expense in the decade after the Paris peace conference. But equally, the new international order that had arisen after 1918–19 provided Britain with significant benefits. Traditional maritime threats disappeared and the Empire's strategic disposition had been improved. Whilst new naval adversaries replaced old ones, readjusting naval policy by holding firmly to the 'one-Power' standard ensured RN supremacy. Ensuing policies at the Washington and Coolidge conferences underscored the resolve to remain first amongst the naval Powers. For narrow national interests, the British took on the role of 'honest broker' in Europe after 1925 – the United States' withdrawal from European affairs offered London a freer hand on the continent and more influence than it would have had if the Anglo-American guarantee had come into force. And, after adjusting to American refusal to join the League, British diplomatists came to exercise a dominating influence at Geneva, using the organisation as another tool in British foreign policy.

---

[93] Vansittart minute, 23 Mar. 1927, FO 371/12038/2249/128.

[94] Wiswould [DOT], 'Memorandum respecting American Financial Penetration of Latin America', 29 Jan. 1926, with minutes, FO 371/11183/590/95.

[95] J. M. Atkin, 'Official British Regulation of Overseas Investment, 1914–1931', *EHR*, 2nd ser., 23(1970); D. B. Kunz, *The Battle for Britain's Gold Standard in 1931* (London, New York, 1987), 8–28. A debate exists about whether it was cheaper to borrow money in New York or London: cf. Aldcroft, *Versailles to Wall Street*, 242; D. E. Moggridge, *British Monetary Policy 1924–1931: The Norman Conquest of $4.86* (Cambridge, 1972), 200.

By mid-1929, therefore, the increase in its national wealth that came with the Great War had not been transformed into concrete political and strategic advantages for the United States. And as Hankow showed – despite Washington enforcing the Monroe Doctrine in Latin America – the British, not the Americans, had the will to use force to protect their interests in the wider world. American wealth spelled potential peril for Britain's pre-eminent position, but wealth means nothing in the hard world of international politics unless translated into tangible expressions of national potency and married to a will to use them. Britain possessed these tangible advantages in the 1920s; its leaders employed them to protect and enhance their country's interests. By capitalising on the strategic preponderance afforded by the Empire, by working to keep the RN as strong as postwar domestic conditions would permit, and by using their capital and expertise deftly in commercial and financial affairs, the foreign-policy-making elite tied British military and economic strength to the exercise of British power in Europe, within the League, and throughout the wider world. As the 1920s ended, settlement of the cruiser question, the only unresolved issue in Anglo-American relations, was at hand. How the foreign-policy-making elite approached the question and, then, constructed their diplomatic strategies would say much about the power and purpose of pre-eminent Britain.

1 The end of Anglo-American naval rivalry, 1929–1930

[Hoover] is, it is generally understood here, much more interested in naval reduction and restriction which he regards as immediately feasible than in the 'Freedom of the Seas' which he is supposed to think will anyhow take a very long time to settle internationally with or by treaties or by conference.

Howard, June 1929[1]

Baldwin and the Conservatives lost the 30 May 1929 General Election and, although Labour lacked a majority in the House of Commons, MacDonald formed a government. Assured of Liberal support because of Lloyd George's antipathy towards Baldwin, the second Labour ministry took office on 7 June.[2] Whilst the new prime minister had an abiding interest in foreign policy – serving as his own foreign secretary in 1924 – intra-party manoeuvring saw him offer the Foreign Office to his chief rival, Arthur Henderson, the party chairman.[3] Yet, despite relinquishing the Foreign Office to Henderson, MacDonald retained control over Britain's American policy. Success here might strengthen the electoral appeal of the party and enhance his position as leader. Moreover, such a course flowed from his interest in Anglo-American relations and, importantly, his public posturing whilst leader of the Opposition after 1924. In terms of the former, he privately reproached American smugness: '[The United States] seems like one of our new rich families that put a heavy and vulgar foot upon our life, that have a big and open purse, but that even in its gifts and in its goodness has an attitude and a spirit that makes one's soul shrink up and shrivel.'[4] But because he was

---

[1] Howard to MacDonald, 6 Jun. 1929, Howard DHW 9/62.
[2] S. Ball, *Baldwin and the Conservative Party. The Crisis of 1929–1931* (New Haven, 1988), 6–7; P. Williamson, 'Safety First: Baldwin, the Conservative Party, and the 1929 General Election', *HJ*, 25(1982), 385–409.
[3] D. Carlton, *MacDonald Versus Henderson. The Foreign Policy of the Second Labour Government* (New York, 1970), 15–17; D. Marquand, *Ramsay MacDonald* (1977), 489–90.
[4] MacDonald to Howard, 8 Feb. 1926, Howard DHW 4/Personal/10.

an atlanticist, removing Anglo-American differences became the focus of his thinking on foreign policy.[5] This informed his utterances whilst in opposition. During that time, he continually criticised Conservative handling of the American question, especially naval limitation. After the Coolidge conference, for instance, he launched a blistering parliamentary attack on the Baldwin government's disarmament policy, holding it responsible for the poor state of Anglo-American relations; and in 1929, just before the election, he wrote for the newspapers of the American press magnate, William Randolph Hearst, arguing that if Labour won office it would move to eliminate the rancour that had grown up since 1927.[6] That Baldwin and Chamberlain had fostered a co-operative spirit in Anglo-American relations by May 1929 would make his task easier.

Within days of becoming prime minister, MacDonald received reports about the American question from Foreign Office and Diplomatic Service experts. On 10 June, Robert Craigie, the head of the Foreign Office American Department, sent memoranda discussing the main points of contention: naval limitation, blockade, and the arbitration treaty.[7] MacDonald learnt of the Belligerent Rights Sub-committee's determination to keep those rights as high as possible, and about not mentioning blockade specifically in any new arbitration agreement. Craigie emphasised that a blockade agreement would benefit both Powers, hence the need for Anglo-American consultation should a conference to codify maritime law be called. He also stressed that the Preparatory Commission had still to produce a single draft disarmament convention and that France would oppose any separate naval arms agreement. At this moment, Howard reported from Washington that Hoover and Stimson wanted a settlement.[8] Believing that ameliorating differences could be achieved by direct discussions at the highest level, the ambassador implored MacDonald to travel to Washington. Craigie's memoranda and Howard's report showed that material for a naval settlement and its attendant problems lay at hand. But others also sought to influence the new premier. Abhorring any strictures on British blockade practices, Hankey dusted off arguments that the hardline

---

[5] Marquand, *MacDonald*, 467–74.
[6] See McKercher, *Baldwin Government*, 88–90; Ritchie [Hearst Newspapers] to MacDonald, 17 Apr. 1929, Rosenberg [MacDonald's secretary] to Ritchie, 22 Apr. 1929, both MacDonald PRO 30/69/1439/1.
[7] Craigie memoranda, 'Naval Disarmament Question', 'Question of an Agreement with the United States in regard to Maritime Belligerent Rights', 'Question of the conclusion of an Anglo-American Arbitration Treaty', all MacDonald PRO 30/69/1/267.
[8] Howard to MacDonald, 6 Jun. 1929, Howard DHW 9/62.

minority in the Belligerent Rights Sub-committee had vainly employed and sent them to his new political master.[9]

Cognisant of British security needs, MacDonald saw the opportunity to transform his rhetoric about settling Anglo-American differences into practical politics. But this could not be done in a vacuum. First, the Preparatory Commission had gone into suspended animation waiting for the particulars of the naval 'yardstick'. Second, as the Washington naval treaty would lapse in December 1931, a new conference would have to be convened to extend its life. Both matters touched the League and French reaction to naval talks outside the Preparatory Commission. Moreover, the Labour Party contained a coterie of pro-League activists who, deprecating bilateral arbitration agreements, wanted Britain to sign a 1920 amendment to the Protocol of the Permanent Court of International Justice (PCIJ), a League appendage. Called the 'Optional Clause' because it was not compulsory until signed, its signatories accepted PCIJ jurisdiction without reservation in disputes involving treaty interpretation, all questions of international law, any 'breach of international obligation', and the level of award should such breach occur.[10] If MacDonald's government signed the 'Optional Clause', Britain and the United States would lack, given the American Congress' opposition to United States membership on the PCIJ, an arbitration mechanism to settle bilateral disputes. Finally, domestic considerations in both countries had to be faced. With Labour in a minority in the Commons, and Borah's thirst for a conference to codify maritime law unslaked, any agreement would have to pass legislative scrutiny. As pressures for a naval settlement and improving relations were building amongst some elements of the press and public opinion in both countries – Edward Price Bell, an anglophile American newspaper correspondent was prominent[11] – raising hopes prematurely had to be avoided.

Dawes' arrival in London on 14 June set in train negotiations lasting until mid-September. Howard had informed MacDonald privately that Dawes received instructions 'not to go too far' concerning the freedom of the seas.[12] This suggested Hoover's inclination to ignore codifying maritime law in achieving a naval agreement. When MacDonald met Dawes on 16 June, Howard's sanguine assessment proved accurate. In

[9] Hankey to MacDonald, 13 Jun. 1929, with enclosures, PREM 1/99; Hankey diary, 18 [but 8] Oct. 1929, HNKY 1/8.
[10] F. P. Walters, *A History of the League of Nations* (1960), 125–6, 274–5.
[11] Bell, 'Private Memorandum for Prime Minister MacDonald', 26 Jun. 1929, Mac-Donald PRO 30/69/673/1; Bell, 'Memorandum for the President', 9 Jul. 1929, HHPP 1031.
[12] Howard to MacDonald, 6 Jun. 1929, Howard DHW 9/62.

friendly conversation, Dawes indicated that a naval settlement was imperative, that the other naval Powers should not be confronted with appearances of an Anglo-American *fait accompli*, that MacDonald's American visit should occur only after the achievement of the lines of a settlement to avoid raising public hopes in Britain and the United States, and that 'questions of belligerent rights, freedom of the seas, and so on, will not rise for the moment'.[13] A naval agreement now took first priority; getting one became the goal of diplomatic efforts over the summer.

These efforts, guided by MacDonald and Hoover, have been chronicled elsewhere.[14] By September, they produced a four-part compromise: MacDonald conceding formal parity in vessels under 10,000 tons; Britain's minimum cruiser requirement reducing to fifty; American heavy cruiser demands dropping to twenty-one, with the possibility that this might be reduced further after discussions with the Japanese; and Hoover allowing Britain an extra 24,000 tons of light cruisers to compensate for the USN having more heavy ones than the RN. Fundamental to the negotiations' success was MacDonald and Hoover's desire to get a settlement, which led them to override their naval experts' advice to achieve a political compromise that downplayed technical considerations. This element of the compromise has been misunderstood. Traditionally, it is argued that a drawn-out resolution of the problem stemmed from MacDonald's domination by the Admiralty and his inability 'to escape the imperatives of Empire and the traditions of a glorious past'.[15] Highlighting the normal give-and-take in the negotiating process, this view belittles the political will in both Downing Street and the White House to break the cruiser stalemate.

Just after MacDonald's 16 June meeting with Dawes, Vice-Admiral Sir William Fisher, the deputy chief of the Naval Staff, expounded the established RN line that 'the Naval Claims of the United States are founded on unsound principles'.[16] Pointing to the doctrine of absolute need and Britain's concession of informal equality in 1927, he opined

---

[13] Henderson despatch to Howard, 24 Jun. 1929, *DBFP II*, I, 8–10; MacDonald diary, 20 Jun. 1929, MacDonald PRO 30/69/1753. The idea that MacDonald was chagrined at not getting an immediate invitation to Washington – O'Connor, *Equilibrium*, 32 – is wrong; cf. '[Dawes] said that America would welcome me but I said I thought that it should be staged as the final & not as the opening act', in MacDonald to Howard, 17 Jun. 1929, Howard DHW 9/62.

[14] W.-H. Bickel, *Die anglo-amerikanischen Beziehungen 1927–1930 im Licht der Flottenfrage* (Zurich, 1970), 100–30; Carlton, *MacDonald Versus Henderson*, 105–14; Hall, *Arms Control*, 69–75; O'Connor, *Equilibrium*, 40–6; Roskill, *Naval Policy*, II, 37–44.

[15] Carlton, *MacDonald Versus Henderson*, 111–12; O'Connor, *Equilibrium*, 32–43.

[16] Fisher draft memorandum, n.d. [but mid-Jun. 1929], FHR 11; emphasis in original. Cf. Field [C-in-C, Mediterranean Fleet] to Hankey, 7 Jun. 1929, HNKY 4/21.

that American-defined parity meant 'each side should possess the same *number* of 8″ and 6″ ships or that each side should have the same 8″ and 6″ *tonnage*'. As RN and USN strategic roles differed, this meant holding to the seventy-vessel minimum, chiefly fifty-five light cruisers for fleet work and patrolling sea lanes. As recent Preparatory Commission discussions had shown, the Americans would not go above a maximum of forty-five, twenty-three of which had to be heavy. Thus, the Admiralty did not see how British and American requirements could be reconciled. In Washington, American experts led by the USN General Board and Admiral Hilary Jones, the chief naval disarmament adviser since 1926, proved reluctant to define the 'yardstick'.[17] The Board argued that only warship ages and displacements be computed in devising a limitation formula; gun calibres should be ignored because determining firepower would be a matter of interpretation on which both sides would surely disagree. Thus, the yardstick's impracticality: 'Any attempt to establish such a value necessarily must be based upon highly technical assumptions and complex computations upon which general agreement is most improbable if not impossible.' Jones asserted that Britain's worldwide network of bases and large merchantmen capable of mounting guns meant the USN could achieve parity only by having more heavy cruisers than the RN. Although Hoover and Stimson looked for a suitable formula, opposition from within the General Board prevented the sending of specific 'yardstick' figures to London.

Given the naval experts' inflexibility and the futility of compromising over the technical issues, MacDonald and Hoover agreed tacitly on a political settlement. In Britain, this conformed to Foreign Office views about Anglo-American differences that arose after the Coolidge conference and, because of Chamberlain's arguments, formed the basis of the Belligerent Rights Sub-committee's reports. Like Baldwin and Chamberlain, therefore, MacDonald reckoned that the naval experts were blocking a cruiser settlement. Hoover concurred; he had a close political adviser, Dwight Morrow, impress this on Howard as early as January – 'a working arrangement could be found and ought to be found without delay provided the matter was handled by real statesmen and not sailors'. Howard reported this to Vansittart, now a private secretary in the prime minister's office advising on foreign policy matters.[18]

In Britain, Downing Street sought Admiralty opinions, and Albert

---

[17] USNGB 438–1, Serial 1427, 10 Jun. 1929; USNGB memorandum, 14 Jun. 1929, with annexes, HHPP 998 [the subsequent quotation is from p. 3]; Jones to Adams [secretary of the Navy], 18 Jun. 1929, Jones 5.

[18] Howard to Vansittart, 24 Jan. 1929, Howard DHW 9/61; Craigie memorandum, 27 Jun. 1929, *DBFP II*, I, 15–16.

Alexander, the first lord, and his advisers were informed of what transpired. This course derived from the consultative nature of Cabinet government in which the premier remained, theoretically at least, first amongst equal ministers. But MacDonald overruled Admiralty advice when difficulties in the negotiations emerged, for instance, when he lowered Britain's cruiser demand to fifty.[19] MacDonald's task was made easier in that unlike the preceding Cabinet, which contained staunch naval hardliners like Baldwin's chancellor of the Exchequer, Winston Churchill, the second Labour ministry lacked equivalent advocates. Urging reform and arms reduction, and wanting British security tied to the League, leading members of the new government supported the prime minister over his navalist opponents in the Admiralty. This does not mean that MacDonald ignored British security in seeking a rapprochement. As he confided to an MP: 'I am keeping my eye upon our relations not only with America, but with the rest of the world, and any agreement which I make with the former will be on condition that it has to be varied if it in any way weakens us dangerously in relation to the latter.'[20] Still, a deal with the United States had to be struck and, whilst other threats were not overlooked, Britain had to make some concession.

Hoover had more freedom of action. This stemmed from the authority that the United States constitution bestowed on the presidency. Cabinet members served at presidential discretion; and, as the various departments and their specialist consulting bodies, like the Navy Department and the USN General Board, only advised, presidents had decided independence in policy-making. Hence, when MacDonald made a public show of good faith in July by cancelling three small auxiliary vessels and slowing down construction of two cruisers, Hoover responded by suspending three vessels authorised by the fifteen cruiser bill.[21] In doing so, he disregarded the expert advisers in his government and weathered criticism from their 'Big Navy' supporters outside. And when Jones and the General Board continued obfuscating over the 'yardstick', Hoover decided on 11 September that USN heavy cruiser

[19] MacDonald to Dawes, 8 Aug. 1929, *DBFP II*, I, 36–8. Cf. Vansittart to Alexander, 3 Jul. 1929, AVAR 5/2/2; MacDonald to Dawes, 24 Jul. 1929, MacDonald PRO 30/69/ 672/1; CC 33(29)1, CAB 23/61. See Fisher to Madden [first sea lord], 31 Aug. 1929, DCNS memorandum, 'Disarmament Conversations', 5 Sep. 1929, both FHR 11.

[20] MacDonald to Bellairs, 30 Jul. 1929, MacDonald PRO 30/69/672/1; MacDonald to Dawes, 8 Aug. 1929, *DBFP II*, I, 36–8; MacDonald diary, 6, 26 Aug., 11 Sep. 1929, MacDonald PRO 30/69/1753. Cf. Fisher minute, 23 Aug. 1929, ADM 116/2686/ 3672.

[21] O'Connor, *Equilibrium*, 37. Cf. Hoover to McNutt [American Legion], 30 Jul. 1929; unsigned memorandum [on favourable US editorial comment on suspending cruiser construction], Aug. 1929, both HHPP 998.

demands would have to be reduced to appease Britain.[22] At that moment, a naval lobbyist, William Shearer, brought a lawsuit against Bethlehem Steel and other large American corporations involved in naval construction, claiming these firms owed him money for successfully disrupting the Coolidge conference. Exploiting adverse public reaction to Shearer's charges, Hoover manipulated the controversy to discredit American 'Big Navy' disciples and win public support for appeasing the British.[23] MacDonald even aided Hoover's bid to conduct unfettered diplomacy. In late August, Howard reported that Borah threatened to block any agreement that did not reduce naval construction to a level he thought appropriate. When MacDonald wrote privately to his friend on the importance to international security of Anglo-American reconciliation, Borah backed off.[24] Thus, as MacDonald left London on 28 September, statesmen rather than sailors had it in their power to settle the naval question.

The importance of MacDonald's mission cannot be overemphasised. As Howard had been predicting since mid-1928, a prime ministerial visit would mend the rift separating the two Powers. Indeed, it inaugurated a period of Anglo-American co-operation that lasted, with difficulty here and there, until Hoover surrendered office in early 1933. Part of this devolved from the MacDonald–Hoover discussions that, if they did not flesh out the September compromise, reaffirmed the principles on which the compromise was based; and, as important, thanks to a public relations triumph engineered by Howard, it saw public American suspicions of British policy begin to be replaced by feelings of trust. Despite a full schedule of public appearances in New York and Washington, MacDonald held private talks with Hoover at the president's country retreat on the Rapidan River on 6–7 October and, afterwards, in the American capital.[25] The two men looked to give

---

[22] USNGB 438–1, Serial 1444A, 11 Sep. 1929; Hoover to Stimson, 11, 12 Sep. 1929, both HHPP 998.

[23] Hall, *Arms Control*, 75–6; O'Connor, *Equilibrium*, 59–60. Cf. Shearer to Hoover, 6 Mar. 1929, Grace [Bethlehem Steel] to Hoover, 9 Sep. 1929, Hoover [Bureau of Investigation] to Richey [President Hoover's secretary], 10 Sep. 1929, with enclosures, O'Brian [assistant to the attorney-general] to Hoover, 17, 20, 23 Sep. 1929, all HHPP 1062. Hoover told Howard: 'I wish you could find a Shearer'; in Howard telegram to Henderson, 12 Sep. 1929, *DBFP II*, I, 78.

[24] Howard to MacDonald, 22, 23 Aug. 1929, Howard DHW 9/63; MacDonald diary, 26 Aug. 1929, MacDonald PRO 30/69/1753; MacDonald to Borah, 26 Aug. 1929, MacDonald PRO 30/69/673/1.

[25] Except where noted, the next three paragraphs are based on 'Memorandum by Mr. MacDonald respecting his Conversations with President Hoover at Washington (October 4 to 10, 1929)', *DBFP II*, I, 106–15; Hoover to Stimson, 9 Oct. 1929, with enclosures, Stimson R79; Hall, *Arms Control*, 77–80; O'Connor, *Equilibrium*, 47–51; Roskill, *Naval Policy*, II, 45–50.

substance to the principles agreed over the summer. For instance, since the Coolidge conference, the Admiralty had wanted to loosen Washington treaty strictures on battleships: extend their lives from twenty to twenty-six years and reduce their displacement to a maximum 25,000 tons and gun calibres to twelve inches.[26] MacDonald pressed this on Hoover who, arguing that 'the days of the battleship were numbered owing to the development of aircraft', countered that battleship numbers be reduced. When MacDonald rejoined about RN reluctance to cut its battlefleet, Hoover accepted reductions to 25,000 tons. His only proviso involved the USN being allowed a 35,000-ton vessel to compensate for two equivalent battleships – the *Nelson* and the *Rodney* – granted Britain by the Washington treaty and commissioned in 1925. Though a final decision on this matter would have to await the anticipated naval conference, MacDonald told the Cabinet that 'elements favourable to a compromise are present'.

Inconclusive discussions touched on destroyers, submarines, and aircraft carriers, together with a British proposal to transfer up to 10 per cent of a class tonnage from one category to another. Still, the elusive 'yardstick' remained the focus of the Rapidan and Washington conversations. By the September compromise, the USN would be permitted 315,000 cruiser tons, 210,000 set aside for heavy vessels. The RN would be allowed 339,000 tons, 150,000 for heavy vessels. With a replacement programme of fourteen cruisers by 1936, the end of a renewed treaty, this would meet Britain's new absolute need. But twenty-one USN heavy cruisers opposed to fifteen British caused concern for MacDonald and his advisers: the Japanese, demanding a cruiser ratio of 5:3.5, might build fifteen. Hoover suggested dropping the American total to eighteen if the British extended the life of their cruiser fleet by delaying their replacement programme until 1937 – this would limit the IJN to twelve heavy cruisers. A decision was made 'to examine ways and means' to reconcile this divergence before the impending naval conference. Obviating an impasse in these discussions, this action had the added benefit of not presenting the other naval Powers with what might be construed as an Anglo-American variant of the 1928 Anglo-French compromise. By 7 October, MacDonald and Hoover agreed that the other three major naval Powers be invited to meet with British and American representatives in London in January 1930. Their brief would be to extend the Washington naval treaty by five years.[27] The invitation outlined four considerations to guide the

[26] London [British Legation, Geneva] telegram (129) to Howard, 24 Jun. 1927, London telegram (133) to Tyrrell [Foreign Office], 25 Jun. 1927, both FO 412/115.
[27] 'Note of Invitation to the Naval Conference', 7 Oct. 1929, *DBFP II*, I, 103–4.

negotiations: the Kellogg Pact would be 'the starting-point of agreement'; the RN and USN would achieve parity by 31 December 1936; the Washington treaty replacement programmes should be re-examined to effect battleship reductions; and London and Washington would urge the abolition of the submarine.[28]

Although dialogue about limiting warships proceeded amicably, potential danger to the growing rapprochement emerged when Hoover suddenly announced that good Anglo-American relations 'could never be fully established until the problems associated with the capture of property at sea in time of war had been squarely faced'.[29] Ignoring the agreement reached at the first MacDonald–Dawes meeting, the president pointed to Borah's desire to preserve 'the freedom of the seas'. Hoover also had a personal interest in belligerent interception of 'food-ships' – during the war, he had headed an organisation that had fed starving European states occupied by the Germans and subject to the British blockade.[30] MacDonald obliquely referred to the Belligerent Rights Sub-committee, which 'found [the question] replete with dangers and complexities of every sort'; but following the sub-committee's recommendation to consult secretly with Washington should a conference to codify international law be in the offing, the prime minister indicated that his government would rather have a separate Anglo-American treaty, that if a conference to codify international law was still called, only the five major naval Powers should attend, and, in either case, private Anglo-American talks should be held to ensure a unified view respecting blockade.

MacDonald telegraphed the Cabinet about his willingness to 'examine this question fully and frankly' with Hoover.[31] This message induced paroxysms of disapproval in Hankey. Whilst Admiralty opinion had been skirted in the political process that produced the September compromise – and Hankey had contributed nothing through his involvement in reparations negotiations beginning in August – he would not allow what he perceived to be an emasculation of British belligerent rights. From his central position in the Cabinet, CID, and COS, he galvanised Henderson and other ministers to block the proposed

---

[28] MacDonald pressed abolition on behalf of the king, who saw the submarine as 'this terrible weapon'. Stamfordham [George V's secretary] to MacDonald, 10 Jul. 1929, Vansittart to Stamfordham, 12 Jul. 1929, both PREM 1/71.
[29] 'Memorandum by Mr. MacDonald', cited in n. 25, above.
[30] Hoover memorandum for MacDonald, 5 Oct. 1929, HHPP 998. Cf. H. C. Hoover, *An American Epic: Famine in Forty-Five Nations: The Battle on the Front Line, 1914–1923*, 3 vols., (Chicago, 1961).
[31] Howard telegram (493, 494) to Henderson, 6 Oct. 1929, *DBFP II*, I, 116–17.

examination.[32] Henderson then wired MacDonald to outline Cabinet opposition, explaining that an Anglo-American arrangement could adversely affect any economic or military sanctions imposed in future to support either the Covenant or the Kellogg Pact.[33] A signatory of both instruments, Britain could not indulge in a bilateral examination: there had to be multilateral talks involving all League members and signatories of the Kellogg Pact. Beyond this, the unspoken and far more important reason involved RN ability to impose future blockades in defence of Britain's narrow national and Imperial interests. Though the Cabinet's action compelled MacDonald to have mention of blockade excluded from the joint communiqué summarising the talks, he promised Hoover that informal examination might occur after he returned to London.[34] The matter went into abeyance.

Cabinet intercession was not unwelcome to MacDonald – Hankey's lobbying conformed to Foreign Office notions about first getting a naval agreement.[35] Determined to keep political rather than technical considerations at the fore in Washington, MacDonald took no naval officers with him. Apart from Thomas Jones, the pro-American deputy secretary of the Cabinet, who handled administrative matters, MacDonald's hand-picked advisers on this mission were the two diplomats most responsible for Britain's American policy: Vansittart and Craigie. With Howard, who shared their ideas about a political resolution of the naval question, Vansittart and Craigie ensured that MacDonald's discussions with Hoover followed Belligerent Rights Sub-committee recommendations. Emphasising this to the Foreign Office on 8 October,[36] Vansittart pointed to MacDonald preventing an international conference and, 'by great exertion', getting a joint Anglo-American examination accepted by Hoover. A Hoover ploy to have the British abandon their naval bases in the Western Hemisphere in return for the Americans building none in the Eastern Hemisphere was also politely, but firmly, rebuffed.[37] There were limits to Britain's desire to resolve Anglo-American naval differences – the fifty cruiser minimum lay at the edge – that Hoover had to accept. This says much about the success of MacDonald's mission.

[32] COS Meetings 81–82, 8–9 Oct. 1929, both CAB 53/3; Hankey memorandum, 'Relations with the United States of America including the Question of Belligerent Rights', 10 Oct. 1929, CAB 53/17; Hankey diary, 8–10 Oct. 1929, HNKY 1/8; Hankey to MacDonald, 11 Oct. 1929, CAB 21/352; Hankey to Snowden [chancellor of the Exchequer], 11 Oct. 1929, with enclosure, Hopkins T 175/36.
[33] Henderson telegram (506) to Howard, 8 Oct. 1929, DBFP II, I, 120–1.
[34] 'Memorandum by Mr. MacDonald', cited in n. 25, above; Craigie to Cotton [US under-secretary of state], 7 Oct. 1929, HHPP 998.
[35] The irony is lost on Roskill, Hankey, II, 490–5, who distorts Hankey's influence.
[36] Howard telegram (499) to Henderson, 8 Oct. 1929, DBFP II, I, 121–2.
[37] Howard telegram (500, 501) to Henderson, 9 Oct. 1929, ibid., 122–3.

Hoover's failure to find an answer to the food-ship question, his inability to overcome British resistance about abandoning bases, and the process of doing no more than reaffirming the principles of the September compromise did not damage the co-operative spirit in relations that had been developing for almost a year. Despite Hoover and Stimson being unhappy about British intransigence, compromise on both sides remained the order of the day.

Howard handled the public side of MacDonald's trip. Judging from Howard's reports, American and British press coverage, plus a deluge of congratulatory messages reaching the Washington embassy,[38] his efforts produced a swell of positive comment that suggested a more favourable British image in the United States. During his tenure as ambassador, which began in 1924, Howard used the public platform, including radio, to great effect in explaining his government's views to the American public on a range of subjects. Aided by the propaganda arm of the embassy at Washington – the British Library of Information at New York (BLINY) – his remarks were disseminated across the United States.[39] Howard had also established personal contacts with leaders of the two major political parties and influential bodies like the Council on Foreign Relations. Given his long-standing arguments favouring a high-level British mission to the United States, he used his connexions to get MacDonald as much public exposure as possible: addresses to the Senate in Washington and six different groups in New York, including the Council on Foreign Relations. MacDonald's central thesis concerned maintaining international peace by co-operative efforts, for which Howard and BLINY achieved the widest possible press coverage, including a national radio audience for MacDonald's speech to the Council. Along with improving relations at the official level,[40] the public tone of the relationship began to change for the better by the time MacDonald left the United States on 13 October to spend two weeks in Canada.

When MacDonald returned to Britain on 1 November, preparations for the London naval conference were underway. Favourable French, Italian, and Japanese replies to the 7 October invitation had been received within ten days.[41] These speedy answers resulted from Paris, Rome, and Tokyo being kept abreast of the summer negotiations and

---

[38] Except where noted, this paragraph is based on Hall, *Arms Control*, 80; McKercher, *Howard*, 348–9; O'Connor, *Equilibrium*, 49–50. Cf. MacDonald diary, 25 Sep. 1929, MacDonald PRO 30/69/1753; Howard to Henderson, 10 Oct. 1929, Henderson FO 800/280.

[39] McKercher, *Howard*, 297–337 *passim*; McKercher, 'Images', 221–48.

[40] See Stimson to Nan [his sister], 1 Nov. 1929, Stimson R79.

[41] *DBFP II*, I, 128–31.

the ensuing MacDonald–Hoover discussions; and, in line with the understanding made at MacDonald's first meeting with Dawes, the Powers were not presented with irreducible Anglo-American limitation proposals. French perceptions, always tinged with suspicion, typified the reaction to the invitation. 'There is now a fairly widespread understanding', Sir William Tyrrell, the ambassador at Paris, reported, 'that, so far as naval matters are concerned, what the conversations and Mr. MacDonald's visit have really secured is the acceptance by the British and American Governments, in principle, of parity between the two fleets.'[42] But agreeing to attend a conference and limiting naval arms were different propositions. Franco-Italian mutual distrust turning on the naval balance in the Mediterranean, which had led both Powers to boycott the Coolidge conference in 1927, remained.[43]

More ominous, Tokyo's desire to increase the IJN cruiser building ratio over that allowed for capital ships could not be ignored. Whilst in the United States, MacDonald approved Hoover's suggestion that Japanese delegates to the conference be invited to stop in Washington for preliminary discussions.[44] To this end, informal talks between Stimson and the Japanese ambassador occurred by the end of October. Stimson expressed his concern about Japanese views to Ronald Ion Campbell, the *chargé* at the British Embassy: the Japanese seemed apprehensive about 'rigid' Anglo-American agreement on limitation; and their desire for a 3.5 ratio for heavy cruisers could affect the naval balance in the southern Pacific.[45] To avoid irritating the Japanese, Stimson asked for information on any Anglo-Japanese talks being held in London. He wanted to avoid any divergence between the English-speaking Powers that might harm the conference. Stressing that the Japanese should be told that London and Washington were examining 'ways and means' to reconcile the 24,000-ton difference in their cruiser requirements, and built around the idea that eighteen American heavy cruisers would limit the IJN to just twelve, Henderson's friendly response hid nothing from the Americans.[46]

The time between MacDonald's return to London and the opening of the conference on 21 January 1930 saw the British and Americans draw closer together. This had two dimensions: the first, the more obvious,

---

[42] Tyrrell despatch to Henderson, 14 Oct. 1929, *ibid.*, 125–7.
[43] Graham [British ambassador, Rome] to Henderson, 18 Oct. 1929, Henderson to Graham, 22 Oct. 1929, both Henderson FO 800/280.
[44] 'Memorandum by Mr. MacDonald', cited in n. 25, above.
[45] Stimson memoranda on conversations with Debuchi [Japanese ambassador, Washington], 16, 23 Oct., SDDF 500. A. 15a3; Campbell telegram (535) to Henderson, 7 Nov. 1929, *DBFP II*, I, 132–3.
[46] Henderson telegram (571) to Campbell, 12 Nov. 1929, *ibid.*, 135–6.

involved smoothing over the unresolved issues that had emerged during MacDonald's trip; the second, hidden from view and a derivative of the first, entailed the evolution of attitudes within the two governments about the need for co-operation. The most important unresolved matter concerned blockade. As MacDonald's Cabinet had not yet seen the Belligerent Rights Sub-committee's reports, these were circulated on 4 November. Although no evidence exists to explain this delay, the premier's desire to have a free hand in pursuing his American policy during the summer probably had much to do with it. Within two days, criticism came from the pro-League section of the Cabinet. Lord Parmoor, the lord president of the council, reproached both reports for being based 'on assumptions which the Labour Party and Labour Government have publicly rejected': that Britain did not want belligerent rights watered down, and that it might impose blockades without reference to the League.[47] MacDonald did not respond. Instead, he wrote to Hoover that his government, mindful of the British people's 'deep sentimental regard for their historical position on the sea', could not agree to an examination of blockade, even concerning food-ships.[48] Raising the spectre of political divisions within Britain that might prevent an Anglo-American agreement, MacDonald cautioned that 'a re-examination is apt to unsettle and stampede' British opinion. Hoover let the matter drop.

Britain's legal right to blockade had also been strengthened in September when the Cabinet decided to sign the 'Optional Clause'.[49] On this single point, MacDonald strayed from the Belligerent Rights Sub-committee recommendations. Nonetheless, this constituted inspired diplomacy on the Labour ministry's part, even if endorsing the 'Clause' occurred because pro-League elements in the Cabinet sought to strengthen the PCIJ rather than improve Anglo-American relations.[50] It meant that the worry about the Americans seeking to arbitrate future blockades, League or otherwise, had evaporated: not only could London now not conclude bilateral arbitration agreements, even with the United States, it could only accept PCIJ adjudication should British orders-in-council and other legal forms be questioned. League wars would be

---

[47] Parmoor memorandum [CP 310(29)], 6 Nov. 1929, CAB 24/206.
[48] The rest of this paragraph is based on MacDonald to Hoover, 19 Nov. 1929, Hoover to MacDonald, 3 Dec. 1929, both HHPP 999.
[49] Cmd. 3452. See discussions of the Cabinet committee, created in July 1929 and on which Henderson and Alexander sat, which formulated arbitration policy: CAB 27/392.
[50] 'Note of a Meeting . . . June 20, 1929', 'Minute by the Secretary of State', 24 Jul. 1929, Dalton [FO parliamentary under-secretary] to Henderson, 20 Aug. 1929, Dalton to Noel-Baker, 21, 27 Aug. 1929, all Dalton II 1/1.

'public' wars, fought under the fiat of the League, because as even Hankey had realised a year earlier:

Once we have a code drawn up for public wars we shall always be able to apply it *mutatis mutandis* to private wars, which by the way, we should always try and induce the world to believe were public wars or else wars like the American operations in Nicaragua, which Phillip [*sic*] Kerr politely designates as police measures.[51]

Although some Admiralty–Foreign Office disagreement developed over elements of the 'Clause', for instance, its legitimacy should League machinery prove inadequate, they concurred that it would not regulate 'naval action in the event of war having broken out'.[52] With Hoover's reluctance to push for an examination of blockade, this meant that the divisive issue of belligerent rights had fallen by the wayside.

Pre-conference exchanges occurred not only between London and Washington. As MacDonald and Hoover had agreed to avoid the appearance of prior Anglo-American commitments, the 7 October invitation solicited the other Powers' views. Beyond Hoover's desire for Japanese–American conversations, this devolved into bilateral discussions between the French and Italians, and between the British and both the Japanese and French. Stretching from 19 November to 18 December, Franco-Italian deliberations were distinguished by France's bid to increase its building ratio over that agreed at Washington whilst denying Italy an equivalent acceleration.[53] Refusing to concede naval supremacy to France, the Italians cunningly called for the abolition of the submarine, a course designed to win support from the British and Americans whilst isolating the French, who saw this warship as a cheap weapon for naval defence. Unable to force the Italians to relent, the French declined to give specific limitation figures.

Although Anglo-French conversations occurred sporadically after MacDonald's return, the Franco-Italian impasse saw the French outline their general goals to the British on 20 December;[54] still foregoing specific figures (Paris wanted an overall tonnage rather than ones for individual categories of vessel), this amounted to pre-conference

---

[51] Hankey to Balfour [Conservative minister], 20 Dec. 1928, CAB 21/320.
[52] Cf. Alexander note [CID 966B], 11 Nov. 1929, enclosing Madden memorandum, 'Optional Clause – British Reservations', 11 Nov. 1929, Henderson memorandum [CID 970B]), 'The Optional Clause', 19 Nov. 1929, both CAB 4/19.
[53] The rest of this paragraph is based on FO–Admiralty memorandum, 'Historical Survey of the Negotiations Since the War for the Limitation of Naval Armament', Jun. 1930, CAB 4/19; Hall, *Arms Control*, 81–83; O'Connor, *Equilibrium*, 57.
[54] 'Memorandum Communicated by the French Ambassador on December 20, 1929', *DBFP II*, I, 173–7. Cf. Craigie memorandum, 18 Dec. 1929, *ibid.*, 167–70; MacDonald diary, 20 Dec. 1929, MacDonald PRO 30/69/1753.

demands that MacDonald and Hoover wanted to avoid. The most important involved using Article 8 – the disarmament article – of the Versailles Treaty as the basis of French naval proposals; this would tie naval limitation to air and land limitation, and ensure that security guarantees accompanied any arms agreement. This put Paris at odds with both London and Washington.[55] The British replied that this translated into pre-conference demands;[56] holding that 'the measure of security' demanded by France had already been achieved through the League, the Washington four-Power treaty, Locarno, the 'Optional Clause', and the Kellogg Pact, MacDonald's government, with American support, refused to bargain before the conference opened.

Whilst the relative weakness of the Italian and French navies allowed MacDonald and Hoover to evade the concerns of Rome and Paris at this stage,[57] such luxury did not exist concerning Tokyo. Japanese overtures to the English-speaking Powers, like those which worried Stimson in late October, showed a determination to achieve a 5:3.5 ratio for IJN auxiliary vessels, mainly cruisers. Although MacDonald spoke for both governments by characterising this privately as an 'impossible position regarding Japan's intentions at [the] 5 Power Conference',[58] Japan's strong naval, military, and political position in East Asia meant that its wishes could not be ignored. In addition, domestic pressures on the Japanese Cabinet by militarist and nationalist opinion suggested that if a compromise proved impossible, any agreement reached at London might see Japan's failure to ratify. Thanks to Stimson's approach to Campbell in early November, London and Washington endeavoured to avoid any divergence when talking to the Japanese.[59] By early

[55] MacDonald diary, 29 Nov. 1929, *ibid*.
[56] Craigie minute, 23 Dec. 1929, enclosing Cadogan [FO Western Department] minute, 18 Dec. 1929, Craigie minute, 19 Dec. 1929, MacDonald minute, 1 Jan. 1930, all FO 371/14256/130/1; 'Memorandum communicated to the French Ambassador', 10 Jan. 1930, *DBFP II*, I, 195–8.
[57] Craigie to Atherton, 3 Dec. 1929, Graham telegram (150) to Henderson, 15 Dec. 1929, Tyrrell despatch (1748) to Henderson, 27 Dec. 1929, Henderson telegram (683) to Howard, 29 Dec. 1929, Howard telegram (619) to Henderson, 31 Dec. 1929, all *ibid*., 157–9, 163–5, 179–83. Cf. 'I instructed our delegation that we did not care whether the French limited their navy or not, and our major purpose of parity with Britain and the extention of the 5–3 ratio with Japan would be accomplished even if France and Italy stayed out of the agreement': in Hoover to Shaw [a friend], 9 Feb. 1946, Hoover Misc. MSS.
[58] MacDonald diary, 29 Nov. 1929, MacDonald PRO 30/69/1753.
[59] Campbell telegram (553) to Henderson, 20 Nov. 1929, Henderson telegram (593) to Campbell, 22 Nov. 1929, both *DBFP II*, I, 144–6. Except where noted, this and next paragraph are based on Henderson telegrams (584, 604, 605, 606) to Campbell, 16, 26 Nov. 1929, Campbell telegrams (550, 559) to Henderson, 19, 23 Nov. 1929, Henderson despatch (1634) to Campbell, 25 Nov. 1929, Henderson telegram (204) to Tilley, 2 Dec. 1929, all *ibid*., 140–1, 144–5, 146–7, 156–7.

December, British and American co-operation had reached new levels. Stimson was fully informed about discussions between MacDonald and Matsudaira Tsuneo, the Japanese ambassador at London, in which cruiser limitation loomed large. Matsudaira learnt that the British 'would accept fifteen 8-inch vessels against 18 for the United States and regard this as parity', the difference being made up by 'certain compensations in the matter of small vessels [light cruisers]'.[60] Though this proposal had not yet been accepted by Washington, it would, if sanctioned, translate into twelve heavy cruisers for Japan, a ratio of 5:3.3 each for the RN and USN *vis-à-vis* the IJN.

Like the French, the Japanese pressed for principles to guide limitation before outlining specific numbers. This entailed setting a precise ratio for heavy cruisers and getting a force of submarines 'necessary for [Japan's] naval purposes', followed by an adjustment regarding 'small cruisers and destroyers'. But as Hoover's Administration had not yet decided whether to accept eighteen heavy cruisers, Tokyo delayed offering precise numbers. This was the situation when the Japanese delegation to the London conference, led by Wakatsuki Reijirō, a former premier, arrived in Washington.[61] Stimson learnt that Japan would not tamper with the Washington treaty capital ship ratio, but that anything less than a 70 per cent ratio for auxiliary vessels would disturb 'Japan's sense of national security'. As neither London nor Washington was prepared to entertain pre-conference commitments – and as the Americans had not determined their heavy cruiser requirements – Stimson won Wakatsuki's approval that the conference 'find a way by which the national feeling of the Japanese people could be protected and their national sensibilities not in any way offended by anything like an attempt to impose upon them or put them in a position of inferiority to other nations'. Once in London, Wakatsuki discovered similar sentiments in talks with Craigie, who reported: 'I gained the impression that both the Japanese delegates [Wakatsuki and Admiral Takerabe Takeshi] are well disposed towards this country and will do their utmost to secure an agreement.'[62] On the eve of the London naval conference, the three major naval Powers understood the requirements of each other – unlike at Geneva in 1927; the problem would be to reconcile their differences over cruisers.

Just after returning from the United States, MacDonald announced a

[60] Henderson telegram (192) to Tilley, 16 Nov. 1929, *ibid.*; Atherton telegram (334) to Stimson, 20 Nov. 1929, HHPP 999.
[61] Campbell despatch (2386) to Henderson, enclosing State Department memorandum, 26 Dec. 1929, with Craigie, Vansittart, MacDonald minutes, all FO 371/14255/72/1.
[62] Craigie minute, 2 Jan. 1930, with MacDonald minute, FO 371/14256/241/1.

major change at the uppermost level of the Foreign Office that strengthened the immediate policy of settling the naval question: Vansittart
would become permanent under-secretary. Done to provide continuing
competence at the administrative and policy-making heart of British
diplomacy, and assuredly to give MacDonald influence in Henderson's
Foreign Office,[63] this action also proved decisive to the course of Anglo-
American relations, in particular, and British foreign policy, in general,
for the next seven years – Vansittart held this post till December 1937.
Sir Ronald Lindsay, the permanent under-secretary since August 1928,
had been at odds with Henderson and his parliamentary under-
secretary, Hugh Dalton, since Labour took office in June.[64] Lindsay's
abilities were unquestioned; but, selected by Chamberlain in reward for
two brilliant years as ambassador at Berlin, he embodied what many
Labour Party supporters disliked about professional diplomats: patri-
cian, wealthy, and possessing a sense of duty to the state that drawing-
room socialists like Dalton confused with 'prejudices' towards them.[65]
Moreover, on two matters – the 'Optional Clause' and Egyptian policy[66]
– Lindsay had gone over Henderson to MacDonald. Using Howard's
long-planned retirement, scheduled for February 1930, as an excuse to
send Lindsay as his replacement, MacDonald chose Vansittart as the
Civil Service head of the Foreign Office. Although some criticism of this
appointment emerged from those passed over, the overwhelming
opinion of both the Foreign Office and Diplomatic Service, as well as
the king, an array of politicians, including Baldwin, and even Dalton,
applauded this promotion.[67]

Just forty-eight when he began his new duties on 7 January 1930,
Vansittart had been at or near the highest levels of the elite for a decade:
Curzon's private secretary from 1920 to 1924; four years as head of
the Foreign Office American Department; and, since February 1928, in
the prime minister's office advising on foreign affairs. He had joined the
Diplomatic Service in 1903 and, by 1911, had entered the Foreign
Office where he remained for the rest of his career. In this process, he

[63] N. Rose, *Vansittart. Study of a Diplomat* (1978), 66–70. Cf. Vansittart to MacDonald,
    24 Dec. 1929, MacDonald PRO 30/69/672/3.
[64] Cf. Lindsay to Dalton, 16 Aug. 1929, Dalton minute, 'Parliamentary Questions', n.d.,
    both Dalton II 1/1; Lindsay to Phipps [British minister, Vienna], 11 Nov. 1929, PHPP
    2/20.
[65] Dalton diary, 8 Nov., 10 Dec. 1929, BLEPS; H. Dalton, *Memoirs*, I (1953), 219.
[66] Dalton diary, 29 Jun., 4 Nov. 1929, BLEPS.
[67] For criticism, see Carlton, *MacDonald Versus Henderson*, 23 n. 2; W. Selby, *Diplomatic
    Twilight* (1953), 4. Selby was Henderson's private secretary. On support, see
    Chamberlain to Vansittart, 13 Nov. 1929, Stamfordham to Vansittart, 2 Jan. 1929 [but
    1930], both VNST II 1/2; R. I. Campbell to Vansittart, 21 Nov. 1929, VNST II 1/3;
    Baldwin to Vansittart, 30 Dec. 1929, VNST II 6/9; Dalton diary, 8 Nov. 1929, BLEPS.

imbibed heavily the 'Edwardian' foreign policy: the absolute importance of maintaining the balances of power in Europe and abroad in concert with other Powers; and, when possible, threatening or using force to support policy.[68] The war only strengthened the utility of these lessons in his mind; and his exposure to their practical application continued into the postwar period as 'Edwardians' dominated the Foreign Office: Curzon and Chamberlain in the foreign secretary's chair; and Sir Eyre Crowe (1920–25), Sir William Tyrrell (1925–28), and Lindsay in that of the permanent under-secretary.[69] Possessing the poise, wit, and charm of the professional diplomat, Vansittart was also atypically pugnacious and competitive, which is shown by his 1927 arguments about sending a gunboat to the Nicaraguan coast; and this was married to cold realism. After the Coolidge conference, he had observed:

A war with America would indeed be the most futile and damnable of all, but it is not 'unthinkable' ... If it is childish – and it is – to suppose that two nations must forever be enemies, it is also childish to stake one's whole existence on the gamble that two must be forever friends (especially when they never have been really.)[70]

Such attitudes permeated Vansittart's advice during his tenure as permanent under-secretary, placing him firmly amongst those British diplomatists who endorsed Palmerston's sage comment about Britain 'having no eternal friends or enemies, only eternal interests'. He provided British diplomacy for most of the 1930s with the indispensable element of *realpolitik*.

During the first six months of the second Labour government, more than anyone else, he served as MacDonald's chief adviser concerning the United States. Apart from his efforts during the summer negotiations, he had made a secret visit to Washington in September to help prepare for the prime minister's visit[71] – this masked by business concerning the estate of his late American wife. After MacDonald returned to London in early November, Vansittart continued to advise him daily.[72] It is significant that the last six years before Vansittart became permanent under-secretary saw him heavily involved in the American question, particularly in his central role in settling the

---

[68] Cf. Lord Vansittart, *Lessons of My Life* (1943), esp. 3–36; Lord Vansittart, *The Mist Procession. The Autobiography of Lord Vansittart* (1958), 43–121. Also important is an unpublished chapter from Vansittart's autobiography, '*Somme Toute*', which discusses the art of diplomacy, in VNST II 3/10.

[69] Cf. Rose, *Vansittart*, 45–65; Collier [FO official] 'Impressions of Sir Eyre Crowe', n.d., Collier Misc. 466.

[70] Vansittart minute, 15 Sep. 1927, Chamberlain FO 800/261.

[71] Howard telegram (407) to Henderson, 4 Sep. 1929, *DBFP II*, I, 65.

[72] MacDonald diary, 4, 5 Nov. 1929, MacDonald PRO 30/69/1753.

blockade claims controversy of 1925–27 and in the year's diplomacy after Coolidge's 1928 Armistice Day speech. This meant that he possessed a knowledge of the issues that provided continuity and consistency to policy. It also meant that he could advance the careers of officials who shared his views, chiefly Craigie, his friend and close colleague since 1925.[73] It was no coincidence that by December 1929, Craigie had emerged as the Foreign Office naval expert who, despite carping from Hankey and others about his 'wrecking the British Empire',[74] accentuated the political dimension of a naval settlement. Equally important problems had to be addressed by the British – reparations, French demands for security and their impact on the Preparatory Commission, and the East Asian balance; thus, like his political master, Vansittart saw the necessity of burying Anglo-American differences to deal better with these threats to Britain's 'eternal interests'.

MacDonald and Hoover kept naval officers in secondary roles in their delegations to the conference.[75] MacDonald led the British delegates and, although Henderson, Alexander, and the Indian secretary, William Wedgewood-Benn, were nominal members, he relied almost solely on Vansittart, Craigie, and two Foreign Office officials, Alexander Cadogan, the League expert, and Herbert Malkin, the chief legal adviser. Admiral Sir Charles Madden, the first sea lord, Fisher, and Captain Roger Bellairs, the Admiralty director of plans, were included to offer technical advice. Stimson headed the American delegation. The senior political delegates who accompanied him were Charles Adams, the navy secretary, and two senators, David Reed, a Republican, and Joseph Robinson, a Democrat; the latter two were selected to ensure bipartisan Senate support for the renewed treaty.[76] The American delegates who corresponded to Vansittart and his Foreign Office retinue were three ambassadors whom Hoover trusted: Dawes, Hugh Gibson, and Dwight Morrow, now the envoy to Mexico City. Assisted by a clutch of naval officers, Jones and Admiral William Veazie Pratt, the chief of naval operations, were to provide technical guidance.

On 5 December, MacDonald had asked that the American delegation reach London early for preliminary talks.[77] Accordingly, although conversations continued with the French, Italians, and Japanese to prevent

---

[73] McKercher, *Baldwin Government, passim.*
[74] Hankey diary, 15 Nov. 1929, HNKY 1/8.
[74] Hoover to Adams, 2 Nov. 1929, Stimson to Atherton, 5 Nov. 1929, Atherton telegram (309) to Stimson, 6 Nov. 1929, all HHPP 999.
[76] Borah declined to join the delegation; Borah to Hoover, 19 Oct. 1929, HHPP 998.
[77] Dawes telegram (362) to Stimson, 5 Dec. 1929, HHPP 999.

any whisper of Anglo-American collusion,[78] MacDonald and Stimson held a lengthy discussion on 17 January.[79] The two men colluded; and the significance of this meeting cannot be stressed too much. Here, the British and Americans ended the naval rivalry that had suffused their relations since the war; the eventual treaty, ready by April, only sealed the deal. Of course, whilst both sides entered the conference with their naval needs defined within the parity principle, both were looking for some advantages. But neither was going to press so hard as to damage Anglo-American accord. In the preceding week, MacDonald had enforced his vision of a political settlement on the Cabinet, chiefly by using the competing interests of the Treasury and the Admiralty to cancel one another.[80] He, thus, ensured that British proposals for reopening the battleship question and extending the building ratio to auxiliary craft would not antagonise Washington. On the American side, earlier informing MacDonald that the United States could accept reduced battleship numbers but not a scaling down in displacement and gun calibres,[81] Hoover and Stimson were moving towards accepting eighteen heavy cruisers for the USN. Whilst this process had yet to be completed before Stimson left Washington on 7 January – it meant side-stepping opposition on the USN General Board – the president understood that compromising over heavy cruisers would be necessary to reach an agreement with the British.[82]

MacDonald and Stimson ranged over a number of issues: conference procedure; Japan's demand for a better cruiser ratio; difficulties presented by France and Italy; and battleship limitation. Significantly cruisers and blockade remained unmentioned. Arguing that Congress would not ratify a treaty giving Japan a 10:7 cruiser ratio, Stimson

---

[78] Tyrrell to Henderson, 20 Dec. 1929, FO 371/14256/244/1; Craigie minute, 6 Jan. 1930, FO 371/14256/336/1; Stimson diary, 19 Jan. 1929, with two Stimson telegrams to State Department, 20 Jan. 1929, all Stimson 12; Cambon to Stimson, 19 Jan. 1929, Stimson R79.

[79] Except where noted the next two paragraphs are based on MacDonald diary, 17 Jan. 1930, MacDonald PRO 30/69/1753; Stimson diary, 17 Jan. 1930, with Stimson memorandum, 'Conference with the Prime Minister of Great Britain', 17 Jan. 1930, both Stimson 12.

[80] Grigg [Snowden's secretary] to Snowden, 13 Dec. 1929, enclosing, Alexander memorandum, 'First Lord's personal and *minimum* proposals', n.d., Upcott [Treasury] memorandum, 'Shipbuilding Programme', 23 Dec. 1929, Snowden minute to Grigg, n.d., all T 172/1693; CC 1(30), CAB 23/63; Madden memorandum, 15 Jan. 1929, [CP 1(30)], CAB 24/209 Parmoor to MacDonald, 9 Jan. 1930, MacDonald PRO 30/69/676; Snowden to MacDonald, 12 Jan. 1930, enclosing Treasury memorandum, 'Naval Conference', 10 Jan. 1930, T 172/1693.

[81] Stimson telegram (3) to US Embassy, London, 3 Jan. 1930, HHPP 987.

[82] Cf. USNGB memorandum, 7 Jan. 1930, GB 438–1; n.a., [but Hoover] memorandum [on instructions to the American delegation], n.d., HHPP 999.

contended that if the Japanese delegation withdrew because they did not get their way:

> we might make a treaty without them and they know that in that case they ran a great danger of having two cruisers laid down to their one by both the United States and Great Britain and that if it was done under those circumstances those four cruisers would be more likely than not to be used against their one in case of trouble.

Whilst it was necessary to find a 'means of saving Japan's face', the desire to achieve Anglo-American agreement above all else emerged in the 17 January meeting. Stimson told MacDonald that 'he was to work with me'. MacDonald recorded afterwards:

> We discussed the attitude of both Japan & France & resolved that neither was to place us in an impossible position with our people if complete co-operation between us could prevent it. 'If the worst comes', [Stimson] said, 'we can make an agreement ourselves two'.

The stage was now set for the London naval conference, which met from 21 January to 22 April.[83] Given all that had passed since the Coolidge conference, the cruiser question occupied a central position in the conference. The British and Americans had reconciled their competing visions of cruiser strength during the MacDonald–Hoover talks at Rapidan and Washington; the only unresolved issue concerned whether the Americans would accept eighteen heavy cruisers. As Tokyo's probing had suggested, and Wakatsuki's discussions in London and Washington confirmed, Anglo-American requirements could not be divorced from those of Japan.[84] Hoover and Stimson had been pressing for the lower figure since late December, but USN General Board deadlock on whether this would meet American strategic requirements prevented a decision before Stimson left for Britain. Accordingly, determining the final bargaining position fell to the delegation after it arrived in London and could survey the situation. Discussions conducted by Reed and Robinson showed that a hard line over twenty-one vessels would prevent a settlement.[85] The Americans would have to accept eighteen to avoid another deadlock. In a tense meeting of American delegates on 28 January, Jones

---

[83] Hall, *Arms Control*, 88–115; O'Connor, *Equilibrium*, 62–108; Roskill, *Naval Policy*, II, 37–70.

[84] Reports from Tilley and Castle, the latter the temporary US ambassador at Tokyo, reinforced this. Tilley despatch (540) to Henderson, 23 Dec. 1930, FO 371/14257/631; Tilley telegram (30) to FO, 30 Jan. 1930, FO 371/14258/856; Castle to Reed, 27 Jan. 1930, Reed to Castle, 20 Feb. 1930, both Castle 71; Castle telegrams (25, 31) to State Department, 10, 19 Feb. 1930, both HHPP 991.

[85] Stimson telegram to Cotton, 5 Feb. 1930, *FRUS 1929*, I, 18.

promoted the higher figure.[86] Pratt overruled him, arguing that the views of Stimson and the civilian representatives had priority – Pratt's appointment as chief of naval operations by Hoover on the eve of the conference suggests the president's determination to outflank the intransigents on the General Board. The decision to accept eighteen vessels was then incorporated in 'The Tentative Plan of the American Delegation', telegraphed to Washington on 4 February;[87] Hoover's approval came the next day. As the conference began its third week, the basis for an Anglo-American compromise had been achieved. All that now needed to be done was, first, to bring this in line with the parity principle as it touched light cruisers for the RN and USN and, then, find some way of blunting the Japanese demand for a 70 per cent ratio. These two goals became the focus of subsequent cruiser negotiations that lasted until 1 April.

Anglo-American agreement proved relatively straightforward. MacDonald and his experts held a series of discussions with Stimson and the Americans after 21 January.[88] By 7 February, after Hoover had approved the 'Tentative Plan', both delegations had circulated memoranda setting out their proposals for limiting all classes of warship.[89] They concurred on eighteen heavy cruisers for the USN and fifteen for the RN, although the American memorandum posited that 'Great Britain would have the option, by reducing the number of its small cruisers, to increase its large cruisers from 15 to 18 so as to give it a total tonnage of 327,000 tons, the exact amount of the tonnage which the United States now asks'. After this, Japan's requirements became the subject of negotiation. Conducted by Reed and Matsudaira, the search for an acceptable compromise took nearly two months.[90] The

---

[86] Jones daily journal, 28 Jan. 1930, plus Jones memoranda, 28 Jan., 5 Feb. 1930, all Jones 5.

[87] Stimson telegram (35) to State Department, 4 Feb. 1930, State Department telegram (55) to American delegation, 5 Feb. 1930, Stimson diary, 5 Feb. 1930, all Stimson 12. Cf. 'Comment by Rear Admiral Moffat [US naval expert]', 29 Jan. 1930, Gibson 109.

[88] Cf. MacDonald diary, 4–6 Feb. 1930, MacDonald PRO 30/69/1753; Jones memorandum, 30 Jan. 1930, Jones 5; Stimson diary, 26, 29 Jan., 3 Feb. 1930, 'Memorandum of conversation', 30 Jan. 1930, 'Memorandum of Conversation', 3 Feb. 1930, Stimson telegram (39) to Washington, 6 Feb. 1930, all Stimson 12. The British and Americans consulted the other delegations: see Stimson diary, 4 Feb. 1930, *ibid.*

[89] 'Statement by Henry L. Stimson ... February 6, 1930', 'Memorandum on the Position at the London Naval Conference, 1930, of His Majesty's Government in the United Kingdom', both in Foreign Office, *Documents of the London Naval Conference 1930* (1930), 513–14, 523–6. Cf. MacDonald diary, 7 Feb. 1929, MacDonald PRO 30/69/1753.

[90] Except where noted, this paragraph is based on minutes of meeting of British and American delegates, 11 Feb. 1930, MacDonald PRO 30/69/679; Henderson telegram (94) to Howard, 11 Feb. 1930, 'Notes of a meeting ... February 17, 1930', Henderson telegram (39) to Tilley, 15 Mar. 1930, 'Notes of a meeting ... April 2, 1930', plus

Americans won a hard-fought campaign to redefine heavy and light
cruisers: the former would conform to the Washington treaty maxima,
10,000 tons with eight-inch weapons; but the latter were now determined by gun calibres. This derived from the Americans having some
vessels exceeding 7,000 tons; hence, by arming them with six-inch guns,
they need not be scrapped. By 31 December 1936, the termination date
of the new treaty, the USN would be allowed eighteen eight-inch-gun
ships, the RN fifteen, and the IJN twelve. But because of tonnage
limitations in this class for the United States, Britain, and Japan –
respectively, 180,000, 146,800, and 108,400 – the Japanese received a
ratio of 66 per cent in numbers but only 60 – per cent in total displacement. Japanese compensation was to come from Britain and the United
States conceding a ratio of 70 per cent in six-inch cruisers, 70 per cent
in destroyers, and 100 per cent in submarines;[91] and to sweeten the deal
further, the Americans would slow down their construction to produce
just fifteen heavy cruisers by 1936.

For their part, the British wrested 50,000 tons more of six-inch-gun
ships than the Americans to compensate for the USN having three more
eight-inch vessels. And MacDonald and his advisers were able to get an
'escalator' clause included in the treaty: if any of the three Powers felt
that 'the requirements of [its] national security' were endangered by the
unanticipated construction of any non-signatory, they could, after
notification, increase tonnages in any category limited by the treaty.[92]
Although Britain might have surrendered the two-Power standard vis-à-
vis the United States and Japan, it had not done so respecting its
potential European rivals, France and Italy. Moreover, as the CID no
longer considered war plans against the United States,[93] the London
conference ratios gave Britain a two-Power standard against Japan
and either France or Italy. Along with the 'escalator' clause, this would
allow the RN the strength to protect British sea-lanes running out to
the Empire and adjacent to the home islands. Although opposition to
the cruiser portion of the treaty surfaced in each country during the
negotiations, particularly in the United States and Japan, it did not
prevent the conclusion of a cruiser agreement.

Appendix I, all *DBFP II*, I, 209, 227–33, 249–51, 282–7; Gibson 'Notes on the
Cruiser Problem', 3 Feb. 1930, Gibson 109; Stimson telegrams (156, 161, 195) to
Cotton, 23, 25 Mar., 2 Apr. 1930, all HHPP 987. Cf. Hall, *Arms Control*, 92–7;
O'Connor, *Equilibrium*, 76–83; Roskill, *Naval Policy*, II, 63–4.
[91] Articles 15 and 16, 'International Treaty for the Limitation and Reduction of Naval
Armament': Foreign Office, *Naval Conference*, 26–8.
[92] Article 21, *ibid.*, 30. Cf. Craigie to MacDonald, 12 Apr. 1930, CAB 21/343.
[93] Report on Defence Exercises, 22 Dec. 1927, CAB 53/15; 'Defence Exercise 2', CAB
53/18–19; COS memorandum, 'Imperial Defence Policy: Annual Review', 21 Jun.
1929, CAB 53/17.

Battleship limitation proved easier. A ten-year construction prohibition for vessels of this class – the 'naval holiday' – had been integral to the Washington treaty; it was to lapse in 1931. As battleships were the most expensive weapons of the time, expanded limitation would not only save the exchequers of the Powers considerable sums, but also aid the ratification of the treaties in each legislature by appeals to retrenchment in arms spending. As late as MacDonald's visit to the United States, Hoover had agreed that the USN might accept a scaling down of battleship displacement and gun calibres and, to compensate for the *Rodney* and *Nelson*, the right to build an equivalent 35,000-ton vessel. In this matter, the Japanese proved willing to follow any compromise worked out by the two English-speaking Powers for, as Stimson remarked to MacDonald on 17 January, 'the chief hold which we had over Japan – to persuade her to make a satisfactory agreement – was her desire to be relieved from the financial pressure of battleship replacement'.[94] Agreement on battleship limitation, therefore, fell to the British and Americans. Pre-conference deliberations within the American government overturned the possibility of scaling down. In the best Mahanian tradition, the USN General Board argued convincingly that the 'backbone of the fleet' should not be diminished.[95] It also asserted that in keeping with the 1921 ratio, battleship numbers should be reduced to fifteen each for Britain and the United States and nine for Japan. (By 1930, Britain had twenty, the United States eighteen, and Japan ten, the latter two Powers having not built to their permitted maxima.) This would mean scrapping five RN warships, three USN ones, and one of the IJN's; and, to counterbalance the RN's two post-Washington battleships, the USN would be allowed two new 35,000-ton vessels, the IJN one. After this, the United States and Japan would scrap an equal number of older vessels to bring full battleship parity into force by 1936.

In general terms, these proposals emerged in the American plan announced on 6 February. They found a receptive audience within MacDonald's ministry. During the pre-conference discussions within the British government, the Admiralty held firm to its demand for no reduction in numbers.[96] But with MacDonald pressing for a political settlement, and pacificists and economists dominating amongst ministers, the Cabinet countered: 'The battleship is simply and solely a ship of war, and as political security is strengthened it must stand to disappear.' Although still affirming the desire to scale down displacement and armament and extend age, the British memorandum of

---

[94] Stimson diary, 17 Jan. 1930, Stimson 12.   [95] O'Connor, *Equilibrium*, 71.
[96] This and the next sentence based on Madden memorandum, 15 Jan. 1930, and CC 1(30), in n. 80, above.

7 February also left room for reducing numbers. This produced discussions in February, March, and early April to find an acceptable limitation formula.[97] The desultory nature of this quest derived from battleship strength being tied to the cruiser question, as well as the problems posed by Franco-Italian differences. In addition, outside pressures were exerted on the British delegation by supporters of the iconoclastic naval thinker, Admiral Sir Herbert Richmond, who saw small battleships as more effective in future exertions of British naval strength.[98] Nonetheless, once cruiser limitation had been arranged in early April, the conference turned to battleships. The five Powers all saw the financial benefits of extending the 'holiday' to 1936, although the French and Italians refused to tie this to any reductions in the numbers of battleships their navies should possess. But while the British were willing to accept fifty cruisers and avoid the scaling down of battleships, they were averse to American and Japanese construction of new 35,000-ton battleships. When MacDonald refused to compromise on this point at the fifth Plenary Session of the conference on 14 April, Stimson withdrew the American demand and the three major Powers, having decided to push on without France and Italy, agreed to establish their battleship strength in the 15:15:9 ratio.[99]

Although MacDonald and Stimson were prepared after their 17 January conversation to ignore the French if need be, serious efforts to bring France into the expanded Washington naval treaty occurred until mid-March. Where the Americans, through Reed, took the lead in negotiating with the Japanese, the British endeavoured to break the Franco-Italian impasse. In initial discussions, the senior French delegates – Briand, the foreign minister in the latest government, and André Tardieu, the premier – seemed flexible despite pre-conference demands centring on the disarmament provisions of Versailles, tying any London agreement to air and land limitation, and arranging security guarantees. Consequently, as the conference began, MacDonald and Stimson

[97] Alexander to MacDonald, 4 Feb. 1930, MacDonald to Madden 11 Feb. 1930, both MacDonald PRO 30/69/676; Stimson telegrams (156, 161, 195) to State Department, 23, 25 Mar., 2 Apr. 1930, all HHPP 987; Morrow memoranda, 8, 28 Mar. 1930, Stimson R79. Then cf. 'Notes of a meeting ... February 13, 1930', 'Notes of a meeting ... February 17, 1930', 'Notes of a meeting ... March 12, 1930', 'Notes of a meeting ... April 2, 1930', with Appendix I, all *DBFP II*, I, 211–18, 227–33, 242–8, 282–7.

[98] On Richmond's ideas, see B. D. Hunt, *Sailor-Scholar. Admiral Sir Herbert Richmond, 1871–1946* (Waterloo, Ont., 1982), 189–207. Cf. Trevelyan [president, Board of Education, and Richmond's brother-in-law] to MacDonald, 27 Mar., 2 Apr. 1930, Alexander to MacDonald, n.d. [but 28 Mar. 1930], MacDonald to Trevelyan, 1 Apr. 1930, all MacDonald PRO 30/69/676; Alexander to Trevelyan, 1 Apr. 1930, AVAR 5/2.

[99] 'Sixth Report of First Committee', 12 Apr. 1930, 'Stenographic Notes of the Fifth Plenary Session of the Conference ... April 14th, 1930', Foreign Office, *Naval Conference*, 229–40, 505–7.

believed that a compromise could be arranged which would see the French accept approximate parity with the Italians in auxiliary craft based on the 1921 ratio.[100] For the first few weeks, progress seemed possible. But on 12 February, the French finally tabled specific figures: a total of nearly 725,000 tons, including provision for three new battleships, a force of ten Washington treaty heavy cruisers, and 100,000 tons of submarines.[101] MacDonald despaired: 'The French mentality is exactly what it was before the war. It allows no value for political security. It thinks in guns & bayonets.'[102] The next day, through Craigie, the British sought to soften French demands by suggesting that a consultative pact for the Mediterranean, akin to the four-Power Pacific treaty that had emerged at Washington in 1921, underpin French security.[103] Whilst MacDonald's government opposed a Mediterranean Locarno, which implied automatic sanctions against a violator of the status quo, it would be willing to do all possible 'within the limits imposed by public opinion [in Britain], to increase France's sense of security'. The collapse of Tardieu's government four days later delayed further negotiations.

When the French delegation returned in early March – again led by Tardieu and Briand – compromise had become impossible. The Italians had finally produced their proposals, which amounted to equality with the French; along with reports from Paris and Rome indicating that neither government would entertain concessions, MacDonald and Stimson concluded that any chances for compromise were slipping away.[104] Confirmation came on 16 March, when Tardieu met separately

---

[100] MacDonald diary, 22, 23, 27 Jan. 1930, MacDonald PRO 30/69/1753; Stimson diary, 21, 23 Jan. 1930, with Morrow memorandum [of a private meeting of senior British, American, and French delegates], 21 Jan. 1930, 'Memorandum of conversation at the Prime Minister's Office [between the British and Americans]', 30 Jan. 1930, both Stimson 12.

[101] 'Statement by the French Delegation', 'Statement by the French Delegation to the Press', both 12 Feb. 1930, Foreign Office, *Naval Conference*, 515–22. Cf. Tyrrell telegram (25) to FO, 10 Feb. 1930, FO 371/14258/1151/1.

[102] MacDonald diary, 14 Feb. 1930, MacDonald PRO 30/69/1753.

[103] This and the next sentence based on 'Note by Mr. Craigie of a Conversation with M. Massigli', 13 Feb. 1930, *DBFP II*, I, 209–11. Cf. Craigie to Hankey, 24 Feb. 1930, CAB 21/339.

[104] 'Memorandum Setting Forth the Position of the Italian Delegation at the London Naval Conference', 'Explanatory Note for the Press Issued by the Italian Delegation', both 19 Feb. 1930, Foreign Office, *Naval Conference*, 527–32. On the lack of compromise, Henderson to Graham, 20 Feb. 1930, Tyrrell to Henderson, 24 Feb., 4 Mar. 1930, all Henderson FO 800/281; Stimson to Nan, 22 Feb. 1930, Morrow memoranda, 24 Feb., 8 Mar. 1930, Reed to Borah, 5 Mar. 1930, Stimson to Hoover, 11 Mar. 1930, all Stimson R79. On MacDonald and Stimson's growing antipathy towards the French, see MacDonald diary, 23 Feb., 7, 11 Mar. 1930, MacDonald PRO 30/69/1753; Morrow memorandum, 27 Feb. 1930, 'Confidential Memorandum of a Conversation Between Prime Minister MacDonald and H. L. S[timson].', 5 Mar. 1930, Stimson diary, 12 Mar. 1930, all Stimson 13.

with MacDonald and Morrow.[105] The British and Americans now recognised that a three-Power treaty would be the goal of the conference. The result was the final settlement of the cruiser and battleship questions involving the British, Americans, and Japanese and confirmed at the fifth Plenary Session on 14 April. That MacDonald and Stimson were intent on removing Anglo-American naval differences regardless of the other Powers can be seen in mid-March when Stimson told Wakatsuki that he and MacDonald were willing to conclude 'a two power treaty' come what may.[106]

On 22 April, after feverish work to bring the disparate elements of the agreed formulae together in acceptable language, the British, their dominion representatives, the Americans, and the Japanese signed the London naval treaty.[107] It extended the 'holiday' for the revised battleship numbers to December 1936; it brought parity in cruisers between the RN and USN whereby the Americans received an extra 30,000 tons of eight-inch-gun ships, and the British 50,000 tons more of six-inch vessels; the Japanese received an improved ratio for auxiliary craft over that which they got in 1921 for capital ships; and the 'escalator' clause allowed each Power, but especially Britain and Japan, to increase tonnages in any category should construction by any non-signatory endanger perceived requirements of national security. The delegates adjourned by agreeing that further discussions would be undertaken by the British to bring the French and Italians into the treaty – although the treaty allowed the French and Italians to construct capital ships authorised at Washington in 1921 but not yet laid down. Like all negotiated settlements, the London naval treaty represented compromise. The British reduced their cruiser number to fifty, a cut of 30 per cent from the seventy demanded since 1927; the American heavy cruiser requirement dropped by one-third compared with that demanded when MacDonald took office; the Americans and Japanese accepted no new battleship construction until 1936; and the Japanese received an improved ratio for vessels under 10,000 tons.

But such compromises should not have been unexpected. Since the twilight months of the second Baldwin government, there had been a realisation on both sides of the Atlantic that Anglo-American naval rivalry should end. The problem was how to do this without repeating 1927. And as the British and Americans understood even before Labour

---

[105] MacDonald diary, 16 Mar. 1930, MacDonald PRO 30/69/1753; Stimson diary, 16 Mar. 1930, with Morrow 'Memorandum of a Conversation', 16 Mar. 1930, Stimson 13.
[106] Stimson diary, 12 Mar. 1930, Stimson 13.
[107] Hankey minutes to MacDonald, 11, 12 Apr. 1930, British Delegation 'Notes for the Chairman', 14 Apr. 1930, all CAB 21/343; 'Stenographic Notes of the Sixth Plenary Session . . . April 22nd, 1930', Foreign Office, *Naval Conference*, 253–78.

took office, any naval settlement would have to be essentially a political one. At the London conference, this translated into accepting restrictions on the RN, USN, and IJN that might not meet the desires of naval officers like Madden and Jones, but which were exchanged for an agreement that obviated discord and reduced government arms spending. Indeed, Jones left London at the end of February because of ill-health; whilst infirmity might have been the reason for his departure, his inability within the American delegation to promote the hardest of hard lines seems equally crucial.[108] But even he could not prevent the ratification of the London treaty once back in the United States, in the same way that die-hards in Britain and Japan could not in their countries.

No one at that time disputed that the London naval treaty was imperfect, that it could be broken, or that it might not prevent the Powers from circumventing it by means fair or foul. There is much truth in Jones' comment that:

While the treaty runs it undoubtedly puts an end to competition, [but] the treaty has merely transferred competition to subjects not mentioned in the treaty, and chiefly to the skill of the naval inventor. For navies are, by their very nature, *competing instruments who have no excuse for existence if they are not able to win* in battle competition.[109]

In this, he shared the views of treaty opponents in Britain like Churchill, who told Baldwin in May 1930, 'the arsenals of all the signatory Powers will be clanging for the next five years with large additions to existing naval strength'.[110] However, Stimson epitomised the temper of the times when he remarked at the sixth Plenary Session: 'We believe that naval limitation is one of the most accurate measures of the world's belief in the possibility of the settlement of all international matters by pacific and rational means.'[111] Here the leaderships in London and Washington were at one, their views supported by domestic opinion, so that in Britain and the United States, as well as in Japan, the treaty was ratified despite powerful opposition.[112] These accomplishments derived largely from Anglo-American co-operation that, although buffeted by minor nuisances like American anxiety over Britain and the dominion governments having six votes in committee,[113] gained strength as the delibera-

---

[108] Jones to Andrew [USN rear-admiral], 17 Feb. 1930, Jones 2.
[109] Jones 'Comment on the Treaty of London', n.d. [but Summer 1930], Jones 5. Emphasis in original.
[110] Churchill to Baldwin, 17 May 1930, Baldwin 117.
[111] Foreign Office, *Naval Conference*, 265.
[112] Hall, *Arms Control*, 105–9; O'Connor, *Equilibrium*, 109–21. The United States ratified in July, Britain in August, and Japan in October.
[113] 'Memorandum of conversation at the Prime Minister's Office', 30 Jan. 1930, Stimson 12.

tions progressed. Of course, on some matters, pre-conference objectives had to be jettisoned. In the British case, submarine abolition proved untenable, though no one in London, except George V, seemed broken-hearted by this development. But it remains that Anglo-American naval rivalry dissipated in a warming transatlantic political atmosphere and, from the perspective of London and Washington, Japanese ambitions were contained. Whilst some impediments remained, like those tied to Franco-Italian rivalry, they were small beer and could be addressed later. The London naval conference removed the emotive issue of naval rivalry that had buffeted Anglo-American relations since the Great War. The question is did Britain's concession of formal parity with the United States weaken London's ability to underpin its foreign policy with strength? The simple answer is no. And this is because the London naval treaty was a political document that sealed a political deal over naval weapons. For instance, whilst the British wanted seventy cruisers, the RN actually had just about fifty at the end of 1929; the USN seventeen; and the IJN thirty-four. The debate at London, and in the two-and-a-half years since the Coolidge conference, had been over theoretical limits to the British, American, and Japanese navies, not over limiting actual vessels.[114] Here, men like Jones in the United States, Churchill in Britain, and Japanese naval hardliners like Admiral Katō Kanji were

114	Britain	United States	Japan
Capital ships			
Battleships and	19	17	10
battlecruisers	550,000 tons	502,000 tons	299,390 tons
Aircraft carriers	6	2 (1)	3 (1)
	104,300 tons	24,400 tons	65,658 tons
Cruisers			
Heavy	17	5 (9)	4 (4)
	165,930 tons	48,150 tons	40,000 tons
Light	32 (4)	12	33
	137,725 tons	76,900 tons	190,572 tons
Destroyers	142 (14)	215	125 (8)
	130,355 tons	240,537 tons	122,950 tons
Submarines	57 (7)	102 (2)	67 (5)
	53,756 tons	82,796 tons	72,525 tons

The numbers in brackets are vessels building; the tonnages of vessels building are not included. From *Jane's Fighting Ships* (1930). Official American figures, differing slightly in total tonnage, ships building, and so on, show the same disparities amongst the three major navies; see tables of fleet strengths built, building, appropriated for or authorised, as of 31 December 1929, in HHPP 999. The 'Summary Table of Fleet Strengths, Built, December 31, 1929' in *ibid.*, shows British total cruiser strength at 54, American at 12, and Japanese at 29.

justified in their criticisms of the London naval treaty. And for Jones, it meant putting a brake on the expansion of the USN, which was already weaker in numbers than either the RN or IJN. But foreign policy, in general, and its variant, arms control, are the art of the possible. The political leaderships in London and Washington had come to understand this even before June 1929. For the British, as the Foreign Office and Esme Howard had been arguing since at least late 1927, a naval agreement would not see the surrender of RN naval pre-eminence. Rather, it would satisfy American *amour propre*, take the wind out of the sails of 'Big Navy' advocates in the United States, and enhance the possibility of Anglo-American co-operation in other international endeavours. On the American side, it would promote Anglo-American co-operation whilst avoiding massive expenditure on warships. Such expenditure would damage American public finances since, as Hoover discovered, it cost twice as much per ton for American shipyards to build warships as it did for British ones; additionally, as Hoover surmised that the British would never allow the United States to surpass them in naval strength, a political settlement had to be the order of the day.[115] Not surprisingly, Hoover prepared American policy on the assumption that the British will to keep the RN at maximum strength would bring little benefit to the United States if hardline policies like those advocated by Jones triumphed within his government.

Thus, in 1930, just as in 1921, the British surrendered the symbol not the substance of sea power to the United States, especially when Britain's massive lead in merchant shipping added to its preponderance in fighting ships.[116] Several senior British naval officers felt that the RN had emerged from the London conference relatively unscathed, given that neither the USN or the IJN was being built to its allowed maximum. Fisher, for one, argued that the American climb-down from twenty-five heavy cruisers to eighteen had been a signal achievement of the negotiations and, given the United States record of never constructing what it was allowed, he posited that 'there is quite a reasonable chance she will only build 15 – the same number as ourselves'.[117] Japan presented problems, but as Fisher told Jellicoe: 'Japan is prohibited from building any more [eight-inch-gun ships] than she now possesses before 1936, so that a halt has been called in the type of cruiser most

---

[115] 'We cannot get parity by naval building; the UK can build for $\frac{1}{2}$ our cost and will continue to build as long as we do'; in unsigned memorandum [in Hoover's hand], n.d. [but Summer 1929], HHPP 998.

[116] See G. C. Kennedy, 'The 1930 London Naval Conference and Anglo-American Maritime Strength, 1927–1930', in McKercher, *Arms Limitation*, 149–71.

[117] The rest of this paragraph is based on Fisher memorandum for Jellicoe, n.d. [but April or May 1930], FHR 11.

dangerous to our sea communications and most ruinous for us to have built in the requisite number.' Representing that of other senior naval officers, Fisher's purpose now became simple: 'All possible pressure and argument should be brought to bear to make the Government lay down a Building Policy which will cover the period of the Treaty and put us in possession of every ton that the Treaty allows.'

In this, he was not unlike other members of the foreign-policy-making elite who had to utilise the diplomatic resources of the state to protect its external interests. Vansittart put this clearly in his first major assessment of the international situation after the conference.[118] Although the London treaty had ended Anglo-American naval rivalry, it did not eliminate other problems that might arise over the competing financial interests of the two Powers. Moreover, other potential threats to Britain remained. French and Italian refusal to sign the treaty might jeopardise British naval security in the Mediterranean. This needed addressing and, even as the ink on the treaty dried, Craigie began efforts in this direction. In addition, problems involving Germany and tied to reparations held the potential for trouble. Outside of Europe, the vehemence of domestic Japanese opposition to the settlement at London – delaying ratification until October 1930 – suggested some uncertainty in the Far East, despite the naval treaty and the four- and nine-Power pacts. But this was an issue that, like those relating to Europe, could now be given more time and energy because of improved Anglo-American relations.

In fact, the co-operative spirit in Anglo-American relations could help to resolve these problems in the interests of the two English-speaking Powers. Exchanging letters in May 1930, MacDonald and Hoover concurred in the desire to work together.[119] 'It has been such a pleasure to me to co-operate with you in this work,' wrote MacDonald. 'The mentalities of Europe will mean much negotiating and persuading on our part yet but we shall go on as best we can.' 'The world makes its progress in short steps,' Hoover responded, 'it is disheartening at times; but the main thing is to keep the light ahead. I do feel that we have laid foundations upon which we or others can build more greatly in times to come.' These sentiments were genuine, but they were now to be tested in Europe and the Far East by a series of financial and political crises spawned by the onset of a global depression that would shake not only the foundations of emerging Anglo-American co-operation, but those of the international order hammered out at Paris in 1919–20.

---

[118] Vansittart memorandum, 'An Aspect of International Relations in 1930' [CID 991–B], 1 May 1930, CAB 4/19.
[119] MacDonald to Hoover, 1 May 1930, Hoover to MacDonald, 14 May 1930, in Hoover to Stimson, 26 May 1930, Stimson R79.

2   The undermining of war debts and reparations, 1929–1932

> The fact is that France and America are both thinking of their forthcoming elections. Any Reparations settlement or adjustment must be accompanied by a corresponding settlement or adjustment of war debts. Hoover knows it but daren't say so.
>
> Neville Chamberlain, December 1931[1]

In October 1929, as MacDonald completed his American trip, the New York Stock Market collapsed. Although indications of Wall Street's weakness had appeared six months before, it was the events of October that precipitated the 'Great Depression'.[2] The capitalist system by the 1920s was a delicate and interlocking structure in which any disruption spread quickly to all its parts. Supply and demand largely determined prices for most basic raw materials, food, and industrialised goods in the global marketplace; and regional division of labour had developed whereby large areas prospered by producing specific materials and goods for sale abroad. Credit financed much of this production, an arrangement based on mutual confidence: lenders and investors would get their funds back; debtors would pay; and producers of food, raw materials, and industrial products would be able to sell at fair prices. Through this process, sellers could purchase from primary and secondary producers, debts could be honoured, and new investment could be undertaken. To ensure smooth financial transactions, there was a stable medium of exchange. Gold underpinned the major currencies, particularly sterling and the dollar. Although London and New York banking houses contested for advantage, this competition occurred within defined rules and was overseen to a degree by co-operation between the Bank of England and the FRBNY.

[1] Chamberlain to Hilda, his sister, 6 Dec. 1931, NC 18/1/764.
[2] The next two paragraphs are based on Aldcroft, *Versailles to Wall Street*; B. Eichengreen, ed., *The Gold Standard in Theory and History* (New York, 1985); Clarke, *Central Bank Cooperation*; J. K. Galbraith, *The Great Crash* (1955); C. P. Kindleberger, *The World in Depression, 1929–1939* (1973); Kunz, *Gold Standard*, 8–28; Moggridge, *British Monetary Policy*; P. Williamson, 'Financiers, the Gold Standard and British Politics, 1925–1931', in J. Turner, ed., *Businessmen and Politics* (1984).

Wall Street's collapse undermined this interlocking system. Technically, it began as a financial problem in the United States – stocks were overvalued. But as stock prices tumbled, the crisis passed from finance to industry. American commodity prices began falling and spread abroad. This situation became complicated when, even before October 1929, the American Congress considered increased customs duties: the Smoot–Hawley tariff. When signed reluctantly by Hoover in June 1930, it raised rates on agricultural raw materials and other goods. Wall Street's weakness constricted American export of capital, as American creditors began calling in their loans. But these were to be paid in dollars, and as European and other debtors confronted higher American tariffs that made acquiring dollars difficult, the confidence that had marked the 1920s declined. International commodity prices fell, debts contracted before 1929 were paid with difficulty, if at all, and unemployment emerged everywhere. Tied to regular liabilities, like capital investment, were special ones incurred in the 1920s: war debts and reparations. In full swing by mid-1930, the general international economic and financial malaise continued for the rest of the decade. It affected Britain and the United States. As naval limitation in the 1920s had shown, it was not solely economic and financial concerns that defined their relationship. But as fiscal dislocation reshaped international politics in the 1930s, the political contours of Anglo-American relations altered. Just as naval limitation was achieved, Anglo-American relations entered a phase quite unlike that either predicted or wanted by MacDonald and Hoover.

In the background, other influences were at work in both countries. Generally, the 'Roaring Twenties' were a time of optimism, of possibilities prompted by prosperity, of beliefs that a new world had been forged on the battlefields of the war, and of increases in material comfort made possible by modern technology and available for those willing to work to acquire them. This optimism is seen best in literature, then dominated by 'modernism': 'aesthetic concentration, imaginative intensity and boldness, a stress on individual sensitivity, a corresponding indifference to purely social values, and a certain contempt for the recent past (which may, however, be associated with attachment to a "tradition" embodying the more remote past)'.[3] Writers from the British Isles like W. B. Yeats, D. H. Lawrence, and Aldous Huxley, joined by Americans such as F. Scott Fitzgerald, Ernest Hemingway, and William Faulkner struck out in new directions. Their work and that

---

[3] This is Spender's definition. Cf. B. Bergonzi, 'The Advent of Modernism 1900–1920', in Bergonzi, ed., *The Twentieth Century* (1970), 17–18; S. Spender, *The Struggle of the Modern* (1963).

of others poked and prodded at politics and social structures, but suggested that hope existed to realise human values.[4]

After October 1929, optimism crumbled. The 'Hungry Thirties' witnessed the general impoverishment of the British and American working and middle classes, the advent of beliefs that the new order created after 1918 was flawed, and the difficulty of hard work achieving material gain. Lawrence, Eliot, Hemingway, Fitzgerald, and the rest saw their comfortable world disappear; more astringent writers, like Christopher Isherwood in Britain and John Steinbeck in the United States, graphically described the Depression's debilitating impact on society, the tensions between returning to older values or pursuing more radical prescriptions and, in Steinbeck's case, the justified use of violence to meet the wrongs of those in authority.[5] In 1925, one of Huxley's characters remarked:

I don't see that it would be possible to live in a more exciting age ... The sense that everything's perfectly provisional and temporary – everything, from social institutions to what we've hitherto regarded as the most sacred scientific truths – the feeling that nothing, from the Treaty of Versailles to the rationally explicable universe, is really safe, the intimate conviction that anything may happen, anything may be discovered – another war, the artificial creation of life, the proof of continued existence after death – why, it's all infinitely exhilarating.[6]

After 1930, exhilaration diminished. Fitzgerald, the most transatlantic of Anglo-American writers, observed as late as 1938: 'Often I have encouraged [that his daughter find a profession] because my generation of radicals and breakers-down never found anything to take the place of the old virtues of work and courage and the old graces of courtesy and politeness.'[7]

The domestic milieu of the 1930s from which both British and American foreign policy sprang differed from that of the 1920s. Baldwin's victory in October 1924 ushered in four-and-a-half years of good, if uninspired, government which not even the 1926 General Strike

[4] M. Bradbury 'The Novel in the 1920s', in Bergonzi, *Twentieth Century*, 180–221; M. Bradbury, 'Style of Life, Style of Art and the American Novelist in the Nineteen Twenties', in M. Bradbury and D. Palmers, eds., *The American Novel and the Nineteen Twenties* (1971), 11–26.

[5] C. Britch, 'Steinbeck's "Breakfast": Godhead and Reflection', in C. L. Lewis and C. Britch, eds., *Rediscovering Steinbeck: Revisionist Views of his Art, Politics, and Intellect* (New York, 1989), 7–32. Cf. V. Cunningham, *British Writers of the Thirties* (Oxford, 1989); S. Hynes, *The Auden Generation. Literature and Politics in England in the 1930s* (1976).

[6] A. Huxley, *Those Barren Leaves* (1925), 34–5.

[7] Fitzgerald to his daughter, July 1938, in A. Turnbull, ed., *The Letters of F. Scott Fitzgerald* (New York, 1963), 36. Cf. P. Fussell, *The Great War and Modern Memory* (1975); R. Wohl, *The Generation of 1914* (Cambridge, MA, 1979), 1–4, 85–121, 203–37.

deflected from its efforts to diminish class tensions and increase prosperity.[8] Labour's election in May 1929 suggested a desire by British voters to spread the wealth more evenly. On the other side of the Atlantic, Hoover's rise to power promised a continuation of Republican 'normalcy' that began in 1920. The Depression changed everything. London and Washington retrenched to keep taxation at acceptable levels. Social policies assumed greater priority, as did alleviating unemployment by increasing industrial production and trade. The problem was that essential British and American foreign policy interests did not change. Internationally, economic dislocation strained the war debt and reparations settlements, leading in part to the rise of Adolf Hitler and the recrudescence of aggressive German foreign policy. It also provided the incubus for discrediting Japan's civilian leaders, who used economic diplomacy to extend Japanese power, and accentuated the rise of militarists who saw armed force as a better method of protecting and enlarging Japanese interests. Hence, the domestic financial and economic impact of the Depression affected international finance and economics and, in turn, the wider political and strategic concerns of the Powers. Such developments played havoc with the Washington and Locarno treaties and the League's quest for disarmament, undercutting the feelings of security that had arisen after 1925. These interconnected issues – domestic politics conditioned by the Depression, changing domestic priorities, and immutable external interests in a volatile international environment – affected the Anglo-American relationship after October 1929.

Given the nature of the crisis, the war debt and reparations regimes came under assault. Actually, in October 1929, the Dawes agreement was being revised. Since the Dawes Plan had not tied German reparations to a fixed schedule of payments, it had been provisional. By the end of 1927, the agreement had helped the German economy recover from the catastrophe of 1922–3. This occurred in several ways: through American loans; through political controls imposed on the German economy to ensure payment (like appointing foreigners to the board of the German National Railroad); and, outside the Plan, as a result of the security offered by Locarno. In late 1927, Germany's economic rejuvenation prompted both Stresemann and Parker Gilbert, an American appointed to administer the agreement in Berlin, to advocate revising Dawes' payment schedule and eliminating foreign

<hr />

[8] B. Pimlott, *Labour and the Left in the 1930s* (1977), 9–20; J. Ramsden, *The Age of Balfour and Baldwin* (1978), 188–294; R. Rhodes James, *The British Revolution: British Politics 1880–1939* (1977), 187–238.

political control.[9] Stresemann did so to overcome domestic critics, who argued that Locarno no longer protected German interests, and to end foreign military occupation of the Rhineland, imposed in 1919 to ensure German fulfilment of Versailles. For his part, Gilbert reckoned that a new reparation scheme would reduce German overborrowing in the United States, augment foreign investor confidence, and commercialise reparation bonds. If revision occurred at a time of calm, Gilbert argued, unlike that in 1924 following the Ruhr occupation, the chances for a lasting settlement would be enhanced.

Since revision hinged on French concurrence, London and Washington had to move carefully. The French had concluded war debt settlements with the British and Americans in April and July 1926. Since payment depended on what France received from Germany in gold and in kind, these agreements had yet to be ratified by the National Assembly. To avoid antagonising the British and Americans, Paris made provisional debt arrangements after 1926; but before ratifying the main agreements, Briand and other ministers wanted assurance that future German transfers covered France's contracted obligations.[10] They did not oppose revision as long as German reparations covered French debt obligations; however, Stresemann wanted the unconditional end of the Rhineland occupation. Here security, tied to Locarno, a purely Anglo-French-German concern, touched reparations and war debts, a wider issue involving the United States.

By June 1929, the diplomatic ground had been prepared to revise Dawes and remove Allied troops from the Rhineland. This had not been easy. In December 1928, Chamberlain and Briand quarrelled with Stresemann's proposal for unconditional evacuation.[11] German gains had to be purchased; the price was an amended reparations agreement. Yielding, Stresemann won the point that any committee struck to produce such an agreement must be composed of non-governmental experts – he wanted to distance reparations from politics. Whilst Coolidge and Hoover supported a committee of private experts, they cleaved to the established American policy that war debts had no link to

---

[9] Jacobson, *Locarno Diplomacy*, 143–7; B. Kent, *The Spoils of War. The Politics, Economics, and Diplomacy of Reparations, 1918–1932* (Oxford, 1989), 272–3; M. Piesche, 'Die Rolle des Reparationsagenten Parker Gilbert während der Weimarer Republik (1924–1930)', *Jahrbuch für Geschichte*, 18(1978), 135–69. Cf. Cmd. 2263; 'Reports of the Expert Committees Appointed by the Reparation Commission (1924)', Reparation R1; 'The Experts' Plan for Reparations Payments (1927)', 'Report of the Agent-General for Reparations Payments (10 December 1927)', both *ibid.*, R2.

[10] D. Artaud, *La question des dettes interalliées et la reconstruction de l'Europe (1917–1929)*, vol. II (Paris, 1978), 774–878.

[11] Chamberlain to Tyrrell, 18 Dec. 1928, to Graham, 18 Dec. 1928, to Rumbold, 19 Dec. 1928, all Chamberlain FO 800/263. Cf. Jacobson, *Locarno Diplomacy*, 232–3.

reparations.[12] Consequently, Washington supported revision as long as the existing debt agreements remained untouched. This ran against the long-standing British argument, outlined in the Balfour note of 1922, that war debts be reduced – even eliminated – to facilitate Europe's economic and financial reconstruction. However, Baldwin's chancellor of the Exchequer, Churchill, had met with Gilbert and Raymond Poincaré, the French premier, in September 1928;[13] convinced that Germany could pay its reparations, which Britain could use to honour its debt agreement with the United States, Churchill persuaded the Cabinet to support revision.

With this settled, a new committee of experts representing Germany, the United States, and the four principal Allied Powers (Belgium, Italy, Britain, and France) met in Paris beginning in January 1929.[14] Chaired by an American industrialist, Owen Young, this committee reported on 7 June 1929, the day MacDonald's Cabinet was sworn in. The 'Young Plan' had five essential parts: Germany's annual payment be reduced to an average of 2 billion marks from the Dawes total of about 2.5 billion; Belgium, Italy, and France should receive indemnities to cover war damages; German transfers to these three Powers, plus Britain, should cover their annual 'outpayments', their war debt payments to the United States; because the United States would not discount its debt claims, to be paid by 1988 in all the debt funding agreements, Germany's schedule of payments should stretch over fifty-nine years; and an independent body, the Bank for International Settlements (BIS), be created to replace the existing control bodies to receive and distribute reparations. The Young Plan succeeded in two ways: by fixing the sum payable by Germany and by making reparations a commercial matter.

As in any negotiation, compromises became necessary and, here, British and American reactions were important. The Young experts reduced Britain's portion of German reparations from 22 to 20 per cent, whilst German payments in kind, particularly coal, which had damaged British continental trade after 1920, were to continue for another decade. The Foreign Office saw this as the price for continental stability; the Treasury felt any reduction damaged Britain's fiscal prestige.[15] This

[12] Howard telegrams (417, 418) to Chamberlain, both 24 Dec. 1928, *DBFP IA*, VI, 6–7. Hoover memorandum, 4 Feb. 1923, HHPP 1006 shows his consistency over the long term. Cf. Borah, 'Note', n.d., Borah 761.

[13] Churchill memorandum, 14 Sep 1928, Churchill [draft] to Poincaré, 24 Oct. 1928, both M. Gilbert, *Winston S. Churchill*, companion vol. V, part 1 (1976), 1337–9, 1363–5. Cf. Artaud, *La question*, II, 897–9; Kent, *Spoils of War*, 282.

[14] Artaud, *La question*, II, 901–8; Jacobson, *Locarno Diplomacy*, 239–76; Kent, *Spoils of War*, 287–303. The 'Young Plan' is in J. W. Wheeler-Bennett and H. Latimer, *Information of the Reparation Settlement* (1930), 173–234.

[15] Sargent [FO] to Wigram [British Embassy, Paris], *DBFP IA*, VI, 333–4; Leith-Ross

divergence led Sir Frederick Leith-Ross, the deputy controller of finance at the Treasury, to minute: 'Locarno &c. ought not to be fundamentally shaken by the British Government defending its interests and calling upon its Allies to fulfil their obligations under existing agreements.' Firm in opposing debt reduction – Washington distanced itself from what it portrayed as a private agreement – Hoover was apprehensive that the debtor Powers were tying war debts and reparations together through the medium of the BIS. To prevent this, he decided that his government would not participate in creating the BIS. Of this Stimson noted: 'we should have drifted into the position of debt-collector against Germany and that would have gone far to prevent any reconciliation between this country and her'.[16] Still, as other Powers had concerns – notably Germany's annoyance that reparations were not further reduced – the reparations issue seemed resolvable just as MacDonald and Hoover began the delicate naval negotiations that occurred during the summer. A conference was to meet in August to give form to the Young proposals.

By the time this conference convened at The Hague on 6 August, British policy concerning reparations and the Rhineland evacuation had undergone profound change. This derived from the advent of the Labour government which, because of MacDonald's concentration on naval policy, saw handling of the Young Plan fall to Henderson and Philip Snowden, the chancellor of the Exchequer. Both men had criticised the Baldwin government's European policies, their attitudes reflecting Labour Party antipathy to the course of British foreign policy since 1925: Locarno's regional focus undermining the ideal of universal League collective security; the lack of progress on arms control; and Britain's failure to sign the 'Optional Clause'. These attitudes surfaced in the Labour Party election manifesto, published in 1928, as well as in the writings of Henderson, Dalton, and Philip Noel-Baker, Henderson's parliamentary private secretary.[17] Suffusing Labour views of Europe was a belief that Baldwin's government had been too ready to appease France; hence, when difficult decisions had to be made, like that over evacuating the Rhineland, Germany had been needlessly antagonised.

The British delegation to The Hague included Snowden, Henderson, Hankey, and Noel-Baker. The delegates met in two commissions: an

minute to Grigg, 11 Jul. [1929], on FO memorandum, 9 Jul. 1929, Craigie minute, 9 Jul. 1929, both T 172/1694.
[16] Stimson diary, 28 Aug. 1929, Stimson 10. Cf. Brown memorandum, 'The Young Reparations Plan. A Hasty Analysis', 24 Jul. 1929, HHPP 1015.
[17] Labour Party, *Labour and the Nation* (1928), 14–15, 41–3. Cf. A. Henderson, *Labour and Foreign Affairs* (1922); H. Dalton, *Towards the Peace of Nations. A Study in International Politics* (1928), esp. 141–66; P. Noel-Baker, *Disarmament* (1926).

economic one, dealing with the Young Plan; and a political one, charged with effecting the Rhineland evacuation. On the first day, Snowden supported fixing the schedule of payments, commercialising Germany's debt, and removing political controls from the German economy.[18] However, he attacked the reduction of Britain's share of reparations and the continuation of deliveries in kind. Opposing increases in German payments, he wanted the annual 2 billion marks proposed in the Young Plan redistributed to meet British requirements. In the Economic Commission on 8 August, he refused to discuss putting the Plan into operation until Britain's share was increased. His ploy angered the French, who had finally ratified the British and American debt agreements on 21 July 1929. Despite French threats to sell their sterling reserves to weaken Bank of England gold holdings, plus pressure from MacDonald and some American bankers to compromise, the chancellor refused to budge.[19] His intransigence forced the other Powers to concede and, by 28 August, Britain received an increase of 83 per cent in payments from Germany over that proposed in the Young Plan. However, because of time constraints, the conference adjourned three days later without giving practical form to the Young proposals. To keep discussions alive, seven committees were struck; the most important dealt with the constitution for the BIS, the amount of reparations that Germany's wartime allies, Austria and Hungary, should pay, and sanctions to be employed against Germany should it again purposely default on its commercialised or other debts.[20]

In the Political Commission, French hedging about evacuating the Rhineland convinced Henderson that Britain should unilaterally withdraw its troops. This conformed to both the election manifesto and Labour's general assertion that continued pressure on the Germans was counterproductive. More importantly, it showed that MacDonald's ministry now pursued foreign policy with greater regard to Labour-defined British interests. In this calculation, less reliance would be placed on regional commitments like Locarno and more on the League – at this juncture, the Cabinet was moving to sign the 'Optional Clause'. Therefore, on 19 August, when Briand evaded a specific date for French

[18] Philip, Viscount Snowden, *An Autobiography* (1934), 789–90. On Cabinet support, Snowden memorandum, 15 Jul. 1929, *DBFP IA*, VI, 420–6; CC 29(29)6 and 30(29), both CAB 23/61.
[19] Carlton, *MacDonald Versus Henderson*, 44–6. Cf. Hankey to MacDonald, 7, 11 Aug. 1929, both CAB 21/317.
[20] Leith-Ross memorandum, 'The Probable Effects of a Failure to Reach Agreement at the Hague Conference', n.d., in Leith-Ross to Grigg, 26 Aug. 1929, T 172/1694; cf. Treasury memorandum, 'The Young Plan and Sanctions', 10 Dec. 1929, T 172/1379, parts 5–7. For a conference summary and work to be done by the committees, see British delegation memorandum [CP 238(29)], 31 Aug. 1929, CAB 24/205.

evacuation, Henderson opened negotiations with Stresemann to have all British forces out of Germany by 31 December 1929.[21] Snowden's actions isolated Briand. Labour diplomatists were not going to court the French by accepting reduced reparations, nor were they about to base a decision about withdrawing British occupation troops on an elastic French timetable. Although Paris opposed modifying the reparations proposals, British and German pressures forced it to negotiate a firm date for pulling Allied troops out of the Rhineland. As the conference adjourned, the French agreed to remove their troops from the Rhineland, which was then to be demilitarised, by 30 June 1930.[22] This would be contingent on putting the Young Plan into practice.

A second Hague conference to this end convened in January 1930. In the interim, two series of events enhanced the emerging spirit of co-operation in Anglo-American relations promoted by the naval negotiations. The first concerned the weakening of the personal relationships that underpinned Locarno. On 3 October 1929, Stresemann died. This removed the one German leader able to balance the demands of the Allied Powers with those of German nationalists like Hitler, who criticised reparations and the strictures imposed by Versailles.[23] Then, three weeks later, political problems in France forced a restructuring of the government there. Though Briand continued holding office until his death in March 1932, younger men like Tardieu and Pierre Laval, less accommodating towards both Britain and Germany, began to dominate French foreign policy.[24] Shaken by Chamberlain's eclipse and the actions of Snowden and Henderson in August, the tripartite collaboration that had distinguished the latter 1920s was evaporating. This did not unduly worry the Labour Cabinet, which was putting the League more at the centre of British foreign policy; and, importantly, Snowden's actions at the first Hague conference had general public support in Britain.[25] By the time the second Hague conference convened in

---

[21] Phipps [The Hague] to Sargent, 20 Aug. 1929, enclosing Henderson to Stresemann, n.d., *DBFP IA*, VI, 552–4; 'Note of a conversation', 21 Aug. 1929, *ibid.*, 556–60. Cf. Jacobson, *Locarno Diplomacy*, 328–9.

[22] British delegation memorandum [CP 238(29)], 31 Aug. 1929, CAB 24/205; Cmd. 3417.

[23] G. A. Craig, *Germany 1866–1945* (Oxford, 1981), 498–524; R. Grathwohl, *Stresemann and the DNVP: Reconciliation or Revenge in German Foreign Policy, 1924–1928* (Lawrence, KS, 1980); P. Krüger, 'Die "Westpolitik" in der Weimarer Republik', in H. Köhler, ed., *Deutschland und der Westen* (Berlin, 1984), 105–30.

[24] J. Néré, *The Foreign Policy of France from 1914 to 1945* (1975), 81–5, 89–92; V. J. Pitts, *France and the German Problem. Politics and Economics in the Locarno Period, 1924–1929* (New York, 1987), 333–44.

[25] Carlton, *MacDonald Versus Henderson*, 53–5.

January, Locarno was ceasing to be the focal point of Britain's European policy.

The second series involved MacDonald and Hoover's approach to the progress of the Young Plan. After MacDonald's visit, Hoover suggested privately to Wilmot Lewis, *The Times'* Washington correspondent, that the moment seemed right to remove all impediments blocking good Anglo-American relations: the naval question, war debts, reparations, liquor smuggling, and 'commercial rivalry'.[26] Hoover would not countenance war debt reduction;[27] but, significantly, beyond blocking American government participation in creating the BIS, the Administration did not raise difficulties over the Young Plan connecting reparations and outpayments. There seems to have been an unspoken agreement by MacDonald and Hoover to avoid controversy over this matter by not discussing it.[28] At London, the Treasury wanted to assert Britain's international fiscal rights despite Foreign Office fear that the political impact of such a policy could rebound unfavourably in Europe.[29] Thus, on 20 November, over policy concerning British seizure of German property during the war, MacDonald forced a compromise between Snowden and Henderson that, more widely applied, ensured that Britain would not break the Young Plan.[30] The result was Anglo-American unity of purpose as the conference approached: Britain would not question the amount of war debt payments; the Americans would not dispute the connexion between reparations and Young Plan outpayments.

The second Hague conference began on 3 January and, because the seven committees had made substantial headway, completed its work within three weeks. In most respects this conference accomplished a

---

[26] Campbell to Lindsay, 24 Oct. 1929, in Campbell to Vansittart, 8 Nov. 1929, VNST II 1/3.

[27] Stimson telegrams (64, 83) to Schurman [US ambassador, Berlin], 14 Sep., 19 Nov. 1929, Castle memorandum, 19 Nov. 1929, all *FRUS 1929*, II, 1083–5, 1094–7, 1101; Campbell despatch (2158) to Henderson, 19 Nov. 1929, Henderson telegram (639) to Howard, 13 Dec. 1929, both *DBFP IA*, VII, 162–3, 242–4.

[28] 'Mr. Hard [a Hoover confidant] told me that there were two or three questions which he felt sure Mr. Hoover would rather not have touched in any conversations during your approaching visit . . . War Debts, the World Court, the League of Nations, and the Recognition of Russia'; in Howard to MacDonald, 28 Aug. 1929, DHW 9/63.

[29] Cf. Snowden to Henderson, in FO telegram (133) to Patteson [British Legation, Geneva], 19 Sep. 1929, Sargent to Phipps, 11 Nov. 1929, enclosing Treasury to FO, 20 Oct. 1929, Sargent to Wigram, 29 Nov. 1929, enclosing Leith-Ross to Sargent, 27 Nov. 1929, all *DBFP IA*, VII, 23, 131–2, 210–12.

[30] MacDonald diary, 20 Nov. 1929, MacDonald PRO 30/69/1753. On American concern, see Edge [US ambassador, Paris] telegram (560) to Stimson, HHPP 987. On Treasury negotiations, see Treasury memorandum, 'The Young Plan and Sanctions', 10 Dec. 1929, Leith-Ross to Grigg, 18 Dec. 1929, Leith-Ross minute to Snowden, 3 Jan. 1930, all T 172/1379. Cf. Sargent to Phipps, 20 Dec. 1929, PHPP 2/8.

great deal: the resultant agreement declared 'a complete and final settlement, so far as Germany is concerned, of the financial questions resulting from the war'; the Rhineland occupation would end on 30 June; future German defaults would be resolved by reference to the PCIJ rather than reliance on armed intervention; Austrian and Hungarian reparations were settled; and the BIS, with headquarters at Basle, was to begin operations in May. Crucially, the final settlement provided for further reductions of German reparations if Washington later agreed to scale down Allied war debts.[31] But beneath the satisfaction of British and American luminaries such as Snowden and Thomas Lamont, the anglophile senior partner of the American banking house J. P. Morgan,[32] difficulties remained. As London and Washington learnt from their embassies in Berlin and Paris, the final agreement generated German and French domestic pressures that might create difficulties outside the realm of international finance.[33]

In Germany, the Reichstag ratified the agreement on 26 March despite the protest resignation of Hjalmar Schacht, the Reichsbank president; the next day, however, under the onslaught of opposition criticism about the inadequacies of its economic programme, Chancellor Hermann Müller's cabinet resigned *en masse*. A new coalition took its place led by a Catholic centrist, Heinrich Brüning.[34] Supported by the Army leadership, Brüning faced down a majority in the Reichstag and, resorting to emergency powers conferred by the Weimar constitution, ruled by decree. To pay reparations and revive Germany's economy, Brüning imposed spending cuts, tight fiscal controls, tax increases, and other deflationary measures that gave additional public support to the opposition parties. Given that anti-Versailles parties like the National Socialists and Communists were focal points for dissatisfied Germans, Brüning confronted decided opposition.

In France, Tardieu faced attacks in the National Assembly concerning the Rhineland evacuation and the dismantling of political control over

[31] Carlton, *MacDonald Versus Henderson*, 59–69; Kent, *Spoils of War*, 313–21; Wheeler-Bennett and Latimer, *Reparation Settlement*, 137–69. The quotation is from Cmd. 3484, 18.
[32] Snowden to Phipps, 25 Jan. 1930, PHPP 3/5; T. W. Lamont, 'The Final Reparations Settlement', *FA*, 8(1930), 336–63. Cf. Egan [J. P. Morgan] to Hoover, 28 Dec. 1929, enclosing Lamont memorandum, 28 Dec. 1929, HHPP 1006.
[33] Tyrrell to Henderson, 13, 24 Feb., 4, 28 Mar. 1930, Henderson to Graham, 20 Feb. 1930, all Henderson FO 800/281; Noel-Baker to Dalton, 12 Mar. 1930, NBKR 4X/87/4; Dalton diary, 21 March 1930, BLEPS; Edge to Hoover, 17 Jan., 24 Feb. 1930, both HHPP 995; Morrow memoranda, 8, 10 Mar. 1930, Stimson to Hoover, all Stimson R79; Moffat [State Department] to Grew [US ambassador, Istanbul], 19 Feb. 1930, Moffat to Wilson, 12 Mar. 1930, both Moffat 1.
[34] Craig, *Germany*, 524–37; E. Eyck, *A History of the Weimar Republic*, vol. II (New York, 1963), 244–62.

the German economy.[35] He could not risk overturning the Young Plan given the developing Anglo-American accord on this matter, especially since France's debt agreements with Britain and the United States had been ratified. Nonetheless, too much has been made of Tardieu's apparent weakness *vis-à-vis* the two English-speaking Powers after October 1929.[36] Tardieu was a realist; whilst he could do little over reparations and war debts – where France's bargaining position was limited – neither he nor his colleagues showed any reluctance when protecting French interests in matters where France had strength.[37] Accordingly, when the London naval conference began just days after the second Hague conference ended, the French adopted the intransigent position that in April led them to refuse to sign the naval treaty. As Tyrrell told Henderson, 'unless the French get additional security either under the Covenant or the Kellogg Pact, reduction of armaments will remain impossible'.[38] Given the improving electoral chances of Hitler's National Socialists, hypercritical of all fetters placed on Germany by the Treaty of Versailles, strained Franco-German relations portended by domestic criticism of the Young Plan in both countries might threaten the balance of power in western Europe. The deepening Depression accentuated such problems.

It has been said of Britain that the 'politics of 1925–31 were ... the politics of unemployment'.[39] Yet these were the politics of all Powers touched by the Depression. Full application of the Smoot-Hawley tariff restricted foreign access to the American market, which brought protests from Powers that either needed dollars to pay their debts or saw United States purchases as crucial for their trade balances.[40] Except for those of Britain, which still adhered to general free trade, these protests were hypocritical. Germany, France, Italy, Japan, and other countries as diverse as Belgium and Canada also used protection to shore up their domestic economies. In addition, the availability of money declined as the London and New York money markets could not float loans to the

---

[35] C. Baechler, 'Une difficile négociation franco-allemande aux conférences de La Haye: Le règlement de la question des sanctions (1929–1930)', *Revue d'Allemagne*, 12(1980), 238–60.

[36] Kent, *Spoils of War*, 314–15.

[37] Cf. M. Claque, 'Vision and Myopia in the New Politics of André Tardieu', *French Historical Studies*, 8(1973), 105–29; J.-B. Duroselle, 'Les "invariants" de la politique étrangère de la France', *Politique Etrangère*, 51(1986), 12–23.

[38] Tyrrell to Henderson, 28 Mar. 1930, Henderson FO 800/281. Cf. Tyrrell despatch (360) to Henderson, 31 Mar. 1930, *British Documents on Foreign Affairs*, part II, ser. J, vol. 3 [hereafter in the form *BDFA*, II, J3], 303.

[39] Rhodes James, *British Revolution*, 479.

[40] Cf. German Embassy to State Department, 12 May 1930, Edge to Stimson, 3 Jul. 1930, enclosing Flandin [French minister of commerce] to Edge, 3 Jul. 1930, both *FRUS 1930*, I, 248–50.

degree they had done in the 1920s. With governments wedded to fiscal orthodoxy, prices for agricultural products, industrial raw materials, and factory-produced commodities depressed, and with even short-term loans difficult to arrange, there was a general recognition by late 1930 that the Depression would take time to overcome. This meant continued high levels of unemployment that threatened social cohesion and political stability. Playing havoc with other major international issues like the ongoing disarmament discussions, the expanding Depression undermined The Hague's 'complete and final settlement ... of the financial questions resulting from the war'.

The Powers saw unemployment, reduced production, and attendant social problems spawned by the Depression as essentially domestic economic questions; this necessitated fiscal measures like retrenchment and boosting trade. Significantly, however, they held war debts and reparations to be international political matters. As these interwoven issues centred on Germany and Young Plan outpayments, they chiefly affected Britain, France, and the United States, and involved whether Berlin would pay its annual 2 billion marks. In Germany by September 1930, the paucity of new loans tied to reduced industrial output had produced 3 million unemployed – a 100 per cent increase over a year before.[41] This strengthened Brüning's opponents. In elections that month for the 577-seat Reichstag, the chancellor's coalition won only 171 places; the National Socialists, whose total rose from 12 to 107, and the Communists, who went from 54 to 77, now were, respectively, the second and third largest parties.[42] During the election campaign, politicians of all stripes, including Brüning, argued that the existing restrictions on Germany had to be revised or removed.[43]

Conditioned by domestic pressures in Britain and the United States where unemployment also reached staggering proportions,[44] British and American diplomatic reactions to the fate of the Young settlement were not unimportant. Until mid-1931, the two Powers adopted a wait-and-see attitude dictated by the belief that the worst of the Depression might pass – and also by the need to concentrate more on domestic policy. In

[41] A. Bullock, *Hitler. A Study in Tyranny*, rev. edn. (Harmondsworth, 1962), 152.
[42] The Social Democrats, also opposed to Brüning, were the largest party (143 seats). E. W. Bennett, *Germany and the Diplomacy of the Financial Crisis, 1931* (Cambridge, MA, 1962), 9–11; Craig, *Germany*, 542–3.
[43] Rumbold [British ambassador, Berlin] despatch (723) to Henderson, 20 Aug. 1930, *DBFP II*, I, 502–4; Gordon [US Embassy, Berlin] telegram to Stimson, 15 Sep. 1930, Gordon despatch (486) to Stimson, 17 Sep. 1930, both *FRUS 1930*, III, 76–9.
[44] In 1929, British unemployment was 1.216 million (11 per cent); American, 1.55 million (3.2 per cent). In 1930, the figures were, respectively, 1.917 million (14.6 per cent) and 4.34 million (8.7 per cent). From Mitchell, *European Historical Statistics*, 167–71; Commerce Department, *Historical Statistics*, 135.

Britain, MacDonald, Snowden, and the Treasury reckoned that reparations should be left alone. The sentiments behind the Balfour declaration had not faded, but to reopen negotiations so soon after the second
Hague conference – and after the disputatious French and German
ratifications – would be counterproductive. In July, therefore, when the
Germans hinted at territorial revisions in the east and an early end to
French control of the Saar (scheduled to lapse in 1935), MacDonald's
government politely rebuffed them.[45] Then after the German elections,
when Julius Curtius, Brüning's foreign minister, suggested a moratorium on all inter-governmental debt payments, the Cabinet, Treasury,
and Foreign Office responded with emphatic opposition to both this and
any idea of revisions.[46] The Young Plan had taken a year to fashion in a
period of relative economic calm; to seek modifications during a time of
crisis, as Parker Gilbert had warned, offered slim chances for success. In
Washington, Hoover and Stimson sympathised with Germany's plight
and the other Powers' determination to link reparations and war debts.[47]
But the White House and the State Department would not reduce the
principal on war debts. Congressional opposition would be immediate,
a revised agreement would meet the same fate as the Versailles Treaty,
and ratification of other White House-sponsored legislation would be
threatened. When Schacht visited Washington in late October whilst
lecturing in the United States, Stimson told him that the Hoover
Administration saw the Young agreement as a contract that Germany
had to fulfil, and, to keep the record straight, he reported his discussion
to Lindsay and Paul Claudel, the French ambassador.[48]

London and Washington's wait-and-see attitude did not mean that
diplomatists of both Powers stood idle. By late 1930, prescient authorities in both the Foreign Office and State Department reckoned that
foreign policy should not ignore economic and financial questions. On
1 December, Sir Victor Wellesley, Vansittart's deputy under-secretary,
circulated a memorandum proposing a 'Politico-Economic Intelligence
Department' within the Foreign Office.[49] Supported by Dalton and

45 Rumbold despatches (546, 548) to Henderson, both 3 Jul. 1930, R.H. Campbell
[British Embassy, Paris] despatch (930) to Henderson, 13 Aug. 1930, all *DBFP IA*, I,
488–91, 493–4.
46 Rumbold despatch (864) to Henderson, 27 Oct. 1930, Henderson despatch (1159) to
Rumbold, 2 Dec. 1930, both *DBFP II*, I, 525–7, 535–9.
47 Stimson diary, 28 Dec. 1930, Stimson 10. Cf. Borah, 'War Debts', 19 Apr. 1932,
Borah 761.
48 Stimson memoranda (2), both 23 Oct. 1930, both *FRUS 1930*, III, 89–90. Cf.
Stimson diary, 19, 23 Oct. 1930, Stimson 10.
49 Wellesley memorandum, 'Proposal for the establishment of a Politico-Economic
Intelligence Department in the Foreign Office', 1 Dec. 1930, FO 371/14939/12855/
12855. Except where noted, this paragraph is based on D. G. Boadle, 'The Formation

Vansittart – Henderson was preoccupied with disarmament – problems quickly arose. Should the head be a career diplomat or an economist from outside government? How would the new division be funded? Would it duplicate the functions of existing agencies like the Department of Overseas Trade (DOT)? And how would this new body work with British embassies and legations abroad and other ministries in Whitehall, particularly the Treasury? After more than a year of discussion within the Foreign Office, plus consultations between Vansittart and Sir Norman Warren Fisher, the Treasury permanent under-secretary, Frank Ashton-Gwatkin, a diplomat, became Foreign Office co-ordinator of economic intelligence sent from British diplomatic posts. In this, Vansittart's desire to have professional diplomats manage this aspect of Foreign Office work triumphed – something helped by the Labour government's collapse in August 1931 and Dalton's return to the opposition benches. Whilst Ashton-Gwatkin believed his work bore fruit by the end of his first year in this post, the Foreign Office's ability to shape economic diplomacy was restricted. Part of the reason derived from the mandates of the economic ministries: the Treasury controlling government expenditure, the Board of Trade supervising trade policy, and the Bank of England overseeing fiscal policy.[50] The rest involved the traditional distaste that British diplomats had for commercial endeavours.[51] Moreover, the crush of traditional political diplomacy saw Ashton-Gwatkin work alone until June 1933, when he finally received an assistant and typist. Still, by early 1932, the Foreign Office had a window on economic and financial issues that it had not had before; and its purely political and strategic advice could now at least be better informed.

The American response was more effective. This devolved from Stimson who, by August 1930, saw the need for an 'Economic Adviser' within the State Department. His difficulty, he confided to Joseph Cotton, the assistant secretary, was a dearth of suitable candidates.[52] He wanted a political economist and, in early 1931, found one after reading a recently published book by Herbert Feis, a research associate on the

of the Foreign Office Economic Relations Section, 1930–1937', *HJ*, 20(1977), 919–36; E. O'Halpin, *Head of the Civil Service. A Study of Sir Warren Fisher* (1989), 184–6.

[50] Ashton-Gwatkin memorandum, 5 Jan. 1933, FO 371/17318/278/278; one of his successes was a circular questionnaire to foreign missions on the impact of tariffs on political policies. On the influence of other ministries and the Bank of England, see G. J. Andeopoulos, 'The International Financial Commission and Anglo-Greek Relations, 1928–1933', *HJ*, 31(1988), 341–64; P. J. Beck, 'The Anglo-Persian Oil Dispute, 1932–1933', *JCH*, (1974), 123–51; Boadle, 'Economic Relations Section', 927; Kunz, *Gold Standard*, 29–52.

[51] D. C. M. Platt, *The Cinderella Service: British Consuls since 1815* (1971).

[52] Stimson to Cotton, 18 Aug. 1930, Stimson R80.

Council of Foreign Relations. Although Feis had earlier examined domestic issues, his *Europe: The World's Banker, 1870–1914* touched a sensitive nerve in the secretary of state.[53] Analysing the connexion between diplomacy and international finance in the half-century before the Great War, Feis argued that the movement of capital abroad increased trade. He asserted that European capital, particularly British capital, gave strength to the investing Power before 1914; crucially, it also helped less developed states – a category into which Feis put the United States – that also sought markets. Feis saw international capitalism as symbiotic rather than exploitive; this prompted Stimson privately to gauge the man. Felix Frankfurter, an anglophile Harvard legal scholar, wrote a glowing reference: 'Work like [Feis's] is not the work of a merely bookish man, and he is not at all a bookish man.'[54] By May, Feis had become Stimson's chief financial adviser.

In this month, Anglo-American detachment from reparations and war debts ended when an Austrian banking crisis spread to Germany and threatened to shatter the fragile German economy. The antecedents of this affair involved French and German diplomatic manoeuvring to enhance their security one against the other. At the League Assembly in September 1929, Briand proposed a pan-European economic union to expand Franco-German reconciliation beyond Locarno. He envisaged a European trading bloc to compete better in the world and, more importantly, through beneficial tariffs and improved trade, obviate German territorial grievances – the impending Rhineland evacuation required a new device to contain German irredentism.[55] Stresemann's death and the politics leading to the rise of Brüning, the reconstruction of the French government, and difficulties attending the Young settlement postponed action until May 1930. Then, with the Young Plan ratified, Briand circulated a memorandum giving form to his original suggestion. However, the advent of Tardieu and pressures from France's eastern European allies saw the economic side of the September

---

[53] H. Feis, *Europe: The World's Banker, 1870–1914* (New Haven, 1930). For earlier work, see his edited *A Collection of Decisions Presenting Principles of Wage Settlements* (New York, 1924).

[54] Stimson to Frankfurter, 9 Apr. 1931, Frankfurter to Stimson, 13 Apr. 1931, both Stimson R81; Stimson diary, 25–27 Apr. 1931, Stimson 16. Frankfurter and Feis had been friends for more than a decade; cf. Frankfurter to Feis, 14 Nov. 1924, Feis to Frankfurter, 1 Feb. 1928, both Frankfurter 54.

[55] The rest of this paragraph is based on D. E. Kaiser, *Economic Diplomacy and the Origins of the Second World War. Germany, Britain, France, and Eastern Europe, 1930–1939* (Princeton, 1980), 13–16; W. Lipgens, 'Europäische Einigungsidee 1923–30 und Briands Europaplan um Urteil der deutschen Akten', *HZ*, 203(1966), 46–89, 316–63; F. J. Murphy, 'The Briand Memorandum and the Quest for European Unity, 1919–1932', *Contemporary French Civilization*, 4(1980), 319–30.

proposal overwhelmed by its political cousin: security needed to be tackled first to affirm the post-1918 European borders. Cognisant of the approaching election and deciding to court nationalist sentiments, yet unwilling to reject Briand's plan outright, Brüning's cabinet sent a non-committal reply in July. This helped beget a 'Commission of Enquiry for a European Union' at the League Assembly in September.

The Brüning government's subsequent response to Briand's May memorandum involved a proposal gestating in Berlin since November 1927: establishing an Austro-German customs union.[56] Such a union would have the double advantage over time of producing a German-dominated bloc of south-eastern European Powers – Austria, Bulgaria, Hungary, Romania, and, perhaps, Yugoslavia; this would strengthen Germany economically and, by weakening France's eastern European alliances, politically. Moreover, it could augment Germany's strategic position in central Europe by laying the basis for political union between Germany and Austria – *anschluss* – prohibited by the treaties of Versailles and Saint-Germain. Bernhard von Bülow, the state secretary in the German Foreign Office, commented baldly that '[w]hen Germany is strong and powerful and need not fear other states, she will be, thanks to her political, economic and moral strength, *the* state to which the new small states will look.' Whilst concern developed in Berlin and Vienna over the ill-favour such revision would generate amongst the other Powers, and whilst controversy exists over its position in Brüning's diplomatic thinking,[57] Curtius, Bülow, and others like Johann Schober, the Austrian foreign minister, won the day. Reasoning that Berlin had a strong bargaining position because neither Paris nor London wished to strengthen radical revisionists in Germany, Curtius believed that a customs union did not violate the treaties. In addition, Anglo-German relations seemed to be entering a new phase as MacDonald had sounded Brüning and Curtius about coming to London for disarmament talks.[58] On 21 March 1931, the Commission of Enquiry received the customs union proposal. Fusion of these two issues in the spring of

---

[56] Bülow memorandum for Brüning, 26 Aug. 1930, quoted in Kaiser, *Economic Diplomacy*, 16. Except where noted, the rest of this paragraph is based on *ibid.*, 23–66 *passim*; Bennett, *Financial Crisis*, 44–81 *passim*; O. Hauser, 'Der Plan einer deutsch-österreichischen Zollunion von 1931 und die europäische Föderation', *HZ*, 179(1955), 45–92; A. Orde, 'The Origins of the German-Austrian Customs Union Project of 1931', *CEH*, 13(1980), 34–59.

[57] Cf. W. Conze, 'Brüning als Reichskanzler: Eine Zwischen bilanz', *HZ*, 214(1972), 310–34; H. Graml, 'Präsidialsystem und Aussenpolitik', *Vierteljahrshefte für Geschichte*, 21(1973), 134–45.

[58] Rumbold to Henderson, 6 Mar. 1931, Rumbold despatch (194) to Henderson, 18 Mar. 1931, both *DBFP II*, I, 579–81.

1931 threatened the political balance of Europe which the Young settlement had helped underwrite. Although earlier reports from their embassies in Berlin suggested that unemployment, reduced production, and the burden of reparations might occasion 'a breakdown in the whole German economic system',[59] London and Washington refused initially to involve themselves in Germany's economic plight.[60] Judging disarmament more important in their diplomacy, Henderson and Stimson concentrated on the Preparatory Commission. With Stimson's support, Craigie had engineered a Franco-Italian compromise preparing the way for France and Italy to sign the London naval treaty.[61] The 'Bases of Agreement' for this compromise reached Parliament on 11 March;[62] but news of the customs proposal ten days later provoked unfavourable reaction in Paris. Suspecting that Austro-German economic union might produce *anschluss*, Paris distanced itself from the Italo-French compromise, in particular, and arms limitation, in general. Alexis St Leger, the political director of the Quai d'Orsay, warned Tyrrell's embassy: 'if the German government persisted in its present policy towards Austria, [France] could go no further in the way of concession'.[63]

Henderson and Stimson reacted strongly. The British foreign secretary moved first. In Paris during 23–25 March for a meeting of a sub-committee of the Commission of Enquiry, he urged referring the Austro-German proposal to the League Council for an opinion on its legality – in practical terms, a submission to the PCIJ.[64] Henderson was buying time. He needed a formula allowing Brüning and Curtius to forsake their scheme without losing face whilst deterring a French hard line that could delay the World Disarmament Conference. Even though the Germans refused to be swayed, the Austrians retreated because of western-Power influence over their economy. This allowed Henderson, working with Briand and Dino Grandi, the Italian foreign minister, to

---

[59] Cf. Rumbold despatch (998) to Henderson, 10 Dec. 1930, *ibid.*, 540–2; Sackett to Hoover, 27 Dec. 1930, HHPP 997.
[60] Sargent to Leigh [Henderson's secretary], 29 Jan. 1931, Henderson to Findlay [British academic], 3 Feb. 1931, both Henderson FO 800/283.
[61] Tyrrell to Henderson, 17 Feb. 1931, Craigie to Vansittart, 20 Feb. 1931, both *ibid.*; MacDonald to Craigie, 2 Mar. 1931, MacDonald PRO 30/69/677; Stimson memorandum, 20 Feb. 1931, Stimson 15; Castle to Gibson, 13 Mar. 1931, Castle 10; Armour [US Embassy, Paris] to Gibson, 2 Apr. 1931, Gibson 103; Mayer [US delegate, Preparatory Commission] memorandum, 5 May 1931, Gibson 107; Stimson to Baker, 8 May 1931, HHPP 1001.
[62] Cmd. 3812.
[63] Wigram memorandum, 27 Mar. 1931, in Tyrrell to Henderson, 27 Mar. 1931, Henderson FO 800/283. Cf. Stimson diary, 25, 29 Mar. 1931, Stimson 15.
[64] Henderson telegram (1) to Rumbold and Phipps, 25 Mar. 1931, *DBFP II*, II, 12–13.

win League Council agreement on 18 May to get a PCIJ ruling on the Austro-German proposal.[65] By securing Schober's assurance that Vienna would not conclude any agreement with Berlin until after the PCIJ decision, Henderson had time to look for his formula. For his part, Stimson planned to visit Rome, Berlin, Paris, and London in late June 'to get a personal survey of the chances of the great disarmament conference next winter'.[66]

Other issues now surfaced that forced American intervention in the war debts and reparations question. A week before the Council decision to approach the PCIJ, the Creditanstalt, Austria's largest private bank, announced massive losses.[67] Here lay Vienna's reason for backing off the customs union proposal, since the bank's looming failure forced the Austrian government to seek a massive BIS credit – 100 million schillings. Both the Bank of England and the FRBNY supported this move because, as Montagu Norman told Benjamin Harrison, his FRBNY opposite, 'a monetary breakdown in Austria might quickly produce a similar result in several countries'.[68] This credit did not staunch the flow of capital from Austria, nor did it prevent the crisis from spreading to Germany with a run on the mark and German creditors, particularly Americans, calling in their short-term loans. By early June, with the BIS credit proving inadequate, Norman and Harrison were considering supporting a new one.

On 6–7 June, Brüning and Curtius made their long-planned visit to Britain, meeting MacDonald, Henderson, Snowden, and Norman at Chequers, the prime minister's country retreat.[69] Whereas the original purpose of the talks had been to make headway on disarmament, the economic crisis dominated discussions. MacDonald and his economic advisers, heretofore reluctant to modify the Young settlement, now thought differently. The impetus for change came from the Treasury. That the German leaders attributed 'all evils [in Germany] to Reparations' – and specifically referred to Hitler – only bolstered Treasury arguments. Prior to the German visit, Leith-Ross had Sir Richard Hopkins, the controller of finance, assess 'the attitude of the German

[65] Henderson telegram (31) to Vansittart, 15 May 1931, 'Resolution of the League of Nations', 18 May 1931', both *ibid.*, 56–7.
[66] Stimson telegrams to US embassies in Rome, London, Paris, Berlin, 16 Apr. 1931, the replies of Dawes (17 Apr. 1931), Edge (17 Apr. 1931), Garrett (18 Apr. 1931), Stimson to Root, 25 May 1931, all Stimson R81.
[67] C. A. Gulick, *Austria from Habsburg to Hitler*, vol. II (Berkeley, 1948), 930–3.
[68] Quoted in Kunz, *Gold Standard*, 48.
[69] Except where noted, this paragraph is based on 'Summary of the Discussion with the German Ministers at "Chequers" ... June 7, 1931', *DBFP II*, II, 71–7. Cf. Bennett, *Financial Crisis*, 122–31.

Ministers' for the Foreign Office and Cabinet.[70] Hopkins accurately predicted that Brüning and Curtius would tie Germany's budget deficit, depressed prices, and more to reparations. Leith-Ross added that if the Germans deferred reparations, the French and Italians would suspend their debt payments.[71] As this would create a shortfall in annual British outpayments – £5.8 million out of £33 million – the Cabinet should postpone this amount of its American remittances, allowed under the 1923 debt agreement, and transfer such monies to other spending. 'One of the chief merits of the Young Plan,' Leith-Ross pointed out, 'was that it established a connection in fact between Reparation receipts and War Debt payments to America.' The critical moment at Chequers arose when Brüning indicated that Germany would seek a moratorium; he wanted it to begin in November 1931. This rekindled strain between MacDonald and his foreign secretary. Cognisant of Treasury concerns, the prime minister assured the Germans that his government would support Berlin diplomatically. However, Henderson was more concerned about arms limitation. Maintaining that the matter could only be resolved by an international conference – French susceptibilities had to be weighed carefully[72] – he argued that the Commission studying the Briand plan would be the best venue for renewed discussion of war debts. MacDonald disagreed. For him, the crucial Power to consider was the United States. Not only were reparations and outpayments linked, but the general question was one where Anglo-American co-operation could bring about a solution. Henderson's advice was brushed aside.

After Brüning and Curtius departed, MacDonald wrote Stimson 'an unvarnished and simple statement of what happened'.[73] Emphasising the immense domestic problems confronting Brüning's government, he also focused on achieving Anglo-American harmony:

I ought further to report to you that of course the United States was frequently mentioned and, in connection with that I took the liberty, which however bold and may be [*sic*] improper it was, I know that both you and the President will pardon because (a) it was purely an expression of personal opinion and (b) it was done with the hope that it would help us all . . . These men are facing a very

[70] Hopkins to FO, 22 May 1931, Leith-Ross T 188/16; the 'evils' comment is in MacDonald diary, 7 Jun. 1931, MacDonald PRO 30/69/1753.

[71] Leith-Ross memorandum, 'Postponement of British War Debt to U.S.A.', n.d. [but late May 1931], Leith-Ross T 188/16.

[72] Tyrrell to Vansittart, 31 May [1931], Henderson to Tyrrell, 1 Jun. 1931, Tyrrell to Henderson, 3, 4 Jun. 1931, all Henderson FO 800/283.

[73] MacDonald to Stimson, 8 Jun. 1931, Stimson R81. Cf. MacDonald diary, 8 Jun. 1931, MacDonald PRO 30/69/1753; and two letters from Boal [State Department] to Newton [Hoover's secretary], both 9 Jun. 1931, with enclosures, HHPP 987.

awful situation and anything which any of us can do to help them discreetly, really ought to be done.

MacDonald asked that Stimson continue characterising his forthcoming European trip as one designed to advance disarmament: 'If you give any sort of expectation that you are coming prepared to discuss economic and financial things, I think you will get badly involved in our troubles, and there will be one country on the Continent [France] which will get into a state of fuss and suspicion.' These tactical considerations aside, Stimson and Hoover were being asked to help settle the European economic crisis. When Stimson received a copy of MacDonald's missive by telegraph, he showed it to Hoover and observed: 'It was an admirable letter, fairminded in its spirit and perfectly frank with us, a model of what relations might be between two foreign offices.'[74]

As Hoover, Stimson, and their advisers, such as Feis, weighed the American response, the European situation worsened. The BIS balked at issuing a second line of credit to Austria. Consistent with the commercialisation of former enemy indebtedness that underpinned the Young settlement – and which created the BIS – it wanted an ordinary loan with adequate guarantees and an agreed schedule of payments. When this created delay, the French government offered a loan on 16 June, conditional on Austria formally rejecting the customs union.[75] Wanting to enhance Britain's financial interests, Norman moved to take the initiative away from the French and, with Snowden's concurrence, offered a 150 million schilling loan to the Austrians on 18 June.[76] Although Vienna backed off the customs union proposal, Berlin seemed loath to follow suit. But buffeted by a massive sell-off of marks, Germany faced a renewed budgetary crisis.[77] Brüning's government was going to ask for a moratorium; its policies in central Europe had antagonised the French; and the whole structure of war debts and reparations was now imperilled.

The Hoover Administration considered possible actions before the Chequers conversations and MacDonald's letter to Stimson. Frederic Sackett, the ambassador at Berlin, and his staff had sent reports since

---

[74] Stimson diary, 9 Jun. 1931, Stimson 16.
[75] Carlton, *MacDonald Versus Henderson*, 194–5; Gulick, *Austria*, II, 933–9.
[76] Feis 'Report, through Governor Harrison[,] of Norman of the Bank of England', 15 Jun. 1931, Stimson R81. Cf. MacDonald diary, 7 Jun. 1931, MacDonald PRO 30/69/ 1753. Kaiser, *Economic Diplomacy*, 38 correctly observes that Norman's move predated the French note; however, this does not diminish Norman's anti-French proclivities.
[77] Thelwall [British Embassy, Berlin] 'Memorandum on the Present Crisis in Germany', 8 Jun. 1931, Newton [British Embassy, Berlin] telegram to Henderson, 18 Jun. 1931, both *DBFP II*, II, 81–4, 85–6.

March about Germany's difficult economic straits.[78] Some State Department officials, like Jay Pierrepont Moffat, head of the Western European Division, thought Sackett too uncritical; but home on leave in early May, the ambassador impressed on Hoover and Stimson his anxiety about the fate of the Young settlement.[79] His apprehension was mirrored by Feis, Department of Commerce assessments, and the counsel, not always appreciated, of Wall Street insiders like Lamont and Frank Altschul, the senior partner of Lazard Frères.[80] Interventionist arguments had additional weight thanks to Dawes and Gibson, both of whom, also at home on leave, supported suspending payments.[81]

On 20 June, Hoover proposed a one-year moratorium on all inter-governmental debts. Two weeks before, on 5 June, thanks to State and Commerce Department information, the ambassadors on leave, and his reading of Wall Street, he had decided to support temporary postpone-ment.[82] Like MacDonald, he encountered divided counsel: where Stimson and his advisers favoured American intervention in the interests of 'psychology and credit', the Treasury secretary, Andrew Mellon, and Ogden Mills, his assistant, saw postponement as a 'breakdown of the debt structure'.[83] Hoover found the State Department view compelling following a private meeting with Stimson, Mellon, and Mills on 5 June.[84] The Chequers meetings over the next two days reinforced Stimson's arguments, and, by 9 June, Mellon and Mills reversed their positions.[85] But the president could not move precipitously. In the two weeks between his decision to support a moratorium and his public announcement, he worked to get domestic public and Congressional

[78] Cf. Sackett to State Department, 23, 24 Mar. 1931, both *FRUS 1931*, I, 566–70; Beitz [US Embassy, Berlin] memorandum, 'Position of German Finances', 22 May 1931, in Feis minute to Stimson, 19 Jun. 1931, Stimson R81. Cf. Kent, *Spoils of War*, 338–42.

[79] Moffat diary, 18, 22 Jan. 1931, Moffat 30. Cf. Stimson diary, 4 May 1931, Stimson 16; Hoover moratorium diary, 6, 8 May 1931, HHPP 1015.

[80] Stimson to Hoover, enclosing Feis memoranda, 5–6 Jun. 1931, Feis to Stimson, n.d. [but *circa* 8 Jun. 1931], enclosing six memoranda, both Stimson R81; Dewhurst [Department of Commerce] memoranda, 9, 12 May 1931; Lamont to Hoover, 5 Jun. 1931, with enclosure; Dulles [Wall Street reparations expert] to Hoover, 12 Jun. 1931, all HHPP 1006.

[81] Hoover moratorium diary, 2–4 Jun. 1931, HHPP 1015; Dawes diary, 4, 18 Jun. 1931, in C. G. Dawes, *Journal as Ambassador to Great Britain* (Westport, CT, 1970 [orig. publ. 1939]), 349–51.

[82] Hoover moratorium diary, 5 Jun. 1931, with 'Proposed statement', HHPP 1015.

[83] Hoover moratorium diary, 5 Jun. 1931, HHPP 1015; Stimson to Hoover, 13 Jun. 1931, with enclosures, Mills to Hoover, 18 Jun. 1931, with enclosure, both HHPP 1006; Stimson diary, 5 Jun. 1931, Stimson 16; Feis minute for Stimson, 13 Jun. 1931; Stimson to Hoover, 14 Jun. 1931; Feis telephone report [conversation with Mills], 15 Jun. 1931, all Stimson R81.

[84] Stimson diary, 5 Jun. 1931, Stimson 16; Stimson minute to Hoover, n.d. [but 6 Jun. 1931], enclosing two memoranda, Stimson R81.

[85] Stimson diary, 9 Jun. 1931, Stimson 16.

support for his action whilst Stimson cleared the diplomatic ground abroad. Hoover wanted to ensure that both Wall Street and Congress appreciated that the government could not stand back from the German crisis.[86] Hoover had Morrow, elected senator for New Jersey in November 1930, approach 'New York bankers', particularly Morgan and Company, 'to find how serious they regarded the condition of the Reichsbank and the Austrian banks'. By 8 June, he, Morrow, Mills, and Stimson began consulting with Congressional leaders and even secured the backing of Borah. The few who did not approve of a moratorium, like Senator James Couzens of Michigan, agreed to 'raise no opposition'. Wider afield, Hoover worked to bring powerful press organs to his side. For instance he had Dawes, in Illinois visiting his family, approach the strongly isolationist owner of the *Chicago Tribune* to ensure 'his favorable attitude'.

Stimson concentrated on keeping the Anglo-American axis firm by meeting with Lindsay and consulting MacDonald.[87] In a telephone conversation with MacDonald on 13 June, Stimson asked two questions: would a one-year moratorium help the European situation? And could the European Powers ask Hoover's administration to make the proposal?[88] After seeing Vansittart and Leith-Ross, MacDonald counselled that getting a speedy decision from the Powers, particularly France, would be difficult. Indicating that his government might announce unilaterally and asking the British to inform him of any difficulties over the next few days that could undermine an American initiative, Stimson next dealt with the other major Powers. France presented the greatest difficulty. He did not want the French to stand back whilst the United States acted. By 15 June, he reckoned 'that France was getting increasingly scared, [and] it might be well to get her even a little more scared before she gained any idea that we might act'.[89] This translated into saying nothing to Paris. But, three days later, after the French ultimatum to the Austrian government, he saw Claudel:

I told him that I had inferred that France had tried to mix politics with that loan, and that I didn't approve of it ... we were not going into any eleemosynary

[86] This paragraph is based on an anonymous chronology of 'Moratorium' [sent to Castle on 7 Jul. 1931], HHPP 1013; Hoover moratorium diary, 6–20 Jun., HHPP 1015; Dawes diary, 21 Jun. 1931, *Dawes Journal*, 352–3.
[87] Stimson diary, 6, 13, 16, 18 Jun. 1931, Stimson 16; Castle memorandum, 12 Jun. 1931, *FRUS 1931*, I, 15–16; Feis to Frankfurter, 26 Jun. 1931, Feis 16; Lindsay telegrams (313, 315) to FO, both 6 Jun. 1931; Henderson telegram (369) to Lindsay, 15 Jun. 1931, all *DBFP II*, II, 69–71, 80–1.
[88] Stimson diary, 13 Jun. 1931, with transcript of first telephone call, *ibid*; MacDonald diary, 14 Jun. 1931, MacDonald PRO 30/69/1753.
[89] Stimson diary, 15 Jun. 1931, Stimson 16.

business towards Germany, while the rest of the Allied Nations stood by and winked at us.[90]

The Italian, German, and Austrian ambassadors received the same message. With domestic support ensured and the European Powers aware that an American-sponsored moratorium must be collective rather than unilateral, Hoover made his public statement that all inter-governmental debt payments would be suspended from 1 July 1931 to 30 June 1932 – because debt payments occurred in June and December, this meant that payments would be deferred until December 1932.[91] He invited the other Powers to give his suggestion form. MacDonald already knew. The day before, Stimson had informed him of the president's announcement, the only leader so treated.[92]

Much has been made of inadequacies in the Hoover moratorium: it should have been for two years; the French were insufficiently sounded; and without revision of the Young settlement, delaying payments only avoided the central problem of Germany's ability to pay.[93] Hoover, however, did not have the luxury of leisurely decision-making. Reports from Europe suggested that Germany and Austria might crack under the economic and financial strain. In Britain on family business on 18 June, and after meeting MacDonald, Henderson, and Norman, Mellon reported that 'the situation had been highly critical two days ago, and that if it had not been for the action taken by the Bank of England on Tuesday [in getting a second loan], Austria would have been broken'.[94] Unless something was done to provide breathing space, the whole reparations–war debts regime might collapse. Hoover had to act and, of the options available, a moratorium seemed the best alternative. Congress, Wall Street, and American voters would not accept debt cancellation. Moreover, cancellation would rebound unfavourably on other American creditors. When rumours circulated in Washington that a war debt moratorium might be offered, some South American Powers seemed prepared 'to default on all of their foreign obligations'.[95]

These were immediate problems. In the longer view, tied to his attitude to protecting American national interests, Hoover had two

90 Stimson diary, 18 Jun. 1931, *ibid.*
91 Lindsay telegrams (333, 334, 335) to FO, all 20 Jun. 1931, *DBFP II*, II, 87–8.
92 'Memorandum of a Trans-Atlantic Telephone Conversation', 19 Jun. 1931, *FRUS 1931*, I, 29–30.
93 Bennett, *Financial Crisis*, 170; Carlton, *MacDonald Versus Henderson*, 198; Marquand, *MacDonald*, 604–5. On Germany's capacity to pay, see S. Marks, 'Reparations Reconsidered: A Reminder', *CEH*, 2(1969), 356–65; D. Felix, 'Reparations Reconsidered with a Vengeance', *CEH*, 4(1971), 171–9.
94 Mills, 'Memorandum of [telephone] conversation with Mr. Mellon ... June 18, 1931', HHPP 1013.
95 Stimson diary, 16 Jun. 1931, Stimson 16.

purposes in offering the moratorium. First, he wanted to thwart a *de jure* link between war debts and reparations. On this issue, he and Stimson disagreed.[96] Stimson argued that 'of course legally [war debts and reparations] were separate; but even legally, in domestic law, as soon as a man became insolvent he and his creditors could not make independent arrangements about their debts'. Hoover countered that connecting the two matters would 'drag us into the European mess'. He wanted the United States isolated from European entanglements even though, as Stimson realistically saw, American foreign policy increasingly had difficulty concentrating on Europe's financial difficulties without considering the political ramifications of such diplomacy. Second, and more important, Hoover connected arms spending with the ability to pay war debts and reparations:

I felt that one of the fundamental difficulties of all Europe was the increasing armament, which now reached the stage where the total expenditure of civilised nations was nearly $5,000,000,000 per annum; that this sum amounted to many times the whole debt weight of the world, but that this did not so much directly concern Germany.[97]

The president encased this sentiment in his 20 June announcement. With the World Disarmament Conference scheduled to begin in February 1932, Hoover probably believed that when inter-governmental debt payments resumed in December 1932, almost a year of deliberation would have produced arms reductions and freed up public money in Europe. That Presidential and Congressional elections would occur in November 1932, in which Hoover could style himself as a defender of American financial interests and a sponsor of improved international security, was probably not far from his mind.

Difficulty in giving the moratorium life arose from predictable quarters. On 24 June the French government, now led by Laval, made counter-proposals that amounted to a demand that the moratorium not be seen as diminishing France's rights granted under the Young settlement.[98] Hoover refused to bargain. Diplomatic exchanges occurred and, on 5 July, he decided enough was enough. With Mills and Castle – Stimson had left for Europe – he drafted a message for Laval that he characterised as 'we do not care what view the French [take] of our formula[,] that we only wanted yes or no, that we proposed to finally test their honesty and to force their hands'.[99] The French retreated, but

---

[96] Stimson diary, 8 Jun. 1931, *ibid.*
[97] Hoover moratorium diary, 6 May 1931, 'Proposed Statement', 5 Jun. 1931, both HHPP 1013.
[98] E. Weill-Raynal, *Les réparations allemandes et la France*, vol. III (Paris, 1947), 620–1.
[99] Chronology of 'Moratorium', 5 Jul. 1931, HHPP 1013. Cf. Edge telegrams (2) to

only after their delayed acceptance of Hoover's proposal produced a further run on the mark, the withdrawal of more German gold, and the failure of some large German banks.

MacDonald's role in this process was one of support for Hoover. Although an element of unjustified self-congratulation dominated his thinking, MacDonald's desire to bolster Anglo-American relations played a large part in this: 'These things I dreamt of when in the U.S. in 1929 but hardly thought they would happen.'[100] Henderson's ideas differed. As at Chequers, he worried about unfavourable French reactions to appeasing Germany over reparations – they might damage concurrent preparations for the disarmament conference. Therefore, in mid-July, whilst in Paris for arms limitation discussions, he played his own game.[101] At that moment, the Powers were considering new German economic aid. Henderson wanted Laval to extend such assistance; and, in return, he sought to induce Brüning and Curtius to offer political concessions. Engineering a visit by Brüning and Curtius to Paris on 18 July, he deliberately ignored instructions from MacDonald not to pressure the Germans to make some compromise in return for financial assistance. The Franco-German talks proved barren because Laval made the impossible demand that in return for a French loan, Brüning's government should agree that Germany would seek no revision of the peace settlement for a decade. Henderson's machinations only heightened tensions between him and MacDonald.

The Paris talks were actually preliminary to a hastily arranged seven-Power conference at London to augment the moratorium by giving Germany short-term relief. For three days beginning on 20 July, MacDonald met with Stimson, Laval, Brüning, and others; their deliberations showed that the time for inventive diplomacy had passed.[102] As the first American secretary of state to attend a European conference since 1919, Stimson joined MacDonald to oppose further loans to Germany – 'I told [Hoover] that what I wanted him principally

Stimson, both 24 Jun. 1931, Castle telegram to Edge, 4 Jul. 1931, Edge telegram to Castle, 5 Jul. 1931, 'Memorandum of a Trans-Atlantic Telephone Conversation', 5 Jul. 1931, all *FRUS 1931*, 57–9, 140–3, 145–50. Cf. Carlton, *MacDonald Versus Henderson*, 198–217; Kunz, *Gold Standard*, 60–71; Marquand, *MacDonald*, 604–8.
[100] MacDonald diary, 21 Jun. 1931, MacDonald PRO 30/69/1753; MacDonald to Norman, 18 Jun. 1931, *ibid.*, PRO 30/69/677.
[101] Carlton, *MacDonald Versus Henderson*, 206–11; Marquand, *MacDonald*, 605–7. Cf. Briand to Henderson, 10 Jul. 1931, Tyrrell to Henderson, 10 Jul. 1931, both Henderson FO 800/283; MacDonald diary, 16 Jul. 1931, MacDonald PRO 30/69/1753; Dalton diary, 20 Jul. 1931, BLEPS.
[102] Except where noted, this paragraph is based on MacDonald diary, 22–23 Jul. 1931, MacDonald PRO 30/69/1753; Stimson memoranda, 18–23 Jul. 1931, all Stimson 17; 'Stenographic Notes of the London Conference', *DBFP II*, II, appendix I.

to know was that I found the British in accord with ourselves and that we were working together like two old shoes.'[103] This unity dashed all hope entertained by Henderson and Laval that political concessions could be wrested from Germany. Significantly, by working with Stimson, MacDonald brought his errant foreign secretary to heel. Although making no innovative decisions, the London conference delegates united on one point: the need for a standstill agreement on non-governmental international credits to Germany. Receiving the details of such an arrangement from Hoover a few days before, Stimson worried initially about French reaction to another unilateral American initiative. At London, however, Stimson discovered MacDonald moving in this direction because it offered stability. By careful manoeuvring, Stimson allowed the standstill proposal to come from the British delegation – which, surprisingly, found support from the French.[104] When the conference ended on 23 July, Germany's financial difficulties as a consequence of the standstill agreement had been relieved within the general moratorium on inter-governmental debt payments.

Anglo-American accord seemed to be the basis for the international effort to meet the reparations–war debts crisis of 1931. In a narrow sense, such appearances were valid. London and Washington saw the moratorium as a way of buying time until the international economy improved; they were disinclined to burden Germany with more debt; and they saw French policy as regressive. In reality, however, the British had surrendered the initiative to the United States. Such a course arose because of the weakness of their economic diplomacy. Since Hoover still resisted a formal link between war debts and reparations, MacDonald's Cabinet could do little beyond endorsing the moratorium as a refinement of the Young settlement. When efforts occurred in the six weeks afterwards to stabilise the German economy, MacDonald understood that his government lacked the resources either to force Berlin to accept new restrictions or to remove existing ones. It shocked the Cabinet that Hoover proposed suspending all inter-governmental debt payments, and not just those tied to reparations.[105] The British would be unable to collect from their debtors, something that tied into the Labour government's domestic economic and financial policies. This domestic dimension assumed decided importance by late July 1931 as the continental crisis spread to Britain. It arose from two associated problems: the

[103] 'Memorandum of the Secretary's Telephone Conversation with the President', 20 Jul. 1931, Stimson 17.
[104] Atherton telegrams (242, 254) to State Department, 17, 20 Jul. 1931, both HHPP 987; Hoover moratorium diary, 20–22 Jul. 1931, HHPP 1013; Stimson diary, 19–23 Jul. 1931, Stimson 17; Stimson to Hoover, 11 Aug. 1931, Stimson R91.
[105] CC 35(31), CAB 23/67; Vansittart to Lindsay, 21 Jun. 1931, T 172/1380.

central European banking crisis which exposed the position of the City of London; and Snowden's prospective budget deficit of £120 million.

As the London conference ended, MacDonald's Cabinet confronted onerous internal problems: unemployment had reached staggering proportions; a balanced budget could not be achieved without cutting social programmes; and the Treasury and Bank of England worried about sterling being driven off the gold standard.[106] Given Labour's minority in the Commons, domestic policy assumed increasing importance. The government had been weakened in May 1931 when Sir Oswald Mosley, the chancellor of the Duchy of Lancaster, resigned after Cabinet rejection of his radical prescription for tackling the Depression: government reform to achieve economies; deficit financing to reduce unemployment through a massive public works programme; and 'mobilisation of national resources on a larger scale than has yet been contemplated'.[107] Neither MacDonald nor his senior ministers would be shaken from their adherence to fiscal orthodoxy and a balanced budget.[108] Under pressure from Snowden in March 1931, and partly in response to Mosley, MacDonald established a Committee on National Expenditure under Sir George May, a businessman. Designed to assess programmes and recommend spending levels, this body became part of 'a cloud of impressive-sounding Commissions and Committees' from which the government sought guidelines for economic and financial revival.[109] Reaching the Cabinet on 30 July, the May Report concluded that the Exchequer faced a shortfall of £120 million in revenues against projected expenditures of about £800 million.[110] Massive economies were required to balance the budget or, at least, bring it near to balance: a cut of £97 million, including £67 million in unemployment assistance. For a socialist ministry riven with faction and supposedly dedicated to the welfare of the under-privileged, the May Report contained explosive political material.

Just as the Cabinet received May's findings, MacDonald, Norman, and Snowden confronted a run on the pound. Britain's short-term liabilities were double its gold reserves and, by July 1931, holders of short-term capital began to lose confidence in sterling. Whilst it has

---

[106] British unemployment now edged past 20 per cent (2.2 million): Mitchell, *European Economic Statistics*, 167–71. Cf. Kunz, *Gold Standard*, 58–71.

[107] R. Skidelsky, *Oswald Mosley* (1975), 199–206.

[108] MacDonald memorandum, 'Re [Mosley's] Memorandum on Unemployment', MacDonald PRO 30/69/1/446.

[109] Rhodes James, *British Revolution*, 513. Other committees included the Macmillan Committee (1929) and the Economic Advisory Committee (1930).

[110] May Committee Report in MacDonald PRO 30/69/5/182. It reached the Commons the next day.

been argued that the Bank of France initiated a sell-off of sterling to force Britain to accept Paris' views on the German question,[111] other reasons were more important. The budget deficit, an adverse balance of payments caused by the decline in trade, and the view that the pound was overvalued combined to produce a sell-off by commercial banks in smaller European countries and a depletion of Bank of England gold reserves.[112] Although daily gold withdrawals averaged £2.5 million in July, MacDonald learnt of a £5 million loss the day the London conference ended.[113] Three days later, Norman obtained a credit of £50 million from the FRBNY and the Bank of France. An increase in the lending rate to $4\frac{1}{2}$ per cent – the rate had been raised to $3\frac{1}{2}$ per cent on 23 July – was thought sufficient to check the outflow of British gold. It failed. On 10 August, MacDonald cut short a vacation in Scotland to rush back to London and meet the crisis.

The events of August 1931 are some of the most analysed in modern British history.[114] For a week – from 12 to 18 August – the Cabinet Economy Committee wrestled with the May Report. Because of Labour's minority position, MacDonald and Snowden conferred simultaneously with Conservative and Liberal leaders to explain the economies being considered: Baldwin, Neville Chamberlain, Baldwin's chief lieutenant who had been chancellor of the Exchequer in 1923, and Sir Herbert Samuel, deputising for the infirm Lloyd George. Beginning on 19 August, the Cabinet met for five days without determining budget cuts that pleased Labour ministers, the trade unions, and the opposition leadership. Because of irreconcilable Cabinet divisions, and because King George V pressured MacDonald, Baldwin, and Samuel, new discussions ensued on 23 and 24 August which led to the resignation of the Labour government and its replacement by a coalition, the National Government, to meet the crisis. MacDonald retained the premiership; Baldwin became lord president; and Samuel took the Home Office. In this process, the Labour and Liberal parties split. Henderson refused to join a coalition dominated by Conservatives and, with Dalton and others, moved to the opposition benches. Likewise, Lloyd George remained in opposition at the head of a rump of Liberals loyal to him; Samuel became leader of a faction called the National Liberals. The new government took office on 25 August. The formation of the

---

[111] Bennett, *Financial Crisis*, 158.
[112] Except where noted, this paragraph is based on Kindleberger, *Depression*, 157–62; Kunz, *Gold Standard*, 77–104.
[113] MacDonald diary, 23 Jul. 1931, MacDonald PRO 30/69/1753.
[114] Ball, *Baldwin*, 172–93; R. Bassett, *1931* (1958); Marquand, *MacDonald*, 608–53; Middlemas and Barnes, *Baldwin*, 618–33; Rhodes James, *British Revolution*, 514–18; K. Rose, *King George V* (New York, 1984), 370–85.

National Government precipitated vicious attacks on MacDonald by his former colleagues over his supposed forsaking of Labour ideals.[115] Nonetheless, those within the new ministry also felt discomfort over governing *à la trois*; Baldwin, who played a leading role in destroying Lloyd George's coalition in 1922, was prominent. But it remains that Labour could not deal with the crisis; fresh ideas and a more pragmatic approach to economic and financial policy at the highest political levels were required. It fell to the National Government to provide such leadership, especially as the gold drain continued.

The immediate difficulty involved defending sterling. This required loans from the United States and France, the only Powers with sufficient gold reserves. Approaches were made to Morgan's and the Bank of France which, on 28 August, produced loans totalling £80 million. A high price was paid for this assistance: the American half of the loan was charged the discount rate in London – $4\frac{1}{2}$ per cent – rather than that at New York – $1\frac{1}{2}$ per cent; and in Paris, French negotiators, particularly Pierre-Etienne Flandin, the minister of finance, 'stressed the necessity of co-operation between the British and French governments' over reparations.[116] Whilst the British had no intention of conceding to French pressures,[117] the high American interest, no matter how justified given the risk involved, began to undermine notions of Anglo-American financial co-operation. But the immediate problem had been met, and the National Government turned to balancing the budget. Snowden, still the chancellor of the Exchequer, introduced an economic plan on 10 September that mixed spending cuts with tax increases.

Neither the Budget nor the Franco-American loan arrested the outflow of gold, a situation deriving from foreign perceptions of British economic weakness. First came shocking news that British sailors at Invergordon refused to muster on 15 September because of pay-cuts in Snowden's Budget.[118] Then uncertainty developed about how long the National Government intended to hold office. MacDonald, Baldwin, and Samuel came together on 24 August with a single purpose: to stabilise the pound and bring in a balanced Budget. With this accomplished, a general election would be called to put a new government in power.[119] Continued pressure on the pound after the Invergordon

[115] Dalton diary, 5 Sep 1931, BLEPS.
[116] Leith-Ross memoranda, 'Conversations with Monsieur Flandin (26–29 August)', 1 Sep. 1931, 'British Policy on Debts and Reparations', n.d. [but Sep. 1931], both Leith-Ross T 188/16; Kunz, *Gold Standard*, 114–17.
[117] Cf. Leith-Ross to Vansittart, 14 Nov. 1931, Leith-Ross T 188/16.
[118] W. N. Medlicott, *Contemporary England, 1914–1964, with epilogue 1964–1974* (1976), 264–65.
[119] S. Ball, 'The Conservative Party and the Formation of the National Government:

mutiny – a loss of £5 million on 16 September, £10 million the next day, and almost £18 million on 18 September – plus reluctance by New York and Paris to advance further credits, changed the situation.[120] On 18 September, the Treasury advised MacDonald that Britain should abandon the gold standard. Three days later, MacDonald and his allies secured the passage of legislation to this end.[121] The leaders of the National Government then decided to call a general election for 27 October and appeal to British voters to return them to office *en bloc* – a coalition could provide a unified front that would dish Henderson and Lloyd George and provide a base for restoring foreign confidence in the economy.[122] By the end of October, a renewed National Government took office with a commanding majority in the Commons. Although MacDonald remained prime minister and Samuel and other Liberals received important Cabinet posts, real power resided with Baldwin and the Conservatives: they controlled 473 out of 554 government seats. British domestic politics had reached a turning-point.

The same held true for foreign policy, especially concerning the United States. In the two months between the seven-Power London conference and Britain abandoning the gold standard, Anglo-American financial co-operation had reached its limits. The United States had sufficient gold holdings to assist Britain unilaterally after early August. In addition, leading members of Hoover's Administration wanted a good working relationship with Britain to make progress on disarmament. Vacationing in Scotland in August after his peregrination through Europe, Stimson impressed this on MacDonald.[123] But as is often the case in American foreign policy, domestic constraints affected the course of diplomatic strategy. Hoover had used as much political capital as he dared to line up domestic support for the moratorium. By September, whilst sympathising with Britain's plight and finally admitting to Stimson that war debts and reparations were connected, he could do no more.[124] The cost to Britain in all of this had been high: abandonment of the gold standard and a significant loss of prestige for the London market.

Debates about the wisdom of going back onto gold in 1925 and the

August 1931', *HJ*, 29(1986); Marquand, *MacDonald*, 628–33, 635–7; Middlemas and Barnes, *Baldwin*, 625–7.
[120] Bassett, *1931*, 237.   [121] Kunz, *Gold Standard*, 129–39.
[122] Marquand, *MacDonald*, 658–70; Middlemas and Barnes, *Baldwin*, 635–48; D. J. Wrench, ' "Cashing In": The Parties and the National Government, August 1931–September 1932', *JBS*, 23(1984).
[123] Stimson diary, 6–7 Aug. 1931, Stimson 17; MacDonald diary, 11 Aug. 1931, MacDonald PRO 30/69/1753.
[124] Kunz, *Gold Standard*, 135–36. Cf. Stimson diary, 8 Sep. 1931, Stimson 18.

problems that overvalued sterling created for British trade thereafter have become interesting academic exercises.[125] But it remains that in the late summer of 1931, MacDonald and his new political allies had to deal with the results of that policy. In this, the American question held extreme importance given its connexion to war debts and reparations; and as the course of economic diplomacy had shown since the first Hague conference, international security and arms limitation could not be divorced from war debts and reparations. This had added piquancy by September 1931. On the nineteenth, as the gold standard and domestic political calculations preoccupied the National Government, a crisis erupted in Manchuria which threatened the East Asian balance of power. With the World Disarmament Conference set to begin on 2 February 1932, the implications of this for security both in Europe and the Far East loomed large. Already strained by the economic and financial crisis in August and September, Anglo-American co-operation would again be tested in wider disarmament and security questions.

[125] Cf. H. F. Fraser, *Great Britain and the Gold Standard* (New York, 1933); R. Skidelsky, *Politicians and the Slump* (1967); P. Q. Wright, ed., *Gold and Monetary Stabilization* (Chicago, 1932).

3 Disarmament and security in Europe and the Far East, 1930–1932

> I asked the United States Ambassador to come and see me this morning in order that I might speak to him about the question of arrangements for the World Disarmament Conference . . . my greatest hopes were based on co-operation with the United States Government, who, with His Majesty's Government, might exercise a decisive influence at the conference.
>
> Henderson, February 1931[1]

Since first meeting in 1926, the Preparatory Commission had made little progress because of the dichotomy between arms limitation and national security.[2] Here lay the root of the different emphases of the British and French draft treaties and the British and American divergence over cruisers. The French and their allies wanted to preserve the security system that had emerged at Locarno, one having at its core their unrestricted land-based military strength and the limited size and nature of the German armed forces. The British sought to balance France and Germany on the Continent and safeguard the naval equilibrium achieved at the Washington conference. The naval treaty allowed the RN a strategic advantage in European and Mediterranean waters and, with the four- and nine-Power treaties, looked to maintain the status quo in the western Pacific Ocean and China. Though supporting the tenor of the British draft treaty – for instance, limiting tonnage by class rather than by a universal total for each Power – Washington and Tokyo pursued modifications to meet their particular security requirements: the USN's desire for a large number of heavy cruisers and the IJN's resolve to increase its cruiser tonnage ratio. Preparatory Commission discussions went into abeyance after April 1929, when Gibson announced the 'yardstick'. Whilst the obstacles to reconciling the competing French and British draft treaties still lurked in the background, Anglo-American naval differences constituted the immediate block to progress. The integrated nature of armed forces meant that considering

[1] Henderson despatch (237) to Lindsay, 19 Feb. 1931, *BDFA*, II, J3, 334.
[2] McKercher, 'Horns and Teeth', 176–9.

air and land disarmament would be fruitless until the two principal naval Powers – and Japan – resolved their divergent requirements. Anglo-American negotiations over the summer revived the Preparatory Commission. By late 1929, supporters of international arms limitation hoped the World Disarmament Conference might soon meet.[3]

MacDonald's government contained an influential group that, clustering around Henderson, wanted to achieve meaningful disarmament. The group comprised Dalton, Noel-Baker, and Robert Cecil, ennobled as Viscount Cecil of Chelwood in 1924. Holding memberships in the LNU, all believed passionately in disarmament.[4] Of these, Cecil was the most important. A Conservative, he had been the minister responsible for disarmament in Baldwin's second government until August 1927, when he resigned to protest at what he regarded as British responsibility for the breakdown of the Coolidge conference. Subsequently attacking his former colleagues from his bench in the Lords, and promoting the League ideal in Britain through his position as LNU president, he was rewarded by MacDonald and Henderson in June 1929 with a place in the Foreign Office to advise on League matters.[5] 'I cannot tell you what a relief it is to me', Cecil wrote to MacDonald, 'to think that a genuine and whole-hearted Peace Ministry is installed in office at this critical time.'[6] Henderson quickly grasped Cecil's commitment to peace when, a week after Labour took office, Cecil begged off representing Britain at a conference to codify rules of war such as those concerning the treatment of prisoners: 'The proposed Conventions deal with the laws of war, that is, the management of the institution which I am anxious to be destroyed.'[7] Despite the idealism reflected by such sentiments, an activist pro-disarmament group was ensconced at the Foreign Office; allied with Parmoor and the pro-League faction in the Cabinet, and the LNU outside government, it looked to make progress when the Preparatory Commission next met.

These British disarmament advocates had allies in the League

[3] Cf. J. H. Bernstorff, 'Der Stand der Abrüstungsfrage', *Europäische Gespräche*, 7(1929), 401–16; Comité National d'Etudes Sociales et Politiques, *L'état actuel du problème du désarmement* (Boulogne-sur-Seine, 1929); P. Kerr, 'Navies and Peace: A British View', *FA*, 7(1929), 20–9; S. de Madariaga, 'Disarmament – American Plan', *Atlantic Monthly* (Apr. 1929), 525–38.
[4] Cf. Lord Robert Cecil, 'Disarmament and the League' [speech delivered in 1923], in Cecil, *The Way of Peace* (1928), 211–32; Dalton, *Peace of Nations*, 141–66; P. J. Noel-Baker, *The League of Nations at Work* (1926).
[5] Cecil of Chelwood, 'Après ma démission', *Revue des vivants*, 1(1927), 611–23; Cecil of Chelwood, 'Case for Disarmament', *Nation* (27 Apr. 1929), 211–32. Cf. Carlton, *MacDonald Versus Henderson*, 18–19; McKercher, *Baldwin Government*, 77–80.
[6] Cecil to MacDonald, 21 Jun. 1929, Cecil BL Add. 51081.
[7] Cecil to Henderson, 14 Jun. 1929, Henderson FO 800/280.

Secretariat, which had responsibility for the day-to-day administration of the Commission and, should it convene, the world conference. They included Sir Eric Drummond, a British career diplomat who had been secretary-general of the organisation since its creation, Frank Walters, his deputy, and Erik Colban, the head of the Secretariat's Disarmament Section.[8] When the invitations to the five major naval Powers to convene in London were issued in October 1929, they lobbied successfully to have Colban attend as an observer 'in view of the important bearing which the forthcoming London Naval Conference is likely to have upon the work of the Preparatory Commission'.[9] More practically, the League Secretariat endeavoured to remove difficulties that might retard the Commission once it reconvened. When Hoover made a public statement in November 1929 about excluding food-ships from future blockades, for instance, Colban had the Secretariat's Economic and Disarmament sections prepare position papers to meet the points raised by the president.[10] Since blockade underpinned the legal application of the Covenant's economic sanctions,[11] League officials wanted to ensure that this powerful weapon in maintaining international peace and security remained undamaged. In this way, by the time the London naval conference began, disarmament advocates in the British government and within the League were preparing for the revival of the Preparatory Commission.

Once naval negotiations at London were under way, the question of how the Commission should fulfil its brief was addressed. Before April 1929, Colban urged other League officials to concentrate on arms limitation above all else, including security.[12] French concerns about Germany and the differing British and French views about limiting

8 Drummond to Noel-Baker, 18 Jun. 1929, Noel-Baker to Drummond, 21 Jun. 1929, Walters to Noel-Baker, 25 Oct. 1929, all NBKR 4X/87/5. Cf. Drummond to Cecil, 11 Jun. 1926, Drummond LNP 33/2; Drummond note, 'Security, Disarmament, etc.', 2 Feb. 1928, Colban minute for Drummond, 1 Mar. 1928, Colban 'Notes sur conversation avec M. Massigli le 11 mars 1929', 'Notes sur conversations avec M. Weizsaecker, le 9 mars et le Comte Bernstorff, le 11 Mars 1929', both 12 Mar. 1929, Drummond minute to Colban, 13 Mar. 1929, all *ibid*. 33/6.
9 Snow [FO] to Colban, 9 Jan. 1930, with Colban and Drummond minutes, LNR 2389/16886/8080.
10 Colban minute to Drummond, 26 Nov. 1929, Drummond minute, 27 Nov. 1929, Hill [Economic Section, Secretariat] to Colban, 5 Dec. 1929, with memorandum, 2 Dec. 1929, all LNR 2389/15991/8080; Colban to Loveday [Economic Section], 26 Nov. 1929, Loveday LNP 11.
11 Cf. Farrar [DOT] memorandum, 'Blockade as a Means of Enforcing Peace', Apr. 1918 [revised 15 Jul. 1919], in Farrar to Lloyd [League Secretariat], n.d. [but Jul. 1919], LNR 289/16/16; Salter [League Secretariat] memorandum, 'The Economic Weapon of the League', 22 Sep. 1919, LNR 289/748/16; Colban 'Memorandum on the Economic Weapon of the League', 22 Jun. 1920, with Drummond minute, LNR 289/1196/16.
12 Colban to Sugimura [under-secretary general], 5 Mar. 1929, Sugimura to Renthe-Fink

naval arms that emerged at London convinced League officials and others like Cecil that security could not be divorced from disarmament.[13] When failure to compromise over extending the Washington capital ship ratios to auxiliary vessels saw Paris and Rome refuse to sign the London naval treaty, it was obvious that the Commission could not concentrate solely on weapons reductions. Furthermore, it suggested that a hasty meeting of the Commission might delay an agreed draft treaty for the consideration of the world conference. Although the Commission chairman, the Dutch diplomat Jonkheer Loudon, wanted a session soon after the London conference ended,[14] more powerful voices urged prudence. Meeting in early April with Cecil and Joseph Paul-Boncour, a senior French arms negotiator, Colban discovered that both thought an autumn meeting would allow time to prepare for delicate negotiations touching reserves, the budgetary limitation of arms, and the organisation of a permanent disarmament commission to oversee the results of the world conference.[15] Although this prompted Colban to despair – 'On the security business I am unfortunately no more enlightened today than before'[16] – a slower pace could not be avoided.

In Britain, this caution derived from the Foreign Office. With MacDonald dominating naval discussions and Snowden leading over reparations, Henderson took control of British disarmament policy. Although he began his tenure as foreign secretary deprecating the hard edge of French policy – seen in his exchanges with Briand at The Hague over the Rhineland evacuation – his attitude changed by the time the London naval conference ended. This odyssey occurred for two reasons. First, advice tendered by Vansittart and key ambassadors like Tyrrell and Sir Horace Rumbold, the ambassador at Berlin, suggested that French security interests could not be treated lightly if the existing European security system built around Locarno was to survive.[17] As Henderson learnt in March from a memorandum that Vansittart had

[Political Section], 12 Mar. 1929, Renthe-Fink to Sugimura, 25 Mar. 1929, Colban minute, 9 Apr. 1929, all LNR 1851/9440/9440.
[13] Cf. 'Note by the Secretariat', 15 Jan. 1930, with enclosures, LNR 2389/16886/8080; Colban to Drummond, 30 Jan. 1930, Colban LNS 5445/1; Cecil to Henderson, 1 Mar. 1930, Henderson FO 800/281.
[14] Colban to Drummond, 3 Mar. 1930, Colban LNS 5445/1.
[15] Colban notes, 'Sur conversation avec Lord Cecil, le 2 avril 1930', 'Date de la prochaine réunion de la Commission Préparatoire', 'Organe du Conseil pour les questions du désarmement après le cession des travaux de la Commission Préparatoire', all 3 Apr. 1930, all Drummond LNP 33/6.
[16] Colban to Drummond, 3 Apr. 1930, *ibid.*
[17] Cf. Rumbold despatches to Henderson, 11 Oct., 12 Dec. 1929, Tyrrell to Lindsay, 4 Nov. 1929, 'Note from the French Ministry of Foreign Affairs to H.M. Embassy (Paris)', 18 Nov. 1929, all *DBFP IA*, VII, 44–7, 92–3, 159–61, 241; Tyrrell to

Orme Sargent, the head of the Foreign Office Central Department, prepare:

However irritating and unadaptable she may sometimes appear, the fact remains that of all the Great Powers of Europe[,] France's objectives resemble most closely our own. Both countries have been satiated by the Peace Settlement: neither is striving to obtain anything more. Both only want to keep and develop what they have got. Both, in fact, are seeking peace and security . . .[18]

And with the widening impact of the Depression, the economic side of Anglo-French relations could not be ignored. 'All the information I gather in commercial and financial circles is to the effect that never was France so economically sound as she is today,' Tyrrell warned in March 1930. 'She has built up huge gold reserves both in America and in England which she imagines give her great strength and means of pressure.'[19] The second reason entailed Henderson being the least francophobic of Labour ministers;[20] therefore, despite some residual concern about the loyalty of Foreign Office officials towards the goals of Labour foreign policy,[21] the foreign secretary came to share the views of his permanent advisers in devising diplomatic strategy. Simply put, as Vansittart and Sargent argued, this involved working with Paris because of the affinity of British and French interests. Such thinking flew in the face of general opinion within the Labour Party about the 'reactionary' Foreign Office being both francophile and germanophobe, attitudes limiting the effectiveness of British diplomacy by making more difficult the reconciliation of Germany.[22] Nonetheless, by July 1930, the Foreign Office could tell the Committee of Imperial Defence, in a memorandum approved by Henderson: 'Generally speaking, it is to the interest of England to see a

Henderson, 1, 24 Feb. 1930, both Henderson FO 800/281; Vansittart minute, 21 Feb. 1930, FO 371/14259/1463/1.

[18] Vansittart minute to Henderson, n.d., enclosing Sargent memorandum, 18 Mar. 1930, with Henderson initials, FO 371/14261/2283/1.

[19] Tyrrell to Henderson, 28 Mar. 1930, Henderson FO 800/281.

[20] Carlton, *MacDonald Versus Henderson*, 31–2; H. R. Winkler, 'Arthur Henderson', in G. A. Craig and F. Gilbert, eds., *The Diplomats, 1919–1939*, vol. II (New York, 1977), 312–19.

[21] '[Henderson] has shouted at Van and Loraine [high commissioner, Egypt] in front of our side of the circus and has said to me several times that "these officials don't seem to want a settlement. They do nothing but raise difficulties." ': in Dalton diary, 7 May 1930, Dalton BLEPS.

[22] Buxton [TUC–Labour Party Advisory Committee on International Questions], 'Memorandum on the Pact of Locarno', Oct. 1925; Angell [TUC–Labour Party Advisory Committee on International Questions], 'Memorandum on the Reactionary Attitude of the Government in International Affairs', Nov. 1925, both MacDonald PRO 30/69/5/139. Cf. W. R. Tucker, *The Attitude of the British Labour Party Towards European and Collective Security Problems, 1920–1939* (Geneva, 1950), 244–6.

strong and prosperous France just as it is to the interest of France to retain the friendship of this country ... their Governments will be obliged to co-operate in the settlement of post-war problems.'[23]

Just as important, a CID sub-committee – the Reduction and Limitation of Armaments Sub-committee (RA) – was created in December 1929 to advise on policy for reducing and limiting armaments. With Henderson as chairman and Dalton, Noel-Baker, and Cecil members, the chief disarmament advocates within the second Labour government learnt quickly the difficulty of squaring Britain's need for effective armed forces with arms reductions. In its first six meetings, concurrent with the naval conference, discussion rested on two proposals to bolster international security: a 'Model Treaty to Strengthen the Means of Preventing War' and a 'Draft Treaty of Financial Assistance'.[24] Emerging from the 1928 League Assembly, the 'Model Treaty' looked to augment the Kellogg Pact by having 'a model which any two or more States might adopt and put into force as between themselves'; whether League members or not, signatories would 'undertake to accept and put in force any directions given by the Council of the League under the provisions of the Covenant with a view to prevent hostilities or restore peace'.[25] The 'Draft Treaty' originated with a Finnish proposal to have the League aid small Powers in raising loans to purchase arms, ammunition, and other implements of war should they suffer attack from larger Powers.[26]

In these deliberations, Cecil, Dalton, and Noel-Baker came to appreciate that Britain required a certain minimum armed strength to cover contingencies from League collective security through aid to the civil power to Imperial policing. At the first meeting, for example, when the Colonial Office argued for unfettered force to defend Kenya from Abyssinian marauders, Cecil acknowledged that 'if [Abyssinia] went to the League and said that as a result of the action we were taking on her borders war might take place, then we could quite easily say that as a matter of fact the Abyssinian tribes were merely raiding British territory and had been driven back'.[27] Over the next three months, although none surrendered the ideal of general arms reduction, Henderson's three assistants saw the connexion between armed strength and

[23] In 'Papers Prepared for the Use of the Chiefs of Staff in their Fifth Annual Review of Imperial Defence (1930)' [CID 1008–B], 29 Jul. 1930, CAB 4/20.

[24] Minutes of the preliminary and first six meetings, 19 Dec. 1929–12 Mar. 1930, CAB 16/98.

[25] *Third Session of the Committee on Arbitration and Security*, LD C.358.M.112.1928.IX, 44–7, 102–6.

[26] *Ibid.*, esp. 108–21.   [27] RA meeting 1, 7 Jan. 1930, CAB 16/98.

security.[28] When the first sub-committee reports reached the CID in March endorsing British support for the two treaties, the need for adequate air, land, and naval strength to maintain internal peace and international security was fundamental to their conclusions;[29] none of the three dissented. The net effect of Henderson's exposure to the intricacies of protecting Britain's 'eternal' interests, and of Cecil, Dalton, and Noel-Baker participating in RA deliberations, was the realisation by Labour's most influential disarmament advocates that rushing towards the World Disarmament Conference could be counter-productive.

By May 1930, following the achievement of the London naval treaty and the Young settlement, disarmament remained the only major foreign policy problem facing MacDonald's government. With Mac-Donald and Snowden preoccupied with domestic problems generated by the Depression, Henderson could direct British disarmament policy with minimum interference from his two chief rivals in the Labour leadership. His immediate concern involved getting ready for the next session of the Preparatory Commission, scheduled for the autumn. With the success of the naval conference, this meant framing specific proposals for limiting air and land forces. In addition, before negotia-tions at Geneva could produce a comprehensive disarmament plan, the Franco-Italian quarrel over auxiliary vessel ratios had to be addressed. To these ends, the Foreign Office saw Anglo-American co-operation as a way to smooth the path to a general arms limitation agreement. '[I] will always happily recall our pleasant association during the past few weeks', Henderson told Stimson as the naval conference ended, 'which I regard as the happiest auguries for our future relations.'[30]

This desire to work with the Americans became central to British arms limitation policies in the period leading to the World Disarmament Conference in February 1932. Importantly, it showed that MacDonald's pro-American sentiments and Henderson's increasing desire to maintain a good working relationship with the French were complementary. As Vansittart pointed out on 1 May 1930, in his first major assessment of the international situation:

If the United States can be persuaded, or, rather, can persuade themselves – and to many it will be collar-work – that of all the European nations we alone are

---

28 Dalton diary, 21 Jan. 1930, Dalton BLEPS; Cecil to Henderson, 1 Mar. 1930, Cecil to MacDonald, 14 Mar. 1930, with enclosure, both Henderson FO 800/281; Noel-Baker to Dalton, 12 Mar. 1930, NBKR 4X/87/4.
29 'Model Treaty to Strengthen the Means of Preventing War. Report' [RA 9], 26 Mar. 1930, 'Draft Treaty for Financial Assistance. Report' [RA 10], 12 Mar. 1930, both CAB 16/98.
30 Henderson to Stimson, 28 Apr. 1930, Stimson R79.

attempting to exert a sane and salutary influence toward the reduction of international friction and the maintenance of peace, Anglo-American relations should be the gainers.[31]

Henderson and the Foreign Office also saw Anglo-American co-operation as having benefits in the Far East. Sir John Tilley, the ambassador at Tokyo, reported during the final stages of the London conference that Japan's willingness to accept less than it wanted over cruisers stemmed from the unity of the British and Americans.[32] Willing to work with the British over general arms limitation after April 1930, Hoover and Stimson could not do much until Congress approved the London treaty; hence, the politics of ratification preoccupied them until July.[33] Once Congress endorsed the treaty, MacDonald and Henderson sent congratulatory letters asserting, in Henderson's phrase, that 'the final ratification of this Treaty will be the prelude to an era of steadily increasing friendship and sympathy between our two nations'.[34] After consulting Hoover, Stimson responded in kind at the end of August.[35]

In Britain, the RA deliberated over the summer. Because the Preparatory Commission's purpose involved producing a single draft treaty as the basis for discussion at the main conference, the Labour government looked for practical proposals to reconcile the competing British and French draft treaties. The discussions had two dimensions: seeking limits on specific kinds of weapons; and searching for a general method of restricting overall forces.[36] Regarding the former, Cecil, Dalton, and Noel-Baker agreed with the service ministries on a series of points. Limiting tanks, heavy guns, and military aircraft would be futile since verification was impossible: these weapons could be easily dispersed or stored in their component parts and quickly assembled in a crisis. On the other hand, restrictions could be placed on manpower given the difficulty of disguising numbers of troops and reserves. Finally, any effort by other Powers to limit British Empire armed forces as a whole could not be accepted without consulting the dominion governments.

---

[31] Vansittart memorandum, 'An Aspect of International Relations in 1930' [CID 991–B], 1 May 1930, CAB 4/19.

[32] Tilley telegram (108) to Henderson, 5 Apr. 1930, *DBFP II*, I, 292–3.

[33] Cf. Stimson 'Memorandum for the President', [?May 1930], Galvin [US Navy League] to Hoover, 21 May 1930, Hoover 'Open Letter', 7 Jul. 1930, Jahncke [Navy Department] to Hoover, 9 Jul. 1930, with enclosure, all HHPP 1000; Stimson to Morrow, 4 Jun. 1930, Stimson to Lippmann [journalist], 7 Jun. 1930, Stimson drafts to Borah, 7 Jul. 1930, Stimson to Hoover, 9 Jul. 1930, with enclosures, all Stimson R80.

[34] MacDonald to Hoover, 25 Jul. 1930, HHPP 1000; Henderson to Stimson, 24 Jul. 1930, Stimson R80.

[35] Stimson to Henderson, 27 Aug. 1930, Stimson R80.

[36] RA meetings 6–7, 11, 28 Jul. 1930, CAB 16/98.

These decisions proved straightforward. Beyond agreeing that Powers should have enough armed strength to provide for national defence – but not enough to take the offensive – finding the principle on which arms limitation should be based was more difficult. Speaking for the disarmament faction, Cecil argued that budgetary ceilings offered the most effective means of control. 'Limitation would be by the total amount of money allotted to each Service,' he pointed out. 'It was in fact a global method.' Other Powers, especially the United States, challenged this approach. At Geneva, Gibson had referred to 'serious objections [in the United States] to the adoption of budgetary limitation ... on constitutional grounds'; and, more importantly, American negotiators made plain after the April 1929 Preparatory Commission that limiting the size of national armouries had to be based on specific figures not 'generalities'.[37] In addition, budgetary restrictions based on existing spending levels would benefit France over Germany. French disbursements allowed reserves for their army; the Versailles treaty prohibition of German conscription would perpetuate the military imbalance that Brüning's government and opposition politicians like Hitler found intolerable. Although Cecil, Noel-Baker, and Dalton refused to abandon budgetary limitation, the report sent to the CID advised that the eventual World Conference should decide on the applicability of the concept, which Britain would support unless there was significant opposition.[38]

Whilst the RA wrestled with these issues, Henderson involved the Foreign Office in the search for a Franco-Italian naval compromise. Craigie's experience at the London conference suggested that domestic political considerations shaped France's naval policies, something seen starkly when Tardieu and Briand left London in late February to deal with the ministerial crisis.[39] The subsequent negotiations at London, as well as Tyrrell's reports, reinforced this perception.[40] The French demanded a larger navy than Italy. Tied to Italy's position as a Mediterranean Power, Benito Mussolini, the Italian dictator's, concept

[37] Gibson memorandum, 6 Aug. 1929, Gibson 109. Cf. Jones, 'Memorandum of Conversation Between Admiral Jones and Admiral Kelly', 19 Apr. 1929, Gibson 103.
[38] 'Report of the Sub-Committee on the Reduction and Limitation of Armaments' [CID 1016–B], CAB 4/20. Cf. Selby minute to Henderson, 14 Oct. 1930, enclosing Cecil to Henderson, 24 Sep. 1930, Cecil memorandum, 24 Sep. 1930, Dalton 'Supplementary Note', n.d., all Henderson FO 800/282.
[39] Craigie to Hankey, 24 Feb. 1930, CAB 21/339. Cf. Colban minute to Drummond, 19 Feb. 1930, Colban LNR 5445/1.
[40] Cf. 'Notes of a Meeting ... March 12, 1930', 'Record of a Conversation between Mr. A. Henderson and M. Briand, 27 Mar. 1930', 'Notes of a meeting ... April 8, 1930', all DBFP II, I, 242–8, 276–9, 293–301; Tyrrell to Henderson, 24 Feb., 4, 28 Mar., 4 Jun. 1930, all Henderson FO 800/281.

of Italian self-esteem had no place for inferiority to France. As Grandi told Sir George Graham, the British ambassador at Rome, French foreign policy seemed designed to make France dominant on the continent, which Italy could not allow.[41] Henderson's conversations with Briand and Grandi at the May 1930 League Council confirmed both French desires to secure a naval march on Italy and Rome's resistance to such a course.[42]

By late September, following unproductive Franco-Italian discussions in which the French opposed British mediation,[43] and with the Preparatory Commission set to meet on 6 November, London and Washington were involving themselves in Franco-Italian discussions. On 20 September, Craigie met with René Massigli, the French naval arms negotiator, who rejected 'a maximum total tonnage figure in each category which would be equal for both France and Italy'.[44] The next week at the League Assembly, when Henderson learnt that the talks had been suspended, he informed the French and Italian representatives that he would 'do anything which either the Italian or French Government felt I could do by way of helping them to reach a satisfactory settlement'.[45] He wanted to reconcile the two Latin Powers in a way that would not affect unfavourably the European and Mediterranean balances of power. This meant careful handling of the French. The American view differed. After consulting Gibson, and two of his advisors, Hugh Wilson and Theodore Marriner, Stimson saw Lindsay to impress on him his distrust of the French.[46] Arguing that 'in naval disarmament [the] aims and interests of His Majesty's Government and [the] United States Government were identical', the secretary of state wanted concerted Anglo-American pressure on Paris to bargain in good faith. When Henderson still advocated caution, which Stimson blamed on Tyrrell for being pro-French,[47] Stimson approached MacDonald through Dawes. By 27 October, the Labour government had agreed to work with Washington to break the Franco-Italian naval stalemate.[48]

[41] Graham to Henderson, 23 Apr. 1930, Henderson FO 800/281.
[42] 'Notes of a conversation ... on May 9', Henderson despatch to Graham, 27 May 1930, Henderson despatch to Vansittart, 17 May 1930, with enclosure, all *DBFP II*, I, 358–62.
[43] Vansittart to MacDonald, 6 Aug. 1930, *ibid.*; Vansittart to Henderson, 25 Aug. 1930, Henderson FO 800/282.
[44] Craigie memorandum, 20 Sep. 1930, *DBFP II*, I, 399–400.
[45] Henderson despatches to Tyrrell and Graham, both 1 Oct. 1930, both *ibid.*, 400–2. Cf. Sissiani [Italian minister of marine] to Alexander, 19 Sep. 1930, AVAR 5/2.
[46] Lindsay telegram to Henderson, 24 Oct. 1930, *DBFP II*, I, 411; Stimson diary, 24 Oct. 1930, Stimson 10.
[47] Stimson diary, 23 Oct. 1930, Stimson 10. Some of Stimson's subordinates appreciated Britain's difficulty; see Marriner to Castle, 19 Aug. 1930, Castle 36.
[48] Stimson diary, 23 Oct. 1929, Stimson 10; *Dawes Journal*, 248–9.

Tyrrell and Graham immediately joined with Gibson to request that Paris and Rome resume naval negotiations.[49] As the French navy was much larger than its Italian counterpart, the British and Americans were prepared to bring France alone into the London treaty. This grated on Italian sensitivities.[50] Nonetheless, the Anglo-American recommendation suggested that during the life of the London naval treaty, 'France should agree on fleet figures acceptable to Great Britain'.[51] At the same time, Paris and Rome should make independent statements about their naval needs – worked out in consultation with the British and Americans and without mentioning the issue of parity. Since these figures would conform to what the British found acceptable – in accordance with the building ratios laid down in Part III of the London treaty, which included the escalator clause[52] – France and Italy could guarantee the naval status quo between them, and their security, until at least 1936. The Anglo-Americans looked to defer discussion of Franco-Italian parity until the anticipated conference convened to extend again the Washington treaty. On 6 November, the day the Preparatory Commission began meeting, Tardieu's ministry endorsed Anglo-French 'conversations' to bring France's naval demands in line with Part III of the London treaty; within twenty-four hours, Mussolini's government followed suit.[53] Craigie travelled immediately to Geneva to meet with Massigli and Augusto Rosso, Grandi's *chef de cabinet*.

For different reasons, this turn of events suited the four Powers. Whilst the French initially looked to American rather than British mediation[54] – probably to divide the two English-speaking Powers – Henderson and Vansittart wanted to be the arbiters in Franco-Italian relations. By getting Washington, Paris, and Rome to accept Craigie's mediation, they provided Britain with a voice in maintaining the European naval balance. No opposition arose in Washington where, apart from the domestic economic crisis, urgent diplomatic problems relating to Philippine independence and difficulties in Central and

---

[49] Graham telegram (177) to Henderson, 27 Oct. 1930, Tyrrell telegram (178) to Henderson, 28 Oct. 1930, both *DBFP II*, I, 414–15; Armour telegrams (324, 345) to Stimson, 27 Oct. 1930, both HHPP 987.
[50] Graham telegram to Henderson, 5 Nov. 1930, Henderson telegram to Graham, 6 Nov. 1930, both *DBFP II*, I, 424–6.
[51] Lindsay telegram to Henderson, 3 Nov. 1930, *ibid.*
[52] Foreign Office, *Naval Conference*, 25–31.
[53] Vansittart telegram (127–128) to Tyrrell, 4 Nov. 1930, Tyrrell telegram (188) to Henderson, 6 Nov. 1930, Henderson telegrams (137, 139) to Graham, both 7 Nov. 1930, Graham to Henderson, 7 Nov. 1930, all *DBFP II*, I, 422–8.
[54] Armour to Gibson, 6 Nov. 1930, Gibson 103; Gibson to Stimson, 6 Nov. 1930, HHPP 987.

South America preoccupied Hoover and Stimson.[55] Besides, since French and Italian naval construction had implications for the security of British sea-lanes running across the Mediterranean, it was politic to let MacDonald's government handle this question. Although accepting the Anglo-American compromise might seem to suggest a climbdown by the French, it constituted *realpolitik*. Tardieu deemed that France's 'naval difficulties with Italy had been allowed to assume as between the two nations an importance out of proportion to its intrinsic importance'; his principal concern in arms limitation, which was conditioned by the German question, related to land-based forces.[56] He would only gain the enmity of the English-speaking Powers, particularly Britain, a Locarno guarantor, by refusing to compromise over naval arms. In Rome, the decision to retreat from the earlier hard line derived from the impact of the Depression. Needing foreign capital and unable to raise money in the United States and Scandinavia, Mussolini's regime in early November was looking to Paris as a source of funds.[57] A month later and to French surprise, the Italians floated their loans in London.[58]

Craigie's efforts stretched over the winter of 1930–1, resulting in the 'Bases of Agreement' published on 11 March 1931. The negotiations demonstrated Craigie's diplomatic skills: he steadily cut away the diplomatic debris, like the emotive concept of 'parity'; he did not let a change of government in France in December overturn initial agreement about a construction holiday for heavy cruisers; and, when the new minister of marine, Pierre Dumont, threatened to authorise an extra battle-cruiser in February in response to a German decision to lay down a pocket battleship – a course that would upset the Mediterranean balance – he got Henderson to intervene successfully in both Paris and Rome.[59] After the London conference, France had seven heavy cruisers built and one building, nine light cruisers, and a total submarine

---

[55] Stimson diary, 10 Oct.–30 Nov. 1930, Stimson 10 *passim*. Cf. '. . . we hope very much that it can be an arrangement between France, Italy and Great Britain, to which we can give our polite assent', in Castle to Gibson, 13 Mar. 1931, Castle 109.
[56] Lindsay telegram (370) to Henderson, 3 Nov. 1930, *DBFP II*, I, 420–1. Cf. Tyrrell to Henderson, 14, 17 Nov. 1930, both Henderson FO 800/282; Ord [US military attaché, Paris] memorandum for Wilson, 'French Military Policy and Disarmament', 24 Oct. 1930, Gibson 104.
[57] Hall, *Arms Control*, 111–12.
[58] Tyrrell to Henderson, 3 Dec. 1930, Tyrrell to Vansittart, 4 Dec. 1930, Norton [FO private secretary] to Tyrrell, 12 Dec. 1930, all Henderson FO 800/282.
[59] Craigie telegram to Vansittart, 18 Dec. 1930, 'Memorandum by Mr. Craigie on his conversations at Geneva, Rome and Paris', 1 Jan. 1931, Craigie telegram to Henderson, 20 Feb. 1930, Briand to Henderson, 21 Feb. 1931, all *DBFP II*, I, 428–6, 448, 453–5, 456–8; Tyrrell to Henderson, 20 Jan., 17 Feb. 1931, Henderson to Tyrrell, 19 Feb. 1931, Craigie to Vansittart, 20 Feb. 1931, all Henderson FO 800/283. Cf. Hall, *Arms Control*, 111–14.

tonnage of 53,017; Italian figures were two heavy cruisers and seven building, twelve light cruisers, and 34,729 submarine tons. Although there seemed to be an Italian advantage in light cruisers, French warships of this class had greater displacement and larger guns. To be in effect for the life of the London treaty, the 'Bases of Agreement' witnessed compromises all round.[60] The French dropped their original demand for ten heavy cruisers, accepting eight until 1936. They reduced their desired submarine tonnage from 100,000 tons to 82,000, which still gave them equality with the USN submarine fleet. Jettisoning the demand for parity, the Italians acquiesced to no building after completing their planned construction. The British agreed to keep their submarine tonnage at the London level of 53,756 – allowing France an advantage in this vessel in European waters; but they reserved the right to expand their destroyer force should the World Disarmament Conference fail 'to arrive at a satisfactory equilibrium between French submarine tonnage and British Commonwealth destroyer tonnage'. Supported by Hoover and Stimson, as well as the Japanese government, the March agreement brought Craigie accolades from MacDonald and Henderson.[61]

The ongoing negotiation of the Franco-Italian agreement did not affect the Preparatory Commission, which met from 6 November to 9 December 1930. Conforming to Henderson and Vansittart's desire for good Anglo-French relations – and probably so as not to endanger the naval talks – MacDonald's ministry rebuffed the Brüning government's demand for German equality of arms with its neighbours.[62] A legitimate grievance because the Allied Powers had not reduced their arms as promised at the Paris peace conference,[63] removing it at that moment would have led the French National Assembly to reject any arms limitation agreement reached at Geneva. On this matter, Foreign Office disarmament advocates divided: Dalton joined Henderson and Vansittart to support a firm Anglo-French axis. Much retrospective

[60] Cmd. 3812. The following figures are from *Jane's Fighting Ships* (1930). France's light cruiser class tonnage was 52,561 tons; that of Italy 44,473.

[61] Stimson diary, 28 Feb., 3 Mar. 1931, Stimson 15; Snow [British Embassy, Tokyo] telegram to Henderson, 28 Feb. 1931, Henderson telegrams to Lindsay and Snow, 4 Mar. 1931, both *DBFP II*, I, 463, 465–6; MacDonald to Craigie, 2 Mar. 1931, MacDonald PRO 30/69/677.

[62] Sargent to Rumbold, 14 Oct. 1930, Rumbold to Sargent, 16 Oct. 1930, both *DBFP II*, I, 517–18; Rumbold despatch (861) to Henderson, 27 Oct. 1930, *BDFA*, II, J3, 306–7.

[63] Committee on Military Clauses memoranda, 'Reply to the German Counter-proposals' [WCP 945], 12 Jun. 1919, 'Allied Reply to the German Counter-proposals' [WCP 945 revise], both CAB 29/16. Cf. E. W. Bennett, *German Rearmament and the West, 1932–1933* (Princeton, 1979), 51–3; J. W. Wheeler-Bennett, *Disarmament and Security Since Locarno, 1925–1931* (1932), 25–7.

criticism from Cecil, Noel-Baker, and their disciples has been levelled at this orientation of British policy prior to the World Disarmament Conference.[64] But the situation in late 1930 dictated that the French could not be bullied into granting equality to the Germans. Tyrrell made this plain, arguing that of all French leaders, Tardieu and Briand were the most conciliatory.[65] It followed that the Commission would be unable to institute sweeping arms reductions. Rather, it would have to lay the basis for the limitation of separate classes of weapons, obtain compromises over ancillary matters like trained reserves, and find means to augment existing security arrangements through initiatives like the 'Model Treaty to Strengthen the Means of Preventing War'.

With British policy determined, Cecil led the British delegation to what proved to be a profitable meeting of the Commission: by 9 December, a single draft treaty had emerged.[66] Success obtained from the two English-speaking Powers indicating the limits to which they would go to placate Paris. Three days after the Commission began deliberating, Henderson wrote to Tyrrell:

I have this moment initialled a pretty lengthy despatch to you endeavouring to set out our position as regards French security in the hope that it may be of assistance to you in meeting French contentions ... I am satisfied that we have gone as far as it is possible to go in the way of meeting France in the matter of security, having regard to our own public opinion.[67]

Shortly afterwards, the American delegation circulated a draft 'derogations article' that constituted an elaborate escalator clause: 'If, during [the] life of [the] present convention, a change of circumstances constitutes, in the opinion of any high contracting party, a menace to its national security, such high contracting party may modify temporarily in so far as concerns itself any article or articles of [the] present convention, other than those expressly designed to apply in the event of war ...'[68] Whilst a means to assure easier Congressional approval of the eventual general treaty, this proposal, Cecil reported, 'afforded satisfaction to the French, not only in regard to the case of actual violation of

---

[64] Cf. Carlton, *MacDonald Versus Henderson*, 93–5; R. Cecil, *A Great Experiment* (1941), 212–13; P. J. Noel-Baker, *The First World Disarmament Conference 1932–33 And Why It Failed* (Oxford, New York, 1979), 47–9.

[65] Tyrrell to Henderson, 7, 14 Nov. 1930, Henderson FO 800/282.

[66] *Preparatory Commission for the Disarmament Conference. Draft Convention* (9 Dec. 1930), LND C.687.M.288.1930.IX.

[67] Henderson to Tyrrell, 10 Nov. 1930, Henderson FO 800/282.

[68] This and the next sentence based on Cecil telegram (150) to Henderson, 24 Nov. 1930, Cadogan despatch (129) to Henderson, 25 Nov. 1930, both *BDFA*, II, J3, 314–18.

the convention, but also in the case of what, for convenience, I may call "changed circumstances"'.

Concerning air and land weapons, the draft treaty amalgamated competing British and French proposals that had lain dormant since late 1927; its naval portion incorporated 'the provisions of the treaties of Washington and London', allowing that the main conference might alter them.[69] After articles outlining the principles for limiting air, land, and sea weapons, for bringing about budgetary limitation, and more, the document comprised a series of blank tables. Covering issues as diverse as 'Maximum Formations organised on a Military Basis stationed in the Home Country' and 'Dirigibles of the Land, Sea and Air Forces', these blanks were to be filled in by the main conference. Progress within the Commission was achieved largely because Paris and Berlin now realised that delay would not further their interests. Henderson's despatch and the American 'derogations article' convinced the French that they could not pry more out of London and Washington to meet their security concerns. Furthermore, with the tripartite naval talks making steady headway, it was difficult to believe that significant concessions to Paris and Rome would be forthcoming. On the German side, chafing at not acquiring equality of treatment in arms limitation, Brüning's government wanted the main conference to convene as soon as possible: 'if the eventual right to re-arm is being increasingly asserted, it is only in order to increase the pressure of the demand for general disarmament, which is what the majority of Germans really want'.[70] Just as critical, both the British and French long knew that the Weimar government had been evading some disarmament strictures, like that on accumulating war materials.[71] Whilst the Foreign Office never perceived these technical violations of Versailles as a threat to the European balance,[72] German moaning about their harsh treatment lacked the innocence necessary to convince others.

Dangers confronting arms limitation did not disappear after December 1930. Dominated by Laval, the new French government that took power

[69] Cecil despatches (115, 128, 132, 133, 142, 143) to Henderson, 15, 23, 29 Nov., 6, 10 Dec. 1930, all *ibid.*, 307–15, 318–27. Cf. *Documents of the Preparatory Commission for the Disarmament Conference* (Jul. 1931), p. 51, LND C.428.M.178.1931.IX.
[70] Newton [British Embassy, Berlin] despatch to Henderson, 14 Nov. 1930, *DBFP II*, I, 533–5.
[71] For instance, Chamberlain despatch (62) to Lindsay, 12 Jan. 1927, *DBFP IA*, II, 716–19. Cf. F. L. Carsten, *The Reichswehr and Politics, 1918–1933* (Oxford, 1966), 220–38, 351–9.
[72] J. P. Fox, 'Britain and the Inter-Allied Military Commission of Control, 1925–26', *JCH*, 4(1969), 143–64; J. Heideking, 'Vom Versailler Vertrag zur Genfer Abrüstungskonferenz: Das Scheitern der alliierten Militärkontrollpolitik gegenüber Deutschland nach dem Ersten Weltkrieg', *Militärgeschichtlichte Mitteilungen*, 28(1980), 45–68.

that month was less conciliatory than its predecessor, a tendency accentuated by the proposed German pocket battleship. In Berlin, Rumbold and his embassy feared that 'an aggressive minority are more likely to prevail over . . . a docile and peaceful majority', unless German grievances about arms limitation were addressed – the September 1930 elections were a fresh memory.[73] Nonetheless, a single draft treaty existed thanks largely to the British and Americans indicating the limits of their tolerance to continued obstruction and offering constructive means to allay French disquiet. The Powers now had to take advantage of the situation to transform the draft treaty into an expression of practical politics.

After the New Year, the Council of the League began preparing for the main conference. At its January meeting, it set 2 February 1932 as the opening date.[74] This was relatively easy. Selecting executive officers to direct the conference and co-ordinate its administration with Drummond's officials was more problematic. Eduard Beneš, the Czechoslovak foreign minister, was first promoted as the 'president' – the chief executive officer. As Czechoslovakia was a French ally, it was suggested that two neutral vice-presidents be appointed for balance: one Danish and one American. Regarding the latter, the names of Morrow and Norman Davis, a Wall Street lawyer with State Department connexions, were mentioned. Opposition to Beneš came from Curtius and Grandi, neither of whom wanted a French ally in such a sensitive post;[75] in Washington, Hoover balked at an American vice-president because of potential domestic disapproval about his government assuming a leadership role in the conference. '[The] United States representatives would as seen from here be thrust into the very forefront', Stimson told Lindsay, 'and most of [the] responsibility for eventual failure would fall on American shoulders.'[76] But with the realism that distinguished his stewardship of the State Department, he posited inevitable failure unless the major Powers concerted together: 'the Conference would not be a success unless Great Britain, France, Italy and Germany participated [with the United States] in preparation for it in the same way as we had worked hard in preparation for the Naval Conference with Great Britain'.[77]

When unhappiness in Berlin, Rome, and Washington scotched a

---

[73] Newton despatch to Henderson, 14 Nov. 1930, *DBFP II*, I, 533–5.
[74] 'Organisation of Peace and Reduction of Armaments', *Monthly Summary of the League of Nations*, 11(Jan. 1931), 5–6.
[75] Rumbold telegram (2) to Henderson, 6 Jan. 1931, Wellesley minute, 9 Jan. 1931, both *DBFP II*, III, 448, 450.
[76] Lindsay telegram (22) to Henderson, 10 Jan. 1931, *ibid.*, 452. Cf. Cotton to Hoover, 10 Jan. 1931, with enclosures, HHPP 1001.
[77] Stimson diary, 6 Jan. 1931, Stimson 15.

Beneš-led executive, new discussions ensued; by May, these had seen Henderson selected as president. His only serious rival appeared to be Briand, whose chance of selection disappeared when Washington joined with Berlin and Rome to deny France such an advantage. Unease in the Hoover Administration with French arms limitation policies *vis-à-vis* Germany was evident by late December 1930.[78] French actions over the next five months concerning the Austro-German customs union proposal, plus rejection of the 'Bases' for a Franco-Italian naval agreement, further eroded any support Briand might have had in Washington. The chief European Powers felt that Henderson had been playing an even hand to achieve arms limitation; for Stimson, the continuation of Anglo-American co-operation would do much to promote the Great Power collaboration that he and Hoover saw as essential for successful arms limitation.[79] Henderson shared this view, something he impressed on Dawes in February.[80] Although MacDonald seemed chagrined at his party rival winning this honour[81] – a personal appointment unrelated to Henderson being British foreign secretary – the political apparatus to guide the World Disarmament Conference had been established by mid-1931. It had the potential to guide the eventual general treaty along lines amenable to British interests.

With the date set and a president selected, the Disarmament Section of the League Secretariat began gathering the Powers' specific arms limitation proposals to fill in the blanks in the draft treaty. These submissions appeared in Commission reports circulated before the main conference convened.[82] Rules of procedure for the conference and its structure were also devised.[83] Here, Colban's hand can be discerned because, even though he left the Secretariat before the main conference began, they reflected lessons he learnt whilst observing the London naval conference.[84] There was to be a general commission, a central co-

---

[78] Gibson to Hoover, 31 Dec. 1930, enclosing undated memorandum, HHPP 1000.
[79] Cf. Tyrrell to Henderson, 3 Mar. 1931, Rumbold to Vansittart, 29 Apr. 1931, both Henderson FO 800/283; 'Note from Sir Eric Drummond recording a conversation with Signor Grandi', 19 Apr. 1931, *DBFP II*, III, 462–4; Stimson diary, 19 Mar. 1931, Stimson 15.
[80] Henderson despatch (237) to Lindsay, 19 Feb. 1931, *BDFA*, II, J3, 334; *Dawes Journal*, 305.
[81] Cf. Dalton diary, 29 Apr., 19–20 May 1931, Dalton BLEPS; Noel-Baker to Vansittart, 16 May 1931, Henderson to MacDonald, 23 May 1931, both Henderson FO 800/283.
[82] Cf. 'Communication from the German Government', 28 Aug. 1931, LNR 2398/27340/25878; 'Communication from the Japanese Government', 10 Sep. 1931, LNR 2402/31060/25878; 'Communication from the French Government', 17 Sep. 1931, LNR 2399/28079/25878.
[83] *Draft Rules of Procedure of the Conference* (21 Dec. 1931), LND C.1002.M.588.1931.IX.
[84] Colban to Drummond, 30 Jan., 1, 10, 11, 13 Feb., 3, 15, 20 Mar. 1930, all Colban LNS 5445/1.

ordinating body, composed of the president, vice-presidents, and chairmen of the special commissions dealing with air, land, and naval disarmament, political questions, and national defence expenditures. To avoid delays, which had occurred at London, the special commissions were to convene simultaneously. Technical committees were to assist the special commissions; and, in contradistinction to London, verbatim minutes of all meetings were to be recorded and circulated to keep the delegations briefed about what was happening. Drummond was made 'responsible for the secretarial work of the Conference and of its commission, sub-commissions and committees as well as of the General Committee of the Conference'. To ensure strong direction, the president received wide powers.[85]

Conference arrangements occurred in a desultory way throughout 1931; such an approach was unintentioned. Financial diplomacy surrounding war debts and reparations deflected the Powers' energies for much of the spring and summer. In Britain, the August crisis that produced the National Government compounded the situation; and as political uncertainty continued in Britain until after the October General Election, arms limitation was not seen as an issue of primary concern for British politicians. Of course, the fashioning of disarmament policy did not go into abeyance in Britain and the United States in this period. Nor did Anglo-American co-operation over this issue cease whilst economic and financial affairs took centre stage in international politics. Henderson and Stimson's ambition to work together, expressed in February, remained a constant during the final seven months of the second Labour government. However, with the Depression in central Europe and Britain threatening the Young settlement, disarmament conference preparations fell to the second rank of foreign policy problems.

In Britain, the RA completed its work by 30 January 1931. With the Commission having arrived at an agreed draft treaty, the British faced only two unresolved matters: controlling the private manufacture of arms and verifying the strength of foreign armed forces. On the first point, Cecil argued that 'there would be every advantage in postponing the discussion of this Convention until after the Disarmament Conference since the results of this Conference must, to a considerable extent, influence the framing of the Private Manufacture Convention'.[86] His colleagues agreed. When the armed services ministries, through the War Office representative, Brigadier A. G. Temperley, brought up

---

[85] For these powers, see *Draft Rules of Procedure*, 1.
[86] RA meeting 9, 30 Jan. 1931, memorandum 'Private Manufacture of Arms, Ammunition and Implements of War' [RA 32], 1 Dec. 1930, both CAB 16/98.

verification – 'the French proposed to camouflage their figures as much as possible'[87] – the sub-committee recognised that technical problems would have to be considered as they arose. A group comprising the representatives of 'the three Fighting Services' was thus instituted to monitor the other Powers' figures and advise the CID.[88] This small body never amounted to much as the service ministries used the main CID as a forum to vent their concerns about the state of British forces relative to those of other Powers.[89] Yet, despite the normal concern expressed about adequate funding for self-defence, these ministries did not worry unduly about arms limitation as long as there occurred, in the words of the War Office, 'the establishment of a more equitable ratio between the over-armed states and those who have disarmed, among whom we are the most prominent'.

Labour disarmament policy since June 1929 had been designed to achieve such a ratio – a naval balance with the United States and Japan; a resolution of Franco-German differences over land-based forces; and limits on air forces to prevent any Power from taking the offensive. With the work of the RA concluded, that policy had been determined. The political side of the equation then dominated: achieving domestic bipartisan support for the government's proposed course of action and, externally, ensuring that difficulties amongst the other Powers did not endanger the main conference before it met. MacDonald addressed the first problem in March 1931 when he sought Conservative and Liberal participation on a special CID sub-committee to establish 'a united national programme to be brought before the Disarmament Confer- ence'.[90] Indeed, MacDonald indicated the Cabinet's desire to have each major party represented on the eventual British delegation. A three- party sub-committee duly convened and, whilst it did not alter Labour policy, accepted that 'France holds the key to disarmament by sea, land and air'.[91] As even the over-prudent Hankey told MacDonald in May, a consensus had developed that supported Henderson and Vansittart's policy towards the Continent: 'We [the British], perhaps, are the only

---

[87] RA meeting 9, 30 Jan. 1931, War Office memorandum, 'Checking the Figures of Foreign Powers' [RA 36], 21 Jan. 1931, both *ibid.*

[88] This sub-committee never submitted a report; see CAB 16/101.

[89] Cf. War Office memorandum, 'Military Appreciation of the Situation in Europe, March 1931' [CID 1046], 31 Mar. 1931, Admiralty memorandum, 'Appreciation of the General Naval Situation in 1931' [CID 1047], 14 Apr. 1931, Air Staff memorandum, 'The General Situation in Respect of Air Armaments' [CID 1048], 27 Apr. 1931, all CAB 4/21.

[90] MacDonald to Baldwin and Lloyd George, 5 Mar. 1931, CAB 21/344.

[91] Hankey minute to MacDonald, 9 May 1931, Hankey to Vansittart, 12 May 1931, both CAB 21/344; Samuel, 'Note on Disarmament', n.d. [but Jun. 1931], Lloyd George notes, n.d. [but Jun. 1931], Hankey to MacDonald, 26 Jun. 1931, all CAB 21/345.

nation in a position to bring any pressure to bear on France in the matter. In doing so, however, it will be necessary to use the utmost caution.' When MacDonald's government sent its proposals about filling in the blanks of the draft treaty to the League Secretariat in early August,[92] the two opposition parties tendered no public criticism.

The external side involved achieving a balance between France and Germany. Brüning and Curtius' invitation to the Chequers meeting in June embraced this strategy, even though by the time the Germans set foot in Britain the financial crisis was dominating discussions. Similarly, Craigie's efforts towards a Franco-Italian naval compromise, which continued after Laval's ministry reneged on the 'Bases of Agreement', was part of Henderson Foreign Office exertions to produce fruitful arms limitation negotiations after February 1932. The foreign secretary's machinations in Paris in late July, prior to the London conference that produced the standstill agreement, represented the high-water mark of this diplomacy. Yet, Anglo-American co-operation was essential in - Labour's diplomatic strategy. By mid-1931, both London and Washington judged that arms limitation and security as they touched the European Powers could not be divorced from war debts and reparations. This was driven home by Berlin's push for an Austro-German union and Laval attaching anti-revisionist conditions to the proposed French loan. These matters convinced those responsible for foreign policy in the MacDonald government and the Hoover Administration that by working together, they could foster a political climate in which the compromises necessary for stability could be achieved. MacDonald's communications with Stimson about the moratorium before and after 20 June, plus Stimson's European tour in July, were indicative. Although Stimson worried about anti-French feelings in Britain – he ascribed these to Montagu Norman – his concern dissipated after private talks with MacDonald and Henderson in early August.[93] To his mind, these discussions were 'very helpful ... on the subject of future policy as to disarmament'. In fact, MacDonald not only mentioned the deliberations of the three-party CID committee, but also gave Stimson the British disarmament proposals to be sent to the League and 'a number of reports made to the committee on which [they were] based'.

Hoover's Administration watched as the British led in seeking a Franco-German disarmament compromise. Although some American diplomatists initially shared Stimson's concern about francophobic

[92] 'Communication from the British Government', 4 Aug. 1931, LNR 2398/26951/25878.
[93] Stimson to Hoover, 11 Aug. 1931, Stimson R81.

sentiments in the British government impeding arms limitation,[94] Washington could do little in the late summer of 1931. Unlike with the financial diplomacy that produced the moratorium, the Americans lacked leverage in arms limitation.[95] And domestically, the tactic of sitting back had benefits for an administration under attack for its inability to bring the United States out of the Depression: European security was a British not an American concern,[96] as Lindsay had learnt in February when Hoover blocked an American vice-president on the conference's executive. Externally, the sacrosanct 1930 naval agreement could not be tampered with since it removed naval rivalry with both Britain and Japan for the foreseeable future. On top of this, American ground and air forces, starved of funds since 1919, were feeble at best.[97] In June 1931, holding the continental United States to be impregnable to attack and that American overseas commitments requiring armed force were minimal, the president enforced brutal budget and manpower cuts on all American armed forces, including the USN.[98] Publicised in the American figures despatched to Geneva for circulation to the other Powers,[99] they highlighted the limits of American influence in arms limitation diplomacy and Washington's need to rely on British initiative.

Anglo-American co-operation, so prized by MacDonald and Hoover, reached its zenith during the summer of 1931. For almost three years, since the immediate aftermath of the 1928 American elections, the relationship had been shaped largely by both leaderships' willingness to compromise over the major political and financial problems that con-

[94] Wilson to Moffat, 16 Jul. 1931, Moffat to Gilbert, 1 Aug. 1931, both Moffat 1.
[95] See Wilson to Gibson, 6 Mar. 1931, and memoranda – 1, 3, 6 Apr. 1931 – recording State, Navy, and War departments' meetings about submitting information to Geneva, all Gibson 105.
[96] Castle to Gibson, 13 Mar. 1931, Castle 10; Armour to Gibson, 2 Apr. 1931, Gibson 103; Marriner telegram (183) to Stimson, 11 Jun. 1931, Castle to Hoover, 31 Jul. 1931, with enclosure, both HHPP 1001.
[97] See the 1928–32 statistics in 'Military Personnel on Active Duty: 1789 to 1970', Department of Commerce, *Historical Statistics*, 1141. Cf. R. Spector, 'The Military Effectiveness of the US Armed Forces, 1919–39', in A. R. Millett and W. Murray, eds., *Military Effectiveness*, vol. II: *The Interwar Period* (Boston, 1988), 70–97; J. R. Wilson, 'The Quaker and the Sword: Herbert Hoover's Relations with the Military', *Military Affairs*, 38(1974), 41–7.
[98] Cf. Hoover to Jahncke, 15 May 1931, unsigned memorandum, 'Naval Conference at Camp Rapidan', 7 Jun. 1931, CNO to Office of Naval Operations, 23 Jul. 1931, enclosing memoranda, 'Plans for Operating and Maintaining the Treaty Navy', 7 Jul. 1931, 'Organization of Naval Forces', n.d., 'Summary of Types', n.d., 'Aircraft Required for the Treaty Navy', 22 Jun. 1931, all HHPP 38. American navalists disagreed; see Knox [retired naval officer and writer] to Johnson [California senator], 23 Jun. 1931, Office of Naval Intelligence to Knox, 3 Jul. 1931, both Knox 3.
[99] 'Communication by the Government of the United States of America', 9 Jun. 1932, LNR 2398/27683/25878.

fronted them. Additionally, as their handling of Japan at London in 1930 and their approach to Franco-German differences demonstrated, there had been a perception about shared interests. Admittedly, residues of suspicion and mistrust remained in some quarters in both capitals.[100] But overall, MacDonald, Hoover, Stimson, and even Henderson recognised that Anglo-American co-operation offered means of underwriting international political and financial security. This consensus related to maintaining the international structures that had emerged in the 1920s. By the autumn of 1931, the systems of security began to face pressures. Thereafter, owing to threats to the balances of power in Europe and the Far East, co-operation began to break down. The reason resided in divergent views about meeting these threats to protect perceived national interests; and, within Britain's foreign-policy-making elite, the belief re-emerged that the United States could not be relied upon to contribute meaningfully to international security.

The first threat emerged on 18 September 1931 in the north-eastern Chinese province of Manchuria.[101] Armed conflict erupted between the Japanese Kwantung Army, which guarded Japanese-controlled railways, and troops loyal to the local warlord, Chang Hseuh-Liang, who owed fealty to the government of the Chinese strongman, Chiang Kai-shek. Within three days of the outbreak of violence in the city of Mukden, the Kwantung Army, supported by additional units from the Japanese army in Korea, commanded the main points along the Southern Manchurian Railway. By mid-October, Japanese forces controlled most of the Manchurian railway system and were spreading out to conquer the province. The Kwantung Army justified its operations outside the railway zone by the need to protect the life and property of Japanese nationals from Chinese brigandage – about which there was some truth; and its success derived from the efficiency of its troops and the effective use of air attacks against cities like Chinchow, a strategic transportation point on the southern route into the province. That Chiang's ostensible national government was weakened by warfare between his forces and other warlords, plus food shortages caused by flooding and other natural calamities, only aided the Japanese. By March 1932, with Japanese mastery over Manchuria complete, a puppet government declared the independence of 'Manchukuo'.

Several reasons underlay Japan's conquest. Manchuria contained

[100] Cf. Bridgeman to Balfour, 12 Apr. 1930, Baldwin 117; Jones to Moffat, 22 Jan. 1931, Moffat 1.
[101] The next two paragraphs are based on J. B. Crowley, *Japan's Quest for Autonomy. National Security and Foreign Policy, 1930–1938* (Princeton, 1966), 82–183; I. C. Y. Hsü, *The Rise of Modern China* (New York, 1975), 656–65; I. H. Nish, *Japan's Struggle With Internationalism. Japan, China, and the League of Nations, 1931–3* (1993), 23–43.

plentiful natural resources, had abundant agriculture, and, thanks to Russian investment before the Russo-Japanese war of 1904–5, and Japanese afterwards, was the most industrialised part of China. Japanese nationalists looked covetously on the province, seeing it as a natural area of economic and strategic expansion through its contiguity with their Korean colony. The intensification of Chinese xenophobia and the advent of the Depression convinced these nationalists, particularly younger officers in the Kwantung Army, that Manchuria might fall from Japan's orbit. Given that anti-Japanese demonstrations and boycotts of Japanese goods were becoming commonplace in China, including Manchuria, the idea emerged that unless the province was seized, Japan's position on the East Asian continent could be weakened. Civilian leaders in Tokyo preferred economic expansion to recourse to arms in establishing Japanese hegemony; but after Mukden, they were outmanoeuvred by militarists in the government. Dominated by military men, a new Cabinet took power in December 1931 and supported what had heretofore been independent Kwantung Army actions that violated the Washington nine-Power treaty and probably the Kellogg Pact and the League Covenant. It constituted a major diplomatic crisis that London and Washington could ignore at their peril.

The British and Americans approached the situation warily. In Britain, domestic problems resulting from the National Government's decision to go off the gold standard on 21 September and subsequent political scheming about how the coalition should contest the antici-pated general election hampered decisive action. Meeting the crisis fell to the Foreign Office, which, beyond agreeing that order should be re-established, divided over how this might be achieved.[102] By the late 1920s, Anglo-Japanese relations in China had been defined by an informal *modus vivendi* that left each Power alone in their spheres of economic interest: Britain chiefly in the south, at Hong Kong and along the Yangtze River; and Japan in the north, in its Liaotung leasehold and Manchuria. A policy of hard realism, it produced balance between the two Powers' interests and even improved Anglo-Chinese relations.[103] After Mukden, Foreign Office East Asian experts led by Wellesley and Sir John Pratt, a senior member of the Far Eastern Department, saw Japan's actions as threatening to the balance of power; they also worried that League intervention would be greeted unfavourably in Tokyo.

---

[102] Except where noted, the next two paragraphs are based on C. Thorne, *The Limits of Foreign Policy. The West, the League and the Far Eastern Crisis of 1931–1933* (New York, 1973), 149–52.

[103] Cf. E. K. S. Fung, 'The Sino-British Rapprochement, 1927–1931', *Modern Asian Studies*, 17(1983), 79–105.

On the other side pro-Leaguers, led by Cadogan, argued that the organisation's ability to meet future crises in the Far East, Europe, or elsewhere would be undermined unless it took a prominent role in bringing about a settlement.

Lord Reading, the caretaker foreign secretary who replaced Henderson, showed initial reluctance to take any initiative that might limit the policy options of the post-election Cabinet. British hands were forced when Chiang's government, using Article 11 of the Covenant, appealed to the League on 21 September to have the Council consider the crisis. Reading understood that Britain now had to support a League-sponsored settlement. 'A failure by the League to find some way round the difficulty would be nothing short of calamity at the present juncture', he told Vansittart, 'and might imperil any hopes we may have of making progress towards a solution in the more immediate field of Europe in which we are so much concerned.'[104] He, therefore, attended a League Council in October that, on the 16th, invited the United States to join its deliberations and, on the 24th, asked Japan to withdraw its troops into the railway zone before the Council reconvened on 16 November. It fell to his successor, Sir John Simon, a Liberal who took office on 5 November, to find a solution that would shield British Far Eastern interests.

American reactions were important in British calculations.[105] It has been argued that after the difficulties Hoover faced from domestic critics and the French over the moratorium, his internationalism waned; first appearing during the Manchurian crisis, his attitude convinced the National Government, dominated by the Conservatives, about the equivocal nature of American foreign policy.[106] There is much truth in this argument, particularly as the new Cabinet, grappling with the manifold challenges confronting Britain, found the Hoover Administration oscillating between action and opposition to Japan with nothing more substantial than words. Incensed at what he held to be Japanese aggression, Hoover reckoned that his government had to do something 'to uphold the moral foundations of international life'.[107] But isolationism militated against both unilateral action and any notion of American participation in collective security. With Geneva involved

---

[104] Reading to Vansittart, 21 Oct. 1931, *DBFP II*, VIII, 810, n. 3. Cf. Reading despatch (126) to Vansittart, with enclosure, 17 Oct. 1931, *BDFA*, II, E10, 350–1.
[105] Vansittart to Simon, 16 Nov. 1931, Simon FO 800/285.
[106] Watt, *John Bull*, 62–3.
[107] In N. Graebner, 'Hoover, Roosevelt, and the Japanese', in D. Borg and S. Kamoto, eds., *Pearl Harbor as History. Japanese-American Relations, 1931–1941* (New York, London, 1973), 25–6. See E. E. Robinson and V. D. Bornet, *Herbert Hoover. President of the United States* (Stanford, 1975), 196–203.

following the Chinese appeal, Administration diplomacy had to proceed prudently. Stimson's assessment differed. Thinking in terms of the global balance, he recognised that the treaties on which Far Eastern and European security found basis were at risk: 'the whole world looks on to see whether the treaties are good for anything or not, and if we lie down and treat them like scraps of paper nothing will happen, and in the future the peace movement will receive a blow that it will not recover from for a long time'.[108] Toying with American support for League sanctions against Japan, he expressed these sentiments after the bombing of Chinchow. Hoover overruled him: '[Stimson] feels deeply and rightly that the whole fabric of international obligations are at stake. I agreed with that, but I could not agree to take any part in economic sanctions. My view was that they would lead to war ...'[109] Given the weakness of United States armed strength accentuated by Hoover's economies in June, American diplomacy had to avoid concrete methods of containing Japan. Bowing to presidential authority, Stimson then pursued a policy that did not first seek to compromise with the British – the hallmark of Anglo-American co-operation since before June 1929.

Accordingly, a gulf began to appear between the two English-speaking Powers in November and December as the League endeavoured to solve the crisis. When the Council reconvened on 16 November, the area of Japanese military operations had expanded. Japanese self-esteem would not allow them to be dictated to by the western Powers, and the rise of the militarist government only entrenched the unyielding elements of Japan's policy.[110] Since 1921, successive Japanese cabinets had co-operated with Britain and the United States, especially over naval arms limitation. Manchuria suggested that a new era marked by a less accommodating Japan had begun. British diplomatists understood this – especially Reading and Simon. Britain lacked the resources to force Japan to retreat, which *ipso facto* meant the League lacked resources. With Washington disinclined to offer practical support, and with the effectiveness of British armed forces in the Far East uncertain, the Cabinet agreed on 11 November that a diplomatic solution that conciliated Japan had become essential.[111] Thus when, on Drummond's

108 Stimson diary, 9 Oct. 1931, Stimson 18. On the top of this page, Stimson later scrawled: 'Trying to wake up H.H.' Cf. Hornbeck [Far Eastern Division, State Department] memorandum, 'Manchuria – American Interests in', 30 Sep. 1931, Hornbeck 453.

109 Hoover memorandum, n.d. [but late 1931] in Hoover to Stimson, 3 Jun. 1936, quoted in Robinson and Bornet, *Hoover*, 199.

110 Lindley despatch (500) to Reading, 21 Oct. 1931, Lindley despatches (559, 586, 593) to Simon, 27 Nov., 12, 15 Dec. 1931, all *BDFA*, II, E10, 378–80, 402–3, 420–1, 422–5.

111 CC 75(31)1, 11 Nov. 1931, CAB 23/69. Cf. COS memorandum, 'Imperial Defence

suggestion, the League Council agreed on 10 December to send a commission of enquiry to the region to investigate and make recommendations for a settlement, London supported it.[112] A commission would buy time whilst some sort of settlement was put together. The impending World Disarmament Conference, plus new threats to the Young Plan created by the worsening Depression, both judged more important for Britain and the European Powers at that juncture, needed to be addressed.[113]

At this moment, American policy wobbled. On 16 October, in a stunning diplomatic departure, Washington instructed Prentiss Gilbert, the American consul at Geneva, to attend the Council as an observer. Three days later his orders were rescinded because some meetings were *in camera*; smacking of secret diplomacy, this created problems with Congressional isolationists.[114] Dawes was then despatched to the Council in November and December but, not joining in its deliberations, he simply paced the lobby to show American solidarity with the League. On top of this, Hoover and Stimson at first opposed a League commission but then not only supported one but allowed an American to join as full member.[115] Stimson selected a friend with Philippine experience, General Frank McCoy, as the United States representative to serve under its chairman, Lord Lytton, a former British viceroy of India. This course of events caused Baldwin, the locus of real power in the National Government, to criticise privately United States policy: 'You will get nothing out of Washington but words, big words, but only words.'[116]

For the Anglo-American relationship, this was a prologue to Stimson's 7 January 1932 announcement that the United States would not recognise

the legality of any situation *de facto*, nor does it intend to recognise any treaty or agreement entered into between those Governments, or agents thereof, which may impair the treaty rights of the United States or its citizens in China ... and

Policy. Annual Review for 1932', 23 Feb. 1932, CAB 53/22 which was being prepared in November–December 1931.

[112] 'Extract from Minutes of the Sixty-Fifth Session of the Council', 10 Dec. 1931, Simon despatch (653) to Lindley, 14 Dec. 1931, both *BDFA*, II, E10, 393, 407–16.
[113] MacDonald to Simon, 14 Nov. 1931, Simon FO 800/285; Leith-Ross to Sargent, 19 Oct. 1931, Leith-Ross to Vansittart, 14 Nov. 1931, both Leith-Ross T 188/16; Neville Chamberlain to Hilda, 6 Dec. 1931, NC 18/1/764.
[114] J. B. Donnelly, 'Prentiss Gilbert's Mission to the League of Nations Council, October 1931', *DH*, 2(1978), 373–87; Thorne, *Limits*, 159–61.
[115] On US policy and the commission, see Stimson diary, 23–25 Sep. 1931, Stimson 18; Stimson diary, 17, 20, 21, 26 Nov., 9 Dec. 1931, Stimson 19; Hornbeck to Castle, 14 Oct. 1931, Hornbeck to Stimson, 18 Nov. 1931, both Hornbeck 453. For justification of US policy, Moffat to Gilbert, 3 Dec. 1931, Moffat 1. Cf. Thorne, *Limits*, 192–9.
[116] Thorne, *Limits*, 247.

that it does not intend to recognise any situation, treaty or agreement which may be brought about by means contrary to the covenants and obligations of the Pact of Paris . . .[117]

The 'Stimson doctrine' – 'the doctrine of non-recognition' – resulted from the growing disfavour with which the Hoover Administration perceived Japan's effort to protect its rights in Manchuria. Japanese arguments about self-defence seemed more a mask hiding expansionism than a legitimate desire to safeguard Japanese commercial investments. The occupation of Chinchow on 2 January proved a watershed: its capture meant that the province had fallen completely under Japanese control.[118] Lacking means to force Japan to disgorge its conquest, the Hoover Administration put on record United States opposition to changes that Japan's actions might make to existing treaty obligations concerning China. Most important was the 'Open Door' which, proposed by the McKinley Administration in September 1899 and accepted by the European Great Powers and Japan, sought to preserve China's political unity and independence whilst attesting that all Powers should enjoy equal commercial and tariff rights there.[119] Reaffirmed at the Washington conference, the 'Open Door' underpinned the American commercial and financial presence in China after 1922.

In limited terms, the Stimson doctrine constituted the sensible diplomatic response of a Power unable to defend its interests in China by force of arms – although Hoover and Stimson soon divided over whether the doctrine involved American disapproval (Hoover's view) or a first step towards stronger statements and, maybe, sanctions (Stimson's view).[120] More widely, apart from raising Japanese hackles, it complicated League efforts to resolve the crisis; and, because there had been no consultation beforehand, it encountered difficulty from Simon and the National Government. First, Stimson did not inform Britain and the other nine-Power signatories of his *démarche* until the day he despatched it.[121] Second, even though the British had formally thrown their support behind the Lytton Commission, Stimson was asking for

---

[117] Stimson note, 7 Jan. 1932, *FRUS Japan, 1931–1941*, I, 76.
[118] D. Borg, *The United States and the Far Eastern Crisis of 1933–1938* (Cambridge, MA, 1964), 7–12; R. N. Current, *Secretary Stimson. A Study in Statecraft* (New Brunswick, NJ, 1954), 85–90; E. E. Morison, *Turmoil and Tradition. A Study of the Life and Times of Henry L. Stimson* (Boston, 1960), 378–88.
[119] Cf. M. Hunt, 'Americans in the China Market: Economic Opportunities and Economic Nationalism, 1890s–1931', *Business History Review*, 51(1977), 277–307; E. R. May, *American Imperialism: A Speculative Essay* (New York, 1968); T. McCormick, *China Market: America's Quest for Informal Empire* (Chicago, 1967).
[120] R. N. Current, 'The Stimson Doctrine and the Hoover Doctrine', *AHR*, 59(1954), 513–42.
[121] Lindsay telegram (12) to Simon, 7 Jan. 1932, *BDFA*, II, E11, 91.

'representations to Tokyo warning the Japanese Government against any infringement of treaty rights' under the nine-Power treaty and the Kellogg Pact.[122] Even before Chinchow fell, the British shared American misgivings about Japan's forward policy in Manchuria.[123] From their perspective, however, the question became how to ensure that British and other foreign interests in China were protected. There were two divergent answers: a policy of armed intervention, or conciliation. The new Cabinet had weighed these alternatives on 11 November and had opted for the latter, which lay at the basis of British policy in January. Offering tough words without force behind them, the Stimson doctrine only antagonised Japan. Simon distanced Britain from the American statement and, though grasping the goal of Japanese policy in Manchuria, took at face value Tokyo's assurances 'that Japan had no territorial ambitions in Manchuria and was the champion in Manchuria of the principle of equal opportunity and the Open Door for economic activities of all nations'.[124] In essence, this meant accepting that a Japanese-controlled Manchuria would not undermine existing foreign treaty rights in the province. On this basis, he and his advisers supported the Lytton Commission. As he minuted on Christmas Day 1931: 'I quite agree that good relations with Japan are of the first order of requisites, & must be safeguarded; but we must, consistently with this, play our part as a member of the League, and use such influence as we have.'[125] Stimson disliked the British response, yet he understood the problems facing them: 'it was not at all unexpected so far as I was concerned, owing to the complications the British are in with India and with their financial situation'.[126]

This suggests that whilst National Government and Hoover Administration tactics differed, Simon and Stimson, and Hoover, for that matter, were at one in their misgivings about Japanese policy. Just as crucial, both leaderships shared a desire to help re-establish stability in East Asia to protect their Chinese interests; and, to a degree, each understood the problems of the other. Therefore, diplomatic means not ends separated London from Washington. In more placid times, similarity of goals might have produced full co-operation, just as at London in 1930 or over the moratorium the preceding June. But by January 1932, the two Powers' inability to shake off the Depression, renewed

[122] Wellesley 'Record ... of a conversation with the French Ambassador', 7 Jan. 1932, *DBFP II*, IX, 87.
[123] Wellesley memorandum, 22 Dec. 1931, *ibid.*, 31–3.
[124] Simon telegram (21) to Lindsay, 9 Jan. 1932, *ibid.*, 101–2.
[125] Simon minute, 25 Dec. 1931, *ibid.*, 33, n. 9.
[126] Stimson diary, 9 Jan. 1932, Stimson 20.

pressures on the war debts and reparations agreements, and the advent of the World Disarmament Conference diffused energies. With a new government in Britain, and Hoover less internationalist in deeds, the gulf that had opened between Britain and the United States had no time to close.

After 18 January, Sino-Japanese conflict spilled out of Manchuria into Shanghai, the financial heart of western interests in China. The Shanghai emergency has been analysed elsewhere.[127] Anti-Japanese demonstrations and a boycott of Japanese goods produced tensions that saw the deaths of some Japanese nationals in the city at the hands of Chinese rioters. Despite Chinese local authorities conceding to Japanese demands for reparations and the dissolution of all anti-Japanese organisations, Tokyo despatched troops, aeroplanes, and ships to the city ostensibly to protect the 'International Settlement' from Chinese outrages but, in reality, to punish the Chinese. By 2 February 1932, the day the World Disarmament Conference opened, Japanese aeroplanes had fire-bombed Chapei, a Chinese sector of the city. RN and USN warships reached Shanghai on 5 February to help defend the 'Settlement'; and the British and American ambassadors in China, Sir Miles Lampson and Nelson Johnson, helped negotiate a settlement once fighting ceased on 3 March – Chinese resistance proved better than expected, preventing a quick Japanese victory. On 4 May, with the withdrawal of Japanese forces, an armistice was achieved. Along with the proclamation of independent Manchukuo two months earlier, the armistice saw a tenuous calm appear.

The Shanghai incident widened the gulf that had opened between the two English-speaking Powers. By 8 February, because the violence there affected all Powers with interests in China – unlike in Manchuria where Japan's were almost exclusive – Hoover and Stimson believed that they could now obtain British support for non-recognition.[128] Stimson then spent from 11 to 15 February making his case personally to Simon on the transatlantic telephone.[129] Despite Geneva having been brought more fully into the crisis – Chiang's government had appealed to the League on 29 January to invoke Articles 10 and 15 of the Covenant[130] –

---

[127] Borg, *Far Eastern Crisis*, 9–12; Nish, *Japan's Struggle*, 90–106; Thorne, *Limits*, 203–10.

[128] Stimson diary, 6–10 Feb. 1932, Stimson 20.

[129] Transcripts of these conversations – 11, 12, (2) 15 Feb. – are in *DBFP II*, IX, 441–4, 460–3, 487, 489–91.

[130] W. W. Willoughby, *The Sino-Japanese Controversy and the League of Nations* (Baltimore, 1935 [1968 reprint]), 218–19. Article 10 sought Council advice in case of 'aggression or in case of any threat or danger of such aggression'; Article 15 appealed to the Council to 'make all necessary arrangements for a full investigation and consideration thereof'. Article 15 had been amended in this sense in 1924; see *ibid.*, 677, 679–80.

Stimson wanted a joint Anglo-American appeal via the nine-Power treaty and the Kellogg Pact. Simon countered that Britain had obligations to the League. After consulting with MacDonald, he agreed to seek Council support for the non-recognition of any changes to China's situation that ran counter to Article 10; Stimson could balance this with an American statement relating to violations of the nine-Power and Kellogg agreements. Agreeing with the argument that joint Anglo-American pressure would be more effective, Stimson responded that Britain should endorse both his initiative and any the League might undertake. At this point, Simon had to depart for Geneva. He had Vansittart inform the American Embassy at London that he would do what he could to get Council support for non-recognition.[131]

Uneasy with this delay, Stimson dropped the matter and decided to seek support from other governments without British blessing. He encapsulated his proposal in an open letter to Borah on 23 February.[132] According to Norman Davis, representing the United States at the disarmament conference, his missive had a good effect at Geneva.[133] In London, however, Vansittart decried it as a rehash of the 7 January declaration.[134] Although Stimson's action pre-empted Council consideration of the proposal he made to Simon, the Assembly adopted a resolution on 11 March that maintained that League members should not 'recognise any situation, treaty or agreement brought about by means contrary to the Covenant ... or to the Pact of Paris'. The resolution also established a 'Committee of Nineteen' to monitor and report on this and other resolutions and to join in searching for a settlement.[135] By then, the Shanghai crisis was receding, Manchukuo was an uncomfortable fact, and the Lytton Commission had embarked for the Far East. And, unexpectedly, division between Britain and the United States had appeared over how to respond to Japan's forward policies in China.

The simple fact was that neither the British nor the Americans had sufficient armed strength in the Far East to take the offensive against Japan. This was driven home to the National Government when it chose conciliation in November 1931, and COS assessments over the next few

---

[131] FO memorandum, 16 Feb. 1932, *DBFP II*, IX, 50–7. Cf. Simon to Atherton, [?5] Feb. 1932, Vansittart to Simon, 8 Feb. 1932, both Simon FO 800/286.

[132] Stimson draft to Borah, 23 Feb. 1932, Stimson R82.

[133] Davis to Stimson, 1 Mar. 1932, *ibid.*

[134] Vansittart to Simon, 26 Feb. 1932, Simon FO 800/286.

[135] 'Resolution Adopted by the Assembly on March 11, 1932', *BDFA*, II, E11, 224–6. The Committee comprised the Assembly president, who doubled as chairman, all Council delegates other than those of Japan and China, and six Assembly members elected by secret ballot.

months disabused Simon and other ministers that it could be otherwise.[136] For London, a political solution in concert with the League remained the only alternative. '*We* are incapable of checking Japan in any way if she really means business and has sized us up, as she certainly has done', Vansittart observed on 1 February 1932. 'Therefore we must eventually be done for in the Far East, unless [the] United States are eventually to use force. It is universally assumed that the United States will never use force.'[137] Here lay the problem which the Stimson doctrine ignored: tough words had to be supported by a show of strength, either economic or military, or both. United States ground and air forces were in no condition to undertake major operations in the Far East in conjunction with those of Britain; and, despite what Stimson might have thought about his government imposing sanctions, Hoover would not do so. The Foreign Office suspected the worst – rightly as it turned out. Admittedly, the British misjudged Stimson to a degree. Of all American leaders at this time, he understood the hard edge of *realpolitik*, and he alone thought in global strategic terms when making policy.[138] However, Stimson misjudged the British, their willingness to accommodate a new situation in the Far East, and their position as leaders within the League. The result was that co-operation between the two English-speaking Powers, at least in responding to Japanese policy in China, proved illusory. Nonetheless, the leaderships in both countries still looked to Anglo-American co-operation in their pursuit of arms limitation and in handling the international economic and financial problems spawned by the continuing Depression. It was these matters that preoccupied them as the crisis in the Far East entered a quiescent phase after March 1932.

[136] Cf. COS Deputies report, 'Situation in the Far East' [COS 295 (DC)], 22 Feb. 1932, COS memorandum, 'The Situation in the Far East' [COS 296], 22 Feb. 1932, both CAB 53/22.

[137] Vansittart minute, 1 Feb. 1932, *DBFP II*, IX, 282, n. 2. Cf. C. Thorne, 'The Shanghai Crisis of 1932: The Basis of British Policy', *AHR*, 75(1970), 1616–39.

[138] For instance, his defence of continued American control of the Philippines: 'Again, our presence in the Philippine Islands has already contributed to the development of a new base of political equilibrium throughout the area of the Western Pacific and Eastern Asia ... withdrawal of American sovereignty from the Philippines and the termination of American responsibility in and for the Islands would profoundly disturb that equilibrium.' In Stimson to Bingham [US senator], 18 Feb. 1932, Stimson R82.

4 The unravelling of co-operation, 1932–1933

> I am trying to avoid a situation which will mean that the United States will go back to the relations they had with us before 1929, when in spite of the Irish Settlement, opposition to us was regarded as very certain proof of patriotism to the United States.
>
> MacDonald, June 1932[1]

Between early 1932 and early 1934, the international order created at the Paris peace conference and modified by the Washington and Locarno treaties and the war debt and reparations settlements came under sustained assault. British foreign policy had to ensure that Britain's economic, political, and strategic interests tied to these arrangements were safeguarded. Generally speaking, since 1921, that policy had been fashioned by finding grounds to co-operate with the major Powers: France, Italy, and Germany in Europe via the League, Locarno, and the war debt and reparations agreements; Japan in the Far East through the three Washington treaties; and, because of its interest in naval affairs and economic diplomacy, the United States by resolving the cruiser question and making the Dawes and Young settlements work. Some division had developed in the foreign-policy-making elite between those like Vansittart, Dalton, and Tyrrell who promoted 'world leadership' policies, whether they focused more on France or more on Germany, and 'atlanticists' like MacDonald. As evidenced by Henderson, these ideas were not mutually exclusive, and this produced a balanced foreign policy in pursuit of the global balance of power. But as the constellation of international power began changing after 1932, so did the equilibrium between the two main wings of the British elite. The 'world leaders' came to dominate policy-making.

Importantly, the National Government did not begin life unwilling to co-operate with the United States, which Dawes' embassy impressed on Hoover and Stimson – as did, after Dawes retired in early 1932, that of his successor, Mellon.[2] Conservative ministers like Baldwin and Neville

[1] MacDonald to Simon, 3 Jun. 1932, Simon FO 800/287.
[2] Dawes telegram to Stimson, 6 Nov. 1932, in Boal to Newton, 6 Nov. 1932, HHPP 988;

Chamberlain had held office in the 1920s when the cruiser question and war debts had strained Anglo-American relations. Whilst some of them thought MacDonald too deferential to Washington,[3] none held implacably hard views about the United States. Even Chamberlain thought that earlier difficulties stemmed from Coolidge, and that Hoover would work with the British rather than against them.[4] As Lindsay impressed on his political masters as late as March 1932, Stimson was trustworthy and had 'a genuine and heartfelt personal love for England'.[5] Within the new Cabinet, apart from MacDonald, some influential ministers were pro-American. Sir Samuel Hoare, the Conservative Indian secretary, for instance, long held ideas about an 'Anglo-American alliance' being 'an inestimable blessing to the world'.[6] Still, compromise between London and Washington became difficult. Overshadowed by Far Eastern troubles, this largely resulted from the course of the World Disarmament Conference and the Depression's impact on war debts and reparations. These matters showed that in Palmerstonian terms, relying on the United States to help protect Britain's 'eternal interests' was misplaced. That Hoover and the Republicans lost the November 1932 American elections and were succeeded in March 1933 by a more isolationist Administration led by a Democrat, Franklin Roosevelt, only showed such reliance to be dangerous. For these reasons, rather than the rise of the National Government, the fissure that opened between Britain and the United States during the initial months of the Manchurian crisis spread quickly and deeply after January 1932.

Although disarmament advocates supposed that the world conference would make quick headway, the delegations met throughout 1932 without result.[7] France's quest for security and Berlin's chagrin over the denial of equality of treatment frustrated even preliminary agreement on minor issues. In this atmosphere, the British and Americans strove to push discussions along and, unable to do so, generated further pressures

Atherton despatch to Stimson, 9 Nov. 1932, in Boal to Newton, 27 Nov. 1932, HHPP 995.
[3] Chamberlain to Hilda, 11 Jun. 1932, NC 18/1/786.
[4] Chamberlain to Hilda, 9 Jun. 1929, NC 18/1/657.
[5] Lindsay to Simon, 3 Mar. 1932, Simon FO 800/286. Cf. Howard to Henderson, 27 Aug. 1929, Henderson FO 800/280.
[6] From Hoare's Harrow prize essay of May 1899, 'The Imperial Mission of the Anglo-Saxon Race', 37, in Templewood P6.
[7] W. E. Arnold-Forster, 'A Policy for the Disarmament Conference', *Political Quarterly*, 2(1931), 378–93; R. Cecil, 'Facing the World Disarmament Conference', *FA*, 10(1931), 13–22; H. W. Harris, 'Towards Disarmament', *CR*, 139(1931), 147–53. On the World Disarmament Conference, see Bennett, *German Rearmament*, 131–304; McKercher, 'Horns and Teeth'; M. Vaïsse, *Sécurité d'abord: La politique française en matière de désarmement, 9 décembre 1930–7 avril 1934* (Paris, 1981).

affecting their ability to co-operate. The genesis of this can be seen in their final – and separate – preparations for the conference. Less than two weeks after taking office, the new Cabinet created an advisory committee on disarmament.[8] Composed of Simon, as chairman, the dominions secretary, J. H. Thomas, and the three service ministers – Lord Londonderry, the air secretary, Viscount Hailsham, the war minister, and Sir Bolton Eyres-Monsell, the first lord of the Admiralty – it submitted two reports by mid-January 1932.[9] Ranging over the problems that confronted Britain, this body determined the figures that Britain wanted inserted into the draft disarmament treaty.[10] It recommended pursuing seven goals at the conference: abolishing the submarine; reducing capital ship displacement and armament; abolishing gas and chemical weapons; abolishing conscription; restricting land guns above a certain calibre; supporting budgetary limitation; and establishing a permanent Disarmament Commission to oversee the implementation of the eventual treaty. On the other side, it opposed prohibitions on both military aircraft and tanks. These decisions proved relatively easy given the work accomplished by the Labour government's limitation of armaments sub-committee, the efforts of the three-party committee, and specialist advice from an inter-departmental group of experts, set up on 7 October.[11]

More burdensome were political and strategic questions. With limitations on the projection of British armed strength in the Far East clear at this point – not through RN weakness, but because previous budget cuts had made Singapore and other bases ill-prepared for either attacking or defending against the Japanese[12] – British armed forces were pared to the operational bone. Simon stressed the problem for the Cabinet:

we cannot hope to persuade other Powers to reduce their armaments by telling them that we cannot reduce ours; and, on the other hand, our previous reductions have made it, in the opinion of our technical advisers, practically impossible to effect very substantial further reductions ourselves.[13]

However, only one Power had to be convinced to reduce its arms:

[8] CC 80(31)4, 20 Nov. 1931, CAB 23/69.
[9] Simon, 'Interim Report', 14 Dec. 1931, Simon note, 'Disarmament Conference', enclosing 'Report', both 11 Jan. 1932, both CAB 27/476.
[10] CDC(31) Meetings 1–4, 6, *ibid.* This produced minor textual amendments to the document sent to Geneva in August 1931; see 'Amendments to the Communication from the British Government', 25 Jan. 1931, LNR 2398/26951/25878.
[11] 'Reports of the Inter-departmental Sub-Committee on Preparation for the Disarmament Conference' [CID 1078B], 27 Nov. 1931, CAB 4/21.
[12] COS Deputies report, 'Situation in the Far East' [COS 295 (DC)], 22 Feb. 1932, CAB 53/22.
[13] Simon note, 11 Jan. 1932, CAB 27/476. Cecil was already complaining; Cecil to Simon, 9 Jan. 1932, with enclosure, Simon FO 800/286.

France. Echoing Vansittart,[14] Simon argued that political guarantees might augment existing security treaties; he had in mind a French suggestion then circulating for a 'Mediterranean Locarno' to diminish Franco-Italian rivalry and allow them to sign the London naval treaty. In this context, American policy remained significant because of the international debt structure: '[the United States] is profoundly mistrustful of the policies and armaments of Europe; and probably only a very real measure of disarmament would convince the United States that the time had come to modify claims which she is fully entitled to press'.

Since a Mediterranean agreement would compound British military and naval obligations, a special group comprised of MacDonald, Chamberlain, and Simon's committee examined the idea. On its recommendation, the Cabinet rejected additional commitments.[15] The chief reasons related to British public opinion hesitating 'to accept a guarantee sufficiently effective to give satisfaction to France', dominion opposition that might 'exercise a detrimental effect on the naval co-operation which Australia and New Zealand now give', and financial costs. The special group understood that unless French security was further bolstered, Paris might reject arms cuts significant enough to impress Berlin. French intransigence might see Germany quit the League: the League, 'even if it survives so shattering a blow, will, for a long time to come, be crippled and emasculated'; and British defence spending would increase significantly. However, the peril in supporting initiatives like a Mediterranean Locarno was precisely the same as doing nothing should the World Conference fail: increased defence spending in a hostile international environment. British policy would have to concentrate on goals delineated by the Simon committee and get the French to accept a measure of disarmament that would enhance the existing security mechanisms provided by the Covenant and Locarno. With French reductions, particularly for their army, Germany's desire for equality of treatment, or, at least, greater equality, could be achieved.

At Washington, Hoover's earlier determination to let the European Powers take the lead in arms limitation weakened. In enforcing cuts on the American armed services in June 1931, he believed that the United States should have minimum forces for defence. Six months later, he decided that this should be the American theme at the World

---

[14] FO memorandum, 'The British Position in relation to European Policy', 1 Jan. 1932, CAB 27/476. Cf. unsigned memorandum, 'Guarantee Pact', n.d. [but Dec. 1931], Simon FO 800/285.
[15] CC 1(30)1E, CAB 23/70. The rest of this paragraph is based on CDC(31) meeting 5, CAB 27/476; MacDonald, 'Report of a Cabinet Committee on a Mediterranean "Locarno"', 18 Jan. 1932 [CP 27(32)], CAB 24/277.

omething he impressed on American delegates before they
ˈɟeneva.[16] Hoover emphasised the 'idea of a basic police
ⁿ German percentage as the standard and considering
ˈ, that as army for offense or defence', and of having 'the
ɟ method [of limitation] apply only to this excess'. In an
ₐₛtonishing departure from traditional American policy, Hoover was
willing to nudge events along the right track by considering war debt
reduction. He broached the matter to Laval in late October, when the
French premier visited Washington, indicating that his purpose was a
corresponding alleviation of German reparations.[17] The president was
suggesting that European good faith could see financial concessions
from the United States beyond the moratorium.

Hoover played to American strength. Because of weak United States
air and ground forces and the inviolability of the 1930 naval treaty,[18] he
lacked the military resources to bargain with the European Powers. This
was highlighted in a series of reports reaching the White House and
State Department in the autumn of 1931.[19] Thus, whereas the British
determined relatively specific goals for the World Conference, the
Americans looked to foster a scheme of general principles to guide arms
cuts.[20] Stimson outlined them in instructions given Gibson, the acting
head of the American delegation – Stimson, the actual head following
Dwight Morrow's sudden death in October, could not leave Washington
for the time being.[21] Consistent with the Kellogg Pact, the Administration wanted to 'preclude any nation retaining armaments likely to be
used for successful aggression particularly initial surprise attacks'; and,
following the logic that dictated American naval limitation policies prior
to 1930, 'the principle of relative strength should apply' to those forces
for the security of the state above those required for preserving 'internal

[16] Stimson diary, 5 Jan. 1932, Stimson 20.
[17] Stimson, 'Memorandum of a conference with Laval' [with Hoover's holograph
corrections], 23 Oct. 1931, Stimson 18. Cf. Feis memorandum, 'Matters that might be
talked over with Premier Laval', 9 Oct. 1931, HHPP 986; Feis memorandum, 20 Oct.
1931, HHPP 1013; Castle to Hoover, 22 Oct. 1931, with enclosure, HHPP 996.
[18] Cf. Moffat and Field [State Department] memoranda for Stimson, both 11 Sep. 1931,
Castle to Hoover, 10 Dec. 1931, with enclosure, all HHPP 1001; unsigned
memoranda, 'National Defence Costs – Land Armaments', 19 Nov. 1931, 'Meeting of
Technical Staff of American Delegation to the General Disarmament Conference,
November 23, 1931', 'Population and Active Army of Powers ratio per 1000 of
population', n.d., all Davis 17; Moffat to Gibson, 17 Sep. 1931, Moffat 1.
[19] Wilson memoranda [on talks with Flandin, Drummond, Rosso, Cecil, Frohwein,
Massigli, Grandi, Bernstorff], 9–12, 15 Sep. 1931, all Gibson 105; Gibson to Moffat,
17 Sep. 1931, Moffat 1; Edge telegram (675) to Stimson, 21 Oct. 1931, HHPP 986;
Sackett to Hoover, 15 Sep. 1931, with enclosures, HHPP 997; Gibson to Castle, Castle
11.
[20] Cf. Bennett, *German Rearmament*, 141–2.
[21] Stimson to Gibson, 19 Jan. 1932, Davis 17.

order'. Beyond this, Gibson and his senior colleagues – Dawes, Norman Davis, and Senator Claude Swanson – could concede to budgetary restriction if it was tied to 'the limitation and reduction of material', extended the life of the 1930 naval agreement within the terms of the resultant treaty, acceded to reductions in capital ship numbers rather than displacement, consented to prohibitions on the use of poisonous gas outside national boundaries, and allowed only for defensive aircraft. They were not to accept trained reserves in determining peacetime force levels or give any authority to the proposed Disarmament Commission that might impinge on national sovereignty (for instance, verification within the United States). Finally, no Power should be compelled to accept the derogatory clause, which played so conspicuous a role in the final deliberations of the Preparatory Commission.

In this way, though willingness to co-operate existed in both capitals,[22] their different approaches towards the conference lessened the chances for accord over arms limitation. The National Government preferred to sustain the existing system of security built around Locarno and the Covenant. With Manchuria laying bare the boundaries of these commitments and those for Imperial defence, Britain could assume no new obligations – here was an echo of the doctrine of absolute need adumbrated in the 1920s. British policy had to focus on reconciling Franco-German differences. Naturally, other Powers were vital to the success of this policy, especially the United States with its stake in the debt settlements. But as the Stimson doctrine showed, American weakness beyond its financial resources, themselves sapped by the Depression, restricted Washington's ability to pursue strong foreign policy. On top of this, the vagaries of American public opinion hindered strong action by the Administration. Hoover and Stimson's approach was more general and, at the same time, more grandiose. With the conference meeting in the midst of the moratorium, they felt that Britain and the European Powers would accept a comprehensive settlement that tied together arms limitation and inter-governmental debts. Hence, Stimson could tell Borah: 'to me it seemed no longer a disarmament conference but a peace conference because it brought up all the underlying political questions which France had previously been unwilling to talk about but as to which she now seemed to be changing in that respect'.[23]

Despite such optimism, three days after the conference opened, the French sought additional security guarantees through the League before

[22] Even Vansittart, who observed: 'we have been careful to cultivate Anglo-American relations to a degree of cordiality never before attained'. Vansittart memorandum, 'The United Kingdom and Europe' [CP 4(32)], 1 Jan. 1932, CAB 27/476.
[23] Stimson, 'Memorandum of a Conversation', 6 Oct. 1931, Stimson 18.

they would discuss specific arms cuts. Tardieu, now minister for war, circulated a plan containing four key points: the internationalisation of civil aviation; all long-range artillery and warships carrying eight-inch guns or bigger, or displacing more than 10,000 tons, be placed under League command; an international police force be put at the League's disposal and placed under its control; and the acceptance of compulsory arbitration in all disputes, with the term 'aggression' specifically defined.[24] The 'Tardieu Plan' met immediate, unfavourable reaction from the major Powers. Surmising Paris' intention to sustain the existing European status quo, integral to which was the weakness of the Reichswehr, Brüning's government rejected continued qualitative deficiencies and demanded equality of treatment.[25] The Hoover Administration had no intention of surrendering United States sovereignty to any international instrument, particularly one entrusting the League with a leading role.[26] Finally, the British, Americans, and Japanese would never allow their battlefleets and heavy cruisers to slip from their control.[27]

Tardieu's plan deflected the conference from its professed purpose, leading to a rush of observations from other delegations,[28] of which the British was the most important. Simon used his opening address on 8 February to seek a political compromise between the French-led faction, on one side, and the Germans, Americans, and Japanese, on the other.[29] He put his weight behind an effective permanent disarmament commission, this to allay American distrust of the League and German concern about the perpetuation of the status quo. Independent of the League, this body would monitor the disarmament treaty and scrutinise arms production so that no Power could steal a march on the others. 'A high level of armaments is no substitute for security,' he remarked. 'At best, it creates the illusion of security in one quarter while at the same time aggravating the sense of insecurity in another.' Then, genuflecting to the French, Simon argued for arms prohibitions or limitations that

---

[24] *Proposal of the French Delegation* (5 Feb. 1932), LND Conf.D.56. Cf. Bennett, *German Rearmament*, 97–9; J. Minart, *Le drame de désarmament français (1919–1939): ses aspects politiques et techniques* (Paris, 1959), 24–6.

[25] *Proposal by the German Delegation Concerning Qualitative Disarmament*, LND Conf.D.124.

[26] Gibson speech, 9 Feb. 1932, *FRUS 1932*, I, 25. Cf. Stimson–Gibson telephone conversation, 8 Feb. 1932, HHPP 1002.

[27] Hankey memorandum, 'The French Proposals', 16 Mar. 1932 [DC(M)(32)4], CAB 27/509.

[28] In order of submission, Spain, Turkey, Germany, Haiti, Italy, Russia [two submissions], Sweden, Holland, the United States, Switzerland, China, Norway, Denmark, Czechoslovakia, Argentina, Japan, the Hedjaz: *Conference Documents*, I, 117–45 *passim*.

[29] *Proposals of the United Kingdom Delegation* (8 Feb. 1932), LND Conf.D.95. Cf. Simon to Henderson, 5 Jan. 1932, Henderson LNS 475/3.

would weaken the ability to take the offensive. But he went no further for, as he told Tardieu, 'British public opinion was definitely opposed to entering into any further commitments or guarantees on the continent of Europe'.[30]

French intransigence over 'security before arms limitation' remained unshaken, something accentuated by Briand's death in March, which robbed the French government of even ostensible affability; and the Depression, which heretofore had by-passed France, began to be felt there with devastating results. Admittedly, discussions occurred in the specialist sub-commissions;[31] the technical committees debated;[32] and the Disarmament Section of the League Secretariat ensured liaison amongst the delegations.[33] Nonetheless, without movement at the top, negotiations below the General Commission foundered.[34] By June, when the specialist commissions tabled their first reports, their labours proved barren. In the interim, the British and the Americans looked for a way around the impasse. The National Government had established a ministerial committee composed of MacDonald, Baldwin, Chamberlain, and a few other senior ministers 'to deal rapidly with messages received from the United Kingdom Delegation during the Disarmament Conference'.[35] From 21 March to 6 June, it focused on reconciling French demands for security with German insistence on equality of treatment. Simon earlier reported that should Berlin persist in pressing its case, Tardieu would 'bring out a number of facts to prove that Germany had, in fact, already broken the Treaty of Versailles'.[36] The

[30] Simon memorandum, 24 Feb. 1932, *DBFP II*, III, 507–10.
[31] Cf. 'Naval Commission. Progress from setting up (25th February, 1932) until adjournment for the Easter recess (19th March, 1932)', 23 Mar. 1932, LNR 2462/35411/35411; Air Commission minutes (27 Feb.–22 Jun. 1932), LNR 2463/37730/35412; minutes [establishing committee on moral disarmament], 15 Mar. 1932, LNR 2461/35608/35409.
[32] For instance, *National Defence Expenditure Commission. Report of the Technical Committee*, I (8 Apr. 1932), LND Conf.D.158.
[33] League Disarmament Section memorandum, 'Naval Commission. Progress from setting up (25th February, 1932) until adjournment for the Easter recess (19th March, 1932)', 23 Mar. 1932, LNR 2462/35411/35411.
[34] For instance, by mid-March, the Land Commission could only report that governments interpreted 'effectives' on differing bases: legal, theoretical, actual, and budgetary, and that there were further problems posed by counting civilian employees in ministries of war and cadets in military academies. See *Land Commission. Report of the Technical Committee of the Definitions Contained in Articles 2 and 3 of the Draft Convention* (16 Mar. 1932), LND Conf.D./C.T./4. See Aghnides [League Disarmament Section] minute to Drummond, 6 Jun. 1932, de Brouckère [chairman, Effectives Sub-committee] to Henderson, both Henderson MSS LNS 475/3.
[35] CC 8(32)8, CAB 23/70.
[36] This and the next paragraph, except where noted, are based on DC(M)(32) meeting 1, 21 Mar. 1932, CAB 27/505. On French plans, see Bennett, *German Rearmament*, 97–9.

situation would transform into a vituperative shouting match that impending elections in both countries would exacerbate to the conference's detriment. Because France would argue that 'she had made her choice and since we had seen fit to reject it, the responsibility for anything she did must lie on our shoulders', the committee searched for means of getting France to compromise.

Given the impossibility of additional security arrangements,[37] the most effective policy would be, in MacDonald's phrase, to 'stand between France and Germany'. Doing so alone might create difficulties – 'we might get bitten'. Accordingly, a consensus emerged that it would be politic to join with the Americans in finding a compromise. This would allow initial criticism to be shared whilst working towards a settlement that both continental Powers could accept. Despite British rejection of 'non-recognition' in January, Anglo-American co-operation seemed possible. In mid-March Simon and Stimson exchanged letters which both emphasised the need to co-operate.[38] Coming just as Davis had told the foreign secretary 'that America and Great Britain ought to try and see whether there was any form of middle position which they could take up', the ground seemed clear for effecting a Franco-German compromise. Following Cabinet instructions, Simon prepared a strategy differentiating between legal disarmament strictures imposed on Germany and its 'moral claim for reconsideration', which was not only 'very strong' but supported by general American opinion.[39] At the same time, although rejecting the Tardieu Plan, the British would not oppose 'regional guarantees between States on the Continent of Europe to meet their special anxieties', and they would seek a definition of 'aggressor' in league with the Americans.

Simon's strategy guided British policy for the next two-and-a-half months; however, Anglo-American co-operation proved illusory through the two English-speaking Powers' different approaches to the conference. In late March, the American delegation began fashioning a 'comprehensive plan' which promoted an American-defined 'security'.[40] It involved going beyond qualitative disarmament by abolishing offensive weapons – which to a large degree the United States

---

[37] Cf. Thomas memorandum, 'Disarmament and Sanctions' [DC(M)2(32)], 10 Mar. 1932, Hankey memorandum, 'The French Proposals' [DC(M)4(32)], 16 Mar. 1932, 'Report of the Interdepartmental Committee' [DC(M)5(32)], 17 Mar. 1932, all CAB 27/509.

[38] Stimson to Simon, 12 Mar. 1932, Simon FO 800/286; Simon to Stimson, 15 Mar. 1932, Stimson R82. Stimson's letter was telegraphed to London.

[39] Simon memorandum, 'Attitude to be Adopted by the United Kingdom Delegation', 31 Mar. 1932, CAB 27/509.

[40] Gibson to Swanson, 25 Mar. 1932, Gibson 118; Stimson diary, 30 Mar. 1932, Stimson 21.

had done already. Gibson told Swanson: 'Although we would not say anything so cynical out loud, its obvious advantage is that it involves no commitments for the United States in regard to security, and obviously no commitment to surrender a single weapon unless and until the agreement has received general acceptance.' Here lay the block to effective Anglo-American lobbying. American words, so eloquent and engaging, lacked force because of the Administration's unwillingness – or inability – to back them with concrete concessions. This was not immediately clear to the British. On 11 April, when Gibson traced the American position, which emphasised security through disarmament, Simon reacted 'with a declaration of support'.[41]

There then followed a series of General Commission resolutions to this end, particularly one proposed by Simon on 22 April:

the Conference declares its approval of the principle of qualitative disarmament – i.e., the selection of certain classes or descriptions of weapons the possession of which should be absolutely prohibited to all States or internationalised by means of a general Convention.[42]

Whilst Brüning's government and that in Paris, with Tardieu now premier, accepted this proposition, giving it form proved impossible. Franco-German deadlock could not be broken when deciding what classes or descriptions of weapons should be prohibited or internationalised. Even the presence of MacDonald and Stimson in Geneva from 16 April to 1 May failed to produce movement, despite Stimson's belief that he had 'accomplished a great deal in my two weeks'.[43] The French remained wary of Anglo-American pressures to force them to make concessions;[44] the Germans would not relent over equality of treatment; and even the major naval Powers could not agree on which warships were 'offensive'. The result was that when the air, military, and naval commissions reported by the first week of June, no specific recommendations for limiting arms came forth.[45]

---

[41] Simon to MacDonald, 16 Apr. 1932, Simon FO 800/286. Cf. Drummond to Aghnides, 27 Apr. 1932, Aghnides to Drummond, 27 Apr. 1932, with Drummond minute, Henderson to Gibson, 29 Apr. 1932, all LNR 2467/37099/36938.

[42] Meetings 13, 14, 16 of the General Commission, 19, 20, 22 Apr. 1932, in League of Nations, *Minutes of the General Commission*, I (Geneva, 1932), 83–93, 110–13. Cf. Hurley (secretary of war) to Borah, 16 Apr. 1932, Adams (secretary of the navy) to Borah, 18 Apr. 1932, both Borah 763.

[43] MacDonald diary, 1 May 1932, MacDonald PRO 30/69/1753; Stimson diary, 16 Apr.– 1 May 1932, Stimson 21. Cf. 'Record of a Meeting', 23 Apr. 1932, *DBFP II*, III, 516–18.

[44] Simon to MacDonald, 16 Apr. 1932, Simon FO 800/286.

[45] *Naval Commission. Report to the General Commission* (28 May 1932), LND Conf.D.121; *Land Commission. Report to the General Commission* (7 Jun. 1932), LND Conf.D.122; *Air Commission. Report to the General Commission* (7 Jun. 1932), LND Conf.D.123.

Continuing stalemate had much to do with the fall of Brüning's ministry on 30 May and its replacement by a more conservative one led by Franz von Papen. Although the Depression and reparations played heavily in this change, Brüning's failure to acquire equality of treatment in disarmament aided his enemies.[46] Papen portended a less accommodating German attitude at Geneva. More importantly, it became clear by late May that London and Washington had different conceptions about what the world conference should accomplish. British policy focused primarily on Europe, specifically on striking a balance between Germany and France; American policy cast a wider net. When the two governments formulated their final disarmament policies six months earlier, they had assumed a spirit of co-operation to bring about an agreement much as had occurred at London in 1930 – the Simon–Stimson exchange in mid-March is indicative. They erred in such thinking. Manchuria had shown that over some crucial matters, shared interests did not exist. Now at Geneva, the British and American inability jointly to force the pace in a multilateral conference had been exposed. The gulf between the Powers had widened further.

With the seeming disarmament deadlock in Europe, and with the Japanese inactive in the deliberations, Hoover attempted to seize the initiative. On 22 June, through Gibson, he suggested that the Powers make massive quantitative and qualitative cuts to their armed forces: after creating a 'police component' – determined by the number of effectives the Paris peace treaties allowed Germany and the other defeated Powers – all armies to be reduced by one-third; the Washington treaty number and class tonnages of battleships, plus submarines, to be cut by one-third; those of aircraft carriers, cruisers and destroyers by one-quarter; and complete prohibition of bombers, chemical and bacteriological weapons, large mobile guns, and armour.[47] Promoting his plan as a chance for the United States to assume 'moral leadership' in international politics,[48] Hoover had baser political reasons for advocating such sweeping cuts. American voters had to understand that limiting arms was possible, and that his Administration could lead whilst the other major Powers, including Britain, seemed unable to do anything. With the presidential election scheduled for November, overshadowed by the poor state of the American economy, a diplomatic success would deflect some criticism of his Administration and the Republican Party. Significantly, the 'Hoover Plan' was announced just

---

[46] Carsten, *Reichswehr*, 338–50; Craig, *Germany*, 553–60.
[47] *Declaration by Mr. Gibson concerning President Hoover's Proposal* (20 Jun. 1932), LND Conf.D.126.
[48] On 'moral leadership', see Hoover, *Cabinet and the Presidency*, 330.

days after his renomination as the Republican presidential candidate.[49] Massive arms cuts, particularly in naval weapons, would translate into substantial retrenchment. If the other Powers decreased arms spending, with debt repayments to resume in December, the possibility of American creditors receiving their money would be enhanced and criticism of Hoover further reduced.[50]

Hoover also issued his plan, in part, because he reckoned that the British were about to suggest cuts and he did not want the initiative to slip away.[51] He was partially correct. In mid-May, Baldwin proposed in Cabinet that abolition of submarines and military and naval aircraft would allow for scaling down capital ships, reducing coastal defence spending, and more.[52] But this had not been translated into policy by June. More important, on 10 June, Simon suggested to the Cabinet that since the conference had 'reached a critical stage', the Great Power delegations should meet privately.[53] Out of the public gaze, they could calmly discuss matters, reach provisional agreement on qualitative and quantitative limitation, and then present the main conference with a solid front. Hence, Simon envisaged a concert of the Great Powers to save the conference. Hoover's suggestion, in contrast, appeared without consultation and, stressing relative need, failed to weigh those Powers' strategic concerns.[54] In this sense, it ran counter to British goals outlined earlier by Simon's ministerial committee. Like the Tardieu Plan, it diverted discussions at Geneva on to another path. Not surprisingly, it was rebuffed, though not immediately. Simon and Joseph Paul-Boncour, a senior French disarmament negotiator, sought clarifications from Gibson, who stressed Washington's disinclination to entertain modifications.[55] French rejection was swift and sarcastic.[56] With MacDonald working to keep Anglo-American relations unsullied, the British responded in a conciliatory fashion.

On 7 July, in identical speeches, Simon in Geneva and Baldwin in London gently restated the British case: arms limitation had to reflect

[49] Lindsay despatch (986) to Simon, 17 Jun. 1932, FO 371/15875/3933/268; Stimson diary, 13–16 Jun. 1932, Stimson 22; Feis minute, 20 Jun. 1932, Feis 123.
[50] See Hoover's holograph drafts of the speech, plus Stimson–Gibson telephone conversation, 20 Jun. 1932 (3.00 p.m.), both HHPP 1002. Cf. Stimson diary, 18–22 Jun. 1932, Stimson 22.
[51] Stimson diary, 7 Jun. 1932, Stimson 22.   [52] CC 26(32)2, CAB 23/71.
[53] Simon memorandum, 'The future proceedings of the Disarmament Conference', 10 Jun. 1932, Simon FO 800/287.
[54] American negotiators earlier complained that Washington's directives ignored strategic issues; see Marriner to Moffat, 9 Apr. 1932, Moffat 1.
[55] Simon, 'Summary of conversation between French[,] American and British Representatives at Geneva,' with annexes, 21 Jun. 1932, Simon FO 800/287.
[56] Bennett, German Rearmament, 168.

the strategic requirements of the Powers. Implying that universal cuts would be unhelpful, they argued that substantive reductions had to be underwritten by general principles allowing an absolute minimum of armed strength for national defence.[57] And reflecting the foreign secretary's 10 June proposals to Cabinet, they suggested that 'detailed discussions' should occur; to get discussions going, they 'set out under the necessary heads of land, sea, and air the manner in which ... these principles could be applied'. At Geneva, Simon immediately lobbied others about private talks to find an acceptable arms limitation formula.[58] With this the 'Hoover Plan' died because of the opposition of the other Great Powers; these Powers looked to other avenues for filling in the blanks of the draft treaty. There would be delay in this until after the American elections, something recognised by Simon, who saw the 7 July speeches as means to keep alive the possibility of agreement.[59] After passing a resolution embodying the principle that its future discussions would be designed 'to reduce the means of attack', the conference adjourned for four months on 23 July; it was surmised that interim private discussions amongst the Powers would produce effective limitation once the conference reconvened. As far as Anglo-American relations were concerned, public professions by Simon and Baldwin about Hoover's plan 'as a contribution to an agreed general programme' did not mirror private attitudes within the British government.[60] The conference had achieved little after six months. To aid deliberations at Geneva, Britain would have to rely more on its own initiative and less on co-operation with the Americans. As even MacDonald recognised after Brüning fell from power, 'we must lead in Europe for some time'.[61]

Although touching arms limitation, MacDonald's comments really referred to war debts and reparations; and, as the World Disarmament Conference prepared to go into recess in late July, this nettled question re-emerged to divide further Britain and the United States. Achieving office because of Labour's inability to act on the May Report, and with Britain off the gold standard, the National Government had to address the country's economic malaise. Within the Cabinet, through their absolute power in the Commons, the Conservatives dominated

<hr>

[57] Simon to MacDonald, 29 Jun. 1932, with enclosure, CAB 21/357; *Statement of Views of His Majesty's Government in the United Kingdom regarding President Hoover's Proposal* (7 Jul. 1932), LND Conf.D.133; 'Statement by Mr. Baldwin in the House of Commons on July 7, 1932', *BDFA*, II, J4, 27–31.
[58] Simon [draft] to Cecil, n.d. [but late Jun. 1932], Simon FO 800/287.
[59] Simon to MacDonald, 18 Jul. 1932, *ibid.*
[60] MacDonald to Baldwin, 24 Jun. 1932, Baldwin 119.
[61] MacDonald to Simon, 31 May 1932, Simon FO 800/286.

economic policy after November 1931.[62] Their objective was Britain's economic revival, and in this equation, as chancellor of the Exchequer, Neville Chamberlain occupied the leading position. Within his formula for revival, which included moderate tariffs and increasing domestic demand for British-produced goods, lay the ending of German reparations and eliminating war debts. 'Reflect on this', he told his sister soon after taking office, '(1) We remitted nearly £400 millions of France's debt to us. (2) If the U.S.A. had agreed to fund our debt on the same terms as she gave to France we should have so overpaid that to put it right we should pay *nothing* for another 9 years!'[63] Such views paralleled opinion outside of government. John Maynard Keynes, the political economist and former Treasury official, had been lobbying to this end since 1919 because of what he argued was the deleterious effect of the Treaty of Versailles on Germany and European stability.[64] Keynes was just the most forceful amongst many,[65] whose admonitions were gaining weight in influential quarters in Britain and Europe because of the terrible conditions in Germany that provided a fillip for extreme nationalist politicians like Hitler.

By November 1931, lengthy discussions involving British, American, French, German, and other experts had occurred in both the BIS and a special committee established at the London conference that created the standstill agreement.[66] Their purpose had been to make the Young Plan reparations regime workable before the Hoover moratorium ended. Increasing German unemployment, reduced German foreign exchange, the relationship between reparations and the payment of German debt to private investors abroad, and sterling's devaluation following the abandonment of the gold standard (which affected Germany's balance of trade and the crumbling international debt settlement) preoccupied these experts. In this process, the Americans and French formed a unified, if uncomfortable bloc. The French resisted any modifications to diminish German reparations. For their part, the Americans opposed changes that would tie Germany's ability to pay reparations to the war debts of the former allies. A joint

---

[62] O'Halpin, *Warren Fisher*, 191.
[63] Chamberlain to Hilda, 6 Dec. 1931, NC 18/1/764.
[64] For instance, J. M. Keynes, *The Economic Consequences of the Peace* (1919).
[65] H. G. Moulton and Leo Paslovsky, *War Debts and World Prosperity* (Washington, 1932), summarises studies by the Institute of Economics after 1923. Such views were not universally shared. Cf. G. P. Auld, *The Dawes Plan and the New Economics* (New York, 1927); B. Ohlin 'The Reparations Problem: A Discussion' [with Keynes' rejoinder], *Economic Journal*, 39(1929), 172–82.
[66] Kent, *Spoils of War*, 353–62. See 'Report of the Special Advisory Committee', 23 Dec. 1931, *DBFP II*, II, 495–514.

communiqué resulting from Laval's Washington visit made Franco-American feelings clear.[67]

Nonetheless, on 20 November, Brüning's ministry appealed to the BIS to shelve Germany's deferable reparations payments and requested that the BIS Advisory Committee recognise that Berlin would have to negotiate a separate agreement with its private creditors by February. When the BIS committee met in early December, the British delegate, Sir Walter Layton, suggested that Brüning's predicament could be overcome if German creditors shared German railway profits.[68] Brüning recoiled from this – ridding foreign interference in the German economy had been hard won at the two Hague conferences – and moved to delay further discussions. Elections were scheduled for France and Germany in the spring and, with the Depression hitting France, he reasoned that Paris might be more willing to negotiate in six months' time. Looking for more immediate results, Chamberlain and the Treasury joined with the Foreign Office to win Cabinet approval for canvassing the Powers to hold a special reparations conference at Lausanne beginning in late January.[69] Chamberlain's strategy involved making 'no public statement which would link up Reparations & War Debts but deal with Reprs first & then go to [the] U.S.A. and ask them to make their contributions'.[70] However, a January meeting proved impossible. Disarmament absorbed energies that otherwise could be directed towards financial diplomacy; though accepting the principle of a conference, the French and Germans argued that delay until the summer would allow them to be better prepared – each obviously hoped for events to unfold in their favour; and Hoover's Administration indicated that it would not partici-pate in any reparations conference, as it was a European matter unrelated to war debts.[71]

Consequently, the Lausanne conference was postponed rather than abandoned. When the conference convened on 16 June, its chances for

---

[67] A copy is in *FRUS 1931*, II, 252–53.
[68] Layton to MacDonald, 28 Dec. 1931, in Leith-Ross to Simon, 29 Dec. 1931, Simon FO 800/285; Layton to Simon, 1, 10 Jan. 1932, both Simon FO 800/286.
[69] Leith-Ross to Vansittart, 14 Nov. 1931, Leith-Ross T 188/16; Treasury memorandum, 'German Reparations', 14 Nov. 1931, Leith-Ross memorandum, 28 Dec. 1931, both Leith-Ross T 188/32; Sargent to Leith-Ross, 16 Nov. 1931, Sargent FO 800/279/Wd/ 31/2; Leith-Ross to Sargent, 16 Nov. 1931, Sargent FO 800/279/Wd/31/3; Simon memorandum, 'Reparations and War Debts – A Bird's Eye View', 29 Dec. 1931, Simon FO 800/285. For the Cabinet's decision, see 'British Proposals for a Reparation Conference', 6 Jan. 1932, *DBFP II*, III, 590–2.
[70] Chamberlain to Hilda, 14 Jan. 1932, NC 18/1/767.
[71] Simon to Tyrrell, 18 Jan. 1932, Tyrrell to Simon, 19 Jan. 1932, Rumbold to Simon, 21 Jan. 1932, all Simon FO 800/286; Rumbold despatch to Simon, 11 Jan. 1932, Simon telegram (38) to Lindsay, 16 Jan. 1932, Lindsay telegram (28) to Simon, 17 Jan. 1932, Tyrrell despatch to Simon, 18 Jan. 1932, all *DBFP II*, III, 17–18, 32–3, 37–40.

success were enhanced by the advent of the new French and German
governments. The new foreign minister in Papen's ministry, Constan-
tine von Neurath, the ambassador at London since 1930, met with
Simon before returning to Berlin to take up his duties.[72] When Simon
observed that 'if Britain was to act as "honest broker" in the impending
discussions, it was necessary that Germany should provide something
more than a list of what she wanted', Neurath gave assurances that 'he
had no intention of going to Lausanne to bang his fist on the table'. May
elections in France saw the eclipse of Tardieu and the advent of
Edouard Herriot as premier of a centre-left government. Although Laval
became foreign minister and Herriot offered token obeisance to the
Tardieu line over collecting reparations, Tyrrell reported the new
premier's clandestine support for prominent journalists who were
preparing French 'public opinion on the necessity of cancellation'.[73]
Therefore, on 11 June, MacDonald and Simon stopped at Paris on the
way to Lausanne to hold pre-conference talks with Herriot. They
discovered that despite Herriot's deep suspicions about Germany's
ultimate intention to upset the European balance, he showed refreshing
flexibility: 'he would not admit any attempt at unilateral cancellation by
the Germans, and he would not, so far as he was concerned, claim that
any agreement reached must be within the limits of the Young Plan and
existing agreements. Between these two extremes he would work for a
final and definitive agreement, subject to a suspensory arrangement
about America.'[74]

A breakthrough at Lausanne seemed possible, though, as Herriot
remarked, the American attitude would determine its ultimate success.
Before the conference was postponed, the French had pushed for an
Anglo-French 'united front vis-à-vis the United States'.[75] London
found such a tactic unacceptable. The Germans had to be mollified,
and no lasting resolution of inter-governmental debts would occur by
estranging the Hoover Administration, Congress, and American voters.
MacDonald implored Simon 'that the utmost care should be exercised
that we should not appear as joining with the French in making any
agreement conditional on America making corresponding concessions
as regards war debts'.[76] Less than two weeks before the Lausanne
conference opened, he cautioned about understanding American

[72] Simon despatch to Newton [British Embassy, Berlin], 6 Jun. 1932, *DBFP II*, III,
152–4.
[73] Simon to MacDonald, 10 Jun. 1932, Simon FO 800/287; on Herriot's covert support
for cancellation, see Tyrrell to Vansittart, 8 Jun. 1932, *ibid.*
[74] 'Notes of a Franco-British conversation . . . on June 11th, 1932', *ibid.*
[75] Tyrrell to Simon, 13, 30 Dec. 1931, both Simon FO 800/285.
[76] Selby to Leith-Ross, 15 Jan. 1931 [but 1932], Simon FO 800/286.

sensitivities so as to prevent a recrudescence of the enmity in Anglo-American relations that had existed before 1929.[77] Importantly, however, London was unwilling to retain the Young agreement. Reparations were dead, and the sooner they disappeared, the sooner an atmosphere of security and stability could be promoted in Europe. This would only benefit the British economy.

After the immediacy of the reparations question had receded earlier in the year following the postponement of Lausanne and the beginning of the World Disarmament Conference, the National Government worked to find common revisionist ground with Hoover's Administration. The high-water mark came when both MacDonald and Stimson were in Geneva in late April. Before the two men met, Simon outlined the results of Foreign Office–Treasury discussions to a private meeting of British experts: 'the essential issue seemed to him to lay between two broad lines of policy: (1) to aim at wiping out reparations completely, regardless of France, or (2) Something less drastic, which France and Germany could both grudgingly accept'.[78] Because Tardieu still held the premiership, the second option guided British policy. MacDonald's discussions with Stimson elicited the usual litany that reparations had no connexion with war debts, debts had to be paid, and the United States government believed that Germany had the capacity to pay. But once this sacred chant was finished, Stimson offered a startling proposition:

If any declaration was made in Europe [about ending war debts and] involving the United States, we must assume that the United States shop windows were closed. Mr. Hoover's Administration had to face Congress in June and then the presidential election. If Europe kept quiet, Mr. Hoover would secure re-election on a domestic policy. After that a very great deal might be done.[79]

As occurred during Laval's Washington visit the previous October, the Americans showed private willingness to work out a compromise with their European debtors. The price entailed the United States not being tied to any formal settlement of reparations at Lausanne.

The changes of government in France and Germany the next month offered hope of a breakthrough or, at least, a resolution that would allow for debt settlement modification sometime in 1933. To this end, more encouragement emanated from Washington. Stimson telephoned

---

[77] MacDonald to Simon, 3 Jun. 1932, Simon FO 800/287. Cf. MacDonald to Stimson, 8 Jan. 1932, Stimson to MacDonald, 27 Jan. 1932, both MacDonald PRO 30/69/678.

[78] 'Notes of a Meeting ... at 10 A.M. on April 23, 1932', Simon FO 800/286.

[79] This conversation was reported in *ibid*. See 'Record of a Conversation at Villa Besinges' [MacDonald, Stimson, Davis, Gibson, and Simon], 23 Apr. 1932, *ibid*. Cf. 'Memorandum of a Meeting, April 15, 1932' [between the State and Treasury departments on foreign defaults], Stimson R82.

MacDonald on 25 May to say 'that the United States Government had been considering the utility of an Economic and Monetary Conference, if the British Government cared to call it'.[80] Stimson candidly remarked that if Washington called the conference, speculation that it did so to maintain the gold standard would be counter-productive. Whilst he cautioned that reparations and war debts could not be discussed, the conference might examine other pressing issues like 'commodity prices, international exchange, trade impediments and kindred subjects', including silver, which had become acute.[81] He also alluded to unsuccessful British, French, German, and Italian talks held in April about aiding the Danubian states by tariff reductions and currency stabilisation.[82] Although willing neither to expand Lausanne's agenda – 'in the public mind Lausanne and reparations were inseparably connected' – nor to consider tariffs other than as a domestic issue, Washington was willing to make a general economic and monetary conference successful.

Following these developments, with MacDonald and Chamberlain leading the British delegation, the Lausanne conference opened with great expectations. Underneath British policy lay a belief that the United States would finally join with Britain and the other Powers to foster international economic recovery. Though tarnished by Manchuria – and despite Treasury uncertainty about Hoover and Stimson delivering on war debts[83] – Anglo-American co-operation could provide a means to this end. In this context, the little more than three weeks of negotiations proved straightforward and – with the twisted history of the question that stretched back before the Ruhr occupation – brisk.[84] The British, French, and others formally accepted that Germany lacked the capacity to pay reparations once the Hoover moratorium ended. In return for cancelling reparations, the Germans agreed to make a one-time payment of 3 billion marks, the equivalent of one-and-a-half

---

[80] Simon despatch (740) to Lindsay, 30 May 1932, *ibid.* Cf. Stimson diary, 24–26 May 1932, Stimson 22; Hoover draft telegram to Mellon, 24 May 1932, with Feis minute to Stimson, n.d. [?24 May 1932], both Stimson R82.

[81] Alleviating the worsening domestic financial situation played heavily in Administration calculations. See Feis to Frankfurter, 15 Jun. 1932, Feis 16; Feis to Davis, 25 Jun. 1932, Feis 15.

[82] Especially sessions 1–2 (6–8 Apr. 1932), T 172/1786. Cf. Tyrrell to Baldwin, 12 Apr. 1932, Baldwin 119; Treasury 'Statement of British Policy in regard to the Danubian Question', n.d., T 172/1381.

[83] Chamberlain minute to Leith-Ross, 25 May 1932, Leith-Ross minute to Chamberlain, 26 May 1932, Leith-Ross to Hankey, 25 Jun. 1932, all Leith-Ross T 188/42.

[84] Cmd. 4126; Cmd. 4129; 'German addition to Political Clause accepted by British and French Delegations ... July 8', *DBFP II*, III, 420. Cf. anonymous minute, 'Undertakings Entered into at Lausanne (other than those contained in the published documents)', n.d., T 172/1788.

annual Young Plan payments, and promised good behaviour.[85] Several
face-saving devices were employed in the settlement. For instance, to
show French opinion that Herriot had not abandoned claims to German
reparations, Papen's government deposited bonds worth £150 million
with the BIS to be redeemed when the international economy recovered
(at Lausanne, the delegations recognised that these would never be
cashed). Nonetheless, the conference achieved its purpose: German
reparations were annulled and inter-governmental debt amongst the
participants repudiated. However, because Britain and the European
Powers refused to divorce war debts from reparations, the agreement
remained provisional, hinging on Washington's willingness to suspend
inter-governmental debts owed the United States. MacDonald remarked with satisfaction as the conference ended: 'No more Reparations! They have gone. No more attempting in a blind and thoughtless
way to heap burdens and burdens upon anybody's shoulders.'[86]
MacDonald's desire for Britain to take the lead in Europe had been
achieved.

Behind the public facade, however, British concern about encouraging European stability remained. Lausanne did not eliminate Franco-
German resentments. During the negotiations, Papen's government had
unexpectedly proposed additional peace treaty revisions, including a
formal nullification of Germany's war guilt and a pledge to equality of
treatment in arms limitation. This prompted one of Chamberlain's
officials to argue that 'the time has come to exercise a ruthless pressure
on the German Delegation to produce the necessary counter-conces-
sions to enable the French to accept the agreement which is already
almost in existence'.[87] Though sundered, the German ruse left a bad
taste in British mouths.[88] Moreover, uncertainty existed about American concessions. 'I also disbelieved in the alleged American attitude',
Chamberlain noted in his diary, 'and as [the French finance minister]
had quoted Stimson I said he did not speak for the American people.'[89]
With the American elections four months away, with the disarmament
conference deadlocked and in recess, and with the Depression as strong
as ever, the strain on Anglo-American relations had not abated.

That strain intensified over the next six months. Following Lausanne,

---

[85] Cmd. 4126, 5.
[86] 'Stenographic Notes of the Fifth Plenary Session of the Conference, Saturday, July 9,
1932', *DBFP II*, III, 433–7.
[87] Dutton minute for Chamberlain and Leith-Ross, 29 Jun. 1932, T 172/1788.
[88] Chamberlain to his wife, 3 Jul. 1932, NC 1/26/464; Chamberlain diary, 4 Jul. 1932,
NC 2/16; MacDonald to Salter [League official], 19 Jul. 1932, MacDonald PRO 30/
69/678.
[89] Chamberlain diary, 18 Jun. 1932, NC 2/16.

Papen's government embarked on a diplomatic campaign to force the Powers to concede equality of treatment in arms limitation as defined by Berlin. Its delegation would boycott Geneva when the disarmament conference resumed on 21 September and stay away until either separate Franco-German discussions broke the deadlock or the other Powers removed Germany's grievance. Central to the German demand, made public on 29 August, was the annulment of Section V of the Treaty of Versailles that restricted German armed forces.[90] This scheme originated with General Kurt von Schleicher, an ambitious army officer. He had played a pivotal role in toppling Brüning, had become Reichswehr minister in Papen's cabinet, and, more than Papen, dominated the machinery of government. Wanting to break the disarmament shackles of Versailles, he had overridden Neurath's concerns to demand equality of treatment at Lausanne. The basis for this resided in a plan promoted by Schleicher, 'The Hidden German Goal at the Disarmament Conference', which sketched nine objectives to increase the strength of the army and navy.[91] How much the other Powers understood about why the Germans issued their *démarche* in late August after being turned down at Lausanne is of little importance. Disarmament discussions at Geneva had reached a crossroads.

Berlin's decision to strike onwards and French discomfort forced the National Government to decide how to meet the German diplomatic offensive. On 15 September, accepting Foreign Office arguments that Britain could not remain silent, the ministerial committee on disarmament considered the effect that a British response would have 'not only on France and on Germany, but on America'.[92] As had been the case since the final Preparatory Commission meetings almost two years before, they decided that British diplomacy should maintain the balance between France and Germany whilst keeping firm the Anglo-American connexion. And following the thinking that had underpinned British actions at Lausanne, the committee looked for Britain to take the lead to assure that any decisions made at Geneva rebounded favourably on the country's interests. The committee decided that Britain would put its reaction on the public record via the press. Under Simon's prompting, a consensus emerged that this statement should champion German equal treatment in terms of legal definitions within the disarmament treaty

---

[90] 'Memorandum handed to French Ambassador in Berlin by German Foreign Secretary on 29 August 1932', *BDFA*, II, J4, 42–4.
[91] On this manoeuvring and the 'Goal', see Bennett, *German Rearmament*, 167–88. Cf. Wilhelm Deist, 'Brüning, Herriot und die Abrüstungsgespräche von Bessinge 1932', *VfZ*, 5(1957), 265–72; Wilhelm Deist, 'Schleicher und die deutsche Abrüstungspolitik in Juni/Juli 1932', *VfZ*, 7(1959), 163–76.
[92] DC(M)(32) Meeting 5, CAB 27/505, plus Appendices A and B.

and in the fact that German arms would be subject to the treaty during its lifetime. However, over increasing the size of German armed forces and expanding the weapons available to them – the certain result of abrogating Section V of Versailles – Britain had to demur. This did not mean that Versailles or the Washington and London naval treaties could not be modified; but the only venue where changes could occur was the disarmament conference. As the approved final draft phrased it: agreement could only come 'by patient discussion through the medium of conference between the States concerned'. The French, it was thought, would be satisfied with the demand that Germany return to the negotiating table, whilst the Germans could appreciate that the British met them part way.

As important would be the impact of Britain's announcement in Washington. The second paragraph of the document, said Simon, was 'intended more particularly for American consumption', and because 'Mr. Stimson was extremely anxious about the situation created by the German demarche ... on the economic recovery of the world'. The key passage read: 'His Majesty's Government most earnestly hope that nothing may be now allowed to intervene which would retard the process of economic recovery, which is so urgently necessary, and which it will be the task of the approaching World Economic Conference to promote by every means in its power.' With the promise of war debt revision after the United States presidential elections, and with Britain having helped derail Hoover's disarmament plan, the National Government needed to convince the Administration, Congressional opinion, and the wider American public that Britain honestly sought arms limitation. The Foreign Office looked to impress Roosevelt, chosen the Democratic Party presidential candidate in July, to the same end. By mid-September, building on Embassy reports that reached London throughout the year stressing the dire straits of the American economy, especially the banking sector, the Foreign Office reckoned that Roosevelt's political capital had increased at Hoover's expense.[93] Thus, Britain had to play to the two major political parties in the United States to safeguard the possibility of war debt revision.

---

[93] Cf. Lindsay despatch (303) to Simon, 24 Mar. 1932, FO 371/15869/2014/187; Lindsay despatch (687) to Simon, 21 Apr. 1932, FO 371/15870/2643/187; Osborne memorandum, 'America in 1918 and 1932', Jun. 1932, with Craigie minute, 15 Jul. 1932, FO 371/15875/4028/268; Lindsay despatch (1123) to Simon, 21 Jul. 1932, with minutes, FO 371/15875/4756/268; Osborne despatch (1389) to Simon, 15 Sep. 1932, with Roberts [FO American Department] minute, 28 Sep. 1929, FO 371/15875/6374/ 268. Some FO officials blamed Hoover for shoddy campaigning: 'This is Mr. Hoover's last, and most devastatingly inept, appearance in the role of the Fat Boy', Roberts minute, 17 Nov. 1932, FO 371/15876/7687/268.

Appearing in the press on 19 September – but circulated to the other Powers the day before – the British response won support from the French and Americans, whilst the Papen government was taken aback.[94] Stimson was particularly impressed: 'in general it followed the policy and feeling that I had been following'.[95] He even admired the anodyne but effective manner in which it addressed Germany's arguments about Section V of Versailles: 'It almost approaches the line of weasel words ... But it is all there and I think will be understood.' At this juncture, domestic politics in Germany and the United States intervened. On 6 November, two days before Americans went to the polls, German elections saw the Communist Party make gains at National Socialist expense and produce almost four weeks of political machinations by which Schleicher emerged as chancellor.[96] Leading a ministry that contained several men who had served under Papen – chiefly Neurath – he confronted mounting pressures from both the Communists and National Socialists, which between them had a majority in the Reichstag. Rumbold thought that the British could work with Schleicher.[97] But he held office only until 30 January 1933 when, his government failing, the economy in tatters, and the president, Paul von Hindenburg, wanting to dish Bolshevism in Germany, Hitler succeeded him. Consequently, for almost three months after 6 November, the exigencies of domestic politics diverted German energies from foreign policy.

In the United States, Roosevelt defeated Hoover, and the Democratic Party won control of both houses of Congress. Republican electoral failure lay in the domestic sphere: the inability to reverse the Depression.[98] The Foreign Office understood why American politicians had concentrated on internal issues during the campaign, but it created uncertainty about the direction United States foreign policy would take under Roosevelt. Earlier in the year, the Foreign Office American Department observed that Roosevelt 'was once an enthusiastic supporter of the League of Nations, but his enthusiasm has waned with the approach of election'.[99] Whilst influential Democrats like Newton Baker, who had been Woodrow Wilson's secretary for war, advocated

---

[94] On French and German reaction, see Bennett, *German Rearmament*, 226–30 which must be read with an eye on its decided anti-British bias.
[95] This and the next quotation from Stimson diary, 18 Sep. 1932, Stimson 23.
[96] Craig, *Germany*, 563–7.
[97] Rumbold despatch (955) to Simon, 7 Dec. 1932, *DBFP II*, IV, 92–9.
[98] W. E. Leuchtenburg, *Franklin D. Roosevelt and the New Deal, 1932–1940* (New York, 1963), 1–17; E. A. Rosen, *Hoover, Roosevelt and the Brain Trust: From Depression to New Deal* (New York, 1977); A. M. Schlesinger, *The Crisis of the Old Order, 1919–1933* (Boston, 1957).
[99] Caccia minute, 12 Feb. 1932, FO 371/15874/790/268.

debt revision,[100] no one could judge how Roosevelt would approach the subject. Unknown to London, Baker advised Roosevelt during the campaign to avoid speaking out on crucial foreign policy issues.[101] Nonetheless, Craigie was optimistic that if Roosevelt could subdue the isolationist wing of his party, he would 'favour a policy of reasonable co-operation with Europe in overcoming the world's difficulties'.[102] But until Roosevelt's inauguration in March 1933, working with a lame duck Administration would complicate British diplomacy.

With Germany still boycotting the disarmament conference and war debt payments to resume in December, matters could not wait. Showing their desire to lead in Europe, the British, on 3 October, invited the French, Germans, and Italians to meet in London eight days later to discuss the impasse at Geneva. The Americans were informed in the hope 'they may be prepared to be associated in some way with this exchange of views'.[103] Nothing of substance emerged from this action – it bogged down over a French counter-proposal to hold the talks in Geneva, a site which was anathema to the Germans who were not participating in the disarmament conference. However, it convinced Herriot that France would have to make concessions at Geneva to forestall German withdrawal and the possibility of subsequent German rearmament. This became clear after Anglo-French discussions in London on 13–14 October during which MacDonald and Simon indicated that they would find some way to give Germany equality of treatment.[104] Although much has been made of French annoyance over British manoeuvring to end the impasse, MacDonald and Simon had tired of Herriot's 'stupid' objections.[105] As Simon told the prime minister:

There is no doubt that [Herriot] is very much opposed to a London meeting, but I entirely agree with you that we should go on with it if we can get the Germans to come. For one thing, it is a proof that we are active in taking a positive step to end this deadlock, and the Government at the moment needs to come out clearly as taking such a step.

[100] Craigie minute, 5 May 1932, FO 371/15875/2641/268.
[101] Baker to Moley [Roosevelt adviser], 10 Sep. 1932, Moley 3.
[102] Craigie minute, n.d. [but probably 23 Jul. 1932], FO 371/15875/4318/268.
[103] Simon telegrams (165, 166) to British ambassadors in Paris, Berlin, Rome, 30 Sep. 1932, Vansittart telegram (170) to British ambassadors in Paris, Berlin, Rome, 3 Oct. 1932, Vansittart telegram (490) to Osborne, 3 Oct. 1932, all *DBFP II*, IV, 204–5, 209–10.
[104] Simon to MacDonald, 6 Oct. 1932, Vansittart to Simon, 6 Oct. 1932, with enclosures, both Simon FO 800/287. Cf. notes of four Anglo-French conversations, 13–14 October, all *DBFP II*, IV, 229–44.
[105] Bennett, *German Rearmament*, 242–3. On the 'stupid' objections, Simon to Mac-Donald, 6 Oct. 1932, Simon FO 800/287.

Sensing French isolation at Geneva, Herriot moved to forestall such an eventuality, as well as the chance that Germany might withdraw from the conference. A week before the German election, he privately circulated a 'Plan' to transform armies into short-term militias.[106] This metamorphosis would occur in stages to assure that no Power would be open to attack and none could take the offensive. The procedure had the double merit of acknowledging Germany's demand for equality and, by bringing the Reichswehr into a universal system of control, providing security for France and its allies. To bolster European security, the 'Herriot Plan' proposed giving the League Council authority to identify and intervene against any transgressor of peace and also arrange an Anglo-American guarantee of the existing status quo. Herriot's 'Plan' ran into predictable difficulty: the Germans wanted clarifications; the Americans would not countenance involvement in European security.[107] But its declaration showed a weakening of French resolve. MacDonald saw an opening. Though wanting to work with the Americans to get Germany back to the negotiating table, he was resigned to do so alone. Not only was American foreign policy uncertain following Hoover's defeat, but Washington seemed more concerned with war debts. Feeling that Simon had lost the initiative in the negotiations, MacDonald had earlier pushed for Britain to be assertive.[108] Thus, before the 'Herriot Plan' was made public on 14 November, Simon outlined a Cabinet-defined scheme in Parliament on 10 November, giving it greater detail at Geneva a week later.[109] The British recommended replacing Section V of the Versailles Treaty with a new convention, binding on all signatories to the disarmament treaty. By this means, arms limitation

[106] Tyrrell to Simon, 30 Oct. 1930, with enclosures, FO 800/287; 'Memorandum on Disarmament communicated to the Conference by the French Delegation' (14 Nov. 1932), CAB 27/509. On French opposition, Tyrrell despatch to Simon, 30 Oct. 1932, BDFA, II, J4, 76–9; Bennett, German Rearmament, 242–9; N. Waites, 'The Depression Years', in N. Waites, ed., Troubled Neighbours: Franco-British Relations in the Twentieth Century (1971), 142–3.

[107] On the Germans, see Newton despatch to Simon, 4 Nov. 1932, with enclosure, DBFP II, IV, 260–1; Newton despatch to Simon, 5 Nov. 1932, BDFA, II, J4, 79–80. For the Americans, Gibson to Davis, 24 Oct. 1932, Davis 26; Moffat to Wilson, 31 Oct. 1932, Moffat 4; Stimson to Davis, 14 Nov. 1932, Stimson R82; Mayer 'Daily Report No.27', 17 Nov. 1932, 'No.28', 21 Nov. 1932, 'No.29', 23 Nov. 1932, all Mayer 1.

[108] 'So soon as Simon's lack of wide & systematised outlook lost him the initiative & placed him under the influence of every current which flowed across the Disarmt. negotiations, he swung hither & thither following in the wake of others & unable to steer his own course': MacDonald diary, 30 Oct. 1932, MacDonald PRO 30/69/1753. Then see CC 56(32)3 and 57(32), both 31 Oct. 1932, CC 60(32)1, 9 Nov. 1932, all CAB 23/72; Chamberlain to Ida, 5 Nov. 1932, NC 18/1/804.

[109] 'Extract from a speech by Sir J. Simon in the House of Commons, Nov. 10, 1932', 'Speech by Sir J. Simon at the Bureau of the Disarmament Conference on November 17, 1932', DBFP II, IV, 263–5, 287–95.

would apply to Germany for the duration of the treaty whilst, without the Versailles strictures, Germany could acquire qualitative parity. Simon stressed that such equality could only come when Germany returned to Geneva and that London opposed increasing armed strength to achieve it.

Given that other treaty revisions had been bandied about in the German election campaign – for instance, the fate of the Polish Corridor – Simon emphasised that there must be 'specific assurance' that the Powers would undertake not 'to resolve any present or future differences between themselves by resorting to force'. His statements broke the deadlock. Within three weeks, Britain's recommendation for four-Power discussions revived and, through American participation, expanded into a five-Power conference at Geneva. Wishing to keep the initiative with Britain, and, perhaps, wanting to ensure that French and German blandishments did not divert Simon, MacDonald led the British delegation. The result was the careful fleshing out of the British November programme that, despite some French and German hedging, formed the basis of a declaration on 11 December: German agreement to return to the main conference; European four-Power rejection of the use of force 'to resolve any present or future differences'; and five-Power affirmation 'to work out a convention which shall effect a substantial reduction and a limitation of armaments with provision for future revision with a view to further reduction'.[110] The World Conference had been meeting without success since 21 September because of Germany's boycott.[111] Although Henderson had undertaken to cajole the Germans into returning and flatter the French about the 'Herriot Plan', he failed to make progress.[112] As had been the case in all Great Power arms limitation and economic diplomacy since 1929, agreement had to occur privately and then be imposed on multilateral meetings. With the five-Power understanding in hand and wanting breathing space, Henderson adjourned the special committees and sub-commissions until 23 January and the General Commission until 31 January.[113]

Hoover's Administration played only a supportive role in helping MacDonald and Simon secure the 11 December declaration. Before the

[110] See records of the meetings between 2–11 Dec. 1932, and the 'declaration', in *ibid.*, 308–78.

[111] Cf. *Report Submitted to the Bureau on the Question of Air Forces* (24 Oct. 1932), LND Conf.D.141; *Committee for the Regulation of Trade in, and Private and State Manufacture of, Arms and Implements of War: Report on the Progress of Work* (12 Nov. 1932), LND Conf.D.145; *Second Report on the Question of Supervision Approved by the Bureau on November 15th, 1932* (17 Nov. 1932), LND Conf.D.148.

[112] Henderson to Neurath, 18 Sep. 1932, Henderson to LeBrun [French president], 4, 10 Nov. 1932, all Henderson LNS 475/6.

[113] Henderson to MacDonald, 13 Dec. 1932, *ibid.*

November election, Davis, heading the American delegation at Geneva, had argued for Anglo-American co-operation in resolving the major issues confronting the Powers.[114] But electoral politics and Roosevelt's victory saw Washington's reluctance to take a leading role in disarmament.[115] Even Roosevelt grasped that it was 'important that we should push the disarmament conference to the fullest extent'.[116] However, with the fate of the 'Hoover Plan' fresh in American minds, the United States delegation made no new proposals. Rather, its contribution to the five-Power conference amounted to refining the British proposals, for example, having the main disarmament treaty lapse on 31 December 1936 to conform to the naval treaties.[117] Therefore, getting the Germans to return to Geneva and overcoming French opposition to equality of treatment were the products of British diplomacy.

As just noted, Washington's focus in the immediate aftermath of the American election centred on the debt settlement. The White House and State Department understood that the European Powers, including Britain, wanted debt revision.[118] Early in the World Disarmament Conference, the French and their allies implied a willingness to make concessions over arms limitation – the French signing the London naval treaty – in return for such revision.[119] On this basis, Stimson's proposition in April that 'a very great deal might be done' after November 1932 if the United States was kept out of the impending reparations settlement was understandable. It eliminated the chance that debt revision would be brought up in the American election campaign, plus it pressured Britain and the European Powers to find a solution to reparations at Lausanne. Yet, these were not empty words. Stimson, Feis, Davis, and others saw the need to adjust war debts. But as Feis' division pointed out in June, American voters would not endorse debt

---

[114] Davis to Atherton, 2 Nov. 1932, Davis 58.
[115] Moffat to Gordon, 6 Oct. 1932, Moffat to Wilson, 1 Dec. 1932, both Moffat 3; Gibson to Davis, 3 Dec. 1932, Davis 26; MacDonald to Davis, 7, 17 Nov. 1932, Davis to MacDonald, 15 Nov. 1932, all Davis 40. On Stimson electioneering, see Moffat to Mayer, 12 Oct. 1932, Mayer 1.
[116] Roosevelt to Davis, 26 Nov. 1932, Davis 51.
[117] Davis memorandum, 28 Nov. 1932, 'Record of a Conversation between Mr. MacDonald, Sir J. Simon, and Mr. N. Davis at Geneva, December 2, 1932', 'Record of a Conversation between Mr. MacDonald, Sir J. Simon, and Mr. N. Davis at Geneva, December 3, 1932', both *DBFP II*, IV, 306–10, 313.
[118] Cf. n.a. [probably Feis], 'Memorandum on the Respective Positions of Germany, Britain and France on the Present Negotiations Respecting Reparations and War Debts', 21 Jan. 1932, Feis memorandum, 'The Reparations and Debt situation as of Today', 27 Jan. 1932, both Stimson R82; Castle memorandum, 3 Jun. 1932, HHPP 988.
[119] Pell [US Embassy, Paris] memorandum, 2 Feb. 1932, Gibson 118; Edge to Gibson, 21 Mar. 1932, Gibson 114.

cancellation; instead, they would accept reduction if the debtor Powers bore some responsibility by meeting their contracted obligations and by cutting arms spending that deflected available funds from more constructive purposes.[120] Stimson probably had such thoughts in supporting a World Economic Conference, where war debts would not be on the agenda, but where a separate debt agreement could be arranged in tandem with accords on commodity prices, international exchange, trade impediments, and other issues like silver. But the Americans lost the initiative.

Two days after Roosevelt's victory, Lindsay officially informed the State Department that debt revision was necessary and that Britain's December payment should be postponed until after this question had been settled.[121] This message was part of the economic recovery strategy that Baldwin and Chamberlain had formulated after November 1931. Apart from tackling reparations and war debts, it comprised initiatives designed to reverse the financial embarrassments of August–September 1931; these included depreciating sterling by 30 per cent to help exports, increasing income tax, retrenching, and balancing the budget.[122] Concurrently, the National Government embarked on policies of economic nationalism to protect industry and agriculture. In practical terms, this meant abandoning free trade by, first, passage of an Import Duties Bill in February and, then, in July, with Baldwin and Chamberlain leading the British delegation, establishing limited tariffs at an Imperial Economic Conference at Ottawa to facilitate intra-Empire trade. Because the National Government looked to protect the pound after its devaluation, there also occurred the strengthening of the Sterling Area, the system whereby various Imperial and other Powers which depended on British trade or credit, or both, maintained sterling reserves in order to stabilise their currencies with the pound. Erecting tariffs produced the resignations of Samuel and other free trade Liberal ministers; however, the vigour of the government's economic policies was unrestrained, and the Conservative majority in the Commons fortified the emerging vision of how Britain should escape the Depression. This strengthened vision underpinned the efforts to annul the war debt settlement.

[120] Feis memorandum, n.d. [but Jun. 1932], Stimson R83.
[121] Simon telegrams (538, 539, 544) to Lindsay, 4, 9 Nov. 1932, *BDFA*, II, C11, 311–13.
[122] The rest of this paragraph is based on Cain and Hopkins, *Deconstruction*, 76–93; I. M. Drummond, *British Economic Policy and the Empire, 1919–1939* (1972), 188–20; S. Howson, *Sterling's Managed Float: The Operation of the Exchange Equalization Account, 1932–9* (Princeton, 1980); Marquand, *MacDonald*, 725–9; Middlemas and Barnes, *Baldwin*, 668–84; Rhodes James, *Revolution*, 519–22.

The decision to pursue debt revision derived from Chamberlain. Prior to the postponement of Lausanne, he had described his objectives to Tyrrell and others.[123] Later, in a Cabinet committee on reparations, he was more forceful.[124] Stimson's April admonition about keeping the United States out of any reparations revision and his intimation about revision after the presidential elections only delayed what, for the chancellor of the Exchequer, was an inevitable restructuring of Anglo-American inter-governmental debt. Most ministers shared Chamberlain's attitudes, though he was concerned about MacDonald's personal ties to Stimson blunting British policy.[125] Nonetheless, in a co-ordinated programme supported by the prime minister, Chamberlain followed Lindsay's presentation of the British note with a press conference to put the government's case before British and American public opinion. Emphasising that 'the present note does not attempt to deal with the ultimate settlement of the British War Debt except in so far as it expresses our desire to begin negotiations on the subject', he stated pointedly that international 'self-confidence has been shaken to its foundations by the events of the last two years, and it will require a considerable period of tranquillity to restore it'.[126]

Hoover and Stimson initially reacted with feelings of betrayal, accentuated when France and other debtor Powers followed Britain's lead about seeking revisions.[127] Stimson told Lindsay that 'the British had made it pretty hard for those of us who were fighting their battles because of the language in which their request was couched'.[128] Part of his discomfort – and that of Hoover and Ogden Mills, who had replaced Mellon as secretary of the Treasury – came from veiled charges about American hypocrisy: that although the Hoover Administration had indicated through public statements like the Laval communiqué of October 1931 that revisions were possible, their policy was to oppose any change. Lindsay convinced Stimson that the British, acting in good faith, had not colluded with the other Powers to delay payment. Stimson

[123] Leith-Ross memorandum [of Chamberlain–Tyrrell meeting], 5 Feb. 1932, T 172/1381. Cf. Chamberlain memorandum [on trade balances], 30 Jan. 1932, NC 8/18/1.
[124] RC(32) Meeting 1, 11 May 1932, plus Treasury memorandum, 'Postponement Clauses in the War Debt Funding Agreements', 9 May 1932, both CAB 27/488.
[125] 'But let us first make up our minds that we are not going to pay America if we are not able to collect from Europe; and let that decision be the basis of our negotiations': Runciman [president of the Board of Trade] memorandum, 23 May 1932, T 172/1382. Cf. Chamberlain to Hilda, 11 Jun. 1932, NC 18/1/786.
[126] Chamberlain press interview, 13 Nov. 1932, BDFA, II, C11, 317–18.
[127] Cf. 'Le problème des dettes de guerre et l'échéance du 15 décembre: La note française aux États-Unis', Temps extract, 15 Nov. 1932, 'Note from the Belgian Government', 15 Nov. 1932, both BDFA, II, C11, 319–20, 322.
[128] Stimson diary, 23 Nov. 1932, Stimson 24; Lindsay telegram (468–469) to Simon, 24 Nov. 1932, BDFA, II, C11, 322–4.

then softened harsh words intended for the American response, which came on 23 November – he showed Lindsay the first draft and changed phrases that the ambassador thought might antagonise British opinion.[129] Stimson's desire to maintain good Anglo-American relations derived as much from his anglophilia as from the desire to have the World Economic Conference meet under the most opportune conditions: 'I can see all the benefits of the good will that we have been laboring so hard for the past three years to build up tumbling in fragments around us'.[130]

The bother was that the debt issue was becoming a matter of American partisan politics. Hoover's personal antipathy to Roosevelt, and the president-elect's desire not to have his hands tied on foreign policy or any other issue before he took office in March, militated against reopening debt negotiations in the near future.[131] Discussions between the two men failed to produce a compromise.[132] Then, in early January 1933, in a meeting arranged by Frankfurter, a Roosevelt adviser, Stimson met the president-elect to explain the foreign policy problems confronting the new Administration; he outlined the debt situation carefully, demonstrated how the war debt question touched preparations for the World Economic Conference, and showed that, if any multilateral approach to end the Depression were to have success, the United States had to be accommodating.[133] Earlier, through correspondence, he had won Roosevelt's agreement that American participation in preparations for the World Economic Conference should continue and that Roosevelt would receive British diplomats to discuss war debts just before his inauguration.[134] But additional lobbying could not dissuade the president-elect from asserting that firm decisions on all matters would have to wait until after 4 March 1933.[135]

[129] Stimson to Lindsay, 23 Nov. 1932, BDFA, II, C12, 26–7. Cf. Stimson diary, 23 Nov. 1932, Stimson 24; Lindsay telegram (468–469) to Simon, 24 Nov. 1932, BDFA, II, C11, 322–4.
[130] Stimson diary, 23 Nov. 1932, Stimson 24.
[131] R. Dallek, Franklin D. Roosevelt and American Foreign Policy, 1932–1945 (Oxford, 1979), 23–9.
[132] Hoover memorandum [of Hoover, Roosevelt, Mills, and Moley meeting], 22 Nov. 1933 [but 1932], HHPP 1013. Cf. E. A. Rosen, 'Intranationalism vs. Internationalism: The Interregnum Struggle for the Sanctity of the New Deal', PSQ, 81(1966), 274–97.
[133] Stimson diary, 4, 9 Jan. 1933, plus Stimson, 'Memorandum of Conversation with Franklin D. Roosevelt, Monday January 9', all Stimson 25; Feis Chronological Notes, 9 Jan. 1933, Feis 123.
[134] Roosevelt to Stimson, 24 Dec. 1932, Stimson R83.
[135] Davis to Stimson, 28 Dec. 1932, Stimson R83; Davis to Roosevelt, 30 Dec. 1932, Davis 32; Tugwell [Roosevelt economic adviser] diary, 27 Dec. 1932, Moley 105/1; Moley diary, 10 Jan. 1933. Cf. Roosevelt to Hoover, 21 Dec. 1932, Hoover HHPP 1013.

By mid-December 1932, several debtor Powers announced that they would suspend indefinitely their payments to the United States.[136] The National Government, however, decided to make its December payment. Whilst Britain had been seen by general American opinion to have a legitimate grievance over war debts in that its gold reserves were low, France's decision to avoid payment was perceived as mean-spirited.[137] French gold reserves and dollar holdings were more than adequate to allow for payment. Through notes exchanged in early December, the British clarified their position about revision and, by making their payment, showed good faith in wanting an equitable solution.[138] But London's decision to pay the December instalment was only a tactical decision in the negotiation process, especially now that Hoover and Stimson were departing and Stimson's April promise could not be delivered. It was a conscious effort to put Britain in a favourable light in the United States whilst pressures were brought to bear on the incoming Administration to cancel the debt. 'At the moment we have earned praise in contrast to those naughty Frenchmen,' Chamberlain wrote to his American step-mother, 'and I am relying on the Americans who understand realities to convert their countrymen whose informa-tion is so limited.'[139] Tinged with criticism of the American position, a range of opinion within Britain saw that the time had come to force debt revision to alleviate British economic and financial difficulties.[140] In Cabinet, MacDonald was almost alone in worrying about the need to foster Anglo-American co-operation. 'In view of the refashioning of the world which is going on,' he wrote to Baldwin, 'it is of great advantage to us to renew political contacts with America, so that we will effectively influence it away from a policy of rather superior isolation.'[141] But by early 1933, the co-operation so arduously built up after Hoover's

[136] 'Le texte de la réponse française à la communication américaine du 23 Novembre', *Temps*, 3 Dec. 1932; 'Note from Belgian Government', 13 Dec. 1932; Erskine [British minister, Warsaw] telegram (25), 19 Dec. 1932, all *BDFA*, II, C12, 15–18, 89, 92.

[137] On American views of Britain, see Lindsay despatches (1714, 1763) to Simon, 17, 30 Nov. 1932, Lindsay telegrams (513, 561) to Simon, 4, 13 Dec. 1932, all *BDFA*, II, C12, 1–2, 18, 69, 71–5; Feis chronological notes, 23 Nov. 1932, Feis 123. On bitterness towards the French, see Moffat to Davis, 19 Dec. 1932, Davis 41.

[138] For the exchanges, see Cmd. 4203, 4210, 4211, 4215, 4216, 4217.

[139] Chamberlain to Mary Carnegie, 17 Dec. 1932, NC 1/20/160. Lindsay had earlier stressed the need to educate American opinion: Lindsay telegram (520–521) to Simon, 5 Dec. 1932, *BDFA*, II, C12, 21–2.

[140] Cf. Leith-Ross memorandum for MacDonald, 25 Nov. 1932, Leith-Ross T 188/49; unsigned memorandum [on Conservative backbench opinion] for Baldwin, 29 Nov. 1932, Baldwin 110; Reading to Chamberlain, 2 Dec. 1932, NC 7/11/25/30; Warren Fisher to Vansittart, 16, 17 Dec. 1932, Vansittart to Warren Fisher, 16 Dec. 1932, all Leith-Ross T 188/58.

[141] MacDonald memorandum, n.d. [but Jan. 1933] for Baldwin, Baldwin 110.

capture of the presidency four years earlier had unravelled to an alarming degree. Beginning with Manchuria and the disarmament and financial diplomacy that followed, it had unravelled further. Still, as Roosevelt prepared to take office in March, in the midst of a major banking crisis in the United States that was far worse for that country's economic solvency than the budget deficit of 1931 had been for Britain, the opportunities to twist the strands of co-operation back in place were there.

5 Moving away from the United States, 1933–1934

> As you know, a very great part of my work has been to create good understanding between America and ourselves, and I regret most profoundly that during the last twelve months, solely owing to the action of the President, that work has been largely undone, which is a great grief to me.
>
> MacDonald, June 1934[1]

From the British viewpoint, Roosevelt's election did not spell the end of Anglo-American co-operation. MacDonald, Chamberlain, and others looked towards an amicable resolution of war debts once general American opinion understood the distress that continued payments created for the British government.[2] Moreover, despite concern about the World Disarmament Conference after Hitler's appointment as German chancellor, hope existed in some quarters that joint efforts by London and Washington might produce headway in arms limitation.[3] Yet, diplomacy differs little from other human enterprise: a willingness to align cannot come from one side alone. Roosevelt refused to follow the more internationalist path taken by Hoover and Stimson. There were compelling reasons, all stemming from the domestic economic crisis that, in his election campaign, he promised to overcome: widespread bank failures menaced the country's fiscal solvency; with the

---

[1] MacDonald to Lindsay [academic], MacDonald PRO 30/69/680/1.
[2] Chamberlain to MacDonald, 4 Jan. 1933, Leith-Ross T 188/58; MacDonald to Astor [British peer], 9 Jan. 1933, MacDonald PRO 30/69/679; Lothian to Baldwin, 16 Feb. 1933, with enclosure, Baldwin 110.
  The British war debt settlement remitted 81 per cent of the debt; that of France, 50 per cent; and that of Italy, 68 per cent. Treasury figures showed: 'United States advances to Great Britain amounted to about 40 per cent. of their total advances ($4,000 millions out of $10,000 millions). But Great Britain has paid since the signature of the Funding Agreement $1,447 millions against an aggregate total of $358 millions paid by all the other debtors combined. Thus Great Britain, whose debt was 40 per cent. of the whole, has paid approximately 80 per cent of the total receipts of the United States and over $1,000 millions more than all the remaining debtors put together': Treasury memorandum, 'The British Case on War Debts', n.d. [but Mar. 1933 from internal evidence], T 172/1512.
[3] MacDonald's comments in DC(M) (32) meeting 12, 2 Mar. 1933, CAB 27/505.

dollar tied to gold, one-half of American gold reserves had drained away in 1932; a high dollar had savaged American exports; reduced demand for consumer goods at home and abroad saw industrial unemployment reach record highs, with attendant social distress; and farm prices and income had declined 40 per cent from their 1929 value.[4] Thus, Roosevelt and his advisers, especially Rexford Tugwell and Raymond Moley, two Columbia University professors, concluded that the United States should solve its problems before tackling international issues.[5]

Although Roosevelt might have held internationalist sentiments during his first term of office,[6] his actions convinced the British otherwise. His pragmatic style of leadership – particularly in foreign policy – militated against Anglo-American co-operation following his capture of the White House. Perhaps this pragmatism is best summarised by his famous comment in 1942:

You may know I am a juggler, and I never let my right hand know what my left hand does . . . I may have one policy for Europe and one diametrically opposite for North and South America. I may be entirely inconsistent, and furthermore I am perfectly willing to mislead and tell untruths if it will help win the war.[7]

This does not mean that Roosevelt lacked a world view. Before 1940, it involved pulling the United States out of the Depression, re-establishing its economic and financial strength, and using every means possible to protect and expand American economic, political, and strategic interests in an increasingly unstable world. Like Stimson, Roosevelt thought in strategic terms; he had been Wilson's assistant secretary of the Navy and helped devise the 1916 and 1918 USN building programmes. But unlike Hoover, the occupant of the White House after March 1933, rather than his chief diplomatic adviser, made foreign policy. Whilst controversy exists amongst American historians about the means Roosevelt employed in pursuing his diplomatic goals – non-Americans are more united in their views about how the leaders of Great Powers act – his desire to enhance and protect the manifold interests of the United

---

[4] Representative of the voluminous literature are T. Ferguson, 'From Normalcy to the New Deal: Industrial Structure, Party Competition, and American Public Policy in the Great Depression', *International Organization*, 38(1984) 41–91; F. Freidel, *Franklin D. Roosevelt. Launching the New Deal* (Boston, 1973), 3–17; K. Louchheim, *The Making of the New Deal* (Cambridge, MA, 1983); V. Perkins, *Crisis in Agriculture: The Agricultural Adjustment Administration and the New Deal, 1933* (Berkeley, 1969); Schlesinger, *Old Order*, 155–269.

[5] 'If we try to rescue the crumbling structure of Europe[,] it seems as though we will be brought tumbling down ourselves', Moley diary, 22 Mar. 1933.

[6] Dallek, *Roosevelt*, 3–20; A. P. N. Erdmann, 'Mining for the Corporate Synthesis: Gold in American Foreign Economic Policy, 1931–1936', *DH*, 17(1993), 171–200.

[7] Morgenthau [secretary of the Treasury] diary, 15 May 1942, quoted in W. F. Kimball, *The Juggler. Franklin Roosevelt as Wartime Statesman* (Princeton, 1991), 7.

States is certain.[8] To this end, although unclear to foreigners early in his presidency, he ran his own foreign policy, often by-passing his secretary of state, Cordell Hull, and the State Department. For the first time, perhaps, the British and others confronted an American president not necessarily constrained by the tug of morality, although Roosevelt certainly believed in the superiority of American civilisation and political culture. Moreover, Roosevelt was an astute politician. If this meant accommodating his foreign policy to appease domestic interests that could stymie his 'New Deal' or, on the other hand, suddenly coddling, beguiling, or assailing another Power for tactical reasons, he would do so unblushingly.

By July 1933, British mistrust of Roosevelt arose over his handling of war debts, arms limitation, and the World Economic Conference. On 21 January, a private emissary from Roosevelt, William Bullitt, saw Mac-Donald secretly at Chequers to lay the ground for official debt negotiations. MacDonald learnt of Roosevelt's wish to cut British war debts by 80 per cent: 'R wishes closest co-operation with us, "more closely than ever" in everything of common interest.'[9] Nine days later, official negotiations began when Lindsay met the president-elect, who stressed that the debt could not be wiped out. Fleshing out Bullitt's overture, Roosevelt contemplated a revised settlement: the British would repay only the principal of their loans. 'He takes total debt as funded, deducts total of payments already made, which he regards as repayment of capital, and suggests that a new agreement be made for repayment of remainder.'[10] Intending to treat other debtor Powers similarly, Roosevelt needed concessions to brandish before American opinion. He wanted debt revision included in 'a comprehensive programme' involving tariff agreements, limitations on tanks and artillery, a scaling down of battleships, and, by prohibiting military aircraft, the elimination of aircraft carriers. To ensure success, Roosevelt asked that the 'British "No. 2 man"' – presumably Baldwin – arrive in Washington by 6 March to

[8] For Americans, cf. C. A. Beard, *American Foreign Policy in the Making, 1932–1940: A Study in Responsibilities* (New Haven, 1946); H. E. Barnes, ed., *Perpetual War for Perpetual Peace: A Critical Examination of the Foreign Policy of Franklin D. Roosevelt and Its Aftermath* (Caldwell, ID, 1953); Freidel, *Roosevelt*, 118–37; F. W. Marks, III, *Wind Over Sand: The Diplomacy of Franklin Roosevelt* (Athens, GA, 1987). For non-Americans, cf. J.-B. Duroselle, *France and the United States. From Beginnings to the Present* (Chicago, 1976), 135–46; H.-J. Schröder, *Deutschland und die Vereinigten Staaten, 1933–1939: Wirtschaft und Politik in der Entwicklung des deutsch-amerikanischen Gegansatzes* (Wiesbaden, 1970); Watt, *John Bull*, 76–84.
[9] MacDonald to Chamberlain, 5 Jan. 1933, NC 7/11/26/25; MacDonald diary, 21 Jan. 1933; Bullitt to Roosevelt, 22 Jan. 1933, in O. H. Bullitt, ed., *For the President. Personal and Secret. Correspondence between Franklin D. Roosevelt and William C. Bullitt* (Boston, 1972), 26–7.
[10] Lindsay telegrams (67–68, 70, 73) to Simon, 30, 31 Jan. 1933, *BDFA*, II, C12, 140–3.

begin negotiations, which would allow for an agreement to be ready for Congress when it convened on 20 April. With the debt question solved, the World Economic Conference would have more chance of success. After this meeting, Davis apprised Lindsay that Roosevelt understood the Powers' difficulty in making payments, even in revised agreements: 'he has it in mind to get out of Congress authority to suspend payments from debtor Governments at his discretion'. Through Davis, Roosevelt proposed a moratorium on war debt payments.

Lindsay immediately travelled to London and, from 6 to 10 February, met with a new Cabinet committee that contained the National Government's five leading ministers – MacDonald, Baldwin, Chamberlain, Simon, and Walter Runciman, the president of the Board of Trade; this committee was to handle the liquidation of the debt. Lindsay and the ministers dissected Roosevelt's suggested settlement, its place in 'a comprehensive programme', and whether a senior minister should travel to Washington.[11] After Lindsay reported that Congress would resist ratifying any agreement that eliminated debts completely, the two Conservatives dominated the discussions. Their essential argument followed a theme developed by Chamberlain in a speech on 24 January: any debt settlement had to be connected with reparations. Lausanne stood at the centre of a new European arrangement that could only be altered to the detriment of Franco-German reconciliation – for which the National Government had worked so hard during its first six months in office. Thus, the debt settlement was as much political as economic, though Chamberlain pointed out that Britain would still have to make annual payments of £5.5 million (about $18 million) under Roosevelt's scheme.

All else in the committee flowed from Chamberlain and Baldwin's judgment: Britain would sanction no alteration to Lausanne; total debtor payments to the United States had to equal the lump sum the German government agreed to pay at Lausanne; World Economic Conference preparations should continue parallel to debt negotiations; and, to avoid the stigma of failure, no British minister would go to Washington unless agreement seemed near. These points were included in instructions for Lindsay, supplemented by Treasury memoranda to aid him in talks with Roosevelt and his advisers.[12] Unmentioned was the desire to arrange a debt settlement after the World Conference met; this delay would allow for some restructuring of the international economy

---

[11] BDA (33) meetings 1–5, 6–10 Feb. 1932, CAB 27/548. Cf. Sargent to Warren Fisher, 26 Jan. 1933, T 172/1512; Chamberlain to Ida, 12 Feb. 1933, NC 18/1/816.

[12] 'Instructions to His Majesty's Ambassador at Washington, February 1933', enclosing Treasury memoranda, *DBFP II*, V, 752–69.

before debts were tackled, and it might make American opinion more understanding about cancellation. Even at this stage the committee, especially Chamberlain, perceived the president-elect to be contradictory: 'He seemed to disclaim any idea of reaching an all-round settlement with the United Kingdom in advance of the World Economic Conference and yet the programme outlined in the conversations with Sir Ronald Lindsay at Warm Springs appeared to contemplate such a settlement.'[13] Having achieved much over the preceding fifteen months, chiefly getting Paris to abandon its reparations claims, the British refused to be rushed into an Anglo-American agreement that could rebound unfavourably on Europe.

Lindsay's subsequent discussions with Roosevelt, Hull, and William Phillips, the new assistant under-secretary of state, emphasised London's desire not to hurry.[14] Amplifying this view in a private letter to the president-elect, MacDonald stressed that 'the American settlement must be a European one as well'; moreover, MacDonald emphasised that the naval settlement following his 1929 American visit occurred only because 'a very full exchange of views between Washington and London' had preceded negotiations. Given Roosevelt's ambitious 'programme' which lumped war debts with tariffs and specific arms limitation proposals, care was needed not to undermine the progress that had occurred in spheres outside debts. Weighing British reaction along with counsel from advisers like Feis and Moley,[15] Roosevelt accepted that there would be no speedy resolution of the debt question; and he would have to find means to reconcile debt revision with Lausanne. Nevertheless, Roosevelt had his own irreducible minima. These were impressed on Lindsay in Washington by Hull, and on MacDonald by Davis, sent to London in March: Congress had to be pacified and a senior British minister had to come to Washington for discussions. These points were put in language that Lindsay characterised as 'nothing cheerful or encouraging'.[16] Still, it resulted in an approach to debts that conformed largely to British wishes. 'It should be remembered', Chamberlain told his colleagues, 'that we had to educate Europe

---

[13] BDA (33) meeting 2, 7 Feb. 1932, CAB 27/548.
[14] MacDonald to Roosevelt, 10 Feb. 1933, in E. B. Nixon and D. B. Schewe, eds. *Franklin D. Roosevelt and Foreign Affairs* (New York, Toronto, 1696–70), vol. I [hereafter in the style *FDRFA*, I], 8–13; Lindsay telegrams (8, 140, 141, 152) to Simon, 21, 27 Feb., 7 Mar. 1933, all *DBFP II*, 669–71, 773–5; Hull memorandum, 23 Mar. 1933, Hull 58.
[15] Moley minute, n.d. [but Feb. 1933], Moley 104/2; Feis memorandum, n.d., in Feis to Hull, 3 Mar. 1933, Hull 33; Feis memorandum, 7 Mar. 1933, Feis 123.
[16] Lindsay telegram (8) to Simon, 21 Feb. 1933, *DBFP II*, V, 769–71.

on the subject of reparations, and we should now have to educate America on the subject of debts.'[17]

On 8 March, speaking for the newly inaugurated Roosevelt, Davis told Lindsay that the 'objective of immediate importance was to arrange somehow that on the 15th June His Majesty's Government should not be compelled either to pay or default'.[18] Over the next few weeks, Hull and Moley indicated that a MacDonald visit would help place 'the whole combination of questions in their proper setting for the American people', and that 'it would not be possible to get any sort of moratorium for [the] June payment through Congress without a visit by the Prime Minister'.[19] The Cabinet committee discussed these and other reports on 31 March.[20] Outwardly, the American position remained unchanged – 'it was a personal debt, that the document had been signed, that [the Americans] had always refused to link [debts] with reparations, and so forth'. But another MacDonald mission might break the deadlock, particularly given what Lindsay had learnt about a moratorium. It might also provide for concerted Anglo-American efforts at the World Economic Conference over currency stabilisation and tariffs. MacDonald agreed to travel to Washington on a visit described publicly as dealing with disarmament and preparations for the World Economic Conference.[21] War debts were to be discussed privately.

From 21 to 26 April MacDonald, with Vansittart and Leith-Ross, met Roosevelt, Hull, Moley, and other officials.[22] Whilst MacDonald found the president charming and open-minded, the mission accomplished little. The Americans would not cancel debts, and they now opposed a moratorium, something made clear when Leith-Ross stayed behind after MacDonald and Vansittart departed. Moley suggested an annual $25 million British payment, almost half as much again as that mentioned by Roosevelt to Lindsay in January.[23] As a diplomatic carrot, the president suggested stabilising the two Powers' currencies by 'linking dollars and pounds'.[24] This issue had decided importance for the

---

[17] BDA (33) meeting 2, 7 Feb. 1933, CAB 27/548.
[18] Lindsay telegram (157) to Simon, 8 Mar. 1933, *BDFA*, II, C12, 168–9.
[19] FO memorandum, 'General Outline of the Main Developments of the War Debt Negotiations since June 1931', 12 Apr. 1933, *ibid.*, 180–3; Feis memoranda of meetings, 27, 29 Mar., 3 Apr. 1933, all Moley 101/6.
[20] BDA (33) meeting 7, 31 Mar. 1933, CAB 27/548.
[21] Cf. American and British press notices, 7 Apr. 1933, *DBFP II*, V, 789, n. 1.
[22] Vansittart telegram (238) to Simon, 22 Apr. 1933, *BDFA*, II, C12, 184; BDA (33) Meeting 8, 4 May 1933, CAB 27/548; Moley diary, 22–25 Apr. 1933.
[23] Leith-Ross telegram (291, 292) for Treasury, 2 May 1933, *BDFA*, II, C12, 186–7.
[24] Leith-Ross telegram (293) to Hopkins, 2 May 1933, *ibid*. Thus, A. M. Schlesinger, *The Coming of the New Deal* (Boston, 1959), 206 is wrong. Also see Feis minute, 'Key Decision', 18 Apr. 1933, Moley 101/6.

forthcoming economic conference because the United States suddenly left the gold standard on 19 April, in part to meet the trade challenge posed by the cheaper British pound.[25] Worried about an American trap, Lindsay and Leith-Ross suspended negotiations on 2 May so as not to be 'rushed' into 'a permanent settlement or to commit ourselves before it is clear that a general agreement can be reached'.[26]

For MacDonald, Baldwin, and their colleagues, the events of April–May suggested that Washington spoke with discrepant voices. Roosevelt offered broad prescriptions for settlement that were contradicted on crucial points by his advisers. Then, the president supported a moratorium only to reverse himself. Moley, appointed an assistant-secretary of state, was locked in a bureaucratic struggle with Hull over the control of policy for the World Economic Conference, which produced conflicting views about tariff revision.[27] Despite his strong anglophilia, Davis, who became a kind of roving ambassador for Roosevelt, had antagonised even MacDonald by spouting views that did not mesh with Washington's pronouncements.[28] That Mellon's replacement, Robert Bingham, had not yet reached London only deprived Whitehall of regular contact with a senior American diplomatist permanently in Britain. Still, an Administration policy had emerged – the debt had to be paid in some way. Additionally, Roosevelt's Washington increasingly perceived the British through an unflattering lens: they were 'self-righteous'; they were 'stupid ... to think this administration would follow this Hoover insanity'; and 'the way the British have been carrying on in matters economic is disturbing me greatly'.[29] With the British wanting cancellation, the prospect of compromise between the two English-speaking Powers was diminishing rapidly as the World Economic Conference neared.

Disarmament exacerbated the situation. Roosevelt's January discussions with Lindsay posited Anglo-American co-operation at Geneva. But as Roosevelt approached economic diplomacy, so he approached arms limitation; nothing would be forthcoming until after his inauguration. Outside events, however, militated against delay. Hitler's rise to

[25] 'The purpose of this move as I see it is two-fold (1) to stop inflationary businesses in Congress by putting this power in the hands of the President, (2) to sock the British especially,' Moley diary, 18–19 Apr. 1933.
[26] Leith-Ross telegram (291, 292) for Treasury, 2 May 1933, *BDFA*, II, C12, 186–7.
[27] Feis to Butterworth [US Legation, Ottawa], 30 Mar. 1933, Feis 11; Feis minutes, 21 Mar., 1 Apr. 1933, Feis 123; Moley diary, 11 Apr. 1933.
[28] MacDonald diary, 30 Mar., 4 Apr. 1933, MacDonald PRO 30/69/1750. Cf. Chamberlain minute, 2 Apr. 1933, on Simon memorandum [on MacDonald, Simon, and Davis discussion], 31 Mar. 1933, T 172/1512.
[29] Feis minute, 'Key Decision', 18 Apr. 1933, Moley 101/6; Moley diary, 22 Apr. 1933; Moffat to Atherton, 8 May 1933, Moffat 2.

power suggested that progress would have to be made quickly to deliver on the 11 December 1932 declaration about equality. Vansittart's pessimism reflected feelings within the British government. 'We should go on trying, with diminished hopes,' he noted, 'though even to *attempt* to deal with such a government as that of Germany (an alarming and insane gang) is now a depressing prospect.'[30] Still, even he saw possibilities of a *modus vivendi* with Washington:

I think it very easy to exaggerate the length of time during which Anglo-American relations will be poisoned by failure to settle the debt problem. Events will dictate to the U.S.A. as well as to us; and the fuller the world is of events (mostly unpleasant ones) the shorter must memories necessarily become.

As important, the Lytton Commission reported on 2 October 1932. Although generally condemning Japanese actions, Lytton and his colleagues suggested a compromise settlement that acknowledged some Japanese justification for their action. Tokyo's rights and interests in Manchuria should be recognised whilst, instead of becoming a separate state, the province received a degree of autonomy under Chinese sovereignty.[31] The Assembly was to consider the report, discuss it, and then, in the new year, vote whether to accept it. However, in early January 1933, the Kwantung Army began operations to conquer all of north-eastern China above the Great Wall. With the Lytton Report vote approaching in February, and since all pretence of Japan protecting its legitimate rights had disappeared, censure of Tokyo's policies seemed certain.

With the Disarmament Conference at another breaking-point, the British decided to make one final effort to keep discussions going. Pushed in the Cabinet by the Foreign Office on 19 January 1933, a draft 'Programme of Work' was discussed by the ministerial disarmament committee over the next few days.[32] Simon outlined the purpose of the submission: 'the object of this "Programme of Work" has been to set out topics for discussion and not to present any new declarations of policy. The situation at Geneva has reached a point where it was necessary for somebody to take charge of the procedure, and unless someone did take charge the Conference was bound to fail.'[33] The Foreign Office view of disarmament negotiations, thus, conformed to the general thrust of British policy articulated by MacDonald the preceding May: to take the

[30] Vansittart memorandum, 26 Feb. 1933, VNST I/2/2.
[31] League of Nations, *Report of the Commission of Enquiry* [with supplements] (Geneva, 1932), LND C.663.M.320.1932.VII. Cf. Nish, *Japan's Struggle*, 190–4; Thorne, *Limits*, 328–45.
[32] DC(M) (32) meetings 6–7, 20, 23 Jan. 1933, CAB 27/505.
[33] Meeting 6, *ibid*.

initiative in Europe to better protect British interests. Tellingly, the Foreign Office reckoned that after almost twelve months of negotiations, the material for an agreement, even a limited one, lay at hand. In the committee deliberations, although the other ministers entertained suspicion of France – 'French policy had always tended towards putting us in the wrong' – the committee endorsed the 'Programme' with minor changes. The only contentious issue concerned Foreign Office willingness to support 'a convention or conventions' for a new regime of European security. Hailsham argued that such agreement ran counter to British interests and that, if a new regime came to pass and the National Government had to oppose it, 'we should be accused of not agreeing with a recommendation which we had originally put forward'. Simon agreed to an equivocal amendment, something he characterised as 'we are not saying we accede to your continental ideas, but we are prepared for you to have them discussed and see what you can do about it'. Still, the point remained that unless prodding occurred, the conference would collapse. It was in Britain's interests to prod.

The 'Programme' was circulated to the conference after it reassembled on 30 January.[34] Hitler's accession to power the same day added urgency and, over the next two weeks, British delegates, chiefly Anthony Eden, the Foreign Office under-secretary deputising for Simon, made speeches in the General Commission to spur the conference into moving.[35] Regardless, work within the specialist commissions and sub-commissions immediately assumed the usual course of interminable discussions without result.[36] This did not happen solely from Hitler's long-espoused desire to rearm Germany. Hitler wanted to ensure that his anti-revisionist neighbours would not launch a preemptive attack on Germany while he was consolidating his regime. Accordingly, German negotiators at Geneva were instructed not to reject proposals out of hand but, instead, to discuss them, seek clarifications, and ensure that any onus for failure fell on the French.[37] Instead, lack of progress at Geneva derived from the Powers' lack of will to find an agreement at a time when uncertainty about European and Far Eastern security increased. German elections in March, called to confirm Hitler's coalition, led to a one-party state in which the National

---

[34] *Draft Proposals by the United Kingdom Delegation dated January 30th, 1933*, LND Conf.D.154.
[35] See Eden speeches, 3, 9, 16 Feb. 1933, *BDFA*, II, J4, 161–8.
[36] Cf. *Minutes of the General Commission*, II, 272, 277–321; *Question of Effectives* (16 Feb. 1933), LND Conf.D.C.G.41; *Air Questions* (Feb. 1933), LND Conf.D.C.G.43; *Pre-Military Training* (28 Feb. 1933), LND Conf.D.C.G.48.
[37] Neurath to Nadolny [chief, German delegation], *Documents on German Foreign Policy*, ser. C. vol. I [hereafter in the form *DGFP*, CI], 42–4.

Socialists completely controlled the levers of government. League acceptance of the Lytton Report on 24 February – only the Japanese delegation voted against it – saw Tokyo announce that Japan would leave the international organisation.[38] Agreeing to stay in the Disarmament Conference, it reserved the right not to sign any agreement that failed to meet its specific requirements.[39] With France finally suffering the full force of the Depression and the lesser Powers disinclined to restrict their means of self-defence, arms limitation had become more difficult to achieve.

Simon and Eden worried sufficiently about the situation to approach the ministerial disarmament committee on 2 March. They circulated two papers: a memorandum by Simon on 'the crisis in Europe' and a 'draft convention' penned by the British delegation at Geneva. The danger, as related by Eden, was 'that the Conference was tottering to failure and this led to the suggestion ... that it might be advisable to have a six months' adjournment'. Over the next week, the committee deliberated, concluding that an adjournment would prove fatal to the conference, that failure would give the Germans the excuse to rearm, and that the British delegation should do all possible to get the conference moving by making suggestions that could keep alive the chances for an agreement, now seen to be limited at best.[40] It produced new British proposals, outlined by MacDonald in Geneva on 16 March, and saw both him and Simon lobbying the other delegations about the importance of not adjourning.[41] Apart from technical questions like restricting artillery calibres to 105 mm, the British plan entailed a five-year period to allow Germany to achieve equality with the other land Powers and the suggestion that the continental Powers look for an additional instrument to effect their security. The private German reaction was unfavourable; but, publicly, following Hitler's bargaining strategy, the chief German delegate, Rudolf Nadolny, took the line that this could be the basis for agreement.[42] The conference did not adjourn. From London's viewpoint, additional pressures were necessary to

---

[38] Nish, *Japan's Struggle*, 223–30; Thorne, *Limits*, 333–6.

[39] *Communication from the Japanese Delegation, dated March 7th, 1933, Concerning its Participation in the Conference* (Mar. 1933), LND Conf.D.155.

[40] DC(M) (32) meetings 12–15, 2–7 Mar. 1933, CAB 27/505; Simon memorandum, Mar. 1933 [CP 52(33)], CAB 24/239. For the convention, see n. 41, below. Cf. Eden to Baldwin, 10, 22 Feb. 1933, Baldwin 129.

[41] *Draft Convention Submitted by the United Kingdom Delegation* (16 Mar. 1933), LND Conf.D.157. Cf. MacDonald–Simon conversations with Nadolny, Aloisi, Politis, Beneš, Paul-Boncour, Daladier, 11–16 Mar. 1933, *BDFA*, II, J4, 179–97.

[42] Nadolny telegram (273) to Neurath, 20 Mar. 1933, *DGFP*, CI, 186–9. Cf. G.L. Weinberg, *The Foreign Policy of Hitler's Germany*, vol. I (Chicago, 1970), 40–6.

achieve results; MacDonald looked for assistance from Roosevelt. It was not forthcoming.

Beyond pious statements about the need to limit arms – and sharing Hoover's view that arms spending diverted Europe's public money away from economic recovery and prevented the honouring of European debts to the United States – Roosevelt promoted nothing of substance at Geneva.[43] Admittedly, within days of his inauguration, he informed MacDonald privately that Anglo-American co-operation at the World Conference should continue.[44] However, the points made to Lindsay in January about abolishing military aircraft, aircraft carriers, and the rest were never offered officially at Geneva. Part of the reason lay with Roosevelt's need to concentrate on the domestic crisis in the United States. The other flowed from the belief that after Hoover's June 1932 *démarche*, the United States could do no more respecting arms limitation and, now, the Europeans should put their affairs in order. Just as crucial was the perception that British and American interests on the related matters of European security and arms limitation were dissimilar. Ray Atherton, the counsellor at the American Embassy at London, reported to the State Department:

In conversations, it is frequently brought out that the British Cabinet is increasingly conscious of England's political responsibilities as a European nation and, after surveying the field of Anglo-American co-operation, has reluctantly come to the conclusion that while Anglo-American aims might coincide with their general outlines, any policy of effective co-operation is practically unobtainable in view of conflicting interests.[45]

Such views found a ready audience.[46] Although misreading the British position concerning the United States, Roosevelt's Washington had some justification for this perception. British war debt policy had the potential of creating inconvenience for the Administration in Congress and the country at large at a time when Roosevelt needed widespread support for his 'New Deal'. Respecting the Far East, the National Government seemed willing to accept Japan's Manchurian conquest as the price to keep Anglo-Japanese relations on an even keel, this despite a public statement by Roosevelt that he would continue Stimson's

[43] Lindsay telegram (165) to Vansittart, 16 Mar. 1933, *DBFP II*, IV, 545–6. Cf. Mayer to Moffat, 28 Mar. 1933, Mayer 1; Davis to Gibson, 12 Apr. 1933, Davis 26; Swanson [secretary of the Navy] to Hull, 27 Apr. 1933, Hull 34; Moffat to Wilson, 31 Jan., 9 May 1933, both Moffat 4.
[44] Mellon to MacDonald, 7 Mar. 1933, MacDonald PRO 30/69/679.
[45] Atherton despatch to Hull, 24 Feb. 1933, SDDF 841.00/1233. Cf. Atherton to Moffat, 28 Mar. 1933, Moffat 2.
[46] Moley diary, 25 Mar. 1933.

doctrine of non-recognition.[47] Consequently, when MacDonald travelled to Washington, neither Roosevelt nor his advisers championed new arms cut proposals.[48] Then, on 16 May, the president announced that whilst his Administration supported continued disarmament discussions at Geneva – he specifically mentioned the British plan – it would avoid taking the initiative to allow other Powers to do so. His only suggestion was that 'all the nations of the world should enter into a solemn and definite pact of non-aggression'.[49] He failed to elaborate and, as disarmament discussions had shown since 1926, non-aggression pacts needed to be supported by more than words.

This was the situation when Britain's next debt payment came due. The general lines of the story are well known.[50] On 15 June, Britain paid the United States $10 million in silver bullion. The intention was to clear the way for the World Economic Conference, which had begun three days earlier. Beneath the surface, however, wariness emerged on each side. Roosevelt's reversal over the moratorium annoyed the National Government which, when it first learnt delayed payments were possible, wanted a three-year suspension.[51] Writing to MacDonald in May, Roosevelt pointed to Congressional opinion as grounds for continuing payments although, under British pressure, he agreed to negotiations to settle the matter before December.[52] For the British, this concession momentarily safeguarded their interests, particularly Lausanne; but it added to the perception of an unco-operative Washington.[53] Before striking upon the final agreement, Roosevelt, Moley, and James Warburg, a New York banker with ties to the Administration, separately made conflicting proposals to the British Embassy about settling the debt issue: non-payment that would not be considered a default; a partial payment; and placing deposit notes with the BIS and up to 25 per cent of the debt payment in gold with the United States Treasury.[54] It was Roosevelt who, after suggesting that he

47 'Press Statement by Roosevelt', 17 Jan. 1933, *FDRFA*, I, 4; Hornbeck memorandum, 'Manchuria Situation. Action by British Government', 12 Jan. 1933, Hornbeck 453; Grew [US ambassador, Tokyo] diary, 11 Feb. 1933, Grew 65.
48 Cf. Phillips memorandum, 24 Apr. 1933, *FDRFA*, I, 68–9, outlining French opposition to the British proposals.
49 'Roosevelt to the Heads of Nations Represented at the London and Geneva Conferences', 16 May 1933, *FDRFA*, I, 126–8. Cf. Vansittart to Simon, 23 May 1933, Simon FO 800/291; Moffat to Mayer, 7 Jun. 1933, Moffat 3.
50 Dallek, *Roosevelt*, 40–1, 44, 48.
51 BDA (33) meeting 10, 17 May 1933, CAB 27/548.
52 Roosevelt to MacDonald, 22 May 1933, *FDRFA*, I, 153–5.
53 CC 39(33)1–2, 9 Jun. 1933, CAB 23/76.
54 Cf. Moley diary, 18–19 Apr. 1933; Leith-Ross telegram (291–292) to Treasury, 2 May 1933, Bewley [commercial counsellor, British Embassy, Washington] telegram (299) to Treasury, 8 May 1933, Lindsay telegram (364–365) to Simon, 4 Jun. 1933, all *BDFA*,

would announce that a partial British payment should be seen 'as a deferment not a default', abandoned the idea, citing Congressional disfavour.[55] The British simply refused to pay more than a token $10 million; and when American opinion barely murmured, Chamberlain remarked: 'I can look back over the whole course of the negotiations without feeling that I should have acted otherwise than I did at any other point . . .'.[56] Hence, not only did American economic diplomacy appear to lack coherence, but Roosevelt seemed also to hide behind Congress to place the blame for default on the British. In Chamberlain's mind, Roosevelt was seeking to divide the British and the other debtors by dealing separately with each Power.[57]

Roosevelt's handling of American policy at the World Economic Conference laid bare any idea that Anglo-American collaboration on crucial international issues could continue. Hoover and Stimson had appointed two academics, Edmund Day and John Williams, to participate in conference preparations, which began at Geneva in October 1932. Following his victory, Roosevelt endorsed their efforts concerning a draft agenda that gave prominence to currency stabilisation, tariff adjustments, and the steadying of silver prices.[58] After 4 March, however, as Day and Williams continued preparatory discussions in London, Administration arrangements for the conference were desultory at best.[59] The domestic crisis and the struggle between Moley and Hull – which Feis intimated to Lindsay[60] – diverted attention away from anything beyond general lines of approach. As late as 16 May, the American delegates had yet to be chosen; and it was only on the boat to Britain that those concerned with currency stabilisation conferred.[61]

II, C12, 186–7, 196–9; Treasury memorandum, 'The Warburg Scheme', n.d. [but May 1933], T 172/1512.
[55] Lindsay telegrams (334, 364–365)) to Simon, 22 May, 4 Jun. 1933, both DBFP II, V, 812, 815–17; Lindsay telegram (375) to Simon, 7 Jun. 1933, T 172/1512. '[Roosevelt] is evidently timid as a hare in regard to debts for all his apparent courage in other directions', Vansittart to Warren Fisher, 6 Jun. 1933, T 172/1512.
[56] Chamberlain to Ida, 17 Jun. 1933, NC 18/1/831.
[57] CC 39(33)2, 9 Jun. 1933, CAB 23/76.
[58] Day to Stoppani, 27 Dec. 1932, LNR 2671/39421/38756; Wilson to Stencek, 28 Dec. 1932, LNR 2669/38880/38039; Feis to Frankfurter, 9 Jan. 1933, Feis 16; Stimson to Roosevelt, 9 Dec. 1932, Feis minute, 23 Dec. 1932, with addendum, 27 Dec. 1932, Feis memorandum, Jan. 1933, Feis memorandum, 24 Jan. 1933, all Feis 123. Cf. Moley diary, 10, 22 Jan., 12 Mar. 1933. The report – The Monetary and Economic Conference . . . An Account of the Preparatory Work – is in LNR 4635/5014/597.
[59] Page [US Tariff Commission] to Hull, 2 Mar. 1933, Hull 33; Moley diary, 25, 27, 31 Mar., 24 Apr., 6 May 1933; Berle [Moley adviser] to Moley, 18 Apr. 1933, with enclosure, Moley 102/2; Feis to Davis, 5 Apr. 1933, with enclosure, Feis 15.
[60] Lindsay telegram (327) to Simon, 19 May 1933, BDFA, II, C12, 195.
[61] Cf. Roosevelt memorandum, 2 May 1933, Hull 34; Moley diary, 16 May 1933; Warburg to Hull, 1 Jun. 1933, SDDF 550.S1 Monetary Stabilization/9.

The National Government, on the other hand, knew what it wanted to achieve. Through the conversations that MacDonald, Lindsay, and Leith-Ross had had in Washington after mid-April, the British believed that Roosevelt's Administration shared the desire to stabilise currencies and adjust tariffs.[62] Therefore, despite the Administration's approach to disarmament and war debts, hope existed that the Americans would work with Britain and the other Powers to bring order to the international economy – other leaders, including Herriot, had trekked to Washington to consult with Roosevelt. The Economic Advisory Council, established by the Labour government in 1931, and which included Keynes, argued that it 'is all the more important, therefore, to find a major project for which Great Britain and the United States can work cordially together at the Conference. A proposal for all-round devaluation would form such a project.'[63] With Preparatory Committee agreement that the conference would discuss monetary and credit policy, prices, and matters like resuming the movement of capital, the Treasury led in formulating the British bargaining position.[64]

After opening on 12 June, the conference became bogged down over currency stabilisation. By leaving the gold standard, the dollar had devalued significantly, which had made American products less expensive. Whilst threatening British and French external trade, cheaper American goods might also penetrate their markets. Roosevelt did nothing to alleviate the anxiety this caused the Europeans because 'he was in no hurry to stabilize until he was sure he was going to get the best bargain there was to be got'.[65] To coerce the Powers further, Roosevelt had Moley write a 'syndicated newspaper column warning against excessive hopes for the Conference'.[66] Still, heading what even Roosevelt's admirers concede was a weak delegation,[67] Hull worked to make the conference successful. Despite having Roosevelt's professed support,[68] he faced several obstacles. After the secretary left Washington, Roosevelt withdrew a trade bill from Congress that Hull

[62] Leith-Ross memorandum, 'Discussions at Washington on the Programme of the World Conference', with appendices, 12 May 1933, T 172/1812.
[63] Economic Advisory Council, 'Seventh Report', 16 May 1933, T 172/1812.
[64] *Account of the Preparatory Work*, 22, LNR 4635/5014/597. Cf. Leith-Ross–Phillips memorandum, 'Money and Prices', May 1933, Treasury memorandum, 'International Lending and Exchange Restrictions', May 1933, BoT memoranda, 'Trade Restrictions and Tariff Policy', 18 May 1933, 'Price Levels – Co-ordination of Production and Marketing', 19 May 1933, 'Government Subsidies', 19 May 1933, all T 172/1812.
[65] Dallek, *Roosevelt*, 45.   [66] *Ibid.*, 45–6.
[67] *Ibid.*, 52–3; Schlesinger, *Coming of the New Deal*, 210. Cf. Moley diary, 1–30 Jun. 1933.
[68] Roosevelt telegram to Hull, 11 Jun. 1933, Hull 34.

felt would have fostered international co-operation at London.[69] Second, Roosevelt wanted all decisions made by the American delegation approved – or disapproved – in Washington.[70] Finally, he and Moley looked to wring every advantage out of the conference for the United States at British expense, not a recipe for success in negotiations with a Power that had already displayed its unwillingness to be blackmailed over debts. As Moley wired the American delegation:

In any negotiations concerning finance between this country and England, the latter will no doubt bear in mind any weak spots in her credit, banking and monetary system. It seems that knowledge of this kind may be used in the general interest by our government, for which reason I venture to trouble you.[71]

Whilst MacDonald created a bad impression by mentioning war debts in his opening speech at the conference, Hull and the American delegation honestly worked to reach an Anglo-American agreement.[72] Then, when currency stabilisation discussions reached an impasse in the second week, Moley travelled to London. Whilst he came to apprise American delegates of 'the latest developments at Washington', and it was emphasised publicly that he served under Hull,[73] his arrival created expectations that he came with means to break the deadlock. Receiving special treatment from the British, which angered Hull, Moley reached an agreement on stabilisation with MacDonald and Chamberlain on 30 June whereby the pound would be pegged at $4.25, a figure Roosevelt had earlier suggested.[74] However, on 2 July, now believing that stabilisation at this level would undermine his domestic monetary policies by depressing prices, Roosevelt sent a telegram that deprecated the conference making any decisions that would impinge on the domestic policies of his government. Made public the next day, this message ended the conference's effectiveness, although Hull managed to keep discussions going without result for three weeks to thwart 'the virtual certainty that the conference would formally fasten upon the President

[69] Dallek, *Roosevelt*, 48–9; C. Hull, *The Memoirs of Cordell Hull*, vol. I (New York, 1948), 250–1.
[70] Phillips telegram to Hull, 15 Jun. 1933, SDDF 550.1 Monetary Stabilization/15.
[71] Moley telegram to Bullitt, 14 Jun. 1933, SDDF 550.1 Monetary Stabilization/16–1, 16–2.
[72] See meetings of the commissions, 20, 23, 26, 27 Jun. 1933, all T 172/1811; meeting 12 (27 Jun. 1933) of the British delegation, to which Hull and other Americans were invited, T 172/1810A.
[73] Cf. Hull to Moley, 26 Jun. 1933, with enclosure, Hull 34; Hull, *Memoirs*, I, 259.
[74] This and the next three sentences are based on Moley telegram to Woodin and Baruch, 30 Jun. 1933, Roosevelt telegram to Hull, 2 Jul. 1933, both *FRUS 1933*, I, 665–6, 673–4; Roosevelt telegrams to Phillips, 30 Jun, 2 Jul. 1933, Phillips telegram to Roosevelt, 1 Jul. 1933, all *FDRFA*, I, 265–7, 268–9. Cf. Hull, *Memoirs*, I, 260–6; R. Moley, *After Seven Years* (New York, 1939), 260–8.

the blame for its failure'.[75] From the British perspective, Roosevelt could not escape culpability – despite comical claims by his defenders that by pressing Hull to keep discussions going, he preserved the 'hope that international co-operation would ultimately take place'.[76] Having spent four years building bridges to the United States, MacDonald felt personally betrayed.[77] For those like Chamberlain, already uncertain about Roosevelt, his actions confirmed the disfavour that had been forming over his approach to war debts and arms limitation: 'The President's latest message was a bombshell ... Its tone was arrogant and it lectured the Conference in a manner and in circumstances which were hardly believable.'[78] Anglo-American co-operation was fast disappearing and, with disarmament negotiations stalemated and the European and Far Eastern balances of power changing, British leaders had to find new means to protect Britain's eternal interests.

Over the next year, the National Government embarked on a re-evaluation of British foreign and defence policy that, when completed, placed the United States in the position it had occupied before June 1929: just another Power to be considered when preserving British external interests. But unlike before 1929, those responsible for British foreign and defence policy after mid-1933 perceived the United States to be a weaker Power. The USN had not been built to anything approaching treaty strength.[79] American economic and financial diplomacy lacked its previous vitality, partly because of the Depression and partly because Britain's economy began to recover through National Government fiscal orthodoxy.[80] At the same time as the Administration's

---

[75] Hull, *Memoirs*, I, 266. Cf. League of Nations, *Reports Approved by the Conference on July 27th, 1933, and Resolutions Adopted by the Bureau of the Executive Committee* (27 Jul. 1933), esp. Appendix 2, 24–9, LND C.435.M.220.1933.II.

[76] Dallek, *Roosevelt*, 57.

[77] MacDonald to Bledisloe [a friend], 31 Jul. 1933, MacDonald PRO 30/69/679.

[78] British Delegation meetings 18–20, 2–4 Jul. 1933, all T 172/1810A. Cf. Chamberlain to Ida, 15 Jul. 1933, NC 18/1/836.

[79] USN authorised construction:

1929	1 aircraft carrier
	14 cruisers
	3 submarines
1930	no construction
1931	no construction
1932	no construction

From Roskill, *Naval Policy*, I, appendix C, 582. The cruiser total for 1929 was reduced by the London naval treaty.

[80] A. Booth, 'Britain in the 1930s: A Managed Economy?', *EcoHR*, 40(1987), 499–521; Howson, *Managed Float*; R. Middleton, *Towards a Managed Economy: Keynes, the Treasury and the Fiscal Debate of the 1930s* (1985); P. Williamson, *National Crisis and*

nationalistic policies suggested a reluctance to become involved in the political and strategic problems of the wider world,[81] the informal entente that had marked the Powers' financial and commercial competition dissolved. Over Middle Eastern oil, Latin American trade and investment, and a desire to profit in China, a rivalry emerged that added stress to the two English-speaking Powers' relationship.[82] Given desires by American commercial and business interests to penetrate dominion markets, chiefly Canada and Australia, the transatlantic relationship had been transformed significantly at the official and unofficial levels by the summer of 1933.

The nature of this new phase in Anglo-American relations can be seen in the British approach to war debts. Whilst the usual flowery rhetoric emanated from Washington after July 1933 about having Britain and the United States work together,[83] MacDonald, Baldwin, and Chamberlain were unwilling to waste effort searching for fresh means of compromise. After letting the dust settle on the World Economic Conference and trying to determine Roosevelt's goals – 'we are all in the dark as to what is in [Roosevelt's] mind, if there is anything in his mind'[84] – Chamberlain took matters in hand. By mid-September, he and Leith-Ross devised a negotiating strategy designed to get an agreement on British terms or, should Roosevelt prove unbending, see Britain render only further token payments.[85] The core of this strategy rested on a scheme

---

National Government. British Politics, the Economy, and Empire, 1926–1932 (Cambridge, 1992), 501–3.

[81] Cf. Jellicoe to Dreyer, 22 Nov. 1933, DRYR 3/2; Hankey to Casey, 12 Dec. 1933, HNKY 5/7; Vansittart to MacDonald, 16 Dec. 1933, MacDonald PRO 30/69/679. The COS 'Annual Review (1933)' [CID 1113–B], 12 Oct. 1933, CAB 4/22 virtually ignores the United States.

[82] Cf. P. G. Beck, 'The Anglo-Persian Oil Dispute, 1932–1933', *JCH*, 9(1974), 123–51; S. E. Hilton, *Brazil and the Great Powers, 1930–1939: The Politics of Trade Rivalry* (Austin, 1975); G. Jones, *The History of the British Bank in the Middle East*, vol. II: *Banking and Oil* (1986); J. Osterhammel, *Britischer Imperialismus im Fernen Osten: Strukturen der Durchdringung und einheimischer Widerstand auf dem chinesischen Markt, 1932–1937* (Bochum, 1982); K. A. Oye, 'The Sterling–Dollar–Franc Triangle: Monetary Diplomacy, 1929–1937', *World Politics*, 38(1985), 173–99; B. M. Rowland, *Commercial Conflict and Foreign Policy: A Study in Anglo-American Relations, 1932–1938* (New York, 1987); H. Shimizu, *Anglo-Japanese Trade Rivalry in the Middle East in the Inter-War Period* (1986).

[83] 'The President Appraises London Conference Results', 26 Jul. 1933, in F. D. Roosevelt, *Roosevelt's Foreign Policy, 1933–1941. Franklin D. Roosevelt's Unedited Speeches and Messages* (New York, 1942), 24–5.

[84] Chamberlain to Hilda, 24 Sep. 1933, NC 18/1/843. MacDonald asked Vansittart, as head of the Secret Service, to see what 'influences must be at work against us' in Washington: MacDonald to Vansittart, 24 Aug. 1933, VNST II 1/5.

[85] Leith-Ross telegram (291–292) to Treasury, Hopkins T 175/79; Leith-Ross minute to Chamberlain, 10 Jul. 1933, T 172/1507; Leith-Ross memorandum for Chamberlain, 'War Debt Position', 25 Jul. 1933, T 172/1511; FO memorandum, 'General Outline of

outlined by Warburg in April 1933 and supported by Moley in private talks at the World Economic Conference: fifty annual payments of $20 million. To avoid continental ideas that London intended to pursue a separate agreement that might endanger Lausanne, Chamberlain informed Paris and Rome of British intentions.[86]

On 3 October 1933, Leith-Ross arrived in Washington. He met with Dean Acheson, the assistant secretary of the Treasury, as well as Warburg and Lewis Douglas, the director of the budget. By 13 October, with Britain's outstanding debt calculated at $2,259 million, Leith-Ross won Acheson's support for two different means of settlement.[87] The first involved Warburg's idea of fifty annual payments of $20 million 'arrived at by eliminating all interest and treating all payments hitherto made as in respect of the capital of the debt'; this would see the British pay slightly less than half of what still was owed. The second approach envisaged reducing the debt to $877 million by deducting British wartime munitions purchases in the United States from the unpaid sum; on this basis, Britain would make fifty annual payments of $17.5 million. Acheson also accepted three other British conditions: 'more favourable terms [given] to any other Government should automatically be applied to the British war debt'; further revision after five years 'if the other debtor countries had not made proportionate payments during that period'; and most-favoured-nation status for British goods entering the United States, a mechanism that would make debt payments easier by giving London better access to American dollars.

Roosevelt rejected the Leith-Ross–Acheson proposals on 17 October. He would not accept a remission of the principal; he wanted fifty annual payments of $40 million; and there could be no most-favoured-nation treatment.[88] This was not unexpected. Leith-Ross revealed to Warren Fisher on 12 October that 'the President adopts a purely negative attitude and turns down every suggestion made. This is perfectly natural as the President obviously wants to get us up to the highest possible

the Main Developments of the War Debt Negotiations since October 1933', BDFA, II, C12, 265–7.

[86] Cf. 'Note of a Conversation between the Chancellor and Monsieur Bonnet on War Debts, 27 July 1933', T 172/1511; Simon telegram (804) to Graham, 22 Sep 1933, BDFA, II, C12, 228. Cf. Chamberlain minute, 18 Aug. 1933, on Lindsay despatch (1088) to Simon, 27 Jul. 1933, T 172/1511.

[87] Leith-Ross to Hopkins, 5 Oct. (3 letters), Leith-Ross to Warren Fisher, 12 Oct. 1933, with enclosures, all Hopkins T 175/79; Warren Fisher telegram (419) to Leith-Ross, 10 Oct. 1933, Hopkins T 175/81; FO memorandum, 'General Outline of the Main Developments of the War Debt Negotiations since October 1933', BDFA, II, C12, 265–7.

[88] Leith-Ross telegram (556, 557, 558, 559, 560) to Warren Fisher, 17 Oct. 1933, BDFA, II, C12, 242–4.

figure.'[89] But the British were not going to budge over a maximum $20 million a year and, as Leith-Ross would reject any American counter-proposal, 'we have some hope that the President will accept our terms with some minor amendments'. When further discussions proved fruit-less, Roosevelt recommended that another token payment be made in December and defended it publicly by citing 'the uncertainties of the present currency situation'.[90] Acceptable to Chamberlain and the Treasury, the arrangement was made sweeter when Roosevelt agreed to British suggestions for a payment of only $7.5 million. With an exchange of notes on 6 November,[91] Leith-Ross departed.

The second token payment evoked little reaction amongst American opinion – although Acheson left the Administration because he and Roosevelt disagreed on war debts and the president's handling of wider questions of domestic and international economic recovery.[92] Never-theless, some American politicians were unhappy with the November agreement, particularly Senator Hiram Johnson, a leading isolationist Republican on the Senate Foreign Relations Committee. He success-fully introduced a bill in Congress that prevented borrowing in the United States by foreign Powers that had defaulted on their debts.[93] Since Roosevelt had stated on 7 November that 'I shall not regard the British Government as in default',[94] Johnson's action did not appear problematical. However, when American legal authorities ruled in early 1934 that token payments were illegal under the terms of the 1923 debt agreement, the Johnson Act came into force against Britain. Despite Chamberlain and the majority of the Cabinet, supported by their back-bench MPs, having consistently opposed default,[95] these events forced their hand. Britain refused to pay anything in June 1934, and all of the

---

[89] This and the next quotation from Leith-Ross to Warren Fisher, 12 Oct. 1933, Hopkins T 175/79.

[90] Leith-Ross to Warren Fisher, 19, 27 Oct., 2 Nov. 1933, all Hopkins T 175/79; FO memorandum, 'General Outline ... of the War Debt Negotiations', *BDFA*, II, C12, 265–7.

[91] Lindsay to Hull, 6 Nov. 1933, Hull to Lindsay, 6 Nov. 1933, both *BDFA*, II, C12, 263–4. Cf. Phillips minute for Hopkins and Warren Fisher, 31 Oct. 1933, with enclosures, T 175/81.

[92] On American opinion, Lindsay to Sargent, 10 Nov. 1933, Sargent FO 800/US/33/4; Lindsay despatch (1636) to Simon, 27 Dec. 1933, *BDFA*, II, C12, 268–70. On Acheson's resignation, cf. Feis to Frankfurter, 15 Nov. 1933, Feis 123; D. S. McLellan, *Dean Acheson. The State Department Years* (New York, 1976), 26–9.

[93] P. G. Boyle, 'The Roots of Isolationism: A Case Study', *Journal of American Studies*, 6(1972), 41–50; H. A. DeWitt, 'Hiram Johnson and Early New Deal Diplomacy, 1933–1934', *California Historical Quarterly*, 53(1974), 377–86.

[94] 'Statement by Roosevelt on the British War Debt', 8 Nov. 1933, *FDRFA*, I, 465–66.

[95] See secretary minutes for Baldwin, 29, 30 Nov. 1932, Baldwin to Mellon, 3 Dec. 1932, Runciman minute, 'Telegram received from the President. 20th October 1933', all Baldwin 110; Hailsham to MacDonald, 17 Feb. 1933, MacDonald PRO 30/69/679;

debtor Powers, except Finland, followed its lead. The war debt structure simply disintegrated. With what amounted to a general default, Lausanne also collapsed. Even this caused little anxiety in London, which understood by mid-1934 that Hitler's government would never pay reparations.

It has been argued that the 1934 debt default was calamitous for Britain in the long run: it weakened the anti-German coalition after European war broke out in September 1939 because the Johnson Act denied Britain and its allies easy access to the American money market.[96] But by avoiding hindsight, Britain's decision to default is understandable. MacDonald's Cabinet had sought a compromise with the Roosevelt Administration for more than a year. They had been rebuffed over war debts and over co-operation at both the world disarmament and economic conferences. It was pointless to seek a settlement when Roosevelt refused to acknowledge the staggering sum the British had rendered over ten years. Moreover, British default showed the limitations of American power. The United States could not collect its debts. It could only try to coerce the debtor Powers by a negative policy: denying them access to the American money market. Whilst giving solace to American nationalists and reinforcing the idea of perfidious foreigners, coercion brought debt payments no nearer. Indeed, it aided the London money market and strengthened the Sterling Bloc, particularly in Europe. It also suggested that if the United States ever needed Britain's assistance or that of other Powers to defend its interests in the wider world, it would have to be more accommodating. British default, therefore, indicated not so much British economic weakness but more the limitations of American external strength. As much as economic and financial muscle, national potency embraces those other elements of strength: capable armed forces, strategic preponderance, and the will to act decisively. It was to these crucial issues that the British elite had already turned by late 1933 to meet threats to Britain's position as the world's pre-eminent Power.

On 14 October 1933, Hitler withdrew Germany from both the League and the World Disarmament Conference – his latter action justified by Germany being denied the promised equality of treatment.[97] German withdrawal made moribund League efforts to construct a system of international arms limitation. Seeking some concrete achievement,

Irwin [president, Board of Education] minute to Chamberlain, n.d., Chamberlain minute to Irwin, n.d. [but both 26 Oct. 1933], NC 7/11/26/16.

[96] Dallek, *Roosevelt*, 74; J. W. Pratt, *A History of United States Foreign Policy*, 3rd edn (New York, 1972), 325.

[97] 'Minutes of the Conferences of Ministers on October 13 ... and October 14, 1933', *DGFP*, CI, 922–6.

Henderson and League officials explored whether existing agreements, like the 1930 London naval treaty, might be extended by other Powers accepting their restrictions.[98] Akin to this, concerted efforts were made to resuscitate a Polish proposal for 'moral disarmament' that had languished since February 1932. Though this proposition excited peace groups in various countries, because of its ambiguous nature – governments would prosecute those within their borders promoting 'war feelings' in broadcasting, the press, education, the cinema and the stage – the major Powers refused to embrace the concept.[99] Consequently, by late 1933, the Disarmament Conference existed in name only: Germany had left; Germany and Japan had renounced their League memberships; the United States refused to make substantive contributions; and the other Great Powers, no matter their public stance, were disinclined to restrict their armed forces when uncertainty existed about what their potential rivals might do. Beyond this, the security systems that had spawned the conference seemed to have weakened. The Washington nine-Power treaty was shown to be ineffectual via the Manchurian crisis, which ended in May 1933 when the Tangku treaty gave Japan dominance in China north of the Great Wall. With Locarno's fate unsure now that Germany had left the League, Britain had to look after its own interests.

Even before Hitler moved, sensing that a watershed in international politics had been reached, Vansittart, Warren Fisher, and Hankey lobbied the Cabinet to examine deficiencies in British armed strength.[100] This came through their support for the COS Annual Review for 1933, circulated just two days before the announcement that Germany would leave the League and the Disarmament Conference.[101] Central to the review was a Foreign Office evaluation of the international situation:

the economic and political situation of the world has for a variety of causes deteriorated, and that the course of events has not only brought to general

[98] Wellesley minute to Baldwin, 16 Oct. 1933, Baldwin 129; Henderson statement, 'Disarmament[.] The Acid Test', n.d. [but late 1933], Henderson LNS 475/2; Henderson to Simon, 22 Nov. 1933, Henderson LNS 475/6. Cf. McKercher, 'Horns and Teeth', 190–1.

[99] *Proposals of the Polish Delegation with regard to the Gradual Attainment of Moral Disarmament* (13 Feb. 1932), LND Conf.D.76. Cf. Gilbert Murray [International Committee on Intellectual Cooperation] to Komarnicki [Polish diplomat], 22 Jul. 1933; Corbett-Ashley [Committee for Moral Disarmament] to Henderson, n.d. [but Dec. 1933], both LNR 4164/440/652.

[100] Pownall [CID assistant-secretary] diary, 9 Nov. 1933, in B. Bond, ed., *Chief of Staff. The Diaries of Lieutenant-General Sir Henry Pownall*, vol. I: *1933–1940* (1972), 23–4. Cf. O'Halpin, *Warren Fisher*, 227; Rose, *Vansittart*, 124–5; Roskill, *Naval Policy*, II, 167–8.

[101] COS 'Annual Review (1933)' [CID 1113–B], 12 Oct. 1933, CAB 4/22.

notice the unsound basis on which international relations rest, but also confronted the world with the inescapable dilemma of finding an urgent solution for the most serious of these questions or of witnessing the further and perhaps rapid deterioration of the situation.[102]

COS concern at that moment lay with the Far East and building up British defences at Singapore and other places. Moreover, in 1932, as a direct result of the Manchurian crisis, the 'ten-year rule' respecting defence spending had been quietly rescinded.[103] Thus, in October 1933, the COS ranged over British commitments in Europe, the Mediterranean, and the Far East to show the difficulty that British forces would confront in meeting them given more than a decade of domestic retrenchment and international arms limitation. They ended by noting: 'No guiding principle has yet been established to replace the "ten-year rule". We ask the Committee of Imperial Defence whether they confirm generally our appreciation of the situation as set forth above, and whether they can give any further guidance to our Government Departments responsible for Imperial Defence.' Hitler's actions two days later underscored the need for re-evaluation. On 9 November 1933, the CID proposed a Defence Requirements Sub-committee (DRC) chaired by Hankey and composed of Vansittart, Warren Fisher, and the three service chiefs, Admiral Sir Ernle Chatfield, General Sir Archibald Montgomery-Massingberd, and Air Chief-Marshal Sir Edward Ellington.[104] First meeting on 14 November, the day before the Cabinet approved its creation,[105] it submitted its first report on 28 February 1934.

Much has been written about the initial deliberations and report of the DRC: that Japan and Germany had become the principal threats to British interests in, respectively, the Far East and continental Europe; that Germany constituted Britain's 'ultimate potential enemy'; and that British defences had to be ready for war by 1939.[106] The DRC

---

[102] FO 'Memorandum on the Foreign Policy of His Majesty's Government in the United Kingdom', 19 May 1933, in 'Papers Prepared for the Use of the Chiefs of Staff in their Annual Review of Imperial Defence (1933)' [CID 112–B], 30 Jun. 1933, *ibid.*

[103] 'No Cabinet Conclusion exists recording [the ten-year rule's] final demise': Roskill, *Naval Policy*, II, 146.

[104] CID Meeting 261, 9 Nov. 1933, CAB 2/6.

[105] CC 62(33), 15 Nov. 1933, CAB 23/77.

[106] 'Defence Requirements Sub-committee. Report' [DRC 14], 28 Feb. 1934, CAB 16/ 109. Because of Hitler's actions at Geneva, the DRC received additional instructions to consider 'the point of view of their effect on German armaments' and 'stipulations ... necessary from the point of view of the United Kingdom'; Hankey memorandum [DRC 4], 23 Nov. 1933, with enclosures, *ibid.* Cf. G. Post, Jr, *Dilemmas of Appeasement. British Deterrence and Defense, 1934–1937* (Ithaca, NY, 1993), 32–8, 43–8; Roskill, *Naval Policy*, II, 169–73; W. K. Wark, *The Ultimate Enemy: British Intelligence and Nazi Germany, 1933–1939* (Ithaca, NY, 1985), 28–34.

recommendations did not advocate rearmament. Rather, they indicated areas, particularly for the RN and RAF, where inadequacies created by retrenchment and the pursuit of arms limitation needed to be addressed. This translated into approximately £71.3 million in extra spending over five years (£61.2 million in capital expenditures and £10.1 million in maintenance costs), 'a minimum for meeting the worst ... deficiencies'.[107] Not surprisingly, these initial recommendations about spending and where it should be directed were adjusted after early 1934 through Cabinet discussion and further DRC review. These subsequent modifications resulted from the domestic fiscal priorities and political concerns of the National Government, which continued in office until May 1940, as well as fluid international circumstances that affected British external interests; and they have been the subject of intense historical debate because of their intimate link to the appeasement diplomacy that British leaders like Chamberlain came to pursue later in the decade.[108] However, in terms of interwar British foreign policy in general, and its Anglo-American variant in particular, the DRC's importance cannot be over-emphasised. By October 1933, the international order that had arisen with the Paris, Washington, and Locarno treaties in the 1920s, and been augmented by efforts to bolster international security through international arms limitation and the resolution of the war debts–reparations imbroglio, had been eroded. A new phase in international politics had begun, with different challenges, something Vansittart, Warren Fisher, Hankey, and the Cabinet recognised. British diplomacy had to adapt so that, just as much as determining arms spending priorities, the DRC became the locus of change in the country's foreign policy.

Vansittart and Warren Fisher dominated the DRC. Although Hankey used his position as chairman to reduce friction between the civilians and military men, and Chatfield represented the RN position with some effect, the service chiefs tended to be marginalised in wide-ranging discussions that, to determine the lacunae in British defence, surveyed the changing pattern of international politics. Part of the reason flowed from the terms of reference set by CID, political directions which, under

---

[107] DRC '[First] Report', 11–12.
[108] Cf. U. Bialer, 'Elite Opinion and Defence Policy: Air Power Advocacy and British Rearmament during the 1930s', *BJIS*, 6(1980), 32–51; W. Murray, 'Munich 1938: The Military Confrontation', *JSS*, 2(1979), 282–302; W. Murray, *The Change in the European Balance of Power, 1938–1939: The Path to Ruin* (Princeton, 1984); R. A. C. Parker, 'Economics, Rearmament and Foreign Policy: The United Kingdom before 1939 – A Preliminary Study', *JCH*, 10(1975), 637–47; G. Peden, *British Rearmament and the Treasury, 1932–1939* (Edinburgh, 1979); R. Shay, *British Rearmament in the Thirties: Politics and Profits* (Princeton, 1977).

Chamberlain's influence, included a modified 'ten-year rule': 'concerning defence questions, account need not be taken of any likelihood of war with the United States, France, or Italy during, say, the next ten years'.[109] Added to this, Vansittart and Warren Fisher represented the leading departments of state in Whitehall, possessed more forceful personalities than their colleagues, particularly Montgomery-Massingberd and Ellington, and served ministers with strong positions in Cabinet. Finally the military commanders were not as well-prepared as the two civilians. As Lieutenant-Colonel Henry Pownall, a CID assistant-secretary assigned to the DRC, recorded privately on the day the first report went to the Cabinet:

After [Ellington] signed [the report] he said to me, almost casually, that his staff had told him he was departing from a previous principle that in a European war an army air force contingent could not be formed from fifty-two squadrons [demanded by the DRC], all, or practically all, of whom would be wanted for home defence.[110]

Vansittart and Warren Fisher shared the belief that the security of British interests in Europe and the Far East depended on discouraging any forward policies that Berlin or Tokyo might contemplate in future. As a recent study shows,[111] this entailed a strategy of deterrence after late 1933 that, though deterrence had never been expunged from the British diplomatic arsenal, meant less reliance on the kind of multilateral collaboration that had produced the Washington and Locarno treaties, the Dawes and Young plans, and Lausanne. Vansittart and Warren Fisher did not forbear international co-operation. Both, for instance, looked to extend the London naval treaty past 1935 – as did Chatfield. But Britain could not rely on hopes that such devices would ameliorate future Anglo-German or Anglo-Japanese differences. Such reliance was unrealistic. '[I]f Germany succeeded in dealing with Austria to her own satisfaction,' Vansittart cautioned, 'she might well turn against Poland who was no longer on very good terms with France. Having dealt with Poland, Germany would at last be free to contemplate a war on a single front, i.e. against ourselves, Belgium and France. He thought it quite possible that Germany would be ready to attack Poland within five years.'[112] Whilst Warren Fisher did not necessarily subscribe to Vansittart's deep distrust of Germany, he shared the 'Edwardian' notion that

---

[109] CID Meeting 261, 9 Nov. 1933, CAB 2/6. See 'Composition and Terms of Reference' [DRC 1], 10 Nov. 1933, CAB 16/109.
[110] Pownall diary, 28 Feb. 1934, Bond, *Pownall*, I, 37. Cf. Ellington's remarks on 'The Field Force' in DRC Meeting 6, 23 Jan. 1933, CAB 16/109.
[111] Post, *Dilemmas*, esp. 1–22.
[112] DRC meeting 7, 25 Jan. 1934, CAB 16/109.

foreign policy was only as effective as the economic and armed strength behind it. Thus, he and Vansittart quarrelled little with COS proposals for modernising weapons, expanding the RAF, building up supplies of war material and petroleum, and the rest. As Pownall observed with surprise: 'It is curious how, all through, the Chiefs of Staff have been the moderating influence in the Committee. The civilians, whose presumable line was to keep down impossible service demands, have continually been the alarmist party, demanding quicker and heavier rearmament, whatever the price.'[113]

Chatfield, Ellington, and Montgomery-Massingberd were concerned mainly with ensuring that the services could fight effectively if called on to do so. Understandable in purely military terms, this narrow focus constituted only the mechanics of national strategy. More important was the wider issue of how that policy should be implemented to sustain Britain and the Empire. Concentrating on this question, Warren Fisher and Vansittart shaped the DRC's re-evaluation of British external policy. They helped set British foreign policy on a course followed until Chamberlain succeeded to the premiership in May 1937; as it touched Anglo-American relations, this re-evaluation produced a major change in policy that affected British diplomatic calculations for even longer.

When the CID set the DRC's terms of reference, Chamberlain and Simon agreed that, despite Manchuria, Anglo-Japanese relations had not suffered irreparable damage. In the foreign secretary's words: 'The Japanese were behaving extremely correctly; but he would remind the Committee that, in any question of trying to approach closer to Japan, they must remember that the strength of Japan's conduct was governed by the fact that she had a definite objective, which was to make herself a great Power in the East.'[114] Caution towards Tokyo suggested itself, something reinforced by Embassy reports from Tokyo. Yet Anglo-Japanese harmony in the Far East was not beyond the realm of possibility. The Japanese question preoccupied Warren Fisher, since protecting British Far Eastern interests necessitated spending on the RN, defences at Singapore, and building up supplies. If diplomatic means could be found to improve Anglo-Japanese relations, then defence requirements – and spending – would ultimately be less because British interests tied to the defence of India, Australia, New Zealand, and the China market would be more secure.[115] Several members of the foreign-policy-making elite shared his views, particularly naval officers and others like Hankey who had always regretted the abrogation of the

[113] Pownall diary, 28 Feb. 1934, Bond, *Pownall*, I, 38.
[114] CID meeting 261, 9 Nov. 1933, CAB 2/6.
[115] Warren Fisher note [DRC 9], 12 Jan. 1934, CAB 16/109.

Anglo-Japanese alliance to win the friendship of the United States.[116] Strengthening Britain's position in the Far East would only create perceptions in Tokyo that it could not endanger British interests with impunity. Warren Fisher calculated that American reactions could be ignored: 'I envisage an ultimate policy of accommodation and friendship with Japan and an immediate and provisional policy of "showing a tooth" for the purpose of recovering the standing which we have sacrificed in our post-war period of subservience to the U.S.A'.[117] Promoting an Anglo-Japanese equilibrium had the added benefit of ensuring that Britain could better meet any challenge mounted by Hitler. Whilst less suspicious of Germany than Vansittart, Warren Fisher recognised the menace it posed in Europe; he, after all, first used the phrase 'ultimate potential enemy'.[118]

Vansittart's vision of British diplomatic strategy centred on Germany and the containment of what he had already termed its preparations for 'external aggression'.[119] His attitude did not belittle the Japanese danger; on 4 December, he confided to the DRC that Foreign Office minutes on the COS Annual Review 'agreed with the priority which had been given'.[120] But, he stressed, his view differed. 'The order of priorities which put Japan first pre-supposed that Japan would attack us after we had got into difficulties elsewhere. "Elsewhere" therefore came first, not second; and elsewhere could only mean Europe, and Europe could only mean Germany.' Not budging from this position over the next two-and-a-half months, Vansittart held that the government's principal concern had to be Germany and that British defence inade- quacies had to be remedied with this in mind. This underlay his support for building up British armed strength, particularly the RAF, but it conformed more widely to his long-held belief about a strong foreign policy by which an effective balance of power could be constructed. Even before the DRC reported, he counselled Simon and MacDonald

---

[116] Churchill to Baldwin, 15 Dec. 1924, in Churchill to Austen Chamberlain, Chamber- lain FO 800/256; Bridgeman to Baldwin, 9 Oct. 1932, Baldwin 118; Hankey memorandum, 10 Nov. 1933, with enclosure, CAB 16/109; Jellicoe to Dreyer, 8 Oct, 22 Nov. 1933, DRYR 3/2. Cf. J. R. Ferris, 'Worthy of Some Better Enemy?: The British Estimate of the Imperial Japanese Army, 1919–1941, and the Fall of Singapore', *CJH*, 28(1993), 223–56.
[117] Warren Fisher note [DRC 9], 12 Jan. 1934, CAB 16/109   [118] *Ibid.*
[119] Vansittart minute, 7 Jul. 1933, VNST I 2/14.
[120] DRC meeting 3, 4 Dec. 1933, CAB 16/109. He later circulated these views in FO 'Situation in the Far East (Memoranda). 1933–34' [DRC 20], *ibid.* Amongst the thirteen memoranda, Pratt, 'British Policy in the Far East', 1 Dec. 1933, Orde [Far Eastern Department] 'Memorandum respecting our Relations with Japan', 14 Dec. 1933, Harcourt-Smith [Far Eastern Department], 'British and Japanese Interests in China and the Prospects of Sino-Japanese Rapprochement', 2 Jan. 1934 are instructive.

that 'Germany will attract friends to her camp if she is allowed to grow, while we remain weak'.[121] For Vansittart, increased defence spending constituted a means to an end: containing Germany via an array of Powers, with Britain in the lead. The only effective way of doing this involved showing other continental Powers, chiefly France and Italy, that Britain had the means and the will to oppose German ambitions.

In this way, although Vansittart and Warren Fisher were both concerned about the wider implications of improving British armed strength and concurred about the ultimate enemy, they disagreed initially about where precisely the immediate threat to Britain's security lay: in Europe or the Far East.[122] Where Warren Fisher argued that the Germans would require several years to revise the European status quo in their favour, Vansittart believed that for the foreseeable future Russo-Japanese rivalry in East Asia precluded a forward policy by Japan that might jeopardise the interests of other Great Powers in the region.[123] But these were not insurmountable differences, and they disappeared by the time the first report was drafted in February 1934. Vansittart acquiesced to the need to ensure that money would be spent on Singapore and the rest to 'show a tooth' to Japan as a precursor to a possible Anglo-Japanese rapprochement. For his part, Warren Fisher did not require much coaxing to sign a report that argued that, by 1939, the deficiencies of British armed forces had to be fixed.

The only point on which the two men differed in a marked way concerned the United States. By the time the DRC began sitting, Anglo-American relations had been buffeted by the bankruptcy of the World Economic Conference, the failure of further debt revison, and Roosevelt's contradictory pronouncements on arms limitation. Since the Treasury had worked to wring positive results from the first two matters, and reckoned that British good faith had been rebuffed by Washington, Warren Fisher assumed an uncompromising attitude concerning the United States. How much this stance showed his own feelings, reflected those of Chamberlain, now hyper-critical of Roosevelt, or represented a departmental viewpoint is moot. In the DRC, he scorned the American ability or desire to pursue a constructive foreign policy in either its political or economic dimension.[124] As he emphasised in a submission in mid-February: 'the U.S.A. are a serious obstacle to our getting on to terms with Japan; and I believe that we have got to

---

[121] Vansittart to Simon, 10 Feb. 1934, VNST I 2/14.
[122] The following disagrees with Post, *Dilemmas*, 35.
[123] Both men's views surface in DRC meeting 3, 4 Dec. 1933, CAB 16/109.
[124] DRC meeting 4, 18 Jan. 1934, *ibid.*

"disentangle" ourselves from the U.S.A. They are no use to us, but make use of us – to our detriment – vis à vis Japan.'[125]

Such strong anti-Americanism worried even Hankey, long a vocal opponent of concessions to the United States. 'Warren Fisher, in Hankey's opinion, is rather mad', Pownall observed.[126] Nonetheless, Warren Fisher and the Treasury perceived little advantage in appeasing the Americans further over naval arms limitation. London had to address actual threats posed by Japan and Germany. The United States could not be trusted to assist Britain in a crisis, especially if Britain faced two first-class Powers simultaneously in Europe and the Far East. But by entrenching their position in the Far East and then moving towards Japan, the British could reduce one threat and be better able to overcome any hazards that might arise from Hitler's regime. Such a tactic meant ignoring American disfavour towards Japan, even though the result would certainly be additional strain to the transatlantic relationship.

Whilst Warren Fisher was prepared to assume this risk, Vansittart was not. Vansittart held little love for the Americans at this juncture, agreeing that 'Anglo-American relations would always be disappointing'; but in the same breath, he pointed out that 'he hoped that the benefits of betterment would not all be thrown away in order to run after the Japanese'.[127] Such beliefs lay at the base of his conception about maintaining the global balance of power. Britain did not have the armed force necessary to oppose both Japan and Germany single-handedly – and would not even after defence deficiencies were met. It had to use other Powers, also fearful of Japanese and German ambitions, to help shore up British interests. In Europe, this meant working with Powers like France – although collaborating with Paris might be difficult.[128] Similarly, especially in the Far East, there would be no profit in Britain purposely antagonising the Americans, even though Vansittart admitted 'that Japan held America in contempt and was of the opinion that, even with a 5:5:3 ratio, they could defeat America at the present moment'.[129] The other members of the DRC, principally Hankey and Chatfield, concurred. Hence, Vansittart's view of how to handle the

[125] Warren Fisher to Hankey [DRC 16], 12 Feb. 1934, *ibid.* Cf. 'Note by Sir Warren Fisher as an addendum to the Defence Requirements Committee Report' [DRC 19], 17 Feb. 1934, *ibid.*

[126] Pownall diary, 15, 19 Feb. 1934, Bond, *Pownall*, I, 36. Cf. DRC meeting 10, 16 Feb. 1934, CAB 16/109.

[127] DRC meeting 3, 4 Dec. 1933, CAB 16/109.

[128] Tyrrell was pressing to move closer to France; see Tyrrell to Baldwin, 6, 19, 29 Nov. 1933, all Baldwin 121. Cf. Drummond [now British ambassador, Rome] to Simon, 27 Nov. 1933, Simon FO 800/288.

[129] DRC meeting 4, 18 Jan. 1934, CAB 16/109.

United States prevailed in the DRC – Hankey even threatened to approach the pro-American MacDonald about Warren Fisher – and Warren Fisher's 'outburst on America' was kept out of its first report.[130]

By the end of February 1934, therefore, British foreign and defence policy had been measured by the government's senior advisers responsible for making it, paying for it, and giving it strength. They had determined that because Britain now confronted threats from two first-class Powers in the Far East and Europe – one actual, one potential, both pregnant with danger to Britain's global position – there had to be significant change. The three armed services, especially the RN and the RAF, required increased public spending to make credible a policy of deterrence and to give strength to the government's overall diplomatic strategy. That strategy, it was posited, should involve less reliance on the 1920s' tendency to pursue multilateral co-operation, which had proved barren over war debts, arms limitation, and general economic and financial questions. Instead, there had to be concerted efforts to work with other Powers that shared British concerns about revisions to the post-1918 international order that might threaten continued peace and security. In these calculations, despite the division between Vansittart and Warren Fisher, the United States had ceased to be as important a consideration as it had been less than twelve months before. The rise of Roosevelt and his departure from the path taken earlier by Hoover and Stimson lay at the bottom of this transformation in official British attitudes. How the Cabinet, especially Simon and Chamberlain, would react to the DRC recommendations and relate them to what was a fast-changing international milieu remained to be seen.

[130] Pownall diary, 19–20 Feb. 1934, Bond, *Pownall*, I, 36.

6 Britain, the United States, and the global balance of power, 1934–1935

> I agree with Van[sittart] to the extent that we do not want to propitiate Japan at the expense of a hostile and jealous United States. At the same time I am entirely with you that we do not want to tie ourselves as we have done in the past to the United States, because she is unreliable and does not know her own mind and her statesmen do not know the mind of their own country.
>
> Chatfield, June 1934[1]

Completed by July 1934, Cabinet examination of the DRC report determined the course of British diplomacy until Neville Chamberlain rose to the premiership three years later. This is because, despite alterations made by the politicians to particular defence spending programmes and the advent of strained Anglo-Italian relations in late 1935 over a crisis in Abyssinia, the one fundamental principle on which the report was founded remained untouched: vigilance concerning Germany and Japan.[2] The economic and naval diplomacy of the Roosevelt Administration meant that the British had to consider American interests when making policy for Europe and the Far East. But because Washington's isolationism meant that the United States fell outside the ambit of improving defence deficiencies, London ignored the Americans in constructing British defence policy. Admittedly, until mid-1936, the threats that had preoccupied the DRC remained muted. In Europe, Hitler concentrated largely on domestic affairs. An attempted fascist putsch in Vienna in July 1934 created brief alarm; but its failure, helped by concerted British, French, and Italian support for the legitimate Austrian government, plus Hitler's claim that he had no connexion with the rebels, saw it recede quickly as an issue of importance.[3] Even after March 1935, when Hitler announced plans to rearm, British diplomatists reckoned that a union of Powers could contain Germany. Although Berlin did not ignore foreign policy, for instance

---

[1] Chatfield to Warren Fisher, 4 Jun. 1934, CHT 3/1.
[2] N. H. Gibbs, *Grand Strategy*, vol. I: *Rearmament Policy* (1976), 93–9.
[3] Weinberg, *Hitler's Germany*, I, 87–107.

Hitler repaired German–Polish relations,[4] an absence of external zeal suggested that the five-year period of grace foreseen by the DRC seemed generous enough. In the Far East, Japan's consolidation of its gains made in northern China between 1931 and 1933 helped dampen concern about impending danger to the eastern reaches of Britain's Empire.[5] With Japanese political life undergoing upheaval, and with Tokyo preoccupied with Russian policies in East Asia, the immediacy of a threat to Britain's position in that region subsided.[6]

These years were also the time when Vansittart dominated the Foreign Office, heavily influencing the direction of foreign policy. This obtained from mounting criticism of Simon that weakened his position in the Cabinet and by MacDonald and Baldwin having full confidence in the permanent under-secretary.[7] Even after Hoare succeeded Simon in June 1935, Vansittart's influence remained undiminished; Hoare relied completely on the advice of Foreign Office permanent officials. Whilst Vansittart had critics, they could not dislodge him as long as he retained the trust of the premier and the leader of the largest party in the coalition; and, in June 1935, Baldwin replaced MacDonald as prime minister. Chamberlain, particularly, did not agree with Vansittart. However, after Cabinet examination of the DRC report, his concentration on domestic economic and political matters saw him do little in foreign policy beyond unsuccessfully seeking to establish an Anglo-Japanese non-aggression pact.[8] Only when the Abyssinian crisis overturned a cardinal precept of the modified ten-year rule – disregarding Italy in British defence preparations – did Vansittart's influence begin to crumble. Foreign Office responsibility for the undermining of good relations with Italy, crucial to both the European balance and Britain's

---

[4] A. Cienciala, 'The Significance of the Declaration of Nonaggression of January 26, 1934, in Polish–German and International Relations: A Reappraisal', *East European Quarterly*, 1(1967), 1–30.

[5] Crowley, *Japan's Quest*, 187–243.

[6] G. M. Berger, 'Politics and Mobilization in Japan, 1931–1945', in J. W. Hall *et al.*, *The Cambridge History of Modern Japan*, vol. VI: *The Twentieth Century* (Cambridge, 1988), 105–18; L. Connors, *The Emperor's Adviser. Saionji Kinmochi and Pre-war Japanese Politics* (London, Oxford, 1987), 135–79.

[7] For criticism of Simon, see Ormsby-Gore [British delegate, Geneva] to Baldwin, 1, 8 Oct. 1933, Tyrrell to Baldwin, 19 Nov. 1933, all Baldwin 121; MacDonald diary, 17, 22 Nov, 11, 17 Dec. 1933, 4 Mar. 1934, MacDonald PRO 30/69/1753; Austen Chamberlain to Neville, 11 Nov. 1934, NC 1/27/119; Neville Chamberlain to Hilda, 17 Nov. 1934, NC 18/1/896. Cf. Dutton, *Simon*, 120–1. On Vansittart's warm relations with MacDonald and Baldwin, see MacDonald to Vansittart and his wife, 27 Dec. 1933, Baldwin to Vansittart, 25 Dec. 1933, both VNST II 1/5.

[8] Cf. 'Committee on Cruiser Allocation': CCA(34) 1st [and only] meeting, 12 Nov. 1934, 'Report', 13 Nov. 1934, both CAB 27/571.

Mediterranean position, was heaped at the permanent under-secretary's door.

The World Disarmament Conference staggered on until June 1934 when Henderson adjourned its deliberations.[9] He intended to reconvene it at a more propitious moment; with his death in 1935 and the Powers' desire to rearm, the conference never met again. To placate public opinion, the National Government had made appropriate public noises in late 1933 and early 1934 about general arms limitation.[10] For instance, just as DRC deliberations began, a Conservative lost a by-election in a safe seat at East Fulham largely because he advocated rearmament; his Labour opponent championed reduced arms spending and a reliance on collective security.[11] Although aware of peace advocacy, Vansittart and his colleagues were undeterred in putting their case for meeting British defence deficiencies before the Cabinet.

Cabinet examination of the DRC report began on 3 May in the ministerial disarmament committee (DCM), now handling arms limitation, rearmament, and ancillary defence policy issues. After two weeks, MacDonald and Baldwin began attending; in a move that lessened Simon's authority, they shared the chairmanship. Criticism exists about this body's tardiness in considering DRC-defined defence deficiencies; but domestic political manoeuvring that spring prompted by home rule for India and intra-coalition friction over whether the National Government as a whole should seek re-election in 1935 preoccupied MacDonald and his senior partners.[12] Yet, once convened, the DCM met regularly over three months and had modified the DRC recommendations by 31 July.[13] These modifications have been carefully examined in other places.[14] The DRC envisaged a balanced strengthening of the armed forces: modernising the RN; ensuring that the Army could defend the home islands and send an expeditionary force to the Continent; and building the RAF to fifty-two squadrons for home

[9] McKercher, 'Horns and Teeth', 191–2.
[10] 'Extracts from House of Commons Debates', 13, 24 Nov. 1933, 6 Feb. 1934, *BDFA*, II, J5, 11–20, 65–71, 205–21; 'Memorandum on Disarmament Communicated by His Majesty's Government in the United Kingdom to the Governments Represented at the Disarmament Conference', 29 Jan. 1934, LND Conf.D.166. Cf. Sargent to Phipps, 2, 9 Dec. 1933, both PHPP 2/10.
[11] R. Heller, 'East Fulham Revisited', *JCH*, 6(1971), 172–96. Cf. M. Pugh, 'Pacifism and Politics in Britain, 1931–1935', *HJ*, 23(1980), 641–56.
[12] For criticism, see Shay, *Rearmament*, 33–4. On the domestic issues, see Marquand, *MacDonald*, 759–60; Middlemas and Barnes, *Baldwin*, 704–15; Rhodes James, *British Revolution*, 504–7.
[13] DC(M)(32) meetings 41–55, and its 'Report', 31 Jul. 1934, both CAB 16/110.
[14] Peden, *Rearmament*, 68–71; Post, *Dilemmas*, 35–40; Shay, *Rearmament*, 34–47; Wark, *Ultimate Enemy*, 28–34.

defence and joint operations on the Continent. Within the DCM, apprehension about the budget, now showing a surplus, and intelligence reports about German air rearmament upset that proposed balance. Promises had been made to reduce taxation, and extra defence spending might compromise the government's electoral appeal *à la* East Fulham – in the spring, National Government candidates lost three more by-elections. Whilst seeing the need to improve each branch of the armed forces, Chamberlain convinced his colleagues to spend more on air defence – Baldwin had told the Commons in March that the RAF 'shall no longer be in a position inferior to any country within striking distance of our shores'.[15] Accepting the deterrent value of air power, the cheapest option, the committee recommended expanding the RAF beyond fifty-two squadrons, reducing RN modernisation spending from £21 million to £13 million, and halving the Army's suggested DRC funding of £40 million. In this way, expenditures recommended by the DRC could be reduced by about one-third.

Despite helping to dilute these recommendations, Chamberlain could not undercut the strategic principles envisaged in the DRC report. This was not for lack of trying. He did not discount meeting the German threat;[16] but he looked to deter a German attack on Britain by expanding the RAF, eschewing joint action with Belgium, Holland, Italy, and France, appeasing Japan, and sundering all connexions with the United States.[17] This amounted to a policy of non-intervention whilst the RAF protected Britain from air attack and the RN prevented a cross-Channel invasion. Thus, Britain would shun involvement in maintaining the European balance, for instance, not despatching an expeditionary force to the Continent; British interests in the Far East would depend on Japanese forbearance after 'showing a tooth'; and the possibility of combining with other Powers, like the United States, in moments of crisis was dismissed.

Chamberlain encountered stiff opposition orchestrated by Vansittart, whose arguments advanced in the DRC appeared in memoranda circulated by Simon and in various comments uttered by MacDonald and Baldwin.[18] More important, the first Foreign Office paper received

---

15 Middlemas and Barnes, *Baldwin*, 754.
16 See his remarks in DC(M)(32) meetings 41–50, CAB 16/110; cf. 'Note by the Chancellor of the Exchequer on the Report of the Defence Requirements Committee' [DC(M)(32) 120], CAB 27/511.
17 DC(M)(32) 45th meeting, 15 May 1934, CAB 27/507.
18 Cf. Vansittart memorandum, 'The Future of Germany' [CP 104(34)], 7 Apr. 1934, CAB 24/248; diary entry, 28 Apr. 1934, in Thomas Jones, *A Diary with Letters 1931–1950* (1954), 126–9; Vansittart to Simon, 14 May 1934, CAB 21/388; Vansittart minute, 2 Jun. 1934, VNST I 1/11; Simon memorandum [DC(M)(32) 118], 14 Jun. 1934, CAB 27/510; Simon memorandum [DC(M)(32) 119], 14 Jun. 1934, CAB 27/

by the DCM as it considered the DRC report was Vansittart's spirited defence of active involvement in the European balance.[19] Using historical arguments drawn from before 1914, he explained that German actions during the 'July crisis' resulted from Berlin not knowing whether Britain would go to war if Germany threatened the continental equilibrium. 'Not only did we keep everyone guessing, until Germany guessed wrong,' he wrote, 'but there was thought in Europe to be little deterrent on our path to a gamble.' He then drove home his main point:

Europe remains in equal doubt both as to our policy and to our capacity. The results are already – or perhaps I should say at last – becoming manifest. Italy, Poland, Yugoslavia, Roumania, are all at varying degrees tending to be drawn into the German orbit; and on Italy's inconstancies now largely depend Austria, Hungary and Bulgaria ... The political map of Europe is, in fact, altering under our eyes and to our disadvantage, if we must look upon Germany as the eventual enemy.

As he had argued in the DRC, Japan would not move unless Britain encountered trouble elsewhere. Elsewhere could only mean Germany. To ensure Britain's position *vis-à-vis* Germany, other Powers, even the United States, might be useful. Vansittart did not concentrate solely on Europe – something missed by his critics then and since. Avoiding regional understandings with other Powers or pursuing policies that suggested British diplomacy lacked force would not protect Britain's global interests: 'The Foreign Office has long endeavoured to make bricks without straw ... In the present temper and material preparations not only of Europe, but of the world – Russia, the United States and Japan as well – British shrinkage will become the more apparent if it continues.' Supported generally by the members of the committee,[20] the Foreign Office prevented Chamberlain from isolating Britain from the swirl of international politics that affected its position in Europe and beyond. With moderate rearmament providing some straw for foreign policy, meeting the new international challenges was the order of the day. The first step concerned naval limitation.

The DRC had avoided recommendations on RN building programmes because, apart from modernisation, these were uncertain until after the conference scheduled for 1935 to renew the London naval treaty. Moreover, French, Italian, and, now, German demands required consideration along with those of the Japanese and Americans. Craigie

---

511. Vansittart advised Baldwin on the Far Eastern situation. MacDonald and Baldwin's comments in DC(M)(32) 50th meeting, 25 Jun. 1934, CAB 16/110 are instructive.

[19] 'Minute by Sir R. Vansittart' [DC(M)(32) 117], 2 Jun. 1934, CAB 27/510.

[20] Hailsham's comments in DC(M)(32) 50th meeting, 25 Jun. 1934, CAB 16/110.

suggested in January 1934 that the Foreign Office and Admiralty prepare a joint Cabinet submission on policy for the 1935 talks.[21] After consulting Warren Fisher, however, agreement was reached whereby Admiralty requirements would be submitted to a new sub-committee formed to co-ordinate planning for the 1935 conference; this body would weigh Foreign Office and Treasury views before the Cabinet became involved.[22] Chatfield detected an opportunity for substantial replacement and new construction funding – the DRC, after all, had just reported;[23] the Admiralty vision of the post-1935 RN reached the Cabinet committee on the naval conference (NCM) in mid-April. Known as the 'Chatfield memorandum', this document argued for a two-Power standard against Japan and 'the strongest European navy'.[24] The Admiralty wanted to limit battleships to 25,000 tons with twelve-inch guns; to secure numerical limitation of these ships but, if impossible, to limit the class tonnage to fifteen vessels; to allow replacement construction to begin in 1937; to give Britain seventy six-inch cruisers whilst abolishing eight-inch ones; and to assure the RN enough strength in other auxiliary classes to deter potential adversaries.

The NCM comprised MacDonald, Baldwin, Chamberlain, Simon, Thomas, Eyres-Monsell and, as expert advisers, Vansittart, Craigie, Chatfield, and Vice-Admiral Charles Little, the deputy chief of the Naval Staff. The Foreign Office and the Treasury each showed concern about the Admiralty scheme.[25] Chamberlain utilised the usual budgetary arguments. Vansittart and Craigie pointed out its political dangers, a return to the demands of 1927: RN expansion whilst the other Powers maintained the status quo. Reports from Tokyo indicated that Japan wanted a significant scaling up of its existing ratios, a result chiefly of the strength and anti-Americanism of an anti-treaty faction of officers in both the government and the IJN.[26] In the United States, the Democrats had sponsored legislation in January, the Vinson–Trammel Bill, to bring the USN to allowed levels; this construction was to occur under the aegis of the National Recovery Administration, a key

---

[21] Craigie memorandum, 9 Jan. 1934, FO 371/17596/1977/1938.
[22] Chatfield to Vansittart, 23 Jan. 1934, FO 371/17596/1978/1938; Hankey to MacDonald, 26 Jan. 1934, Craigie to Hankey, 27 Jan. 1934, both CAB 21/404.
[23] Chatfield to Fisher [C-in-C Mediterranean Fleet], 11 May 1934, CHT 4/5.
[24] 'Memorandum by the Chief of the Naval Staff in Preparation for the 1935 Naval Conference' [NCM(35) 1], 14 Mar. 1934, CAB 29/148.
[25] Except where noted, this paragraph is based on NCM(35) meetings 1–5, CAB 29/147.
[26] Cf. Snow [British Embassy, Tokyo] despatch (562) to Simon, 28 Sep. 1933, Lindley despatch (2) to Simon, 3 Jan. 1934, both BDFA, II, J6, 385–7, 388–9. On IJN factions, see I. Gow, 'Admiral Kato Kanji: Heretic, Hero, or the Unorthodox in the Pursuit of an Orthodox Naval Policy', in B. J. C. McKercher and A. H. Ion, eds., Military Heretics: The Unorthodox in Policy and Strategy (Westport, CT, 1993), 161–4.

mechanism in the president's New Deal.[27] Accordingly, shipyard and ancillary employment as much as Roosevelt's advocacy of a strengthened USN would guide American policy in 1935.

The NCM report reached the DCM as it assessed the DRC recommendations.[28] Appended was the 'Chatfield memorandum', to which were added Craigie and Vansittart's comments about the political likelihood of agreement on each bargaining point: battleships, cruisers, and the rest.[29] The NCM presented the DCM with several objectives for the conference: Britain could accept IJN increases in return for 'some substantial *quid pro quo*'; 'the principle of separate quotas' for the Dominions had to be honoured; capital ship limitation should be pursued, especially the replacement programme, along with the new two-Power standard; the cruiser requirements were acceptable if large six-inch gun ships – over 8,000 tons – were limited in a 5:5:3 ratio; the Washington treaty ratio, with some increase for France and Italy, should be maintained in other craft; and the treaty should last at least six years, by when British defence deficiencies were to have been remedied.

With the course the DCM was taking about danger in Europe – emphasising a strengthened RAF – the naval question centred on the Far East. Treasury and Admiralty views were disparate to say the least, the rationale behind their arguments centring on differing judgments about the United States. Chamberlain adumbrated the by-now-familiar theme that British security lay with the Japanese and not the Americans. Reflecting the hard anti-Americanism of his ministry – Warren Fisher had circulated a stinging critique of American policy to the NCM along the lines of his DRC 'outburst'[30] – the chancellor disentombed the idea of an opening to Tokyo. Concerned about defending the Empire in the aftermath of Manchuria, the Admiralty looked for an Anglo-American naval condominium in the Pacific. Contrary to the view in the late 1920s, some influential naval officers were beginning to perceive the USN in a more favourable light.[31] In the DCM, given defence requirements against Germany, proposed Admiralty spending for new construction, which the 'Chatfield memorandum' pegged at £67 million,

---

[27] State Department memorandum, 22 Sep. 1933, Lindsay despatch (1572) to Simon, 8 Dec. 1933, both *BDFA*, II, J6, 383–5, 387–8. Then cf. Dallek, *Roosevelt*, 75–6; Waldo Heinrichs, Jr, 'The Role of the United States Navy', in Borg and Okamoto, *Pearl Harbor*, 207–8.

[28] 'Preparations for the 1935 Naval Conference. Draft Report' [DC(M)(32) 121], 11 Jun. 1934, CAB 27/511.

[29] Vansittart–Chatfield memorandum, 'Preparations for the 1935 Naval Conference', 23 Mar. 1934, *ibid.*

[30] Fisher memorandum [NCM(35) 3], 23 Apr. 1934, CAB 29/149.

[31] Cf. Drax [C-in-C, America and West Indies Station] to Admiralty, 9 Oct. 1932, Drax, 'Notes on the Present Situation in the United States', 11 Mar. 1933, both DRAX 2/4.

was reduced to £55.5 million. Since construction programmes for 1932–3 and 1933–4 had been suspended, Eyres-Monsell and Chatfield were obligated to spend £21.7 million over the next two fiscal years to rectify those deficiencies: £11.9 million in 1935–6 and £9.8 million in 1936–7. This sum was to be deducted from the authorised £55.5 million, so that funding dedicated solely to new construction would not occur until 1937–8. Controversy exists over this decision: on one hand, Eyres-Monsell is castigated for not defending the Admiralty's position adequately; on the other, blame is put on the committee for ignoring Britain's wider naval needs.[32]

Regardless, the possibility existed that the 1935 conference might modify the Washington naval system to allow for increased security and incur less spending. Craigie and Little met in April with Norman Davis, passing through London on his way to Geneva. In friendly discussion, Davis indicated that the Roosevelt Administration would oppose increasing Japan's ratio; Craigie and Little referred to seventy cruisers and mentioned the battleship limitation proposals.[33] Exposing potential difficulties, this informal exchange suggested that exploratory talks with the other naval Powers would be profitable. Consequently, under NCM authorisation, invitations were despatched to Washington and Tokyo asking them to send delegations to London for preliminary conversations. This diplomacy persuaded the DCM to reduce RN modernisation and construction spending programmes suggested by the DRC and NCM. Once the main naval conference met in 1935, RN requirements could be gauged more precisely; and, in the interim, the delayed 1932–4 programmes could be fulfilled. Such an approach conformed to Foreign Office views about eliminating the diplomatic disadvantages confronting Britain: it would not be isolated from the other Powers; naval discussions might provide Britain with leverage in other international questions; and such leverage could help sustain the balances of power in the Mediterranean, the Far East, and, most importantly, in western Europe where the German question remained paramount.

Though the pre-conference conversations were to be held in October, the British, chiefly Craigie, met with representatives of the four major naval Powers over the summer. Mussolini's government adhered to the arguments maintained since 1930: Italy's navy had to have parity with

---

[32] Cf. Hall, *Arms Control*, 160; Roskill, *Naval Policy*, II, 171–2.
[33] Cf. Craigie memorandum [NCM(35) 2], 12 Apr. 1934, CAB 29/148; 'Memorandum of a Conversation', 12 Apr. 1934, Davis 9. Craigie's memorandum mentions seventy cruisers; Davis' does not. The suggestion that the former was inserted after the fact – Hall, *Arms Control*, 151 – is unwarranted; Davis' omission probably resulted from an effort to convince Hull and Roosevelt that a basis for agreement was closer than it was.

France. But its fleet remained small, even after it announced plans to lay down two battleships in the autumn.[34] Paris, conversely, saw benefit in compromising, partly because of domestic political problems and partly because of concern about the Germans. François Piétri, the minister of marine, endorsed Chatfield's battleship and cruiser proposals.[35] More important, Paris was not seeking upward revision of existing building ratios; in fact, Piétri proposed reducing the French submarine tonnage to 80,000 from the 100,000 figure offered in the ill-starred 1931 'Bases of Agreement'. France might even go below this if compensated in other classes of vessel. Having superiority over the combined Italian and German fleets, the French could be tolerant in seeking common ground with the British.

For London, Japanese and American attitudes remained more important. In late June–early July, Craigie met with Matsudaira just as Japan's new government, headed by Admiral Okada Keisuke, took office. Whilst Okada represented a compromise between pro- and anti-treaty factions, a hardline admiral, Ōsumi Mineo, became navy minister. Sir Robert Clive, the British ambassador at Tokyo, reported that Okada's ministry 'will be unyielding on the "unrestricted" navy view, although this does not necessarily imply a navy equal in size of tonnage to the British or American navies'.[36] Matsudaira indicated that existing ratios had to be altered and, if the Americans resisted, it might be better to avoid a conference. Beyond this *pro forma* position, Craigie detected a willingness to work with the British. Matsudaira suggested that if some concessions were granted Japan, chiefly allowances to build what it felt necessary within the existing tonnage limitations given adjustments for specific classes of vessel, a settlement amongst the three Powers could be reached.[37] Craigie minuted:

The statements that no difficulty should arise between Great Britain and Japan with regard to ratio and, further, that some form of tripartite political entente between Great Britain, the United States and Japan might assist a solution of

[34] Craigie memorandum, 17 Jul. 1934, with Vansittart minute, 19 Jul. 1934, FO 371/17599/6055/1938.
[35] Craigie memorandum, 28 Jun. 1934, FO 371/17598/5383/1938; minutes of meetings, 9, 10 (2), 11, 12 Jul. 1934, all FO 371/17598/5504/1938; Simon to George V, 3 Jul. 1934, Simon FO 800/289.
[36] Clive despatch (5369) to Simon, 5 Jul. 1934, *BDFA*, II, E13, 229–31. Cf. *Saionji-Harada Memoirs*, 899–932; S. Pelz, *Race to Pearl Harbor. The Failure of the Second London Naval Conference and the Onset of World War II* (Cambridge, MA, 1974), 50–1.
[37] Craigie memorandum, 28 Jun. 1934, FO 371/17598/5428/1938; Craigie memorandum, 2 Jul. 1934, FO 371/17598/5430/1938. Hall, *Arms Control*, 154–5 says an IJN officer, Captain Shimomura Shosuke, held talks with the British in July. There is no evidence of this; see Kelly [FO American Department] to Clive, 16 Aug. 1934, FO 371/17598/5167/1938.

the United States–Japan ratio difficulty[,] seemed to me important, even though they may at the moment only represent the opinion of the Ambassador.[38]

The success of the 1935 conference, it seemed, hinged on American policy. Discussions with Davis and Bingham were not encouraging. Davis' April conversations with Craigie and Little led Washington to believe that there would be Anglo-American co-operation against any Japanese effort to revise the existing ratios. Obviously, Davis either ignored or did not understand the British proposals for new battleship limitation and the demand for seventy cruisers.[39] Bingham, conversely, after meeting privately with Vansittart, warned Roosevelt: '[the British] are not willing to adopt any Anglo-American policy that might be interpreted as coercion in Japan and solidify the control of the military element'.[40] Davis returned to London in mid-June and confronted the awkward fact that the British intended to remedy their naval deficiencies in a way that might see co-operation with the Japanese.[41] Lacking precise details of what the Roosevelt Administration looked to achieve in 1935, Davis talked generally about maintaining the existing ratios and tonnages with, perhaps, reductions in the latter. The lack of definite proposals annoyed the British, who were specific: willing to reduce battleship displacement and gun calibres, they looked to replace older vessels in this class beginning in 1936; they sought seventy cruisers; and they wanted adjustments within other classes that retained the 1930 ratios agreed.

'Mr. Norman Davis', reported Craigie, 'said that he and his colleagues had been completely taken aback by the scale of the increases which we were now proposing. Mr. Bingham was particularly upset.'[42] Vansittart reckoned Davis and Bingham feigned annoyance 'as part of a bargaining manoeuvre'.[43] When Roosevelt sent a personal message to MacDonald that 'the world demands for the social and economic good of human beings a reduction in armaments and not an increase', Vansittart observed: 'Mr. Roosevelt is playing politics at home and shutting his eyes to everything abroad – a habit not only of Mr. Roosevelt but of most other U.S. politicians.'[44] The November 1934

---

[38] Craigie minute, 28 Jun. 1934, FO 371/17598/5428/1938.
[39] See note 33, above; Bingham diary, 12 Apr. 1934, Bingham 1.
[40] Bingham to Roosevelt, 8 May 1934, Roosevelt PSF GB 1934.
[41] See NC(USA) minutes, CAB 29/149. Cf. MacDonald diary, 18, 20 Jun. 1934, MacDonald PRO 30/69/1753; Vansittart minute, 26 Jun. 1934, FO 371/17598/5184/1938.
[42] Craigie minute, 23 Jun. 1934, FO 371/17598/5184/1938.
[43] Vansittart minute, 26 Jun. 1934, *ibid*. Cf. Davis and Bingham to Roosevelt and Hull, 29 Jun. 1934, in Bingham diary, 22 Jun. 1934, Bingham 1.
[44] Roosevelt to Davis, in Hull to Davis, 26 Jun. 1934, *FDRFA*, II, 160–1; Vansittart minute, 15 Jul. 1934, FO 371/17598/5315/1938.

American mid-term elections were approaching. With the French and
Japanese showing a willingness to compromise in ways that would
augment RN strength in an increasingly hostile world, the National
Government had no need to chase the Americans. Davis departed in
mid-July empty-handed. Importantly, the Roosevelt Administration
sought to avoid public perceptions of Anglo-American disagreement,
especially if this could shift responsibility for failure to Japan.[45] Hull
issued a statement on 16 July that 'the suspension of the talks did not
mean that there had been a breakdown'; and Davis won Simon's
agreement that no communiqué would be issued summarising the
talks.[46]

Matsudaira's warm words about Anglo-Japanese co-operation came
just as Hirota Kōki, the Japanese foreign minister, suggested to Clive
'that Japan would be only too ready to conclude non-aggression pacts
with America and Britain'.[47] The possibility of an Anglo-Japanese
rapprochement loomed. As MacDonald and Baldwin were both vacationing in early August, Clive's report reached the desk of the acting
prime minister, Chamberlain. Pouncing on it as a means to achieve an
Anglo-Japanese understanding, he requested a Foreign Office assessment.[48] Vansittart asked for American and Far Eastern department
views on the intertwined questions of naval limitation and the non-
aggression proposal. Conditioned by the knowledge that Washington
had spurned Hirota's offer,[49] their reactions were divided. The Far
Eastern Department head, Charles Orde, acknowledged that the foreign
minister might sincerely want to ameliorate Anglo-Japanese differences.
But regarding naval limitation, Hirota, a civilian, would have difficulty
in getting 'the higher naval authorities' to accept limitation within the
existing ratios.[50] Additionally, any Anglo-Japanese non-aggression pact
would vex the Americans, Chinese, and Russians, let alone the Dutch
and Portuguese, both of whom had Far Eastern colonies. Through
Craigie, the American Department argued that granting 'equality of
status' over naval arms would better protect British interests than a

[45] Moffat to Davis, 20 Jul. 1934, Davis 41.
[46] Bingham diary, 16, 18, 19 Jul. 1934, Bingham 1; Bingham to Hull, 23 Jul. 1934, Hull
37; Kelly to Clive, 16 Aug. 1934, FO 371/17598/5167/1938.
[47] Clive despatch (369) to Simon, 5 Jul. 1934, BDFA, II, E13, 229–31.
[48] '[T]he Chancellor has written to me a letter of very strong advocacy': in Vansittart
minute, 25 Aug. 1934, FO 371/17599/7695/938. Chamberlain's letter cannot be
located.
[49] Vansittart minute, 22 Aug. 1934, FO 371/17599/7695/1938. Cf. Clive despatch (438)
to Simon, 15 Aug. 1934, BDFA, II, E13, 245–7; Hull to Roosevelt, 9 Jun. 1934, with
enclosure, Roosevelt PSF Japan 1933–1934.
[50] Orde minute, 28 Aug. 1934, FO 371/17599/7695/1938.

fruitless search for common ground with the Americans.[51] He also supported Hirota's proposal as long as 'non-aggression' could be adequately defined, and if Britain retained the right of self-defence. 'This would, in practice', he noted with icy realism, 'be mere camouflage – but heavy applications of political camouflage may be necessary if we are to prevent naval limitation from going by the board next year.'

Vansittart sided with Orde.[52] Granting 'equality of status' would allow Tokyo to 'estimate [its] needs at a figure which will entirely alter the status quo', whilst a bilateral non-aggression pact would provide Japan with 'a free hand in China', weakening Britain's links to those other Powers with Far Eastern interests. Weakening those links would undermine Britain's ability to influence the East Asian balance. Vansittart advised Simon on 29 August to discourage Cabinet support for a non-aggression pact. Chamberlain, however, forced the issue. Before seeing Clive's report, he drafted a memorandum on 'The Naval Conference and Our Relations with Japan'.[53] Returning to the proposition that 'it is essential that we should not find ourselves in a few years time confronted simultaneously with a hostile Germany and an unfriendly Japan', he repeated the standard Treasury argument: appease Japan over naval arms; conclude an Anglo-Japanese non-aggression pact; do nothing respecting the Americans beyond keeping Washington informed of what was transpiring; take a soft line in naval negotiations with Paris to keep the Germans in line; and conduct a public education campaign in Britain to explain why the government was meeting British defence deficiencies. His reasoning was based on Roosevelt's reluctance to co-operate. Mirroring his experiences in economic diplomacy since November 1931 as much as those over arms limitation and security, he commented: 'American representatives lay stress in private upon the immense advantages which would accrue to the world if only we worked together … When we have laid all our cards on the table they shake their heads sadly and express their regretful conviction that Congress will have nothing to do with us unless we can make an offer that will suit them better.' Clive's report assured him about the merit of his bargaining strategy. He sent copies of his draft to Baldwin, Simon, Hoare, and Thomas in early September.[54]

This precipitated an exchange between Chamberlain and Simon who, bolstered by Vansittart, prevented an immediate approach to the

[51] Craigie minute, 23 Aug. 1934, *ibid.*
[52] Vansittart minute, 25 Aug. 1934, Vansittart minute to Simon, 29 Aug. 1934, both *ibid.*
[53] Chamberlain memorandum, 'The Naval Conference and Our Relations with Japan', n.d. [but early Aug. 1934], NC 8/19/1.
[54] Chamberlain minutes (2), both n.d., *ibid.*

Cabinet.[55] Simon argued that the Anglo-Japanese non-aggression pact would threaten the East Asian balance by provoking ill-favour amongst the Americans, Chinese, Russians, and Dutch. Indeed, giving the Japanese increased security might lead them to pursue a forward policy in the region. Simon, thus, suggested a joint submission; on 16 October, a week before the preliminary naval talks began, a memorandum signed by Simon and Chamberlain reached the Cabinet.[56] Whilst Chamberlain's arguments from his August draft remained, Foreign Office anxiety about an Anglo-Japanese pact giving Tokyo 'a free hand' were emphasised. Added to this, as Manchuria had shown, the risk existed that the Japanese might not honour the guarantee.[57] By this time, additional conversations between Clive and Hirota indicated that Okada's government saw a non-aggression pact as a replacement for the naval treaty should the latter prove impossible to extend.[58] In these circumstances, even though the most favourable light had been placed on a non-aggression pact, the Cabinet delayed formal discussions with the Japanese.[59]

Beginning on 18 October, the naval talks involved the British, Americans, and Japanese and, lasting until 20 December, with the Japanese delegation unbending over continuing the existing ratios, they were adjourned rather than ended.[60] The British confronted two antithetical bargaining positions. Led by Davis and Admiral William Standley, the American CNO, American delegates were adamant that existing ratios be maintained. Their arguments reflected British ones concerning the RN: the USN was a two-ocean navy; the IJN was a regional force;

---

[55] Based on Chamberlain to Simon, 10 Sep. 1934, Simon to MacDonald, 3 Oct. 1934, both Simon FO 800/291; Chamberlain to Simon, 1 Sep. 1934, *DBFP II*, XIII, 24–5; Simon to Chamberlain, 7 Sep. 1934, SP 79. In my article 'No Eternal Friends or Enemies: British Defence Policy and the Problem of the United States, 1919–1939', *CJH*, 28(1993), 284 n. 103, the references to these documents are incorrect: *horresco referens*.

[56] Simon–Chamberlain memorandum [CP 223(34)], 16 Oct. 1934, CAB 24/250. On its drafting, see A. Trotter, *Britain and East Asia* (Cambridge, 1975), 101–5; Dutton, *Simon*, 192–3. Cf. A. Trotter, 'Tentative Steps for an Anglo-Japanese Rapprochement in 1934', *Modern Asian Studies*, 8(1974), 59–83.

[57] The notion that Simon caved in to Chamberlain on this issue – Dutton, *Simon*, 192–3 – is misplaced. Cf. Orde memorandum, 4 Sep. 1934, *DBFP II*, XIII, 31–4 [original removed from FO 371 records]; Craigie minute, 2 Oct. 1934, Vansittart minute, 2 Oct. 1934, FO 371/18184/5846/591; Allen [Far Eastern Department] minute, 3 Oct. 1934, Randall [Far Eastern Department] minute, 3 Oct. 1934, FO 371/18184/5859/591; Craigie minute, 5 Oct. 1934, Wellesley minute, 5 Oct. 1934, FO 371/18184/6192/591.

[58] Clive telegram (232) to Simon, 29 Sep. 1934, FO 371/18184/5846/591.

[59] CC (35)7, CAB 23/80. Cf. Madden to Chatfield, 19 Oct. 1934, Warren Fisher to Chatfield, n.d. [but Oct. 1934], both CHT 3/2.

[60] Except where noted, the next two paragraphs are based on Hall, *Arms Control*, 162–70; Pelz, *Race*, 132–51; Roskill, *Naval Policy*, II, 295–9; Trotter, *East Asia*, 104–14.

consequently, conceding quantitative parity to Japan would give the IJN pre-eminence in Far Eastern waters. The senior Japanese delegates, Matsudaira and Rear-Admiral Yamamoto Isoruko, adhered to the line laid down by Okada's cabinet: the IJN had to have quantitative equality with the RN and USN; this constituted a matter of 'national feelings and prestige'; and, if Japanese demands were denied, Japan would withdraw from the Washington naval system. Despite these competing positions, a glimmer of compromise appeared. The Americans seemed agreeable to 20 per cent cuts for each Power below the 1930 tonnage figures if the existing ratios were maintained. If such reductions proved impossible, Washington could live with the 1930 tonnages. For their part, Matsudaira and Yamamoto suggested a 'common upper limit' for overall warship tonnage whereby each Power could decide its specific requirements. They tied this proposal to a suggestion that offensive warships – battleships, aircraft carriers, and heavy cruisers – be abolished or their numbers reduced significantly; either avenue would augment security by enhancing defence and allow for a low 'common upper limit'. But these bargaining positions remained nothing more than diplomatic eye-wash; Japan and America were each prepared to see the naval treaty lapse, especially if the odium for failure could be put on the other's shoulders.[61] Roosevelt's Administration entertained deep suspicions about Japanese ambitions in China, especially since in April 1934, Amau Eiji, a spokesman for Hirota's ministry, declared publicly: 'Owing to [the] special position of Japan in her relations with China, her views and attitude respecting matters that concern China may not agree in every point with those of foreign nations; but it must be realised that Japan is called upon to exert the utmost effort in carrying out her mission and in fulfilling her special responsibilities in East Asia.'[62]

Although it might create difficulty with Japan in other matters, for instance, over cotton exports to China, the Foreign Office advised Simon that Britain must not acknowledge Tokyo's assertion that it could unilaterally determine threats to China's political stability and then move to resolve them.[63] Like other signatories of the Washington nine-Power treaty, Japan could only draw attention to such threats. Whilst

---

[61] Cf. Roosevelt memorandum to Swanson [secretary of the Navy], 17 Dec. 1934, *FDRFA*, II, 322–3.

[62] For Amau's statement, see Lindley telegram (83), 20 Apr. 1934, *BDFA*, II, E13, 161–2. Cf. Hornbeck to Hull, 14 Apr. 1934, enclosing Hornbeck memorandum, 'Problem of Japanese–American Relations', 5 Apr. 1934, 'Draft of Possible Statement in Rejoinder to Japanese Statement', 26 Apr. 1934, 'Memorandum of Conversation Between Secretary Hull and the Japanese Ambassador, Mr. Hirosi Saito', 19 May 1934, all Roosevelt PSF Japan; Grew to Hornbeck, 29 Jun. 1934, Grew 69; Grew diary, 20 Apr. 1934, Grew 71.

[63] Louis, *British Strategy*, 222; Trotter, *East Asia*, 71–3.

the Amau declaration was not the overriding concern for the British in Anglo-Japanese relations – the naval balance remained more important – subsequent policy discussions looked for means to obviate Anglo-Japanese differences; this desire partially informed NCM and DCM deliberations and the discussions surrounding Chamberlain's draft memorandum. At the preliminary talks beginning in October, the National Government looked to balance between the Americans and Japanese. Davis agreed that the British should explore a compromise with the Japanese – he surmised that inevitable Japanese rejection would push Britain towards the United States. Simon accordingly outlined a 'middle course' to the Japanese: the 'common upper limit' was acceptable as long as the IJN remained quantitatively inferior to the RN and USN; although Britain could not accept the distinction between 'offensive' and 'defensive' warships, an arrangement on qualitative limitation was possible; and to meet Japanese concerns about their security, some type of non-aggression pact should be pursued. Matsudaira politely rejected the British offer on 19 November, asserting that the IJN could not accept quantitative inferiority. For the next month, the British probed the Japanese position, making further suggestions like allowing the IJN full equality after 1942. The Japanese refused to perpetuate the existing ratios in any form, whilst the Americans had no intention of accepting formal equality between the USN and the IJN. On 29 December 1934, Tokyo gave formal notice that when the London treaty lapsed twelve months hence, Japan would no longer be bound by its restrictions.

Tokyo's intransigence precluded an Anglo-Japanese agreement,[64] putting paid to Chamberlain's notion that strengthening the RN could be slowed whilst home air defences were improved. However, Japan's denunciation did not spell the end to naval limitation. The London naval treaty dictated that the three Powers would have to meet in a formal conference in 1935; hence, a new treaty was still possible. To this end, the British gave Yamamoto proposals for submission to the proper authorities at Tokyo that could serve as a basis for new negotiations.[65] 'It is precisely to avoid the staking out of incompatible claims based on a fixed ratio', Craigie observed, 'that we have suggested . . . the making by each naval Power of a unilateral declaration as to its building programme over a fixed period of years.'[66] British requirements for all classes of

---

[64] I agree with Trotter, *East Asia*, 107–8. Cf. D. C. Watt, 'Britain, the United States and Japan in 1934', in Watt, *Personalities*, 83–99.

[65] FO–Admiralty memorandum, 'Notes on the minimum British Naval Strength necessary for security', 15 Jan. 1935, plus Craigie and Vansittart minutes, both 11 Jan. 1935, Simon minute, 12 Jan. 1935, all FO 371/18731/478/22.

[66] Craigie minute, 19 Mar. 1935, FO 371/18732/2878/22. Cf. Warren Fisher memo-

vessel were restated; they were justified in the 'sense of security' necessary for Imperial defence; and they referred to the laying down of German capital ships. Unlike Japan's, British naval planning had to consider more than the Far Eastern naval balance. Following the Foreign Office line that British policy should maintain regional understandings with other Powers, the American delegation also received the proposal for programme declarations. With this diplomacy, the naval question went into abeyance whilst the British waited for responses from Washington and Tokyo.[67]

Subsequent judgment of Britain's strategic position arising from the preliminary talks concludes that 'Britain was not relevant to the Japanese–American rivalry in the Pacific', that 'some kind of condominium over China at the expense of third parties (and the Chinese) was now ruled out by Britain's weakness', and that 'Britain was incapable of dealing effectively with the two [threats in Europe and the Far East] simultaneously'.[68] Made with hindsight, such an assessment ignores contemporary factors suggesting neither that Britain was weak nor that its diplomatists had lost the initiative in concurrently protecting the country's interests in Europe and the Far East. First, the modified DRC proposals were being implemented to meet defence deficiencies. Central to this process was ensuring that a European crisis did not arise that, in diverting British attention away from the outer reaches of the Empire, would allow the Japanese to move with impunity in the Far East. Admittedly, in November 1934, the CID accepted that the danger period for Britain in the Far East would last until 1936, when Japan would complete its fleet modernisation, including the IJN Fleet Air Arm.[69] But with both the RN and Singapore being strengthened as a result of the DCM report, British regional interests could be secured until then by diplomatic efforts 'to avoid incidents which might lead Japan to take precipitate action'. Second, the non-aggression pact's demise reinforced Vansittart's arguments about how best to protect Britain's external position. With an Anglo-Japanese agreement dead, he and his advisers reckoned that other Powers concerned about Japanese policy might be willing to join with Britain in maintaining the

randum, 'Naval Discussions, 1934', 7 Nov. 1934, Warren Fisher to Chatfield, 1 Jan. 1935, both CHT 3/2.
[67] Simon telegram (304–305) to Lindsay, 20 Dec. 1934, *DBFP II*, XIII, 155.
[68] Hall, *Arms Control*, 169–70.
[69] CID 266th meeting, 22 Nov. 1934, CAB 2/6. Cf. COS Report, 'Defence Plans' [CID 1149B], 23 Oct. 1934, COS 'Imperial Defence Policy. Annual Review' [CID 1154B], 30 Nov. 1934, with Appendix, 'Japanese Naval Preparations', both CAB 4/23; COS Report, 'Strategic Position in the Far East' [399C], 29 Oct. 1934, CAB 5/7.

international status quo.[70] Finally, Britain's position as an East Asian Power was not ignored by either Washington or Tokyo. During the preliminary naval discussions, the possibility of an Anglo-Japanese settlement rattled the White House because its conclusion would weaken American influence in the region. As Roosevelt told Davis:

Simon and a few other Tories must be constantly impressed with the simple fact that if Great Britain is even suspected of preferring to play with Japan to playing with us, I shall be compelled, in the interest of American security, to approach public sentiment in Canada, Australia, New Zealand and South Africa in a definite effort to make these Dominions understand clearly that their future security is linked with us in the United States.[71]

While displaying Roosevelt's ignorance about Imperial sentiment, this outburst also shows that Britain's strategic position had not been diminished nor its weaknesses exposed.

Despite Treasury pressure for some East Asian *modus vivendi* with Japan that excluded the United States,[72] Foreign Office views dominated policy. 'It seems to me', Simon told the Cabinet in January 1935, 'that the true aim of our policy should be to remain on good terms not only with Japan but with China and the United States as well.'[73] This meant searching for means to balance British, American, and Japanese interests in East Asia. By mid-February, the Cabinet established a committee on political and economic relations with Japan (PEJ) that focused on China and its relations with those Powers which enjoyed control over its economy.[74] Naturally, vigilance in Europe remained essential. Vansittart's iron logic expressed in the DRC a year earlier remained untarnished: 'Japan would attack us [only] after we had got into difficulties elsewhere ... elsewhere could only mean Europe, and Europe could only mean Germany.' More than ever, the European and Far Eastern balances were connected in British diplomatic strategy.

Throughout 1935, therefore, British foreign policy sought to maintain the global balance of power; in this process, a major Cabinet shuffle in June enhanced Vansittart's leading role in the foreign-policy-making elite when Hoare replaced Simon. As Baldwin, who took the premiership, had as much confidence as his predecessor in the permanent under-secretary, and as the ministers of the restructured National

---

[70] See Vansittart minute, 11 Jan. 1935, FO 371/18731/127/22; notes of meeting held in Vansittart's FO room, 15 Jan. 1935, FO 371/18823/409/55.
[71] Roosevelt to Davis, 9 Nov. 1934, Davis 51.
[72] Cf. Warren Fisher minute to Chamberlain, 12 Nov. 1934, CHT 3/2; Warren Fisher memorandum for Chamberlain, 21 Jan. 1935, *DBFP II*, XX, 404–6.
[73] Simon memorandum, 'Anglo-Japanese Relations', 21 Jan. 1935, Simon FO 800/290.
[74] Extract from CC 9(35), in *DBFP II*, XX, 424.

Government concentrated on preparing for an autumn election, Vansittart dominated the day-to-day running of the Foreign Office. The specific issues preoccupying British foreign policy in those twelve months had the potential to subvert Britain's interests: Hitler's announcement in March that Germany would rearm regardless of the Treaty of Versailles; financial trouble in the Far East related to China and silver; the Italo-Abyssinian crisis beginning in October; and the advent of the second London naval conference that, sitting from 9 December 1935 to 26 March 1936, saw Japan remove itself from any system of naval limitation. These matters were intertwined in terms of the global balance of power; in each, the United States impinged on British diplomatic tactics. 'With Anglo-American relations in particular there is nothing wrong', Vansittart later wrote, 'except that we get farther from each other whenever we try to get nearer.'[75] Such sentiments permeated his diplomatic thinking after the 1934 naval talks. Needlessly offending the Americans would complicate the more important problems confronting Britain. Whilst London needed to remain wary of Roosevelt, an unhostile United States would make Foreign Office tasks less burdensome. With Craigie appointed an assistant under-secretary in January, Britain's policy towards the United States lay in the hands of the two senior Foreign Office officials who had been handling Anglo-American relations for more than a decade.

Vansittart's aim of strengthening the European balance to contain Germany was helped in early 1935 when the French and Italians moved to end their rivalry. After meeting in Rome in the first week of January, Laval, again the French foreign minister, and Mussolini signed agreements to settle future Franco-Italian disputes by arbitration, to bury their differences in Africa, promote the territorial status quo in central Europe and the Danubian basin, and outline their opposition to unilateral revision of existing arms limitation treaties.[76] Their purpose derived from a shared concern about German ambitions that, although the Austrian putsch had failed, were seen in Vienna the preceding summer. Via Drummond, who had left the League to become British ambassador in Rome, the Foreign Office understood that Mussolini looked covetously on Abyssinia and that Paris encouraged his longing to

---

[75] Lord Vansittart, *Events and Shadows. A Policy for the Remnants of a Century* (1947), 86.
[76] E. M. Robertson, *Mussolini as Empire Builder: Europe and Africa, 1932–36* (New York, 1977), 114–17; D. C. Watt, 'The Secret Laval–Mussolini Agreements of 1935 on Ethiopia', in E. M. Robertson, ed., *The Origins of the Second World War* (1971), 19–20. Cf. M. Knox, *Mussolini Unleashed, 1939–1941. Politics and Strategy in Fascist Italy's Last War* (Cambridge, 1982), 19–20.

expand Italy's East African empire.[77] On the basis of public statements and communications from the French, and following the dictates of *realpolitik*, Vansittart reasoned that Britain would benefit by acquiescing to Italian penetration of Abyssinia.[78] All that Britain should do was ensure that Italy did so peacefully, by negotiation with Haile Selassie, the Abyssinian emperor. To this end, Britain and France could act as mediators.

Vansittart saw the Franco-Italian *entente* as a device that Britain could exploit to contain Germany on the Continent. The French seemed willing to co-operate. From 1 to 3 February, Laval and the French premier, Flandin, visited London.[79] Their discussions with MacDonald, Simon, and other senior ministers spawned the publicly expressed hope that Germany would agree to non-intervention pacts for central Europe and the Danubian basin, and that it would join an air agreement supplementary to Locarno – no aerial bombardment of cities. Regarding the latter, each signatory would agree to support whichever Power might be subject to attack. In these talks, the British showed willingness to accept moderate German rearmament as a fact of life, since continued frustration of Germany's claim for 'equality of treatment' would only buttress Hitler. This willingness translated into a proposal to ignore German violations of Versailles and seek means to negotiate an end to that portion of the treaty denying German equality. Just as critical for the impending naval conference, the Laval–Mussolini agreement suggested that France and Italy might sign a new naval limitation treaty. Piétri's compromise, broached the preceding summer, remained on the table, though Laval would not discuss future naval limitation until German policy was known. Accordingly, by mid-February, the British opened lines of communication to Hitler's government. Preparations began to have Simon visit Berlin to examine the 'air Locarno', general issues of security, and Germany's return to the League.[80]

The visit was delayed. On 4 March the National Government released a White Paper that, explaining increased estimates to meet British defence deficiencies in an election year, referred to Germany's illegal rearmament.[81] Hitler caught a diplomatic cold but recovered sufficiently

[77] Cf. Perth telegrams (38, 39–40) to Simon, 14, 15 Jan. 1935, *DBFP II*, XIV, 99–100, 105–7.
[78] Vansittart minute, 25 Feb. 1935, *DBFP II*, XIV, 166–7; Vansittart memorandum, 25 Feb. 1935, FO 371/18828/1632/55; Vansittart minute, 2 Mar. 1935, FO 371/19105/974/1.
[79] N. Rostow, *Anglo-French Relations, 1934–36* (1984), 83–119. A copy of the resultant communiqué, 3 Feb. 1935, is in *DBFP II*, XII, 482–4.
[80] Craigie memorandum, 'Visit to Berlin. Naval Armaments', 7 Mar. 1935, FO 371/18732/2843/22.
[81] Cmd. 5114. Cf. Weinberg, *Hitler's Germany*, I, 204–6.

by 16 March, a week after announcing that the German air force, the
Luftwaffe, had come into existence, to proclaim that Germany would no
longer be restricted in providing for its terrene defence. A decree
establishing an army of thirty-six divisions and the reintroduction of
conscription accompanied his statement. Hitler's action immediately
brought the British, French, and Italians together. At Stresa from 11 to
14 April, MacDonald and Simon conferred with Flandin, Laval, and
Mussolini. They reaffirmed the need for central European and Danubian pacts and issued a resolution censuring Hitler's unilateral repudiation of the disarmament provisions of Versailles. This resolution
immediately received unanimous support from the League Council,
though in a more condemnatory way.[82] Hugh Wilson, the American
observer at the League, told Hull that Massigli thought Vansittart had
'played the decisive role' in bringing the three anti-revisionist Powers
together.[83] Certainly, within the British government, Vansittart led in
convincing Simon and the Cabinet about finding common ground with
the French; he cleared the way with Paris and Rome; and he did so for
balance-of-power reasons.[84] A recent critic of Vansittart has argued that
he 'forgot that military strength is relative. His service on the Defence
Requirements Committee led him to exaggerate British weakness by
ignoring Germany's unpreparedness for major war in 1934–5.'[85] Not
only does this misrepresent Vansittart's views – let alone show complete
misunderstanding of the first DRC report – it ignores the domestic
milieu from which British foreign policy sprang. The National Government had suffered further by-election defeats, British peace advocates
were promoting the so-called 'Peace Ballot', and the National Government had to face the electorate within the year. Voters would not
countenance forward action against Germany. However, an alignment
with France and Italy, whose military strength combined with that of
Britain could deter Germany, was not only palatable to domestic
opinion, but conformed to the successful traditions of British diplomacy
and the continental balance of power which had informed policy for
more than two centuries. In fact, throughout 1935, in terms of the
global balance, Vansittart was moving towards the idea that Bolshevik

---

[82] Simon telegram (74) to Baldwin, 18 Apr. 1935, *DBFP II*, XII, 927–8.
[83] Wilson to Hull, 20 Apr. 1935, Wilson 3. Cf. A. L. Goldman, 'Sir Robert Vansittart's
Search for Italian Cooperation against Hitler, 1933–1936', *JCH*, 9(1974), 93–130.
[84] Vansittart minutes, 19 Mar. 1935, FO 371/18830/2214/55; 29 Mar. 1935, FO 371/
19106/1139/1; 1 Apr. 1935, FO 371/18833/2656/55; Vansittart to Phipps, 5 Mar., 26
Apr. 1935, both PHPP 2/17; CC 20(35), 8 Apr. 1935, CAB 23/81.
[85] Rostow, *Anglo-French Relations*, 81.

Russia might be useful in helping to contain both Germany in Europe and Japan in the Far East.[86] Whilst Roosevelt entertained private concerns about the European situation, the British saw Washington as unhelpful in ensuring the continental balance. Hull responded to the Anglo-French talks by telling Simon that 'I do not see how I could usefully comment in a public statement on what is in the first instance a European political development'.[87] For the Foreign Office, if not the Cabinet, his attitude corresponded to the thrust of American foreign policy since Roosevelt's rise to the White House. 'I think the [FO American] Dept. is aware of the view which I have now long held', Vansittart observed early in 1935, 'that, if anything is to come of Anglo-American relations, the U.S.A. will for some time to come have to make something over 50 per cent of the running instead of zero.'[88] By 1935, as they had shown consistently since 1920, the Americans had no intention of getting involved in European political affairs; and the reason had not changed: no vital United States interests were involved. Moreover, with the debt default and the effective end of reparations, official Washington had no desire to enmesh itself in a substantive way in European security. The British response was to ignore the United States in constructing a counter-balance to Germany, though, if Roosevelt and his advisers later felt a desire to co-operate – or, rather, if American Congressional and public opinion would allow them to do so – so much the better. But this appeared unlikely. United States opinion seemed increasingly isolationist as American revisionist historians argued that German 'war guilt' was a myth, as popular books with titles like *Merchants of Death* received wide distribution, and as prominent Americans like Borah now denounced the decision to go to war in 1917.[89] Consequently, beginning

---

[86] In this respect, the final words are those of the insightful S. Bourette-Knowles, 'The Global Micawber: Sir Robert Vansittart, the Treasury, and the Global Balance of Power, 1933–1935', and M. L. Roi, 'From the Stresa Front to the Triple Entente: Sir Robert Vansittart, the Abyssinian Crisis, and the Containment of Germany', both *DS*, 6(1995), 91–121 and 61–90.

[87] Hull to Simon, 7 Feb. 1935, Simon FO 800/290. Cf. Simon to MacDonald, 11 Feb. 1935, *ibid.*

[88] Vansittart minute, 14 Jan. 1935, FO 371/18760/531/531.

[89] On revisionism, see H. E. Barnes, *The Genesis of the World War*, 2nd edn (New York, 1927); S. B. Fay, *The Origins of the World War*, 2 vols. (New York, 1928); for popular books, see H. C. Engelbrecht and F. C. Hanighen, *Merchants of Death. A Study of the International Armaments Industry* (New York, 1934); F. H. Simonds, *Can Europe Keep the Peace?* (New York, 1931); more generally, see S. Adler, *The Isolationist Impulse: Its Twentieth Century Reaction* (New York, 1957); C. A. Beard and G. H. E. Smith, *The Idea of National Interest. An Analytical Study in American Foreign Relations* (New York, 1934); W. I. Cohen, *The American Revisionists. The Lessons of Intervention in World War I* (Chicago, 1967).

in 1934, a Senate committee investigated the United States arms and munitions industry and its supposed connexion with American entry into the Great War. Presided over by Senator Gerald Nye, this committee stirred up latent American xenophobia by charging – but never proving – that the Wilson Administration joined the war to safeguard its Allied loans.[90]

German rearmament remained, therefore, a situation which Britain and the other European Powers had to confront on their own. Stresa constituted a co-operative political approach, underpinned by the deterrent value of British, French, and Italian collective armed strength.[91] Beyond this, other diplomatic tools were available. For Paris, containing Germany in the west had to be balanced by a similar arrangement in the east. By early 1935, the French alliances concluded with Poland and the 'Little *Entente*' in the 1920s had been fractured as much by Hitler, through initiatives like the German–Polish Non-Aggression Pact of 1934, as by the French government's defensive mentality seen with the 1929 decision to construct the Maginot Line. This saw Paris pursue a Russian alliance that, signed on 2 May 1935, bound both Powers to act together if either suffered attack from a third European Power. Such action would not be automatic: the two Powers would appeal to the League Council – Russia had joined the League in 1934; and to align the treaty with Locarno, French compliance would depend on British, Belgian, and Italian sanction.[92] At Stresa, Laval announced French intentions to find an arrangement with Moscow; the British reaction involved making certain that Locarno would not be endangered.[93] MacDonald's Cabinet accepted Foreign Office legal views that the Franco-Russian alliance did not jeopardise the security treaty, whilst the Italians were reported ready to follow the French 'over any major European proposals involving Germany'.[94]

This set the stage for the conclusion of the Anglo-German naval agreement of 18 June 1935. Controversy exists about the British

[90] Cf. W. S. Cole, *Senator Gerald P. Nye and American Foreign Relations* (Minneapolis, 1962); J. E. Wiltz, *In Search of Peace. The Senate Munitions Enquiry, 1934–1936* (Baton Rouge, 1963).
[91] The following disagrees profoundly with Rostow, *Anglo-French Relations*, 150–1, for instance: 'The solidarity of Stresa was a public relations sham.' My analysis is informed by Roi, 'Stresa Front'.
[92] H. Azeua, *Le pacte franco-soviétique, 2 mai 1935* (Paris, 1968); J.-B. Duroselle, *La décadence* (Paris, 1979), 139–42.
[93] Cf. Simon telegram (108) to Clerk [British ambassador, Paris], 18 Apr. 1935, Malkin [FO legal adviser] minute, 25 Apr. 1935, Simon telegram (109) to Clerk, 26 Apr. 1935, all *DBFP II*, XIII, 190, 204–6, 210.
[94] On Cabinet views, CC 31(35)1: CAB 23/81; on the Italians, Phipps telegram (185) to Simon, 11 May 1935, Drummond telegram (296) to Simon, 13 May 1935, both *DBFP II*, XIII, 249, 250.

decision to establish a naval condominium with the Germans two months after Stresa: that it showed Britain's disloyalty towards its Stresa partners and was the beginning of the discredited 'appeasement' of Hitler that resulted in the outbreak of general European war in 1939.[95] More balanced analysis suggests that a complex series of considerations influenced policy: controlling arms spending; reducing British naval commitments in Europe to allow flexibility in the Far East; creating a basis for renewed European arms control and security; and meeting domestic concerns about rearmament.[96] These intricate problems convinced ministers to support an Anglo-German naval agreement as the National Government reorganised before the anticipated 1935 election – the agreement was signed eleven days after the Cabinet shuffle. But what needs to be made clear is that, first, the agreement with the Germans conformed to the Foreign Office vision of maintaining the global balance of power and, second, consideration of the American question in British thinking played a key part in creating what amounted to a European naval equilibrium.

Foreign Office influence in the negotiation of the agreement is seen by the fact that Craigie, the acknowledged expert on naval arms limitation, supported by Vansittart, received responsibility for co-ordinating British policy. It was Craigie's suggestion that when Simon visited Berlin in early March 1935, naval matters be raised in conversations with German leaders. Prior to this, after Japan gave notice that it would no longer be bound by the London naval treaty, Vansittart, Craigie, and several senior Foreign Office officials began considering how to ensure that the RN would not weaken because of the breakdown of the Washington–London naval system. As Craigie stressed, 'satisfactory progress towards a European [naval] agreement amongst the European Powers will undoubtedly exercise a sobering influence at Tokyo'.[97] Therefore a new naval system had to be constructed, including the Japanese if possible, and balanced by a mechanism that brought France, Italy, and Germany into play. If potential RN adversaries in European and Mediterranean waters could be neutralised diplomatically, RN

[95] Cf. R. A. Best, 'The Anglo-German Naval Agreement of 1935: An Aspect of Appeasement', *Naval War College Review*, vol. 34, no. 2(1981), 68–85; C. Bloch, 'Great Britain, German Rearmament, and the Naval Agreement of 1935', in H. Gatzke, ed., *European Diplomacy Between the Two Wars, 1919–1939* (Chicago, 1972), 125–51; E. Haraszti, *Treaty-Breakers or 'Realpolitiker'? The Anglo-German Naval Agreement of 1935* (Boppard am Rhein, 1974).

[96] H. H. Hall III, 'The Foreign Policy-Making Process in Britain, 1934–1935, and the Origins of the Anglo-German Naval Agreement', *HJ*, 19(1976), 477–99. Cf. D. C. Watt, 'The Anglo-German Naval Agreement of 1935: An Interim Judgement', *JMH*, 28(1956), 155–76.

[97] Craigie minute, 17 Jan. 1935, FO 371/18731/901/22.

ability to protect British Far Eastern interests would be amplified, whether or not Japanese leaders accepted limitation of the IJN at the impending naval conference. This was the context in which British policy concerning the German navy evolved in the first six months of 1935: a political willingness to accept moderate German rearmament as a fact of life; a belief that Anglo-German agreement could lead to a general European naval settlement; and an expectation that this settlement would bolster Britain's position in the Far East where the British relationship with the United States and Japan was being redefined. Until the Flandin–Laval visit to London, Foreign Office concern about naval matters centred on providing Washington and Tokyo with Britain's minimum requirements for the forthcoming conference.[98] Then, given French misgivings about discussing naval limitation until Berlin's attitude was known, the matter of Germany had to be faced. Admittedly, when consideration had earlier been given to bringing Germany into a system of naval limitation, Simon had observed: 'The main difficulty which occurs to me about this scheme is that Germany may reply to suggestions that she should define ... her building programme, that she must first have conceded to her the right to build what she pleases & then she might be prepared to consider what voluntary limitations are possible for the next few years. She will then raise *gleichberichtigung* as a preliminary question.'[99] The Flandin–Laval visit convinced the Foreign Office that German naval aspirations could not be ignored if agreement amongst Britain and the European Powers had any hope of achievement. Here lay the origins of Craigie's proposal for Simon raising naval limitation in Berlin. Admittedly, by the time that Anglo-German talks occurred on 25–26 March, the situation had altered substantially. Simon found the German chancellor disinclined to bring Germany back into the League, that he was uninterested in an eastern European security system, and that he would provide no guarantees for Austrian independence.[100] And, tellingly, Hitler emphasised that *Luftwaffe* strength now equalled that of the RAF, which, with his intention to expand the *Wehrmacht*, illustrated his commitment to strengthen German foreign policy. However, when the British delegation broached the idea of German participation 'in any general conference of naval Powers that might be held in the near

[98] Cf. note 65, above; Craigie to Lindsay and Clive, 5 Feb. 1935, FO 371/18732/1478/22.
[99] Simon minute, 20 Jan. 1935, FO 371/18731/901/22.
[100] See the notes of the four meetings held on 25–26 March, as well as German note, 'Eastern Pact', 26 Mar. 1935, and Phipps telegram (139) to Vansittart, 26 Mar. 1935, all *DBFP II*, XII, 702–46. Cf. Dutton, *Simon*, 196–200, which is good on intra-Cabinet machinations.

future', Hitler saw merit in the idea.[101] He laid 'claim to 35 per cent of the British fleet [and] implied unequivocal recognition of British naval superiority'.

Despite the problems posed by German air and land rearmament – the COS and CID began considering British reactions[102] – the possibility of an Anglo-German naval agreement suggested that Britain could still find diplomatic means of containing German strength. Stresa provided a political mechanism showing that limits to treaty revision existed. Although Simon and Vansittart initially opposed the League's denunciation of Hitler's unilateral repudiation of the disarmament provisions of Versailles – a French initiative – supporting it stood as the price to maintain good Anglo-French relations. 'The dilemma was not an easy one to solve', Vansittart told Phipps, 'because, as you know, we had never been enthusiastic about the French recourse to the League, on the score of German introduction of conscription – indeed, we thought it rather a tactical error. There was, however, really no choice in regard to the balance of advantage.'[103] Similarly, Hitler's willingness to bury Anglo-German naval differences, despite the displeasure this might engender in Paris, could benefit Britain in Europe and the Far East. Hitler avowed no naval *gleichberichtigung*; the problem then became one of finding a basis for agreement to ensure the RN's ability to gird British foreign policy, or, in Vansittart's earlier words, to make bricks with straw.

Despite varying interpretations, the general lines of the agreement of 18 June are familiar.[104] After Simon's March visit to Berlin, and although the 'Stresa Front' had been formed, the British and Germans prepared for naval limitation talks. By the time the German delegation arrived in London to begin discussions on 4 June, Craigie and the British experts assumed some reductions were possible in the German total suggested by Hitler in March;[105] however, refusing to reduce their

---

[101] This and the next sentence are from the minutes of the third meeting; see note 100, above.

[102] COS meetings 139–44, 9–29 Apr. 1935, CAB 53/5; Air Ministry memorandum, 'The German Air Programme and Its Bearing on British Air Strength' [COS 373], 17 Apr. 1935, COS Report, 'The German Air Programme and Its Bearing on British Air Strength' [COS 374], 29 Apr. 1935, COS Report, 'Re-orientation of the Air Defence System of Great Britain' [COS 376], 14 May 1935, all CAB 53/24; Sub-Committee on Industrial Intelligence in Foreign Countries memorandum, 'German Aircraft Industry' [CID 1170B], 11 Apr. 1935, COS memorandum, 'Proposed Aerial Convention. Possible inclusion of Holland' [CID 1176B], 6 Jun. 1935, Air Staff memorandum, 'German Air Rearmament' [CID 1180B], 14 Jun. 1935, all CAB 4/23.

[103] Vansittart to Phipps, 26 Apr. 1935, PHPP 2/17.

[104] See notes 95–6, above. Cf. Roskill, *Naval Policy*, II, 302–6.

[105] For instance, Craigie minute, 8 May 1935, FO 371/18733/3894/22; Little to Craigie, 4 May 1935, FO 371/18733/4333/22.

requirements below 35 per cent of RN strength, the Germans sought equality in submarine tonnage with the entire Commonwealth. Whilst causing consternation in the Cabinet and the Foreign Office, the belief emerged that a hard line would obviate a much-needed agreement.[106] The Admiralty reckoned that these concessions would allow the RN a two-Power standard in European waters and a one-Power standard against Japan in the Far East – it would take Germany until the early 1940s to reach Hitler's goal. As Vansittart learnt from Chatfield: 'it will be the greatest mistake not to clinch the agreement now definitely. It will be the first Naval agreement in Europe that will have been achieved and[,] if we take a strong attitude and present Europe with a courageous decision[,] it will much more likely, in our opinion, lead to something decisive in Europe generally.'[107] The revamped National Government accepted the German proposals.[108]

This agreement harmonised with the Foreign Office vision of maintaining the global balance of power, and, importantly, the American question played a key part in British thinking about creating what amounted to a European naval equilibrium. European naval limitation was intimately connected with that in the Far East, which Craigie stressed in a perceptive comment after Simon met with Hitler:

The attitude taken up by the German Government in this matter is very similar to that adopted by the Japanese Government and if we succeed in over-coming the Japanese difficulty I should not despair of solving the German problem. Conversely, agreement by Germany to negotiate on the basis of a programme arrangement would strengthen our hands considerably in securing Japanese assent to the same basis of negotiation.[109]

Simon's visit occurred just as the CID and COS evaluated Britain's East Asian strategic difficulties. In this early discussion, the Foreign Office and Admiralty divided over the immediacy of a Japanese threat. 'We cannot afford to impair our relations with the United States for the sake of friendship with Japan', the Foreign Office admitted, 'nor can we afford to jeopardise our position, present and potential, in China by supporting Japanese ambitions in that country in their full scope.'[110] But a *modus vivendi* remained possible: 'Within these limits, however, there is room for friendly relations and the evident anxiety of Japan for

[106] Craigie minute, 4 Jun. 1935, FO 371/18733/5214/22; Simon memorandum [CP 119(35)], 7 Jun. 1935, CAB 24/255; Report on 'Anglo-German Naval Discussions' [NCM(35) 50], 5 Jun. 1935, with annexes, CAB 29/148
[107] Chatfield to Vansittart, 13 Jun. 1935, FO 371/18734/5414/22.
[108] Simon draft memorandum, Jul. 1935, with annexes, FO 371/18735/5987/22.
[109] Craigie minute, 29 Mar. 1935, FO 371/18732/3190/22.
[110] FO memorandum, 'The Situation in the Far East' [COS 368], 16 Mar. 1935, CAB 53/24.

such relations is a happy indication that we can at least expect some regard for our own interests in all that she does.' 'The situation is the more disquieting', the Admiralty countered, 'as the state of unrest in Europe might well react unfavourably on Far Eastern affairs and vice versa.'[111] But here lay the value of an Anglo-German agreement. It reduced the possibility of confronting naval adversaries simultaneously in European and Far Eastern waters. Thus, whilst disagreeing about the immediacy of the Japanese threat, the Foreign Office and Admiralty were united in believing that a European settlement strengthened Britain's hand in the Pacific. In short, it provided British diplomatists with material to maintain better the global balance of power.

The British did not ignore the European balance in this diplomacy. In early January, the French had indicated a desire to include 'all the Naval Powers' in a second London naval conference.[112] By 1 March, anticipating his Berlin trip, Simon had informed Charles Corbin, the French ambassador at London, 'that we now propose to go ahead with the Germans'.[113] Yet the delicacy of the European situation following Hitler's announcement of German rearmament and the Foreign Office's quest to create a unified bloc at Stresa witnessed British hesitation to inform Paris and Rome about Hitler's naval proposals.[114] Judging that these could be scaled down through negotiation, it would be better to wait until more specific figures were known. However, German reluctance to accept a figure below 35 per cent or relent over submarine equality confronted the National Government and its foreign and defence policy advisers with a dilemma: either accept the German figures or hazard the chance that Hitler would expand his navy as he was then expanding the *Wehrmacht* and *Luftwaffe*.[115] The Foreign Office and Admiralty saw merit in limiting German naval strength; coupled with the new Cabinet's desire to keep spending in line, their counsel swayed the politicians to endorse the agreement.[116] The Foreign Office believed that after their initial anger subsided, both the French and Italians could be convinced of the value of limiting German naval strength – this in stark contrast to the situation after Hitler's rearmament

---

[111] Naval Staff, 'Memorandum on the Memorandum Prepared by the Foreign Office on the Situation in the Far East' [COS 370], 6 Apr. 1935, *ibid.*
[112] Craigie minute, 8 Jan. 1935, FO 371/18731/104/22.
[113] Craigie minute 1 Mar. 1935, FO 371/18732/2877/22.
[114] Sargent minute, 1 Apr. 1935, Vansittart minute, n.d., both FO 371/18732/3190/22.
[115] Hall, *Arms Control*, 177–9.
[116] Admiralty memorandum [NCM(35) 49], 3 Jun. 1935, Chatfield memorandum [NCM(35) 50], 5 Jun. 1935, both CAB 29/148; Craigie memorandum, 4 Jun. 1935, FO 371/18733/5214/22; Simon memorandum, 'Anglo-German Naval Discussions' [CP119(35)], 7 Jun. 1935, CAB 24/255; NC(G) meetings 4–10, 6–20 Jun. 1935, CAB 29/150.

speech in March. This argument played heavily in the explanation of the agreement circulated to the other naval Powers – one of Hoare's first actions as foreign secretary involved allaying French concerns.[117] The governments in Paris and Rome dutifully criticised the settlement,[118] as did their newspapers. But as Craigie commented about French press reaction: 'this is to be expected until such time as it calms down sufficiently to study the text and the real implications of the agreement'.[119]

As this was a European settlement with East Asian implications, American reaction did not lack weight. In early January 1935, the British proposals for renewed naval discussions had been published in American newspapers without London's concurrence. The Foreign Office saw Hull's unfriendly hand in this publicity, whose purpose Craigie surmised was to undercut Davis within the Administration.[120] Nonetheless, the Foreign Office believed that as a result of the preliminary discussions in 1934, the Navy Department in Washington was converted 'to the view that our demand for 70 cruisers was in circumstances a reasonable one'.[121] Over the following months, whilst the British gaze fixed on Japan and the three chief European Powers, London concluded that an Anglo-American naval agreement was possible.[122] Of course, unresolved issues remained – the Administration's unwillingness to reduce battleship size or eliminate eight-inch guns on cruisers[123] – but on other matters, London's and Washington's views converged. For instance, responding to a query from Craigie, Atherton reported that his government might accept a maximum of fourteen inches for battleship gun calibres if France and Italy were induced 'to abandon or suspend' construction of such guns.[124] Although some officials like Moffat disparaged Stresa and British efforts to balance between France and Germany, the Roosevelt Administration could do little but avoid quarrels with Britain. American policy, Moffat told

---

[117] Hoare minute, 13 Jun. 1935, Hoare FO 800/295.
[118] See the French and Italian replies in Hoare draft memorandum, 1 Jul. 1935, Annex II, FO 371/18735/5971/22. Cf. Hoare to Laval and Mussolini, both 20 Jun. 1935, Hoare FO 800/295.
[119] Craigie minute, 20 Jun. 1935, FO 371/18734/5460/22. Cf. Hoare to Laval and Mussolini, both 20 Jun. 1935, Hoare FO 800/295. Corbin saw advantages in that the French fleet would be larger than its German counterpart; Craigie to Clerk, 12 Jun. 1935, FO 371/18734/572/22.
[120] Craigie minute, 11 Jan. 1935, FO 371/18731/343/22.
[121] Craigie minute, 11 Jan. 1935, FO 371/18731/478/22.
[122] FO–Admiralty memorandum, 'Questions of Naval Limitation, with Relation to the Possible Holding of a Conference for the Limitation of Naval Armament', 30 Mar. 1935, FO 371/18732/3205/22.
[123] See 'Qualitative Limitation' in *ibid.*
[124] Atherton to Craigie, 10 May 1935, FO 371/18733/4531/22.

Mayer, was 'to continue just as you are doing, in other words to maintain our position and if possible to prevent any dramatic disagreements'.[125] The Foreign Office suspected that official American reaction to the Anglo-German agreement would be at the worst grudging acceptance – this given the course of the naval discussions in late 1934 and the fact that any settlement would now have to be arranged outside the confines of the World Disarmament Conference.

Thus, the British looked for a rapprochement with Berlin that did not upset the rough condominium of Anglo-American naval interests that had emerged in the talks that ended in December 1934. Their policy involved establishing a basis of discussion at the second London naval conference by which Anglo-American unity of purpose could produce a general agreement that would extend into the 1940s. Corresponding to the DRC surmise that the United States could be ignored in meeting British defence deficiencies, this attitude can be seen in British assessments in the spring of 1935 that saw American naval policy concerned more with the Far East and Japan.[126] The RN and the USN no longer worried about each other but, instead, had to consider other potential rivals. Thus, it was not surprising that when news of the Anglo-German naval agreement reached Washington, the American official response was favourable. Privately reactions were less sanguine.[127] Roosevelt feared 'that the British have, in the German Naval agreement, let themselves in for real resentment on the Continent, and also for much trouble to themselves in the days to come'. But having cut themselves adrift from Europe, the Americans could do little but embrace this *fait accompli*.

It has been charged that the British agreement with the Germans showed 'an apparently high and naïve level of trust in Hitler', given that the German threat to Britain was 'a land and air problem'.[128] This sort of retrospective indictment belittles the global strategic problems confronting Britain in 1935. The DRC and DCM understood the risks. Since the National Government could not rely on Washington in

---

[125] Moffat to Mayer, 8 Mar. 1935, Moffat 9. On criticism of Stresa, Moffat to Dunn, 19 Apr. 1935, Moffat 8; Long [US ambassador, Rome] to Roosevelt, 19 Apr. 1935, *FDRFA*, II, 486–8.

[126] FO–Admiralty 'Survey of the Present Position of Naval Conversations and Recommendations as to Future Policy' [NCM(35) 46], Jan. 1935; CAB 29/148; Craigie minute [on conversation with Matsudaira], 4 Mar. 1935, FO 371/18732/2968/22. Cf. Craigie minute [on conversation with Atherton], 5 Apr. 1935, FO 371/18733/3755/22.

[127] Bingham to Roosevelt, 28 Jun. 1935, Roosevelt to Bingham, 11 Jul. 1935, both *FDRFA*, II, 553–4; Moffat to Atherton, 24 Jun. 1935, Moffat 8. American criticism was not universal; cf. Phillips diary, 11 Jun. 1935, Phillips 7.

[128] Hall, *Arms Control*, 179.

matters relating to European security, London had to preserve the
position of Britain and the Empire the best it could. Generally speaking,
this involved maintaining the balances of power in Europe, the Mediterranean, and the Far East whilst rectifying defence deficiencies. For
Britain, these balances were connected, especially as they touched
Germany, the 'ultimate potential enemy', and Japan, which would
certainly seek to profit in East Asia if the European balance wobbled.

For the British, the international situation had steadied by June 1935.
Stresa appeared not only to lay a basis for co-operation on the
Continent, it had decided Mediterranean implications. Negotiating the
naval agreement with Germany, although it meant short-term problems
with France and Italy, suggested the possibility of success at the second
London naval conference. And, significantly, the Anglo-German naval
agreement conformed to a long-standing element of British arms limitation policies that went back to the World Disarmament Conference –
meeting legitimate German grievances respecting equality of treatment;
at the moment when Hitler's government was eliminating that grievance
unilaterally on land and in the air, a naval settlement portended much
for future stability. Of course, British action concerning Germany in
June 1935 was 'appeasement' – but 'appeasement' had long been
integral to the British diplomatic arsenal.[129] Designed to protect Britain's narrow national interests, it also lacked altruism of any sort –
again, this evokes little surprise as British diplomatists were in the
business of protecting the country's 'eternal' interests. Stresa and the
Anglo-German naval agreement were a beginning not an end to meeting
the new challenges in international politics that marked the post-1933
period, one that began with the collapse of the World Disarmament
Conference, the end of war debts and reparations, and the advent of
aggressive regimes in Berlin and Tokyo. What all of this meant for the
Anglo-American relationship, however, remained uncertain.

[129] M. Gilbert, *The Roots of Appeasement* (London, 1966); P. Kennedy, 'The Tradition of
Appeasement in British Foreign Policy, 1865–1939', *BJIS*, 2(1976), 195–215; D. C.
Watt, 'The Historiography of Appeasement', in A. Sked and C. Cook, eds., *Crisis and
Controversy: Essays in Honour of A. J. P. Taylor* (London, 1976).

7 From Abyssinia to Brussels via London, Madrid, and Peking, 1935–1937

> Japan had a strong appetite and it would be difficult to stop that policy
> in this way, more so as now Japan was perhaps not so afraid of America
> as she had been. All evidence shewed that the United States was
> withdrawing more and more into its own shell.
>
> Vansittart, October 1935[1]

In the two-and-a-half years following the conclusion of the Anglo-German naval agreement, the Locarno and Washington treaties joined the war debts and reparations agreements on the diplomatic scrap heap. These changes resulted from Hitler, Mussolini, amd militarist Japanese leaders working to alter the European, Mediterranean, amd Far Eastern balances in their favour. British perceptions of the United States, based on the lessons drawn from the bilateral relationship, affected London's general global policy in the period 1935–7. The same was true for Washington. In this, there was discordance. As the DRC showed, the British thought about external policy chiefly in political and military terms, doing so in relation to the competing interests of other Powers. For Americans, or at least those who thought in terms of global policy, Britain presented the primary difficulty. Wherever they looked, they saw Britain – blocking access to raw materials, air routes, cable networks; involving itself deeply in Venezuelan oil and investment in Argentina; seeking to control access to Middle Eastern oil; regulating three-quarters of world rubber production.[2] In the Far East, the State Department remained convinced that British policy was designed to

---

[1] DRC meeting 17, 10 Oct. 1935, CAB 16/112.

[2] Cf. P. J. Baram, 'Undermining the British: Department of State Policies in Egypt and the Suez Canal before and during World War II', *Historian*, 40(1978), 631–49; J. DeNovo, *American Interests and Policies in the Middle East, 1900–1939* (Minneapolis, 1963); R. Gravil, *The Anglo-Argentine Connection, 1900–1939* (Boulder, CO, 1985); Hilton, *Trade Rivalry*; M. R. Megaw, 'The Scramble for the Pacific: Anglo-United States Rivalry in the 1930s', *Historical Studies*, 17(1977), 458–73; R. M. Moore, *Commercial Conflict and Foreign Policy: A Study in Anglo-American Relations, 1932–38* (New York, 1987); F. Venn, 'A Futile Paper Chase: Anglo-American Relations and Middle East Oil, 1918–1934', *DS*, 1(1990), 165–84.

enlist American aid to protect British investments in China against the Japanese. In Europe, they saw Britain working to maintain the continental balance, even though this sometimes meant compromising with the enemies of democracy, like fascist Italy, in the interests of the City of London. Hence, American perceptions of Britain were based chiefly on economic and financial issues and, through this lens, the White House, the Administration, and Congress, plus powerful pressure groups outside, such as oil companies, fashioned policy towards Britain. International politics were transformed significantly at mid-decade; Anglo-American co-operation of any sort remained an impossibility.

By late June 1935, domestic and international reaction to the Anglo-German agreement had died down. Deft handling of the parliamentary debate by Baldwin, Hoare, Chamberlain, and others saw the treaty recede as a domestic issue of first-class importance.[3] Denying that their actions undermined Versailles, they promoted the agreement as showing the possibilities of Anglo-German co-operation and improved Imperial defence. With a General Election looming, more pressing issues, tied to the economy, unemployment, and social policy, preoccupied politicians canvassing for votes. Outside of Britain, Craigie's earlier suspicion that calm would return after the initial reaction proved accurate – although 'calming down' did not hide Paris' rankling at the agreement's *de facto* recognition that the Versailles Treaty was ending.[4] As Laval remarked on 26 June after meeting Eden: 'Keeping within the framework of the communiqué of the 3rd February [following the Laval–Flandin visit to London] we concentrated on finding the best line of negotiation to bring about a rapid solution of the problems raised therein. We shall continue to examine by the diplomatic channel those questions which the shortness of our conversations made it impossible to deal with exhaustively.'[5] With preparations for the second London naval conference underway, an inclusive naval agreement remained possible.

Difficulty arose from Mussolini's decision to expand Italy's East African empire.[6] An area of Italian interest for fifty years, Abyssinia had defeated Italy in 1896 at the Battle of Adowa. By the early 1930s, with reputed mineral wealth also beckoning, Abyssinia re-emerged as a goal

---

[3] Haraszti, 'Realpolitiker', 119–33. Cf. Craigie memorandum, 'Effect on France of the Anglo-German Naval Agreement of June, 1935', Jun. 1935, Templewood VIII/I.

[4] Rostow, *Anglo-French Relations*, 170–1.

[5] 'Record of Anglo-French Conversation ... June 27', Clerk telegram to Hoare, 28 Jun. 1935, *DBFP II*, XII, 488–94.

[6] G. W. Baer, *The Coming of the Italian–Ethiopian War* (Cambridge, MA, 1967); D. Mack Smith, *Mussolini* (New York, 1982), 188–95; Robertson, *Mussolini as Empire-Builder*, 93–131.

of Italian conquest for reasons of national honour and material gain. A clash of arms provoked by a frontier dispute between Italian Somaliland and Abyssinia had occurred on 5 December 1934; although the matter came before the League the next month, Mussolini ordered his service chiefs on 30 December to plan for an invasion. With military preparations underway, the Italian dictator laid the diplomatic groundwork for his conquest. His January 1935 conversations with Laval were a beginning. Then, at Stresa, he subtly intimated his ambitions and drew no objections. Although unsure about the British – London promoted the appeal to the League, provoking an anti-British press campaign in Italy – Mussolini came to believe that his Stresa partners would acquiesce in Italy's absorption of Abyssinia. In Britain's case, he reckoned that a fixation with Germany would free his hands.

Mussolini's optimism about Britain lasted until mid-May 1935. Until then, neither the Foreign Office nor Cabinet saw the East African question as grave.[7] But Italian military preparations coupled with probing by Italian diplomats in London convinced the Foreign Office that a crisis was near. Expecting Italian forces would be ready by the autumn, the Foreign Office impressed on the Cabinet the need for action. This produced a strategy that guided British policy for the next several months: British diplomatists should seek a settlement before September between Mussolini and Haile Selassie; and they should safeguard firm Anglo-Italian ties.[8] Hoare and Vansittart understood that war in East Africa could adversely affect the European, Mediterranean, and Far Eastern balances of power. Vansittart even considered purchasing Italian goodwill with the currency of British Somaliland.[9] The high-water mark of this conciliation came in August: the British and French offered the Italians a privileged economic position in Abyssinia with the right to appoint advisers to Haile Selassie's army, civil service, and police.[10] Mussolini remained unmoved. On 3 October, the Italians attacked Abyssinia from their East African colony of Eritrea.

British policy after October was simple: to prevent Italian action from undermining Britain's ability to influence the balances of power in Europe and the Far East. But whilst the goal was uncomplicated,

---

[7] For example, CC 20(35), 8 Apr. 1935, CAB 23/81. The COS evinced little concern; see COS Annual Review of Imperial Defence Policy [COS 372], 29 Apr. 1935, CAB 53/24.

[8] Simon memorandum [CP 98(35)], 11 May 1935, CAB 24/55; CC 27(35), 15 May 1935, 28(35), 17 May 1935, both CAB 23/81.

[9] Goldman, 'Vansittart's Search', 114.

[10] Eden telegram to Barton [British minister, Addis Ababa], 15 Aug. 1935; Clerk despatch to Hoare, 16 Aug. 1935, both *DBFP II*, XIV, 488, 496–7; Vansittart to Hoare, 19 Aug. 1935, Hoare FO 800/295.

achieving it was not. Domestic constraints imposed themselves on the Cabinet. The LNU and other peace groups had announced the results of their 'Peace Ballot' in June.[11] In responding to a nationally distributed questionnaire, more than 80 per cent of British households supported all-round arms reductions and League collective security; regarding the latter point, however, nearly seven million favoured military sanctions. With the General Election scheduled for 14 November, Baldwin and his ministers genuflected to these sentiments. This suited Vansittart and Hoare. Confident that Britain could defeat Italy in a single-handed war, the COS believed that such a struggle would encourage German and Japanese actions detrimental to British interests.[12] The CID Defence Policy and Requirements sub-committee (the DPR), created in July 1935 to replace the old ministerial disarmament committee, reached the same conclusion.[13] It became Vansittart's policy, through Hoare, to support League economic sanctions to persuade the Italians to accept a political settlement – in the Foreign Office mind, if the League succeeded, the lesson for Hitler would be obvious.[14] One part of this strategy involved Anglo-French collaboration; the other entailed co-operation with the Roosevelt Administration, since League economic sanctions would work only if the United States supported Geneva.

By November, ineffective League sanctions, primarily embargoing petroleum exports to Italy, led Vansittart towards clandestine negotiations with the French.[15] Ready by 8 December, and based on the August offer, the 'Hoare–Laval plan' proposed that Italy be ceded seven-eighths of Abyssinia and that the remainder, controlled by Haile Selassie, have access to the Red Sea via a corridor through British Somaliland. A leak in the French Foreign Ministry before a publicity campaign could be undertaken to support the agreement led to Laval's fall; in Britain, the Plan's contents produced such disfavour in Parliament, including amongst recently re-elected National Government backbenchers, that Hoare also resigned. Eden, the minister responsible

[11] A. Livingstone, *The Peace Ballot* (1935); M. Ceadl, 'The First British Referendum: The Peace Ballot, 1934–1935', *EHR*, 95(1980), 810–39.
[12] COS memorandum [COS 397], 16 Sep. 1935, CAB 53/25. Cf. Chatfield to Dreyer, 16 Sep. 1935, CHT 4/4.
[13] DPR meetings 5 (23 Aug.), 6 (5 Sep.), 7 (11 Sep.), 8 (17 Sep.), 9 (23 Sep.), CAB 16/136.
[14] CC 40(35), 24 Jul. 1935, and 'ministerial meeting', 6 Aug. 1935, both CAB 23/82; Vansittart to Hoare, 9, 19 Aug. 1935, Hoare to Eden, 15, 17 Sep. 1935, all Hoare FO 800/295.
[15] G. W. Baer, *Test Case: Italy, Ethiopia, and the League of Nations* (Stanford, 1976); R. A. C. Parker, 'Great Britain, France and the Ethiopian Crisis', *EHR*, 89(1974), 293–332; R. Quartararo, 'Le origini del piano Hoare–Laval', *Storia contemporanea*, 8(1977), 749–90; J. C. Robertson, 'The Hoare–Laval Plan', *JCH*, 10(1975), 433–65.

for League affairs, became foreign secretary on 22 December. Committed to the League, he pursued stiff policies against Italy, continuing them even after Abyssinian defeat in May 1936 by withholding Britain's formal recognition of the conquest. The immediate result of the crisis was the destruction of Stresa; in the longer term, Mussolini was drawn into Hitler's diplomatic orbit. Moreover, in March 1936, whilst the British, French, and Italians were preoccupied with East Africa, Hitler engineered a major blow against Versailles by remilitarising the Rhineland.[16]

Until recently, the American factor in British policy has been unclear; too much has been written with hindsight, distorting events through the prism of the 'appeasement' debate.[17] New work, however, shows that the attitudes of the Roosevelt Administration during the summer and autumn of 1935 had decided influence on the evolution of British policy leading to the Hoare–Laval Plan; in this, appeasing Italy was not a consideration.[18] After May 1935, the British approached the State Department and the American Embassy in London several times to determine Washington's attitude towards League-imposed economic sanctions against Italy. Beyond seeking to have Italy respect the Kellogg–Briand Pact, Washington would do nothing.[19] Hull told Lindsay on 5 July: 'the United States had no disposition to get in the way of the British Government but would let it proceed with the leadership it had already assumed'.[20]

The ambassador's assessment in mid-August held 'that there is every disposition to help; that help would be moral only; and that there will always be much timidity'.[21] Such timidity flowed from American isolationists getting Congress to pass neutrality legislation on 31 August.

---

[16] J. T. Emmerson, *The Rhineland Crisis, 7 March 1936: A Study in Multilateral Diplomacy* (Ames, IA, 1977); D. C. Watt, 'German Plans for the Reoccupation of the Rhineland: A Note', *JCH*, 1(1966), 193–9.

[17] Cf. S. U. Chukumba, *The Big Powers against Ethiopia: Anglo-French-American Maneuvers during the Italo-Ethiopian Dispute, 1934–1938* (Washington, DC, 1977); R. A. Friedlander, 'New Light on the Anglo-American Reaction to the Ethiopian War, 1935–1936', *Mid-America*, 45(1963), 115–25; B. Harris, *The United States and the Italo-Ethiopian Crisis* (Stanford, 1964); D. F. Schmitz, *The United States and Fascist Italy, 1922–1940* (Chapel Hill, 1988).

[18] M. Roi, ' "A completely immoral and cowardly attitude": the British Foreign Office, American neutrality, and the Hoare–Laval Plan', *CJH* (1994), 331–51.

[19] Bingham telegram (310) to Hull, 9 Jul. 1935, SDDF 741.65/72; Bingham diary, 9, 29 Jul, 25 Sep. 1935, Bingham 1; Atherton telegram (384) to Hull, 20 Aug. 1935, SDDF 711.41/314; Hoare despatch to Lindsay, 29 Jul. 1935, Lindsay despatch to Hoare, 12 Aug. 1935, Lindsay telegram (226) to Hoare, 14 Aug. 1935, Hoare telegram (235) to Lindsay, 17 Aug. 1935, all *DBFP II*, XIV, 439–40, 477–8, 479, 498.

[20] Hull memorandum, 5 Jul. 1935, Hull 58. Cf. Lindsay telegram (165) to Hoare, 5 Jul. 1935, *DBFP II*, XIV, 363.

[21] Lindsay telegram (200) to Hoare, 12 Aug. 1935, *DBFP II*, XIV, 477.

Resulting from general American disfavour towards European power politics, Nye Committee sensationalism, and xenophobic sentiments lurking behind the Johnson Act, these decrees were to last six months.[22] They blocked American arms trading with all belligerents and authorised the president to warn American citizens about travelling on belligerent ships. As Lindsay's embassy and the Foreign Office watched the passage of this legislation with apprehension, Hoare worried that a legally neutral United States would undermine League effectiveness.[23] When Roosevelt failed to get authority to determine the aggressor in a conflict so as to aid the victim, the isolationists had won. Craigie worried that in defending itself in future from an unprovoked attack or by honouring its League and other treaty commitments, Britain might be considered a belligerent.[24]

Once the invasion began, however, efforts centred on ending the crisis quickly. These initially involved League pressures on Rome. On 7 October, the Council condemned Italy as an aggressor; twelve days later, it imposed limited sanctions (embargoing arms and ammunition, prohibiting loans and credits, restricting imports of Italian goods, and banning trade in certain war-related materials).[25] By 6 November, hostilities had not ended. The League's Sanctions Committee then endorsed an oil embargo – Italy was a net importer of petroleum and its armed forces could not continue operations without adequate supplies. Several reasons delayed imposing the embargo until the end of the month. One was the British election; another, more important, was the attitude of the United States, the world's largest producer of petroleum. On 9 October, although tentatively approving British support for League oil sanctions, Baldwin's Cabinet understood that their effectiveness depended on American willingness to co-operate.[26] Until early December, Vansittart and Hoare worked vainly for such co-operation.[27]

[22] R. A. Divine, *The Illusion of Neutrality* (Chicago, 1962), 81–121; M. Jonas, *Isolationism in America, 1935–1941* (Ithaca, 1966), 136–68; S. L. Weiss, 'American Foreign Policy and Presidential Power: The Neutrality Act of 1935', *Journal of Politics*, 30(1968), 672–95.

[23] Hoare to Drummond, 31 Aug. 1935, Hoare FO 800/295; Osborne [*chargé d'affaires*, Washington] telegram (212) to Hoare, 22 Aug. 1935, FO 371/18772/7421/3483/45. Cf. Lindsay telegram (203) to Hoare, 14 Aug. 1935, Hoare telegram (235) to Lindsay, 17 Aug. 1935, both *DBFP II*, XIV, 479, 498.

[24] Craigie minute, 20 Sep. 1935, FO 371/18772/7968/45.

[25] Walters, *League*, 652–63.

[26] CC 45(35), 9 Oct. 1935, CAB 23/82. Cf. Sargent to Warren Fisher, 3 Sep. 1935, Treasury memorandum, 26 Aug. 1935, Chamberlain minute, 24 Aug. 1935, all T 172/1838; CID Report on Trade Questions in Time of War [CP 186(35)], 30 Sep. 1935, CAB 24/257.

[27] Bingham memorandum, 8 Oct. 1935, Bingham to Hull, 17 Oct. 1935, both Bingham 1; Feis diary, 23 Oct. 1935, Feis 124; Phillips diary, 9 Oct. 1935, Phillips 8; Craigie

As late as 4 December, with Hoare and Vansittart negotiating secretly with the French, the foreign secretary asked Lindsay one last time whether the Americans would respect League sanctions. Receiving a negative reply, Hoare had no option but to work with Laval.[28] Their 'Plan' was not appeasement. From Britain's vantage-point, given ineffective oil sanctions, the agreement was designed to ensure Anglo-French solidarity and prevent a war with Italy; both were essential to avoid disequilibria in Europe and the Far East. Michael Roi shows that whilst British support of the Plan was 'immoral', such support remained necessary to protect narrow British national interests.

The oil issue was profoundly important to the evolving Anglo-American relationship: it exhumed the old question of belligerent versus neutral rights. Roosevelt wished for Italian defeat. Yet, he could not assist the League because of the neutrality legislation. Just as critical, he knew that influential isolationist senators like Johnson, essential to his domestic recovery programme, wanted no truck with the League. Added to this, there is some truth in the charge made by Roosevelt's critics that, generally, he held the British and French to be no better than the Italians or Germans.[29] Accordingly, Roosevelt pursued an independent policy. On 5 October, before the League acted, he embargoed arms, ammunition, and implements of war to both belligerents.[30] But beyond threatening to publicise the names of Americans who travelled on Italian ships and those of oil companies trading with Italy, he did nothing except ask those companies not to sell their products to Italy.[31] The argument that the 'accord between American and League actions, and the domestic problems it threatened to pose for FDR, disappeared quickly between November 25 and December 12 when France and Britain crippled League actions'[32] is incorrect on two points. From the Anglo-French perspective, there

minute, 8 Oct. 1935, FO 371/18772/8480/3483; Lindsay despatch (1218) to Hoare, 18 Nov. 1935, FO 371/18772/9713/3483; Hoare to Eden, 9 Oct. 1935, Hoare to Runciman, 22 Nov. 1935, both Hoare FO 800/295. Cf. Ashton-Gwatkin memorandum, 'Raw Materials', 7 Sep. 1935, Hoare FO 800/295; BoT memorandum [CP 212(35)], 27 Nov. 1935, CAB 24/257.
[28] Hoare telegram to Lindsay, 4 Dec. 1935, Lindsay telegram to Hoare, 6 Dec. 1935, both *DBFP II*, XV, 377–8, 383–4. Cf. Hoare memorandum, 8 Dec. 1935, Templewood VIII/I.
[29] F. W. Marks III, *Wind Over Sand. The Diplomacy of Franklin Roosevelt* (Athens, GA, 1988), 123–8; Watt, *John Bull*, 80–2.
[30] 'Proclamation', 5 Oct. 1935, *FDRFA*, III, 16.
[31] Cf. Roosevelt telegram to Hull, 10 Oct. 1935, Hull to Roosevelt, 13 Nov. 1935, Roosevelt to Hull, 23 Nov. 1935, *ibid.*, 17–18, 67–8, 90–1; Feis diary, 26, 30 Oct. 1935, both Feis 124. Stimson supported the British: Stimson to Baldwin, 11 Oct. 1935, Baldwin 123.
[32] Dallek, *Roosevelt*, 116.

was no accord. More telling, the Hoare–Laval Plan only became a reality when Roosevelt's government would not embargo oil. At Geneva, Hugh Wilson understood that London acted for balance-of-power reasons: 'the primary impulse of Hoare's decision lay in a sudden realization of the exposed and dangerous isolation of Great Britain if something were not done to bring the States of the League into a sharing of the risk'.[33] Washington lacked Wilson's shrewdness. Short of a full League naval blockade of Italy, which the RN would have to impose on the eve of the impending naval conference, London and Paris fell back upon the Hoare–Laval Plan. In February 1936, the neutrality laws were extended by compelling the president to enforce American embargoes against new belligerents in any conflict.[34] Before this, Vansittart saw clearly that reliance on Powers that did not share Britain's interests was misguided. Afterwards, until its defence deficiencies were met, Britain had to utilise whatever diplomatic means were available to protect its global position.[35]

The first opportunity came when the second London naval conference began on 9 December, the day the press learnt about the Hoare–Laval Plan. Given the 1934 naval conversations, and despite Craigie lobbying the Japanese and Americans in January 1935 about 'a unilateral declaration' of their future building programmes, the possibility of extending the existing quantitative ratios seemed remote. Whilst some Americans like Davis wanted greater Anglo-American co-operation, Roosevelt, Hull, and Swanson were disinclined to make early commitments. Their concern lay with Tokyo's attitudes; and the Japanese refused to make their bargaining position known. On 7 August 1935, the British finally asked the Washington treaty Powers, as well as Germany and Bolshevik Russia, to consider programme declarations as a first step for a new naval conference.[36]

By October, London had concluded that the chances for conserving quantitative limitation remained slim at best. Although Paris sought assurances about Germany honouring the Anglo-German naval agreement before it made specific commitments, and Rome would participate only if all the Powers accepted qualitative limitation,[37] the crucial reactions were those of Washington and Tokyo. The Americans first

---

[33] Wilson to Hull, 16 Dec. 1935, Wilson 3.
[34] Divine, *Neutrality*, 151–8; Jonas, *Isolationism*, 180–4.
[35] Vansittart to Phipps, 20 Dec. 1935, PHPP 2/17.
[36] Hoare despatch (714) to Lindsay, 7 Aug. 1935, enclosing FO memorandum, 2 Aug. 1935, FO 371/18737/6954/22. Cf. FO–Admiralty memorandum, 'Future Course of Naval Negotiations', 18 Jul. 1935, FO 371/18737/6525/22.
[37] Craigie memorandum, 11 Sep. 1935, FO 371/18739/8071/22; 'Memorandum communicated by Italian Embassy', 4 Sep. 1935, FO 371/18739/7833/22.

surmised that London looked to build on the Anglo-German agreement to establish a united European negotiation front that was 'unacceptable to the United States Government'.[38] Although Craigie dispelled these suspicions in private talks with Atherton, Roosevelt's Administration stood firm on three points: it wanted battleship displacement minima of 35,000 tons; it would not eliminate 10,000-ton cruisers with eight-inch guns; and it opposed Japanese claims for parity.[39] For its part, Tokyo demanded acceptance of the 'common upper limit'.[40] On 18 October, as the Abyssinian crisis heated up, the Japanese informed Craigie that they would attend a conference but not declare their building programme.[41] Under Foreign Office pressure, the NCM advised the Cabinet to call a conference.[42] Craigie reckoned there could be 'a qualitative agreement without [Japan], subject to the usual let-out clause'.[43] Vansittart was more direct; if the conference failed, he wanted Japan held responsible and placed in the prisoner's dock of international opinion.[44]

This was the context in which the second London naval conference deliberated until March 1936.[45] Delegations from Britain, the United States, Japan, France, and Italy attended, aware that Germany and Bolshevik Russia would be asked to accede to the treaty. The Japanese immediately sought the 'common upper limit', proposing this be achieved by British and American reductions; as a bargaining tactic, they advocated eliminating aircraft carriers and battleships. When compromise proved impossible, they withdrew on 15 January 1936. Whilst Japan's withdrawal destroyed any possibility of quantitative limitation, it opened the way for productive negotiations by the remaining four Powers. Encased in a treaty initialled on 25 March, their salient achievements were: annual proclamations of building programmes; capital ship displacement fixed at 35,000 tons, with gun calibres reduced from sixteen to fourteen inches contingent upon Japanese – and, later, Italian – acquiescence; aircraft carriers limited to

---

[38] Atherton to Broad [FO American Department], 19 Aug. 1935, FO 371/18738/7286/22.
[39] 'Record of a Meeting', 27 Sep. 1935, FO 371/18739/8361/22.
[40] Japanese *aide-mémoire*, 26 Aug. 1935, *BDFA*, II, E14, 200; Craigie memorandum, 7 Sep. 1935, FO 371/18739/8397/22.
[41] Craigie memorandum, 18 Oct. 1935, with enclosure, FO 371/18740/9070/22.
[42] CC 48(35), 23 Oct. 1935, CAB 23/83; NCM memorandum, 'The Naval Conference, 1935' [CP 201(35)], 11 Oct. 1935, CAB 24/257.
[43] Craigie minute, 5 Oct. 1935, FO 371/18739/8599/22.
[44] Vansittart minute, 4 Oct. 1935, FO 371/18740/8758/22.
[45] M. W. Berg, 'Protecting National Interests by Treaty: The Second London Naval Conference, 1934–1936', in McKercher, *Disarmament*, 203–27; Pelz, *Race*, 159–64; Roskill, *Naval Policy*, II, 284–321.

23,000 tons; cruisers exceeding 10,000 tons banned until 31 December 1942, the end of the treaty; prototype vessels between 10,000 and 17,500 tons prohibited; and an 'escalator' clause 'in case of war' or should building occur 'outside the qualitative limits by non-contracting Powers'.[46] The treaty was not unblemished. The Italians suddenly withdrew at the end of February, ostensibly protesting League sanctions but, really, avoiding encumbrances to their naval construction. Nonetheless, for reasons having little to do with promoting international arms limitation, other Powers – Germany, Poland, Bolshevik Russia, and the Scandinavian states – later signed the treaty.[47]

Subsequent assessments of the conference are two-fold: it showed a Britain weakening relative to the United States, Japan, and changing circumstances in Europe;[48] and the British, chiefly the Foreign Office and NCM, were so devoid of originality that they could not find a workable limitation formula.[49] Neither evaluation rings true. Those responsible for British foreign policy believed by December 1935 that Anglo-American political co-operation in confronting changing international circumstances remained unlikely – oil sanctions remained fresh in British minds. Davis told Craigie in early March 1936 that 'the only argument that would have weight with [Japan's] realistic statesmen was that England and the United States intended to work closely together in naval matters and to allow no misunderstandings to arise between them'.[50] Such sentiments were grist for 'atlanticist' mills in each country. However, Baldwin's government and Roosevelt's Administration each approached the conference intent on protecting their separate narrow national interests. Anglo-American concordance arose as a by-product of disparate policies designed to ensure that neither Power's strategic position in the wider world weakened. Prior to the conference, the British had no delusion that quantitative ratios could continue. This realistic assessment produced the suggestion for programme declarations. It did not mean that Craigie, Chatfield, Vansittart, and the rest abandoned the attempt to find a workable formula. But after the Japanese *démarche* of 18 October, they realised that progress would be slow. Craigie even proposed ambassadorial discussions rather than a full conference. Roosevelt demurred, wanting 'nothing that would make it appear that we are taking this naval conference casually and less

---

[46] Cmd. 5136.
[47] For Hitler's reasons, cf. A. Hillgruber, 'England in Hitlers Aussen-politischer Konzeption', *HZ*, 218(1974), 65–84; Weinberg, *Foreign Policy*, I, 271–2.
[48] Hall, *Arms Control*, 184–92 *passim*.   [49] Pelz, *Race*, 152–64 *passim*.
[50] Craigie memorandum, 4 Mar. 1936, FO 371/19809/2021/4.

seriously than we have taken previous naval conferences and thus run the risk of being blamed for failure'.[51]

British bargaining strategy after December 1935, as before, looked to avoid anything smacking of an Anglo-American front that would adversely affect Anglo-Japanese relations and the Far Eastern balance.[52] Craigie, Chatfield, and Eden worked honestly with Bingham, Davis, Standley, and Phillips, the nominal head of the American delegation; the Americans followed Roosevelt's dictate that London and Washington should co-operate as much as possible. Yet, there was no equivalent of the MacDonald–Stimson axis of six years before. For the British, times had changed: American isolationism seemed stronger than ever; and a post-conference *modus vivendi* with Japan remained crucial for Britain's Far Eastern position. Consequently, whilst the new treaty papered over the cracks in the Anglo-American relationship and had domestic benefits for the National Government so soon after the 'Peace Ballot', it existed as tangible proof that Britain would not sacrifice the RN on the altar of international arms limitation. Despite paper parity, the Americans had yet to build to treaty levels; and, taking into account announced building programmes, the RN retained a rough two-Power standard against the IJN and the new German navy.[53]

In fact, whilst publicly resolving the naval question, the National Government worked behind the scenes to strengthen the British armed forces. Further German rearmament and Japanese naval policy required

---

[51] FO–Admiralty memorandum, 'Course of Naval Negotiations', 11 Oct. 1935, FO 371/ 18740/8758/22; Roosevelt to Bingham, 1 Nov. 1935, *FDRFA*, III, 45–7.

[52] Craigie minute, 5 Nov. 1935, FO 371/18740/9218/22; FO telegram 9(2) to Clive, 6 Jan. 1936, Eden telegram (6) to Lindsay, 10 Jan. 1936, both FO 371/19803/4; Phillips diary, 8, 14 Jan. 1936, Phillips 9.

[53]

	Britain	United States	Japan	Germany
Capital ships				
Battleships and	14 (2)	15 (2)	10	6 (2)
battlecruisers	474,350 tons	464,000 tons	301,400 tons	69,120 tons
Aircraft carriers	5 (3)	4 (3)	4 (2)	(2)
	100,900 tons	92,000 tons	68,370 tons	
Cruisers				
Heavy	13	16 (2)	12 (4)	(3)
	124,250 tons	151,950 tons	107,800 tons	
Light	28 (17)	10 (9)	23 (2)	6
	176,800 tons	70,500 tons	124,255 tons	35,400 tons
Destroyers	143 (38)	187 (52)	109 (26)	30 (22)
	176,025 tons	216,825 tons	126,093 tons	21,330 tons
Submarines	54 (12)	88 (15)	63 (4)	18 (18)
	55,299 tons	74,545 tons	77,167 tons	5,424 tons

The numbers in brackets are vessels building; the tonnages of vessels building are not included. From *Jane's Fighting Ships* (1936).

a reassessment of British defence requirements. On 8 July 1935, the DRC was revived.[54] By November, it had reported twice to the DPR. An 'Interim Report' of 24 July discussed when British forces should be ready for war.[55] There was no unity of opinion. Attempting to see the world from the vantage-point of their German opposites, the COS believed that 1942 seemed likely; Vansittart and Warren Fisher opted for 1939, their argument being that Germany might provoke war 'by miscalculation or political error of judgement'. Thanks to Hoare's lobbying, the DPR endorsed the Vansittart–Warren Fisher assessment.[56] Given European developments and the need to maintain the Far Eastern naval and political balance, the DPR's action meant that the National Government had to go beyond meeting defence deficiencies and expand the armed forces.[57] Circulated on 21 November, the 'Third Report' addressed the nature of this expansion.[58]

Mirroring those in 1933–4, the DRC discussions that produced the 'Third Report' divided into two parts: a narrow one pertaining to the technical side of armed forces expansion – although, now, the dilemma of whether increased taxes or a loan should be used to finance arms spending was addressed; and a broader one about how those forces should be arrayed for home and Imperial defence. And the old pattern re-emerged. Chatfield, Ellington, and Montgomery-Massingberd concentrated on the 'Programme and Requirements' for each branch of the services; backed by Warren Fisher, Vansittart provided the strategic basis for policy.[59] The DRC reaffirmed the need for balanced armed strength. Responding to Hitler's build-up of the *Luftwaffe*, the March 1935 White Paper had modified spending programmes set by the ministerial committee in 1934, weighting them in favour of the RAF. Therefore, the 'Third Report' called for a two-Power naval standard against Japan and Germany; it advocated Army expansion to provide adequate Imperial garrisons, ensure home defence, and 'enable us to honour our international obligations ... [including] the occupation for ourselves and the denial to the enemy of an advanced air base in the Low Countries'; it sought additional air strength to permit operations against Japan, strengthen the Fleet Air Arm, and ensure cover for the

---

[54] Pownall memorandum, 9 Jul. 1935, CAB 16/112.
[55] DRC meetings 13–14, 'Interim Report' [DRC 25], 24 Jul. 1935, *ibid.*
[56] CC 40(35), 24 Jul. 1935, CAB 23/82, DPR meeting 4, 29 Jul. 1935, CAB 16/136.
[57] Vansittart to Hoare, 9, 19 Aug. 1935, Hoare to Eden, 15 Sep. 1935, all Hoare FO 800/ 295.
[58] DRC meetings 15–26 (3 Oct.–14 Nov. 1935), DRC 'Third Report' [DRC 37], 21 Nov. 1935, CAB 16/112.
[59] 'The soldiers, sailors and airmen are gradually beginning to show signs of no longer being the worst pacifists and defeatists in the country': Hoare to Eden, 17 Sep. 1935, Hoare FO 800/295.

continental 'Field Force'.[60] The projected cost by 1 January 1939 was estimated at £239 million; additional spending for upgrading and replacement, another £178.5 million (totalling £417.5 million), was required by the end of 1940. The DRC also recognised that British industry, with regard to both manning and retooling, had to be readied for arms and ancillary production.

The meat of the 1935 deliberations concerned the strategic basis of foreign and defence policy. Unshaken in his conviction about the German threat, Vansittart did not think in purely European terms.[61] '[I am] sure the tendency in the next few years would be for Germany and Japan to draw closer together', he said in July, 'and Japan would take advantage of the complications in Europe to erode our position in the Far East.'[62] By October, with Abyssinia unfolding, his assessment remained unchanged.[63] With Warren Fisher's support, these arguments again showed the strength of a united Foreign Office–Treasury view in bureaucratic struggles over foreign and defence policy. Germany and Japan, in that order of priority, persisted as the principal dangers to international stability and, hence, British security. But Italy now seemed likely to use its Abyssinian success as 'a stepping stone' for greater influence in the Mediterranean. Discounting imminent Italo-German rapprochement, Vansittart guessed that isolated Italy might later help Hitler realise his ambitions in Central and Eastern Europe, especially in Austria. He deprecated COS suggestions that Britain allow Hitler a free hand in these regions; Germany would only strengthen to Britain's detriment. Whilst Britain might co-operate with Germany on particular issues – unmentioned, the naval agreement certainly stood at the fore in his thinking – Hitler had to be deterred from bold actions. Strong British armed forces tied to 'the *Entente*' with France would go far in achieving this goal. But it was impossible to divorce European and Mediterranean questions from Far Eastern problems. Vansittart opined about 'a policy of friendliness towards Japan' backed by a regional military presence to deter Japanese covetousness towards British

---

[60] 'Summary of Conclusions and Recommendations', 'Third Report', 38–44, CAB 16/112. Cf. War Office memorandum, 'Army Requirements' [DRC 28], 2 Oct. 1935, Air Ministry memorandum, 'Royal Air Force Requirements additional to the Expansion of First Line Strength for Home Defence' [DRC 30], 2 Oct. 1935, Admiralty memorandum, 'Naval Requirements' [DRC 33], 9 Oct. 1935, all *ibid.* For balanced analysis of the report, see Gibbs, *Grand Strategy*, 254–68; Post, *Dilemmas*, 107–15.

[61] Cf. I. Colvin, *Vansittart in Office* (London, 1965); A. L. Goldman, 'Two Views of Germany: Nevile Henderson vs. Vansittart and the Foreign Office, 1937–1939,' *BJIS*, 6(1980), 247–77; Post, *Dilemmas*, 107–15; Rose, *Vansittart*.

[62] DRC meeting 14, 19 Jul. 1935, CAB 16/112.

[63] DRC meetings 15–18, 20, 22–4, *ibid.* Vansittart to Hoare, 19 Aug. 1935, Hoare FO 800/295, uses the 'bricks without straw' metaphor.

markets, colonies, and the two South Pacific dominions. Britain should only support League collective security if sanctions gave legal cover to the protection of British strategic or economic interests.

The 'Third Report' reached the Cabinet on 4 December and passed to the DPR(DR), a special DPR sub-committee (Baldwin, Chamberlain, Eden, the service ministers,[64] and Lord Weir, an industrialist tied to the Conservative Party; Vansittart, Warren Fisher, and the COS served as expert advisers). It held nine meetings in January 1936.[65] Abyssinia, Japan's rejection of naval limitation, and uncertainty about Hitler saw the politicians accept most of the DRC's recommendations. They slightly modified DRC budgetary proposals, agreeing to spend £394.5 million (£241 million by 1 January 1939 and £153.5 million by 1 January 1941). However, whilst these amended allocations still constituted significant spending increases,[66] the notion of balanced forces was again deflected. The RN and RAF received most of what the DRC recommended. For instance, the DPR(DR) maintained the RN's two-Power standard *vis-à-vis* Germany and Japan, the heart of the Anglo-German naval agreement. Should this naval equilibrium later be tipped to British disadvantage, the London naval treaty's escalator clause would justify RN expansion. But the 'Field Force', crucial in DRC thinking, would not be augmented by reservists; and strengthening the Territorial Army, estimated at £45 million, would be determined after three years.

Beyond this, the Foreign Office–Treasury view about the direction of foreign policy underpinned by rearmament was not subject to major debate. At the 25 February Cabinet that approved the DRP(DR) report, no difficulties emerged about the strategic basis of policy. The ministers simply made the sensible decision that changes to programmes and requirements might result from 'the priority in which the requirements of the several Services are to be provided in view of the international situation and other factors'.[67] On 13 March, Baldwin appointed a minister, Sir Thomas Inskip, to oversee rearmament. Vigilance towards Germany and Japan remained imperative. Italy might present future problems if its Mediterranean policies affected the transit of the fleet to and from Far Eastern waters. As unreliable as it was –

[64] In the new National Government, Eyres-Monsell, created Viscount Monsell earlier in the year, remained first lord of the Admiralty; Lord Swinton became air minister; and Alfred Duff Cooper became war minister.
[65] See DPR(DR) meetings in CAB 16/123.
[66] DPR(DR) Report [CP 26(36)], 12 Feb. 1936, CAB 24/259. These funds would be added to the totals projected in the 1935 White Paper. The 1936 budget was already established at £124 million: Cmd. 5114.
[67] CC 10(36), 25 Feb. 1936, CAB 23/83.

Laval's fall precipitated a political crisis in Paris – France existed as the principal British ally.

Most striking in these discussions was the absence of any consideration of the United States. Vansittart avoided the American question when painting the diplomatic horizon; neither Warren Fisher nor Chamberlain felt moved to issue anti-American diatribes; and other ministers concentrated on the problems surrounding force levels, paying for them, and co-ordinating industrial capability with the government's defence requirements. The only serious mention of Anglo-American relations came from Chatfield; but rather than defence planning over the next three to five years, his interest touched bargaining tactics on ending quantitative limitation.[68] Still, the new naval treaty prevented an embittering of relations beyond that which had occurred over Abyssinia and oil sanctions. The RN's strength remained undiminished, and Cabinet endorsement of rearmament meant that means were available to amplify that strength. Whereas American neutrality laws might create future problems, fashioning effective deterrence against Germany and Japan, with Italy prowling in the background, was more important.

Such policies were pursued until late 1937 to maintain the European, Mediterranean, and Far Eastern balances of power. This devolved from Vansittart, whose concept of diplomatic strategy was supported by Baldwin and MacDonald. However, the permanent under-secretary's role in the Hoare–Laval Plan produced Foreign Office critics within the government. In a Cabinet held just before Hoare's resignation, Chamberlain charged that 'the Foreign Secretary had been greatly misled by his Staff'.[69] Although Baldwin and MacDonald said nothing, a silence supportive of the permanent officials, Vansittart and his senior advisers had made enemies. Disfavour towards them increased beneath the political surface as a series of new international problems arose following the collapse of the Washington naval treaty and, through Hitler's remilitarisation of the Rhineland, the end of Locarno: maintaining good Anglo-French relations in the face of growing German strength; confronting improved Italo-German relations; seeing anti-Bolshevik regimes in Eastern Europe gravitate towards Berlin; dealing with civil war in Spain; and responding to renewed crisis in China after July 1937. Vansittart had placed men who thought like him – all 'Edwardians' – in leading positions in the Foreign Office: Craigie, Sargent, who became a deputy under-secretary in March 1936, Lancelot Oliphant, an assistant under-secretary, Orde, Lawrence Collier, the head of the Northern

[68] DRC meeting 25, 12 Nov. 1935, CAB 16/112.   [69] CC 56(35), CAB 23/90B.

Department, and Ralph Wigram and William Strang, successive heads of the Central Department. Although differing on diplomatic tactics, these officials endorsed the strategy of maintaining the global balance.[70] For Vansittart, his series of 'Old Adam' papers – 'Old Adam' was the spectre of militarism abroad – were spirited defences of using foreign policy, backed by allies and the economic and military resources of the state, to offset German, Italian, and Japanese threats to the international status quo.[71]

But the Hoare–Laval debacle and the advent of political leaders with a different world-view fostered resistance to the Foreign Office vision of how to meet external threats. Chamberlain increasingly judged that a willingness to meet the legitimate grievances of the totalitarian Powers constituted a better recipe for international peace and security – and, believing in the deterrent value of air power, the cheap defence option, for domestic reform unburdened by avoiding vast expenditure of public funds on arms.[72] Other ministers shared his belief, chiefly Hoare after his return to the Cabinet as first lord of the Admiralty in April 1936. As late as March 1937, he warned Chamberlain about the Foreign Office's pro-French attitudes preventing productive dialogue with Hitler and Mussolini.[73] But the most important critic of the 'Edwardian' Foreign Office establishment came from within. Just thirty-eight when appointed foreign secretary, Eden believed, as his approach to Abyssinia showed, that collective security could better eliminate threats to international stability.[74] Such attitudes had suffused his disarmament work from 1931 to 1933 and, thereafter, as the minister responsible for League affairs. 'The [League] experiment might have appeared hazardous, but it aroused brave hopes for me also', he later recorded. 'It seemed an

---

[70] Cf. Collier minute, 20 Feb. 1935, FO 371/19460/927/135; Collier memorandum, 16 May 1935, VNST I/2/21; Orde minute, 16 Feb. 1934, FO 371/18176/823/316; Orde memorandum, 12 Feb. 1935, FO 371/19460/927/135; Sargent memorandum, 17 Jan. 1935, FO 371/18825/1009/55; Sargent minute, 9 Jan. 1936, FO 371/20338/479/20; Wigram memorandum, 29 Mar. 1935, FO 371/18825/1090/55; Wigram 'Note on Interim Report', 16 Jul. 1935, *DBFP II*, XIII, 524–5.
[71] For examples of three Vansittart memoranda, see 'An Aspect of International Relations in 1931', 1 May 1931, FO 371/15205/3277/321/61; 'The Crisis in Europe' [CP 52(33)], 2 Mar. 1933, CAB 24/239; 'The World Situation and British Rearmament', 31 Dec. 1936, FO 371/19949/8998/8998/18.
[72] CC 31(36), 29 Apr. 1936, CC 39(36), 27 May 1936, CC 40(36), 9 May 1936, all CAB 23/84. Cf. Warren Fisher to Chamberlain, 15 Sep. 1936, NC 7/11/29/19. See D. Dilks, '"We Must Hope for the Best and Prepare for the Worst": The Prime Minister, the Cabinet and Hitler's Germany, 1937–1939', *Proceedings of the British Academy*, 73(1987), 309–52; D. Reynolds, *The Creation of the Anglo-American Alliance 1937–1941: A Study in Competitive Cooperation* (Chapel Hill, 1982), 8–9.
[73] Hoare to Chamberlain, 17 Mar. 1937, NC 7/11/30/74.
[74] On his world-view, see A. Eden, *Foreign Affairs* (1939), 54–61. Cf. S. Aster, *Anthony Eden* (1976), 16–35; A. R. Peters, *Anthony Eden at the Foreign Office 1931–1938*, 1–20.

opportunity to escape from a balance of power, which had failed to keep the peace [before 1914], to an international authority which might have the collective strength to do so.'[75] He also chafed at Vansittart's dominance in policy-making, which translated into criticism of the permanent under-secretary's diplomatic style:

[Vansittart] clearly saw the growing military power and political ambition of Nazi Germany as the principal danger. To meet this he was determined to keep the rest of Europe in line against Germany, and would pay almost any price to do so ... he expressed himself with such repetitive fervour that all except those who agreed with him were liable to discount his views as too extreme.[76]

As London confronted new international difficulties, the traditional methods of meeting them began to be questioned.

In this process, until late 1937, the Anglo-American relationship affected the evolution of British global strategy. It found tangible expression in two crises: the Spanish civil war and Japan's renewed attempt to extend its empire in China. On 18 July 1936, Spanish Army commanders in Morocco rebelled against their government.[77] Antagonistic towards the socialist policies and anti-clerical bent of the left-wing regime in Madrid, the insurgents sought to engineer a *coup d'état* to establish ultra-rightist order in the country. Despite early successes and winning control of western mainland Spain by the end of the year, the rebels were denied victory. With the Basques in the north and the Catalans in the east joining forces loyal to the government, the war became one of attrition marked by brutality on each side. And the struggle adopted ideological hues. Bolshevik Russia supported the 'Loyalists'; the Italians and Germans backed the 'Nationalists', led by the pro-fascist general, Francisco Franco. Amongst the Powers, this war proved emotive for the public who cared about politics, polarising opinion along partisan lines and producing a range of writings and motion pictures stark in their portrayal of good and evil on both sides.[78] A diverse group of British and American writers, including George Orwell, Graham Greene, Ernest Hemingway, and Lillian Hellman, saw the Spanish conflict as a defining moment in international politics. Hemingway had the protagonist of his novel *For Whom the Bell Tolls* say: 'as long as we can hold them here we keep the fascists tied up. They

[75] Earl of Avon, *Facing the Dictators* (1962), 8.
[76] *Ibid.*, 242–3.
[77] P. Preston, *The Coming of the Spanish Civil War. Reform, Reaction and Revolution in the Second Republic 1931–1936* (1978); H. Thomas, *The Spanish Civil War*, 2nd edn (1977).
[78] Cf. F. R. Benson, *Writers in Arms. The Literary Impact of the Spanish Civil War* (New York, 1967); T. Christensen, *Reel Politics. American Political Movies from* Birth of a Nation *to* Platoon (New York, 1987), 56–8.

can't attack any other country until they finish with us and they can never finish with us.'[79] Orwell, whose service with Loyalist forces saw an early idealism tarnished by the realities of combat, remarked that this 'war, in which I played so ineffectual a part, has left me with memories that are mostly evil'.[80]

For Britain's foreign-policy-making elite, emotional responses were inimical both to general European peace and British strategic interests in the western Mediterranean. Whilst some opposition MPs sympathised with the Loyalists, Hoare's remark 'that he hoped for a war in which the Fascists and Bolsheviks would kill each other off' exemplies the general attitude of the Cabinet and Foreign Office.[81] Still, facing the reality of armed struggle on the Continent, the British aim throughout the crisis – it ended in March 1939 with Nationalist victory – involved preventing the fighting from escalating into a general European war. In practical terms, this meant fostering a policy of non-intervention.[82] Despite desires to support the legitimate regime in Madrid, the new French government, the 'Popular Front' of leftist parties led by a socialist, Léon Blum, was convinced by Eden to underwrite non-intervention; by late August, Berlin, Rome, and Moscow also accepted the principle.[83] This, however, constituted a diplomatic placebo: Italy and Germany clandestinely supplied Franco with arms and 'volunteers'; Mussolini and Hitler recognised the Nationalist government in November 1936; and Russian aid prevented a Loyalist collapse in December. As the war stretched into 1937, the British did not waver. Restraint was essential, despite Nationalist blockades of Loyalist ports, the bombing of Guernica, a Basque city, by German 'volunteers', and attacks on neutral merchantmen in the Mediterranean by unmarked Italian aircraft and submarines. By September 1937, a conference at Nyon, boycotted by Italy and Germany because Bolshevik Russia attended, produced agreement about defending sea routes by armed

---

[79] E. Hemingway, *For Whom the Bell Tolls* (New York, 1940), 432.
[80] G. Orwell, *Homage to Catalonia* (1951 [orig. 1939]), 247. Cf. J. Fyrth, *The Signal was Spain: The Spanish Aid Movement in Britain, 1936–1939* (1986).
[81] W. N. Medlicott, *British Foreign Policy Since Versailles, 1919–1963*, 2nd edn (1968), 150. Such sentiments were shared by that critic of National Government foreign policy, Winston Churchill; see Churchill to Eden, 7 Aug. 1936, Eden FO 954/27/SP/36/8.
[82] M. Alpert, 'Humanitarianism and Politics in the British Response to the Spanish Civil War, 1936–1939', *European History Quarterly*, 14(1984), 423–40; J. Edwards, *The British Government and the Spanish Civil War, 1936–1939* (1979).
[83] D. Blumé, 'Contribution à l'histoire de la politique de la non-intervention (en Espagne): documents inédits de Léon Blum', *Cahiers de Léon Blum* (1977–8), 5–93; D. Carlton, 'Eden, Blum and the Origins of Non-Intervention', *JCH*, 6(1971), 40–55.

force.[84] Thereafter, the situation stabilised outside of Spain, whilst the struggle inside continued.

Anglo-American relations were not strained by London's advocacy of non-intervention, or by non-intervention allowing Italo-German support for Franco to enervate slowly Loyalist military muscle. Some American radicals censured the failure of western Powers to assist a democratically elected government.[85] Claude Bowers, the American minister in Spain, resented what he saw as condonation of fascist aggression.[86] However, non-intervention commended itself to Roosevelt. Like British leaders, he wanted to prevent the fighting in Spain from escalating into a general war; and domestic considerations loomed large in White House thinking. During the first months of the Spanish crisis, the 1936 presidential election, scheduled for 3 November, imposed itself on Roosevelt. It became necessary to flourish before voters his support for neutrality. In mid-August, he declared:

We can keep out of war if those who watch and decide have a sufficiently detailed understanding of international affairs to make certain that the small decisions of each day do not lead toward war and if, at the same time, they possess the courage to say 'no' to those who selfishly or unwisely would get us into war.[87]

Accordingly, he blocked export licences for Nationalist arms purchases, lobbied pacifist leaders about his opposition to war, and suggested to the *New York Times* that following the election he might call a meeting of 'the heads of the most important nations in an effort to assure the peace of the world'.[88] After 3 November, whilst a conference proved elusive, his resolution to avoid involvement in Spanish affairs continued.[89] Hull stressed Roosevelt's domestic success: 'Isolationists approved because we were keeping aloof from the conflict. Internationalists approved because we were cooperating with Britain and France.'[90]

The British became concerned over what the neutrality laws portended should they become embroiled in armed conflict. On 1 May 1937, Congress extended the existing statutes indefinitely. Still forbidding American travel on belligerent ships and proscribing loans and selling munitions, the new bill contained two amendments: the

---

[84] P. Gretton, 'The Nyon Conference – the Naval Aspect', *EHR*, 90(1975), 103–12.
[85] Thomas [American socialist] to Roosevelt, 31 Aug. 1936, *FDRFA*, III, 408–9; N. Thomas, 'In Defense of Free Spain', *New Masses*, 20(8 Sep. 1936).
[86] C. Bowers, *My Mission to Spain: Watching the Rehearsal for World War II* (New York, 1954). Cf. Bowers to Hull, 11 Aug, 23 Sep. 1936, both Hull 39; Bowers to Roosevelt, 26 Aug. 1936, Roosevelt PSF Spain 1936.
[87] Roosevelt speech, 14 Aug. 1936, *FDRFA*, III, 377–83.
[88] Dallek, *Roosevelt*, 128–30.
[89] Roosevelt memorandum, 3 Jul. 1937, *FDRFA*, IV, 32.   [90] Hull, *Memoirs*, I, 479.

president could invoke neutrality in a foreign civil war if selling arms to either side endangered American interests; and foreign belligerents could buy American non-military products with hard currency and carry them away in non-American merchantmen. The former was Roosevelt's response to domestic disquiet about Spain; for the State Department, the latter, the 'cash and carry' provision, would 'relieve our Government of the duty of sponsoring claims for the loss of cargoes, and ... it will relieve it of the duty of sponsoring claims for the loss of American ships'.[91] Whilst the Foreign Office and CID saw that Britain could draw upon the American market in wartime given RN strength and the predominance of British merchant shipping, renewing the neutrality legislation still meant that Washington might not assist Britain or its allies in a moment of crisis.[92]

By March 1937, Anglo-American relations at the highest political levels were exceptionally good after Chamberlain and Henry Morgenthau, Roosevelt's Treasury secretary, co-operated to meet a devaluation of the franc. '[T]he Americans are as pleased as Punch at the way I have kept them au fait', Chamberlain told his sister, 'and Morgenthau triumphantly declares that this shows how the two Treasuries can work together ... for the common good.'[93] In fact, the British and the Americans were in the midst of negotiations to liberalise their trade. This obtained from Hull who, following the World Economic Conference, pursued a diplomacy to lower tariffs by bilateral agreements. He reckoned that easier access to markets and raw materials would lessen the chance of war by reviving the international economy.[94] In June 1934, his efforts saw Congress pass the Trade Agreements Act, authorising the president to conclude agreements with other Powers for reducing specific duties by as much as 50 per cent. Desultory conversations through Lindsay and Bingham's embassies followed, but progress proved difficult. Hull, Feis, and others in Washington railed at the Ottawa preferences; Leith-Ross, Runciman, and John Troutbeck, the head of the Foreign Office American Department, rankled at Hull's criticisms of moderate British protection.[95] Suggestions of British

[91] Moore to Roosevelt, 4 Mar. 1937, *FDRFA*, IV, 321–2.
[92] Troutbeck minute, 22 Jun. 1937, Cadogan [deputy under-secretary] minute, 23 Jun. 1937, both FO 371/20666/3992/448.
[93] Chamberlain to Hilda, 13 Mar. 1937, NC 18/1/998. Cf. Feis to Butterworth [US Embassy, London], 26 Feb. 1937, Feis 11; Morgenthau to Hull, 3 Mar. 1937, Klotz [Treasury] to Hull, 8 Mar. 1937, both Hull 40.
[94] D. F. Drummond, 'Cordell Hull', in N. Graebner, ed., *An Uncertain Tradition: American Secretaries of State in the Twentieth Century* (New York, 1961), 184–209; A. W. Schatz, 'The Anglo-American Trade Agreement and Cordell Hull's Search for Peace, 1936–1938', *JAH*, 57(1970), 85–103.
[95] Cf. Hull memoranda [conversations with Lindsay], 28 Nov. 1934, 4 Apr. 1935,

hypocrisy in this diplomacy – refusing to surrender advantages but demanding American concessions[96] – are misleading. As a senior State Department official told the anglophobe Moffat: 'I cannot myself see that we are in much of a position to throw stones at Empire preference, in view of our own course [Smoot–Hawley] prior to the present administration.'[97] By early 1937, given Abyssinia, the Rhineland, and the Spanish civil war, Foreign Office officials and leading Cabinet ministers saw trade negotiations as means to strengthen transatlantic ties and augment British diplomatic strength. In March, Lindsay advised, 'a trade agreement is the only important active measure that we can take to predispose America favourably in the manner we desire'.[98]

Trade discussions had become more serious by early 1937 because the British recognised that whilst the Americans might be ignored in defence calculations, little would be gained in fostering needless political strains. In January, Runciman travelled privately to Washington and, meeting Roosevelt and others, discussed exchanging information on military matters and other political issues.[99] But American neutrality could not be ignored. Baldwin's government wanted to avoid undue optimism about Anglo-American co-operation in non-economic matters.[100] Roosevelt and his advisers worried that substantial arms spending by the European Powers and Japan would undermine trade recovery – pressure on the franc had occurred partly as a result of Blum's government seeking a loan to underwrite French rearmament. However, given trade discussions and collaboration over the franc – an American perception of Britain based on economic and financial issues – Morgenthau won Roosevelt's permission to ask Chamberlain 'if he has any suggestions to make as to how we can keep the world from going financially broke due to constant increased cost of armaments?'[101] This approach was doubly important as Baldwin had announced his decision to retire, and Chamberlain was to succeed him in May.

22 Jan., 22 Oct. 1936, all Hull 58; Feis to Butterworth, 2 May 1934, 16 Mar. 1935, 28 Aug. 1936, all Feis 11; Leith-Ross to Boothby [Conservative MP], 8 Jan. 1935, Leith-Ross T 188/300; Troutbeck to Waley, 8 Oct. 1936, T 160/750;

[96] I. Drummond and N. Hillmer, *Negotiating Freer Trade. The United Kingdom, the United States, Canada, and the Trade Agreements of 1938* (Waterloo, Ont., 1989), 41.
[97] Miller to Moffat, 21 Oct. 1936, Moffat 11.
[98] Lindsay to Eden, 17 Mar. 1937, Eden FO 954/29/US/37/1.
[99] R. A. Harrison, 'The Runciman Visit to Washington in January 1937: Presidential Diplomacy and the Non-Commercial Implications of Anglo-American Trade Negotiations', *CJH*, 19(1984), 217–39.
[100] Early [Roosevelt's secretary] memorandum, 26 Jan. 1937, Roosevelt PSF GB.
[101] Morgenthau diary, 9 Feb. 1937, in J. M. Blum, ed., *From the Morgenthau Diaries*, vol. I: *Years of Crisis, 1928–1938* (Boston, 1959), 458.

Morgenthau's query was delivered orally through a British diplomat who was returning to London – wanting nothing in writing, Roosevelt and Morgenthau asked that Chamberlain be told that only they knew about the enquiry.[102] Chamberlain welcomed an opportunity of 'giving an appreciation of the European situation & showing what [the] U.S.A. can do to help'.[103] He responded with a memorandum drafted in the Foreign Office.[104] In anodyne language, Morgenthau was informed that the sources of danger in Europe were 'both political and economic and it is sometimes difficult to disentangle them from one another'. Britain laid the responsibility on Germany's 'desire to make herself so strong that no-one will venture to withstand whatever demands she may make whether for European or colonial territory'. Chamberlain added:

It is because of the belief that British forces would be available against German aggression that British rearmament plans have been welcomed by so many nations in Europe with a sigh of relief, and if they still feel anxious, their anxiety arises from their doubts whether this country's rearmament will be adequate or will be completed in time to act as a deterrent to German ambitions.

Roosevelt and Morgenthau were also instructed on the Far Eastern balance being connected to that in Europe. Germany and Japan had concluded an 'anti-Comintern' pact in November 1936. Echoing Vansittart's long-standing worry, Chamberlain argued: 'Anything therefore which would tend to stabilise the position in the Far East would *pro tanto* ease our position there and safeguard us against added embarrassment in the event of trouble in Europe.' Pointing to restrictions in the 1935 neutrality laws against both aggressors and victims alike, he thought more good would be accomplished if the president received wider latitude 'to deal with each case on its merits'. Acknowledging that the reconsideration of the neutrality laws constituted 'a matter of domestic controversy', Chamberlain believed that 'in view of Mr. Morgenthau's request for the Chancellor's views he has thought that the U.S.A. Government would wish to have them expressed without reserve'.

Roosevelt and Morgenthau could do little beyond amending the 1937 neutrality laws by the 'cash and carry' provisions. Congress and public opinion constrained presidential flexibility. More importantly, despite co-operating over issues like the franc, London and Washington had

---

[102] Bewley, 'Record ... of a conversation with Mr. H. Morgenthau', 23 Feb. 1937, *DBFP II*, XVIII, 279–81.
[103] Chamberlain to Hilda, 13 Mar. 1937, NC 18/1/998.
[104] Eden to Chamberlain, 5 Mar. 1937, with enclosure, Woods [Treasury] to Harvey [Eden's private secretary], 11 Mar. 1937, with enclosure, Eden to Chamberlain, 13 Mar. 1937, Chamberlain to Eden, 15 Mar. 1937, all *DBFP II*, XVIII, 348–52, 381–8, 415–16, 428. A copy of Chamberlain's memorandum, n.d., is in Roosevelt PSF GB.

differing conceptions about how to preserve international security. The Americans reckoned that economic initiatives would reduce friction; the British believed in policies of deterrence backed by armed strength. Any chance to resolve these disparate views vanished in the summer;[105] this included the admittedly slim possibility of Chamberlain visiting Washington, a project promoted by Norman Davis.[106] On 7 July 1937, at the Marco Polo Bridge near Peking, the Japanese provoked a crisis with China and sent their armies south of the Great Wall to destroy Chiang Kai-shek's government, weaken Western influence in that country, and add more territory, population, and resources to their empire.[107]

The period in the Far East from the Tangku truce to the Marco Polo Bridge incident was one of equilibrium amongst Britain, Japan, and China. But stability did not signal a lack of diplomatic manoeuvring; for Britain, this entailed looking for a *modus vivendi* with Japan whilst fostering Kuomintang friendship – a strong Kuomintang government would better safeguard British trading interests. Thanks to the DRC, the British were 'showing a tooth' in the region by strengthening Singapore and ensuring rough RN–IJN equivalency. The Japanese, conversely, worked to undermine Western influence in China and enfeeble Kuomintang authority. In May and June 1935, after an ultimatum from Tokyo, Kuomintang political and military authorities were withdrawn from the five northernmost provinces; Japan then undertook to establish pliant administrations *à la* Manchukuo.

Beneath these currents lay the American question. By early 1935, the Chinese economy had worsened as a consequence of rising silver bullion prices. A year earlier, American politicians from silver-producing states had lobbied to raise silver prices. It produced legislation in June 1934 compelling United States Treasury purchases of domestic and foreign silver to maintain a quarter of American monetary stocks in the precious metal.[108] Silver prices inflated and, with China on the silver standard, there were outflows of Chinese bullion to America. China's prices appreciated, Chinese trade weakened whilst a depression gripped the

---

[105] Welles to Roosevelt, 27 May 1937, enclosing memorandum for Chamberlain, n.d., Roosevelt memorandum, 28 Apr. [but May] 1937, both Roosevelt PSF GB.

[106] Davis to Chamberlain, 10 Jun. 1937, with Troutbeck and Vansittart minutes, both 23 Jun. 1937, FO 371/20661/4412/228; Eden telegram to Lindsay, 24 Jun. 1937, Eden FO 954/29/US/37/16; Roosevelt minute on Hull to Roosevelt, 29 Jun. 1937, Hull 41.

[107] A. D. Coox, 'The Kwantung Army Dimension', in P. Duus *et al.*, *The Japanese Informal Empire in China, 1895–1937* (Princeton, 1989), 395–428; Crowley, *Japan's Quest*, 301–78.

[108] P. S. Ghosh, 'Passage of the Silver Purchase Act of 1934: The China Lobby and the Issue of China Trade', *Indian Journal of American Studies*, 6(1976), 18–29.

country, and Chiang's government scrambled to prevent its currency from collapsing. Chinese officials looked for loans in New York and London; British trading interests, chiefly from Hong Kong and Shanghai, pressured the National Government to protect their investments and, by extrapolation, Britain's general East Asian position.[109] On 31 December 1934, Chiang's government proposed a consortium loan of £20 million to resuscitate China's economy.

In London, the matter assumed a political tint. The Treasury reckoned 'that any loan or credit must form part of a reasonable scheme of currency reform, including a link with sterling and a fixed rate of exchange to correct the balance of [Chinese] payments'. But unilateral British action proved impossible. Because of Washington's unwillingness to lower silver prices or help underwrite a loan, Treasury–Foreign Office division arose over what policy to pursue. Worried about trade and investment in China, the Treasury argued that Anglo-Japanese co-operation could reverse China's economic fortunes and, politically, help restrain Japan from using its military strength to rearrange Chinese affairs to Britain's detriment.[110] The Foreign Office countered that Anglo-Japanese collaboration would rebound unfavourably on the Far Eastern balance: Chinese opinion would be inflamed; Washington would react unfavourably; and Russia, important for both the East Asian and European balances, would be suspicious if Britain aligned with its principal Far Eastern adversary.[111]

It took five months for the British to determine their response. Delay came partly from European problems relating to Stresa; the rest obtained from how to balance British, American, and Japanese interests. Finding that balance became the goal of the PEJ. On 4 June, it made two decisions: first, as a sop to Chinese nationalism, the British Embassy would move to Nanking, Chiang's capital; second, Leith-Ross would go to China as the temporary financial expert in the embassy.[112] Leith-Ross' mission proved successful in reorganising the Chinese currency and in exploring means for a new loan – he reported in June 1936;[113] it also demonstrated to Tokyo that London would not acquiesce to Amau's claim about Japan's sole guardianship in East Asia. However, in searching for a financial *modus vivendi* with Japan, Leith-

---

[109] Borg, *Far Eastern Crisis*, 121–2; Trotter, *East Asia*, 133–5.
[110] Fergusson minute for Chamberlain, 15 Jan. 1935, Warren Fisher minute for Chamberlain, 21 Jan. 1935, both T 172/1831. Waley memorandum, 15 Jan. 1935, *ibid.*, calculated British investment in China at £300 million.
[111] Collier–Ashton-Gwatkin memorandum, 7 Jan. 1935, Orde memorandum, 7 Jan. 1935, both *DBFP II*, XX, 381–8.
[112] PEJ conclusions (18 Feb., 14 May, 4 Jun.), CAB 27/596.
[113] Leith-Ross, 'Financial Mission to China', 4 Sep. 1936, Appendix, CAB 27/596.

Ross failed.[114] Treasury–Foreign Office division – the Treasury was prepared to call Tokyo's bluff – prevented a resolute response to Japanese ambitions. From June 1936 to July 1937, Anglo-Japanese relations oscillated between poor and not so poor. Anti-British feelings emerged in Japan, for instance, after the signature of the anti-Comintern pact. Along with Tokyo's naval aspirations, these events were compounded by a Japanese economic offensive in traditional British markets and strong British efforts to protect India, Australia, and other markets by tariffs.[115] By early 1937, however, the Japanese ambassador at London, Yoshida Shigeru, was canvassing the Foreign Office about a possible rapprochement. Although the Foreign Office warily approached this overture,[116] it suggested that Far Eastern stability might be possible, the more so as RN manoeuvres at Singapore in February highlighted a reassertion of British strength.

During this period, Roosevelt's Administration refused active involvement in Far Eastern affairs. True, it continued Stimson's doctrine of non-recognition. But beyond this, Washington lacked the will to use its influence to help contain Japanese zeal. It refused to staunch the outflow of Chinese silver; it pressed forward over Philippine independence; Roosevelt prevented Morgenthau from meeting Leith-Ross in Canada on the latter's journey to the Far East on the specious grounds that Leith-Ross was too junior an official; the Treasury and State departments quarrelled over whether to support the Chinese loan; and the USN did not build to its allotted level allowed under the existing naval treaties.[117] Low-level contacts had occurred to establish some kind of Anglo-American co-operation in both Europe and the Far East – some fostered by the Foreign Office, some by Roosevelt. These never amounted to much because, when difficulty emerged, Washington backed off supporting Britain and its confederates. Through a dialectical

---

[114] Cf. V. Rothwell, 'The Mission of Sir Fredrick Leith-Ross to the Far East, 1935–1936', *HJ*, 18(1975), 147–69; Trotter, *East Asia*, 148–87 *passim*.

[115] S. L. Endicott, *Diplomacy and Enterprise: British China Policy, 1933–1937* (Vancouver, 1975); J. Osterhammel, 'Imperialism in Transition: British Big Business and the Chinese Authorities, 1931–1937', *China Quarterly*, 98(1984), 250–86; Shimizu, *Trade Rivalry.*

[116] S. O. Agbi, 'The Foreign Office and Yoshida's Bid for Rapprochement with Britain in 1936–1937: A Critical Reconsideration of the Anglo-Japanese Conversations', *HJ*, 21(1978), 173–9.

[117] On silver, Hull memorandum, 2 Oct. 1934, *FRUS 1934*, II, 443–5. On the Philippines, Roosevelt to Swanson, 3 May 1935, *FDRFA*, II, 495–6; Grew diary, 7 Dec. 1935, Grew 75. On Morgenthau–Leith-Ross meeting, Roosevelt to Bingham,, 11 Jul. 1935, Roosevelt PSF Bingham. On the loan, Roosevelt to Morgenthau, 6 Dec. 1934, *FDRFA*, II, 305–6; Blum, *Morgenthau Diaries*, 211–20. On the USN, see Appendix C in Roskill, *Naval Policy*, I, 584; between 1935 and 1937, there were no appropriations for destroyers and above.

process known only to himself, Roosevelt justified American policy by arguing that he was waiting for London to make the first move. In July 1935, he told Bingham: 'Many years ago I came to the reluctant conclusion that it is a mistake to make advances to the British Government; practical results can be accomplished only when they make the advances themselves.'[118] Subsequent British openings to Washington over oil sanctions, Chinese silver, and the Leith-Ross mission, plus gentle nudging over the neutrality laws, only confirmed London's perceptions about American isolationism that had been forming since before the World Economic Conference.

Yet, by early 1937, even Chamberlain seemed prepared to find a basis for Anglo-American political co-operation to deter Japan. He had amended the Foreign Office draft reply to Morgenthau's enquiry by proposing 'a Regional Pact in the Far East in which our two countries would join with China, Japan, and the U.S.S.R. in guaranteeing the territorial status quo'.[119] The Foreign Office objected: '[American] contemplated withdrawal from the Philippines is an indication of their determination to be free of entanglements even in the Far East – and to ask them something that we cannot hope that they will give might be, I suggest, unwise.' Nonetheless, Eden remained:

alive to the necessity of doing everything that may be possible to prevent Japan causing additional complications for us at a time when we might be involved in trouble in Europe, and if we can get the United States Government to take a practical interest in the Far East and to discuss with us and the Japanese an alignment of our respective policies there, that will be as much as I think we can hope to get from them, and would in fact constitute a considerable deterrent and warning to Japan.

The opportunity to do so arose after the Marco Polo Bridge incident. The ensuing crisis escalated incrementally.[120] Intransigence in the two Far Eastern capitals prevented a peaceful solution pressed by Eden and the Foreign Office; by late July, following the withdrawal of Kuomintang forces, the Japanese army had extended its control in the region around Tientsin and Peking. A relative calm ensued until 17 August when, echoing the Manchurian crisis in 1931–2, Sino-Japanese tensions saw the outbreak of fighting in Shanghai. Whereas British economic and trading interests in northern China were minimal, those in the south were substantial. On 13 September, Chiang's government approached

---

118 Roosevelt to Bingham, 11 Jul. 1935, Roosevelt PSF Bingham.
119 Woods [Treasury] to Harvey [Eden's private secretary], 11 Mar. 1937, with enclosure, Eden to Chamberlain, 13 Mar. 1937, both *DBFP II*, XVIII, 381–5, 415–16.
120 Cf. Lee, *Sino-Japanese War*, 23–49; P. Lowe, *Great Britain and the Origins of the Pacific War. A Study of British Policy in East Asia 1937–1941* (Oxford, 1977), 14–32.

Geneva where, under British pressure, its appeal was directed to a standing Far Eastern Advisory Committee rather than the Council or Assembly – following Abyssinia, London believed that American support for League sanctions would not be forthcoming. On 5 October, the Advisory Committee issued two reports. Thanks to British guidance, neither report pilloried Japan as an 'aggressor', although the Committee sympathised with China and found Japan's reaction excessive given the minor nature of the Marco Polo Bridge incident. A crucial recommendation supported an Australian proposal made in late September: a conference of the Washington nine-Power signatories to find a settlement.[121] After nettled diplomacy, it was agreed that such a conference should convene at Brussels in early November.

British policy during these months looked to arrange a negotiated settlement by mediating between Tokyo and Nanking. With rearmament incomplete, using armed force to re-establish the pre-July 1937 status quo could not be entertained.[122] And, anyway, as Vansittart, Warren Fisher, and the COS had been arguing since November 1933, a military engagement in East Asia would simply encourage Germany to rearrange the European balance in its favour. However, Britain could not countenance a rapprochement when Japan threatened Britain's strategic and economic interests in China. Following Foreign Office advice, Chamberlain's new Cabinet broke off the Eden–Yoshida discussions.[123] Although junior Foreign Office officials and diplomats divided over culpability for the initial clash of arms, senior officials like Cadogan, recently appointed deputy under-secretary after three years as ambassador in China, held Tokyo responsible.[124] Events surrounding Shanghai and the wounding of Cadogan's successor at Nanking, Sir Hughe Knatchbull-Hugessen, in a Japanese air attack on his car, accentuated Foreign Office anti-Japanese feelings.

It has been suggested that until late September, Britain lacked 'a comprehensive, as opposed to a day-to-day, response to Japan's actions in China'.[125] This is disingenuous. Once fighting in northern China

[121] Walters, *League*, 735–6.
[122] COS memorandum, 'Far East Appreciation, 1937' [COS 591], 1 Jun. 1937, CAB 53/32.
[123] Eden telegram to Dodds [British Embassy, Tokyo], 12 Jul. 1937, *BDFA*, II, E16, 81–2.
[124] On divisions, see Knatchbull-Hugessen diary, 25 Jul. 1937, KNAT 1/11; Thomas [FO Far Eastern Department] minute, 1 Sep. 1937, FO 371/21039/5864/233; Orde minute, 29 Jul. 1937, FO 371/20951/4562/9; Piggott [British military *attaché*, Tokyo] despatch to Craigie, 8 Sep. 1937, FO 371/21029/7662/28. On Cadogan, see Cadogan minute, 14 Jul. 1937, FO 371/20950/4130/9; Cadogan minute, 1 Nov. 1937, FO 371/21040/8754/414. Cf. Knatchbull-Hugessen to Cadogan, 22 May 1937, KNAT 2/64.
[125] Lee, *Sino-Japanese War*, 49.

threatened to disrupt the Far Eastern equilibrium, Chamberlain, Eden, and the Foreign Office looked to end hostilities quickly and preserve as much Chinese sovereignty as possible. With armed intervention impossible, political involvement – mediation – existed as the only effective response. But this diplomacy hinged on American support for a unified front that went beyond toothless declarations like 'non-recognition'. From mid-July to late August, London pressed Washington to help arrange a negotiated settlement. Whilst American policy mirrored that of Britain (sympathy for China's predicament despite any guilt that Chiang's regime bore for the escalation of the fighting, whilst avoiding an outright breach with Japan[126]), the British laboured vainly to achieve even the pretence of Anglo-American unity. Some glimmers of promise appeared, notably a Bingham proposal in mid-July for joint economic pressures on Tokyo. Although the British were equally reluctant to impose sanctions against Japan, Eden thought Bingham's suggestion might be transformed into an Anglo-American political front.[127] In July and August, he supported at least four separate approaches to Washington to help urge restraint on Tokyo. Each was rebuffed.[128] Hull argued that 'liberalizing the international economic situation' would be more effective than armed force in preserving peace – this reflected private American criticisms about British economic foreign policy being autarkic.[129] Lindsay's embassy also learnt that Washington would pursue separate but 'parallel action'.

In early September, a special Cabinet committee confirmed that increasing RN strength in Far Eastern waters spelled danger for Britain's strategic interests in the Mediterranean – the Nyon conference was about to meet.[130] Roosevelt had written to Chamberlain on 28 July to delay Davis' proposal for a prime ministerial visit until the diplomatic

---

[126] Hull memorandum [conversation with Japanese ambassador], 12 Jul. 1937, Roosevelt to Kung [Kuomintang finance minister], n.d. [but 2 Aug. 1937], both Roosevelt PSF Japan; Hornbeck memorandum, 31 Jul. 1937, Hornbeck 456; Moffat [now head, European Division, State Department] to Davis, 8 Sep. 1937, Moffat 12.

[127] Eden telegram to Lindsay, 21 Jul. 1937, Eden FO 954/29/US/37/17.

[128] Eden telegram to Lindsay, 13 Jul. 1937, FO 371/20950/4086/9; Lindsay telegram to Eden, 14 Jul. 1937, FO 371/20950/4087/9; Eden telegram to Lindsay, 20 Jul. 1937, FO 371/20950/4130/9; Lindsay to Eden, 21 Jul. 1937, FO 371/20950/4317/9; Eden memorandum [conversation with Bingham], 28 Jul. 1937, FO 371/20951/4620/9; Hull memorandum [conversation with Chalkley], 9 Aug. 1937, Hull 58; Eden to British Embassy, Washington, 30 Aug. 1937, FO 371/20954/9; Mallet [counsellor] telegram to Eden, 31 Aug. 1937, FO 371/20955/6303/9; Mallet telegram to Eden, 7 Sep. 1937, FO 371/20955/6284/9.

[129] Cf. Moffat to Armour [US minister, Ottawa], 10 Aug. 1937, Moffat 12; Feis to Frankfurter, 6 Oct. 1937, Frankfurter 54.

[130] Meeting 1, 8 Sep. 1937, CAB 27/626.

ground could be 'properly prepared'.[131] After the special Cabinet committee deliberated, Chamberlain responded:

Perhaps the community of sentiment between our two countries as to the events in the Far East and the developments in the European situation may be doing something to create a favourable atmosphere[,] and the conclusion of an Anglo[-]American commercial agreement[,] when we have found ways of overcoming its obvious difficulties[,] will undoubtedly be an important step in the right direction.'[132]

With their diplomatic advances spurned and the Chamberlain–Roosevelt talks on hold, British efforts at mediation had to be directed elsewhere. As Chiang had appealed to Geneva, these efforts centred on the League's Advisory Committee and the convening of the Brussels conference.

To be fair to Roosevelt, he avoided invoking the neutrality laws in this crisis to ensure Chinese access to American supplies – this occurred on the legal grounds that there were no declarations of war.[133] But on 5 October, he muddied the situation by delivering his so-called 'quarantine' speech.[134] Without specifically mentioning Germany, Italy, or Japan, he observed that 'peace-loving nations must make a concerted effort in opposition to those violations of treaties and those ignorings of humane instincts which today are creating a state of international anarchy and instability from which there is no escape through mere isolation or neutrality'. The president probably wanted to educate Americans about the false security of isolationism and pacificism in an uncertain world.[135] But when isolationists immediately chided any suggestion that the United States should involve itself in international security questions, Roosevelt obfuscated. Saying he cast no aspersions about Japanese policy, he fell back on explaining his ideas by repeating hoary truisms like: 'We seek peace, not only for our generation but also for the generation of our children.'[136]

The Americans were compelled to attend the Brussels conference – Roosevelt ended his speech by saying 'America actively engages in the search for peace'. However, in divining Roosevelt's real intent, the British saw little substance beyond a veiled, and dangerous, warning of economic blockade against Japan. Foreign Office consensus about the speech was: 'It seems to amount to the usual attitude that America will

---

[131] Roosevelt to Chamberlain, 28 Jul. 1937, Roosevelt PSF GB.
[132] Chamberlain to Roosevelt, 28 Sep. 1937, *ibid.*   [133] Dallek, *Roosevelt*, 146–7.
[134] 'Speech by the President', 5 Oct. 1937, *FDRFA*, 7, 10–21.
[135] D. Borg, 'Notes on Roosevelt's Quarantine Speech', *PSQ*, 72(1957), 405–33; Dallek, *Roosevelt*, 147–52.
[136] Cf. Press Conference, 8 Oct. 1937, 'Radio Speech of the President', 12 Oct. 1937, both *FDRFA*, 53–4, 86–9.

talk but not act, or at least not act in a manner that can be relied on.'[137]
Vansittart took the line that it would be politically imprudent to 'cold-
water' the speech in public since 'we must see how far we can develop
this change of tone in the U.S.A. '.[138] The Cabinet concurred. Meeting
on 6 October, no one dissented when Chamberlain observed: 'If this
country were to become involved in the Far East the temptation to the
Dictator States to take action whether in Eastern Europe or in Spain
might be irresistible.'[139] To his sister, he confided that Roosevelt
unintentionally laid a trap for the new National Government. 'Of course
our opposition have interpreted [the speech] as I knew they would, as
meaning that U.S.A. would put economic sanctions on Japan if we do
the same and they are preparing the way for an accusation that we as
usual are standing in the way and preventing the courageous and
altruistic Americans from saving the Chinks from aerial bombs.'[140]
Chamberlain's government, thus, looked on the Brussels conference as
a means of demonstrating that it had not abdicated its responsibilities in
looking for a peaceful solution to the Sino-Japanese war. As rearmament
was incomplete, and it was certain by mid-October that Roosevelt
would avoid concrete measures to meet Japanese aggression, the British
would do nothing at Brussels beyond seeking mediation between
Nanking and Tokyo.

Pressures for mediation issued forth from the British Embassy at
Tokyo. Craigie had assumed the post of ambassador to Japan in
August. Apprised by his staff of growing anti-British sentiments
amongst Japanese political and military leaders, he advocated reconciliation in a stream of reports over the next two months.[141] Eden was
swayed;[142] he saw in the Brussels conference a device to achieve
stability in China and establish closer Anglo-American ties – the
Japanese had announced they would not attend. British policy towards
the conference emerged in Cabinet on 13 October, a result of
Chamberlain and Eden agreeing that there had to be conciliation, that
Chiang could avoid Haile Selassie's fate only by such a policy, and that
economic sanctions against Japan would be useless unless the other

[137] Holman [FO American Department], Orde, Sargent minutes, all 7 Oct. 1937, all FO
371/20667/7185/448; Allen [FO American Department] minute, 7 Oct. 1937, FO
371/20667/7236/448.
[138] Vansittart minute, 7 Oct. 1937, FO 371/20667/7185/448.
[139] CC 36(37)5, CAB 23/89.
[140] Chamberlain to Hilda, 9 Oct. 1937, NC 18/1/1023.
[141] Cf. Craigie telegram to Eden, 6 Sep. 1937, FO 371/20955/6169/9; Craigie telegram to
Eden, 25 Sep. 1937, FO 371/20956/6972/9; Craigie despatch to Eden, 6 Oct. 1937,
enclosing 'Political Diary No.9', BDFA, II, E16, 163–5; Craigie telegram to Eden,
30 Oct. 1937, FO 371/21016/8783/6799.
[142] Eden to Craigie, 27 Sep. 1937, FO 371/20956/6972/9.

nine-Power signatories, including the Americans, supported them.[143] But, critically, division between Eden and Chamberlain developed over the American question. Where Chamberlain had little faith in Roosevelt using American strength to bolster Far Eastern stability, Eden wanted to use Brussels to improve Anglo-American relations, important for Europe and the Far East. Although the Cabinet sided with Chamberlain in rejecting sanctions, Eden succeeded in having Lindsay's embassy explain the British attitude to the State Department. This occurred on 18 October.[144] Three alternatives existed. Two of them – waiting for the situation to improve or censuring Japan without imposing sanctions – might reward Japanese adventurism. The third – either aiding China outright or imposing economic sanctions against Japan – would antagonise Tokyo without any certainty of success. Within a day, the State Department affirmed that sanctions were beyond the purview of the Brussels conference.[145]

With this knowledge, Chamberlain's government told Parliament that it would go as far as the United States in finding a solution to the crisis[146] – hence, British policy did not change after the 13 October Cabinet. On his side, Roosevelt spelled out the American position to Davis: rejecting joint action with the League, not wanting the United States 'as the leader in, or suggestor of, future action', and having his government avoid being seen as 'a tail to the British kite'.[147] Reviving Hull's 'parallel lines' argument, Roosevelt wanted the British to understand that American policy would be one of 'independent co-operation'. On this basis, discussions occurred on 2 November, the day before the conference opened, between the senior British and American delegates: Eden, Malcolm MacDonald, the dominions secretary, Davis, and Stanley Hornbeck, the chief of the State Department Far Eastern Division.[148] Annoyed at Davis' suggestion that the British had 'had enough of sanctions', Eden retorted that 'we had so far shown ourselves more ready for action than the United States Government'. Nonetheless, he stressed that 'while the present business of the Conference was mediation, [Davis] must not assume that we were unwilling to take part in any international action'. Seeking to build bridges to Washing-

[143] CC 37(37)5, CAB 23/89.
[144] Eden telegram to Mallet, 18 Oct. 1937, FO 371/21015/8013/6799.
[145] Mallet telegram to Eden 19 Oct. 1937, *ibid.*   [146] Lee, *Sino-Japanese War*, 70.
[147] Roosevelt memorandum, n.d. [?19 Oct. 1937], *FDRFA*, 7, 129. Cf. Moffat to Davis, 8 Sep. 1937, Moffat 12; Hornbeck memorandum 'A Nine Power Conference: Reflections on Situation and Problems', 13 Oct. 1937, Hornbeck 457; Davis to Welles, 1 Nov. 1937, Davis 63.
[148] Davis to Eden, n.d., Eden FO 954/29/US/37/21, and subsequent correspondence, *ibid.*, US/37/22 to US/37/25; Avon, *Facing the Dictators*, 536–7.

ton, Eden observed that whilst Chamberlain's government had to weigh the Far Eastern situation with that in Europe, it would willingly take such action in concert with the United States. Evading the strictures Roosevelt had placed on him, Davis indicated that the president worried that if Britain faced trouble elsewhere, the United States 'might some day have to deal, maybe alone, with a greatly strengthened Japanese power across the Pacific'. Roosevelt, Eden learnt, wanted 'to do something to check the tendency now'.

The Brussels conference began with Eden believing that Britain and the United States might find a basis for collaboration.[149] Hopes for such consolidation proved barren by the time the conference adjourned on 24 November.[150] Several factors robbed the discussions of practical results: Japanese refusal to attend; French concern more with protecting their Indochina holdings than salvaging Chiang's claims to sovereignty; British resistance to the application of economic sanctions without American support; and American resistance to being a 'suggestor' of future action. There is great truth in the assessment that: 'The conference meandered along in the hope that Japan could be persuaded to behave constructively towards it. The hope gradually faded, as it was realized that Japan regarded it with contempt.'[151] Besides showing the British and American inability to find common interests, the conference's only achievement was a report 'which merely affirmed general principles'. The Japanese remained entrenched in northern China; and, following overtures from Tokyo in October, Berlin was moving to mediate between the warring Powers. With Italian signature of the anti-Comintern pact on 3 November, the seeming alignment of the three totalitarian Powers presented major problems for the British. The intertwined issues of British security in Europe and East Asia confronted Chamberlain and his ministers with difficult decisions. It was obvious to London that the Roosevelt Administration, trussed by the neutrality laws and sensitive to domestic isolationist pressures, could only make a minimal contribution to international stability.

149 Eden to George VI, n.d. [?14–15 Nov. 1937], Eden FO 800/954/FE/37/10.
150 On the conference, see Lee, *Sino-Japanese-War*, 70–8; Lowe, *Pacific War*, 30–1.
151 *Ibid.*

8 Appeasement, deterrence, and Anglo-American relations, 1938–1939

> It is always best & safest to count on *nothing* from the Americans
> except words but at this moment they are nearer 'doing something'
> than I have ever known them and I cant [*sic*] altogether repress hopes.
>
> Chamberlain, December 1937[1]

Chamberlain made this famous statement about Americans, their 'words', and international security during a flashpoint spawned by the fighting in China.[2] On 12 December 1937, Japanese aircraft operating along the Yangtze River attacked a USN gunboat, the *Panay*, whilst Japanese shore batteries shelled two RN riverboats, the *Ladybird* and the *Bee*. In the case of the *Panay*, escorting American-owned tankers and evacuating American embassy staff, those swimming to safety were machine-gunned: three were killed and almost fifty were wounded. Roosevelt immediately demanded an apology and reparations.[3] Although Tokyo claimed the attack was unintentional, Grew received formal regrets from Hirota, and the Japanese government agreed to pay $2 million in restitution. Roosevelt's initial reaction to the '*Panay* incident' prompted Chamberlain's comment, a hope that Washington would finally use American strength to help show the totalitarian Powers that limits existed to their ambitions. However, when the British approached Washington about a joint reaction to the Japanese attack, they met refusal.[4] Roosevelt did talk about an Anglo-American blockade in the event of a future Japanese indiscretion, but he phrased it in vague terms.[5] Added to this, Congressional isolationists moved quickly to

---

[1] Chamberlain to Hilda, 17 Dec. 1937, NC 18/1/1032; emphasis in original.
[2] Except for the excellent Reynolds, *Alliance*, 297, n. 29, who troubled to examine the Chamberlain papers, most historians have used the quotation cited in Feiling, *Chamberlain*, 325. It deletes the crucial phrase coming after 'words', which completely changes Chamberlain's meaning. Cf. Lee, *Sino-Japanese War*, 54; Pelz, *Race*, 193.
[3] Roosevelt memorandum, 13 Dec. 1937, Roosevelt PSF Japan. Cf. H. D. Perry, *The Panay Incident: Prelude to Pearl Harbor* (New York, 1969).
[4] Hull memorandum, 14 Dec. 1937, Hull 58; CC 47(37)4 (15 Dec.), CC 48(37)5 (22 Dec.), both CAB 23/90.
[5] Dallek, *Roosevelt*, 154; Lee, *Sino-Japanese War*, 90–3.

prevent the president from using armed force to defend American interests beyond the continental United States. On 14 December, Representative Louis Ludlow introduced a bill to ensure that, except in meeting an invasion, the United States could only go to war if American citizens agreed to do so in a national plebiscite. Debate on the 'Ludlow War Referendum Bill' stretched into the New Year: the bill was defeated on 10 January 1938 by a slim margin and after heavy Administration lobbying.[6] '[W]hen all allowance for these factors has been made', Lindsay counselled, the 'size of [the] minority shows that isolationist elements in Congress are impressively strong.'[7] Admittedly, some Foreign Office officials surmised that 'Japanese aggressiveness, intentional or uncontrolled, may break down America's natural isolationism'.[8] But Roosevelt's narrow legislative victory suggested that any hope of his Administration 'doing something' practical in terms of international security had disappeared.[9]

The '*Panay* crisis' occurred precisely when Chamberlain moved to control British foreign policy. In the first week of December 1937, he and Eden felt strong enough to oust Vansittart as permanent undersecretary – with Baldwin retired and MacDonald having died suddenly in November, Vansittart had lost his political patrons.[10] On 1 January 1938, Vansittart became the government's 'chief diplomatic adviser', an impressive-sounding but powerless post; Cadogan succeeded him. Despite Warren Fisher being long-prepared to offer himself as Vansittart's successor,[11] Eden favoured Cadogan, a result of their close working relationship when Cadogan served as the Foreign Office adviser for League affairs. Then fending off prime ministerial interference in foreign policy – Lord Halifax, the lord president and Chamberlain's friend, had met with Hitler and his henchmen in November with the prime minister's support[12] – Eden wanted someone trustworthy as his senior counsellor.

Neutering Vansittart remained central to Chamberlain's determination to set a different course for British foreign policy. By December

---

6   E. C. Bolt, Jr, *Ballots before Bullets: The War Referendum Approach to Peace in America, 1914–1941* (Charlottesville, VA, 1977), ch. 20.
7   Lindsay telegram to Eden, 10 Jan. 1938, FO 371/21525/196/64.
8   Beith [FO American Department] minute, 19 Jan. 1938, FO 371/21525/383/64.
9   Holman [FO American Department] minute, 12 Feb. 1938, FO 371/21525/1081/64.
10 Chamberlain to Hilda, 6 Nov. 1937, Chamberlain to Ida, 14 Nov., 12 Dec. 1937, NC 18/1/1027, 1028, 1031. Cf. Carlton, *Eden*, 105; V. Rothwell, *Anthony Eden. A Political Biography, 1931–57* (Manchester, 1992), 40.
11 Warren Fisher to Chamberlain, 15 Sep. 1936, NC 7/11/29/19.
12 'Account by Lord Halifax of his visit to Germany, November 17–21, 1937', *DBFP II*, XIX, 540–56. Cf. Halifax to Chamberlain, 6, 9 Nov. 1937, NC 7/11/30/65, 66; Chamberlain to Ida, 26 Nov. 1937, NC 18/1/1030.

1937, Chamberlain believed it dangerous to rely on the balance of power to protect Britain's global interests.[13] By the same token, he seems to have felt that international conferences were unproductive, something confirmed by his experience with the Disarmament Conference, Lausanne, the World Economic Conference, and the second London naval conference. The League could at best provide only 'moral pressure' to reconcile antagonistic Powers. He, thus, concluded that British security would be enhanced by meeting the legitimate grievances of the totalitarian Powers, or, at least, those grievances whereby concessions did not imperil British interests. There also existed the possibility that such a policy, by removing points of contention, might augment British diplomatic capital by dividing the 'Axis' Powers. In a word, it was appeasement, which in different guises had long been a weapon in Britain's diplomatic arsenal. This does not mean that Chamberlain and his ministers would forego rearmament – whilst the totalitarian Powers might be appeased, they still had to be deterred from being too adventurous. 'I believe the double policy of rearmament and better relations with Germany and Italy', he recorded before Vansittart's ouster, 'will carry us safely through the danger period, if only the Foreign Office will play up.'[14]

Chamberlain also believed that mounting defence expenditures were as lethal to British security as an attack by another Power because they sapped the country's economic vitality. Senior members of his Cabinet, including Eden, Halifax, Inskip, and Simon, now the chancellor of the Exchequer, shared his view that reducing tensions by appeasing the dictators would slacken defence spending increases. In the summer and autumn of 1937, the government initiated a fresh review of defence spending. It became clear during these months, despite the outbreak of fighting in China, that the consensus that had existed when the third DRC Report was circulated had broken down. Simon argued that the government had to balance defence spending with the economic and financial resources available to it.[15] The COS made plain that although Britain could fight Germany, Italy, or Japan singly, it could not fight two or all three simultaneously.[16] Indeed, the service chiefs did not see

[13] This and the next three sentences are based on Chamberlain to Ida, 4 Jul., 30 Oct., 26 Nov. 1937, NC 18/1/1010, 1026, 1030; Chamberlain to Hilda, 24 Oct. 1937, 5 Dec. 1937, NC 18/1/1025, 1030a.
[14] I. Colvin, *The Chamberlain Cabinet* (New York, 1971), 46.
[15] Simon memorandum [CP 165(37)], 25 Jun. 1937, CAB 24/270.
[16] COS 'Comparison of the Strength of Great Britain with that of Other Nations as at January, 1938' [CP 296(37)], 12 Nov. 1937, CAB 24/273; COS memorandum, 'Planning for War with Germany' [COS 644JP], 13 Nov. 1937, CAB 53/34. Cf. COS meetings 216, 221, both CAB 53/8.

Germany as the Power with which Britain might necessarily have to fight. For his part, Inskip stressed the need to balance economic health with effective armed force.[17] The Cabinet agreed, deciding that defence programmes already approved would not be touched, whilst those accepted in principle were open to Treasury scrutiny. Again, the Army was the big loser:

The actual recommendation of the interim [Inskip] report was that the Army's continental role be eliminated. The reasons were given that France no longer expected Britain to contribute a large continental force in their alliance, that the recent German guarantee of Belgian neutrality eliminated the need for a British force to secure that area, and that the demands for the presence of the Army in the Empire were of a higher priority than its commitment to the Continent. The unstated, but dominant reason, of course, was cost.[18]

Here lay the basis of the blend of appeasement and deterrence that distinguished British foreign policy for most of the remaining twenty months of the interwar period. It is one of the most intensely studied periods in British diplomatic history, one distinguished by a corpus of studies marked by charges of 'guilt' against Chamberlain and his supporters for failing to oppose the dictators, by vicious character assassinations of leading British statesmen, and by far-fetched counterfactual historiography that argues how easily war could have been avoided.[19] More balanced appreciations of 'appeasement' have been produced over the past thirty years in contradistinction to those lurid exercises in finger-pointing. Although differing over the culpability shared by Chamberlain and others for the outbreak of war in September 1939, they are concerned more with understanding how and why war came – and avoiding hindsight.[20] They show that the government's

---

[17] Inskip 'Interim Report on Defence Expenditure in Future Years' [CP 316(37)], 15 Dec. 1937, CAB 24/273. Cf. Warren Fisher memorandum, 'Defence. Sir T. Inskip's New Report', 18 Dec. 1937, Warren Fisher 1.

[18] Shay, *Rearmament*, 170.

[19] 'Cato', *Guilty Men* (1940) began casting stones. Cf. A. L. Kennedy, 'Munich: The Disintegration of British Statesmanship', *Quarterly Review*, 286(1948), 425–44; R. Lamb, *The Drift to War* (1989); W. Murray, *The Change in the European Balance of Power, 1938–1939: The Path to Ruin* (Princeton, 1984); L. B. Namier, *Diplomatic Prelude, 1938–1939* (1948); W. R. Rock, *Appeasement on Trial: British Foreign Policy and Its Critics, 1938–1939* (Hamden, CT, 1966); A. Rothstein, *The Munich Conspiracy* (1958); D. F. Schmitz and R. D. Challener, eds., *Appeasement in Europe: A Reassessment of US Policies* (Westport, 1990).

[20] S. Aster, *1939: The Making of the Second World War* (1973); D. Dilks, 'Appeasement Revisited', *University of Leeds Review*, 15(1972), 28–56; P. M. Kennedy, 'The Tradition of Appeasement in British Foreign Policy, 1865–1939', *BJIS*, 2(1976), 195–215; W. N. Medlicott, *Britain and Germany: The Search for Agreement, 1930–1937* (1969); W. J. Mommsen and L. Kettenacker, eds., *The Fascist Challenge and the Policy of Appeasement* (1983); C. Webster, 'Munich Reconsidered: A Survey of British Policy', *International Affairs*, 37(1961), 137–53. The efforts of D. Cameron Watt must stand

foreign policy found basis on a rational response to the triple threat to
international security that lay in Europe, the Mediterranean, and the
Far East. Of course, reliance on 'appeasement' ultimately failed whilst
equally rational diplomatic strategies, like the balance of power, were
discarded. However, protecting Britain's global position involved as-
suring the security of the home islands and defending the Empire and
access to overseas markets. In Chamberlain's mind, as in those of
MacDonald and Baldwin before him, in those of the ministers who
served them, and in those outside of government who endeavoured to
influence foreign policy, Britain's external position was tied intimately to
its domestic social and economic health. By December 1937, Inskip
estimated the bill for adequate defence by 1941 at £1,500 million.[21]
Unless checked, further arms spending might damage the state's fiscal
solvency, see a return to the internal dislocation of the early 1930s, and
produce a weakened Britain unable to ensure either home or Imperial
security. Foreign and defence policies, accordingly, were complex.
Chamberlain decided that appeasement tied to sizable armed forces
could reduce tensions with the totalitarian Powers and deter them from
creating a crisis that could lead to war and diminish Britain's international position. In this process, the American question had significance, for just as British perceptions of the United States affected their
general global policy in the period 1935–7, so, too, did they affect that
policy in 1938–9.

Early in 1938, following the Ludlow bill's defeat, Hull delivered a radio
speech on 'Trade, Prosperity, and Peace'. He intimated that international economic initiatives could not sometimes be divorced from
political questions. In assessing Hull's message, the Foreign Office
American Department observed: 'A political, as distinct from an economic, interest in foreign affairs is something new in the U.S. And it is
still in an embryonic state.'[22] This attitude suffused British policy
concerning the United States until the Germans marched into Prague
thirteen months later. Chamberlain and those ministers and their
advisers clustering around him reckoned that Roosevelt's Administration, whilst waking to the strategic nature of problems in international
security, felt disinclined to co-operate with Britain even in circumstances
where innocent American blood had been spilled. Thus, Chamberlain
did not plan on assistance from Washington. For over two years, he and

above all else in this respect. See the apotheosis of his work: *How War Came. The
Immediate Origins of the Second World War, 1938–1939* (1989).
[21] Inskip 'Interim Report'.
[22] Hull speech, 7 Feb. 1938, with Beith minute, 19 Feb. 1938, FO 371/21515/1226/64.

other British diplomatists had struggled vainly to convince Roosevelt, Hull, and other Americans about moving beyond 'words' to contain the totalitarian Powers. Neutrality legislation made no distinction between the aggressor and the victim of aggression. Whilst the desire to liberalise trade might have some benefit to international peace, American intransigence over silver had not helped China. Most importantly, any success in pressuring the ambitious – for instance, applying oil sanctions against Italy or responding to the *Panay* and *Ladybird* attacks – required collective not parallel efforts. By January 1938, finding a basis for Anglo-American co-operation became secondary to the more crucial diplomatic problems of reducing the threats posed by Germany, Italy, and Japan. Chamberlain's government continued the Anglo-American trade negotiations for tactical reasons: in Lindsay's earlier expressed view, 'to predispose America favourably in the manner we desire'.[23] However, the reality of the situation as 1938 began meant concentrating on what was possible rather than what was not.

It was disconcerting, therefore, when, two days after the Ludlow bill's defeat, Roosevelt secretly approached London with a 'Peace Plan'. Uneasy over both the Far Eastern crisis and uncertainty in Europe created by Spain and strain in Austro-German relations, the president wanted to reduce international tensions within the domestic political strictures placed on him.[24] At the time of the quarantine speech, Sumner Welles, the new under-secretary of state, had proposed that Roosevelt call 'a world conference' to establish 'basic principles' of international law, establish rules for land and naval war, including neutral rights, and guarantee freedom of access 'on the part of all peoples to raw materials'.[25] On 12 January 1938, Roosevelt acted on Welles' proposal, having Welles explain its contents to Lindsay and indicate that the president 'was communicating his scheme to His Majesty's Government alone'.[26] If supported by the British, he would invite the governments of several smaller European Powers, plus some Latin American states, to meet in Washington and then 'warn' Paris, Berlin, and Rome of 'the general lines of his scheme'. With Eden

---

[23] Cf. 'I reckoned [the treaty] would help to educate American opinion to act more & more with us and because I felt sure it would frighten the totalitarians': Chamberlain to Hilda, 21 Nov. 1937, NC 18/1/1029. See Drummond and Hillmer, *Freer Trade*, 97–122.

[24] Dallek, *Roosevelt*, 144. But, as the British case from 1935 to 1937 shows, if he believed that London felt he could 'provide effective leadership', Roosevelt suffered self-delusion.

[25] Welles memorandum, 6 Oct. 1937, *FDRFA*, VII, 29–32.

[26] Lindsay telegrams (37–40) to FO, 11–12 Jan. 1937, Cadogan minute for Chamberlain, 13 Jan. 1938, all FO 371/21526/2127/64; narrative of events, 12 Jan.–7 Mar. 1937, Eden FO 954/30/US/43/2.

vacationing in France, Chamberlain responded. Avoiding outright rejection, he suggested a delay: 'the President may consider – what has occurred to me – whether there is not a risk of his proposal cutting across our efforts here'.[27] Regarding the latter point, he allowed that his government contemplated the appeasement of Mussolini by offering *de jure* recognition of the Italian conquest of Abyssinia – behind the scenes, Chamberlain was also preparing for conversations with the Germans about returning some of their colonies lost during the Great War.[28] Feeling 'a little disappointed' with the British response, Roosevelt agreed to wait.

Eden's return on 15 January began a dispute with Chamberlain that, on 20 February, saw the foreign secretary's resignation. There were two intertwined matters of contention: Roosevelt's initiative and formal British recognition of Italy's absorption of Abyssinia. Of all Chamberlain's ministers, only Eden remained willing to continue expending energy towards building strong political ties with the United States. He emphasised the deleterious effect that treating the 'Peace Plan' lightly would have on Anglo-American relations – 'we shall have committed the greatest mistake';[29] and, behind Chamberlain's back, he telephoned Lindsay to inform the Americans that he would do all possible to get the Cabinet to accept an international conference. But neither Chamberlain nor other ministers were enamoured of the idea, especially since they believed that it could damage the openings they were hoping to make to Hitler and Mussolini.

The matter simmered into February. The Cabinet Foreign Policy Committee (FPC) followed Chamberlain's lead in encouraging Washington, but it wanted to avoid the appearance of a joint Anglo-American enterprise. 'While the Dictators and Japan may decide it to be impolitic to reject the scheme out of hand', Chamberlain instructed Lindsay, 'they are almost sure in their hearts to dislike it.'[30] He added:

In any case to miss such an opportunity of relaxing the tension brought about by Italy's activities in the Mediterranean and of establishing relations with that country which might enable us to influence her in the right direction in future would seem to me to be incurring a grave responsibility especially at a time

---

[27] Chamberlain to Roosevelt, 14 Jan. 1938, Roosevelt PSF GB; narrative of events, 12 Jan.–7 Mar. 1937, Eden FO 954/30/US/43/2.
[28] On 5 November 1937, Hitler had outlined his plans for German expansion in Europe to his senior diplomatic and military advisers; he seemed prepared for war with Britain, France, and Russia to achieve his plans. See Weinberg, *Hitler's Germany*, II, 34–43.
[29] Eden to Chamberlain, 17 Jan. 1937, Eden FO 954/US/38/2; Eden memorandum (unsigned), 17 Jan. 1937, Eden FO 954/US/38/4. Cf. Cadogan to Eden, 13 Jan. 1938, FO 371/21525/2127/64.
[30] FPC meetings 19–20, both 21 Jan. 1938, FO 27/622; Chamberlain telegram (59) to Lindsay, 21 Jan. 1938, FO 371/21526/2127/64.

when events in the Far East may at any moment make new demands on our resources.[31]

Chamberlain made the same point to Roosevelt.[32] On 18 February, when the president went on a five-day vacation, Lindsay learnt that the plan would be announced on his return. By 23 February, events had got away from Roosevelt.

First, Hitler had met the Austrian chancellor, Kurt von Schuschnigg, on 12 February to pressure him into supporting Austro-German *anschluss* – political union. A direct violation of the treaties of both Versailles and St Germain, Hitler's demands prompted Schuschnigg to outmanoeuvre Berlin by having the Austrian people decide on *anschluss* by plebiscite. A crisis ensued that was resolved on 12 March when, with Schuschnigg admitting defeat and calling off the plebiscite, the Germans marched into Vienna and annexed Austria.[33] More important, Eden resigned. Though earlier telling Chamberlain that he saw no interference by Downing Street in the administration of foreign policy,[34] Eden opposed the prime minister's intention to give *de jure* recognition to Italy's Abyssinian conquest. The reason was not opposition to appeasement as a diplomatic strategy – Eden supported the opening to Germany[35] – but, rather, his intense dislike of Mussolini. Eden wanted a sign of Mussolini's good faith before recognition occurred, specifically the withdrawal of Italian 'volunteers' from Spain. Believing that poor Anglo-Italian relations had driven Mussolini into the German orbit, Chamberlain demurred. Here, the Austrian question intervened. Eden felt that although Mussolini had long opposed *anschluss*, he 'has, or thinks he has, some kind of *quid pro quo* from Berlin in return for his acquiescence in Austrian events'.[36] Chamberlain accepted private Italian assurances from Count Galeazzo Ciano, Mussolini's foreign minister, that there was no Italo-German collusion over Austria.[37] The issue was resolved at Cabinets on 19–20 February when Eden found little support for his position.[38] On 21 February 1938, Halifax became foreign secretary. Chamberlain now dominated British foreign policy.

For Chamberlain, the twisted events of January–February 1938

---

[31] Chamberlain telegram (60) to Lindsay, 21 Jan. 1938, *ibid.*
[32] Chamberlain to Roosevelt, 21 Jan. 1938, Hull 42; Eden telegram (115) to Lindsay, 11 Feb. 1938, with FO draft and revisions, Eden minutes to Chamberlain, 10, 11 Feb. 1938, all FO 371/21625/2127/64.
[33] N. Schausberger, *Der Griff nach Österreich: Der Anschluss* (Vienna, 1979).
[34] Eden to Chamberlain, 9 Jan. 1938, NC 7/11/31/100.
[35] Eden memorandum, 'German Contribution Towards General Appeasement' [FP(36)43], 25 Jan. 1938, CAB 27/626.
[36] Eden to Chamberlain, 18 Feb. 1938, Eden FO 954/IT/38/10.
[37] Chamberlain diary, 19–27 Feb. 1938, NC 2/24A.
[38] Carlton, *Eden*, 124–33; Rhodes James, *Eden*, 190–4.

demonstrated the impossibility of the two English-speaking Powers combining to influence the course of international politics. David Reynolds has perceptively observed that once Chamberlain succeeded Baldwin, he 'wanted Anglo-American co-operation in principle, but only where it was consonant with his overall diplomatic goals and where U.S. support could be guaranteed'.[39] This is somewhat unfair to Chamberlain in the first six months of his premiership – he and Eden worked honestly to bring the Americans into the mediation process over the Far Eastern crisis. But by the time Roosevelt mooted his 'Peace Plan', Chamberlain saw little profit in running after Washington. The British had disregarded the Americans in their defence calculations since the first DRC meetings in 1933–4; now, they were prepared to ignore them in their political policies as they set about appeasing the dictators. Chamberlain's attitude towards the Roosevelt Administration and its failure to support practical responses to meet security threats is best summarised in his view of the 'Peace Plan' after the *anschluss*:

What a fool Roosevelt would have looked if he launched his precious proposal. What would he have thought of us if we had encouraged him to publish it, as Anthony was so eager to do? And how we too would have made ourselves the laughing stock of the world.'[40]

The British had long realised that Hitler sought the *anschluss*; if this occurred, the Foreign Office and the intelligence services predicted, the German dictator's gaze would then fall on Czechoslovakia where several million 'Germans' lived in its western reaches.[41] In Vansittart's concept of the European balance, Austria had to remain independent to weaken Germany's position in Central Europe. To this end, he supported Stresa in 1935. Even after Anglo-Italian estrangement, he resisted suggestions about abandoning Austria; his opposition to this idea when floated by the COS during the 1935 DRC meetings is indicative. By early 1938, however, Chamberlain's Cabinet was willing to acquiesce in Austria's disappearance, provided it occurred peacefully. Britain lacked the military resources to support Vienna; French assistance was uncertain; and the possibility of local fighting escalating into general war could not be discounted.[42] Hitler's possible use of armed force to settle the question disconcerted Chamberlain.[43] Nonetheless, in Cabinet and

[39] Reynolds, *Alliance*, 17.
[40] Chamberlain to Hilda, 13 Mar. 1938, NC 18/1/1041.
[41] Wark, *Ultimate Enemy*, 102–3.
[42] See Halifax's comments in CC 5(38), 16 Feb. 1938, CC 11(38), 9 Mar. 1938, both CAB 23/92. Cf. CID meeting 312(4), 4 Mar. 1938, CAB 2/7; COS memorandum, 'Appreciation of the Situation in the Event of War with Germany. New Terms of Reference' [COS (678JP)], 4 Feb. 1938, CAB 53/36.
[43] Chamberlain to Hilda, 13 Mar. 1938, NC 18/1/1041.

FPC examination of German actions, the premier and his senior ministers agreed that remaining calm was crucial if appeasement was to have any chance of success.[44] Concern now shifted to Czechoslovakia, a problem made more piquant by the Cabinet having accepted Inskip's final estimate of defence expenditures by 1941: £1,650 million.[45]

For the British, the six months after the *anschluss* were a time of increasing concern about Hitler's determination to resolve the Czech question in his favour. Using the excuse of bringing the German-speaking population of western Czechoslovakia – the Sudetenland – into the Reich, he looked to destroy Czechoslovakia. This would remove a military threat on Germany's eastern flank and establish German strategic and economic dominance in Central and Eastern Europe. Chamberlain decided that abandoning the Czechs would eliminate Hitler's last grievance about Versailles. On 30 September 1938, at a conference in Munich to which it was not invited, Czechoslovakia was forced to cede the Sudetenland to Germany. Chamberlain convinced a reluctant Edouard Daladier, the French premier, about the merit of this course, despite the existence of a long-standing Franco-Czech defensive alliance; Britain, France, Germany, and Italy guaranteed the rump of Czechoslovakia; and Hitler signed an Anglo-German agreement 'never to go to war with one another again'.

Munich was the apotheosis of appeasement. Subsequent criticism of Chamberlain is manifold: he allowed himself to be manoeuvred into a poor bargaining position; Hitler duped him; he demonstrated weakness by failing to confront Hitler militarily; he showed the Russians that they could not rely on the British; and his policy was not only immoral, it delayed the eventual war to a time when Germany had increased in strength.[46] On the other side, defenders of British policy show that British rearmament was incomplete, that British public opinion depre-cated war, that the dominions, especially Canada, would be loath to join in the fighting, that a war to maintain Czech control of the Sudetenland would be fought in Western not Central Europe, and that French wavering affected Chamberlain's willingness to resist Hitler's

---

[44] CC 12(38), 12 Mar. 1938, CAB 24/93; FPC meeting 26, 18 Mar. 1938, CAB 27/623.
[45] Inskip 'Report on Defence Expenditure in Future Years' [CP 24(38)], 8 Feb. 1938, CAB 24/274; CC 5(38)9, 16 Feb. 1938, CAB 23/92. Cf. Warren Fisher minute, 15 Feb. 1938, Warren Fisher 1.
[46] See note 19, above. Cf. T. Gilbert, *Treachery at Munich* (1989); D. N. Lammers, *Explaining Munich: The Search for Motive in British Policy* (Stanford, 1966); W. Murray, 'German Air Power and the Munich Crisis', in B. Bond and I. Roy, eds., *War and Society: A Yearbook of Military History*, vol. II (1977).

belligerence.[47] The conclusions of the latter group have greater merit. They look forwards down the time arrow into the unknown future, not backwards with the certitude of hindsight. Chamberlain certainly misjudged Hitler; and, of course, sacrificing Czechoslovakia was immoral. However, war was possible in September 1938 and, like many leaders, Chamberlain could rationalise the immorality of his own actions: he was not forsaking 'the double policy' of rearmament and appeasement; war would have been disastrous in 1938 – as it was in 1939; supported by the majority of British public opinion, he had bought peace by paying Hitler's price. He was only disabused of this belief, as was most British opinion, after the Germans occupied Prague and the rump of Czechoslovakia in March 1939.

The unfolding Czech crisis after March 1938, culminating in the German occupation of Prague a year later, touched Anglo-American relations. It had two strands: a visible one tied to the continuing negotiations over the trade agreement, finally signed in November 1938; and a less obvious one relating to mutual perceptions that affected each Power's evolving global policy. The trade negotiations had been desultory until spring 1938, although a Canadian–American trade agreement, which respected the Ottawa preferences, had been concluded in 1935. Whilst the Foreign Office and Lindsay's embassy saw the political benefits of co-operating over trade,[48] Treasury and Board of Trade officials resisted making concessions. Although arguing that an Anglo-American agreement would damage Britain's economic relationship with South Africa, Australia, and New Zealand, these officials' real purpose lay in not giving the Americans advantages at British expense.[49] As Chamberlain told a Cabinet committee when still chancellor: 'the Minister of Agriculture was probably right in suggesting that Mr. Cordell Hull's intention was to make a breach in the Ottawa Agreements. If so, Mr. Hull must not be allowed to have his own way.'[50] London showed no hesitation in withstanding what it saw as Washington's aggressive economic diplomacy. In 1936–7, for instance, the two

<hr/>

[47] See note 20, above. Cf. D. Carlton, 'Against the Grain: In Defense of Appeasement', *Policy Review*, 4(1980), 134–50; C. Thorne, *The Approach of War, 1938–39* (1967), 54–91; D. C. Watt, 'Der Einfluss der Dominions auf die britische Aussenpolitik vor München 1938', *VfZ*, 8(1960), 64–74.
[48] Cf. Ashton-Gwatkin minute, 24 Feb. 1937, FO 371/20659/1759/228; Ashton-Gwatkin minute, 11 Mar. 1937, FO 371/20659/2847/228.
[49] See Treasury–BoT comments in minutes of meeting, 23 Mar. 1937, FO 371/20659/2473/228; BoT memorandum, 20 Mar. 1937, FO 371/20659/2253/228; Simon minute, 7 Jun. 1937, T 172/1858. Concern also existed amongst all political parties; see Grigg [for an all-party RIIA group] to Chamberlain, 27 Sep. 1937, NC 7/11/30/57.
[50] Meeting 11, Committee of Trade and Agriculture, 12 Apr. 1937, FO 371/20659/2964/225.

Powers disputed each other's claims to the Phoenix Islands in the southern Pacific Ocean, islands critical in the competition over air routes and radio transmissions.[51] Yet, the central issue in the trade talks was that Britain was an industrial Power needing to export finished goods and import raw materials and foodstuffs. The United States wanted to export its large surplus of primary products whilst limiting the ingress of secondary commodities. But those primary products (chiefly tobacco, timber products, and meat), the export of which the Americans wished to increase to Britain, were largely satisfied in Britain by trade with the Empire and other countries (but not excluding the United States).

It was clear by early 1938 that the Ottawa agreements were not benefiting Britain, something underscored by renewed pressure on the pound.[52] The British knew that an agreement would not much alter imbalances in Anglo-American and Anglo-Canadian trade; they also knew that even with a trade agreement, these imbalances could be offset by existing surpluses with the Empire and Britain's European trading partners.[53] Accordingly, by spring 1938, Chamberlain's government was willing to pursue an Anglo-American trade accord because of its political implications. This does not mean that the final negotiations, stretching from May to November 1938, lacked hard bargaining: Chamberlain's government pushed for every British advantage; near the end of the negotiations, with Washington confronting an unexpected recession that threatened to undermine the New Deal, Hull suddenly demanded further tariff reductions. Nor does it suggest that opposition to unencumbering trade disappeared in both Britain and the United States. In Britain, Leopold Amery, a staunch Imperial isolationist who had been Baldwin's colonial and dominions secretary in the 1920s, created discomfort for the government front bench; in the United States, lobby groups like those for the lumber and textile industries pressured the White House to get more than it gave away.

Still, thanks to Chamberlain's impregnable political position, two

[51] For instance, the files FO 371/19831/223/223 to FO 371/19832/8035/223.
[52] R. A. C. Parker, 'The Pound Sterling, the American Treasury and British Preparations for War, 1938–9', *EHR*, 98(1983), 261–79. Except where noted, the next two paragraphs are based on Drummond and Hillmer, *Freer Trade*, 97–150; R. N. Kottman, *Reciprocity and the North Atlantic Triangle 1932–1938* (Ithaca, 1968), 183–271.
[53] And the emergence of the 'sterling area' also helped. By the mid-1930s, all the Imperial governments and several smaller European Powers, including Latvia, Estonia, Portugal, and the Scandinavians, held sterling reserves in London to maintain a fixed currency relationship with the pound and use sterling as an international means of payment. See Drummond, *Economic Policy*, 118–20; B. Thomas, 'The Evolution of the Sterling Area and its Prospects', in Manseargh, *Commonwealth Perspectives*, esp. 179–82.

trade agreements were concluded in the third week of November – one between Canada and Britain and one between Britain and the United States, both of which balanced the Canadian–American one of 1935. As the best recent study of the post-1914 British economy stresses: 'It certainly implied no real trust in the Roosevelt administration, since the British authorities were well aware that the American campaign for reciprocity was rooted in a virulent hostility to the preferential system and the imperialism which supposedly lay behind it.'[54] For London, the trade agreement's merit was political and strategic. For instance, following Hull's last-minute push for additional tariff reductions, Chamberlain would probably have been willing to let the negotiations lapse. However, to create an image of Anglo-American unity – the better to help deter Germany and Italy – his Cabinet accepted a less than perfect deal.[55] The agreement might not only create the appearance of closer Anglo-American relations in the aftermath of Munich, but, perhaps, also allow for British borrowing in the United States in a moment of crisis. For his part, Roosevelt's purpose in pursuing this diplomacy had less to do with Europe and more with augmenting the American penetration of the Canadian market.[56]

Against the backdrop of the Czech crisis in 1938, the very visible trade negotiations obscured the more important aspect of Anglo-American relations at this juncture: mutual perceptions that affected each Power's evolving global policy. Chamberlain and his senior advisers were not dissuaded from believing that whilst the Americans might legitimately be concerned about preserving international peace and security, they could offer nothing militarily to deter either Hitler or Mussolini. Roosevelt's 'Peace Plan' existed as persuasive confirmation. Thus, when the FPC assessed the *anschluss* on 18 March 1938 and the question was raised of 'whether any useful purpose would be served by trying to enlist the support of the United States against policies of violence', Chamberlain contended that there was 'no reason to suppose that the United States were prepared to intervene actively in Europe whatever Mr. Cordell Hull may say by way of general and pious aspirations'.[57] Such attitudes held sway at the upper levels of the government for the next twelve months. 'All this time anxious looks were directed to [the] U.S.A. hoping something might be said', Inskip recorded in his diary just prior to Munich. 'Roosevelt told someone we

[54] Cain and Hopkins, *British Imperialism*, II, 102.
[55] CC 49(38)9, CAB 23/96. Cf. C. A. MacDonald, *The United States, Britain, and Appeasement, 1936–1939* (1980), 109–10.
[56] Drummond and Hillmer, *Freer Trade*, 147. Cf. Feis to Bullitt [now US ambassador, Paris], 6 Sep. 1938, Feis 12; Feis to Schuster, 7 Jul. 1938, Feis 26.
[57] FPC meeting 26, 18 Mar. 1939, CAB 27/623.

could have everything except "troops and loans". He ought to have added "or lethal weapons".'[58] Perhaps, most critical of all, the COS acknowledged that American supplies to Britain and its allies in the event of a crisis would be helpful; however, whilst the Americans might wish to help, any assistance that Washington might give would be severely constrained by the neutrality laws.[59]

Of course, the idea of finding common Anglo-American ground still animated some members of the foreign-policy-making elite. On the back benches, Eden continued to champion transatlantic accord. He went to the United States in December 1938, met with Roosevelt, and privately 'was horrified at the atmosphere I found ... 90 per cent of the US is firmly persuaded that [Baldwin] and I are the only Tories who are not fascists in disguise. Certainly HMG have contrived to lose American sympathy utterly.'[60] After returning to Britain, he worked to rebuild political bridges to Washington.[61] A diverse group of individuals did the same: these included Churchill, the emerging critic of 'appeasement' in the Commons who had long been demoted to the government back benches, Hankey, now retired and in the Lords, and Kerr, who had become the Marquess of Lothian in 1930.[62] But their influence was minimal until after March 1939 because, apart from lacking political authority, they constituted a relatively small and disunited group. In addition, senior Foreign Office officials saw the importance of not dismissing possible American help out of hand. Cadogan and Vansittart impressed such sentiments on the FPC in January 1939, when it considered contingencies in the event that Germany invaded Holland.[63]

[58] Quoted in W. R. Rock, *Chamberlain and Roosevelt. British Foreign Policy and the United States, 1937–1940* (Columbus, OH, 1988), 114.
[59] COS memorandum, 'Mediterranean, Middle East and North-East Africa Appreciation' [COS 691], 21 Feb. 1938, sections 32, 162, CAB 53/37; COS memorandum, 'Situation in the Event of War Against Germany' [COS 716], 26 Apr. 1938, Annex (2)(ii), CAB 53/38; COS memorandum, 'German Aggression Against Holland' [COS 830], 25 Jan. 1939, section 22, CAB 53/44.
[60] Eden to Baldwin, 19 Dec. 1938, Baldwin 124. Eden's American efforts produced a mixed reaction. Cf. the positive views of Kennedy [US ambassador, London] telegram to Halifax, 18 Dec. 1938, and the negative ones of Lister Kaye to Halifax, 18 Dec. 1938, both Halifax FO 800/324.
[61] Harvey diary, 25 Dec. 1938, Harvey, *Harvey Diary*, 229–30.
[62] Churchill speech, 'Defence of Freedom and Peace' [radio broadcast to the USA], 16 Oct. 1938, in R. Rhodes James, ed., *Winston Churchill: His Complete Speeches, 1897–1963*, vol. VI (1974), 6015–17; Hankey diary [conversation with Bullitt], 2 Oct. 1938, HNKY 1/16; Anon. [but Lothian], 'The Commonwealth and the Dictators', *Round Table*, 111(Jun. 1938), 435–52.
[63] Halifax memorandum, 'Possible German Intentions' [FP 74], 19 Jan. 1939, enclosing Cadogan, Jebb [Cadogan's secretary], Vansittart, Strang [head, FO Central Department] memoranda, CAB 27/627; Vansittart and Cadogan comments at FPC meeting 35, 23 Jan. 1939, CAB 27/624.

Although the FPC agreed to inform Roosevelt about British intentions should the Germans invade – armed intervention if an attempt at arbitration failed – and the premier concurred, Chamberlain remained doubtful of any assistance.[64]

On the American side by early 1938, changes in the State Department and, because of Bingham's sudden death, the appointment of a new ambassador to London brought forward three men who shared Roosevelt and Hull's wariness about involvement in European political affairs.[65] Welles, a Latin American expert, had become under-secretary in May 1937 following William Phillips' appointment to the American Embassy in Rome. Charming, urbane, and effective in implementing the president's 'Good Neighbor' policy in South and Central America, his experience confirmed for him the paramount importance of concentrating diplomatic energy on entrenching American interests in these regions.[66] For at least his first two years as under-secretary, probably because he had little considered diplomatic questions beyond the Western Hemisphere, he lacked an appreciation of the complexities of European Great Power politics. His promotion of Roosevelt's 'Peace Plan' is a case in point. Should Hitler and Mussolini reject the president's overture, he argued:

The rallying of public opinion on a world scale to those policies which alone can make for peace and economic progress would in itself be productive of practical good because of its inevitable repercussions on the German and Italian populations, as well as upon those smaller countries of Europe which have been feeling increasingly during these past three years that the great democracies have surrendered their leadership and consequently they themselves, as a means of self protection, must align themselves with Rome and Berlin.[67]

Thus, Welles thought about diplomacy in economic terms; he failed to grasp British and French strategic difficulties; and he assumed that sage American words alone would weaken German and Italian influence over their smaller neighbours.

In mid-1937, after two years as the American minister in Australia, Moffat returned to Washington to head the State Department's new Division of European Affairs. Critical of Britain before leaving the

---

[64] 'It might well be', Chamberlain said, 'that Hitler would in the circumstances refuse to regard the United States as a neutral country, and it would by no means follow that a refusal by him to accept an American arbitrator would put him in the wrong with his own people'; in FPC meeting 35, 23 Jan. 1939, CAB 27/624. Cf. Halifax telegram (37) to Mallet, 24 Jan. 1939, *DBFP III*, IV, 4–6.

[65] As the following discussion shows, I do not share Reynolds, *Alliance*, 27–8 view that these men were 'realists'. Cf. Watt, *John Bull*, 83.

[66] Welles to Roosevelt, 7, 16 Aug. 1937, *FDRFA*, VI, 261–3, 302; Welles to Roosevelt, 13 Nov., 21 Dec. 1937, *ibid.*, VII, 222–3, 437–8.

[67] Welles memorandum, 10 Jan. 1938, Roosevelt PSF GB.

United States, his time in Sydney only deepened his mistrust of British foreign policy. Much of his efforts in Australia had centred on trade questions and the competing British and American claims to those small islands in the southern Pacific Ocean. He castigated Anglo-Australian attempts to defend their economic interests as 'anti-American', British bargaining strategies as 'ruthless' and 'unscrupulous', and any Australian newspaper articles critical of American trade policies as being 'under British inspiration'.[68] Such sentiments suffused his perceptions of British foreign policy after he returned to Washington. Assessing British claims that Hitler was 'insane', he charged: 'It was not so long ago that Mussolini was "insane", and before that the Kaiser, and before that other people who have happened to cross the path of British policy.'[69] He despaired of negotiating with London: it was 'an extraordinary thing how the Briton, once he has made up his mind, considers that if he budges 10 per cent he has gone more than half way to meet the other fellow'.[70] As head of the State Department division responsible for monitoring Anglo-American relations after mid-1937, he consistently advocated circumspection: 'Britain's interest in principles and in democracy was skin deep – something to be played up when it coincided with Britain's material interests and to be discarded as soon as it no longer served a useful purpose.'[71]

In January 1938, following Bingham's death the month before, Roosevelt appointed a Boston Irish businessman, Joseph Kennedy, as ambassador at London.[72] A self-made man who, as chairman of the federal Securities and Exchange Commission after 1934, had helped better regulate Wall Street, Kennedy arrived in London at the time of the *anschluss*. One of his first analyses of British policy concerning Europe held: 'Whether this is averting or merely deferring war, I don't believe we, or they, can tell at this moment.'[73] Despite understanding Britain's diplomatic plight – 'I can talk Chamberlain's language and Lord Halifax's language' – he saw little benefit in American involvement in European Great Power politics.[74] Improving trade had first priority. Hence, whilst reporting on political and strategic elements of British policy towards the Continent – even becoming supportive of

[68] Moffat to Jacobs [US mission, Pretoria], 9 Jun. 1936, Moffat to Phillips, 24 Aug. 1936, both Moffat 11; Moffat diary, 26 Jan. 1937, Moffat 38.

[69] Moffat to Gilbert [US Embassy, Berlin], 3 Oct. 1938, Moffat 13.

[70] Moffat to Johnson [US Embassy, London], 11 May 1938, *ibid.*

[71] Moffat to Wilson, 21 Feb. 1938, Moffat 14.

[72] J. K. Veith, 'Joseph P. Kennedy and British Appeasement: The Diplomacy of a Boston Irishman', in K. P. Jones, ed., *U.S. Diplomats in Europe, 1919–1941* (Santa Barbara, 1981), 165–82.

[73] Kennedy to Moffat, 14 Apr. 1938, Moffat 13.

[74] Kennedy to Hull, 11, 22 Mar. 1938, both Hull 42.

appeasement – he spent most of his first year in London concentrating on the trade negotiations and their immediate aftermath.[75] Predictably, when the Sudeten crisis arose in September 1938, he considered that Chamberlain's policy leading to Munich was the practical response to a dangerous situation; nevertheless, it only profited Washington to remain aloof from the European diplomatic fray.[76]

As in Britain during this period, some members of the American foreign-policy-making elite believed in promoting closer Anglo-American relations or, because of their abhorrence of fascism, in supporting any deterrence of totalitarian aggressiveness. Davis lobbied the White House and State Department 'that a policy of isolation and non-cooperation will not only increase our economic insecurity and endanger our peace and political security but will necessitate an ever increasing burden of armaments in proportion to the spread of lawlessness'.[77] Within Roosevelt's cabinet, Morgenthau and the secretary of the interior, Harold Ickes, saw danger in Europe from 'fascist' Germany and Italy. A Jew, Morgenthau was angered by the official anti-semitism of Hitler's regime; for Ickes, although he, too, found Nazi anti-semitism rebarbative, the problem was one where democratic ideals were under siege.[78] Although both men held that 'appeasement' weakened the British and French ability to meet the totalitarian threat, each used his authority to support policies designed to assist Britain and France.[79] Yet, Roosevelt's caution, which both Morgenthau and Ickes laid at Hull's door, prevented strong interventionist action by Washington in the year after the *anschluss*. Just before the final phase of the Czech crisis in September 1938, Lindsay saw Roosevelt who 'confessed himself impotent in the present crisis and "spoke in a friendly and appreciative manner of the Prime Minister's policy and efforts for

[75] See Kennedy to Moffat, 14 Apr., 3, 17, 31 May 1938, all Moffat 13; Kennedy telegram (412) to Hull, 16 May 1938, SDDF 741.62/270; Kennedy telegram (1167) to Hull, 12 Oct. 1938, SDDF 741.00/202; for economic issues, Feis to Kennedy, 21 Dec. 1937, Feis 20; Butterworth to Feis, 31 Aug. 1938, Feis 11; Kennedy to Moffat, 14 Apr., 31 May 1938, both Moffat 13; Kennedy to Hull, 22 Jul. 1938, Hull 43. Cf. Borah to Lippman, 18 Oct. 1938, Borah 765.

[76] Cf. Kennedy telegram to Hull, 14 Sep. 1938, Kennedy to Roosevelt, 19 Dec. 1938, both Roosevelt PSF GB; Kennedy to Moffat, 27 Sep., 18 Oct. 1938, both Moffat 13; Halifax despatch to Lindsay, 5 Sep. 1938, *BDFA*, II, C6, 190–1.

[77] Davis to Hull, 28 Feb. 1938, Hull 42. Cf. Davis to Hull, 7 Aug. 1938, Hull 43; Davis to Lothian, 31 Mar. 1939, Davis 40.

[78] For instance, Ickes diary, 30 Mar., 2 Apr. 1938, in H. L. Ickes, *The Secret Diary of Harold L. Ickes*, vol. II (New York, 1954), 47–9, 351–2.

[79] On appeasement, see Ickes diary, 2 Apr. 1938, Ickes, *Diary*, 352; Morgenthau to Roosevelt, 17 Oct. 1938, Morgenthau R1. On Ickes restricting the sale of strategic raw materials to Germany, see Ickes diary, 23 Feb. 1938, Ickes, *Diary*, 324–5; on Morgenthau trying to support sterling and the franc to allow for British and French defence spending, Blum, *Morgenthau Diaries*, 514–16.

peace."'[80] Although Roosevelt talked about his willingness to attend any international conference to effect frontier revisions, about the need for Britain and France to follow a defensive strategy built around blockade if war broke out, and, should war occur, about his government circumventing the neutrality laws by trans-shipping American supplies to Britain and France via Canada, London thought this discussion a thin reed on which to tie a British hard line towards Germany.

In such circumstances, London's response to Hitler's revisionist diplomacy between the *anschluss* and the Prague crisis developed with little reference to the United States – beyond the image of solidarity achieved by the trade agreement. Chamberlain's government did not dismiss the possibility of co-operation; but, whilst seeing possible strategic benefits from such a course – perhaps, access to American economic and financial resources should war break out – they refused to rely on it unless American support could be assured. At Washington, Roosevelt and the State Department thought in terms of protecting narrow American interests, interests dominated by achieving economic and political security in the Western Hemisphere and avoiding intervention in European Great Power politics.[81] It is a testament to both Chamberlain and Roosevelt that relations between the two English-speaking Powers were bereft of the poison that could easily have flowed from mutual recriminations and criticism over the Powers' differing approach to the Austrian and Czech crises in 1938. Yet, Anglo-American relations were not close; and, as the final phase of trade agreement negotiations showed, Britain and the United States were competitors. Each of the two governments had little understanding about the other's position. In early 1939, Roosevelt repeated to Lothian his by-now-hoary excuse for inaction: 'while he was willing to help all that he could, he would do nothing if Great Britain cringed like a coward'.[82] Chamberlain's uncertainty at the same time can be seen in his reaction to the FPC decision to tell the Americans about British options should the Germans invade Holland.[83]

Chamberlain's attitude was important. After Munich, adhering to his ideas about bilateral agreements with the totalitarians, he looked to use the absence of crisis to improve relations with the dictators. An

---

[80] This and the rest of this paragraph is based on Reynolds, *Alliance*, 35–6.
[81] Cf. D. Haglund, *Latin America and the Transformation of U.S. Strategic Thought, 1936–1940* (Albuquerque, 1984).
[82] Ickes diary, 29 Jan. 1939, Ickes, *Diary*, 571. Cf. Moffat to Wilson [now US ambassador, Berlin], 20 Oct. 1938, Moffat 14.
[83] Cf. Chamberlain to Hilda, 5 Feb. 1939, NC 18/1/1084; 'Conference with the Senate Military Affairs Committee', 31 Jan. 1939, *FDRFA*, XIII, 197–223; and extract of the latter in Halifax FO 800/324.

Anglo-Italian convention had been concluded the preceding April whereby, if Italian troop levels in Spain were reduced, Britain would recognise Mussolini's Abyssinian conquest.[84] In early January, two months after 10,000 Italian troops had been pulled out of Spain, Chamberlain travelled to Rome with Halifax and Cadogan. Although going ostensibly to formalise the April agreement, the prime minister looked for common ground between Britain and Italy in opening fresh discussions for a general European settlement. Such hopes stemmed from positive reports from Perth, who, it is suggested, wanted Anglo-Italian rapprochement so badly that he 'was driven to the edge of misrepresentation'.[85] Chamberlain left empty-handed. Mussolini and Ciano could not convince the British to join in preventing German economic encroachments in Hungary and Yugoslavia; Chamberlain and Halifax failed to persuade the Italians to open the way for further Anglo-German reconciliation.

The occupation of Prague changed everything.[86] Chamberlain saw that appeasement had failed, admittedly with some reluctance given that his political career had come to be defined by the diplomacy that he had pursued for over a year. Moreover Halifax, whose support for the premier's policy had cooled considerably after Munich, became convinced that a demonstration of resolve to deter Hitler from further coercion in Eastern Europe had become essential. Cognisant that a diplomatic Rubicon had been crossed, the Cabinet understood that rearmament had to be pushed forward with even greater vigour, a task now resting with Chatfield, who, having retired from the RN and been made a peer, succeeded Inskip on 29 January 1939. Perhaps the most telling assessment of the failure of appeasement came from Cadogan, who lamented: 'I must say it is turning out – at present – as Van predicted and as I never believed it would.'[87]

The recognition of changed circumstances produced another major shift in British diplomatic strategy: a return to the precepts of the balance of power long promoted by Vansittart and his supporters – although Vansittart, as a punishment for being correct, remained isolated as chief diplomatic adviser. In essence, Chamberlain's 'double policy' was replaced by a 'single' one: deterrence. The idea was to

---

[84] D. C. Watt, 'Gli accordi mediterranei anglo-italiani del 16 aprile 1938', *Rivista di Studi Politici Internazionali*, 26(1959), 51–96.

[85] Watt, *How War Came*, 94. On the visit, cf. R. Quartararo, *Roma tra Londra e Berlino: La politica estera fascista dal 1930 al 1940* (Rome, 1980), 404–23; P. Stafford, 'The Chamberlain–Halifax Visit to Rome: A Reappraisal', *EHR*, 98(1983), 61–100.

[86] Except where noted, the next two paragraphs are based on Aster, *1939*; Watt, *How War Came*, 141–87; Weinberg, *Hitler's Germany*, II, 535–56.

[87] Cadogan diary, 26 Mar. 1939, Dilks, *Cadogan Diary*, 163.

prevent war by continuing to rearm and, in Europe, by organising a group of Powers to contain German and Italian ambitions. At the end of March, Chamberlain's government combined with Daladier's ministry to guarantee the sovereignty of Poland, to which Hitler's interest now turned; and, with Mussolini formally annexing his Albanian client on 7 April, they followed with guarantees for Romania and Greece.[88] In May, conscription was introduced for the first time in peacetime Britain.[89] This decision derived from the need, recognised before Prague, to commit ground forces to the Continent to show that Britain would support France in the event of a German attack. The quest to find Powers that could assist the Anglo-French exertions to contain Germany came to rest on the possibility of working with Bolshevik Russia. This tactic proved barren as Hitler, pragmatic in his diplomatic strategies, competed to buy Russian favour; and he was willing to pay the territorial price demanded by Joseph Stalin, the Bolshevik dictator: a free hand in eastern Poland, the absorption of Estonia and Latvia, and the humbling of Finland.[90] Chamberlain's desire to work with the Russians was lukewarm at best, a result of his antipathy towards communism as much as of his refusing to sacrifice Poland after having guaranteed its sovereignty only months before.[91] With the signing of the 'Nazi–Soviet' non-aggression pact on 23 August 1939, Hitler felt emboldened to move against Poland. He did so on 1 September 1939, believing that London and Paris would concede his conquest. They did not. When an Anglo-French ultimatum to Germany to withdraw from Poland by 3 September expired, Britain and France were at war with Germany.

For Anglo-American relations, the German occupation of Prague ended the British ignoring of the United States in their foreign and defence strategies – this was part of the general bid to contain Germany and Italy. But, importantly, until August 1939, British policy relating to the American question was based on two suppositions: that British foreign policy could prevent war; and that, given Roosevelt's record of avoiding an active role in matters of international security, the image of

---

[88] S. Conkov, 'The British Policy of Guarantees and Greece (March–April 1939)', *Studia Balcanica*, 4(1971), 187–202; D. Lungau, 'The European Crisis of March–April 1939: The Romanian Dimension', *IHR*, 7(1985), 390–414; S. Newman, *The British Guarantee to Poland: A Study in the Continuity of British Foreign Policy* (1976).

[89] Colvin, *Cabinet*, 217–21; P. Dennis, *Decision by Default. Peacetime Conscription and British Defence Policy 1919–1939* (1972).

[90] M. Light, 'The Soviet View', in R. Douglas, ed., *1939: A Retrospect Forty Years After* (1983), 74–89; G. Roberts, *The Unholy Alliance: Stalin's Pact with Hitler* (1989).

[91] Cf. R. Manne, 'The British Decision for Alliance with Russia, May 1939', *JCH*, 9(1974), 3–26; A. Prazmowska, *Britain, Poland, and the Eastern Front, 1939* (1987); Watt, *How War Came*, 447–61.

Anglo-American solidarity had to be actively pursued. Regarding the latter point, the British approach to the United States underwent a subtle change from that followed since just before the *anschluss*. Where previously Chamberlain, Halifax, and other British diplomatists had hoped that an appearance of Anglo-American solidarity might emerge from supposedly co-operative ventures, after Prague they consciously worked to create such an image and, by this, laid the ground for as much practical co-operation as possible.

For Halifax, this endeavour began immediately after Munich with the selection of Lindsay's replacement. During the summer of 1938, Lindsay indicated his desire to retire. Having turned sixty, he was approaching the end of his ninth year as ambassador. On 29 July 1938, Halifax confided his 'choices' as a successor to Cadogan, '1 Lothian, 2 Lytton, 3 Chatfield, 4 Grigg [an MP and former governor of Kenya]'.[92] Although Cadogan convinced Halifax to drop Grigg from his list, the issue fell into abeyance as London grappled with the Czech crisis. When the time for a decision came in December 1938, Halifax promoted Lothian's candidacy. Criticism of Lothian surfaced privately from within the Diplomatic Service and publicly in the Commons – he was not a professional diplomat and had been a prominent 'appeaser'.[93] Nevertheless, Halifax believed that Lothian's appointment would strengthen transatlantic bonds. Such beliefs did not reflect unfavourably on Lindsay. Instead, they embraced Halifax's desire to utilise Lothian and his well-publicised 'atlanticism' to bolster Anglo-American ties.[94] Just as important, the Munich agreement had unsettled Halifax. Increasingly wary of Chamberlain's strategy for handling the dictators, he looked for more practical ways of deterring Germany.[95] The announcement of Lothian's appointment was delayed until April 1939 – George VI and his consort were to visit the United States in June, and Lindsay would remain in Washington to crown his embassy with this event. Lothian would begin his duties at the end of August 1939.

The royal visit to the United States, the first by a reigning British monarch, was promoted by the Chamberlain government, first, to reinforce the impression of an improving relationship and, second, to strengthen co-operative ties. The original plan had been for George VI to travel only to Canada.[96] But after the Munich agreement, under

---

[92] Cadogan diary, 29 Jul. 1938, Dilks, *Cadogan Diary*, 88–9.
[93] Cf. Cadogan diary, 15 Dec. 1938, *ibid.*, 130; minutes on parliamentary questions, 26, 28 Apr. 1939, FO 371/22823/3108/707 and FO 371/22823/3170/707.
[94] Reynolds, *Alliance*, 46–7; D. Reynolds, *Lord Lothian and Anglo-American Relations, 1939–1940* (Philadelphia, 1982), 2–3; Rock, *Chamberlain and Roosevelt*, 160–1.
[95] A. Roberts, *'The Holy Fox'. A Biography of Lord Halifax* (1991), 123–38.
[96] Beith minute, 9 Mar. 1939, FO 371/22800/1698/27.

some pressure from Roosevelt's Administration, it was decided to have him spend a few days in the eastern United States. Following Prague, the importance of his meeting Roosevelt put the Canadian leg of his journey into the political shadows.[97] With Roosevelt also wanting to show the totalitarian Powers the image of Anglo-American solidarity, the visit proved successful in British eyes.[98] Lindsay's embassy played down the visit's obvious diplomatic purpose by using royal public appearances to emphasise the 'personal charm of Their Majesties whose unaffected simplicity and graciousness was obviously of the type to draw [a] response from the Great American public'.[99] Capped by a stay at Roosevelt's estate at Hyde Park, New York, where the royal couple relaxed and ate hot dogs, 'Their Majesties "debunked" personally the last suspicion that may have existed . . . that the British monarchy was in any way "stuffed shirt"'.[100] In terms of the real reason for the visit, the Foreign Office American Department observed: 'The political results of the visit are probably best summed up in the words of Mr. Henry L. Stimson in his letter to Sir R. Lindsay – "a quiet, solid influence towards good understanding on both sides of the Atlantic".'[101] Whilst Lindsay observed that isolationism still gripped large sections of American public opinion, he argued that '[i]n the event of a very grave crisis this [visit] might have decisive results'.[102]

Other initiatives to enhance the image of Anglo-American solidarity and improve the prospects for co-operation were undertaken by both the government and those outside of it like Eden and Churchill. Within the government, the Foreign Office stood at the fore in this regard. To prevent the kind of discord that had occurred in January–February 1938 over the 'Peace Plan', Halifax ensured that Roosevelt received up-to-date intelligence on the relative strengths of the RAF and the *Luftwaffe*.[103] In early 1939, the president had mentioned figures that grossly misrepresented the disparity between the two air forces. Concurrently, Halifax used the public platform to embellish the idea that the British and American peoples shared a common morality in international politics. Thus, when Mussolini annexed Albania, Halifax spoke in

---

[97] Cf. D. Reynolds, 'FDR's Foreign Policy and the British Royal Visit to the USA, 1939', *Historian*, 45(1983), 461–72; B. D. Rhodes, 'The British Royal Visit of 1939 and the "Psychological Approach" to the United States', *DH*, 2(1978), 197–211.

[98] Lindsay despatch (660) to Halifax, 16 Jun. 1939, FO 371/22801/4435/27; Lindsay despatch (663) to Halifax, 16 Jun. 1939, FO 371/22801/4437/27; Lindsay despatch (677) to Halifax, 20 Jun. 1939, FO 371/22801/4441/27; Lindsay despatch (679) to Halifax, 20 Jun. 1939, with minutes, FO 371/22801/4443/27.

[99] Gage [FO American Department] minute, 3 Jul. 1939, FO 371/22801/4443/27.

[100] *Ibid.*   [101] *Ibid.*   [102] Lindsay despatch (679); see note 98, above.

[103] Reynolds, *Alliance*, 48–9. Cf. 'Record of an Anglo-French Conversation', 22 Mar. 1939, *DBFP III*, IV, 462–3.

Parliament about the unfavourable reaction this generated amongst 'the overwhelming mass of opinion in this country, by most of the states of Europe, and by the United States of America'.[104] He told the FPC that if 'we did nothing[,] this in itself would mean a great accession to Germany's strength and a great loss to ourselves of sympathy and support in the United States, in the Balkan countries, and in other parts of the world'.[105] He, therefore, kept the White House abreast of British efforts with regard to the guarantees to Poland, Greece, and Romania.[106] Behind the scenes, both Kennedy and the American military attaché in London, Lieutenant-Colonel Bradley Chynoweth, were being consulted by the War Office and the Air Ministry on a number of technological matters, including early British developments in radar.[107] Such consultations were not new. In January 1938, the USN director of plans, Captain Royal Ingersoll, had travelled to London for exploratory talks with his British opposite, Captain Thomas Phillips.[108] Their meeting arose in response to growing concerns, especially in the Admiralty, about Japanese aggressiveness; despite American insistence that these discussions were non-committal, they led to periodic exchanges of technical information about naval construction, tactics, and Japanese and German naval policies. Admittedly, isolationist fury in Congress when Ingersoll's mission was discovered limited the value of these exchanges. But for the British after mid-March 1939, concern about the reactions of American isolationists had receded in importance. As Halifax told Kennedy two days after Prague:

> It ought, so it seemed to me, to be the object of our two Governments to bend all their efforts, as discreetly as they might, to the task of making it plain to the German people that we were animated by no hostile motives towards them, but that our attitude was dictated wholly by the extent to which the moral sense of civilisation was outraged by the present rulers of Germany.[109]

Unofficial overtures to the Americans became the domain of those like Churchill and Eden who wanted to harness latent American power to Britain's deterrence of Germany and Italy. Although Churchill had been decidedly anti-American during the 1920s, a function of Anglo-American naval and economic rivalry, his attitudes had changed by the

[104] Kennedy telegram (479) to Hull, 14 Apr. 1939, SDDF 711.41/441.
[105] FPC meeting 38, 27 Mar. 1939, CAB 27/624.
[106] Cf. Halifax to Roosevelt, 21, 23 Mar., 5 Apr. 1939, all Roosevelt PSF GB.
[107] For example, Chynoweth reports (13, 14, 16), 19, 28 Apr., 5 May 1939, all Chynoweth MSS. Cf. Chynoweth to McCabe [assistant chief, Army Staff, Washington], 9 May 1939, ibid.
[108] L. Pratt, 'Anglo-American Naval Conversations on the Far East of January 1938', JRIIA, 47(1971), 745–63.
[109] Halifax despatch to Lindsay, 17 Mar. 1939, DBFP III, IV, 364–5.

late 1930s. Far from being animated by genuine feelings of kinship between the two major English-speaking Powers, his transformation was purely pragmatic: Britain needed allies to maintain the European balance and defend the Empire; any successes to these ends that he could claim for himself would aid in his effort to discredit Chamberlain and so succeed him as prime minister and leader of the Conservative Party.[110] Nonetheless, he used his eloquence to speak publicly about 'nothing [being] more vital to the safety and peace of the world than the increasing unity of sentiment and principle between the peoples of the English-speaking world'.[111] Behind the scenes, as part of an effort to force Chamberlain to bring him into the Cabinet, he pressed his ideas about foreign and defence policy on as many ministers as possible.[112] Eden, especially after his December 1938 trip to the United States, seems to have established a personal relationship with Kennedy and leading members of the American Embassy at London as a calculated move to rebuild those political bridges to Washington. Letters from these American diplomats sympathetic to the British dilemma in Europe in turn reached the White House and State Department.[113]

Sympathy, however, did not translate into concrete support for Britain during the spring and summer of 1939. Washington's evaluation of the European situation reflected the cautious attitudes that had distinguished the non-economic diplomacy pursued by the president and his principal advisers since early 1938. From British entreaties, Kennedy's reports, and analyses from other American diplomats in Europe, Roosevelt, Hull, Moffat, and Welles were not ignorant of the instability on the continent after Prague.[114] But divisions existed amongst American diplomatists over how the United States might

[110] B. J. C. McKercher, 'Churchill, the European Balance of Powers and the USA', in R. A. C. Parker, ed., *Sir Winston Churchill. Studies in Statesmanship* (1995).
[111] Churchill speech, 25 Nov. 1925, in M. Gilbert, ed., *Winston S. Churchill*, companion vol. V, part 3: *1936–1939* (1982), 1257, n. 2. Cf. his radio speeches to the USA, 16 Oct. 1938, 28 Apr. 1939, in *ibid.*, 1216–27, 1478–80.
[112] Churchill to Wood [air minister], 29 Oct. 1938, to Chatfield, 16 Mar. 1939, to Hore-Belisha [war minister], 27 Mar. 1939, enclosing 'Memorandum on Sea-Power, 1939', to Chamberlain, 9 Apr. 1939, to Halifax, 17 Apr. 1939, all *ibid.*, 1246, 1392, 1413–17, 1438–9, 1460–1.
[113] For example, Johnson [*chargé*, US Embassy, London] to Moffat, 29 Dec. 1938, 27 Apr. 1939, both Moffat 15; Kennedy to Roosevelt, 20 Jul. 1939, Roosevelt PSF GB Kennedy. Johnson's letters were written so as not to compromise his source, though this was clearly Eden. Kennedy actually sympathised with Chamberlain's political problems, rather than the Churchill–Eden effort to broaden the government.
[114] Cf. Hull memoranda [conversations with Lindsay], 11, 17 Apr. 1939, Hull 58; Biddle [US minister, Warsaw] to Hull, all with enclosures, 7, 18 Apr., 13, 16, 20 May 1938, Hull 44; Kennedy telegram to Hull, 4 Apr. 1939, SDDF 740.00/736; Bullitt telegram to Hull, 10 May 1939, SDDF 740.00/1416; Welles to Roosevelt, 29 Mar. 1939, with enclosure, *FDRFA*, XIV, 218–28; Davies [US ambassador, Brussels] to Roosevelt, 5

respond to the European danger. Senior American ambassadors in Europe disagreed on the line Washington should take. Thinking that Warsaw could be pressured into yielding to Hitler over Danzig and the Polish Corridor, Kennedy continued advocating appeasement even after Chamberlain's Cabinet had rejected it.[115] At Rome, Phillips surmised 'that Mussolini is so anxious to avoid war that we may hope for his calming influence on Hitler'.[116] Bullitt, on the other hand, now the ambassador at Paris, argued that American support of Britain and its French ally would give Hitler cause to think; his proposals included a strengthening of the United States armed forces and finding means to allow for the payment of the French war debt so as to circumvent the Johnson Act.[117] In Berlin, Hugh Wilson, the ambassador since mid-1938, wishfully suggested in May 1939 that '[Hitler's] problem now is … shall he measure swords with the British Empire, with the potential of the United States behind them and the possible eventual participation of the United States in the conflict'.[118] Washington was not blind to the Anglo-French predicament. For instance, on 28 April 1939, in response to the Polish guarantee, Hitler renounced both the German–Polish Non-Aggression Pact of January 1934 and the Anglo-German naval agreement. Assessing the German chancellor's motives – 'the real hate, the real jealousy, the real antagonism of Germany was toward England' – Moffat reckoned: 'Germany completely freed her hands so that she could move in any direction'.[119] Such attitudes echoed in the State and other departments of the American government.[120] Still, Welles continued focusing on improving the American position in South and Central America.[121] Whilst not belittling the problems in Europe, Moffat saw his brief as pursuing narrow American interests, for example, telling Atherton, appointed ambassador to Denmark in August, that his main concern would be trade promotion.[122] There was

Apr. 1939, with enclosure, *ibid.*, 258–61; Davies to Roosevelt, 8 Jun. 1939, *ibid.*, XV, 237–9; Gunther [US minister, Bucharest] to Roosevelt, 19 Jun. 1939, *ibid.*, 273–5.

[115] Kennedy telegram to Hull, 16 May 1939, SDDF 740.00/1501.

[116] Phillips to Moffat, 1 Mar. 1939, Moffat 16; Phillips to Roosevelt, 26 May 1939, *FDRFA*, XV, 196–200.

[117] Cf. Bullitt to Roosevelt, 23 Mar., 4 Apr., 13 Jul. 1939, Roosevelt to Hull, 26 Jul. 1939, Roosevelt PSF Bullitt.

[118] Wilson to Hull, 19 May 1939, Wilson 3.

[119] Moffat diary, 28 Apr. 1939, Moffat 42.

[120] Feis to Butterworth, 9, 31 May 1939, Feis 11; Ickes diary, 6 Apr., 13 May, 2 Jul. 1939, Ickes, *Diary*, 611–12, 634–5, 675–6; Treasury 'Preliminary report on the possibilities of depriving the aggressor countries of needed strategic war materials', 10 Apr. 1939, Morgenthau Diary.

[121] Cf. Welles to Roosevelt, 6, 17 May, 17 Jun. 1939, all *FDRFA*, XV, 44–5, 119–20, 258–62.

[122] Moffat to Atherton, 12 Aug. 1939, Moffat 15.

a feeling in Washington that the British, especially, were manoeuvring to inveigle the United States into active intervention in Europe to help deter Hitler.[123] Apart from the need to weigh domestic isolationist opinion and the criticisms of his political adversaries, Roosevelt was not immune to such suspicions.

Roosevelt's attitudes were crucial to the evolving American policies towards Europe in the year after Munich. The president was uneasy about the European situation as it touched American security. An indication of his concern involved his support for American rearmament, especially the USN and the United States Air Force.[124] In 1938, he put his weight behind a second Vinson–Trammel bill in Congress to expand the USN. Later in the year, he pushed for the construction of a 10,000-aircraft air force and the industrial capacity to produce 20,000 planes a year. Although these goals were unrealistic, American resources began to be directed to building up American armed strength. Since these programmes would not bear fruit until after 1940, Roosevelt and his advisers, chiefly Welles, endeavoured to improve American relations with Latin America. But these policies collectively were designed to improve security in the Western Hemisphere. After Munich, the chief threat to international stability resided in Europe. It was Europe that increasingly preoccupied Roosevelt.

He judged Chamberlain's government to be less than earnest in its venture to contain German ambitions. Although his attitude reflected a misreading of British policy, the president adopted truculence towards the British to force them to be more direct in blocking Hitler's enthusiasms. This explains his remark to Lothian in January about cowardly Britain. With his selection to replace Lindsay still secret, Lothian had travelled to the United States as a private citizen. He brought a memorandum which, prepared by Hankey after a discussion between Lothian and Kennedy, outlined 'the effect on the United States of America of a collapse of the British Empire'.[125] To avoid being 'the sole survivor of democracy', Hankey argued that the 'question for [the Americans] is whether one of these rare moments is not at hand when prudence, foresight and self-interest, combine in rendering action

---

[123] Moffat diary, 2 May 1939.
[124] Cf. P. E. Coletta, *The American Naval Heritage*, 3rd edn (New York, 1987), 288–90; Dallek, *Roosevelt*, 172–5; J. L. McVoy *et al.*, 'The Roosevelt Resurgence (1933–1941), in R. W. King, ed., *Naval Engineering and American Seapower* (Baltimore, 1989), 161–200; J. D. Millett, *The Army Service Forces. The Organization and Role of the Army Service Forces* (Washington, 1954), 18–22; S. E. Morison, *The Two-Ocean War. A Short History of the United States Navy in the Second World War* (Boston, 1963), 20–5.
[125] Hankey memorandum, 8 Dec. 1938, HNKY 4/30. A copy is in Roosevelt PSF GB Kennedy. Cf. Hankey to Phipps, 13 Feb. 1939, HNKY 4/31.

desirable which may change the history of mankind'. Roosevelt responded by telling Lothian that 'as long as he or Britishers like him took that attitude of complete despair, the British would not be worth saving anyway'[126] – and this is when Roosevelt questioned British mettle. Roosevelt explained his attitude to a British friend: 'What the British need today is a good stiff grog, inducing not only the desire to save civilization but the continued belief that they can do it. In such an event they will have a lot more support from their American cousins ...'. This pugnacity, however, represented the censuring half of a carrot-and-stick approach towards Britain and its European predicament. The carrot appeared a few days after he saw Lothian. Roosevelt told the Senate Armed Services Committee in a confidential meeting that the United States could not avoid supporting Britain and France in a crisis; he then had his comments leaked to show his resolve.[127]

Roosevelt wanted to stiffen British resistance to Hitler in the year after Munich. But the argument that he had vainly sought to do so since the Abyssinian crisis is flimsy.[128] His inability to comprehend Britain's strategic dilemma after the onset of Anglo-Italian estrangement in late 1935 (three first-class Powers threatening home and Imperial security), his cutting his diplomatic cloth to appease domestic isolationist and commercial interests, and the constant disparity between his words and his actions combined to weaken his influence in London. That he used private contacts like Lothian to make his case, rather than official channels through the British Embassy, diluted his message. No question exists that by late 1938, he believed that London's problem was not so much *matériel* weakness in opposing Nazi Germany, though this consideration had importance; rather, as he told Lothian, it was one of resolve. In Roosevelt's mind, however, the problem was to be solved by the European Great Powers. Willing to have his country serve as a source of supply for Anglo-French resistance to the totalitarian Powers,[129] he wanted to avoid having the United States brought into another European war.

The British understood this reluctance. After the Prague crisis, Roosevelt met another British friend visiting the United States, Sir Arthur Willert, the former head of the Foreign Office News Department.[130] Continuing his carrot-and-stick diplomacy through unofficial

---

[126] Roosevelt to Merriman [British friend], 15 Feb. 1939, Roosevelt PSF GB.
[127] 'Conference with the Senate Military Affairs Committee', 31 Jan. 1939, *FDRFA*, XIII, 197–223.
[128] The argument of Dallek, *Roosevelt*, 101–68. Cf. Watt, *John Bull*, 77–83.
[129] Reynolds, *Alliance*, 43–4.
[130] Halifax memorandum, 'Conversation between President Roosevelt and Sir Arthur Willert, March 25 and 26, 1939' [FP(36)80], 20 Apr. 1939, CAB 27/627.

mediaries – he wanted Willert to report his views to London[131] – he first admonished British foreign policy: 'Why did we not have conscription? Why did we let the Germans have a monopoly of intimidation? . . . Why did we not let stories leak out about the tremendous preparations on foot to bomb Germany?' Then, he produced the carrot by elaborating his intention 'to leave nothing undone to make the dictators understand that if they challenged [the British] they would have to reckon with a maximum of hostility from the United States'. Halifax circulated these comments to the FPC. Yet, Roosevelt's actions seemed to belie his words. After being informed of the president's earlier statements to the Senate Armed Services Committee, Chamberlain remarked that 'Roosevelt is saying Heaven knows what but . . . there is an uneasy feeling that in the case of trouble[,] it would not do much to bring [the] U.S. in on the side of the democracies'.[132] Thus, when the Germans marched into Prague, beyond imposing already planned import duties on German goods and giving a presidential lecture to the Italian ambassador at Washington, the Roosevelt Administration remained remarkably quiet. Not surprisingly, when the FPC considered Britain's reaction to this crisis, which produced the Polish guarantee, the United States went without mention in its deliberations.[133] This does not mean that London was unconcerned about American opinion: the Foreign Office saw the need to avoid provoking an isolationist reaction against British policy.[134] This is why at the time of the Albanian annexation, Halifax spoke to Kennedy about 'the object of our two Governments' being to show the dictators that 'the moral sense of civilisation was outraged' by its leaders. It is also why he had Lindsay primed with the latest information about the Polish, Romanian, and Greek guarantees; and why he agreed with the Air Ministry that Roosevelt be informed of issues like the latest developments in British short-wave radio transmissions.[135]

To give Roosevelt his due, he did attempt to strengthen Anglo-French deterrence of the dictator Powers after the Prague crisis. It came with his

[131] Scott [FO American Department] minute, 17 Apr. 1939, FO 371/122828/2856/1292.
[132] Chamberlain to Hilda, 5 Feb. 1939, NC 18/1/1084.
[133] FP(36) meetings 38–40, 27, 30, 31 Mar. 1939, CAB 27/624. Rock, *Chamberlain and Roosevelt*, 172 alludes to this absence.
[134] Scott minute, 6 Apr. 1939, FO 371/22829/2693/1292. Cf. Cadogan minute, 6 Apr. 1939, Vansittart minute, 8 Apr. 1939, Halifax minute, 8 Apr. 1939, all *ibid.*; Balfour minute, 9 May 1939, FO 371/122829/3125/1292.
[135] Halifax to Roosevelt, 21, 23 Mar., 5 Apr. 1939, British Embassy to Roosevelt, 29 Mar. 1939, Kennedy to Roosevelt, 6 Apr. 1939, all Roosevelt PSF GB; Hull memorandum [conversation with Lindsay], 11 Apr. 1939, Hull 58; Halifax to Lindsay, 11 Apr. 1939, *DBFP III*, V, 169; Wood [air minister] to Halifax, and reply, 27, 28 Apr. 1939, Halifax FO 800/324

determination to amend the 1937 Neutrality Act, set to expire on 30 April 1939. Although he judged that it might be best to repeal legal neutrality, such a course was politically impossible given the temper of domestic American opinion. In this way, he chose the next best option: amending the existing statute by jettisoning the arms embargo and making permanent the temporary cash-and-carry provisions concerning trade with future belligerents. Given British wealth and RN pre-eminence, these changes would benefit Britain and France whilst, hope-fully, convincing Hitler of the futility of further expansion. Roosevelt, however, failed to realise his ambitions. He confronted decided opposi-tion in Congress, including from conservative Democrats, over a range of issues: his domestic economic policies; a 1937 attempt to pack the US Supreme Court with political appointees to ensure that New Deal programmes were not declared unconstitutional; and isolationist furore over French purchases of American-produced military aircraft. After a tedious legislative process that lasted until Congress recessed in mid-July, the Senate Foreign Relations Committee delayed considering the law until the Senate reconvened in January 1940. This meant two things: the cash-and-carry provisions, which were experimental and had legal force only until 30 April, were not extended; and the arms embargo, not subject to any time limit, remained on the books. Although the responsibility for failure did not reside solely with Roose-velt – Pittman and other Democratic Party leaders in Congress were equally culpable – the result of failure is what mattered.

The British observed the attempted amendment of the neutrality laws with interest. Understanding that American public opinion had begun to depart from strict isolationism, the Foreign Office thought it would be counter-productive to lobby the Administration for specific changes to the legislation.[136] Nonetheless, London seemed uncertain about whether Roosevelt's efforts would succeed. 'Isolationist sentiment in Congress', observed the Foreign Office American Department, 'stimu-lated by opposition to the President's internal policies, is extremely

---

[136] This shift in opinion was clear in a 9 April 1939 Gallup Poll received by the Foreign Office: in FO 371/22813/2982/98.

	Sell Britain food supplies (per cent)	Sell Britain war materials (per cent)	Send troops (per cent)
Before 30 Sep. 1938	57	34	5
Before 15 Mar. 1939	76	55	17
9 Apr. 1939	82	66	16

The Admiralty wanted to lobby for lifting certain restrictions on merchantmen in American ports, but the Foreign Office demurred. See Jarrett [Admiralty] to Balfour, 3 May 1939, Scott minute, 5 May 1939, both FO 371/22814/3311/98.

strong & we must not reckon with any certainty on any fundamental change in the law which the bill would at least leave as it was before May 1.'[137] But when the Senate Foreign Relations Committee delayed consideration of the law, its action caused consternation in London. It was understood that 'antagonism to the President, timidity, weakness of the administration's leadership in both houses, and isolationism [were] the main reasons for Congress's negative attitude'.[138] When Perth reported from Rome that Phillips thought the rejection of the president's formula 'would lead Hitler to hold that he could go ahead with adventure without the risk of American intervention on the side of Great Britain and France', R. A. B. Butler, the Foreign Office parliamentary under-secretary, commented acidly: 'I think the ambassador is [?a] defeatist.'[139]

On the eve of general European war, such sentiments towards the Roosevelt Administration were common in London.[140] But the diplomatic and strategic exigencies of the summer of 1939 saw the British work to achieve the image of Anglo-American solidarity. George VI's visit in June offered a 'psychological' approach to the United States upon which closer Anglo-American relations could be pursued given the willingness of general American opinion to support Britain materially in a war. More substantively, Halifax was keeping official Washington informed of developments in British policy through Lindsay and Kennedy. There were even renewed – and secret – discussions by naval staff officers about possible Anglo-American naval co-operation in the Far East. Still, as the European balance of power shifted to British disadvantage between March and August 1939, the United States was not a priority in British strategic thinking. Working on combined operations with the French, planning to protect the Low Countries, deciding on how best to defend Mediterranean sea routes against the Italians, and devising means like blockade to hamper the economic and financial side of Germany's military strength preoccupied London. The expiry of the Anglo-French ultimatum to Germany on 3 September inaugurated a new and deadly phase in Britain's history as the greatest of the Great Powers. It also inaugurated a phase in which Roosevelt and his advisers would have to decide the extent to which the United States should involve itself in another European war.

---

[137] Balfour minute, 1 Jun. 1939, FO 371/22814/3498/98. Cf. Balfour minute, 8 Jun. 1939, FO 371/22814/3875/98; Scott minute, 21 Jun. 1939, FO 371/22814/4156/98; Gage minute, 4 Jul. 1939, FO 371/22814/4450/98.
[138] Gage minute, 24 Jul. 1939, on Lindsay telegram (329) to FO, 22 Jul. 1939, FO 371/22815/5062/98. Cf. Lindsay despatch (777) to Halifax, 14 Jul. 1939, FO 371/22815/5051/98; Balfour minute, 18 Jul. 1939, FO 371/22815/4890/98.
[139] Perth minute, 12 Jul. 1939, Butler minute, n.d., both FO 371/22815/4991/98.
[140] Reynolds, *Alliance*, 57–8.

9 Belligerent Britain and the neutral United States, 1939–1941

> We are entering upon a sombre phase of what must evidently be a protracted and broadening war, and I look forward to being able to interchange my thoughts with you in all that confidence and good will which has grown up between us since I went to the Admiralty at the outbreak.
>
> Churchill, November 1940[1]

The outbreak of European war forced Chamberlain to restructure his government. With appeasement in ruins and deterrence a failure, the political temper of both his party and Parliament compelled him to bring the two chief critics of his foreign policy into a newly created War Cabinet. On 3 September, Churchill was appointed first lord of the Admiralty and Eden became dominions secretary. Because Churchill had consistently and publicly criticised British diplomatic strategy since before Munich – suggesting to general British opinion that he grasped better the international situation than Chamberlain[2] – Churchill could probably have declined to join Chamberlain and formed his own ministry as his friend, Alfred Duff Cooper, confided to his diary: 'Was it better to split the country at such a moment or bolster up Chamberlain?'[3] Clearly, Churchill thought it necessary to maintain national unity. He accepted Chamberlain's leadership and threw himself into his duties with a gusto suggesting that the restructured National Government had been infused with badly needed vitality.

Apart from revitalising the government and unifying the direction of war policy, Churchill and Eden's readmission to Britain's foreign-

---

[1] Churchill to Roosevelt, 6 Nov. 1940, in W. F. Kimball, ed., *Churchill and Roosevelt. The Complete Correspondence*, vol. I [hereafter in the style *Churchill–Roosevelt*, I] (Princeton, 1984), 81.

[2] Cf. G. C. Peden, 'Winston Churchill, Neville Chamberlain and the Defence of the Empire', in J. B. Hattendorf and M. Murfett, eds., *The Limitations of Military Power* (1990), 160–72.

[3] Duff Cooper diary, 2 Sep. 1939, in Gilbert, *Churchill*, Companion vol. V, part 3, 1603–4. Cf. Feiling, *Chamberlain*, 420–2; Gilbert, *Churchill*, V, 1106–15; Rhodes James, *British Revolution*, 331; N. Thompson, *The Anti-Appeasers. Conservative Opposition to Appeasement in the 1930s* (Oxford, 1971), 220–3.

policy-making elite proved vital to the Anglo-American relationship. With Lothian having presented his credentials to Roosevelt on 31 August, the political strength of those who had long advocated closer Anglo-American relations suddenly increased. However, the initiative for high-level Anglo-American contact came from Roosevelt who, eight days after the Anglo-French declaration of war, wrote to both Chamberlain and Churchill (his letters did not reach London till 3 October).[4] Beneath expressions of good wishes – he congratulated Churchill on his appointment – was a desire to be informed about the naval and strategic side of British war policy: 'What I want you and the Prime Minister to know is that I shall at all times welcome it if you will keep me in touch personally with anything you want me to know about.' At this time, Roosevelt had little personal regard for either Chamberlain or Churchill.[5] But in line with his endeavour to stiffen British resistance to Hitler – this time with the carrot of a favourable ear without the stick of unflattering comments about the British character – the gravity of the situation required a direct opening to assure Chamberlain's government of American concern for Britain's plight. He seems to have believed that Churchill's rise to the Cabinet meant that there was finally a political leader in office in London who could cope with the threat in Europe presented by Hitler. Like Chamberlain, Churchill understood the importance of American material support for the Anglo-French war effort, although he, too, seems to have had little initial personal regard for the president.[6] Still, Churchill took up Roosevelt's offer of keeping him informed. Over the winter of 1939–40, supported by Chamberlain and Halifax – the premier let Churchill deal with Roosevelt – Churchill established a secret correspondence with the president ostensibly designed to keep him abreast of naval developments. More practically, it was designed to build political bridges to the centre of the American government that would abet Britain's effort to defeat Germany.

It is crucial to understand the nature of the Churchill–Roosevelt wartime relationship that began with that first exchange of letters and lasted until Roosevelt's death in April 1945. For a long while the personal ties that developed between these two men, ties that became genuinely friendly, were portrayed as the basis of an Anglo-American

4 Roosevelt to Churchill, 11 Sep. 1939, *Churchill–Roosevelt*, I, 24; Roosevelt to Chamberlain, 11 Sep. 1939, Roosevelt PSF GB.
5 Reynolds, *Alliance*, 85–7, esp. n. 134.
6 Chamberlain to Lothian, 15 Sep. 1939, FO 800/397. On Churchill and Roosevelt, see W. F. Kimball, *Forged in War. Roosevelt, Churchill, and the Second World War* (New York, 1996), 1–61. Cf. Churchill to Roosevelt, 5 Oct. 1939, *Churchill–Roosevelt*, I, 26–7; W. S. Churchill, *The Second World War*, vol. I (1948) [hereafter in the style *SWW*, I), 440–1.

'special relationship'.[7] Emerging during the war years and continuing afterwards, this relationship supposedly lay at the heart of what one diehard atlanticist termed 'one of the most decisive forces in modern history'.[8] During the Cold War, for instance, Churchill embroidered on this theme. The personal side of this transatlantic diplomacy must be approached cautiously. In the first place, between October 1939 and May 1940, there were only twelve messages: eight from Churchill, three from Roosevelt, and one telephone call.[9] Moreover, Roosevelt and Chamberlain wrote to one another in this same period.[10] Second, although these early communications suggest emerging Anglo-American co-operation, they dealt with minor matters like British efforts to sink the German pocket battleship *Graf Spee*. Third, because of more pressing problems that arose during the 'Phoney War' – the time from September 1939 until April 1940, when the German attack in the West began with the descent on Scandinavia – the question of the United States remained in the second rank of British strategic calculations.

Only after France surrendered to Germany on 22 June 1940 and Britain faced the Axis alone did Churchill begin serious communications with Roosevelt. The reason was simple: he needed to court friendly Powers to sustain Britain's war effort. For his part, after June 1940, Roosevelt appreciated that a German-dominated Europe presented grave strategic problems for the United States, including some in the Western Hemisphere. On both sides of the Atlantic, the cold calculation of national interests brought Britain and the United States – and Churchill and Roosevelt – closer together. In the first twenty-seven months of the war, from Germany's attack on Poland to Japan's

[7] H. C. Allen, 'Anti-Americanism in Britain', *CR*, 200(1961), 625–9; G. W. Ball, 'The "Special Relationship" in Today's World', in W. E. Leuchtenberg *et al.*, eds. *Britain and the United States* (1979), 47–59; S. G. Putt, *View from Atlantis: The Americans and Ourselves* (London, 1955); A. C. Turner, *The Unique Partnership: Britain and the United States* (New York, 1971).

[8] M. Greene, 'American Kinship with Britain', *Quarterly Review*, 301(1963), 383–93. Cf. *SWW*, I, and W. S. Churchill, *The Unwritten Alliance: Speeches, 1953 to 1959* (1961). Cf. M. Weidhorn, 'America Through Churchill's Eyes', *Thought*, 50(1975), 5–34. Then see M. Beloff, 'The "Special Relationship" in Today's World', in M. Gilbert, ed., *A Century of Conflict, 1850–1950: Essays for A. J. P. Taylor* (1966), 149–71; W. F. Kimball, 'Thirty Years After, or the Two Musketeers', *DH*, 18(1995), 161–76; D. Reynolds, 'A "Special Relationship"? America, Britain and the International Order Since the Second World War', *IA*, 62(1985/6), 1–20; D. Reynolds, 'Roosevelt, Churchill, and the Wartime Anglo-American Alliance, 1939–1945: Towards a New Synthesis', in W. R. Louis and H. Bull, eds., *The 'Special Relationship': Anglo-American Relations Since 1945* (Oxford, 1986), 17–41.

[9] *Churchill–Roosevelt*, I, 24–35.

[10] Chamberlain to Roosevelt, 4 Oct., 8 Nov. 1939, Roosevelt PSF GB; Chamberlain to Lothian [for Roosevelt], 4, 7 Feb. 1940, Roosevelt PSF Welles; Chamberlain to Roosevelt, 13 Mar. 1940, NC 7/11/33/142.

co-ordinated assault on the European East Asian empires and the American colonies of Hawaii and the Philippines, those interests merged. For the British, this period spelled the end of their country's global pre-eminence as Roosevelt's United States finally fused American economic and financial wealth to political involvement in the wider world, a desire to achieve strategic preponderance outside the Western Hemisphere, and a will to shape the world in an American-defined image.

During the Phoney War, the Chamberlain government pursued military and foreign policies that mirrored Britain's experience between 1914 and 1918. In the military field, these efforts concentrated on building up adequate armed force and strengthening the alliance with France to confront the Germans in the West. Anglo-French staff talks were desultory in 1936–8 but after Munich, and especially after Prague, they focused on creating a combined military response to the Germans on the Great War model: a Supreme War Council (the SWC), a Joint Staff of military advisers, and a secretariat.[11] Attended by Chamberlain and Daladier, SWC first met on 12 September 1939 'to advertise Franco-British unity and supply mutual encouragement [so as] to forestall the enemy's efforts to divide the Allies'.[12] Thereafter, it met regularly until June 1940 to co-ordinate Allied military strategy.[13] Recognising that the French would contribute most to the land war, Chamberlain's government agreed that the British Field Force commander, General Lord Gort, would be subordinate to the French commander-in-chief, General Maurice Gamelin.[14] However, London kept control over its own naval and air forces, a decision having as much to do with meeting the German threat in Europe as defending the Empire.[15]

Lord Grey, the foreign secretary until December 1916, had argued that wartime diplomacy existed to sustain the armed forces engaged in fighting.[16] During the winter of 1939–40, chiefly via the SWC, British

---

[11] French, *British Way*, 195–200; Gibbs, *Grand Strategy*, 607–80. Cf. COS memorandum, 'Anglo-French Staff Conversations 1939' [COS 856], 31 Mar. 1939, CAB 53/46; COS report, 'Staff Conversations with the French' [COS 877], 13 Apr. 1939, CAB 53/47.

[12] J. R. M. Butler, *Grand Strategy*, vol. II: *September 1939–June 1941* (1957), 20.

[13] *Ibid.*, 43, 76–80, 119–20, 169.

[14] B. Bond, 'Gort', in J. Keegan, ed., *Churchill's Generals* (1991), 37–8.

[15] Gibbs, *Grand Strategy*, 681–4. Cf. COS reports, 'Reinforcements for Egypt' [CID 1561], 4 Jul. 1939, 'Reinforcements for places abroad other than Egypt' [CID 1562], 5 Jul. 1939, both CAB 4/30; COS note, 'Strategical Planning Progress Report No.1' [COS 948], 1 Jul. 1939, CAB 53/52.

[16] Grey of Fallodon, *Twenty-Five Years*, vol. II (1926), 153–60. This paragraph is based on B. Bond, *Britain, France, and Belgium, 1939–1940*, 2nd edn (1990); L. H. Cutright, 'Great Britain, the Balkans and Turkey in the Autumn of 1939', *IHR*, 10(1988), 433–55; R. A. C. Parker, 'Britain, France, and Scandinavia, 1939–1940', *History*,

foreign policy followed this dictum by working with allied and neutral Powers to achieve the optimum conditions possible for waging war. Beyond Allied collaboration, efforts were made to entice the lesser neutral Powers in Europe – in the Low Countries, the Balkans, and Scandinavia – to align with Britain and France. This diplomacy proved unsuccessful. The Belgians refused to enter staff talks from fear of inciting a German attack. Despite the guarantees of April 1939, the possibility of a 'Balkan bloc' evaporated because of Romanian anxiety about Bolshevik Russia and Yugoslavian and Greek apprehensions about Italy. In Scandinavia, the Swedish government's pro-German sentiments, Norwegian nervousness about a German attack, and the outbreak of a Russo-Finnish war (which might divert Allied troops from western Europe if Britain and France intervened) militated against a pro-Allied bloc in this region. Still, there were some successes. By mid-October, an Anglo-Franco-Turkish treaty was concluded, though it would not come into operation until Ankara received sufficient supplies of arms and other war material. And a cautious policy towards Mussolini's Italy, such as avoiding provocative actions like imposing a blockade, seemed to play on Rome's initial concern that Germany might be defeated by the two Allies.

Ultimately, Anglo-French efforts proved inadequate to stem the German attack when it came in the spring of 1940.[17] Norway and Denmark were overrun in April; Holland and Belgium fell between 10 and 14 May; and, after failing to stop the German juggernaut at Sedan on 14–15 May, British and French forces in eastern France were forced to retreat. The collapse of the French Army saw the creation of a new government in Paris, led by Marshal Henri Pétain, which surrendered on 22 June; before this, although encircled at the port of Dunkerque, the British Army with some French and Belgian units was able to retreat across the Channel in late May and early June to regroup in Britain. Another casualty of the German onslaught was Chamberlain. On 10 May 1940, he fell from office over German success in Norway, and Churchill rose to the premiership.

Against the setting of the Phoney War, Anglo-American relations were

61(1976), 369–87; G. L. Weinberg, *A World at Arms. A Global History of World War II* (Cambridge, 1994), 73–89; L. Woodward, *British Foreign Policy in the Second World War*, vol. I (1970), 1–80.
[17] This paragraph is based on Butler, *Grand Strategy*, 119–207; J. D. Fair, 'The Norwegian Campaign and Winston Churchill's Rise to Power in 1940: A Study of Perception and Attribution', *IHR*, 9(1987), 410–37; Gilbert, *Churchill*, VI, 174–648; B. Stegemann, 'Operation Weserübung', H. Umbreit, 'The Battle for Hegemony in Western Europe', both in K. A. Maier *et al.*, *Germany and the Second World War*, vol. II: *Germany's Initial Conquests in Europe* (Oxford, 1991), 206–19, 229–316.

defined, on one hand, by the British government's effort to get the maximum United States material support for Britain's armed forces and, on the other, by Roosevelt's desire not to have the United States drawn into any fighting. However, the Phoney War period was not viewed by contemporaries as preliminary to an unavoidable German attack.[18] Since warfare had not broken out on the Franco-German border and as London had yet to suffer attack by the *Luftwaffe*, a range of opinion in Britain and the United States was uncertain whether Hitler felt he could win a war in the West. Accordingly, whilst Chamberlain's government laboured to build up adequate armed forces should they be needed, it employed a diplomacy towards the neutral United States designed to enhance Allied war-making potential. In Washington, Roosevelt and his advisers were willing to assist Britain and France as much as they could without making military commitments; at the same time, they looked to ensure American hemispheric security through their own military and foreign policies.

Lothian needed little encouragement to lobby Roosevelt and Hull about applying the neutrality laws favourably towards Britain.[19] On 12 September, Roosevelt adhered to that legislation and announced an embargo on arms sales and restrictions on American travel on belligerent ships. But at a special session of Congress on 21 September, after digesting reports reaching him from Lothian, Kennedy, Bullitt, and others, he announced that he wanted the embargo repealed and amendments introduced, including the revival of the cash-and-carry provisions.[20] Pittman brought a bill to this effect to the Senate on 2 October. After concerted White House lobbying and bipartisan support from internationalist Republicans like Stimson, a revised neutrality law passed both houses of Congress by 2 November. Loans to governments that had defaulted on war debts were still prohibited, and belligerent Powers could not use American harbours as supply bases; but the embargo on arms exports vanished, allowing belligerent purchases on a cash-and-carry basis. Over the next eight months, Allied purchases in the United States rose rapidly;[21] to assist the British and French,

---

[18] Reynolds, *Alliance*, 64.

[19] Lothian to Halifax, 5, 15 Sep. 1939, Halifax to Lothian, 27 Sep. 1939, Lothian speech to the NY Pilgrim's Society, 25 Oct. 1939, all Halifax FO 800/324. Cf. Hull memoranda [conversations with Lothian], 4, 11, 19 Sep. 1939, Hull 58.

[20] Dallek, *Roosevelt*, 200–5. Cf. Morgenthau diary, 28 Sep. 1939; Borah, 'Cash-and-Carry-Brief', n.d., Borah 759.

[21] Between July 1939 and June 1940, the British alone spent $1,892 million on goods (including aircraft, aircraft materials, munitions, iron, steel, manufactures, food, and petroleum): Morgenthau diary, 17 Jul. 1940. In 1938, £1 equalled $4.95; by 1940, £1 equalled $4.03: Butler and Sloman, *Political Facts*, 310. Then, compare:

Roosevelt had Morgenthau prevent the Germans and Russians from 'buying up [the] principal sources of supplies needed by France or England'.[22] These purchases created difficulties for London by devaluing sterling and depleting British dollar and gold holdings. On the American side, London's decision to buy only goods necessary for the war effort reduced exports to Britain in important commodities like agricultural products; farm and other interest groups lobbied the Administration about the seeming unfairness of British policy.[23] Yet, despite these difficulties, a basis for Anglo-American collaboration had been established by June 1940. It had occurred largely because the leadership of both Powers saw it in their interests to co-operate.

Co-operation also emerged over naval matters. Sensing the imminence of the European crisis in June 1939, Roosevelt conceived of a 'security zone' in the Atlantic to ensure the protection of North America. He mentioned this during George VI's visit and, on 5 September, announced that American naval and air forces would patrol the Atlantic Ocean to a distance of 300 miles from the coast.[24] Moreover, he asked for refuelling and other rights at British bases in the West Indies and the Canadian port of Halifax. Churchill immediately saw value in making this concession – 'we should welcome any such scheme, and it would be of the highest importance to our safety and success'; and he used the opportunity of his correspondence with Roosevelt over the winter to show the president that the RN was respecting American neutral rights in the 'security zone' and to seek Roosevelt's help in imposing the British blockade outside of it.[25] Roosevelt understood the need to assist the British, and he even acquiesced in the British arrest in May 1940 of a cipher clerk in Kennedy's embassy, Tyler Kent, who was preparing to leak the Churchill–Roosevelt correspondence because he thought it compromised American neutrality.[26]

Significantly, Britain's blockade against Germany after September

	British GNP	British exports	British imports
1938	4,671	532.3	919.5
1940	5,980	437.2	1,152.1

Figures are millions of pounds. From Mitchell, 'Overseas Trade 3', 'Prest's Estimates [National Income], 1915–1946', *British Historical Statistics*, 284, 368.

[22] Morgenthau diary, 1 Dec. 1939.

[23] A. P. Dobson, *US Wartime Aid to Britain, 1940–1946* (New York, 1986), 15–18.

[24] Lothian telegram (440) to Halifax, 6 Sep. 1939, FO 371/22837/6062/6061; Woodward, *Foreign Policy*, I, 158. On telling the king, Lindsay telegram (293) to Halifax, 1 Jul. 1939, FO 371/23901/10081/9805.

[25] Churchill to Pound [first sea lord], 7 Sep. 1939, ADM 116/922. Cf. Churchill to Roosevelt, 29, 30 Jan., 28 Feb. 1940, *Churchill–Roosevelt*, I, 33–5.

[26] Leutze, *Bargaining*, 47–55; W. F. Kimball and B. Bartlett, 'Roosevelt and Prewar Commitments to Churchill: The Tyler Kent Affair', *DH*, 5(1981), 291–311.

1939 did not evince the kind of emotive American reaction it had in 1914–17. Lothian delivered a note to Hull on 3 September 1939 explaining that British actions would be 'in conformity with the recognised rules applicable to the exercise of maritime belligerent rights by warships'. At Hull's suggestion, an Anglo-American committee of experts (diplomats from Lothian's embassy and Feis) was formed to establish 'something like the certificate system that was in operation during the last part of the World War' to reduce interference with 'American commerce'.[27] Though opposition emerged from isolationists and others, like Borah, who promoted the freedom of the seas, general American opinion seemed to sympathise with Britain's action. In a series of despatches over the winter, Lothian argued that only intemperate policies and an attitude of indifference to American goodwill would swing opinion into the camp of the opponents of the blockade.[28] By early 1940, the embassy held that American fears of being drawn into the war were receding, but with an eye to Nye's investigation in the mid-1930s, Lothian advised that overt British propaganda in the United States might be ill-received by the American public.[29] In this atmosphere of general American distaste for Hitler's regime and a growing sympathy for Britain's position, prudence by Chamberlain's government would only benefit the Allied war effort. Whilst British critics in the United States began to coalesce around staunch isolationists like the celebrity-aviator, Charles Lindbergh, Roosevelt, most of his advisers, an array of politicians, some important elements of the American media, the Roman Catholic hierarchy, and influential British *emigrés* supported British efforts to meet the German threat during the Phoney War.[30] As a recent study suggests, the majority of American opinion saw it in the United States' interest to provide material and moral support to Britain

[27] Lothian to Hull, 3 Sep. 1939, Roosevelt PSF GB; Hull memoranda [conversations with Lothian], 4, 11 Sep. 1939, Hull 58. Cf. W. N. Medlicott, *The Economic Blockade* (1952), 43–62.
[28] Woodward, *Foreign Policy*, I, 161–4. Cf. Lothian to Halifax, 15 Sep. 1939, Hoare to Lothian, 25 Sep. 1939, Chatfield to Lothian, 26 Sep. 1939, all FO 800/397; Lothian to Chamberlain, 28 Nov. 1939, NC 7/11/32/172; Lothian to Hoare, 3 Nov. 1939, 3 Feb. 1940, both Templewood XI/5.
[29] Lothian to Halifax, 11 Mar. 1940, Halifax FO 800/324.
[30] W. S. Cole, *America First: The Battle Against Intervention, 1940–1941* (Madison, WI, 1953); W. S. Cole, *Charles A. Lindbergh and the Battle Against American Intervention in World War II* (New York, 1974). Cf. Morgenthau diary, 29 Apr. 1940; J. Davis, 'Notes on Warner Brothers Foreign Policy, 1918–1948', *Velvet Light Trap*, 17(1977); W. M. Turtle, 'Aid to the Allies Short-of-War versus American Intervention, 1940: A Reappraisal of William Allen White's Leadership', *JAH*, 56(1970), 840–58; T. E. Hachey, 'Anglophile Sentiments in American Catholicism in 1940: A British Official's Confidential Assessment', *Records of the American Catholic Historical Society of Philadelphia*, 85(1974), 70–83; Rathbone [British actor] to Chamberlain, 11 Apr. 1939, NC 7/11/32/200A.

after September 1939 for the most realistic of reasons: it was better that Britain, rather than the United States, fight Germany.[31] Naturally, in pursuing their own narrow national interests, the British and Americans did not see every element of their emerging co-operation as beneficial. In the economic sphere, London recognised that the outflow of gold and the depletion of British dollar reserves were creating a dangerous imbalance in favour of the United States. Such an imbalance threatened British control over its informal economic empire, something driven home when Roosevelt met with Sir Frederick Phillips, the senior British Treasury representative in Washington, shortly after the fall of France: 'How about selling some of these securities that you have in the Argentine, such as Street Railway and so forth?'[32] An obvious price had to be paid in seeking American economic assistance. This tendency in American policy was especially pronounced in relation to Western Hemispheric security, where economic diplomacy and American national security overlapped.[33] A case in point touched the Danish colony of Greenland. After Denmark fell to Germany, the Canadian government sent a small force to secure aluminium mines on the island. However, Washington despatched a force of its own and displaced the Canadians.[34] Although Eden chafed at the American desire to control these mines, London made no formal protest over the American action.

Before Hitler's Germany launched its offensive in Western Europe, the Cabinet held concerns about American expectations that the Anglo-French alliance could meet the German threat. British concerns reached a peak in February–March 1940. On 2 February, Roosevelt announced that Welles would travel to Berlin, Rome, Paris, and London seeking information on the possibility of a negotiated settlement to end the crisis.[35] Roosevelt actually proposed the Welles mission more for domestic political reasons – he was considering running for an unprecedented third term as president in the November 1940 elections, and the

---

[31] M. A. Ramsay, '*Vox Populi*: Some Notes on US Public Opinion, Great Britain, and US Foreign Policy, 1937–1941' (forthcoming).

[32] Morgenthau diary, 17 Jul. 1940, with Morgenthau memorandum, 'Dollar Requirements of the United Kingdom Exchange Control', n.d.

[33] Cf. D. Green, *The Containment of Latin America: A History of the Myths and Realities of the Good Neighbor Policy* (Chicago, 1971); Haglund, *Transformation*; R. Pommerin, *Das Dritte Reich und Lateinamerika: Die deutsche Politik gegenüber Süd- und Mittelamerika, 1939–1942* (Düsseldorf, 1977).

[34] J. A. English, 'Not an Equilateral Triangle: Canada's Strategic Relationship with the United States and Britain, 1939–1945', in B. J. C. McKercher and L. Aronsen, eds., *The North Atlantic Triangle in a Changing World: Anglo-American-Canadian Relations, 1902–1956* (Toronto, 1996), 147–50.

[35] Lothian telegram to Halifax, 2 Feb. 1940, Halifax FO 800/324.

mantle of peacemaker would help him with American voters.[36] But the British greeted Welles' mission with apprehension. The Foreign Office American Department encapsulated these anxieties with the argument that the 'President and those surrounding him think that we can't win', adding:

The United States cannot afford to let us lose and would not like to see us defeated ... [Roosevelt] has decided to send Mr Sumner Welles and even if we assure him that the mere mention of the visit will affect our interests injuriously he will no doubt, secure in his conviction that we can't win, disregard our remonstrances and feel that he is saving us from ourselves.[37]

After consulting Halifax, Chamberlain officially welcomed Welles' mission, but he cautioned Roosevelt that 'there would be the utmost difficulty in persuading the people of this country and, I believe of France, that any settlement is worth signing with Hitler or the present regime'.[38] Building on Lothian's assessments about the volatility of general American opinion, the Cabinet and the Foreign Office made every effort to convince Welles, and Moffat, who accompanied him, of British resolve.[39] Additionally, British financial weakness had to be minimised; any suggestion of a need for American financial aid would rattle American isolationists who, looking back to 1914–17, saw such aid as the precursor to intervention. British disquiet was allayed after Welles met with the king, Chamberlain, senior Cabinet ministers, and Opposition MPs on 11–13 March.[40] First, German arrogance had seen Welles leave Berlin with a critical view of German policy. Second, especially after meeting with Chamberlain and Churchill, Welles sympathised with the British predicament. He began to believe in German culpability for the crisis, and that American support for the British could help to restrain Hitler. The only difficulty was that Hitler could not be restrained.

The British way in warfare since at least the late seventeenth century had involved finding allies that shared British interests and then, providing the bulk of financing and a contribution of armed force,

[36] Dallek, *Roosevelt*, 215–17.
[37] Scott minute, 7 Feb. 1940, FO 371/24238/1309/131.
[38] Chamberlain telegram to Lothian, 4 Feb. 1940, Halifax FO 800/324.
[39] On US opinion, see Lothian to Halifax, 5 Feb. 1940, with enclosure, *ibid.*; on preparations, Lothian telegram to Scott, 29 Feb. 1940; Eden minute to Halifax, n.d., Stevenson [Halifax's secretary] memorandum, 'Entertainment of Mr. Sumner Welles', 1 Mar. 1940; Stevenson memorandum, 'Mr. Sumner Welles' Visit', 9 Mar. 1940, all *ibid.*
[40] See Chamberlain and Churchill's favourable reports to the War Cabinet, WM 67(40)7, 13 Mar. 1940, CAB 65. Cf. Record of meeting, 13 Mar. 1940, Halifax FO 800/326; Welles memorandum, 11 Mar. 1940, Roosevelt PSF Welles.

288 Transition of power

fighting enemy Powers.[41] This approach sometimes ran aground, for instance, in maintaining the first three coalitions against revolutionary and Napoleonic France after 1792.[42] Yet, geography, the Royal Navy, British financial and industrial capacity, and the ability to find overseas supplies of raw materials and markets traditionally had given Britain decided strategic advantages. In large degree, British involvement against the Central Powers between 1914 and 1918 had been predicated on this approach to warfare. And in the interwar period, the general assumption by a range of statesmen, from Ramsay MacDonald to Austen Chamberlain, was that Britain would have allies to assist in any continental struggle. The European crisis after 1 September 1939 suggested that war, if it broke out, would be limited to the Anglo-French alliance, on one side, and Germany, on the other: Mussolini remained neutral, unsure of Hitler's chances for victory; Bolshevik Russia was more concerned with securing its position against the Baltic states and Finland; and the minor Powers, especially Holland and Belgium, were frantically working to keep aloof from any potential fighting. Even outside of Europe, in the Far East, the Japanese were waiting to see how the European crisis would be resolved – another indication that Vansittart's iron logic expressed in the first DRC still had validity. With American policy since September 1939, in tandem with the Welles mission, showing that the United States would be benevolently neutral towards Britain and France in a conflict with Germany, Chamberlain's government by March 1940 reckoned that a major war might still be averted.

Hitler's actions after April 1940, leading to the fall of France on 22 June, dramatically changed the situation.[43] Regardless of the reasons for Anglo-French defeat, the fact remains that on 22 June 1940, Britain suddenly and unexpectedly found itself alone against the Axis Powers. Mussolini unearthed the courage to attack stricken France on 10 June and, from the Italian colony of Libya, looked covetously on Egypt. With the *Luftwaffe* able to cross the Channel to bomb British targets, with British economic, financial, and industrial strength stretched to the limit, and with access to overseas supplies of raw materials and markets constricted by the possibility of a German submarine offensive, the traditional strategic advantages of the British way in warfare were melting away. The French collapse presented Churchill's new War

[41] French, *British Way.*
[42] A. Bryant, *The Years of Endurance, 1793–1802* (New York, 1942); C. D. Hall, *British Naval Strategy in the Napoleonic Wars, 1803–15* (Manchester, 1992); P. Mackesy, *War Without Victory: The Downfall of Pitt, 1799–1802* (Oxford, 1984).
[43] D. Reynolds, '1940: Fulcrum of the Twentieth Century', *IA*, 66(1990), 325–50 is instructive.

Cabinet with a disaster that threatened the foundations of British global power. Less obviously, it was the turning-point in the evolving Anglo-American relationship.

In his memoirs, Churchill related: 'Future generations may deem it noteworthy that the supreme question of whether we should fight on alone never found a place upon the War Cabinet agenda ... we were much too busy to waste time upon such unreal, academic issues.'[44] He was disingenuous, seeking retrospectively to sustain Britain's Cold War image as a resolute enemy of totalitarianism. On 26 May 1940, during the Dunkerque evacuation, Churchill asked the COS 'what are the prospects of our continuing the war alone against Germany and probably Italy'. He couched this request in terms of the defeat of France and Belgium leaving Britain alone, and 'in the event of terms being offered to Britain which would place her entirely at the mercy of Germany'.[45] Over the next few days the Cabinet assessed the military position. Their discussion was based on COS assessments that if British forces could be evacuated from Dunkerque, the home islands could be defended against a German attack: the RN could safeguard the Channel, the RAF could defend the skies, and ground forces could garrison the coast.[46] No minister advocated surrender, but Halifax argued that Italian support might be bought to help Britain achieve security 'from the point of view of the balance of power'. Churchill countered with the argument that the 'only thing to do was to show [Hitler] that he could not conquer this country'.[47] The Cabinet endorsed his view and, despite some ministers, such as Lord Beaverbrook, who opposed making major concessions to Washington, it became clear that Britain would have to rely on American support to continue the war.

Halifax also advocated a direct appeal to the American people; this idea had been broached privately by Jan Smuts, the South African statesman, who suggested a declaration stating: 'We are only concerned with the defence of world liberty against what will undoubtedly mean the domination of the world by Nazi power. Will the United States help or will they stand aside and take no action in defence of the rights of man?'[48] Two weeks earlier, Roosevelt had declined Churchill's request

[44] *SWW*, II, 177–8.
[45] WM 139(40)1, Confidential Annex, 26 May 1940, CAB 65.
[46] WM 140(40), Confidential Annex, 26 May 1940, WM 141(40)9, Confidential Annex, WM 142(40), Confidential Annex, both 27 May 1940, WM 145(40)1, Confidential Annex, 28 May 1940, WM 146(40)1, Confidential Annex, 29 May 1940, all *ibid*.
[47] See the exchanges in WM 140(40), Confidential Annex, 26 May 1940, *ibid*. Cf. Vansittart minute, 14 Jun. 1940, Scott minute, 17 Jun. 1940, on Lothian to Halifax, 3 Jun. 1940, Halifax FO 800/324.
[48] For this discussion and excerpts of Smuts' letters, see WM 145(40)1, Confidential Minute, 28 May 1940, *ibid*. Churchill's comment, quoted below, is from this meeting.

for the loan of fifty USN destroyers to bolster the RN.[49] Whilst the president cited the problem of Congressional approval blocking such a loan, Churchill understood that Roosevelt was not about to squander American warships until the dust cleared in Europe. Realising that a direct appeal would do little at that moment, Churchill won the day in the Cabinet with the argument: 'If we made a bold stand against Germany, that would command [American] admiration and respect; but a grovelling appeal, if made now, would have the worst possible effect.' Britain would have to fight on to survive.[50]

Britain's position was not completely hopeless. The dominions were ready to offer what assistance they could. Despite British prewar apprehension about isolationist sentiment in Ottawa, Mackenzie King's government had declared war on Germany on 10 September 1939.[51] In Britain, the Admiralty believed as late as January 1938 that even if Canada remained neutral, Canadian harbours and 'intelligence organisations' would be made available to the RN.[52] It went without saying that the always avaricious Canadians would be only too willing to sell food and industrial raw materials to Britain. Therefore, Canadian military participation in war was an added bonus; and, by the summer of 1940, Canadian troops were helping to garrison Britain against a possible German invasion. By the same token, Australia and New Zealand also declared war on Germany and, though uneasy about Japanese ambitions in the Pacific, were willing to send troops to the Mediterranean. After September 1940, when Italian forces in Libya attacked Egypt, Australian and New Zealand soldiers helped repel this assault. Also in Britain at this time were the political remnants of the states overrun by the Germans – governments-in-exile – which had brought with them some of their armed forces;[53] admittedly, however,

[49] Churchill to Roosevelt, 15 May 1940, and reply, 16 May 1940, *Churchill–Roosevelt*, I, 37–9.
[50] Roberts, *Halifax*, 220 – Churchill 'was not fighting so much for victory as for better terms in the near future' – is erroneous.
[51] Cf. J. Granatstein and R. Bothwell, '"A Self-Evident National Duty": Canadian Foreign Policy, 1935–1939', *JCIH*, 3(1975), 212–33; B. J. C. McKercher, 'World Power and Isolationism: The North Atlantic Triangle and the Crises of the 1930s', in McKercher and Aronsen, *Triangle*, esp. 133–7.
[52] Barnes [Admiralty] to Batterbee [Board of Trade], 22 Nov. 1937, 11 Feb. 1938, Phillips [director of plans, Admiralty] minute, 5 Jan. 1938, Troup [Naval Intelligence] minute, 12 Jan. 1938, all ADM 1/9488.
[53] J. L. Ready, *Forgotten Allies: The Military Contribution of the Colonies, Exiled Governments, and Lesser Powers to the Allied Victory in World War II*, 2 vols. (Jefferson, NC, 1985). Cf. F. Kersaudy, *Churchill and De Gaulle* (1981); P. Ludlow, 'Britain and Northern Europe, 1940–1945', *Scandinavian Journal of History*, 4(1979), 123–69; S. K. Pavlowitch, 'Out of Context: The Yugoslav Government in London, 1941–1945', *JCH*, 16(1981), 89–118; A. Prazmowska, *Britain and Poland, 1939–1943: The Betrayed Ally* (Cambridge, 1995).

these exiled forces were small and lacked adequate equipment. Augmented by these additional forces and access to outside supply, the RN, RAF, and British Army could defend the home islands and maintain a presence in key strategic areas like Egypt.[54] The strength of the RN, with bases like Malta, Gibraltar, and Alexandria, allowed for the supply of British and Imperial forces and harassment of German and Italian shipping. Moreover, thanks to Polish intelligence having broken the Germans' most confidential Enigma codes, the secrets of which came to British intelligence, Churchill had daily information on German tactical, operational, and strategic moves.[55] Yet, whilst a solitary Britain and its dominion allies could defend their position against Germany in the summer of 1940 and, after September, against Italy in North Africa, there was little chance that it could launch an offensive capable of defeating the two European Axis Powers. Indeed, as Sir Howard Kingsley Wood, Churchill's chancellor of the Exchequer, reminded his colleagues during this difficult time, all the government could hope to do was to finance a defensive strategy not an offensive one.

In this context, the United States emerged in Churchill's mind – as well as that of his Cabinet – as the one Power that could help underwrite the British war effort and, perhaps, even join the struggle on Britain's side. Given the subsequent mythology surrounding the Anglo-American 'special relationship', it must be realised that what eventually became the Anglo-American wartime alliance was a close-run thing. Churchill understood that only effective British opposition to the Axis would convince Roosevelt and American opinion generally that United States support would not be wasted. Such resistance, therefore, became the order of the day. As it turned out, the ambitions of Hitler and Mussolini, rather than any initiative by Churchill's government, provided the British with opportunities over the remaining six months of 1940 to show the Americans British resolve.

In late August, Hitler unleashed the *Luftwaffe* on Britain to prepare

---

[54] D. W. Braddock, *The Campaigns in Egypt and Libya, 1940–1942* (Aldershot, 1964); B. Maughan, *Tobruk and Alamein* (Sydney, 1987); W. A. Miller, *The 9th Australian Division Versus the Africa Corps: An Infantry Division Against Tanks – Tobruk, Libya, 1941* (Ft. Leavenworth, KS, 1986); New Zealand, War History Branch, *New Zealand in the Second World War, 1939–1945* (Wellington, 1950); New Zealand, War History Branch, *The Relief of Tobruk* (Wellington, 1961); B. Pitt, *The Crucible of War*, vol. I: *Western Desert, 1941* (London, 1980); Stacey, *Canada*, 270–323; C. P. Stacey, *Arms, Men and Governments. The War Policies of Canada, 1939–1945* (Ottawa, 1970), 146–59.
[55] F. H. Hinsley, *British Intelligence in the Second World War*, abridged edn (Cambridge, 1993), 14–29 *passim*. Cf. C. Andrew, 'Churchill and Intelligence', in M. Handel, ed., *Leaders and Intelligence* (1989); R. A. Woytak, *On the Border of War and Peace: Polish Intelligence and Diplomacy in 1937–1939 and the Origins of the Ultra Secret* (Boulder, CO, 1979).

the way for a German invasion. This air battle over the Channel and southern England – the Battle of Britain – was extremely intense until late October.[56] Thanks to courageous British and Imperial airmen, good intelligence, and modern fighter aircraft, the latter the result of the Chamberlain government's rearmament policies before September 1939, the *Luftwaffe* failed to break British resolve. Postponing the invasion, Hitler directed the German Navy to step up its submarine offensive against British shipping lanes; known as the Battle of the Atlantic, this struggle involved a German economic strategy to starve Britain of essential food and raw materials and destroy its overseas trade.[57] Although the British initially had difficulty in meeting this German offensive, the RN and the Royal Canadian Navy (RCN) began to utilise their naval supremacy to meet the submarine offensive. In addition, in early July 1940, to prevent the French Fleet from falling into German hands, the RN sank the flower of the French navy at Oran.[58]

Britain's resistance to the Axis offensive in summer–autumn 1940 did as Churchill surmised: it began to create feelings amongst crucial members of Roosevelt's Administration that Britain had the desire and will to oppose Germany and Italy. However, the American decision to support Britain's war effort after mid-June was not straightforward. During the Phoney War, Roosevelt's attitude concerning the British and French ability to avoid defeat fluctuated.[59] At times he seemed optimistic but, when events seemed to go against the two Allies, he would become discouraged. This vacillation reflected divisions within his Administration. On one extreme was Hull, whose legalistic approach to foreign policy suggested a line of complete neutrality in the conflict.[60] On the other was Harry Woodring, the secretary of war, an

[56] H. Boog, *Die Deutsche Luftwaffenführung, 1935–1945: Führungsprobleme, Spitzengliederung, Generalstabsausbildung* (Stuttgart, 1982); B. Collier, *The Defence of the United Kingdom* (1957); W. Murray, *Strategy for Defeat: The Luftwaffe, 1933–1945* (Maxwell, AL, 1983).

[57] 'Conference of the C.-in-C., Navy, with the Fuehrer on October 14, 1940', in Anonymous, *Fuehrer Conferences on Naval Affairs 1939–1945* (1990), 143–5. Cf. J. Brennecke, *Die Wende im U-Boot-Krieg: Ursachen und Folgen, 1939–1943* (Herford, West Germany, 1984); U. Elfrath, *Die Deutsche Kriegsmarine, 1935–1945* (Friedberg, 1985), esp. vol. III; T. Hughes, *The Battle of the Atlantic* (New York, 1977); S. Roskill, *The War at Sea 1939–1945*, vol. I: *The Defensive* (1954).

[58] Butler, *Grand Strategy*, 221–7.

[59] Cf. Morgenthau diary, 3 Oct., 14 Oct. 1939, 3 Mar., 29 Apr. 1940; Ickes diary, 14 Oct. 1939, Ickes, *Diary*, 352

[60] See the papers Hull requested from his officials about modifying the Neutrality Act: for instance, Green memorandum, 2 Oct. 1939, Savage memorandum, 'Change of Neutrality Policies in Time of War', 4 Oct. 1939, Hackworth memorandum, 'Arms, Ammunition, and Implements of War', 17 Oct. 1939, all Hull 84. Cf. his discussions with British diplomats over trade and ancillary questions in memoranda, 4, 11 Sep.

unreconstructed isolationist.[61] In the middle were ministers like Morgenthau and Ickes, each of whom, despite some reservations about the
British ability to meet the Axis threat, wanted to help underwrite
Britain's war effort.[62] This divergence was reflected in the State Department and diplomatic service. After his mission when he confronted the
stark differences between Nazi Germany and liberal Britain and France,
Welles argued for as much American support as possible. Conversely,
other officials like Moffat and one of his subordinates, Adolf Berle,
tended to see little difference between the Anglo-French Powers, on one
hand, and their Axis foes, on the other. But whilst they held both
equally guilty for the outbreak of the war, they did everything possible to
help the British blockade of Germany.[63] Amongst the ambassadors,
Bullitt continued his earlier line of argument that as much aid as
possible had to flow to the anti-German coalition.[64] His arguments were
countered by Kennedy, who believed that inevitable German victory
meant that the United States should do nothing to sustain Britain's war
effort.[65]

German victory over France changed everything. Vacillation in
Washington ended as Roosevelt, the guiding hand of American foreign
and defence policy, was forced to decide whether the United States
should aid Britain in its war against the Axis. On 10 June 1940, just after
Italy's attack on France, Roosevelt delivered a speech at Charlottesville,
Virginia. He proclaimed:

we will pursue two obvious and simultaneous causes: We will extend to the
opponents of force, the material resources of this nation, and harness and speed
up the use of those resources in order that we ourselves may have the equipment
and training equal to the task in an emergency.[66]

1939, 22 Jan., 6 Mar., 20 Mar. 1940, all Hull 58. Cf. Borchard (Yale Law School) to
Borah, 29 Sep., 3 Oct. 1939, Borah 774.
[61] K. D. McFarland, *Harry H. Woodring: A Political Biography of FDR's Controversial
Secretary of War* (Lawrence, KS, 1975).
[62] Morgenthau diary, 28 Sep. 1939, 3, 14 Mar. 1940, including Treasury memorandum,
13 Oct. 1939; Ickes diary, 16, 23 Sep., 28 Oct. 1939, Ickes, *Diary*, 9, 18, 51.
[63] Moffat diary, 12 Sep. 1939; Berle diary, 8 Sep. 1939, 4, 28 Jan. 1940, in B. B. Berle
and T. B. Jacobs, eds., *Navigating the Rapids, 1918–1971. From the Papers of Adolf A.
Berle* (New York, 1973), 254, 281, 288. Then see Moffat to Johnson, 4 Jan. 1940,
Moffat 16; Reynolds, *Alliance*, 68 about the blockade. Cf. Feis to Brand, 22 Apr. 1940,
Feis 11.
[64] 'Bullitt practically sleeps with the French Cabinet': Ickes diary, 4 Feb. 1940, Ickes,
Diary, 124.
[65] '[Kennedy] cheerfully entered into the conversation and before long he was saying that
Germany would win, that everything in France and England would go to hell, and that
his one interest was in saving his money for his children': Ickes diary, 10 Mar. 1940,
ibid., 147. Cf. Lothian to Halifax, 27 Feb. 1940, Halifax FO 800/324.
[66] Roosevelt speech, 10 Jun. 1940, in G. Beckles, ed., *America Chooses! In the Words of
President Roosevelt [June 1940–June 1941]* (1941), 16.

But American opinion still seemed resistant to American involvement outside of the Western Hemisphere. Roosevelt began to back-track, probably because he had now decided to seek an unprecedented third term and needed to assure his position with the voters. On 14 June, he cautioned Churchill 'that while our efforts will be exerted towards making available an ever increasing amount of materials and supplies[,] a certain amount of time must pass before our efforts in this sense can be successful to the extent desired'.[67] He also indicated that the British Fleet must not fall into enemy hands. The next day the French government fled Paris; almost two months were to pass till his next message to Churchill.

This two-month period proved crucial to the Anglo-American relationship. Several interpretations exist about why Roosevelt did not communicate with Churchill – in the same period, Churchill sent four messages, three seeking material and diplomatic support. One flattering interpretation suggests that the president perceived the European crisis as means to sunder totalitarian threats to liberal democracy, and that he needed a little time to establish a basis for this.[68] Looking more broadly at American policy in the eighteen months between June 1940 and December 1941, some of his thoughtful critics argue that he was simply 'slow' in confronting the strategic problems confronting the United States.[69] His two most empathetic chroniclers assert that whilst cognisant of the danger to American interests but constrained by isolationism, 'he cast about for ways to "sell" the American people, and his own military, on aid to Britain'.[70] Grains of truth are in each of these judgments. Roosevelt's actions conformed to the precepts of his Charlottesville speech. Until the fall of France, and despite their fluctuating views about British resolve, Roosevelt and most of his advisers reckoned that Britain and France could withstand the German onslaught and, as they did between 1914 and 1918, gradually weaken Germany by blockade and armed strength. The events of June 1940 came as an unpalatable surprise. Ickes said in early May that 'the Allied cause [is something] in which I am perfectly sure we are more intimately concerned than the great majority of our people believe'.[71] This was true – for economic, political, strategic, and ideological reasons.

---

[67] Roosevelt to Churchill, 14 Jun. 1940, *Churchill–Roosevelt*, I, 47–8.

[68] J. P. Lash, *Churchill and Roosevelt 1939–1941. The Partnership that Saved the West* (New York, 1976), 129–67.

[69] Watt, *John Bull*, 91. Polemics like Marks, *Wind Over Sand*, 163 ('From the opening gun of September 1939 ... Roosevelt acted to maximize American involvement') can be safely discarded.

[70] Kimball, *Forged*, 57; Reynolds, *Alliance*, 65.

[71] Ickes diary, 4 May 1940, Ickes, *Diary*, 171.

Whether or not he grasped the full strategic implications of Germany's threat to Britain,[72] Roosevelt resolved in the crucial two months after 14 June 1940 to do all he could to assist the British war effort. He gave practical form to his own resolve by adding strong-willed interventionists to his Cabinet. Woodring and Charles Edison, the secretary of the Navy, were replaced on 19 June; the anglophile Stimson became secretary of war, and Frank Knox, a Chicago newspaper publisher and the Republican vice-presidential candidate in 1936, succeeded Edison. This surprising act – Stimson had long been critical of Roosevelt – had the double merit of bringing vitality to the policy-making process and of giving that policy an aura of bipartisan support.[73] Roosevelt then got his military chiefs, notably General George Marshall, the Army chief of staff, to accept that material support of Britain would not endanger the American ability to defend its Western Hemispheric interests.[74] Similar pressures were put on other sections of his Administration, especially the War Department and State Department, to remove impediments to British access to American war *matériel*.[75] He also began moves to improve North American defence. On 27 May, he had selected Moffat as the new American minister in Ottawa. Taking up his post on 12 June, Moffat immediately began discussions with Mackenzie King, who wanted to establish contacts between the Canadian and American military staffs.[76] American authorities appeared cool to the idea but, on 3 July, Roosevelt supported such contacts as long as there were no formal commitments. A month later, the president was prepared to go further. On 17–18 August 1940, Roosevelt, Mackenzie King, and their advisers met at Ogdensburg, New York;[77] they created the Permanent Joint Board on Defence, supposedly an advisory committee. By the end of August, a series of its recommendations were being put into action. Akin to these developments, and partly because of Stimson's determination to strengthen American external policy,

---

[72] See the files (daily reports sent to the White House by the British Embassy) 'Great Britain; Military Situation: June 1940' and 'July 1940', in Roosevelt PSF GB.

[73] Roosevelt had been considering removing Woodring since late 1939: Ickes diary, 19 Nov. 1939, 17 Feb., 19 May 1940, Ickes, *Diary*, 64–5, 136, 180.

[74] D. G. Haglund, 'George C. Marshall and the Question of Military Aid to England, May–June 1940', *JCH*, 15(1980), 745–60.

[75] Morgenthau diary, 17 Jun., 11, 17 Jul., 14 Aug. 1940 is instructive.

[76] Moffat diary, 14, 29 Jun. 1940; Moffat to Welles, 14 Aug. 1940, Roosevelt PSF Canada; Mackenzie King memorandum, 27 Jun. 1940, Department of External Affairs, *Documents on Canadian External Relations: 1931–1941*, part 2, vol. VII (Ottawa, 1974), 100–1.

[77] '[Roosevelt] also got the idea on the spot that he would see McKenzie King [*sic*]': Morgenthau diary, 16 Aug. 1940. Cf. Dallek, *Roosevelt*, 245; English, 'Triangle', 163–6; F. E. Pollock, 'Roosevelt, the Ogdensburg Agreement, and the British Fleet: All Done with Mirrors', *DH*, 5(1981), 203–19; Stacey, *Canada*, 310–14.

Roosevelt gave public support on 2 August to legislation – the Selective Service Act – providing for conscription.[78] Finally, Roosevelt decided to run for a third term as president and, at the Democratic National Convention in Chicago on 16 July, he easily won his party's nomination on the first ballot.[79]

Thus, by the time he telegraphed Churchill after the two-month silence, Roosevelt had reinvigorated military policy-making in his Administration, moved to strengthen the American armed forces, begun to improve North American defence, and solidified his political domestic position so as to capture a third – and crucial – term as president. His purpose was to do all possible to prevent Germany and Italy from defeating Britain. After the fall of France, Roosevelt knew he had to go beyond the material and moral support that his Administration had been willing to give between September 1939 and June 1940. His decision to go further meant pursuing foreign and defence policies that would mark the United States as an interventionist Power beyond the Western Hemisphere. More important, this decision would unlock the latent political and military power of the United States and wed it to the economic, financial, and industrial strength that it had long possessed. Although Roosevelt's long-term political, strategic, and economic goals will be dealt with later, the exposed position of Britain and its Empire by autumn 1940 gave the United States an additional advantage in seeking to pursue external policies that would strengthen and enhance American interests.

Reflecting the new direction in American strategy, Roosevelt's first message to Churchill in two months proposed that the United States transfer fifty older destroyers to Britain in return for, first, leases to build naval and air bases in British possessions in the Caribbean and Newfoundland and, second, a promise that if 'the waters of Great Britain become untenable for British ships of war', the RN would be transferred to 'other parts of the Empire [probably Canada]'. The matter had long been discussed within the Administration, but the August offer resulted from both Roosevelt's resolve to assist Britain and, more importantly, the Churchill government's demonstration over two months that it would resist the Axis pressure – for instance, the action at Oran denying the Germans the French Fleet.[80] Anglo-American discussions over a

---

[78] Dallek, *Roosevelt*, 248–9; J. A. Huston, 'Selective Service in World War II', *Current History*, 54(1968), 345–50.

[79] J. M. Burns, *Roosevelt: The Lion and the Fox* (New York, 1956), 426–30; B. F. Donahoe, *Private Plans and Public Dangers* (Notre Dame, 1965).

[80] On 14 August, to show British goodwill, a mission led by Sir Henry Tizard went to the United States 'to make available virtually all of Britain's technical and scientific secrets'. See D. Zimmerman, *Top Secret Exchange. The Tizard Mission and the Scientific*

destroyer transfer had occurred intermittently since Churchill first raised the matter in mid-May.[81] It has been suggested that 'both governments were engaged in an uneasy bargaining game that summer, exploring in a rather heavy-handed way how best to obtain support from the other'.[82] The story of 'the destroyers-for-bases deal' is well known.[83] In negotiations that stretched throughout August, the British and Americans manoeuvred within their established practice of 'competitive co-operation' to achieve the best agreement possible for themselves. Needing as many warships as possible, especially because of Italian ambitions in the Mediterranean, Churchill had to accept Roosevelt's chief demands. The first involved ninety-nine-year leases allowing the Americans to build eight bases in Newfoundland and the Caribbean – Churchill wanted the destroyers as a gift. The second was a public statement by Churchill that the RN would 'in no event be surrendered or sunk' – Churchill complied on 5 September, though he told Roosevelt privately that 'these hypothetical contingencies seem more likely to concern the German Fleet or what is left of it than our own'.[84]

However, the results of the agreement are most telling in terms of the Anglo-American relationship at that moment. Churchill had tied the neutral United States to belligerent Britain in a way that ostensibly saw greater American involvement in the military side of British war effort. 'The effects in Europe', he later wrote, 'were profound.'[85] Roosevelt showed American opinion that having broken some isolationist bonds that constrained his diplomacy, he had acquired tangible rewards for sending destroyers to Britain – and his Republican adversary in the impending election, Wendell Willkie, was playing on this shift in American opinion to advocate increased American support

---

War (Montreal, Kingston, Buffalo, 1996). Zimmerman's argument that this mission was 'one of the key events in the forging of the Anglo-American alliance' is wide of the mark.

[81] Churchill to Roosevelt, 15 Jun., 31 Jul. 1940, *Churchill–Roosevelt*, I, 49–51, 56–7. A draft telegram with the same request, dated 5 July, was not sent: *ibid.*, 54.

[82] Reynolds, *Alliance*, 116. Memoranda of conversations, 24 Jun., 5, 15 Jul. 1940, Hull and Lothian; memorandum of conversation 4 Aug. 1940, Hull, Lothian, Welles, Hackworth; Lothian memorandum, 26 Jun. 1940, British Embassy memorandum, 3 Jul. 1940, all Hull 58.

[83] Dallek, *Roosevelt*, 243–7; W. H. Langenberg, 'Destroyers for British Bases: Highlights of an Unprecedented Trade', *Naval War College Review*, vol. 22, no. 9(1970), 80–92; Leutze, *Bargaining*, 115–27; Reynolds, *Alliance*, 113–31.

[84] Lothian telegram to Churchill, 16 Aug. 1940, FO 371/24241/3793/131; Lothian telegrams to Churchill, 27, 28 Aug. 1940, FO 371/24241/3980/3742; WM 220(40)1, 6 Aug. 1940, 227(40)1, 14 Aug. 1940, WM 239(40)7, 2 Sep. 1940, all CAB 65; Churchill to Roosevelt, 25, (2) 27, 31 Aug. 1940, Roosevelt to Churchill, 30 Aug. 1940, all *Churchill–Roosevelt*, I, 65–9; *SWW*, II, 415.

[85] *SWW*, II, 416.

of Britain.[86] More important, Roosevelt had taken an overt step in aligning with Britain against the Axis Powers; and he did so in a way that, by acquiring bases at British expense, had strengthened the American armed forces strategically for a possible struggle against Nazi Germany.

Between 2 September 1940, when the 'destroyers-for-bases' deal was signed, and 7 December 1941, when the Japanese air attack on the US naval base at Pearl Harbor occurred, Churchill's government and the Roosevelt Administration drew closer together. The growing friendship between the two leaders had some influence here, but more important was the confluence of British and American national interests involving the defeat of the Axis Powers in Europe and, until the unexpected Pearl Harbor attack, in containing Japanese ambitions in East Asia. The broad brushstrokes and the fine detail of this portrait of increasing Anglo-American co-operation are well known.[87] Britain's essential problem for most of this period lay in its need for food, raw materials, war *matériel*, and other supplies to meet the Axis threat to the home islands and the British position in the Mediterranean. Hence, adhering to the general precepts of his Charlottesville speech, Roosevelt worked to supply Britain with 'material resources' to conduct the war and, simultaneously, rearm the United States. His short-term goal after 2 September was re-election to a third term. Foreign policy was not the only issue of concern for Roosevelt and Willkie; still, that the two presidential contenders and the majority of American voters believed that the United States should support Britain made Roosevelt's double task easier once he secured re-election on 5 November.[88]

For Churchill, the destroyers-for-bases deal was a singular achievement. Just after Churchill assumed the premiership, his son asked him how Britain could defeat Germany. Churchill responded: 'I shall drag the United States in.'[89] Four months later, although Roosevelt needed little dragging, Britain had a major ally, albeit one only beginning to transform its potential strength into real national power. Even before signing the destroyers deal, Churchill's government stepped up its pressure on the Roosevelt Administration to increase its support of the

[86] W. L. Willkie, *We, the People* (1940); W. L. Willkie, *This is Wendell Willkie: A Collection of Speeches and Writings on Present-day Issues* (1940).
[87] Dallek, *Roosevelt*, 252–72; Dobson, *Wartime Aid*, 14–92; W. F. Kimball, *The Most Unsordid Act: Lend-Lease, 1939–1941* (Baltimore, 1969); Reynolds, *Alliance*, 145–68. Cf. R. Shogan, *Hard Bargain: How FDR Twisted Churchill's Arm, Evaded the Law, and Changed the Role of the American Presidency* (New York, 1995).
[88] H. S. Parmet and M. B. Hecht, *Never Again: A President Runs for a Third Term* (New York, 1968).
[89] Randolph Churchill recollection, 18 May 1940, M. Gilbert, ed., *The Churchill War Papers*, vol. II: *Never Surrender, May 1940–December 1940* (New York, 1995), 70–1.

British war effort. With the Battle of Britain as a backdrop to this diplomacy, Churchill used his personal connexion with Roosevelt to make the case for increased assistance; Lothian lobbied in Washington for the same end; and the British Purchasing Commission in the United States worked feverishly to acquire as many supplies as possible.[90] In comparison to the earlier period, Churchill, Lothian, and the others found Washington more helpful.[91] To show Washington the co-operative nature of British policies, the British Embassy and Tizard's Mission began to transfer 'important and highly secret technical information' to the American army and navy.[92] London initially greeted Roosevelt's re-election with the expectation of eventual American intervention; this ran counter to Lothian's prediction that full American involvement would not occur until American rearmament neared completion in a year or so, or if American interests were threatened in a major way.[93] Roosevelt's apparent desire to facilitate aid saw observers in London overestimate his commitment to go to war – the carrot of his long-established policy to stir Britain to fight. By mid-November, however, British optimism was fading.

Lothian had returned to London in October.[94] With his Washington experience, Lothian understood that whilst the ship of American public opinion was moving towards greater intervention in the war, it had yet to reach its destination. After the American election, supported by Halifax and the Foreign Office, he pressed a reluctant Churchill to send a frank message to Roosevelt outlining the parlous situation confronting Britain as the Battle of Britain was ending and the Battle of the Atlantic was heating up. Churchill worried about being so forthright. Still, before Lothian departed for Washington on 15 November, a draft letter had been prepared, something Cadogan called 'putting all our cards on the

---

90 Cf. Churchill to Roosevelt, 22 Sep., 4, 25 Oct. 1940, *Churchill–Roosevelt*, I, 71, 74, 78; Leith-Ross minute, 25 Oct. 1940, Leith-Ross T 188/300; Hull memoranda of conversations, 16, 30 Sep., 25 Nov. 1940, Hull 58; British Purchasing Commission, 'Statement of the Estimated Value of Additional Orders ...', 28 Nov. 1940, in Morgenthau diary; 'Memorandum of Important Points Relating to Production Problems Contained in the Brief of the "Survey of Britain's Wartime Economic Organization"', 8 Oct. 1940, Roosevelt PSF GB.

91 Morgenthau, 'Memorandum for the President', 19 Sep., 3 Oct. 1940; 'Statement of British Aircraft Requirements', 29 Oct. 1929, 'Statement of British Army Requirements', n.d., 'Statement of Naval Requirements', with Morgenthau diary, 14 Aug. 1940.

92 Zimmerman, *Tizard*, 96–129. Cf. British Technical Mission memorandum, 28 Oct. 1940, in Morgenthau diary.

93 The rest of this paragraph is based on Reynolds, *Alliance*, 147–50. Cf. Lothian to Hoare, 19 Oct. 1940, Templewood XII/17.

94 Except where noted, the next two paragraphs are based on Kimball, *Unsordid Act*, 91–9; Reynolds, *Alliance*, 150–3; E. R. Stettinius, Jr, *Lend-Lease. Weapon for Victory* (New York, 1944), 57–85.

table'.[95] Churchill delayed for ten days, till Halifax and the Foreign Office rekindled their pressure. With Lothian having already told American reporters on his return that 'Britain's broke; it's your money we want', and with the requirement of American assistance increasing, Churchill sent a twenty-page missive to Roosevelt on 7 December 1940.[96]

There had been last-minute wrangling in London over its contents. Halifax and the Foreign Office wanted an honest assessment of the difficult position Britain faced in terms of war finance, shipping, and the military position in Europe, the Mediterranean, and Far East. Not wanting to expose completely Britain's strategic problems, Churchill wanted to concentrate on shipping because of the U-boat attacks on British Atlantic sea-lanes. His desire prevailed, although he did address financial and strategic issues, munitions supply, and British war production. Roosevelt was already moving in this direction, but this message and further lobbying by Lothian galvanised the White House into action. It encouraged Roosevelt's decision to introduce a bill into Congress to lend or lease American-produced war *matériel* to any Power that the president reckoned was important in helping defend the United States. Roosevelt had a tough time with the isolationists but, on 8 March 1941, a majority in the American Congress passed the Lend-Lease Bill.[97] Whilst the legislation did not mention Britain specifically – with the Chiang Kai-shek and other pro-American regimes in mind, the cunning Roosevelt wanted as much latitude as possible in doling out aid – Churchill was ecstatic:

[The bill] made us free to shape by agreement long-term plans of vast extent for all our needs. There was no need for repayment. There was not even to be a formal account kept in dollars or sterling. What we had was lent or leased to us because our continued resistance to the Hitler tyranny was deemed to be of vital interest to the great Republic.[98]

Roosevelt put a positive spin on Lend-Lease publicly on 17 March: 'History cannot be made or written by wishful thinking. We American people are writing new history to-day.'[99] Whether American opinion understood Roosevelt's motives, he had committed the United States to Britain's anti-Axis war effort. His commitment was seen in tangible ways.[100] In January 1941, secret Anglo-American staff talks were held in

[95] Cadogan diary, 11 Nov. 1940, Dilks, *Cadogan Diary*, 335. The draft letter, 12 Nov. 1940, is in *Churchill–Roosevelt*, I, 89–95.
[96] Churchill to Roosevelt, 7 Dec. 1940, Roosevelt PSF GB.
[97] Kimball, *Unsordid Act*, 132.   [98] *SWW*, II, 569.
[99] Roosevelt speech, 17 Mar. 1941, in Beckles, *America Chooses*, 90.
[100] The rest of this paragraph is based on Butler, *Grand Strategy*, II, 423–7; Leutze, *Bargaining*, 218–52; Reynolds, *Alliance*, 182–91.

Washington that sought, first, a combined global strategy and, second, a plan for the defence of the Atlantic. By April, as a result of these talks, Washington announced a security zone that ran the length of the North Atlantic from the Azores to Greenland. Within this expanded zone, American vessels helped the RN anti-submarine campaign by reporting sightings of German U-boats to Washington, which were then relayed to London.

Over the next eight months, until Pearl Harbor, Churchill's government increasingly found itself with an American ally determined to safeguard its own interests as much as help Britain defend itself against Germany and Italy. This determination was especially pronounced in the economic sphere. The pro-American Lothian had argued as early as April 1940 that Americans would 'make loans or give credits or even gifts to the Allies' to help defeat the Axis; but, he cautioned: 'The United States will not do much in this direction until she is sure she has got our investments, our gold and any assets Overseas which are saleable in the United States of America.'[101] American policy towards Britain in 1940–1 lacked altruism. On a range of economic and financial issues ancillary to Lend-Lease and which involved British spending – for instance, wheat exports, the sterling–dollar balance, and merchant shipping – Washington drove hard bargains with London that added markedly to American political strength within the Anglo-American relationship.[102] American success rankled with some British observers. Thus, in negotiations over American rights in establishing the agreed bases in the West Indies, Churchill's private secretary, John Colville, remarked: 'The West Indian Colonies themselves … are resentful, and their feelings are shared by many people here in view of the conditions which the Americans have demanded and which amount to capitulations.'[103]

Churchill found mounting disaffection towards the United States in his Cabinet. Leo Amery, the Indian secretary, held that trade issues tied to Lend-Lease threatened Imperial Preference, thereby weakening the economic bonds holding the Empire together.[104] Beaverbrook believed

---

[101] Lothian despatch to Halifax, 29 Apr. 1940, FO 800/324.
[102] A. P. Dobson, ' "A Mess of Pottage for Your Economic Birthright?" The 1941–42 Wheat Negotiations and Anglo-American Economic Diplomacy', *HJ*, 28(1985), 739–50; W. F. Kimball, ' "Beggar My Neighbour": America and the British Interim Finance Crisis, 1940–1941', *JEH*, 29(1969), 758–72; K. Smith, *Conflict Over Convoys: Anglo-American Logistics Diplomacy in the Second World War* (Cambridge, 1996).
[103] Colville diary, 5 Mar. 1941, J. Colville, *The Fringes of Power. 10 Downing Street Diaries 1939–1955* (1985), 360.
[104] Amery diary, 9, 11 Aug. 1941, J. Barnes and D. Nicholson, eds., *The Empire at Bay. The Leo Amery Diaries 1929–1945* (1988), 709–10.

the Americans conceded nothing: 'They have taken our bases without valuable consideration. They have taken our gold. They have been given our secrets and offered us a thoroughly inadequate service in return.'[105] 'The Colonial Office are frightened that in the heat of the conflict,' Colville reported, 'we shall cede much that will afterwards be regrettable.'[106] Yet, as Colville noted:

the P.M. is ill-satisfied with the point of view expressed by his colleagues. He believes that the safety of the state is at stake, that America in providing us with credits that will enable us to win the war which we could not otherwise do, and that we cannot afford to risk the major issue in order to maintain our pride and to preserve the dignity of a few small islands.

Churchill was realistic. Britain was in an exposed position. To protect the home islands from German conquest, to fight the Italians in North Africa, and to hold as much of the Empire as possible, Britain needed American support; to acquire that support, it had to pay the American price. Both Britain and the United States shared the same interest in meeting Axis aggression; but, unlike before June 1940 in relation to the French, the British lacked the power to enforce their will on the Americans. Amery, Beaverbrook, and others should not have been surprised that Britain was becoming a supplicant to the United States, since Britain for the most part had traditionally been dominant – and never altruistic – in its relations with other Powers. Perhaps they recognised this situation, and this is what agitated them. As Churchill had long argued, however, to defeat the Axis and preserve the Empire, Britain had to purchase American help with its economic, political, and strategic capital.

Passage of Lend-Lease brought the United States into Britain's anti-Axis war effort just as the course of the war changed.[107] In October 1940, Mussolini's armies had tried to overrun Greece from Italy's Albanian colony. They failed and, by early 1941, with Italy facing a successful Greek counter-attack in the Balkans and a British one in North Africa, Hitler had to despatch German forces to help his erstwhile ally. Additional problems in Belgrade in March 1941 led to the German occupation of Yugoslavia and the expansion of the war into Greece and

---

[105] Beaverbrook to Churchill, 26 Dec. 1940, in A. J. P. Taylor, *Beaverbrook. A Biography* (New York, 1972), 439.

[106] Colville diary, 5 Mar. 1941.

[107] This paragraph is based on Braddock, *Campaigns*; J. Erickson, *The Road to Stalingrad* (1975); J. Erickson and D. Dilks, eds., *Barbarossa: The Axis and the Allies* (Edinburgh, 1994); R. D. S. Higham, *Diary of a Disaster: British Aid to Greece, 1940–1941* (Lexington, KY, 1986); Pitt, *Crucible*, I; H. Umbreit, 'The Return to an Indirect Strategy Against Britain', in Maier, *Germany*, II, 408–15; A. L. Zapantis, *Hitler's Balkan Campaign and the Invasion of the USSR* (Boulder, CO, 1987).

Crete, where Churchill diverted some of his North African forces to fight the Germans. The Germans were victorious in the Balkans by the end of May. Sensing that Britain could be dealt with later, after further weakening by the U-boat offensive, Hitler turned his attention towards achieving his long-cherished goal of defeating and occupying Bolshevik Russia – the planning for which began in late June 1940. Feeling secure in Western Europe, the Balkans, and North Africa, Hitler stupidly ordered his armies to attack Russia on 21–22 June 1941. After a year of facing the Axis alone, Churchill's government had a major ally on the Continent that could also fight the Germans. Admittedly, the initial months of the German offensive drove the Red Army back hundreds of miles. But distance, the advent of an early winter, and Russian resistance saw the German offensive halt by December on a line that ran from Leningrad and Moscow to the Crimea in the south. Also receiving Lend-Lease by the autumn of 1941, Stalin's forces began to regroup, rearm, and plan for the 1942 campaigning season. Red Army success would only assist British efforts to revive their fortunes in Western Europe and the Mediterranean.

1941 also proved a period of change in the Far Eastern balance of power. Whilst Japanese forces had occupied Chinese territory along the entire coastline and the major river systems by mid-1939, much of Chinese territory remained outside Japanese control. Moreover, they faced armed opposition from both Chiang and his nationalist army based in the south-western city of Chungking and Mao Tse-tung and communist forces operating out of northern Shensi province. Although Japan's conquest of China was not yet realised, Tokyo's ambitions in East Asia were unslaked. Looking covetously on the resources of Russian Siberia, Japan went to war briefly and unsuccessfully with Russia in 1939.[108] After an armistice, the Japanese then looked southwards to consolidate their position in China and, watching the developments in Europe, exploit the weakness of the White Imperial Powers caused by the outbreak of the war in September 1939. In June 1939, the Japanese threatened the British concession at Tientsin, supposedly neutral territory.[109] Silver reserves from the Bank of China were deposited there, and some Chinese patriots used it as a refuge whilst conducting guerrilla actions against the Japanese. Unable to get American or French support, Craigie began negotiations on an agreement whereby Tokyo tried to wrest Britain's formal recognition of Japan's

---

[108] A. D. Coox, *Nomonhan: Japan against Russia, 1939* (Stanford, 1985).
[109] Lowe, *Pacific War*, 127–34; A. Shai, 'Le conflit anglo-japonais de Tientsin, 1939', *Revue d'histoire moderne et contemporaine*, 22(1975), 293–302; Watt, *How War Came*, 339–60.

special position in China. The negotiations dragged on. By August, thanks to the intrusion of other issues, chiefly Washington's denunciation of the Japanese–American trade treaty, the granting of export credits by Britain, and the announcement of the Nazi–Soviet non-aggression pact, the Japanese government resigned and Japan entered another quiescent period respecting Britain, the United States, and the other White Imperial Powers.

British willingness to negotiate over Tientsin derived from COS assessments that the concession could not be defended.[110] Though diplomatically difficult to swallow, COS guidance conformed to the Far Eastern strategy that the COS and CID had been pursuing since before the Marco Polo Bridge incident. Recognising after the second London naval conference that the Japanese dominated Korea, Taiwan, and eastern and northern China, the British worked to establish a defensive perimeter along the southern edge of this region. This element of Imperial defence centred on improving Singapore's defences and, further south, seeking agreements with Australia and New Zealand.[111] British political and military leaders endeavoured to deter Japan's ambitions beyond its immediate sphere of interest in the western Pacific north of the equator. As late as March 1939, Craigie counselled: 'The presence of [an] adequate fleet and air force, based at Singapore, would, by removing the chance of a rapid attack on the fortress, also remove one of the prizes of war and so enhance in Japanese eyes, the advantages of neutrality.'[112]

A central canon of this strategy was that if ever Japanese forces threatened the perimeter, moving either into South-east Asia or the wider Pacific, Britain's ability to resist such advances would be augmented by the USN. Craigie and others felt confident that the Americans would not countenance an expansion of the Japanese Empire into these regions. 'His Majesty's Government', Halifax told Lindsay after the Prague crisis, 'cannot leave out of account the fact that if they are involved in a European conflict, they might not be able at once to

[110] COS memorandum, 'The Situation in the Far East' [FP(39)96], 18 Jun. 1939, CAB 27/627.
[111] For instance, COS memorandum, 'Strategic Importance of the Pacific Islands' [CID 1455B], 23 Jul. 1938, CID memorandum, 'Strategic Importance of the Pacific Islands' [CID 1463B], 23 Jul. 1938, both CAB 4/28; COS memorandum, 'New Zealand: Conference on Pacific Questions' [CID 1542B], 31 Mar. 1939, CAB 4/29. Cf. Drax [Admiralty War Plans] 'Notes', 17 Feb. 1939, DRAX 2/17; Dreyer [C-in-C, China Station] memorandum for first sea lord, 'Some Strategical Notes – Western Pacific', 10 Feb. 1939, Dreyer memorandum, 'An Admiralty Far Eastern Committee (F.E.C.)', 12 Jun. 1939, both DRYR 9/2; Chatfield to Dreyer, 20 Jan. 1938, CHT 4/4.
[112] Craigie telegram to FO, 23 Mar. 1939, FO 371/23560/2885/456.

reinforce on a large scale their naval forces in the Far East, and that might affect United States naval dispositions.'[113] At the same moment Churchill, still a backbencher, saw the soundness of this idea.[114] If war broke out in Europe, he surmised, Britain's main strategic weakness would lie in the Far East. With the bulk of the RN concentrated west of Suez, he argued that the 'farthest point we can hold in the conditions imagined is Singapore'. But should the Japanese decide to exploit Britain's entanglement in Europe – Hong Kong and Shanghai would fall but Singapore could hold out – Britain could probably rely on the Americans to prevent Japan from restructuring the western Pacific balance of power to American disadvantage. This attitude informed his strategic thinking concerning the Far East after September 1939, when he became first lord of the Admiralty, and after May 1940, when he rose to the premiership.[115]

It is true that Churchill showed caution in handling the Japanese after May 1940. A basic tenet of British global strategy since the Washington conference had been to send a fleet to Singapore in the event of a Far Eastern crisis.[116] After May 1940, and especially after the fall of France and the Italian attack on Egypt, British ground, air, and naval forces had to be concentrated in the Mediterranean and in home waters. As the DRC, the CID, and the Cabinet had recognised since 1933–5, Britain could not simultaneously fight and defeat three first-class Powers. Therefore, a minimum of RN warships and available funds for building up Singapore's defences were diverted eastward to deter Japan.[117] Even after the Japanese exploited France's defeat by occupying French Indochina in July 1940, Churchill continued to be prudent. In July 1940, his government bent to pressures from Tokyo and closed the Burma Road, a supply route between India and south-western China, built in 1938 and, by 1940, Chiang's chief source of war *matériel*.[118] The closing created an unfavourable diplomatic odour in Washington where it was seen as British appeasement of Japan. After the destroyers-for-bases deal,

[113] Halifax telegram (131) to Lindsay, 19 Mar. 1939, FO 371/23560/2879/456.
[114] 'Memorandum on Sea-Power, 1939', 27 Mar. 1939, Gilbert, *Churchill* Companion vol. V, part 3, 1414–17.
[115] Churchill memorandum on Australian naval defence, 17 Nov. 1939, quoted in Murfett, *Fool-proof Relations*, 277–8; Churchill to Australian and New Zealand premiers, 11 Aug. 1940, *SWW*, II, 435–7; Churchill minute, 4 Oct. 1940, FO 371/24729/4632/60.
[116] I. Hamill, *The Strategic Illusion: The Singapore Strategy and the Defence of Australia and New Zealand, 1919–1942* (Singapore, 1981); J. Neidpath, *The Singapore Naval Base and the Defence of Britain's Eastern Empire, 1919–1941* (1981).
[117] R. O'Neill, 'Japan and British Security in the Far East', in R. Blake and W. R. Louis, eds., *Churchill* (Oxford, 1992), 275–89.
[118] Dallek, *Roosevelt*, 238–9, 242; Reynolds, *Alliance*, 133–5; C. Thorne, *Allies of a Kind. The United States, Britain, and the War Against Japan, 1941–1945* (1978), 66–8.

Churchill raised with Roosevelt the possibility of reopening the Burma Road in tandem with a visit by a USN fleet to Singapore.[119] Although a fleet visit did not materialise, the Burma Road reopened in mid-October. The Burma Road issue typified the British approach to maintaining the Far Eastern balance in the eighteen months before Pearl Harbor. The war in Europe and the Mediterranean put the Far East in third place in British strategic priorities. Indeed, until the day of the Pearl Harbor attack, Churchill supposed that a Japanese offensive was virtually impossible.[120] Although not all his advisers shared his attitude, Churchill believed that the Japanese could largely be deterred by probable American armed intervention. This belief lay at the bottom of his pursuit of a USN visit to Singapore. To a large extent, the necessities of fighting Germany and Italy in Europe and the Mediterranean forced Churchill's government to abdicate the chief responsibility for containing Japan in East Asia and the western Pacific to the Roosevelt Administration. Not surprisingly, British influence in the region declined, whilst that of the United States increased.

The Roosevelt Administration appeared willing to take up the challenge and confront the Japanese question.[121] Since 8 March 1941, Japanese–American negotiations for a Far Eastern settlement had been in progress; conducted mainly by Hull and Admiral Nomura Kichisaburo, the Japanese ambassador in Washington, they continued until the Pearl Harbor attack. Importantly, the Americans had broken Japanese codes, so that the State Department knew at every stage what transpired between Nomura and Tokyo. War in the Pacific was not inevitable: Roosevelt, Hull, and their advisers understood American naval weakness in the Far East; if Tokyo had shown a willingness to withdraw back behind the Great Wall and abjure further expansion, the Roosevelt Administration might have accepted the absorption of Manchukuo and recognised Japan's leading position in China.[122] But dominated by

---

[119] Churchill to Roosevelt, 4 Oct. 1940, *Churchill–Roosevelt*, I, 74–5.
[120] Reynolds, *Alliance*, 246–7; Thorne, *Allies*, 91–127.
[121] Except where noted, this paragraph is based on L. H. Brune, 'Considerations of Force in Cordell Hull's Diplomacy, July 26 to November 26, 1941', *DH*, 2(1978), 389–405; Dallek, *Roosevelt*, 269–313; H. Feis, *The Road to Pearl Harbor* (Princeton, 1950); G. Prange, *At Dawn We Slept: The Untold Story of Pearl Harbor* (New York, 1981); J. G. Utley, *Going to War with Japan, 1937–1941* (Knoxville, 1985); Weinberg, *Arms*, 245–63; R. Wohlstetter, *Pearl Harbor: Warning and Decision* (Stanford, 1962).
[122] I disagree with the conspiracy theorists who argue that Roosevelt manoeuvred the United States into the European war by provoking Japan. See Barnes, *Perpetual War*; C. A. Beard, *President Roosevelt and the Coming of the War, 1941: A Study in Appearances and Realities* (New Haven, 1948); C. C. Tansill, *Back Door to War: The Roosevelt Foreign Policy, 1933–1941* (Chicago, 1952). Cf. the reasoned critique of the above: R. H. Ferrell, 'Pearl Harbor and the Revisionists', *Historian*, 17(1955), 215–33.

chauvinistic civilians and military officers, Japan's leadership could not brook any retreat. As Saito Yoshie, the emperor's adviser, warned:

America's intention is to bring about peace between Japan and China by means of an agreement between Japan and the United States ... This procedure will transfer leadership in East Asia to the United States. It will interfere with the implementation of an independent policy by our Empire.[123]

In the minds of Japanese leaders, a basis for agreement did not exist. Washington wanted Japan to withdraw from French Indochina and southern China; Tokyo saw the conquest of China as integral to their national survival and central to their desire to create the 'Greater East Asia Co-prosperity Sphere', a new order in East Asia dominated by Japan. Similarly, Japanese leaders wanted access to crucial raw materials, especially oil, something that made the Dutch East Indies a potential prize of the first magnitude. Compromise proved an elusive commodity, but both sides continued to negotiate. The Japanese braced for war; on 20 October, the IJN planners were ordered to plan an air attack on Pearl Harbor as final preparations were made for a descent on Malaya, Singapore, the Philippines, and the Dutch East Indies. In Washington, Roosevelt tried to get the Japanese to compromise by imposing economic sanctions, freezing Japanese assets in the United States and embargoing step-by-step crucial strategic commodities like pig iron and oil. This only confirmed Tokyo's decision for war, at the base of which was the argument that Japan was only doing in East Asia what the White Imperial Powers had long done. On 7 December 1941, it launched its surprise attack on Pearl Harbor and struck south against Malaya, the Philippines, and the Dutch East Indies. The United States was at war in the Pacific; on 11 December, following the dictates of the September 1940 German–Italian–Japanese Tripartite Pact, Germany and Italy declared war on the United States. Churchill's dream of American involvement in the European war was now realised. Henceforth, the Anglo-American relationship would never be the same.

[123] '38th Liaison Conference', 10 Jul. 1941, Ike Nobutaka, ed. and trans., *Japan's Decision for War. Records of the 1941 Policy Conferences* (Stanford, 1967), 95–6.

Epilogue
'A new order of things', 1941–1945

> But, unless appearances are deceptive, the United States is also now
> groping towards a new order of things in which Great Britain, whilst
> occupying a highly important position as a bastion of Western
> European security and as the focal point of a far-flung oceanic system,
> will nevertheless be expected to take her place as junior partner in an
> orbit of power predominantly under American aegis.
>
> Balfour, August 1945[1]

Churchill accepted the heavy economic and political price that American assistance after June 1940 necessitated. For Britain to survive
Germany's onslaught, retain its Empire, and seek means to defeat the
Axis, the United States had to join the war on Britain's side. Lately,
however, the United States' position in Churchill's wartime grand
strategy has been questioned. Building on criticisms of Churchill's
diplomacy that emerged as early as 1944, it is argued that Anglo-
American alignment – along with British partnership with Bolshevik
Russia – eroded Britain's power, squandered its freedom of action in
foreign policy, and, thereby, because Britain by 1945 became secondary
to the United States (and Russia), destroyed Britain as the greatest of
the Great Powers.[2] The most recent critique argues that Britain's
interests would have been better served by settling with Germany in
either 1940 or, after Hitler turned on Russia, 1941. Hitler and Stalin
could then have torn themselves to pieces, Britain would not have
become beholden to the United States, and, once the Russo-German

---

[1] Balfour [British Embassy, Washington] to Bevin [foreign secretary], 9 Aug. 1945,
Foreign Office, *Documents on British Policy Overseas*, ser. I, vol. III (1986), 17.
[2] J. Charmley, *Churchill: The End of Glory. A Political Biography* (London, New York, San
Diego, 1993), 559–70. For early critiques, see D. Reynolds, 'Churchill the Appeaser?
Between Hitler, Roosevelt, and Stalin in World War Two', in M. L. Dockrill and B. J. C.
McKercher, eds., *Diplomacy and World Power. Studies in British Foreign Policy,
1890–1950* (Cambridge, 1996), 198, n. 3. For similar arguments, see M. Cowling, *The
Impact of Hitler: British Politics and British Policy, 1933–1940* (1975); A. J. P. Taylor, *The
Origins of the Second World War* (1961).

war ended, Britain and its Empire would have been intact, with London retaining decided influence in establishing the postwar order.

Yet, as a perceptive response to this fanciful musing demonstrates, and apart from the British public's obvious anti-Germanism, Hitler could not be trusted; despite the German leader wanting to destroy and then colonise Bolshevik Russia, Britain existed as 'a prime target of Hitler's malevolence'.[3] Since London would have had to make concessions in any Anglo-German peace settlement, Britain's power would still have diminished, its freedom of action been constrained, and its position of pre-eminence lost by inclusion in a Nazi *imperium*. Britain would have gained nothing by seeking peace in 1940–1 and, given the experience of Austria, Czechoslovakia, France, the Low Countries, and other German-dominated states, lost much. Churchill's strategy was determined neither by ideology – Stalin's regime was as barbarous as Hitler's – nor kinship – the special Anglo-American relationship was largely mythological. Rather, it was shaped by the cold dictates of *realpolitik*. After September 1939 and, especially, after June 1940, Anglo-American interests coincided: prevent German domination of Europe, protect North Atlantic lifelines, and ensure Britain's national survival. The reasons animating these interests might differ – for the British, survival was an end in itself; for the Americans, these interests were the means with which any strategy of defeating Germany had to be implemented. Still, each Power's interests coincided.

However, Roosevelt and his advisers had the upper hand following their decision to support Britain after the fall of France. They began to translate the vast wealth and industrial capacity of the United States into the tangible expressions of power: troops, ships, aeroplanes, and other implements of war. They demanded concessions from London. They acquired bases essential to national security and the wider projection of their strength. They chanced war to assist Britain through destroyers-for-bases, Lend-Lease, staff talks, and extending the Atlantic security zone. Most important, Roosevelt, Morgenthau, and others were finding the will to exercise American power to achieve specific strategic, financial, and political goals beyond the Western Hemisphere – Stimson had long believed in such diplomacy. By late 1940, for the first time since Hoover's disarmament plan, American leaders were undertaking bold initiatives in foreign policy. Part of the reason involved the waning strength of isolationism; the larger part stemmed from the European war threatening American security and interests abroad.

Earlier American policy-makers – Coolidge, Hoover, and Roosevelt

---

[3] This and the next two sentences are based on Reynolds, 'Churchill the Appeaser?'.

until September 1939 – pursued interventionist economic diplomacy whilst largely abjuring its political cousin. After 1939, war in Europe and Far Eastern problems changed everything. America's position as a Great Power was being challenged; ignoring this challenge courted great risk. The British had a role in pushing Roosevelt to this realisation, although Roosevelt was moving in this direction before Lend-Lease. He and his advisers were committed to helping the British, but their confronting the Axis and Japan would occur so that American strategic, economic, and other interests benefited. If this meant driving hard bargains with London, or weakening Britain, so be it. This does not mean that they avoided mistakes in the early going; they did not: for example, thinking the Japanese could be deterred by the carrot of the Hull–Nomura conversations and the stick of embargoes. American sailors at Pearl Harbor paid the price. By late 1941, however, Roosevelt's America was beginning to flex its muscles. Churchill understood its growing power. After the Americans entered the struggle, he looked to exploit that power to defend British interests. Until the war ended, this understanding and the intention to capitalise on growing American power became central to his efforts and those of his advisers in making Britain's American policy, in inter-Allied relations, and in fashioning wartime strategy and war aims.

It is not the purpose of this study to examine the military course of the Second World War from Pearl Harbor till its end in the summer of 1945. Instead, emphasis lies with the diplomacy of Anglo-American relations and the shift in power that marked the relationship. By late 1941, Britain had survived a dangerous year-and-a-half. It had weathered the fall of France and a year alone fighting the Axis Powers. It had courted the United States to find a major ally, when Hitler's ambitions in the East suddenly presented a second in Russia. But Britain's position as the leading Great Power was being eroded as 1941 ended. No one in London knew in the days after 7 December how the war would develop. Would Russia resist the anticipated German offensive in 1942? With the ghost of the Nazi–Soviet pact in the background, would an eastern stalemate produce a separate Russo-German peace settlement so that Hitler's forces could turn their full strength against Britain? Following the Crete disaster and *Afrika Korps* success in North Africa, could British forces defend the Suez lifeline? In the Far East, would the Japanese be successful in dislodging the White Imperial Powers and then create and hold the Greater East Asia Co-prosperity Sphere? Within the emerging Allied alliance, what would Moscow and Washington demand for their part in the struggle? Britain was losing its leading position amongst the Great Powers, indeed, given the situation in East Asia, its global pre-eminence. Which amongst the other belligerents would profit most from this erosion of power?

In a critical sense, Anglo-American relations had a new face even before Pearl Harbor. On the British side, Lothian died in December 1940. Churchill chose Halifax as the new ambassador – his original choice, Lloyd George, begged off. Putting Halifax in Washington had the double merit of having a senior British statesman in the American capital whilst removing a political threat to Churchill within the Cabinet.[4] Eden again became foreign secretary. Although a member of the Conservative Party's Churchillian wing, Eden now distrusted American policy. He thought Churchill showed too much 'sentiment for his transatlantic allies'.[5] 'I accepted the fact', he recorded with sorrow, 'that the United States must in time become the dominant partner in Anglo-American councils.' Hence, by early 1941, although Churchill's authority had not diminished, the foreign-policy-making elite was less pro-American than that after September 1939. On the American side, a series of events enhanced White House domination of American external policy. Roosevelt replaced Kennedy with John Winant, a loyal New Dealer, an anti-Nazi committed to the war, and a politician of left-wing sympathies. In Roosevelt's calculations, Winant's appointment would appeal to both Conservatives and Labour within Churchill's coalition, thereby improving Anglo-American relations – Roosevelt also reckoned that Labour would form the immediate postwar government.[6] Winant, importantly, was more pliant than Kennedy. At the State Department, Welles and Hull were locked in a continual bureaucratic duel over policy-making. Because of these problems, and preferring informal diplomatic channels to official ones, Roosevelt gave increasing authority in foreign policy matters to a White House adviser, Harry Hopkins. Like Colonel House during the Great War, Hopkins became a roving presidential envoy.[7] This development meant that more than ever, Roosevelt controlled American policy towards Britain; and though open to guidance from his diplomatic and military advisers, he was going to ensure that American policy on all its facets bore his stamp.

Two weeks after Pearl Harbor, Churchill was in Washington to consult with Roosevelt. Known as the 'Arcadia' conference and lasting until January 1942, these discussions created the Anglo-American

---

[4] On Lloyd George, Cadogan diary, 13, 16 Dec. 1940, *Cadogan Diary*, 339–41.
[5] Earl of Avon, *The Reckoning* (1965), 367–8.
[6] D. Reynolds, 'Roosevelt, the British Left, and the Appointment of John G. Winant as United States Ambassador to Britain in 1941', *IHR*, 4(1982), 393–413.
[7] See M. Gilbert, *Winston S. Churchill*, vol. VI: *Finest Hour, 1939–1941* (1983), 981–1000.

wartime alliance. Their genesis lay in August 1941, when Churchill and Roosevelt met at Placentia Bay, Newfoundland and issued the 'Atlantic Charter', a statement genuflecting to both Wilsonian idealism and the lessons supposedly learnt during the Great Depression.[8] Countering Axis propaganda that Germany and Italy were oppressed, have-not Powers fighting for national existence, this document stressed that 'after the final destruction of Nazi tyranny', there had to be freedom of the seas, the pursuit of true international security, and, with a new organisation to replace the League, effective disarmament. The Charter also contained concepts like the right of peoples to choose their own systems of governance, that access to trade and raw materials was the right of all states, and that, after the war, states should collaborate economically. Over the next few months, the Charter was signed by all of the Allies, including Russia but not France – Churchill and Roosevelt argued that there was no French government fighting the Axis, since French *emigré* leaders had failed to create a single political union. In essence, the Placentia Bay meeting outlined the war aims of belligerent Britain and the neutral United States.

Arcadia determined the practical means by which the Charter could be realised. These means had two dimensions: organising effective decision-making and determining western Allied strategy.[9] The first element developed out of Churchill and Roosevelt's shared desire for real co-operation in directing their half of the struggle. The Russians would conduct their war independently, though every effort would be made to co-ordinate Anglo-American and Russian operations; and Churchill and Roosevelt agreed to keep Stalin continually informed of their decisions. Giving form to an American suggestion, Churchill and Roosevelt established the Combined Chiefs of Staff Committee (CCS). Headquartered in Washington, this body comprised the American chiefs of staff and, because the British chiefs could not be long away from London, British deputies with authority to make decisions. If the CCS became deadlocked, the issue would be referred to Churchill and Roosevelt for a final decision. It is impossible to overestimate the CCS's importance in the wartime Anglo-American relationship. Admittedly, early growing pains appeared in the decision-making process, for instance, in mid-January 1942, the matter of American reinforcements for the Far East denuding

[8] Gilbert, *Churchill*, VI, 1154–68; T. A. Wilson, *The First Summit. Roosevelt and Churchill at Placentia Bay, 1941*, rev. edn (Lawrence, KS, 1991); Woodward, *Foreign Policy*, II, 198–203. Cf. Cadogan diary, 9–12 Aug. 1941, which includes a copy of the Charter, *Cadogan Diary*, 397–401.
[9] Dallek, *Roosevelt*, 321–2; M. Gilbert, *Winston S. Churchill*, vol. VII: *Road to Victory, 1941–1945* (1986), 23–44; J. M. A. Gwyer, *Grand Strategy*, vol. III, part 1 (1964), chs. 14–15; M. A. Stoler, *The Politics of the Second Front* (Westport, CT, 1978), 22–6.

the European theatre of ships, troops, aeroplanes, and other war materials.[10] But by mid-1942 this body functioned relatively effectively,
helped by Field-Marshal Sir John Dill, the senior British representative
until his death in 1944, and General Marshall working well together.[11] In
April 1942, the CCS received authority over all Anglo-American operations subject to the wider strategic decisions that might emerge when
Churchill and Roosevelt consulted.

More important at Arcadia was the basic strategy that the two
English-speaking Powers should pursue. After 7 December 1941,
Churchill worried that the galvanising affect of the Pearl Harbor attack
on American opinion might compel Roosevelt to concentrate his forces
in the Far East.[12] Such fears were allayed when Roosevelt confirmed
that the Anglo-Americans would pursue a 'Europe first' strategy.[13]
Churchill and Roosevelt both believed that Japan's offensive would fall
short if its forces dared attack Singapore and the Philippines. Mirroring
prewar COS thinking, the Anglo-American response should be to
mount defensive operations and, after Germany and Italy were defeated,
the Far Eastern defensive could be transformed into the offensive. Yet,
Roosevelt had to agree to defeat the European Axis before turning all
Allied resources on Japan. Not only was it essential for British survival,
it would help the Russians, who were tying down something like two
hundred German divisions in the East.

After determining the goal of 'Europe first', the question became how
to achieve it? At Arcadia, Churchill advocated a peripheral strategy.[14]
He argued for wearing down the Axis on Europe's periphery tied to the
aerial bombardment of Germany's industry and economic infrastructure. A direct attack against the Continent was risky. If it did not
succeed or if the western Allies were worn down in achieving victory, the
Russians might overshadow the Allies in the aftermath of the war.
Conversely, once Germany and its Italian ally were weakened by

---

[10] Chiefs of Staff Conference 10 [hereafter CCS], 12 Jan. 1942, *American–British Joint
     Chiefs of Staff Conferences* [microfilm edition: National Archives, Washington DC]. Cf.
     C. Barnett, 'Anglo-American Strategy in Europe', in A. Lane and H. Temperley, eds.,
     The Rise and Fall of the Grand Alliance (1995).
[11] A. Danchev, 'A Special Relationship: Field-Marshal Sir John Dill and George
     C. Marshall', *JRUSI*, 130(1985), 56–61; A. Danchev, *Very Special Relationship: Field-
     Marshal Sir John Dill and the Anglo-American Alliance, 1941–1944* (1986).
[12] Despatch, 17 Dec. 1941, in H. G. Nicholas, ed., *Washington Despatches 1941–1945.
     Weekly Political Reports from the British Embassy* (1981), 4–7.
[13] Churchill to War Cabinet and COS, 23 Dec. 1941, *SWW*, III, 664–5; COS
     memorandum [revised by US Joint Chiefs] n.d., CCS meeting 1, 24 Dec. 1941, Annex I.
[14] Churchill memoranda, 'Part I – The Atlantic Front', 16 Dec. 1941, 'Part II – The
     Pacific Front', 17 Dec. 1941, 'Part III – 1943', 18 Dec. 1941, 'Part IV – Notes on the
     Pacific', 20 Dec. 1941, *Churchill–Roosevelt*, I, 294–308. Cf. Gilbert, *Churchill*, VII,
     23–44; T. Ben-Moshe, *Churchill. Strategy and History* (Boulder, CO, 1992), 179–80.

peripheral operations – tied to Russian pressures from the East – Hitler's *Festung Europa* could be invaded, Nazi Germany defeated, and the western Allies could bargain effectively with Stalin. Adoption of the peripheral strategy drew on British strengths. Based on ideas that had informed his thinking as first lord of the Admiralty in the Great War – the failure of which had driven him from office in 1915 – Churchill pressed for clearing Axis forces out of North Africa as preparatory to invading Italy. Successful Allied operations in North Africa would safeguard Britain's position in Egypt, in particular, and in the Mediterranean, generally. Anglo-American forces could then invade Italy, advance up the peninsula and, expanding into the Balkans, launch a final offensive against Germany from what Churchill called 'the soft under-belly of Europe'. Of course, there was nothing 'soft' about either the Italian or Balkan peninsulas – the problem in 1915 – but such a campaign would safeguard Britain's Imperial position in the Mediterranean. Supporting the air offensive against Germany, Roosevelt's military chiefs opposed moving American forces and equipment across the Atlantic to augment the British strategic position in North Africa and the Mediterranean.[15] They argued that these forces would be better used to attack the Continent; and with the Russian ability to withstand a German offensive in 1942 unknown, to relieve pressure on the Red Army. Here the matter rested for the moment. Since the bulk of the USN was needed in the Pacific, the RN and RCN would sweep the North Atlantic free of U-boats, a problem increasingly important because Lend-Lease convoys now had to reach the northern Russian port of Murmansk.[16] American forces and supplies would be sent to Britain, but where those forces would be employed would have to be determined later in 1942.

Arcadia inaugurated a phase in Anglo-American relations that lasted until November 1943, a phase when strategy largely dominated transatlantic deliberations. It was also when the British used the opportunities presented by the vagaries of the struggle to bolster their position within the Anglo-American-Russian triplice. London and Washington confronted two major problems in the six months after Arcadia: when and where to attack Axis Europe; and how to handle Japan after its forces unexpectedly conquered Malaya, Singapore, Burma, and the Philippines and, then, began campaigns westwards towards India and further

---

[15] Dallek, *Roosevelt*, 322.
[16] Admiralty, *Convoy and Anti-submarine Warfare Reports* (1952); N. R. L. Franks, *Search, Find, and Kill: Coastal Command's U-boat Successes* (Harvest Hill, Bucks., 1990); M. Milner, *The U-boat Hunters: The Royal Canadian Navy and the Offensive against Germany's Submarines* (Toronto, 1994); D. Syrett, *The Defeat of German U-boats: The Battle of the Atlantic* (Columbia, SC, 1994).

south towards Australia and New Zealand.[17] The second was largely resolved by the Americans. In May and June 1942, with the air power afforded by its aircraft carriers, the USN defeated the IJN in two crucial battles: the Battle of Midway, which prevented the Japanese from threatening the Hawaiian Islands; and the Battle of the Coral Sea, which blocked Japan's surge southwards towards Australia.[18] The British contribution in these actions was virtually non-existent. Two warships that Churchill sent to assist Singapore's defence – the battleship *Prince of Wales* and battle-cruiser *Repulse* – were sunk by Japanese aircraft *en route*. These developments resulted in the Americans beginning to mass supplies and troops in Australia for a push northwards against the Japanese. In India, under General Sir Archibald Wavell, British forces, including those which retreated from Burma, undertook to shore up defences to safeguard India and Ceylon, and to prevent any possibility of the Germans in North Africa and the Japanese in South-east Asia hooking up in South Asia. Accordingly, whilst the war in East Asia and the Pacific had taken an unexpected turn, the situation had stabilised for the Anglo-Americans by June 1942.

The issue of when and where the attack on Axis Europe would occur was more difficult given not only British and American differences over the Mediterranean strategy, but also because of the Russian question. Eden met with Stalin and his foreign minister, Vyacheslav Molotov, in December 1941.[19] Despite the *Wehrmacht* sitting on the outskirts of Moscow, Stalin demanded British recognition of postwar territorial adjustments in Russia's favour, including the Baltic states and eastern Poland. Eden sought a formal military agreement, 'but not a treaty until the Dominions had been consulted'. He also refused to conclude any agreements without consulting Washington. Discussions ranged over the advent of the Far Eastern war, the North African campaign, and other issues. The tone seemed friendly, but British reluctance to accept Russian demands for Polish territory – Britain had gone to war in 1939 honouring the Polish guarantee – annoyed Stalin. 'We have allayed some at least of the past suspicions', Eden told Churchill. 'Stalin, I believe, sincerely wants military agreements but he will not sign until we recognize his

[17] L. Allen, *Singapore 1941–1942* (1984); A. Draper, *Dawns Like Thunder: The Retreat from Burma 1942* (1987); M. Hauner, *India in Axis Strategy* (Stuttgart, 1982); H. P. Willmott, *The Barrier and the Javelin: Japanese and Allied Pacific Strategies, February to June 1942* (Annapolis, 1983).
[18] Admiralty, *Battles of Coral Sea and Midway* (1952); E. P. Hoyt, *Blue Skies and Blood: The Battle of the Coral Sea* (New York, 1975); G. Prange, *Miracle at Midway* (New York, 1982).
[19] Avon, *Reckoning*, 334–52; Cadogan diary, 15–29 Dec. 1941, *Cadogan Diary*, 420–4; Woodward, *Foreign Policy*, II, 220–36.

frontiers, and we must expect continued badgering on this issue. Meanwhile our position and that of America is completely safeguarded.'[20]

In May 1942, Molotov travelled to London and Washington.[21] In Britain, he learnt that whilst Churchill's government would accept Soviet control of the Baltic states, it was unprepared to do the same for eastern Poland. Invoking the principles of the Atlantic Charter, Roosevelt supported the British position. With Stalin's blessing, Molotov relented over Poland and signed an Anglo-Russian mutual assistance treaty that promised postwar co-operation. Though the treaty papered over Anglo-Russian differences, the Polish question had yet to be resolved. In Washington, Molotov discovered that Roosevelt and his military advisers supported an attack on Europe as soon as possible.[22] Playing on the problems of supply via Murmansk – almost constant daylight marked the Arctic summer – and the Russian difficulty in alone meeting the 1942 German offensive, Molotov convinced Roosevelt to endorse a 'Second Front' in Europe that year. In April 1942, at London, Hopkins and Marshall had discussed with Churchill and the British chiefs the assembling of American air and ground forces in Britain.[23] Explicit in these talks, and apart from launching the strategic bombing offensive against Germany, was the idea that these forces would be used for an assault against the Continent no later than 1943. Still wanting to clear North Africa of the Axis, troubled about Japanese successes, and even considering an invasion of Norway to protect better Allied convoys on the Murmansk run, Churchill did not demur. But this was waffling. When Washington issued a public statement on 11 June that 'full understanding was reached with regard to the urgent tasks of creating a Second Front in Europe in 1942', the British told Molotov that they could give 'no promise in the matter'.[24] An impasse had developed with the British, on one side, and the Russians and Americans, on the other. Events then conspired to give Churchill a diplomatic victory over his allies.

In June–July 1942, the war in Russia and in North Africa, and the

---

[20] Eden to Churchill, 21 Dec. 1941, in Avon, *Reckoning*, 351–2. Cf. S. M. Miner, *Between Churchill and Stalin: The Soviet Union, Great Britain, and the Origins of the Grand Alliance* (Chapel Hill, 1988).

[21] Avon, *Reckoning*, 380–3; Gilbert, *Churchill*, VII, 110–13; Woodward, *Foreign Policy*, II, 244–54. Cf. D. Kirby, 'Morality or Expediency?: The Baltic Question in British–Soviet Relations, 1941–1942', in V. S. Vardys and R. J. Misiunas, eds., *The Baltic States in Peace and War, 1917–1945* (1978); K. Sainsbury, ' "Second Front in 1942": A Strategic Controversy Revisited', *BJIS*, 4(1978), 47–58.

[22] Dallek, *Roosevelt*, 341–4. Cf. Roosevelt to Churchill, 31 May, 6 Jun. 1942, *Churchill–Roosevelt*, I, 503–4, 507–8.

[23] Gilbert, *Churchill*, VII, 85–92; F. C. Pogue, *George C. Marshall*, vol. II (New York, 1966), 308–20.

[24] *SWW*, IV, 341–2, which includes the 'Aide-Mémoire' given to Molotov. Cf. Pogue, *Marshall*, II, 305–6.

Battle of the Atlantic, seemed to turn in German favour. Just days after Washington's 11 June announcement about a Second Front, the *Wehrmacht* overran southern Russian lines in the Crimea; this victory meant that the road to the Volga now lay open.[25] By the end of June, the *Afrika Korps* inflicted a heavy defeat on British forces, decimating their armour. Egypt and Suez seemed suddenly within Hitler's grasp. Finally, in the North Atlantic, U-boat successes saw almost 2 million tons a month of merchant shipping sent to the bottom, a figure exceeding the productive capacity of British and American shipyards – losses increased to a peak of over 4 million tons by November.[26] These events together killed any chance of a Second Front in 1942. Apparent Russian weakness meant that an invasion of northern France or the Low Countries would meet strong German resistance. To meet the North African crisis, Churchill's government shifted all available manpower, armour, and aeroplanes to defend Egypt, weakening any possible Anglo-American invasion force. And the U-boat offensive suggested lack of security in crucial Allied sea-lanes. A cross-Channel attack would have to wait till at least 1943.

In Washington, on 10 July, delay of the Anglo-American invasion of the Continent led the American military chiefs to advocate shifting their forces and military resources for a major offensive against the Japanese. Roosevelt overruled them. Discussing the situation with Hopkins, he remarked: 'I do not believe we can wait until 1943 to strike at Germany. If we cannot strike at SLEDGEHAMMER [the Anglo-American invasion of Western Europe], then we must take the second best – and that is not in the Pacific.'[27] Germany remained the principal enemy. Anglo-American resources had to be directed to its defeat. Approved by Churchill who had travelled again to Washington in the latter half of June to press the British case after the Molotov mission,[28] this decision meant that political manoeuvring began to merge with the purely military side of war-making. The Russians would have to fight the Germans alone for at least another year. Additionally, almost an entire convoy *en route* to Murmansk had been lost to U-boat attacks. Further convoys would be delayed till the autumn, when the return of Arctic darkness and augmented naval strength would give greater security to Allied

[25] Weinberg, *Arms*, 348–51, 411–17.
[26] Table 4 ('Tonnage of British-controlled ships lost to submarines') and table 7 ('Monthly comparison of British-controlled merchant shipping tonnage under repair and lost to submarines, 1942'), Smith, *Convoys*, 250, 252.
[27] R. E. Sherwood, *The White House Papers of Harry L. Hopkins*, vol. II (1949), 604. Cf. M. A. Stoler, 'The "Pacific-First" Alternative in American World War II Strategy', *IHR*, 2(1980), 432–52.
[28] Danchev, *Dill*, 66–8; Gilbert, *Churchill*, VII, 126–34; Pogue, *Marshall*, II, 332–3; Stoler, *Second Front*, 52–7.

merchantmen. It was decided that Churchill should give Stalin this message in a face-to-face meeting. He did so in August, arguing with some justification in strained conversations that an offensive in North Africa constituted a Second Front.[29]

Despite Russian charges of Anglo-American infidelity and the unquenched desire of Roosevelt's military advisers to launch a major offensive against the Japanese,[30] Churchill had been handed the opportunity to realise the peripheral strategy in the Mediterranean. With Roosevelt's support, preparations began even before Churchill's Moscow trip to rid North Africa of Axis forces. On 26 July, General Dwight Eisenhower, Marshall's protégé, became Supreme Allied Commander of Operation Torch, the invasion of French North Africa. On 8 August, General Bernard Montgomery assumed command of the British Eighth Army in Egypt. These appointments set in train planning and preparation for what became in October–November a giant pincer movement to crush the *Afrika Korps*:[31] Montgomery driving from the east and Eisenhower from the west. On 23 October, the heavily reinforced Eighth Army attacked the Germans at El Alamein; after twelve days fighting, the German retreat began. Three months later, on 23 January, the Eighth Army occupied Tripoli. Between 8 and 11 November, after German resolve broke at El Alamein, Eisenhower's troops landed in French North Africa at Casablanca, Algiers, and Oran. They immediately pushed towards Tunisia.

Despite British and American forces containing the Germans in Tunisia by early January 1943, victory was unattainable till May, five months later than Allied planners anticipated.[32] Delay arose from several factors, chiefly effective German rearguard action designed to get the maximum men, weapons, and supplies back to Italy, and Allied inability to interdict German lines of communication. Belated Allied success in Tunisia created a major diplomatic dilemma for the British and Americans: a cross-Channel invasion could not occur in 1943. It would be impossible to build up enough troops, war materials, and shipping, including landing-craft, to mount an operation before winter.[33] Since Stalin would be displeased, further postponement would

[29] Gilbert, *Churchill*, VII, 172–208.
[30] Dallek, *Roosevelt*, 345–7; Kimball, *Forged*, 150–2.
[31] N. Hamilton, *Monty*, vol. I: *The Making of a General* (Toronto, 1982), 559–774; G. F. Howe, *North Africa: Seizing the Initiative in the West*, United States Army in World War II: The Mediterranean Theatre of Operations series (Washington, 1957).
[32] N. Hamilton, *Master of the Battlefield. Monty's War Years 1942–1944* (1983), 64–241.
[33] K. Smith, 'Logistics Diplomacy and the Second Front: The Unintended Consequences of Franklin Roosevelt's Management Style, 1942–1943', unpublished paper, National Policy History Conference, Bowling Green University, Ohio, 6 Jun. 1997.

damage intra-alliance bonds. Anglo-American forces had to continue fighting on the Axis periphery. At a conference at Washington in May, code-named Trident, it was decided to invade Italy.[34] Not only were adequate troops, supplies, and shipping available to cross the narrow waters between Tunisia and Sicily but, after three years of military defeat, with its economy deteriorating, and the political basis of Mussolini's regime being eroded, Italy seemed ripe for the taking. Churchill reckoned, moreover, that moving onto the Italian peninsula might augment the peripheral strategy by enticing Turkey into the struggle on the Allied side. Of course, victory in Italy could also be a springboard for operations in the Balkans. The case was made to Stalin that a viable Second Front on the Continent via Italy would be established.

The Russians were unimpressed, this producing a bitter exchange of messages between Stalin and Churchill, the temporary withdrawal of Moscow's ambassadors from London and Washington, and the advent of controversy about the Russian-defined Second Front in 1943 that has not yet abated.[35] Nonetheless, despite the low point to which Russia's relations with its Allies fell in summer 1943, western planning commenced for an invasion of Italy. Anglo-American objectives were helped by the collapse of the Fascist regime: Mussolini fell in a *coup d'état* on 25 July, and a retired army general, Pietro Badoglio, led a provisional government.[36] Badoglio immediately began secret negotiations with the Allies to remove Italy from the war. With this diplomacy in the background, Anglo-American forces bolstered by Canadian and other Imperial troops invaded and captured Sicily by late August.[37] A complex series of missed opportunities and miscalculations saw the Allied invasion of Italy, which began on 3 September, bog down. By December 1943, when Allied planners assumed their forces would control most of Italy, the Germans had not been dislodged from a line that ran across the peninsula from a point about fifty miles south of Rome; and two

[34] Dallek, *Roosevelt*, 345–7; Gilbert, *Churchill*, VII, 402–19.
[35] P. Böttger, *Winston Churchill und die Zweite Front, 1941–1943: Ein Aspekte der britischen Strategie im Zweiten Weltkrieg* (Frankfurt, 1984); N. Gelb, *Desperate Venture: The Story of Operation Torch* (New York, 1992); J. Grigg, *1943: The Victory that Never Was* (1980); I. N. Zemskov, 'Diplomatic History of the Second Front', *International Affairs* [Moscow], 7(1961), 49–57.
[36] A. Brissaud, *La Tragédie de Vérone. Grandi et Ciano contre Mussolini, 1943–1944* (Paris, 1971); R. De Felice, *Mussolini*, vol. IV, part 1, book 2: *Crisi e agonia del regime* (Turin, 1981); B. Mussolini, *The Fall of Mussolini: His Own Story* (Westport, CT, 1975 [orig. pub. 1948]).
[37] G. F. Botjer, *Sideshow War: The Italian Campaign, 1943–1945* (College Station, TX, 1996); D. J. Dancocks, *The D-Day Dodgers: The Canadians in Italy, 1943–1945* (Toronto, 1991); D. Graham and M. Tugwell, *Tug of War: The Battle for Italy, 1943–1945* (1986); Hamilton, *Master*, 297–356; R. Lamb, *War in Italy, 1943–1945: A Brutal Story* (1993).

Italian governments competed for the loyalty of Italians: Badoglio's pro-Allied regime in the south and a pro-German one in the north. The chance to deliver a knock-out blow in Italy had failed, and this undermined the supposed efficacy of the peripheral strategy. Churchill was now in a difficult political position with his two alliance partners. The changing nature of the war compounded this difficulty. A year earlier, in the period November 1942–January 1943, Stalin's armies had fought and defeated the *Wehrmacht* at Stalingrad. Not only had the Red Army achieved battlefield mastery, it had completely destroyed the attacking German forces.[38] Using this triumph as the basis for a counter-attack, and utilising armour and artillery that had been manufactured and built up in 1942, the Red Army forced the overextended Germans to retreat back across southern Russia. By late autumn 1943, when the western Allies found the Italian prize beyond their grasp, the Russians routed the Germans, emasculated *Wehrmacht* vitality, and prepared for a major offensive in 1944 with the potential of driving the Germans further back and bringing all of Eastern Europe under Moscow's control. In the Pacific theatre, American forces under General Douglas MacArthur in the South Pacific and Admiral Chester Nimitz in the eastern Pacific built on the Coral Sea and Midway triumphs with successful counter-attacks designed to drive the Japanese back towards their home islands.[39] Although complete victory in both Eastern Europe and the Pacific still required major exertion, the tide of battle had turned in Allied favour.

It is axiomatic that in wartime, success on the battlefield translates into greater diplomatic strength; similarly, weakness constrains diplomacy. Churchill's problem by late 1943 derived from the limited success of British forces in Italy; and, increasingly important, difficulties facing the British Tenth Army in India in pushing the Japanese out of Burma. The British quandary in South-east Asia, shared by the Americans because of Roosevelt's long-standing support of Chiang's regime, derived in part from the Kuomintang contributing little to fighting the Japanese.[40] Although the anglophobic General Joseph Stillwell, commanding

---

[38] W. Craig, *Enemy at the Gates: The Battle for Stalingrad* (1973); R. Cross, *Citadel: The Battle of Kursk* (1993); J. Förster, *Stalingrad: Ereignis, Wirkung, Symbol* (Munich, 1992); J. Piekalkiewicz, *Operation 'Citadel': Kursk and Orel. The Greatest Tank Battle of the Second World War* (1987); L. C. Rotundu, ed., *Battle for Stalingrad: The 1943 Soviet General Staff Study* (1973);

[39] R. B. Frank, *Guadalcanal* (New York, 1990); L. McAulay, *Battle of the Bismarck Sea* (New York, 1991); W. C. Mullins, ed., *1942: Issue in Doubt. Symposium on the War in the Pacific by the Admiral Nimitz Museum* (Annapolis, 1995); A. Stuart, *Guadalcanal: World War II's Fiercest Naval Campaign* (1985).

[40] E. Fischer, *The Chancey War: Winning China, Burma, and India in World War II* (New York, 1991); W. Morwood, *Duel for the Middle Kingdom: The Struggle between Chiang*

American forces in the China-Burma-India Theatre, blamed the British for many of the problems in dislodging the Japanese,[41] Chiang proved reluctant to mount a major offensive. Looking to the postwar period, he stockpiled his arms and other supplies, including Lend-Lease aid, which he needed to fight Mao's Communists for control of China.

Allied successes in 1943 occurred with virtually no British participation. Admittedly, the strategic bomber offensive was beginning to affect Germany's economic infrastructure – but not enough to enervate German war production.[42] And for Britain, the unanticipated delays in the Torch and Italian operations caused by concentrating Allied shipping in the Mediterranean were damaging the British economy. With so many merchantmen diverted from the North Atlantic, British import totals declined markedly in 1943 (about 30 per cent less than 1942), so that pressure on both the Exchequer and the British public was mounting.[43] Tied to the stand-off in Italy, further economic and financial distress undercut British diplomacy as 1943 drew to a close.

In 1942–3, intra-Allied diplomacy concentrated on military efforts to stymie the German and Japanese offensives and, if possible, force them to retreat. This had been accomplished by the end of 1943, even to a degree in Italy. In 1944–5, the issue became one of determining war aims that could be imposed on defeated Germany and Japan. In November 1943, Churchill met with Roosevelt and Stalin at Teheran. This first 'Big Three' meeting stands as a crucial moment in the war. It was when the Allies saw the strategy of their operational response to the Axis and Japan transform into one dominated by the development of war aims and the beginning of putting them into practice to ensure international security once peace returned. Roosevelt told Stalin later in the war: '[Postwar international politics] ought to spell the end of the system of unilateral action, the exclusive alliances, the spheres of influence, the balances of power, and all the other expedients that have been tried for centuries – and have always failed.'[44] Yet, for Roosevelt 'the juggler', Churchill, and Stalin, one enduring truth about *realpolitik* existed of which each never

Kai-shek and Mao Tse-Tung for Control of China (1980); P. Zeigler, *Mountbatten* (New York, 1985), 227–59.

[41] See C. Romanus and S. Riley, *Stillwell's Mission to China* (Washington, DC, 1953); B. Tuchman, *Stillwell and the American Experience in China, 1911–1945* (New York, 1979).

[42] R. Beaumont, 'The Bomber Offensive as a Second Front', *JCH*, 22(1987), 21–44; E. R. Beck, *Under the Bombs: The German Home Front, 1942–1945* (Lexington, KY, 1986); N. Frankland, *The Bombing Offensive Against Germany: Outlines and Perspectives* (1965). Cf. A. Speer, *Inside the Third Reich. Memoirs* (New York, 1970), 284–6.

[43] Central Statistical Office, *Statistical Digest of the War* (1951), table 161. Cf. Smith, *Convoys*, 13–27; Smith, 'Logistics Diplomacy'.

[44] In G. Hess, *The United States at War, 1941–1945* (Arlington Heights, 1986), 109.

lost sight: protecting and extending national interests. Churchill understood Britain's grand strategic interests to be security of the home islands and defence of the Empire. In terms of Europe, his policies at Teheran and after looked to re-establish the balance of power on the continent. Further afield, he sought to recapture what Britain had lost in the Far East. Only on this basis – a revived European balance in which Britain had influence, and the recrudescence of a strong Empire – could Britain hope to remain a Power of the first rank.

He tasted the task before him in two series of meetings with Roosevelt in 1943. The first occurred at Casablanca in January. Ostensibly, the two leaders met to co-ordinate grand strategy, as the battles of North Africa, Stalingrad, and the Atlantic seemed near to victory.[45] However, the Tunisian delay suggested that the contemplated cross-Channel invasion in 1943 might suffer. Stalin needed to be mollified. Therefore, the two leaders dealt with matters tied to the prosecution of the Tunisian campaign; and they sought to reconcile the two chief contenders for leadership of pro-Allied French forces outside Vichy France – General Charles de Gaulle and General Henri Giraud. The problems with Tunisia are outlined above. In terms of the French question, important given the Torch landings in Algeria, Churchill and Roosevelt helped create a French Committee of National Liberation in Algiers in May, of which the two generals became co-presidents. By November 1943, de Gaulle had out-manoeuvred Giraud to become sole leader of the Committee, though neither Churchill nor Roosevelt recognised it as a government-in-exile.[46]

More generally at Casablanca, Churchill pressed for operations against Sicily after North Africa was cleared; given the American military chiefs' antipathy to this proposal, the matter was held in abeyance until the Tunisian campaign ended.[47] Only at Trident in May was it decided to invade Italy. More important at Casablanca was Roosevelt's sudden public announcement that the Allies would pursue 'the unconditional surrender' of the Axis Powers and Japan.[48] Part of the reason for his

---

[45] Dallek, *Roosevelt*, 369–85; Gilbert, *Churchill*, VII, 292–315; Kimball, *Juggler*, 63–81.

[46] P. M. H. Bell, 'War, Foreign Policy, and Public Opinion: Britain and the Darlan Affair, November–December 1942', *JSS*, 5(1982), 393–415; J. Charmley, 'Harold Macmillan and the Making of the French Committee of Liberation', *IHR*, 4(1982), 533–67; A. B. Gauson, 'Churchill, Spears and the Levant Affair, 1941', *HJ*, 27(1984), 697–713.

[47] Gilbert, *Churchill*, VII, 294–313. Cf. A. Danchev, 'Being Friends: The Combined Chiefs of Staff and the Making of Allied Strategy in the Second World War', and J. Gooch, '"Hidden in a Rock": American Military Perceptions of Great Britain, 1919–1940', both in L. Freedman *et al.*, eds., *War, Strategy, and International Politics: Essays in Honour of Sir Michael Howard* (Oxford, 1992), 155–73, 195–210.

[48] A. Armstrong, *Unconditional Surrender: The Impact of Casablanca Policy upon World War II* (New Brunswick, NJ, 1961); Dallek, *Roosevelt*, 373–6; Lord Hankey, 'Unconditional Surrender', *CR*, 176(1949), 193–8.

action stemmed from Allied negotiations with Vichy officials prior to and after the Torch landings. But his main ground for making this statement probably derived from the need to reassure Stalin that the western Allies would not abandon Russia. Controversy exists about this statement because the phrase did not appear in the final communiqué of the conference, and the president suggested that Churchill knew nothing beforehand about his intention. Yet, Churchill did know, telling the Cabinet almost a week earlier that he supported such a statement.[49] Reacting to American concern that the British might not fight against Japan after Germany's defeat, Churchill was willing to reassure his partner. His reassurance tied Britain, bloodied and financially drained by the war,[50] firmly to the American wagon for potential long-term operations in the Far East.

[49] Gilbert, *Churchill*, VII, 300, 309.

[50]

	Britain			
	1939	1941	1943	1945
Domestic exports (millions of US$)	2,057	1,472	1,359	1,751
Trade imports (millions of US$)	4,144	4,615	7,598	6,113
Coal production (millions of tons)	231	206	199	183
Pig iron production (thousands of tons)	7,980	7,393	7,187	7,107
Steel production (thousands of tons)	13,221	12,312	13,031	11,824
National wealth (GNP) (current prices, billions of US$)	23.0	27.1	31.9	33.2
	United States			
Domestic exports (millions of US$)	3,192	5,153	13,028	10,097
Trade imports (millions of US$)	5,978	4,375	3,511	4,280
Coal production (thousands of short tons)	394,855	514,149	590,177	577,617
Pig iron production (thousands of long tons)	32,091	49,307	54,272	47,558
Steel production (thousands of short tons)	52,799	82,839	88,837	79,702
National wealth (GNP) (current prices, billions of US$)	90.5	124.5	191.6	211.9

Source: From Mitchell, *British Historical Statistics*, 249, 283, 284, 289, 453, 454, 829, 830; US Department of Commerce, *Historical Statistics*, 224, 589, 599, 693, 884. The £/$ conversion is based on Sloman and Butler, *Political Facts*, 310 (table of 'Foreign Exchange Rates'). Cf. Bairoch, 'Industrialization Levels', 275; Bairoch, 'Gross National Product', 280–1.

Formal confirmation that Britain would contribute to the final push against Japan amounted to another fee that Churchill had to pay to win the war in Europe. It also meant that British forces would be in a position to reoccupy key Far Eastern Imperial possessions, like Singapore and Shanghai, following Japan's collapse. Yet, Churchill's support for unconditional surrender indicated Britain's waning political leverage within the alliance. Trident masked this development as, outwardly, Roosevelt's decision to support the Italian invasion conformed to Churchill's notion of the peripheral strategy. However, circumstances created by delayed victory in the Tunisian operations rather than Churchill's power of persuasion lay behind Roosevelt's backing of operations against Italy. The changing dynamic of Anglo-American relations became clearer when the two leaders met at Quebec City in August 1943, with a side visit to Roosevelt's Hyde Park estate. Thanks to Trident, preliminary planning for a cross-Channel invasion had begun and, tentatively scheduled to begin in spring 1944, the operation received its code-name: Overlord.[51] CCS consideration of how it could be achieved involved transferring troops and shipping, including precious landing-craft, from the Mediterranean to Britain.

In the Quebec-Hyde Park discussions, Churchill and Roosevelt addressed the issue of who would command Allied forces for both Overlord and the South-east Asian theatre of operations.[52] Churchill proposed General Alan Brooke, the chief of the Imperial General Staff, for the cross-Channel attack. Roosevelt countered that 'Commands should go to which ever country has the largest number of troops employed'; Churchill relented, agreeing that an American should command – Eisenhower received this plum. On the same principle, Roosevelt accepted Churchill's nomination of Admiral Louis Mountbatten, the chief of British Combined Operations, for the South-east Asia command. Beyond this question, both men and their advisers reached several conclusions that determined western Allied strategy for the rest of the war. Despite Churchill's fear that sanctioning a cross-Channel invasion would weaken the offensive in Italy, the date for Overlord was set for May 1944. For his part, Roosevelt conceded that the Italian campaign would not become a defensive operation on the western Allies' part. On a completely different level, they discussed the production of a new weapon, the atomic bomb. For two years, Roosevelt's Administration had funded secret research on and development of this device, to which Britain and Canada contributed materials and

[51] G. Harrison, *Cross-Channel Attack* (Washington, DC, 1951), Chapters 2–3.
[52] Dallek, *Roosevelt*, 408–21; Gilbert, *Churchill*, VII, 470–88; Zeigler, *Mountbatten*, 216–26.

scientific knowledge.[53] The two leaders promised to exchange 'information and ideas' concerning atomic research, never to use this weapon against each other, and never to use it against other Powers 'without each other's consent'.

Churchill achieved some crucial goals at Quebec, notably getting American support for the invasion of Italy and a promise that these operations would continue after the amphibious assault on France. And British command in South-east Asia would make more certain the re-establishment of Britain's Imperial presence in Burma, Malaya, and Singapore. Churchill had even received assurances that the Americans would share atomic knowledge. On the bigger issue in western Allied grand strategy, however, Roosevelt had put his political weight behind a cross-Channel invasion in 1944. He had demanded and forced Churchill's acquiescence in an American commander for Overlord. Roosevelt had accomplished this major strategic shift with the telling argument about those who contributed more troops. Quebec showed the United States' growing political dominance within the Anglo-American relationship.

Three months later at Teheran, British influence decreased further.[54] The major military decision made by the 'Big Three' concerned the precise date for D-Day; this would be in mid-May 1944. This decision resulted from a hard line pursued by Stalin that, because Roosevelt sided with him, diminished British influence within the alliance. Stalin suggested that his armies would not begin their summer 1944 offensive until after the western Allies had landed on French beaches. By November 1943, Stalin understood his political strength within the alliance: the Red Army had inflicted massive casualty and material losses on the *Wehrmacht* and had driven the Germans out of Russia. He could delay the Russian attack on Germany and its Eastern European allies, which might strengthen German military resistance in the West. Mouthing support for Overlord, Churchill attempted to put conditions on a May operation, for instance, that 'landings depended upon the Germans not bringing into France "larger forces than the British and

[53] *FRUS. Conference at Washington and Quebec, 1943* (Washington, DC, 1972), 1123. Cf. M. Gowing, *Independence and Deterrence: Britain and Atomic Energy, 1945–1952*, vol. I (1974), 69–73; D. Holloway, 'The Atomic Bomb and the End of the Wartime Alliance', in Lane and Temperley, *Grand Alliance*, 207–10.
[54] Except where noted, this and the next two paragraphs are based on V. Berezhkov, *Tehran: Lessons of Victory* (Moscow, 1988); K. Eubank, *Summit at Teheran* (1985); V. Mastny, 'Soviet War Aims at the Moscow and Teheran Conferences of 1943', *JMH*, 47(1975); P. D. Mayle, *Eureka Summit: Agreement in Principle and the Big Three at Tehran, 1943* (1987); K. Sainsbury, *The Turning Point: Roosevelt, Stalin, Churchill, and Chiang Kai-shek, 1943: the Moscow, Cairo, and Teheran Conferences* (1985). Cf. R. Edmonds, *Churchill, Roosevelt, and Stalin in Peace and War* (1991).

Americans could gather there"'.[55] Looking both to end the war in
Europe quickly and to ensure good Russian–American relations once
peace returned, Roosevelt confirmed that Overlord would occur as
promised. Churchill grudgingly agreed, a condition of the evolving
Anglo-American alliance captured by Cadogan: 'the President promises
everything that Stalin wants in the way of attack in the West, with the
result that Winston, who has to be more honest, is becoming an object
of suspicion to Stalin'.[56]

As noted earlier, intra-Allied diplomacy after 1943 centred increasingly on determining war aims. Teheran initiated this phase of coalition
warfare as the 'Big Three' began charting the postwar international
order. On the western side Roosevelt, rather than Churchill, led in these
matters, for example, in lobbying Stalin about a new international
organisation to replace the League. Within this organisation, Roosevelt
advocated the concept of 'four policemen' (Britain, Chiang's China,
Russia, and the United States) to ensure international peace and
security. Endorsing a new League, Stalin's comments reflected a desire
to use the new body to keep postwar Germany in check. Nonetheless, it
was a beginning. These talks at Teheran led to the creation of an intra-
Allied committee in August 1944, which met at Dumbarton Oaks in the
United States, to draft a constitution for what Roosevelt called the
'United Nations'[57] – genuflecting to American opinion, he refused to
speak of an Allied alliance after December 1941 but, instead, talked of
the United Nations fighting the Axis and Japan. In these discussions,
even over China as a 'policeman' and despite Chiang's failure to
participate actively against Japan, Churchill stood as an interested but
largely silent observer.[58]

The other major war aim considered at Teheran concerned Germany
and its eastern neighbours. Each leader agreed that defeated Germany
would be occupied and dismembered, although the degree of dismem-
berment differed according to their perceived national interests.
Churchill wanted a viable German state in the heart of Central Europe
for balance of power purposes; Stalin seemed to want several smaller
states that, because of disunity, could never again threaten his country;
Roosevelt stood somewhere in the middle. Ultimately, handling the
German question fell to a body established by Eden, Hull, and Molotov

---

[55] Gilbert, *Churchill*, VII, 584.
[56] Cadogan diary, 29 Nov. 1943, *Cadogan Diary*, 580.
[57] R. C. Hilderbrand, *Dumbarton Oaks. The Origins of the United Nations and the Search for Postwar Security* (Chapel Hill, 1990), 5–66; Woodward, *Foreign Policy*, V, 70–134.
[58] E. J. Hughes, 'Winston Churchill and the Formation of the United Nations Organisation', *JCH*, 9(1974), 177–94.

at Moscow in October 1943, the European Advisory Commission [EAC]. Its mandate was to determine the details of a European settlement.[59] At Teheran, the 'Big Three' agreed to consider its recommendations later in the war. Respecting Eastern Europe, Stalin made proposals that would recognise both Russia's contribution to the war and its future security. He wanted a slice of eastern Poland promised to Russia after the Russo-Polish war of 1920–1 but taken by the Poles. Poland would be compensated by being ceded part of eastern Germany, whilst Moscow retained control of the port of Königsberg – in the summer of 1943, relations between Russia and the Polish government-in-exile were broken when the Germans discovered the graves of massacred Polish officers in former Russian territory.[60] Churchill and Roosevelt were not opposed to this territorial transfer, but concurred that it would require further study. Then, Roosevelt went further by enquiring about Russian territorial objectives in the Far East. Stalin commented generally about giving security to Siberia and the Pacific Maritime Provinces but, probably because he had not thought much about the matter, made no specific demands. This issue, too, would have to be dealt with later. In summary, and tied to the Overlord decision, political discussions at Teheran showed a growing intimacy between Roosevelt and Stalin, reflecting desires to build a *modus vivendi* that could last into the postwar period. British interests were not necessarily ignored in this process; yet, with the changing nature of the war, Roosevelt showed determination to safeguard American interests regardless of Churchill's desires.

This is why Teheran is important. It precipitated a new departure in intra-alliance relations, in general, and the Anglo-American relationship, in particular. Churchill's abiding ambition in 1944 involved protecting his Mediterranean strategy from being whittled down by the requirements of Overlord. He knew that Britain's role in the cross-Channel operation would be less than that offered in southern Europe. British forces had a prominent role in Italy and, when Italy fell, he surmised that a British-led advance into Yugoslavia would provide for a successful assault on southern Germany.[61] British support for anti-German Yugoslav partisans, led by the communist, Josip Tito, had been fundamental

---

[59] B. Kuklick, 'The Genesis of the European Advisory Commission', *JCH*, 4(1969), 189–201; H.-G. Kowalski, 'Die "European Advisory Commission" als Instrument alliierter Deutschland-Planung, 1943–1945', *VfZ*, 19(1971), 261–93.

[60] A. Polonsky, *The Great Powers and the Polish Question 1941–45. A Documentary Study in Cold War Origins* (1976), 31–37; A. Polonsky, 'Polish Failure in Wartime London: Attempts to Forge a European Alliance, 1940–1944', *IHR*, 7(1985), 519–60.

[61] WM(44)88, 7 Jul. 1944, CAB/65.

to Britain's Mediterranean strategy.[62] Moreover, London was taking the lead in supporting the Greek government-in-exile in driving German occupation forces out of Greece and re-establishing itself in Athens.[63] If Britain was to influence the development of war aims after Teheran, it needed success on the battlefield. These were the dual elements of a foreign policy designed to ensure Britain's international influence as the Second World War ended.

However, Roosevelt used American material strength and expanding military and diplomatic muscle to pursue war aims that he increasingly argued were those of the western half of the alliance. A basic tenet of American beliefs was that colonialism was antithetical to American ideals, this despite American colonies existing in everything but name in Puerto Rico, Hawaii, and even the prewar Philippines. Although anti-colonialism had lain near the surface of American external policy since the Spanish-American war – and had materialised periodically thereafter, for instance, during the 1932 Ottawa conference – it bubbled to the top in 1944 and early 1945. Admittedly, Roosevelt and his advisers were not critical solely of British colonialism; they also were distressed by that embodied by the French, Dutch, and other White empires. Roosevelt had always sympathised with Marshall, Admiral Ernest King, the naval chief, and others who deplored the use of American forces to prop up the British Empire in the Mediterranean and the Far East. Roosevelt had only overruled their reluctance to participate in the Mediterranean campaign for pragmatic reasons. After Teheran, when Allied victory became a question of 'when' rather than 'if', Roosevelt moved to ensure that the United States would not be a party to reviving the Imperial presence of Britain, France, and the other colonial Powers.[64] Churchill's response was to do all possible to win in the Mediterranean and launch an offensive against southern Germany; then, using what men and supplies he could garner, especially landing-craft, he would shift them to Mountbatten to recapture Burma, Malaya, and, the main prize, Singapore:

[Singapore] is the Supreme British objective in the whole of the Indian and Far Eastern theatres. It is the only prize that will restore British prestige in this

---

[62] E. Barker, *British Policy in Southeast Europe in the Second World War* (1976); A. Lane, *Britain, the Cold War, and Yugoslav Unity, 1941–1949* (Brighton, 1996), 7–38.

[63] Weinberg, *Arms*, 727.

[64] W. R. Louis, *Imperialism at Bay. The United States and the Decolonization of the British Empire, 1941–1945* (Oxford, 1978); J. J. Sbrega, *Anglo-American Relations and Colonialism in East Asia, 1941–1945* (New York, 1983); Thorne, *Allies of a Kind*. Cf. W. LaFeber, 'Roosevelt, Churchill and Indochina, 1941–1945', *AHR*, 80(1975), 1277–94; C. Thorne, 'Indochina and Anglo-American Relations, 1942–1945', *PHR*, 45(1976), 73–96.

region, and in pursuing it we render the maximum aid to the United States operations by engaging the largest number of the enemy in the most intense degree possible and at the earliest moment.[65]

At the same time, Churchill endeavoured to secure a leading British role in re-establishing and maintaining the postwar European balance. His diplomacy from Teheran till the end of the war was designed to achieve these dual goals. Roosevelt's dominance within the western alliance gradually came to block Churchill's ambitions. As an instance, in the months prior to D-Day, pushed back to 6 June 1944 because of inclement weather, Churchill pressed for private talks with Roosevelt. His ostensible reason was 'not so much [because] ... there are new departures in policy to be taken but there is a need after more than 90 days of separation [since Teheran] for checking up and shaking together'. Roosevelt refused to meet, citing slight infirmity but, really, wanting to avoid a disagreement with Churchill over carrying out the cross-Channel invasion.[66] Although Churchill continued asking for a meeting, nothing came of his overtures until late June – well after D-Day and a western Allied beach-head had been established in Normandy.[67] At that time, the CCS were deliberating in London, the better to be near the fighting; the British and American staffs divided over essential Allied strategy in Western Europe and the Mediterranean. Based on assessments from Eisenhower's headquarters, the Americans were concerned about the success of both the operations in Normandy and proposed landings in southern France.[68] To this end, the Americans advocated stripping the Allied armies in Italy of manpower and resources, transferring them to the other two fronts, and leaving only enough forces to defend the gains made. The British disagreed. Churchill informed Roosevelt on 28 June:

The deadlock between our Chiefs of Staff raise most serious issues. Our first wish is to help General Eisenhower in the most speedy and effective manner.

---

[65] Churchill minute, 12 Sep. 1944, quoted in Gilbert, *Churchill*, VII, 955.

[66] Churchill to Roosevelt, 18 Mar. 1944, and reply, 20 Mar. 1944, both *FRUS. The Conference at Quebec 1944* (Washington, 1972), 3–4. Cf. Dallek, *Roosevelt*, 468.

[67] C. D'Este, *Decision in Normandy* (New York, 1983); J. A. English, *The Canadian Army and the Normandy Campaign: A Study of Failure in High Command* (New York, 1991); M. Hastings, *Overlord: D-Day and the Battle for Normandy* (1984); T. A. Wilson, ed., *D-Day, 1944* (Lawrence, KS, 1994).

[68] SHAEF Memoranda, 'Release of Shipping and Craft from Operation "Neptune"', 12 Jun. 1944, 'The Employment of Mediterranean Forces in Aid of "Neptune"', 12 Jun. 1944, are both annexes in CCS Meeting 164, 13 Jun. 1944, in CCS 'Octagon Conference September 1944'. *Papers and Minutes of Meetings, Octagon Conference and Minutes of Combined Chiefs of Staff Meetings in London, June 1944* [microfilm edition: National Archives, Washington DC]. 'Neptune' was the code-name of the assault phase of 'Overlord'.

But, we do not think this necessarily involves the complete ruin of all our great affairs in the Mediterranean, and we take it hard that this should be demanded of us.[69]

He had already broached another face-to-face meeting with the president, his apprehension about the seeming muddle in which the western Allies found themselves also being impressed on both Hopkins and Winant.[70] Though the immediacy of this problem abated somewhat by early July, the broad strategic problem of where western Allied forces should fight – and in what strength – needed to be addressed at the highest level. Roosevelt accepted Churchill's invitation, and planning began for what became a second Anglo-American summit at Quebec.

This meeting occurred on 11–17 September 1944, with two days of discussions at Hyde Park afterwards.[71] Second Quebec provided Churchill with an opportunity to push for British-led military operations in Italy and the Balkans that could be translated into strengthening his diplomatic hand when the occupation of Germany, the structure of the new international security and financial organisations, the general European settlement, and the plans for defeating Japan were finalised. At Quebec, he ensured that Allied landing-craft in Italy, after amphibious operations against Yugoslavia's Istrian peninsula, would be sent on to Mountbatten; and Roosevelt agreed that British forces could participate in the final push against Japan. He also won Roosevelt's agreement that Anglo-American control of atomic research and development would continue after the war. Second Quebec, however, did not alter basic Anglo-American strategy. Its main decisions concerned the fate of defeated Germany and whether Britain would receive additional American economic aid once peace returned. The two were connected.

The EAC had devised a scheme for postwar control of Germany, in which there would be American, British, and Russian zones of military occupation.[72] The Americans accepted this scheme but, on 13 September, suddenly proposed a plan conceived by Morgenthau that

---

[69] Churchill to Roosevelt, 28 Jun. 1944, in *Churchill–Roosevelt*, III, 212–13. Cf. Churchill to Roosevelt, 28 Jun. 1944, enclosing Prime Minister and Minister of Defence memorandum, 'Operations in the European Theatres', n.d., and reply, 29 Jun. 1944, ibid., 214–23.

[70] Churchill to Roosevelt, 20 Jun. 1944, *FRUS Quebec 1944*, 8. See Winant to Roosevelt, 3 Jul. 1944, Churchill to Hopkins, 19 Jul. 1944, both Roosevelt MR [Roosevelt Map Room MSS, Roosevelt Library, Hyde Park, NY] 11.

[71] *FRUS Quebec 1944*. Cf. Dallek, *Roosevelt*, 467–78; Gilbert, *Churchill*, VII, 954–70; Kimball, *Forged*, 274–81; B. J. C. McKercher, 'Towards the Post-War Settlement: Winston Churchill and the Second Quebec Conference', in D. Woolner, ed., *The Second Quebec Conference Revisited* (New York, forthcoming).

[72] L. Kettenacker, 'The Anglo-Soviet Alliance and the Problem of Germany, 1941–1945', *JCH*, 17(1982), 435–58; T. Sharp, *The Wartime Alliance and the Zonal Division of Germany* (1975), 56–89.

envisaged Germany's complete disarmament. Most German heavy industry would be dismantled and removed to destroy the country's war-making potential. Industrial components would be transferred to those states that Germany had devastated in the war. Of the remaining industry, largely in the Ruhr Valley, part would be internationalised and part would be turned over to the French. Outside the Ruhr, the rest of the country would be divided into a northern and a southern state, each with agricultural economies.[73] Over Eden's objections, Churchill accepted the plan because Roosevelt promised to continue Lend-Lease aid to Britain after Germany's defeat.[74] In his mind, British support of the plan was a *quid pro quo* for this aid, crucial for the final phase of the war against Japan and re-establishing the Empire in East Asia. Ultimately, Morgenthau's plan suffered a bureaucratic death. Stimson and others in Washington marshalled strong strategic arguments to convince Roosevelt that a viable Germany was 'a natural and necessary asset for the [postwar] productivity of Europe'.[75]

Nonetheless, Churchill acquiesced in Roosevelt's support of a plan that ran counter to the concept of the postwar balance of power that he had pursued since before Teheran. Britain's emerging strategic predicament in late 1944 centred on Russian military victories in Eastern Europe, which indicated as early as August that Stalin intended to impose pro-Russian communist regimes in the states liberated from the Germans in that region. The litmus was Poland, where an uprising began in Warsaw under the aegis of the Polish government-in-exile.[76] The Russians refused to allow Anglo-American air supply of the insurgents – transport planes would have to land behind Russian lines to refuel – so that by the end of September the uprising had failed. Then the Red Army advanced, defeated the weakened Germans, and allowed communist Poles to assert their authority. Churchill had implored Roosevelt to pressure Stalin to aid the insurgents;[77] when Roosevelt refused to do so to keep Russo-American relations on an even keel,

---

[73] Treasury Department memorandum, 'Suggested Post-Surrender Program for Germany', 1 Sep. 1944, *FRUS Quebec 1944*, 86–90. Cf. White [US Treasury] minute to Morgenthau, 1 Sep. 1944, with enclosures, esp. 'Directive for Military Government in Germany under Phase I', 'Political Guide', 'Economic Guide for Germany', in Morgenthau Diary.

[74] See Gilbert, *Churchill*, VII, 961–2. Cf. 'Roosevelt–Churchill Meeting, September 15, 1944', *FRUS Quebec 1944*, 362; *SWW*, VI, 156–57.

[75] Stimson, 'Memorandum for the President', 9 Sep. 1944, in Morgenthau Diary.

[76] J. Coutouvidis and J. Reynolds, *Poland 1939–1947* (New York, 1986), 91–102; Polonsky, 'Polish Failure'; J. T. Tomasz, *Revolution From Abroad: The Soviet Conquest of Poland's Western Ukraine and Western Byelorussia* (Princeton, 1988).

[77] Churchill to Roosevelt, (3) 18 Aug., 23 Aug., (3) 4 Sep. 1944, and replies, 26 Aug., 5 Sep. 1944, *Churchill–Roosevelt*, III, 281–3, 292–3, 296, 309–13.

Churchill understood that Washington and Moscow were taking the leading role in shaping postwar Europe. With Roosevelt suggesting that American troops might be removed from Europe after German defeat – he was seeking a fourth term as president in the November 1944 elections[78] – Churchill did not want Britain to be left alone to face a menacing Russia once peace returned.

Churchill looked, therefore, to balance his American policy with that involving Russia. With Roosevelt's knowledge, he and Eden travelled to Moscow in October 1944.[79] Meeting with Stalin and Molotov, they moved to settle the Polish problem; they discussed the war against Japan; and they gave preliminary shape to postwar spheres of influence in Central and Eastern Europe and the Balkans. This latter issue was most important, suggesting British political and strategic advantages in the Mediterranean and Southern Europe once peace returned. The crucial moment came when Churchill proposed that the three major Allies determine 'percentages' of dominance in Romania, Greece, Yugoslavia, Hungary, and Bulgaria. Despite the odd nature of dividing influence by 'percentages',[80] the proposal constituted a simple matter of *realpolitik* for Churchill, who recognised both the Red Army's successes by 1944 and the fact that Stalin was going to ensure pliant, pro-Soviet regimes in regions liberated by Russian force of arms. The Russians would dominate the continental interior, including that of the Balkans and along the Black Sea coast of Bulgaria to the Straits but not beyond. With American concurrence, the British would dominate on the Balkan littoral, including the Yugoslav coast. Although some adjustment of the original percentages occurred, and although Stalin promised to support democratic elections in the liberated states, the die was cast. Reaching an equivalent compromise concerning Poland proved more difficult. Bowing to the inevitable and swallowing his distaste for Stalin's response to the Warsaw uprising, Churchill forced the head of the Polish government-in-exile in London to find political means to create a coalition government in liberated Poland with pro-Russian Poles. Churchill had washed his hands of the Polish problem.

By late October 1944, Churchill believed he had accomplished a great

---

[78] Dallek, *Roosevelt*, 433.
[79] *SWW*, VI, 226–43; P. G. H. Holdich, 'A Policy of Percentages? British Policy and the Balkans after the Moscow Conference of October 1944', *IHR*, 9(1987), 28–47; J. M. Siracusa, 'The Meaning of TOLSTOY: Churchill, Stalin, and the Balkans, Moscow, October 1944', *DH*, 3(1979), 443–63; J. M. Siracusa, 'The Night Stalin and Hitler Divided Europe: The View from Washington', *RP*, 43(1981), 381–410.
[80] Romania (Russia 90%; the others, 10%); Greece (Britain, in accord with the United States, 90%; Russia 10%); Yugoslavia and Hungary (50% each); and Bulgaria (Russia 75%; the others 25%). In *SWW*, VI, 227.

deal. He had won breathing space for the Mediterranean strategy, guaranteed landing-craft for Mountbatten's assault on Singapore, assured continued Lend-Lease assistance, and influenced the emerging order in Eastern Europe and the Balkans. Britain would have a role in establishing and influencing the postwar settlement. He put his feelings about this role in his congratulations on Roosevelt's re-election:

I feel that you will not mind my saying that I prayed for your success and that I am truly thankful for it. This does not mean that I seek or wish for anything more than the full, fair and free play of your mind upon the world issues now at stake in which our two nations have to discharge their respective duties.[81]

Here was the focus of Churchill's diplomacy as the defeat of Allied enemies in Europe and the Far East loomed: Britain and the United States should continue to work together to bring about effective international peace and security, and they should do so as full partners.

Churchill's difficulty after November 1944 was that his ability to influence alliance policy ebbed as each day passed. This became clear at the second 'Big Three' summit, held at Yalta, in the Crimea, in early February 1945.[82] By this time, with victory in Europe certain and victory in the Far East inescapable, war aims had become fundamentally important. Yalta produced a series of bilateral arrangements amongst the three leaders designed to safeguard their narrow national interests after German surrender. The EAC had finally determined how occupied Germany should be divided into occupation zones and how, in general terms, it should be governed till it could be made peaceable. Stalin sought British and American recognition of Eastern Europe, including Poland, as a Russian sphere of influence. Not knowing whether the atomic bomb would be ready for use in the Pacific theatre after the 'Europe first' strategy was realised, Roosevelt wanted the Russians to enter the struggle against Japan as soon as possible – Russia and Japan were not at war thanks to a non-aggression pact concluded in April 1941. Russian participation would hasten the end of the struggle and save American lives. With Morgenthau's plan dead, Churchill returned to the problem of maintaining the postwar balance in Europe; with the ground for this prepared in the autumn of 1944, when de Gaulle was recognised as the head of a provisional

[81] Churchill to Roosevelt, 8 Nov. 1944, *Churchill–Roosevelt*, III, 383.
[82] Except where noted, the next three paragraphs are based on *FRUS. The Conferences at Malta and Yalta, 1945* (Washington, DC, 1955). Cf. R. D. Buhite, *Decisions at Yalta: An Appraisal of Summit Diplomacy* (Wilmington, DE, 1986); D. S. Clemens, *Yalta* (New York, 1970); Dallek, *Roosevelt*, 506–25; Gilbert, *Churchill*, VII, 1171–218; R. C. Lukas, *The Strange Allies. The United States and Poland, 1941–1945* (Knoxville, 1978); J. L. Snell, *The Meaning of Yalta* (Baton Rouge, LA, 1956); A. G. Theoharis, *The Yalta Myths: An Issue in U.S. Politics, 1945–1955* (Columbia, MO, 1979).

French government, he lobbied for a French occupation zone in Germany. As a result of these general desires, Stalin agreed to enter the war against Japan three months after the end of hostilities in Europe and to accept a French zone of occupation as long as it was not constructed from part of the Russian zone. Wary of de Gaulle, Roosevelt agreed to fashion a French zone out of the assigned British and American ones. For their part, Churchill and Roosevelt conceded to Eastern Europe falling under Russian sway, though they got Stalin to conform to the Atlantic Charter by agreeing that 'democratic' elections occur in Eastern Europe. Potential problems resided with the Marxist concept of 'democracy' that, in a single-party state, was anathema to 'liberal' concepts of the term defined by the two English-speaking Powers. Nonetheless, deals were struck that seemed to establish a new postwar order in Europe.

Beyond these decisions, however, stood the British dilemma that had emerged at Teheran. Roosevelt and Stalin settled a range of issues without reference to their British partner. In terms of proposals that emanated from Dumbarton Oaks, Roosevelt and Stalin determined how the two chief impediments to an agreement on the United Nations Organisation (UN) – voting procedure in the Security Council, the centre of decision-making, and membership – should be removed. On procedural matters within the Security Council, a majority of the votes of permanent and non-permanent members would be required. On all other matters, an advance on the League's procedures, each permanent member would have the right of veto. Respecting membership, Stalin wanted separate representation for the seventeen republics of the Soviet Union. When Roosevelt countered that all forty-eight states of the American union should have the same right, it was agreed that there would be only three Soviet members – Byelorussia, the Ukraine, and the remainder led by Russia. Isolated from these deliberations, but to preserve British ties to the United States, Churchill accepted Roosevelt's lead. Preparations immediately began for a conference, which began at San Francisco in late April 1945, to give the Dumbarton Oaks–Yalta agreements legal form.

In terms of the Far East, Stalin now had specific Russian demands designed to restore advantages that tsarist Russia had won from Peking in the nineteenth century and lost to Tokyo in the Russo-Japanese war of 1904–5. In private discussions by-passing both Churchill and Chiang, Roosevelt and Stalin agreed that communist Outer Mongolia would remain intact, that the Kurile Islands and the southern half of the Sakhalin Peninsula would be transferred to Russia, and that the Russians would regain economic advantages in Manchuria, as well as

control of the naval base at Port Arthur.[83] Apart from believing that the
Russians had legitimate demands in East Asia, Roosevelt's motive in
these talks seems to have been a desire to ensure a smooth Russo-
American relationship after the war. In this equation, Churchill had to
accept what Roosevelt and Stalin decided – as did Chiang. Politically,
the Russo-American arrangement constituted 'old diplomacy' of the
pre-1914 variety that the British had long practised. In the context of
1945, given the Atlantic Charter and supposedly close Anglo-American
relations, it meant that Britain had been unable to affect a political
settlement in East Asia that would markedly influence its postwar
Imperial prestige in China. Its chief partners were economically (the
United States) and militarily (the United States and Russia) in the
ascendant. Whilst not weak *vis-à-vis* other Great Powers like newly
liberated France or Italy, Britain lacked the military and economic
power of the United States and Russia. And the Russians and Americans
were making decisions that in crucial ways were anathema to Britain's
survival as a Power of the first rank.

The pattern of intra-alliance relations as it reflected on British power
became more stark as the war in Europe and the Far East ground to a
halt. In both theatres, American and Russian strength increased, whilst
that of Britain declined relative to its two partners. A watershed was
reached on 12 April 1945, when Roosevelt died unexpectedly. A new
president, Harry Truman, was in the White House; his preoccupation
was Russo-American relations, tensions in which had emerged even
before Yalta.[84] Truman had been vice-president just three months; he
knew little of the grand strategy of the war – and nothing about the
atomic bomb – so that he relied on the advice of Roosevelt's political
and military advisers in Washington and in the theatres of war. These
advisers were increasingly suspicious of Russian ambitions, chiefly in
Europe, and they argued for using American political strength to keep
Stalin in line.[85] In May, Truman cancelled Lend-Lease, which affected

---

[83] *FRUS Yalta*, 984.

[84] Cf. J. L. Gaddis, *The Long Peace. Enquiries into the History of the Cold War* (Oxford,
1987), 3–19; G. F. Kennan and J. Lukacs, *G. F. Kennan and the Origins of Containment,
1944–1946* (Columbia, MO, 1997); A. Perlmutter, *FDR & Stalin: A Not So Grand
Alliance, 1943–1945* (Columbia, MO, 1993); D. W. Tuttle, *Harry L. Hopkins and
Anglo-American-Soviet Relations, 1941–1945* (New York, 1983). For a wider perspec-
tive, D. Reynolds, W. F. Kimball, and A. O. Chubarian, eds., *Allies at War: The Soviet,
American, and British Experience, 1939–1945* (New York, 1994); and D. Reynolds, ed.,
The Origins of the Cold War in Europe: International Perspectives (New Haven, 1994).

[85] Cf. R. J. Maddox, *From War to Cold War: The Education of Harry S. Truman* (Boulder,
CO, 1988); R. Moskin, *Mr. Truman's War: The Final Victories of World War II and the
Birth of the Postwar World* (New York, 1996); R. L. Messer, *The End of an Alliance:
James F. Byrnes, Roosevelt, Truman, and the Origins of the Cold War* (Chapel Hill, 1982);
R. J. Walton, *Henry Wallace, Harry Truman, and the Cold War* (New York, 1976).

Britain as much as it did Russia. Shortly before, opposing the advice of Marshall and Eisenhower, Churchill advocated that the Anglo-American armies in Germany drive east of the Elbe River to capture Berlin before the Red Army – this ran counter to an earlier agreement that Anglo-American forces would stop at the Elbe. Truman supported his generals.[86] Churchill's ability to make Britain's case to the highest levels of American policy-making had lessened substantially by 8 May 1945, when the Germans surrendered, over even that limited strength that he had enjoyed at Yalta. Britain was irretrievably America's junior partner.

Britain's place in what John Balfour, a senior diplomat at the British Embassy in Washington, called 'the new order of things' was confirmed at the final 'Big Three' meeting of the war, held at Potsdam between 17 July and 2 August 1945.[87] Two major issues engaged Churchill, Truman, and Stalin: the occupation of Germany and defeating Japan. The latter was especially important for the United States. Just before the conference began, and suffering great losses, American forces had captured Okinawa, to the south of the Japanese home islands. With the invasion of Kyushu, the southernmost of Japan's islands, scheduled for November, Truman wanted the Red Army to move into northern China as quickly as possible to tie down Japanese forces. In his first meeting with Stalin, Truman learnt that the Russians would enter the war by 15 August. He immediately reckoned that 'we'll end the war a year sooner now'.[88] From Britain's perspective, however, Russian entry into the Far Eastern struggle constituted a strategic issue of decided importance.[89] Following the lines of Roosevelt's dictum that 'Commands should go to which ever country has the largest number of troops employed', Truman and his advisers were moving to emplace an American occupation regime in Japan. Although this regime allowed for some foreign occupation forces, Washington had no intention of permitting London or Moscow to influence policy towards defeated Japan. And with the Russians given a free hand in northern China, including Manchuria – the Red Army began operations on 8 August – Britain's postwar position

[86] S. E. Ambrose, *Eisenhower and Berlin, 1945: The Decision to Halt at the Elbe* (New York, 1986); F. C. Pogue, *The Decision to Halt at the Elbe* (Washington, DC, 1990).
[87] Except where noted, the next four paragraphs are based on J. L. Gormly, *From Potsdam to the Cold War: Big Three Diplomacy, 1945–1947* (Wilmington, DE, 1990); C. L. Mee, *Meeting at Potsdam* (New York, 1996); H. Thomas, *Armed Truce. The Beginnings of the Cold War 1945–46* (1986), 123–45; Woodward, *Foreign Policy*, V, 401–99. Cf. V. O. Pechatnov, *The Big Three after World War II: New Documents on Soviet Thinking about Postwar Relations with the United States and Great Britain* (Washington, DC, 1995).
[88] Truman to his wife, 18 Jul. 1945, in R. H. Ferrell, ed., *Dear Bess: The Letters from Harry Truman to Bess Truman 1910–1959* (New York, 1983), 519.
[89] Eden to Churchill, 17 Jul. 1945, Avon, *Reckoning*, 545–7.

in both China and, more generally, East Asia was more precarious than before the 1939 Tientsin incident. The postwar United States would certainly be less truculent towards Britain in East Asia than had prewar Japan; but at Potsdam, it was clear that Truman's Administration intended to translate America's military victory into a strategic preponderance in the Far East that safeguarded American political, economic, and financial interests there. Weakened by the war, needing to revive its Imperial authority in South-east Asia, and having reduced economic means to re-establish its financial and trading presence in places like Hong Kong and Shanghai, Britain's vulnerability to American inroads was now an unpleasant circumstance in the new East Asian order. Then, on 24 July, Truman informed Churchill that the atomic bomb had been tested successfully in New Mexico. Telling Churchill that it would be used against Japan as soon as possible – a pretence of the consultation Roosevelt promised at Quebec in 1943 – the president forced his British ally to endorse his plan. Since the Americans controlled the bomb and its production, Churchill could do little else. And, importantly, Truman's concern about East Asia after 24 July had little to do with the British. Anxious to save American lives in the final conquest of Japan, animated by a degree of revenge for Pearl Harbor, and certainly wishing to signal to Stalin that the United States was a Power to be reckoned with in both East Asia and Europe, Truman saw the use of the bomb as a tangible expression of the preponderance of American power in the postwar world. On 2 September 1945, after two of its cities had been decimated with atomic weapons,[90] Japan surrendered. The Americans occupied Japan and continued support for the Kuomintang as the legitimate government of China. In contrast to the Americans, and coupled with its financial and economic weakness, Britain's minimal military contribution to the final Allied victory in East Asia meant that Britain had only a small postwar voice in a region crucial to Britain's standing as a global Power.

Disposing of the relics of German power followed on Yalta's refinements of the EAC plan. The 'Big Three' – or as Cadogan called them, the Big '$2\frac{1}{2}$'[91] – dealt with the administrative regime, a decision-making apparatus, reparations, denazification, and border adjustments, chiefly the always thorny Polish–German frontier. The results produced military governments in each zone, separate German and Berlin control commissions comprising the four zonal military commanders, and,

---

[90] Cf. G. Alperovitz, *Atomic Diplomacy: Hiroshima and Potsdam: The Use of the Atomic Bomb and the American Confrontation with Soviet Power* (Boulder, CO, 1994); D. D. Wainstock, *The Decision to Drop the Atomic Bomb* (Westport, CT, 1996).
[91] Cadogan diary, 2 Aug. 1945, *Cadogan Diary*, 278.

above them, reflecting the wartime CCS, a Council of Foreign Ministers to resolve deadlocks within the control commissions. Similar regimes were established for Austria, resuscitated by the Allies, and Vienna. Immediate problems involved getting adequate food supplies, medical care, and housing for both the German people and millions of displaced people within the country. Within the strictures of denazification – former Nazi Party members, including competent technocrats, skilled executives, and others, could not hold administrative or managerial posts – there was also the problem of reviving German economic life.

Apart from these technical issues of peacemaking, there loomed the larger political questions important to achieving security. Providing an overarching framework for postwar international politics, the San Francisco conference had already devised the UN Charter. Flowing from this development, the 'Big Three' agreed at Potsdam that the Council of Foreign Ministers would draft peace treaties. On this basis, Italy would be invited to join the UN following an Italian peace settlement, whilst normalising relations with Nazi Germany's former Eastern European allies like Bulgaria and Hungary, now under Russian sway, would follow peace treaties with them. But tensions within the alliance that had been building since 1941–2 spilled into the open and undermined the sought-for security.[92] Russia's long-held ambition to secure access to the Mediterranean, evidenced by renewed pressure on Turkey, was rebuffed, as was its desire to occupy the former Italian colony of Libya. The British and Americans also withstood Stalin's call to restructure the Greek government; civil war had erupted in Greece between the British-supported regime and pro-communist insurgents. Similarly, having suffered horrendously in the war – although Stalin conveniently forgot the Nazi–Soviet pact – the Russians perceived western Allied interference in their attempt to construct a defensive *glacis* on their European perimeter. They wanted pliant, pro-Russian states in the region and, with Stalinist brutality, had begun to create them; their endeavours here created a western perception of aggrandising Russian power with the potential to disrupt the European balance. Hence, over the central question at Potsdam, the future of Germany, the three Powers had completely different interests. The Russians wanted an economically and militarily weak German state to remove once and for all the major threat to their security. The Americans sought a militarily weak but economically strong Germany that could serve as the sheet-anchor for a

---

[92] M. Kessel, *Westeuropa und die deutsche Teilung: englische und französische Deutschlandpolitik auf den Aussenministerkonferenzen von 1945 bis 1947* (Munich, 1989); Mastny, 'Soviet War Aims'; P. D. Ward, *The Threat of Peace: James F. Byrnes and the Council of Foreign Ministers, 1945–1946* (Kent, OH, 1979).

revived European economy within the capitalist world. Sharing American desires for German economic vitality, the British saw a denazified Germany as pivotal to the postwar balance on the continent of Europe. Whether Potsdam offered a real possibility for continued 'Big Three' co-operation is moot – they had also to contend with a de Gaulle apparently humiliated by not being invited to the conference. The essential economic, political, and strategic interests of the three Powers, and now France, were largely antithetical. With ideological divisions thrown into the mix, hopes of perpetuating the wartime alliance into the postwar era were illusory. And during Potsdam, the nature of the 'Big Three' suffered another radical change when Churchill and the Conservatives suffered defeat in a General Election on 25 July; a Labour government took office led by Clement Attlee. Although Attlee and his foreign secretary, Ernest Bevin, shared Churchill's views about the European balance, and were deeply suspicious of Russian policy, it did not matter who led Britain's return to peace. The Americans were now in the ascendant at the moment in Europe when western leaders, including Attlee and Bevin, reckoned they were witnessing Nazi German totalitarianism being replaced by a Bolshevik Russian variant. Because of their overwhelming material and military power, and the will to utilise it to defend and extend United States interests, the Americans were leading Britain and its other western allies in opposing perceived Russian aggression. It constituted the tangible postwar expression of Roosevelt's 1943 axiom about command going to the most powerful state. The transition was complete. With the 'new order of things' increasingly defined by western tensions with the Russians in Europe, the Far East, and elsewhere – in short, the Cold War – Truman, Marshall, and other American leaders were going to guide the western response.[93] Facing the Russian threat, financially drained, and confronting the difficult task of consolidating an eroding Empire, Britain grudgingly took its role in this new order as the junior partner of the United States.

The fifteen years after 1930 proved decisive in the history of Britain as the greatest of the Great Powers. In that crucial decade and a half, tied to Britain's domestic political and economic structure, its leaders' response to the changing constellation of international politics resulted in the surrender of its pre-eminence to the United States. Although American primacy might well have been pre-destined because of the

---

[93] Dawson, *Byrnes*; R. M. Hathaway, *Ambiguous Partnership: Britain and America, 1944–1947* (New York, 1981); M. P. Leffler, *A Preponderance of Power: National Security, the Truman Administration, and the Cold War* (Stanford, 1992).

wealth, industrial capacity, and population of the United States, the degree to which British power waned and that of the United States waxed was not predetermined. In the interwar period, British diplomacy looked to safeguard Britain's 'eternal interests'. This was especially so after 1930, when the international economic and financial crisis undermined the Great Power equilibria in Europe and the Far East that had been created by the Washington and Locarno treaties and the Dawes and Young war debt agreements. Utilising the country's financial muscle, its armed strength (resting on the potency of the RN), and its prestige, those responsible for foreign policy worked to preserve national and Imperial security. Their will to shape events rather than let events limit or damage the state's interests gave them decided influence in international politics. The situation was helped, first, by 'world leaders' within the foreign-policy-making elite dominating the machinery of government until at least late 1937, and second, from flaws in 'imperial isolationism' and 'atlanticism' that made their strategic concepts impractical in protecting British interests in the new order that emerged after 1918. Part stemmed from the other Great Powers being regional Powers with regional interests that undermined any pretence they might have had of global Power status.

Until the fall of France in June 1940, the United States was such a Power. Admittedly, interwar America had decided financial, economic, naval, and political strength. So, despite the Wall Street collapse, the New York money market remained important throughout the interwar period; and American pursuit of overseas markets and investment saw determined United States competition with Britain, the Europeans, and Japan in both hemispheres. At the same time, tied to the shrill cries of American navalists for 'parity' with Britain, American industrial and financial capacity allowed the USN to remain strong enough to worry its two chief rivals, the RN and IJN. Over particular political issues such as those spawned by the Manchurian crisis, Washington's sensitivities could not be dismissed by the chancelleries of the other Powers. Yet, America's writ remained strong only within the Western Hemisphere. Outside of this region, Washington had little real influence; indeed, in many respects it pursued what can most charitably be called negative foreign policies. The doctrine of 'non-recognition' did not force Japan to disgorge Manchuria, and the strictures of neutrality legislation abetted Mussolini's conquest of Abyssinia. The hard line over war debt collection and reparations produced the collapse of the Dawes–Young agreements, the unproductive Johnson Act, and deadlock at the World Economic Conference. Winning paper parity at the Washington and first London naval conferences, the United States failed to build the

USN to its allotted levels; at the World Disarmament Conference, it produced arms limitation proposals that ignored the legitimate strategic fears of the other Great Powers. Whilst these policies might all have occupied the moral high ground – important for American voters – they did little to help preserve international peace and security. In this sense, Britain's ignoring of the United States after 1934 in, first, its military planning and, then, its diplomatic calculations shows the poor perception that other governments had of the United States as a Great Power.

British leaders in the 1930s from MacDonald and Henderson to Neville Chamberlain and Halifax understood that Britain's international influence derived from its economic and financial solvency, the ability of the armed forces to defend the home islands and the Empire, and their willingness to meet external threats. However, they disagreed on the tactics and strategy that underpinned foreign policy. One element of this disagreement concerned the context in which foreign policy was being pursued: for instance, Chamberlain's government confronted three aggressive first-class Powers in three regions vital to British security; MacDonald's did not. The second element centred on the abilities of these leaders to meet perceived threats, the fundamentally important issue of personality and policy. In the early 1930s, the major issues confronting the British related to resolving the war debts and reparations imbroglio and finding a workable regime of international arms control. After mid-1937, they were more prosaic, tied to finding means to maintain European security and ensure the survival of Imperial interests in the Mediterranean and the Far East. Accordingly, MacDonald, Henderson, and Simon pursued interventionist diplomacy at places like The Hague and Geneva whilst, in response to the Manchurian crisis, endeavouring to maintain the Imperial status quo. Neville Chamberlain, on the other hand, at least until March 1939, was much less interventionist, looking to limit British liabilities by seeking accommodations with the totalitarian Powers. Simply put, British power in the 1930s existed in a changing international climate, the changes brought about by the realities of international politics shaped by prestige, perception, will, and human agency.

American power existed in the same climate. Hoover and Stimson brought a fresh approach to American foreign policy by seeking to work with Britain over the nettled issue of naval arms limitation. MacDonald and the Foreign Office saw the possibilities of co-operation. Building on this rapprochement, the Hoover Administration saw a means by which American policy at the World Disarmament Conference could be pursued profitably. Additionally, as the international financial crisis

proved unremitting, a London–Washington axis offered means to miti-
gate the impact of the crisis, something seen in Stimson's proposal for a
World Economic Conference. Still, the domestic strength of isolationism
constricted United States foreign policy. The doctrine of non-recognition as a response to the Manchurian crisis exists as a case in point, as
does the Hoover disarmament plan. When Roosevelt took office, any
notion of continued Anglo-American co-operation faded. Domestic
economic and financial problems preoccupied the new Administration;
the demise of the war debt–reparations agreements and the torpedoing
of the World Economic Conference were an immediate result. When the
international horizon darkened after 1935, because of Abyssinia, the
renewal of Sino-Japanese fighting, and Hitler's aggressiveness, Roosevelt
and his advisers saw little American advantage in helping to underwrite
efforts to preserve European and East Asian security. Both the American
government and American voters were determined to stay aloof from
any international crisis outside of the Western Hemisphere. The problems in 1938–9 were the problems of Britain and the other Great
Powers. Roosevelt might attempt to give the British 'a good stiff grog';
he might indicate that the United States would give some support to
Britain and its French ally in a moment of crisis. But there was no
question of effective American intervention against the totalitarian
Powers. Such a tack represented *realpolitik* – Britain could fight on
behalf of the United States – as much as it did the fact that the United
States was incapable of being anything but a regional Great Power.

The fall of France changed the equation. After 1918, and certainly
after 1930, Britain had arrogated for itself the leading position in
resolving a range of financial, political, and strategic questions. It had
not done this alone, always finding ways to align with other Powers in
multilateral venues or by bilateral arrangements. Most often British
diplomatists had success. Sometimes, they did not. Power is relative
according to circumstance; and not even the greatest of the interwar
Great Powers could obtain everything it sought, when it sought it, or in
the manner it sought it. But German success in summer 1940 changed
everything. On the defensive, Britain faced defeat by Nazi Germany
whilst Italy and Japan manoeuvred to poach the British Empire. American security and America's growing interests were imperilled. Roosevelt
had to act, although American rearmament was incomplete and the
neutrality legislation had been amended to help the anti-German
Powers. It resulted in 'destroyers for bases', Lend-Lease, and increasing
Anglo-American naval co-operation. Helping the situation was Winston
Churchill's rise to the premiership in Britain. Although rarely warm to
the United States before the late 1930s, he understood after June 1940

that Britain's survival as a Great Power depended on both aligning with the United States and gaining access to American arms, supplies, and war materials. There then emerged an Anglo-American coalition that, following the Japanese attack on Pearl Harbor, transformed into a wartime alliance.

The evolution of this alliance – with summit meetings, the CCS, the devising of joint strategy, and the need to work with Stalin's Russia – proved decisive in Allied victory over the European Axis Powers and Japan. It was at once the saviour of Britain and the reason for the loss of British global pre-eminence. Roosevelt's America did not enter the Second World War to save its British ally. It did so to preserve and extend American financial, political, and strategic interests. As the struggle progressed, British influence over Allied strategy and the determination of the shape of the postwar world dwindled; that of the Americans expanded. The reason was simple. The United States contributed more to the war, especially the material requirements of the Allied war effort; and its forces dominated in critical theatres of war, which was translated into American Supreme Allied Commanders in Europe and the Pacific. Churchill fought for every British advantage, chiefly in keeping alive the Mediterranean strategy as a means to strengthen Britain's hand in the final determination of war aims. But Roosevelt – and Stalin – were just as determined; the American and Russian economic and military contributions to victory dwarfed that of the British. At Teheran and Yalta, as well as at Casablanca, the two Quebec conferences, and more, Churchill found his influence on war- and peace-making diminishing. Admittedly, he kept alive the peripheral strategy until the end of the war; he won a zone of occupation for France in defeated Germany; and he seemed to contain Russian ambitions in the Balkans. But this amounted to small beer, as Roosevelt, and Truman after him, put an American stamp on the western part of the 'new order of things' that emerged with the defeat of Germany, Italy, and Japan. As the wartime alliance began to shatter, even before Potsdam, and Russia began to emerge as a threat to western interests, Churchill and his Labour successors were compelled to follow the American diplomatic lead. They lacked the material and military resources to do otherwise. Their recognition of American leadership was the act of men who knew that Britain needed a stronger Power as an ally. Churchill might have thought in 1940 that Britain's weakness was temporary, and that its former status could be revived after the war. But as Balfour remarked in August 1945, the United States expected Britain 'to take her place as junior partner in an orbit of power predominantly under American aegis'. He was correct. The transition was complete.

Select bibliography

PRIVATE MSS COLLECTIONS

A. V. Alexander
    (AVAR) Roskill Archives, Churchill College, Cambridge
Earl Baldwin of Bewdley
    University Library, University of Cambridge
Robert Bingham
    Library of Congress, Washington, DC
Senator William Borah
    Library of Congress, Washington, DC
William Castle
    Herbert Hoover Presidential Library, West Branch, Iowa
Viscount Cecil of Chelwood
    (BL Add MSS) British Library, London
Sir Austen Chamberlain
    FO 800 Series, Public Record Office, Kew
    AC Series, University Library, University of Birmingham
Sir Neville Chamberlain
    NC Series, University Library, University of Birmingham
Admiral Baron Chatfield
    (CHT) National Maritime Museum, Greenwich
Col. Bradley Chynoweth
    US Army Historical Center, Carlisle Barracks, Pennsylvania
Erik Colban
    League of Nations Section Files, Palais des Nations, Geneva
Hugh Dalton
    British Library of Economic and Political Science, London
Norman Davis
    Library of Congress, Washington, DC
Admiral Sir Ernle Drax
    (DRAX) Roskill Archives, Churchill College, Cambridge
Admiral Sir Frederick Dreyer
    (DRYR) Roskill Archives, Churchill College, Cambridge
Sir Eric Drummond
    League of Nations Private Papers, Palais des Nations, Geneva
Sir Anthony Eden
    FO 800 Series, Public Record Office, Kew
    FO 954 Series, Public Record Office, Kew

Herbert Feis
    Library of Congress, Washington, DC
Sir N. Warren Fisher
    British Library of Economic and Political Science, London
Admiral Sir W. W. Fisher
    (FHR) National Maritime Museum, Greenwich
Foreign Office Miscellaneous
    FO 800 Series, Public Record Office, Kew
Felix Frankfurter
    Library of Congress, Washington, DC
Hugh Gibson
    Herbert Hoover Presidential Library, West Branch, Iowa
Joseph Grew
    Houghton Library, Harvard University, Cambridge, Massachusetts
Earl of Halifax
    FO 800 Series, Public Record Office, Kew
Baron Hankey
    (HNKY) Roskill Archives, Churchill College, Cambridge
Arthur Henderson
    FO 800 Series, Public Record Office, Kew
    League of Nations Section Files, Palais des Nations, Geneva
Sir Samuel Hoare (Viscount Templewood)
    FO 800 Series, Public Record Office, Kew
    Templewood MSS, University Library, University of Cambridge
Herbert Hoover
    (HHPP) Presidential Papers Series, Herbert Hoover Presidential
    Library, West Branch, Iowa
    Misc. MSS Series, Hoover Institute of War and Revolution, Stanford
    University, Palo Alto, California
Sir Richard Hopkins
    T 172 Series, Public Record Office, Kew
Stanley Hornbeck
    Hoover Institute of War and Revolution, Stanford University, Palo Alto,
    California
Baron Howard of Penrith
    DHW Series, Cumbria County Record Office, Carlisle
Cordell Hull
    Library of Congress, Washington, DC
Admiral Hilary Jones
    Library of Congress, Washington, DC
Sir Hughe Knatchbull-Huggesson
    (KNAT) Roskill Archives, Churchill College, Cambridge
Admiral Dudley Knox
    Library of Congress, Washington, DC
Sir Frederick Leith-Ross
    T 188 Series, Public Record Office, Kew
Frank Loveday
    League of Nations Private Papers, Palais des Nations, Geneva

J. Ramsay MacDonald
   PRO 30/69 Series, Public Record Office, Kew
Ferdinand Meyer
   Herbert Hoover Presidential Library, West Branch, Iowa
J. Pierrepont Moffat
   Houghton Library, Harvard University, Cambridge, Massachusetts
Raymond Moley
   Hoover Institute of War and Revolution, Stanford University, Palo Alto,
   California
Henry Morgenthau, Jr.
   Microfilmed Diary. Franklin D. Roosevelt Presidential Library, Hyde
   Park, New York
Philip Noel-Baker
   (NBKR) Roskill Archives, Churchill College, Cambridge
Sir Eric Phipps
   (PHPP) Roskill Archives, Churchill College, Cambridge
Sir Frederick Phillips
   T 177 Series, Public Record Office, Kew
William Phillips
   Houghton Library, Harvard University, Cambridge, Massachusetts
Franklin D. Roosevelt
   PSF Series, Franklin D. Roosevelt Presidential Library, Hyde Park, New
   York
Sir Orme Sargent
   FO 800 Series, Public Record Office, Kew
Sir John Simon
   FO 800 Series, Public Record Office, Kew
Henry Stimson
   Sterling Library, Yale University, New Haven, Connecticut
Baron Vansittart
   (VNST) Roskill Archives, Churchill College, Cambridge
Hugh Wilson
   Herbert Hoover Presidential Library, West Branch, Iowa

PUBLIC ARCHIVES

ALLIED POWERS REPARATION COMMISSION

A microfilm project of University Publications of America, Inc. (Arlington, VA,
   1975)
Official Documents of the Allied Powers Reparation Commission

LEAGUE OF NATIONS ARCHIVES, PALAIS DES NATIONS, GENEVA

League of Nations Registered Files: LNR Series
League of Nations Section Files: LNS Series
League of Nations Published Documents: LND

NATIONAL ARCHIVES, WASHINGTON, DC

State Department
Decimal Files

United States Navy
General Board

Chiefs of Staff
American-British Joint Chiefs of Staff Conferences (microfilm edition)
Papers and Minutes of Meetings, Octagon Conference and Minutes of Combined Chiefs of Staff Meetings in London, June 1944 (microfilm edition)

PUBLIC RECORD OFFICE, KEW

Admiralty
ADM 1   Admiralty and Secretariat Papers
ADM 116   Admiralty and Secretariat Case Books

Cabinet
CAB 21   Registered Files
CAB 23   Cabinet Minutes
CAB 24   Cabinet Memoranda
CAB 27   *Ad Hoc* Committees
CAB 65   War Cabinet Minutes (microfiche edition, 1989)

Chiefs of Staff Committee
CAB 53   Minutes and Memoranda

Committee of Imperial Defence
CAB 2   CID Minutes
CAB 4   CID Memoranda
CAB 5   CID Colonial Defence Memoranda
CAB 16   CID Sub-Committees

Foreign Office
FO 371   General Correspondence
FO 412   Confidential Print Miscellaneous

Treasury
T 172   Chancellor of the Exchequer's Office Miscellaneous Papers

OFFICIAL PUBLICATIONS

Canada. Department of External Affairs. *Documents on Canadian External Relations: 1931–1941*, part 2, vol. VII (Ottawa, 1974).

Great Britain. Admiralty. *Battles of Coral Sea and Midway* (1952).
Convoy and Anti-Submarine Warfare Reports (1952).
Great Britain. Central Statistical Office. *Statistical Digest of the War* (1951).
Great Britain. Foreign Office. *Documents of the London Naval Conference 1930* (1930).
Documents on British Policy Overseas, ser. I, vol. III (1986).
Ike Nobutaka, ed. and trans. *Japan's Decision for War. Records of the 1941 Policy Conferences* (Stanford, 1967).
League of Nations. *Monthly Summary of the League of Nations.*
New Zealand. Department of Internal Affairs. War History Branch. *New Zealand in the Second World War, 1939–1945* (Wellington, 1950).
The Relief of Tobruk (Wellington, 1961).
United States. Department of Commerce. *Historical Statistics of the United States. Colonial Times to 1970* (Washington, DC, 1975).
United States. Department of State. *Papers Relating to the Foreign Policy of the United States* (Washington, DC, 1861–).
United States. Department of State. *FRUS. The Conferences at Malta and Yalta, 1945* (Washington, DC, 1955).
FRUS. The Conferences at Washington and Quebec, 1943 (Washington, DC, 1972).
FRUS. The Conference at Quebec 1944 (Washington, DC, 1972).
United States. Office of the President. *Address of President Coolidge at the Observance of the 10th Anniversary of the Armistice, Under the Auspices of the American Legion* (Washington, DC, 1928).
Watt, D. Cameron, and Bourne, K., gen. eds., *British Documents on Foreign Affairs* (Wilmington, DE, on-going).

OTHER PUBLICATIONS

Adams, F. C. *Economic Diplomacy: The Export–Import Bank and American Foreign Policy, 1934–1939* (Columbia, MO, 1976).
Adler, S. *The Isolationist Impulse: Its Twentieth Century Reaction* (New York, 1957).
Agbi, S.O. 'The Foreign Office and Yoshida's Bid for Rapprochement with Britain in 1936–1937: A Critical Reconsideration of the Anglo-Japanese Conversations', *HJ*, 21(1978).
Aldcroft, D. H. *From Versailles to Wall Street, 1919–1929* (Berkeley, Los Angeles, 1977).
The British Economy, vol. I: *The Years of Turmoil 1920–1951* (Brighton, 1986).
Alexandroff, A., and Rosencrance, R. 'Deterrence in 1939', *World Politics*, 29(1977).
Allen, H. C. 'Anti-Americanism in Britain', *CR*, 200(1961).
Allen, L. *Singapore 1941–1942* (1984).
Alpert, M. 'Humanitarianism and Politics in the British Response to the Spanish Civil War, 1936–1939', *European History Quarterly*, 14(1984).
Ambrosius, L. E. *Woodrow Wilson and the American Diplomatic Tradition. The Treaty Fight in Perspective* (New York, 1987).

Anonymous. 'The Commonwealth and the Dictators', *Round Table*, 111(Jun. 1938).

Fuehrer Conferences on Naval Affairs 1939–1945 (1990).

Armstrong, A. *Unconditional Surrender: The Impact of Casablanca Policy upon World War II* (New Brunswick, NJ, 1961).

Arnold-Forster, W. E. 'A Policy for the Disarmament Conference', *Political Quarterly*, 2(1931).

Artaud, D. *La question des dettes interalliées et la reconstruction de l'Europe (1917–1929)* (Paris, 1978).

Ashton-Gwatkin, F. T. A. 'Thoughts on the Foreign Office, 1918–1939', *CR*, 188(1955).

Aster, S. *Anthony Eden* (1976).

Atkin, J. M. 'Official British Regulation of Overseas Investment, 1914–1931', *EHR*, 2nd. ser., 23(1970).

Avon, Earl of. [A. Eden]. *Foreign Affairs* (1939).

Facing the Dictators (1962).

The Reckoning (1965).

Baechler, C. 'Une difficile négotiation franco-allemande aux conférences de La Haye: Le règlement de la question des sanctions (1929–1930)', *Revue d'Allemagne*, 12(1980).

Baer, G. W. *The Coming of the Italian–Ethiopian War* (Cambridge, MA, 1967).

Test Case: Italy, Ethiopia, and the League of Nations (Stanford, 1976).

Bairoch, P. 'Europe's Gross National Product: 1800–1975', *JEEH*, 5(1976).

'International Industrialization Levels from 1750 to 1980', *JEEH*, 11(1982).

Ball, S. 'The Conservative Party and the Formation of the National Government: August 1931', *HJ*, 29(1986).

Baldwin and the Conservative Party. The Crisis of 1929–1931 (New Haven, 1988).

Baram, P. J. 'Undermining the British: Department of State Policies in Egypt and the Suez Canal Before and During World War II', *Historian*, 40(1978).

Barker, E. *British Policy in Southeast Europe in the Second World War* (1976).

Barnes, H. E. *The Genesis of the World War*, 2nd edn (New York, 1927).

Barnes, H. E., ed. *Perpetual War for Perpetual Peace: A Critical Examination of the Foreign Policy of Franklin D. Roosevelt and Its Aftermath* (Caldwell, ID, 1953).

Barnes, J., and Nicholson, D., eds. *The Empire at Bay. The Leo Amery Diaries 1929–1945* (1988).

Barnett, C. *The Audit of War. The Illusion and Reality of Britain as a Great Nation* (1986).

Beard, C. A. *American Foreign Policy in the Making, 1932–1940: A Study in Responsibilities* (New Haven, 1946).

President Roosevelt and the Coming of the War, 1941: A Study in Appearances and Realities (New Haven, 1948).

Beard, C. A., and Smith, G. H. E. *The Idea of National Interest: An Analytical Study in American Foreign Relations* (New York, 1934).

Beaumont, R. 'The Bomber Offensive as a Second Front', *JCH*, 22(1987).

Beck, P. G. 'The Anglo-Persian Oil Dispute, 1932–1933', *JCH*, 9(1974).

Beckles, G., ed. *America Chooses! In the Words of President Roosevelt [June 1940–June 1941]* (1941).

Bell, P. M. H. 'War, Foreign Policy, and Public Opinion: Britain and the Darlan Affair, November–December 1942', *JSS*, 5(1982).

Ben-Moshe, T. *Churchill. Strategy and History* (Boulder, CO, 1992).

Bennett, E. W. *Germany and the Diplomacy of the Financial Crisis, 1931* (Cambridge, MA, 1962).

German Rearmament and the West, 1932–1933 (Princeton, 1979).

Berezhkov, V. *Tehran: Lessons of Victory* (Moscow, 1988).

Berle, B. B., and Jacobs, T. B., eds. *Navigating the Rapids, 1918–1971. From the Papers of Adolf A. Berle* (New York, 1973).

Best, R. A. 'The Anglo-German Naval Agreement of 1935: An Aspect of Appeasement', *Naval War College Review*, 34(1981).

Bialer, U. 'Elite Opinion and Defence Policy: Air Power Advocacy and British Rearmament during the 1930s', *BJIS*, 6(1980).

Bickel, W.-H. *Die anglo-amerikanischen Beziehungen 1927–1930 im Licht der Flottenfrage* (Zurich, 1970).

Birn, D. *The League of Nations Union, 1918–1945* (1981).

Blake, R., and Louis, W. R., eds. *Churchill* (Oxford, 1992).

Blum, J. M., ed. *From the Morgenthau Diaries*, 2 vols. (Boston, 1959, 1965).

Boadle, D. G. 'The Formation of the Foreign Office Economic Relations Section, 1930–1937', *HJ*, 20(1977).

Bolt, E. C., Jr. *Ballots before Bullets: The War Referendum Approach to Peace in America, 1914–1941* (Charlottesville, VA, 1977).

Bond, B. *British Military Policy between the Two World Wars* (Oxford, 1980).

Britain, France, and Belgium, 1939–1940, 2nd edn (1990).

Bond, B., ed. *Chief of Staff. The Diaries of Lieutenant-General Sir Henry Pownall*, vol. I: *1933–1940* (1972).

Boog, H. *Die Deutsche Luftwaffenführung, 1935–1945: Führungsprobleme, Spitzengliederung, Generalstabsausbildung* (Stuttgart, 1982).

Booth, A. 'Britain in the 1930s: A Managed Economy?', *EcoHR*, 40(1987).

Borg, D. *The United States and the Far Eastern Crisis of 1933–1938* (Cambridge, MA, 1964).

Borg, D., and Okamoto, S., eds. *Pearl Harbor as History. Japanese–American Relations, 1931–1941* (New York, London, 1973).

Botjer, G. F. *Sideshow War: The Italian Campaign, 1943–1945* (College Station, TX, 1996).

Böttger, P. *Winston Churchill und die Zweite Front, 1941–1943: Ein Aspekte der britischen Strategie im Zweiten Weltkrieg* (Frankfurt, 1984).

Bourette-Knowles, S. 'The Global Micawber: Sir Robert Vansittart, the Treasury, and the Global Balance of Power, 1933–1935', *DS*, 6(1995).

Bowers, C. *My Mission to Spain: Watching the Rehearsal for World War II* (New York, 1954).

Boyle, P. G. 'The Roots of Isolationism: A Case Study', *JAS*, 6(1972).

Braddock, D. W. *The Campaigns in Egypt and Libya: 1940–1942* (Aldershot, 1964).

Braisted, W. E. *The United States Navy in the Pacific, 1909–1922* (Austin, 1971).

Brandes, J. *Herbert Hoover and Economic Diplomacy: Department of Commerce Policy, 1921–1928* (Pittsburgh, 1962).

Brennecke, J. *Die Wende im U-Boot-Krieg: Ursachen und Folgen, 1939–1943* (Herford, West Germany, 1984).

Brown, J. C. 'Why Foreign Oil Companies Shifted Their Production from Mexico to Venezuela during the 1920s', *AHR*, 90(1985).

Brune, L. H. 'Considerations of Force in Cordell Hull's Diplomacy, July 26 to November 26, 1941', *DH*, 2(1978).

Bryant, A. *The Years of Endurance, 1793–1802* (New York, 1942).

Buckley, T. *The United States and the Washington Conference, 1921–1922* (Knoxville, 1970).

Buhite, R. D. *Decisions at Yalta: An Appraisal of Summit Diplomacy* (Wilmington, DE, 1986).

Bullitt, O. H., ed. *For the President. Personal and Secret. Correspondence between Franklin D. Roosevelt and William C. Bullitt* (Boston, 1972).

Bullock, A. *Hitler. A Study in Tyranny*, rev. edn (Harmondsworth, 1962).

Burks, D. D. 'The United States and the Geneva Protocol of 1924', *AHR*, 64(1959).

Burns, J. M. *Roosevelt: The Lion and the Fox* (New York, 1956).

Burns, R. D., and Dixon, W. A. 'Foreign Policy and the "Democratic Myth": The Debate on the Ludlow Amendment', *Mid-America*, 47(1965).

Butler, J. R. M. *Grand Strategy*, vol. II: *September 1939–June 1941* (1957).

Lord Lothian (Philip Kerr) 1882–1940 (1960).

Cain, P. J., and Hopkins, A. G. *British Imperialism*, 2 vols. (London, New York, 1993).

Carlton, D. 'Great Britain and the Coolidge Naval Conference of 1927', *PSQ*, 83(1968).

'The Anglo-French Compromise on Arms Limitation, 1928', *JBS*, 8(1969).

MacDonald Versus Henderson. The Foreign Policy of the Second Labour Government (New York, 1970).

'Eden, Blum and the Origins of Non-Intervention', *JCH*, 6(1971).

'Against the Grain: In Defense of Appeasement', *Policy Review*, 4(1980).

Carr, R. *The Spanish Tragedy: The Civil War in Perspective* (1977).

Carsten, F. L. *The Reichswehr and Politics, 1918–1933* (Oxford, 1966).

Cassels, A. 'Repairing the *Entente Cordiale* and the New Diplomacy', *HJ*, 23(1980).

Cato, *Guilty Men* (1940).

Ceadel, M. *Pacifism in Britain, 1914–1945: The Defining of a Faith* (1980).

'The First British Referendum: The Peace Ballot, 1934–1935', *EHR*, 95(1980).

Cecil, R. [Lord Cecil of Chelwood]. 'The Draft Treaty of Mutual Assistance', *JRIIA*, 4(1924).

'Après ma démission', *Revue des vivants*, 1(1927).

The Way of Peace (1928).

'Case for Disarmament', *Nation* (27 Apr. 1929).

'Facing the World Disarmament Conference', *FA*, 10(1931).

A Great Experiment (1941).

Chamberlain, A. *The League* (1926).

'Britain as a European Power', *JRIIA*, 9(1930).

Charmley, J. 'Harold Macmillan and the Making of the French Committee of Liberation', *IHR*, 4(1982).

Churchill: The End of Glory. A Political Biography (London, New York, San Diego, 1993).

Christensen, T. *Reel Politics. American Political Movies from 'Birth of a Nation' to 'Platoon'* (New York, 1987).

Chukumba, S. U. *The Big Powers Against Ethiopia: Anglo-French-American Maneuvers during the Italo-Ethiopian Dispute, 1934–1938* (Washington, DC, 1977).

Churchill, W. S. *The Unwritten Alliance: Speeches, 1953 to 1959* (1961).

Clarke, S. V. O. *Central Bank Cooperation, 1924–1931* (New York, 1967).

Clemens, D. S. *Yalta* (New York, 1970).

Cohen, W. I. *The American Revisionists: The Lessons of Intervention in World War I* (Chicago, 1967).

Cole, W. S. *America First: The Battle Against Intervention, 1940–1941* (Madison, WI, 1953).

Senator Gerald P. Nye and American Foreign Relations (Minneapolis, 1962).

Charles A. Lindbergh and the Battle Against American Intervention in World War II (New York, 1974).

Collier, B. *The Defence of the United Kingdom* (1957).

Colville, J. *The Fringes of Power. 10 Downing Street Diaries 1939–1955* (1985).

Colvin, I. *Vansittart in Office* (1965).

The Chamberlain Cabinet (New York, 1971).

Conkov, S. 'The British Policy of Guarantees and Greece (March–April 1939)', *Studia Balcanica*, 4(1971).

Conze, W. 'Brüning als Reichskanzler: Eine zwischen Bilanz', *HZ*, 214(1972).

Corbett, J. S. *Some Principles of Maritime Strategy* (1911).

Costigliola, F. C. 'Anglo-American Financial Rivalry in the 1920s', *JEH*, 27(1977).

Council on Foreign Relations. *The United States in World Affairs. An Account of American Foreign Relations 1936* (New York, 1937).

Coutouvidis, J., and Reynolds, J. *Poland 1939–1947* (New York, 1986).

Cowling, M. *The Impact of Hitler: British Politics and British Policy, 1933–1940* (1975)

Craig, G. A. *Germany 1866–1945* (Oxford, 1981).

Craig, G. A., and Gilbert, F., eds. *The Diplomats, 1919–1939*, vol. II (New York, 1977).

Craig, H. *Enemy at the Gates: The Battle for Stalingrad* (1973).

Cross, R. *Citadel: The Battle of Kursk* (1993).

Crowley, J. B. *Japan's Quest for Autonomy. National Security and Foreign Policy, 1930–1938* (Princeton, 1966).

Current, R. N. *Secretary Stimson. A Study in Statecraft* (New Brunswick, NJ, 1954).

'The Stimson Doctrine and the Hoover Doctrine', *AHR*, 59(1954).

Cutright, L. H. 'Great Britain, the Balkans and Turkey in the Autumn of 1939', *IHR*, 10(1988).

D'Este, C. *Decision in Normandy* (New York, 1983).

Dallek, R. *Franklin D. Roosevelt and American Foreign Policy, 1932–1945* (Oxford, 1979).

Dalton, H. *Towards the Peace of Nations. A Study in International Politics* (1928). *Memoirs*, vol. I (1953).

Danchev, A. 'A Special Relationship: Field-Marshal Sir John Dill and George C. Marshall', *JRUSI*, 130(1985).

Very Special Relationship: Field-Marshal Sir John Dill and the Anglo-American Alliance, 1941–1944 (1986).

'Being Friends: The Combined Chiefs of Staff and the Making of Allied Strategy in the Second World War', in Freedman, *et al. War, Strategy*.

Davis, J. 'Notes on Warner Brothers Foreign Policy, 1918–1948', *Velvet Light Trap*, 17(1977).

Dawes, C. G. *Journal as Ambassador to Great Britain* (Westport, CT, 1970 [orig. publ. 1939]), 349–51.

Dayer, R. A. *Finance and Empire: Sir Charles Addis, 1861–1945* (New York, 1988).

'Anglo-American Monetary Policy and Rivalry in Europe and the Far East, 1919–1931', in McKercher, *Anglo-American Relations*.

Deist, W. 'Brüning, Herriot und die Abrüstungsgespräche von Bessinge 1932', *VfZ*, 5(1957).

'Schleicher und die deutsche Abrüstungspolitik in Juni/Juli 1932', *VfZ*, 7(1959).

Dennis, P. *Decision by Default. Peacetime Conscription and British Defence Policy 1919–1939* (1972).

DeNovo, J. *American Interests and Policies in the Middle East, 1900–1939* (Minneapolis, 1963).

DeWitt, H. A. 'Hiram Johnson and Early New Deal Diplomacy, 1933–1934', *California Historical Quarterly*, 53(1974).

Dilks, D. 'Appeasement Revisited', *University of Leeds Review*, 15(1972).

'The British Foreign Office Between the Wars', in McKercher and Moss, *Shadow and Substance*.

' "We Must Hope for the Best and Prepare for the Worst": The Prime Minister, the Cabinet and Hitler's Germany, 1937–1939', *Proceedings of the British Academy*, 73(1987).

Divine, R. A. *The Illusion of Neutrality* (Chicago, 1962).

Dobson, A. P. ' "A Mess of Pottage for Your Economic Birthright?" The 1941–42 Wheat Negotiations and Anglo-American Economic Diplomacy', *HJ*, 28(1985).

Dockrill, M. L. 'The Foreign Office and the Proposed Institute of International Affairs', *IJ*, 50(1980).

Dockrill, M. L., and Goold, J. D. *Peace Without Promise. Britain and the Peace Conferences 1919–23* (1981).

Dockrill, M. L., and McKercher, B. J. C., eds. *Diplomacy and World Power. Studies in British Foreign Policy, 1890–1950* (Cambridge, 1996).

Dohrmann, B. *Die englische Europapolitik in der Wirtschaftskrise, 1921–1923: Zur Interdependenz von Wirtschaftsinteressen und Aussenpolitik* (Munich, 1980).

Donahoe, B. F. *Private Plans and Public Dangers* (Notre Dame, IN, 1965).

Donnelly, J. B. 'Prentiss Gilbert's Mission to the League of Nations Council, October 1931', *DH*, 2(1978).

Douglas, R., ed. *1939: A Retrospect Forty Years After* (1983).

Draper, A. *Dawns Like Thunder: The Retreat from Burma 1942* (1987).

Drummond, I. M. *British Economic Policy and the Empire, 1919–1939* (1972).

Drummond, I. M., and Hillmer, N. *Negotiating Freer Trade. The United Kingdom, the United States, Canada, and the Trade Agreements of 1938* (Waterloo, Ont., 1989).

Du Réau, E. 'Enjeux stratégiques et redéploiement diplomatique français: novembre 1938–septembre 1939', *Relations Internationales*, 35(1983).

Dukes, J. R. 'The Soviet Union and Britain: The Alliance Negotiations of March–August, 1939', *East European Quarterly*, 19(1985).

Duroselle, J.-B. *France and the United States. From Beginnings to the Present* (Chicago, 1976).

La décadence (Paris, 1979).

'Les "invariants" de la politique étrangère de la France', *Politique Etrangère*, 51(1986).

Duus, P., *et al. The Japanese Informal Empire in China, 1895–1937* (Princeton, 1989).

Edwards, J. *The British Government and the Spanish Civil War, 1936–1939* (1979).

Egerton, G. W. *Great Britain and the Creation of the League of Nations: Strategy, Politics and International Organization, 1914–1919* (Chapel Hill, 1978).

'Britain and the "Great Betrayal": Anglo-American Relations and the Struggle for the United States Ratification of the Treaty of Versailles, 1919–1920', *HJ*, 21(1978).

'Diplomacy, Scandal, and Military Intelligence: The Craufurd–Stuart Affair and Anglo-American Relations, 1918–1920', *INS*, 2(1987).

'Ideology, Diplomacy, and International Organisation: Wilsonism and the League of Nations in Anglo-American Relations, 1918–1920', in McKercher, *Anglo-American Relations*.

Eichengreen, B., ed. *The Gold Standard in Theory and History* (New York, 1985).

Emmerson, J. T. *The Rhineland Crisis, 7 March 1936: A Study in Multilateral Diplomacy* (Ames, IA, 1977).

Endicott, S. L. *Diplomacy and Enterprise: British China Policy, 1933–1937* (Vancouver, BC, 1975).

Engelbrecht, H. C., and Hanighen, F. C. *Merchants of Death. A Study of the International Armaments Industry* (New York, 1934).

English, J. A. *The Canadian Army and the Normandy Campaign: A Study of Failure in High Command* (New York, 1991).

Erdmann, A. P. N. 'Mining for the Corporate Synthesis: Gold in American Foreign Economic Policy, 1931–1936', *DH*, 17(1993).

Erickson, J. *The Road to Stalingrad* (1975).

Erickson, J., and Dilks, D., eds. *Barbarossa: The Axis and the Allies* (Edinburgh, 1994).

Eubank, K. *Summit at Teheran* (1985).

Fair, J. D. 'The Norwegian Campaign and Winston Churchill's Rise to Power in 1940: A Study of Perception and Attribution', *IHR*, 9(1987).

Fanning, R. 'The Coolidge Conference of 1927: Disarmament in Disarray', in McKercher, *Arms Limitation*.

Fay, S. B. *The Origins of the World War*, 2 vols. (New York, 1928).

Feis, H. *Europe: The World's Banker, 1870–1914* (New Haven, 1930).

The Road to Pearl Harbor (Princeton, 1950).

Felix, D. 'Reparations Reconsidered with a Vengeance', *CEH*, 4(1971).

Ferguson, T. 'From Normalcy to the New Deal: Industrial Structure, Party Competition, and American Public Policy in the Great Depression', *International Organization*, 38(1984).

Ferrell, R. H. 'Pearl Harbor and the Revisionists', *Historian*, 17(1955).

Ferris, J. R. 'A British "Unofficial" Aviation Mission and Japanese Naval Developments, 1919–1929', *JSS*, 5(1982).

Men, Money, and Diplomacy: The Evolution of British Strategic Policy, 1919–1926 (Ithaca, NY, 1989).

'"The Greatest Power on Earth": Great Britain in the 1920s', *IHR*, 13(1991).

'The Symbol and Substance of Seapower: Great Britain, the United States, and the One-Power Standard, 1919–1921', in McKercher, *Anglo-American Relations*.

'Worthy of Some Better Enemy?: The British Estimate of the Imperial Japanese Army, 1919–1941, and the Fall of Singapore', *CJH*, 28(1993).

Fischer, E. *The Chancey War: Winning China, Burma, and India in World War II* (New York, 1991).

Fletcher, W. M. *The Search for a New Order. Intellectuals and Fascism in Prewar Japan* (Chapel Hill, 1982).

Förster, J. *Stalingrad: Ereignis, Wirkung, Symbol* (Munich, 1992).

Fox, J. P. 'Britain and the Inter-Allied Military Commission of Control, 1925–26', *JCH*, 4(1969).

Frank, R. B. *Guadalcanal* (New York, 1990).

Frankland, N. *The Bombing Offensive Against Germany: Outlines and Perspectives* (1965).

Franks, N. R. L. *Search, Find, and Kill: Coastal Command's U-boat Successes* (Harvest Hill, Bucks., 1990).

Fraser, H. F. *Great Britain and the Gold Standard* (New York, 1933).

Freedman, L., *et al.*, eds. *War, Strategy, and International Politics: Essays in Honour of Sir Michael Howard* (Oxford, 1992).

Freidel, F. *Franklin D. Roosevelt. Launching the New Deal* (Boston, 1973).

French, D. *The British Way in Warfare, 1688–2000* (1990).

Friedberg, A. L. *The Weary Titan. Britain and the Experience of Relative Decline, 1895–1905* (Princeton, 1988).

Friedlander, R. A. 'New Light on the Anglo-American Reaction to the Ethiopian War, 1935–1936', *Mid-America*, 45(1963).

Fung, E. K. S. 'The Sino-British Rapprochement, 1927–1931', *Modern Asian Studies*, 17(1983).

Fussell, P. *The Great War and Modern Memory* (1975).

Fyrth, J. *The Signal was Spain: The Spanish Aid Movement in Britain, 1936–1939* (1986).

Gaddis, J. L. *The Long Peace. Enquiries into the History of the Cold War* (Oxford, 1987).

Gardner, L. C. *Economic Aspects of New Deal Diplomacy* (Madison, WI, 1964).

Gauson, A. B. 'Churchill, Spears and the Levant Affair, 1941', *HJ*, 27(1984).

Gelb, N. *Desperate Venture: The Story of Operation Torch* (New York, 1992).

Ghosh, P. S. 'Passage of the Silver Purchase Act of 1934: The China Lobby and the Issue of China Trade', *Indian Journal of American Studies*, 6(1976).

Gibbs, N. H. *Grand Strategy*, vol. I: *Rearmament Policy* (1976).

Gifford P., and Louis, W. R., eds. *France and Britain in Africa: Imperial Rivalry and Colonial Rule* (New Haven, 1971).

Gilbert, M. *The Roots of Appeasement* (London, 1966).

Winston S. Churchill, 6 vols. (1976–86).

Gilbert, M., ed. *A Century of Conflict, 1850–1950: Essays for A. J. P. Taylor* (1966).

The Churchill War Papers, vol. II: *Never Surrender, May 1940–December 1940* (New York, 1995).

Gilbert, T. *Treachery at Munich* (1989).

Goldberg, M. D. 'Anglo-American Economic Competition 1920–1930', *Economy and History*, 16(1973).

Goldman, A. L. 'Sir Robert Vansittart's Search for Italian Cooperation against Hitler, 1933–1936', *JCH*, 9(1974).

'Two Views of Germany: Nevile Henderson vs. Vansittart and the Foreign Office, 1937–1939', *BJIS*, 6(1980).

Gooch, J. '"Hidden in a Rock": American Military Perceptions of Great Britain, 1919–1940', in Freedman, *et al. War, Strategy.*

Gowing, M. *Independence and Deterrence: Britain and Atomic Energy, 1945–1952*, vol. I (1974).

Graebner, N., ed. *An Uncertain Tradition: American Secretaries of State in the Twentieth Century* (New York, 1961).

Graham, D., and Tugwell, M. *Tug of War: The Battle for Italy, 1943–1945* (1986).

Granatstein, J., and Bothwell, R. '"A Self-Evident National Duty": Canadian Foreign Policy, 1935–1939', *JCIH*, 3(1975).

Grant, J. E. *The Problem of War and Its Solution* (1922).

Grathwohl, R. *Stresemann and the DNVP: Reconciliation or Revenge in German Foreign Policy, 1924–1928* (Lawrence, KS, 1980).

Green, D. *The Containment of Latin America: A History of the Myths and Realities of the Good Neighbor Policy* (Chicago, 1971).

Greene, M. 'American Kinship with Britain', *Quarterly Review*, 301(1963).

Gretton, P. 'The Nyon Conference – the Naval Aspect', *EHR*, 90(1975).

Grey of Fallodon, *Twenty-Five Years*, vol. II (1926).

Grigg, J. *1943: The Victory that Never Was* (1980).

Gwyer, J. M. A. *Grand Strategy*, vol. III, part 1 (1964).

Hachey, T. E. 'Anglophile Sentiments in American Catholicism in 1940: A British Official's Confidential Assessment', *Records of the American Catholic Historical Society of Philadelphia*, 85(1974).

Hagan, K. J. *This People's Navy. The Making of American Sea Power* (New York, 1991).

Haglund, D. G. 'George C. Marshall and the Question of Military Aid to England, May–June 1940', *JCH*, 15(1980).
Latin America and the Transformation of U.S. Strategic Thought, 1936–1940 (Albuquerque, 1984).
Hall, C. *Britain, America, and Arms Control, 1921–37* (1987).
Hall, H. H., III. 'The Foreign Policy-Making Process in Britain, 1934–1935, and the Origins of the Anglo-German Naval Agreement', *HJ*, 19(1976).
Hall, J. W. *et al. The Cambridge History of Modern Japan*, vol. VI: *The Twentieth Century* (Cambridge, 1988).
Hamill, I. *The Strategic Illusion: The Singapore Strategy and the Defence of Australia and New Zealand, 1919–1942* (Singapore, 1981).
Hamilton, N. *Monty*, vol. I: *The Making of a General* (Toronto, 1982).
Master of the Battlefield. Monty's War Years 1942–1944 (1983).
Handel, M., ed. *Leaders and Intelligence* (1989).
Hankey, Lord. 'Unconditional Surrender', *CR*, 176(1949).
Haraszti, E. *Treaty-Breakers or 'Realpolitiker'? The Anglo-German Naval Agreement of 1935* (Boppard am Rhein, 1974).
Hardie, F. M. *The Abyssinian Crisis* (1974).
Harkness, D. *The Restless Dominion: The Irish Free State and the British Commonwealth of Nations, 1921–31* (London, Dublin, 1969).
Harris, B. *The United States and the Italo-Ethiopian Crisis* (Stanford, 1964).
Harris, H. W. 'Towards Disarmament', *CR*, 139(1931).
Harrison, G. *Cross-Channel Attack* (Washington, DC, 1951).
Harrison, R. A. 'The Runciman Visit to Washington in January 1937: Presidential Diplomacy and the Non-Commercial Implications of Anglo-American Trade Negotiations', *CJH*, 19(1984).
Hastings, M. *Overlord: D-Day and the Battle for Normandy* (1984).
Hattendorf, J. B., and Murfett, M., eds. *The Limitations of Military Power* (1990).
Hauser, O. 'Der Plan einer deutsch-österreichischen Zollunion von 1931 und die europäische Föderation', *HZ*, 179(1955).
Heller, R. 'East Fulham Revisited', *JCH*, 6(1971).
Henderson, A. *Labour and Foreign Affairs* (1922).
Labour and the Geneva Protocol (1925).
Hess, G. *The United States at War, 1941–1945* (Arlington Heights, 1986).
Higham, R. D. S. *Diary of a Disaster: British Aid to Greece, 1940–1941* (Lexington, KY, 1986).
Hilderbrand, R. C. *Dumbarton Oaks. The Origins of the United Nations and the Search for Postwar Security* (Chapel Hill, 1990).
Hillgruber, A. 'England in Hitlers Aussenpolitischer Konzeption', *HZ*, 218(1974).
Hilton, S. E. *Brazil and the Great Powers, 1930–1939: The Politics of Trade Rivalry* (Austin, 1975).
Hinsley, F. H. *British Intelligence in the Second World War*, abridged edn (Cambridge, 1993).
Hogan, M. J. *Informal Entente. The Private Structure of Cooperation in Anglo-American Economy Diplomacy, 1918–1928* (Columbia, 1977).
Holdich, P. G. H. 'A Policy of Percentages? British Policy and the Balkans after the Moscow Conference of October 1944', *IHR*, 9(1987).

Holloway, D. 'The Atomic Bomb and the End of the Wartime Alliance', in Lane and Temperley, *Grand Alliance*.

Hoover, H. C. *An American Epic: Famine in Forty-Five Nations: The Battle on the Front Line, 1914–1923*, 3 vols. (Chicago, 1961).

Howe, G. F. *North Africa: Seizing the Initiative in the West*, United States Army in World War II: The Mediterranean Theatre of Operations Series (Washington, DC, 1957).

Howson, S. *Sterling's Managed Float: The Operations of the Exchange Equalisation Account, 1932–39* (Princeton Studies in International Finance, 46, 1980).

Hoyt, E. P. *Blue Skies and Blood: The Battle of the Coral Sea* (New York, 1975).

Hudson, W. J., and North, J., eds. *My Dear P.M. R.G. Casey's Letters to S.M. Bruce 1924–1929* (Canberra, 1980).

Hughes, E. J. 'Winston Churchill and the Formation of the United Nations Organisation', *JCH*, 9(1974).

Hughes, T. *The Battle of the Atlantic* (New York, 1977).

Hull, C. *The Memoirs of Cordell Hull*, 2 vols. (New York, 1948).

Hunt, B. D. *Sailor-Scholar. Admiral Sir Herbert Richmond, 1871–1946* (Waterloo, Ont., 1982).

Hunt, M. 'Americans in the China Market: Economic Opportunities and Economic Nationalism, 1890s–1931', *Business History Review*, 51(1977).

Ickes, H. L. *The Secret Diary of Harold L. Ickes*, 3 vols. (New York, 1954).

Ikuhiko Hata. *Reality and Illusion: The Hidden Crisis between Japan and the U.S.S.R., 1932–1934* (New York, 1967).

Jacobson, J. 'The Conduct of Locarno Diplomacy', *RP*, 34(1972).
   Locarno Diplomacy. Germany and the West, 1925–1929 (Princeton, 1972).

Jaffe, L. S. *The Decision to Disarm Germany. British Policy towards Postwar German Disarmament, 1914–1919* (Boston, 1985).

Jane's Fighting Ships (1930).

Johnson, P. B. *Land Fit for Heroes. The Planning of British Reconstruction 1916–1919* (Chicago, 1968).

Jonas, M. *Isolationism in America, 1935–1941* (Ithaca, 1966).

Jones, G. *The History of the British Bank in the Middle East*, vol. II: *Banking and Oil* (1986).

Jones, K. P., ed. *U.S. Diplomats in Europe, 1919–1941* (Santa Barbara, 1981).

Kaiser, D. E. *Economic Diplomacy and the Origins of the Second World War. Germany, Britain, France, and Eastern Europe, 1930–1939* (Princeton, 1980).

Kamman, W. *A Search for Stability: United States Diplomacy toward Nicaragua, 1925–1933* (Notre Dame, 1968).

Kaufman, B. I. 'United States Trade and Latin America: The Wilson Years', *JAH*, 58(1971).

Keegan, J., ed. *Churchill's Generals* (1991).

Keeton, E. *Briand's Locarno Policy. French Economics, Politics, and Diplomacy, 1925–1929* (New York, 1987).

Kennan, G. F., and Lukacs, J. *G. F. Kennan and the Origins of Containment, 1944–1946* (Columbia, MO, 1997).

Kennedy, A. L. 'Munich: The Disintegration of British Statesmanship', *Quarterly Review*, 286(1948).

Kennedy, G. C. 'The 1930 London Naval Conference and Anglo-American Maritime Strength, 1927–1930', in McKercher, *Arms Limitation*.

Kennedy, M. D. *The Estrangement of Great Britain and Japan 1917–35* (Manchester, 1969).

Kennedy, P. M. 'The Tradition of Appeasement in British Foreign Policy, 1865–1939', *BJIS*, 2(1976).

The Rise and Fall of the Great Powers. Economic Change and Military Conflict from 1500 to 2000 (New York, 1987).

Kent, B. *The Spoils of War. The Politics, Economics, and Diplomacy of Reparations, 1918–1932* (Oxford, 1989).

Kernek, S. J. 'The British Government's Reactions to President Wilson's "Peace Note" of December 1916', *HJ*, 13(1970).

Kerr, P. 'Navies and Peace: A British View', *FA*, 7(1929).

Kerr, P., and Howland, C. P. 'Navies and Peace: Two Views', *FA*, 8(1929).

Kettenacker, L. 'The Anglo-Soviet Alliance and the Problem of Germany, 1941–1945', *JCH*, 17(1982).

Keynes, J. M. *The Economic Consequences of the Peace* (1919).

The Revision of the Treaty (1919).

Kimball, W. F. *The Most Unsordid Act: Lend-Lease, 1939–1941* (Baltimore, 1969).

'"Beggar My Neighbour": America and the British Interim Finance Crisis, 1940–1941', *JEH*, 29(1969).

'Thirty Years After, or the Two Musketeers', *DH*, 18(1995)

Forged in War. Roosevelt, Churchill, and the Second World War (New York, 1996).

Kimball, W. F., ed. *Churchill and Roosevelt. The Complete Correspondence*, 3 vols. (Princeton, 1984).

The Juggler. Franklin Roosevelt as Wartime Statesman (Princeton, 1991).

Kimball, W. F., and Bartlett, B. 'Roosevelt and Prewar Commitments to Churchill: The Tyler Kent Affair', *DH*, 5(1981).

Kindleberger, C. P. *The World in Depression, 1929–1939* (1973).

King, R. W., ed. *Naval Engineering and American Seapower* (Baltimore, 1989).

Kirby, D. 'Morality or Expediency?: The Baltic Question in British–Soviet Relations, 1941–1942', in V. S. Vardys and R. J. Misiunas, eds., *The Baltic States in Peace and War, 1917–1945* (1978).

Knox, M. *Mussolini Unleashed, 1939–1941. Politics and Strategy in Fascist Italy's Last War* (Cambridge, 1982).

Kolko, G. 'American Business and Germany, 1930–1941', *Western Political Quarterly*, 15(1962).

Kottman, R. N. *Reciprocity and the North Atlantic Triangle 1932–1938* (Ithaca, NY, 1968).

Kowalski, H.-G. 'Die "European Advisory Commission" als Instrument alliierter Deutschland-Planung, 1943–1945', *VfZ*, 19(1971).

Kuklick, B. 'The Genesis of the European Advisory Commission', *JCH*, 4(1969).

Kunz, D. B. *The Battle for Britain's Gold Standard in 1931* (London, New York, 1987).

Labour Party. *Labour and the Nation* (1928).

LaFeber, W. 'Roosevelt, Churchill and Indochina, 1941–1945', *AHR*, 80(1975).

Lamb, R. *The Drift to War* (1989).

Lammers, D. N. *Explaining Munich: The Search for Motive in British Policy* (Stanford, 1966).

Lamont, T. W. 'The Final Reparations Settlement', *FA*, 8(1930).

Lane, A. *Britain, the Cold War, and Yugoslav Unity, 1941–1949* (Brighton, 1996).

Lane, A., and H. Temperley, eds. *The Rise and Fall of the Grand Alliance* (1995).

Langenberg, W. H. 'Destroyers for British Bases: Highlights of an Unprecedented Trade', *Naval War College Review*, 22(1970).

Larner, C. 'The Amalgamation of the Diplomatic Service with the Foreign Office', *JCH*, 7(1972).

Lash, J. P. *Churchill and Roosevelt 1939–1941. The Partnership that Saved the West* (New York, 1976).

Layton, W. T. 'The Forthcoming Economic Conference of the League of Nations and Its Possibilities', *JRIIA*, 6(1927).

Leffler, M. P. *The Elusive Quest. America's Pursuit of European Stability and French Security, 1919–1933* (Chapel Hill, 1979).

  A Preponderance of Power: National Security, the Truman Administration, and the Cold War (Stanford, 1992).

Lenton, A. *Lloyd George, Woodrow Wilson, and the Guilt of Germany: An Essay in the Prehistory of Appeasement* (Baton Rouge, 1985).

Leuchtenburg, W. E. *Franklin D. Roosevelt and the New Deal, 1932–1940* (New York, 1963).

Leuchtenberg, W. E., *et al. Britain and the United States* (1979).

Link, A. S. *President Wilson and His English Critics* (Oxford, 1959).

Lipgens, W. 'Europäische Einigungsidee 1923–30 und Briands Europaplan um Urtiel der deutschen Akten', *HZ*, 203(1966).

Louchheim, K. *The Making of the New Deal* (Cambridge, MA, 1983).

Louis, W. R. *British Strategy in the Far East 1919–1939* (Oxford, 1971).

  Imperialism at Bay. The United States and the Decolonization of the British Empire, 1941–1945 (Oxford, 1978).

Louis, W. R., and Bull, H., eds. *The 'Special Relationship': Anglo-American Relations Since 1945* (Oxford, 1986).

Lowe, P. *Great Britain and the Origins of the Pacific War. A Study of British Policy in East Asia 1937–1941* (Oxford, 1977).

Ludlow, P. 'Britain and Northern Europe, 1940–1945', *Scandinavian Journal of History*, 4(1979).

Lukas, R. C. *The Strange Allies. The United States and Poland, 1941–1945* (Knoxville, 1978).

Lungau, D. 'The European Crisis of March–April 1939: The Romanian Dimension', *IHR*, 7(1985).

MacDonald, C. A. 'Britain and the April Crisis of 1939', *European Studies Review*, 21(1972).

  The United States, Britain, and Appeasement, 1936–1939 (1980).

Madariaga, S. de. 'Disarmament – American Plan', *Atlantic Monthly* (Apr. 1929).

Maddox, R. J. *From War to Cold War: The Education of Harry S. Truman* (Boulder, CO, 1988).

Mahan, A. T. *The Influence of Sea Power Upon the French Revolution and Empire, 1793–1812*, vol. II (1892).

Maier, K. A., *et al. Germany and the Second World War*, vols. I and II (Oxford, 1990–1).

Manne, R. 'The British Decision for Alliance with Russia, May 1939', *JCH*, 9(1974).

Manseargh, N., *et al. Commonwealth Perspectives* (Durham, NC, 1958).

Marder, A. J. *From Dreadnought to Scapa Flow: The Royal Navy in the Fisher Era 1904–1918*, 5 vols. (1961–70).

Marks, F. W., III. *Wind Over Sand: The Diplomacy of Franklin Roosevelt* (Athens, GA, 1987).

Marks, S. 'Reparations Reconsidered: A Rejoinder', *CEH*, 5(1972).

Marquand, D. *Ramsay MacDonald* (1977).

Martel, G. 'The Meaning of Power: Rethinking the Decline and Fall of Great Britain', *IHR*, 13(1991).

Martin, L. W. *Peace Without Victory: Woodrow Wilson and the British Liberals* (Port Washington, NY, 1958).

Mastny, V. 'Soviet War Aims at the Moscow and Teheran Conferences of 1943', *JMH*, 47(1975).

Maughan, B. *Tobruk and Alamein* (Sydney, 1987).

May, E. R. *American Imperialism: A Speculative Essay* (New York, 1968).

Mayle, P. D. *Eureka Summit: Agreement in Principle and the Big Three at Tehran, 1943* (1987).

McAulay, L. *Battle of the Bismarck Sea* (New York, 1991).

McCormick, T. *China Market: America's Quest for Informal Empire* (Chicago, 1967).

McDougall, W. A. *France's Rhineland Diplomacy, 1914–1924: The Last Bid for a Balance of Power in Europe* (Princeton, 1978).

McKercher, B. J. C. *The Second Baldwin Government and the United States, 1924–1929: Attitudes and Diplomacy* (Cambridge, 1984).

'The British Diplomatic Service in the United States and the Chamberlain Foreign Office's Perceptions of Domestic America, 1924–1927: Images, Reality, and Diplomacy', in McKercher and Moss, *Shadow and Substance*.

'Austen Chamberlain's Control of British Foreign Policy, 1924–1929', *IHR*, 6(1984).

'A Sane and Sensible Diplomacy: Austen Chamberlain, Japan, and the Naval Balance of Power in the Pacific Ocean, 1924–29', *CJH*, 21(1985).

'Belligerent Rights in 1927–1929: Foreign Policy Versus Naval Policy in the Second Baldwin Government', *HJ*, 29(1986).

'Wealth, Power, and the New International Order: Britain and the American Challenge in the 1920s', *DH*, 12(1988).

Esme Howard. A Diplomatic Biography (Cambridge, 1989).

'"Our Most Dangerous Enemy": Great Britain Pre-eminent in the 1930s', *IHR*, 13(1991).

'"The Deep and Latent Distrust": The British Official Mind and the United States, 1919–1929', in McKercher, *Anglo-American Relations*.

'Of Horns and Teeth: The Preparatory Commission and the World Disarmament Conference, 1926–1934', in McKercher, *Arms Limitation.*

'From Enmity to Cooperation: The Second Baldwin Government and the Improvement of Anglo-American Relations, November 1928–June 1929', *Albion*, 24(1992).

'No Eternal Friends or Enemies: British Defence Policy and the Problem of the United States, 1919–1939', *CJH*, 28(1993).

'Old Diplomacy and New: The Foreign Office and Foreign Policy, 1919–1939', in Dockrill and McKercher, *Diplomacy and World Power.*

'Towards the Post-War Settlement: Winston Churchill and the Second Quebec Conference', in D. Woolner, ed., *The Second Quebec Conference Revisited* (New York, forthcoming).

McKercher, B. J. C., ed. *Anglo-American Relations in the 1920s: The Struggle for Supremacy* (London, Edmonton, 1991).

Arms Limitation and Disarmament, 1899–1939: Restraints on War (New York, 1992).

McKercher, B. J. C., and Aronsen, L., eds. *The North Atlantic Triangle in a Changing World: Anglo-American-Canadian Relations, 1902–1956* (Toronto, 1996).

McKercher, B. J. C., and Ion, A. H., eds. *Military Heretics: The Unorthodox in Policy and Strategy* (Westport, CT, 1993).

McKercher, B. J. C., and Moss, D. J., eds. *Shadow and Substance in British Foreign Policy, 1895–1939. Memorial Essays Honouring C. J. Lowe* (Edmonton, 1984).

McLellan, D. S. *Dean Acheson. The State Department Years* (New York, 1976).

Medlicott, W. N. *The Economic Blockade* (1952).

British Foreign Policy Since Versailles, 1919–1963, 2nd edn (1968).

Britain and Germany: The Search for Agreement, 1930–1937 (1969).

Contemporary England, 1914–1964, with Epilogue 1964–1974 (1976).

Megaw, M. R. 'The Scramble for the Pacific: Anglo-United States Rivalry in the 1930s', *Historical Studies*, 17(1977).

Messer, R. L. *The End of an Alliance: James F. Byrnes, Roosevelt, Truman, and the Origins of the Cold War* (Chapel Hill, 1982).

Meyer, R. H. *Bankers' Diplomacy: Monetary Stabilization in the Twenties* (New York, 1970).

Middlemas, K., ed. *Thomas Jones. Whitehall Diary*, 2 vols. (1969).

Middlemas, K., and Barnes, J. *Baldwin. A Biography* (1969).

Middleton, R. *Towards a Managed Economy: Keynes, the Treasury and the Fiscal Debate of the 1930s* (1985).

Millett, A. R., and Murray, W., eds. *Military Effectiveness*, vol. II: *The Interwar Period* (Boston, 1988).

Milner, M. *The U-boat Hunters: The Royal Canadian Navy and the Offensive Against Germany's Submarines* (Toronto, 1994).

Minart, J. *Le drame de désarmament français (1919–1939): ses aspects politiques et techniques* (Paris, 1959).

Miner, S. M. *Between Churchill and Stalin: The Soviet Union, Great Britain, and the Origins of the Grand Alliance* (Chapel Hill, 1988).

Mitchell, B. R. *European Historical Statistics 1750–1970* (1975).

British Historical Statistics (Cambridge, 1990).
Moggridge, D. E. *British Monetary Policy 1924–1931: The Norman Conquest of $4.86* (Cambridge, 1972).
Moley, R. *After Seven Years* (New York, 1939).
Mommsen, W. J., and Kettenacker, L., eds. *The Fascist Challenge and the Policy of Appeasement* (1983).
Moore, J. R. 'Sources of New Deal Economic Policy: The International Dimension', *JAH*, 61(1974).
Moore, R. M. *Commercial Conflict and Foreign Policy: A Study in Anglo-American Relations, 1932–38* (New York, 1987).
Morison, E. E. *Turmoil and Tradition. A Study of the Life and Times of Henry L. Stimson* (Boston, 1960).
Morison, S. E. *The Two-Ocean War. A Short History of the United States Navy in the Second World War* (Boston, 1963).
Morwood, W. *Duel for the Middle Kingdom: The Struggle Between Chiang Kai-shek and Mao Tse-Tung for Control of China* (1980).
Moskin, R. *Mr. Truman's War: The Final Victories of World War II and the Birth of the Postwar World* (New York, 1996).
Moulton, H. G., *et al.* 'Economic Problems Involved in the Payment of International Debts' [roundtable discussion], *American Economic Association Papers and Proceedings*, 16(1926).
Murphy, F. J. 'The Briand Memorandum and the Quest for European Unity, 1919–1932', *Contemporary French Civilization*, 4(1980).
Murray, W. 'German Air Power and the Munich Crisis', in B. Bond and I. Roy, eds., *War and Society: A Yearbook of Military History*, vol. II (1977).
'Munich 1938: The Military Confrontation', *JSS*, 2(1979).
Strategy for Defeat: The Luftwaffe, 1933–1945 (Maxwell, AL, 1983).
The Change in the European Balance of Power, 1938–1939: The Path to Ruin (Princeton, 1984).
Namier, L. B. *Diplomatic Prelude, 1938–1939* (1948).
Neidpath, J. *The Singapore Naval Base and the Defence of Britain's Eastern Empire, 1919–1941* (1981).
Neilson, K. E. *Strategy and Supply. Anglo-Russian Relations, 1914–1917* (1985).
'"Greatly Exaggerated": The Myth of the Decline of Great Britain before 1914', *IHR*, 13(1991).
Britain and the Last Tsar: Anglo-Russian Relations, 1894–1917 (Oxford, 1996).
Newman, S. *The British Guarantee to Poland: A Study in the Continuity of British Foreign Policy* (1976).
Nicholas, H. G., ed. *Washington Despatches 1941–1945. Weekly Political Reports from the British Embassy* (1981).
Nish, I. H. *Alliance in Decline. A Study in Anglo-Japanese Relations 1908–23* (1972).
Japan's Struggle With Internationalism. Japan, China, and the League of Nations, 1931–3 (1993).
Nixon, E. B., and Schewe, D. B., eds. *Franklin D. Roosevelt and Foreign Affairs*, 17 vols. (New York, Toronto, 1969–70).
Noel-Baker, P. J. 'Menace of Armaments', *Nation*, 35(1924).
The Geneva Protocol for the Pacific Settlement of International Disputes (1925).

The League of Nations at Work (1926).

Disarmament (1926).

The First World Disarmament Conference 1932–33 And Why It Failed (Oxford, New York, 1979).

O'Connor, R. G. *Perilous Equilibrium. The United States and the London Naval Conference of 1930* (Lawrence, KS, 1962).

O'Halpin, E. *Head of the Civil Service. A Study of Sir Warren Fisher* (1989).

Ohlin, B. 'The Reparations Problem: A Discussion', *Economic Journal*, 39(1929).

Orde, A. *Great Britain and International Security, 1920–1926* (1977).

'The Origins of the German-Austrian Customs Union Project of 1931', *Central European History*, 13(1980).

British Policy and European Reconstruction After the First World War (1990).

The Eclipse of Great Britain. The United States and British Imperial Decline, 1895–1956 (New York, 1996).

Osborn, G. C. *Woodrow Wilson in British Opinion and Thought* (Gainesville, FL, 1980).

Osterhammel, J. *Britischer Imperialismus im Fernen Osten: Strukturen der Durchdringung und einheimischer Widerstand auf dem chinesischen Markt, 1932–1937* (Bochum, 1982).

'Imperialism in Transition: British Big Business and the Chinese Authorities, 1931–1937', *China Quarterly*, 98(1984).

Oye, K. A. 'The Sterling–Dollar–Franc Triangle: Monetary Diplomacy, 1929–1937', *World Politics*, 38(1985).

Page, K. *War: Its Causes, Consequence and Cure* (1924).

Parker, R. A. C. 'Great Britain, France and the Ethiopian Crisis', *EHR*, 89(1974).

'Economics, Rearmament and Foreign Policy: The United Kingdom Before 1939 – A Preliminary Study', *JCH*, 10(1975).

'The Pound Sterling, the American Treasury and British Preparations for War, 1938–9', *EHR*, 98(1983).

Chamberlain and Appeasement. British Policy and the Coming of the Second World War (1993).

Parker, R. A. C., ed. *Sir Winston Churchill. Studies in Statesmanship* (1995).

Parmet, H. S., and Hecht, M. B. *Never Again: A President Runs for a Third Term* (New York, 1968).

Parrini, C. P. *Heir to Empire: United States Economic Diplomacy, 1916–1923* (Pittsburgh, 1969).

Parsons, E. B. 'Why the British Reduced the Flow of American Troops to Europe in August–October 1918', *CJH*, 12(1977).

Peden, G. *British Rearmament and the Treasury, 1932–1939* (Edinburgh, 1979).

Pelz, S. *Race to Pearl Harbor. The Failure of the Second London Naval Conference and the Onset of World War II* (Cambridge, MA, 1974).

Perett, W. G. 'Naval Policy in French Foreign Affairs, 1930–1939', *Proceedings of the Annual Meeting of the Western Society for French History*, 4(1976).

Perlmutter, A. *FDR & Stalin: A Not So Grand Alliance, 1943–1945* (Columbia, MO, 1993).

Perry, H. D. *The Panay Incident: Prelude to Pearl Harbor* (New York, 1969).

Peters, A. R. *Anthony Eden at the Foreign Office 1931–1938* (1986).

Piekalkiewicz, J. *Operation 'Citadel': Kursk and Orel. The Greatest Tank Battle of the Second World War* (1987).

Piesche, M. 'Die Rolle des Reparationsagenten Parker Gilbert während der Weimarer Republik (1924–1930)', *Jahrbuch für Geschichte*, 18(1978).

Pimlott, B. *Labour and the Left in the 1930s* (1977).

Pitt, P. *The Crucible of War*, vol. I: *Western Desert, 1941* (London, 1980).

Pitts, V. J. *France and the German Problem. Politics and Economics in the Locarno Period, 1924–1929* (New York, 1987).

Platt, D. C. M. *The Cinderella Service: British Consuls Since 1815* (1971).

Pogue, F. C. *George C. Marshall*, vol. II (New York, 1966).

The Decision to Halt at the Elbe (Washington, DC, 1990).

Pollard, S. *The Development of the British Economy 1914–1950* (1962).

Pollock, F. E. 'Roosevelt, the Ogdensburg Agreement, and the British Fleet: All Done with Mirrors', *DH*, 5(1981).

Polonsky, A. *The Great Powers and the Polish Question 1941–45. A Documentary Study in Cold War Origins* (1976).

'Polish Failure in Wartime London: Attempts to Forge a European Alliance, 1940–1944', *IHR*, 7(1985).

Pommerin, R. *Das Dritte Reich und Lateinamerika: Die deutsche Politik gegenüber Süd- und Mittelamerika, 1939–1942* (Düsseldorf, 1977).

Post, G. Jr. *Dilemmas of Appeasement. British Deterrence and Defense, 1934–1937* (Ithaca, NY, 1993).

Prange, G. *At Dawn We Slept: The Untold Story of Pearl Harbor* (New York, 1981).

Miracle at Midway (New York, 1982).

Pratt, J. W. *A History of United States Foreign Policy*, 3rd edn (New York, 1972).

Pratt, L. 'Anglo-American Naval Conversations on the Far East of January 1938', *JRIIA*, 47(1971).

Prazmowska, A. *Britain, Poland, and the Eastern Front, 1939* (1987).

Britain and Poland, 1939–1943: The Betrayed Ally (Cambridge, 1995).

Preston, P. *The Coming of the Spanish Civil War. Reform, Reaction and Revolution in the Second Republic 1931–1936* (1978).

Pugh, M. 'Pacifism and Politics in Britain, 1931–1935', *HJ*, 23(1980).

Putt, S. G. *View from Atlantis: The Americans and Ourselves* (London, 1955)

Quartararo, R. 'Le origini del piano Hoare–Laval', *Storia contemporanea*, 8(1977).

Roma tra Londra e Berlino: La politica estera fascista dal 1930 al 1940 (Rome, 1980).

Rabe, S. G. 'Anglo-American Rivalry for Venezuelan Oil, 1919–1929', *Mid-America*, 58(1976).

Randall, S. J. 'The International Corporation and American Foreign Policy: The United States and Colombian Petroleum, 1920–1940', *CJH*, 9(1974).

Rapson, R. L. *Britons View America: Travel Commentary, 1860–1935* (Seattle, 1971).

Ready, J. L. *Forgotten Allies: The Military Contribution of the Colonies, Exiled Governments, and Lesser Powers to the Allied Victory in World War II*, 2 vols. (Jefferson, NC, 1985).

Renouvin, P. *Histoire des relations internationales*, vol. VIII: *Les crises du XXe siècle*, part 2: *1929–1945* (Paris, 1958).

Reynolds, D. *Lord Lothian and Anglo-American Relations, 1939–1940* (Philadelphia, 1982).

The Creation of the Anglo-American Alliance 1937–1941: A Study in Competitive Cooperation (Chapel Hill, 1982).

'Roosevelt, the British Left, and the Appointment of John G. Winant as United States Ambassador to Britain in 1941', *IHR*, 4(1982).

'FDR's Foreign Policy and the British Royal Visit to the USA, 1939', *Historian*, 45(1983).

'A "Special Relationship"? America, Britain and the International Order Since the Second World War', *IA*, 62(1985/6).

'1940: Fulcrum of the Twentieth Century', *IA*, 66(1990).

Britannia Overruled. British Policy and World Power in the Twentieth Century (1991).

'Churchill the Appeaser? Between Hitler, Roosevelt, and Stalin in World War Two', in Dockrill and McKercher, *Diplomacy and World Power*.

Reynolds, D., ed. *The Origins of the Cold War in Europe: International Perspectives* (New Haven, 1994).

Reynolds, D., Kimball, W. F., and Chubarian, A. O., eds. *Allies at War: The Soviet, American, and British Experience, 1939–1945* (New York, 1994).

Rhodes, B. D. 'The British Royal Visit of 1939 and the "Psychological Approach" to the United States', *DH*, 2(1978).

Rhodes James, R. *The British Revolution: British Politics 1880–1939* (1977).

Rhodes James, R., ed. *Winston Churchill: His Complete Speeches, 1897–1963*, vol. VI (1974).

Richardson, D. *The Evolution of British Disarmament Policy in the 1920s* (1989).

RIIA. *International Sanctions* (London, New York, Toronto, 1938).

Robbins, K. *The Abolition of War. The 'Peace Movement' in Britain, 1914–1919* (Cardiff, 1976).

Roberts, A. *'The Holy Fox'. A Biography of Lord Halifax* (1991).

Roberts, G. *The Unholy Alliance: Stalin's Pact with Hitler* (1989).

Robertson, E. M. 'Zur Wiederbesetzung des Rheinlandes, 1936', *VfZ*, 10(1962).

Mussolini as Empire-Builder. Europe and Africa, 1932–36 (New York, 1977).

Robertson, E. M., ed. *The Origins of the Second World War* (1971).

Robertson, J. C. 'The Hoare–Laval Plan', *JCH*, 10(1975).

Robinson, E. E., and Bornet, V. D. *Herbert Hoover. President of the United States* (Stanford, 1975).

Rock, W. R. *Appeasement on Trial: British Foreign Policy and Its Critics, 1938–1939* (Hamden, CT, 1966).

Chamberlain and Roosevelt. British Foreign Policy and the United States, 1937–1940 (Columbus, OH, 1988).

Roi, M. '"A Completely Immoral and Cowardly Attitude": the British Foreign Office, American Neutrality, and the Hoare–Laval Plan', *CJH*, 29(1994).

'From the Stresa Front to the Triple Entente: Sir Robert Vansittart, the Abyssinian Crisis, and the Containment of Germany', *DS*, 6(1995).

Romanus, C., and Riley, S. *Stillwell's Mission to China* (Washington, DC, 1953).

Roosevelt, F. D. *Roosevelt's Foreign Policy, 1933–1941. Franklin D. Roosevelt's Unedited Speeches and Messages* (New York, 1942).

Rose, N. *Vansittart. Study of a Diplomat* (1978).

Rosen, E. A. 'Intranationalism vs. Internationalism: The Interregnum Struggle for the Sanctity of the New Deal', *Political Science Quarterly*, 81(1966).

Hoover, Roosevelt and the Brain Trust: From Depression to New Deal (New York, 1977).

Roskill, S. W. *The War at Sea 1939–1945*, vol. I: *The Defensive* (1954).

Naval Policy Between the Wars, 2 vols. (1968, 1976).

Hankey. Man of Secrets, 3 vols. (1970–4).

Rostow, N. *Anglo-French Relations, 1934–36* (1984).

Rothstein, A. *The Munich Conspiracy* (1958).

Rothwell, V. 'The Mission of Sir Fredrick Leith-Ross to the Far East, 1935–1936', *HJ*, 18(1975).

Anthony Eden. A Political Biography, 1931–57 (Manchester, 1992).

Rotundu, L. C., ed. *Battle for Stalingrad: The 1943 Soviet General Staff Study* (1973).

Rowland, B. M. *Commercial Conflict and Foreign Policy: A Study in Anglo-American Relations, 1932–1938* (New York, 1987).

Sabahi, H. *British Policy in Persia, 1918–1925* (1990).

Sainsbury, K. ' "Second Front in 1942": A Strategic Controversy Revisited', *BJIS*, 4(1978).

The Turning Point: Roosevelt, Stalin, Churchill, and Chiang Kai-shek, 1943: The Moscow, Cairo, and Teheran Conferences (1985).

Salter, A. 'The Economic Conference: Prospects of Practical Results', *JRIIA*, 6(1927).

Schatz, A. W. 'The Anglo-American Trade Agreement and Cordell Hull's Search for Peace, 1936–1938', *JAH*, 57(1970).

Schausberger, N. *Der Griff nach Österreich: Der Anschluss* (Vienna, 1979).

Schlesinger, A. M. *The Crisis of the Old Order, 1919–1933* (Boston, 1957).

The Coming of the New Deal (Boston, 1959).

Schmitz, D. F. *The United States and Fascist Italy, 1922–1940* (Chapel Hill, 1988).

Schmitz, D. F., and Challener, R. D., eds. *Appeasement in Europe: A Reassessment of US Policies* (Westport, CT, 1990).

Schröder, H.-J. *Deutschland und die Vereinigten Staaten, 1933–1939: Wirtschaft und Politik in der Entwicklung des deutsch-amerikanischen Gegansatzes* (Wiesbaden, 1970).

Schuker, S. A. *The End of French Predominance in Europe. The Financial Crisis of 1924 and the Adoption of the Dawes Plan* (Chapel Hill, 1976).

Schwabe, K. *Woodrow Wilson, Revolutionary Germany, and Peace-making, 1918–1919: Missionary Diplomacy and the Realities of Power* (Chapel Hill, 1985).

Seeds of Conflict. Series 3. The Spanish Civil War, 1936–1939 (Nendeln, Liechtenstein, 1975 reprint).

Seidel, R. N. 'American Reformers Abroad: The Kemmerer Missions in South America, 1921–1931', *JEH*, 32(1972).

Selby, W. *Diplomatic Twilight* (1953).

Sewall, A. F. 'Key Pittman and the Quest for the China Market, 1933–1940', *PHR*, 44(1975).

Shai, A. 'Le conflit anglo-japonais de Tientsin, 1939', *Revue d'histoire moderne et contemporaine*, 22(1975).

Sharp, T. *The Wartime Alliance and the Zonal Division of Germany* (1975).

Shay, R. *British Rearmament in the Thirties: Politics and Profits* (Princeton, 1977).

Sherwood, R. E. *The White House Papers of Harry L. Hopkins*, vol. II (1949).

Shimizu, H. *Anglo-Japanese Trade Rivalry in the Middle East in the Inter-War Period* (1986).

Shogan, R. *Hard Bargain: How FDR Twisted Churchill's Arm, Evaded the Law, and Changed the Role of the American Presidency* (New York, 1995).

Silverman, D. P. *Reconstructing Europe after the Great War* (Cambridge, MA, 1982).

Simonds, F. H. *Can Europe Keep the Peace?* (New York, 1931).

Siracusa, J. M. 'The Meaning of TOLSTOY: Churchill, Stalin, and the Balkans, Moscow, October 1944', *DH*, 3(1979).

  'The Night Stalin and Hitler Divided Europe: The View from Washington', *RP*, 43(1981).

Sked, A., and Cook, C., eds. *Crisis and Controversy: Essays in Honour of A. J. P. Taylor* (London, 1976).

Skidelsky, R. *Politicians and the Slump* (1967).

  Oswald Mosley (1975).

Sloman, A., and Butler, D. *British Historical Facts, 1900–1975*, 4th edn (1975).

Smith, K. *Conflict Over Convoys: Anglo-American Logistics Diplomacy in the Second World War* (Cambridge, 1996).

Smith, M. S. *British Air Strategy Between the Wars* (Oxford, 1984).

Snell, J. L. *The Meaning of Yalta* (Baton Rouge, 1956).

Snowden, Philip, Viscount. *An Autobiography* (1934).

Stacey, C. P. *Arms, Men and Governments. The War Policies of Canada, 1939–1945* (Ottawa, 1970).

Stafford, P. 'The Chamberlain–Halifax Visit to Rome: A Reappraisal', *EHR*, 98(1983).

Steiner, Z. S. *The Foreign Office and Policy, 1898–1914* (Cambridge, 1969).

Stettinius, E. R., Jr. *Lend-Lease. Weapon for Victory* (New York, 1944).

Stivers, W. *Supremacy and Oil. Iraq, Turkey, and the Anglo-American World Order, 1918–1930* (Ithaca, NY, 1982).

Stoler, M. A. *The Politics of the Second Front* (Westport, CT, 1978).

  'The "Pacific-First" Alternative in American World War II Strategy', *IHR*, 2(1980).

Stone, G. A. 'Britain, Non-Intervention and the Spanish Civil War', *European Studies Review*, 9(1979).

Strang, Lord. 'The Formulation and Control of Foreign Policy', *Durham University Journal*, 49(1957).

Stuart, A. *Guadalcanal: World War II's Fiercest Naval Campaign* (1985).

Syrett, D. *The Defeat of German U-Boats: The Battle of the Atlantic* (Columbia, SC, 1994).

Tansill, C. C. *Back Door to War: The Roosevelt Foreign Policy, 1933–1941* (Chicago, 1952).

Taylor, A. J. P. *The Origins of the Second World War* (1961).
Beaverbrook. A Biography (New York, 1972).
Taylor, A. J. P., ed. *Lloyd George: Twelve Essays* (1971).
Theoharis, A. G. *The Yalta Myths: An Issue in U.S. Politics, 1945–1955* (Columbia, MO, 1979).
Thomas, H. *The Spanish Civil War*, 2nd edn (1977).
Thompson, J. A. 'The League of Nations Union and the Promotion of the League Idea in Great Britain', *AJPH*, 18(1972).
Thompson, N. *The Anti-Appeasers. Conservative Opposition to Appeasement in the 1930s* (Oxford, 1971).
Thorne, C. *The Approach of War, 1938–39* (1967).
'The Shanghai Crisis of 1932: The Basis of British Policy', *AHR*, 75(1970).
The Limits of Foreign Policy. The West, the League and the Far Eastern Crisis of 1931–1933 (New York, 1973).
'Indochina and Anglo-American Relations, 1942–1945', *PHR*, 45(1976).
Allies of a Kind. The United States, Britain, and the War Against Japan, 1941–1945 (1978).
Border Crossings. Studies in International History (New York, 1988).
Trotter, A. 'Tentative Steps for an Anglo-Japanese Rapprochement in 1934', *Modern Asian Studies*, 8(1974).
Britain and East Asia, 1933–1937 (Cambridge, 1975).
Tuchman, B. *Stillwell and the American Experience in China, 1911–1945* (New York, 1979).
Tucker, W. R. *The Attitude of the British Labour Party Towards European and Collective Security Problems, 1920–1939* (Geneva, 1950).
Turner, A. C. *The Unique Partnership: Britain and the United States* (New York, 1971).
Turner, J., ed. *Businessmen and Politics* (1984).
Turtle, W. M. 'Aid to the Allies Short-of-War versus American Intervention, 1940: A Reappraisal of William Allen White's Leadership', *JAH*, 56(1970).
Tuttle, D. W. *Harry L. Hopkins and Anglo-American-Soviet Relations, 1941–1945* (New York, 1983).
Utley, J. G. *Going to War with Japan, 1937–1941* (Knoxville, 1985).
V. 'An English View of Anglo-American Relations', *FA*, 1(1922).
Vaïsse, M. *Sécurité d'abord: La politique française en matière de désarmament, 9 décembre 1930–7 avril 1934* (Paris, 1981).
Vansittart, Lord. *Lessons of My Life* (1943).
Events and Shadows. A Policy for the Remnants of a Century (1947).
The Mist Procession. The Autobiography of Lord Vansittart (1958).
Venn, F. 'A Futile Paper Chase: Anglo-American Relations and Middle East Oil, 1918–1934', *DS*, 1(1990).
Waites, N., ed. *Troubled Neighbours: Franco-British Relations in the Twentieth Century* (1971).
Walters, F. P. *A History of the League of Nations* (1960).
Walton, R. J. *Henry Wallace, Harry Truman, and the Cold War* (New York, 1976).
Wark, W. K. *The Ultimate Enemy: British Intelligence and Nazi Germany, 1933–1939* (Ithaca, NY, 1985).

Watt, D. C. 'The Anglo-German Naval Agreement of 1935: An Interim Judgement', *JMH*, 28(1956).

'Gli accordi mediterranei anglo-italiani del 16 aprile 1938', *Rivista di Studi Politici Internazionali*, 26(1959).

'Der Einfluss der Dominions auf die britische Aussenpolitik vor München 1938', *VfZ*, 8(1960).

Personalities and Policies. Studies in the Formulation of British Foreign Policy in the Twentieth Century (1965).

'German Plans for the Reoccupation of the Rhineland: A Note', *JCH*, 1(1966).

Succeeding John Bull. America in Britain's Place, 1900–1975 (Cambridge, 1984).

How War Came. The Immediate Origins of the Second World War, 1938–1939 (1989).

Webster, C. 'Munich Reconsidered: A Survey of British Policy', *IA*, 37(1961).

Weidhorn, M. 'America Through Churchill's Eyes', *Thought*, 50(1975).

Weill-Raynal, E. *Les réparations allemandes et la France*, 3 vols. (Paris, 1947).

Weinberg, G. L. *The Foreign Policy of Hitler's Germany*, vol. I (Chicago, 1970).

A World at Arms. A Global History of World War II (Cambridge, 1994).

Weiss, S. L. 'American Foreign Policy and Presidential Power: The Neutrality Act of 1935', *Journal of Politics*, 30(1968).

Wheeler-Bennett, J. W. *Disarmament and Security Since Locarno, 1925–1931* (1932).

Wheeler-Bennett, J. W., and Latimer, H. *Information of the Reparation Settlement* (1930).

Wigley, P. *Canada and the Transition to Commonwealth: British–Canadian Relations 1917–1926* (Cambridge, 1977).

Williams, M. 'German Imperialism and Austria, 1938', *JCH*, 14(1979).

Williams, W. A. *The Tragedy of American Diplomacy* (Cleveland, 1959).

Williamson, P. 'Safety First: Baldwin, the Conservative Party, and the 1929 General Election', *HJ*, 25(1982).

National Crisis and National Government. British Politics, the Economy, and Empire, 1926–1932 (Cambridge, 1992).

Willkie, W. L. *This is Wendell Willkie: A Collection of Speeches and Writings on Present-Day Issues* (1940).

We, the People (1940).

Willmott, H. P. *The Barrier and the Javelin: Japanese and Allied Pacific Strategies, February to June 1942* (Annapolis, MD, 1983).

Willoughby, W. W. *The Sino-Japanese Controversy and the League of Nations* (Baltimore, 1935 [1968 reprint]).

Wilson, J. R. 'The Quaker and the Sword: Herbert Hoover's Relations with the Military', *Military Affairs*, 38(1974).

Wilson, T. A. *The First Summit. Roosevelt and Churchill at Placentia Bay, 1941*, rev. edn (Lawrence, KS, 1991).

Wilson, T. A., ed. *D-Day, 1944* (Lawrence, KS, 1994).

Wiltz, J. E. *In Search of Peace: The Senate Munitions Enquiry, 1934–1936* (Baton Rouge, 1963).

Wohlstetter, R. *Pearl Harbor: Warning and Decision* (Stanford, 1962).

Woodward, L. *British Foreign Policy in the Second World War*, 5 vols. (1970–6).
Woytak, R. A. *On the Border of War and Peace: Polish Intelligence and Diplomacy in 1937–1939 and the Origins of the Ultra Secret* (Boulder, CO, 1979).
Wrench, D. J. '"Cashing In": The Parties and the National Government, August 1931–September 1932', *JBS*, 23(1984).
Wright, P. Q., ed. *Gold and Monetary Stabilization* (Chicago, 1932).
Zapantis, A. L. *Hitler's Balkan Campaign and the Invasion of the USSR* (Boulder, CO, 1987).
Zeigler, P. *Mountbatten* (New York, 1985).
Zemskov, I. N. 'Diplomatic History of the Second Front', *International Affairs* [Moscow], 7(1961).
Zimmerman, D. *Top Secret Exchange. The Tizard Mission and the Scientific War* (Montreal, Kingston, Buffalo, 1996).

UNPUBLISHED WORK

Chalk, F. R. 'The United States and the International Struggle for Rubber, 1914–41', unpublished Ph.D. dissertation, University of Wisconsin, 1970.
Forster, R. de V. 'The British Image of the United States', unpublished Ph.D. dissertation, Yale University, 1956.
Ramsay, M. A. '*Vox Populi*: Some Notes on US Public Opinion, Great Britain, and US Foreign Policy, 1937–1941' (forthcoming).
Rowe, E. A. 'The British General Election of 1929', unpublished B.Litt. thesis, Oxford University, 1960.
Smith, K. 'Logistics Diplomacy and the Second Front: The Unintended Consequences of Franklin Roosevelt's Management Style, 1942–1943', unpublished paper, National Policy History Conference, Bowling Green University, Ohio, 6 June 1997.

Index

As this study deals on every page with Britain and the United States, only the most important points in their bilateral relationship are referenced here.

Chynoweth, Lieutenant-Colonel Bradley (American military attaché, London, 1938–9), 270
Ciano, Count Galeazzo (Italian foreign minister), 255, 266
Claudel, Paul (French ambassador, Washington), 76, 85–6
Clive, Sir Robert (British ambassador, Tokyo), 194, 196, 197, 198
Colban, Erik (head, League Disarmament Section, 1919–30), 97–8, 111–12
Collier, Lawrence, (head, Foreign Office Northern Department, 1932–41), 230
Colonial Office, 302
Colville, John (Churchill's private secretary), 301, 302
Combined Chiefs of Staff (CCS), 312–13, 324, 329–30, 338
Committee of Imperial Defence (CID), 8, 14, 18, 22, 40, 54, 99–100, 113–14, 201, 210, 211–12, 235, 304–5
  Belligerent Rights Sub-committee (1928–9), 25, 26, 27, 33–4, 36, 40, 44
  Defence Policy and Requirements Sub-committee (DPR) (1935), 219, 226–7
  Defence Requirements Sub-committee (DRC) (1933–4), 177–85, 202, 214–15, 238, 256, 305
    Cabinet consideration, 186, 188–90, 192–3, 305
    Report (Feb. 1934), 178–9, 183, 185, 201
  Defence Requirements Sub-committee (DRC) (1935), 226–30, 238, 250–1, 256; 'Interim [second] Report' (Jul. 1935), 227; Third Report (Nov. 1935), 227–8, 229–30
  Reduction and Limitation of Armaments Sub-committee (RA), 100–1, 102–3, 112–13, 128
    three-party sub-committee (1931), 113, 114, 128
Committee on National Expenditure (1931), see May Report
Coolidge, Calvin (American president, 1923–9), 25, 26, 67–8, 96, 127, 309
Coolidge naval conference (1927), 24–5, 30, 33, 39, 49, 60
Corbett, Sir Julian (naval thinker), 23–4
Corbin, Charles (French ambassador, London, 1935), 212, 213 n.119

Cotton, Joseph (assistant secretary, State Department, 1929–31), 77
Council on Foreign Relations, 42, 77–8
Couzens, James (American senator), 85
Craigie, Sir Robert, 33, 41, 47, 50, 57, 62, 148, 190–2, 196
  head, Foreign Office American Department (1928–35)
  and Franco-Italian 'Bases of Agreement' (1931), 80, 103–7, 111
  and Japan, 196–7, 198–201; Amau declaration (1934), 199
  and London naval conference (1935–6), 203, 217, 223–6; and IJN quantitative equality, 199, 224; preparations, 193–5, 195–6, 196–8, 198–201
  assistant secretary, Foreign Office (1935–7), 203, 211, 221
  Anglo-German naval agreement (1935), 208–15
  and London naval conference (1935–6), 203, 217, 223–6; Treaty, 224–5
  ambassador, Tokyo (1937–41), 245
  Tientsin incident (1939), 303–4, 337
Crowe, Sir Eyre (permanent under-secretary, Foreign Office, 1920–5), 49
cruiser question (1922–30), 23–5, 31, 27
  Anglo-American solution, 1929–30, 35–7, 41, 43, 46–7, 51, 52–4, 60
Curtius, Julius (German foreign minister, 1930–2), 76, 79, 81–2, 88, 110, 114
  proposed moratorium on inter-governmental debt (1930), 76
Curzon, George Marquess of (Unionist and Conservative foreign secretary, 1919–23), 15, 49
Czechoslovakia, 15, 110, 309
  Munich agreement (1938), 257–66 passim

Daladier, Edouard (sometime French premier and cabinet minister), 257, 267, 281
Dalton, Hugh (Labour parliamentary under-secretary, Foreign Office, 1929–31), 48, 69, 76–7, 91, 96, 99 n.21, 126
  and disarmament, 100–1, 102–3, 107–8
Danzig, 272
Davis, Norman (American diplomatist), 110, 124, 131, 134, 151, 163, 202, 213, 264

    Standstill Agreement (1931), 88–9,
        114, 139
    and Rhineland, 67, 70–1, 73, 78, 220
    and Romania, 267, 270, 275, 332
    and Russia, 288, 333–4
    Franco-Russian alliance (1935), 207
    security, 46, 56, 95, 97, 108, 127,
        128–9, 165
    and Spanish civil war (1936–9), 232–4,
        265–6
    Nyon Conference (1937), 233
    and United States, 13–14, 15, 18, 42–3,
        45–6, 50–1, 56–8, 60, 76, 80,
        85–6, 87–90, 103–7, 127–8, 131,
        139–40, 150–1, 151–5, 170, 272,
        311, 328, 333–4
    and war debts, 67, 68, 75, 76, 89–90,
        150–5, 157 n.2, 176, 272
    Hoover moratorium on inter-
        governmental debt (1931), 84–7,
        131, 139, 143; London Conference
        (Jul. 1931), 88–9, 93; Paris talks
        (Jul. 1931), 88
    Lausanne Conference (1932), 140–2,
        143–4, 151, 160, 168, 174, 176
Franco, General Francisco (Spanish fascist
    leader), 232–3
Franco-Russian alliance (1935), 207
Frankfurter, Felix (anglophile American
    jurist), 78, 154
freedom of the seas, 11, 13, 25, 35, 40

Gamelin, General Maurice (French
    commander-in-chief, 1939–40),
    281
Gandhi, Mahatma (Indian nationalist), 8
Geneva Protocol (1924), 18
George V (British monarch, 1910–36), 40
    n.28, 60, 91
George VI (British monarch, 1936–52),
    268–9, 277, 284, 287
German–Polish Non-Aggression Pact
    (1934), 207, 272
Germany, 1, 13, 16, 17–18, 22, 66, 73, 75,
    78, 80–1, 109, 129, 165–6, 215,
    253
    and Austria, 209, 228, 338
    anschluss (political union) with
        Austria, 79, 80, 255–6, 260
    and Austrian banking crisis (1931),
        78, 81, 85
    and Austro-German customs union,
        proposed (1931), 79–80
    Nazi putsch (1934), 186
    and colonies, 13, 254

    and Czechoslovakia, 257–66 *passim*
    and Dawes Plan, 18, 19, 66–7
    and disarmament, 24, 68–71, 73–4, 76,
        78, 80, 103, 107, 109, 110–11, 129,
        132, 156, 166, 177
    'equality of treatment', 107–8, 127,
        129, 133–6, 144–5, 147–8,
        148–50, 164, 204
    World Disarmament Conference
        (1932–5), 126, 127–8, 129, 131,
        133–6, 138, 146–8, 150–1, 156,
        164–6, 176–7; British 'Programme
        of Work' (1933), 164–5; Herriot
        Plan (1932), 149–50; MacDonald
        Plan (1933), 166; 'moral
        disarmament', 17; Simon Plan
        (1932), 149–50
    and France, 11, 15, 17–18, 19, 24,
        68–71, 73–4, 76, 78, 80, 103,
        107–8, 110–11, 114, 127, 129,
        131, 133–6, 139–40, 144–6,
        148–50, 151, 160, 165, 186, 194,
        204–5, 207, 230, 266–7, 281–2,
        288–9, 333–4
    defeat (1940), 280, 282, 288–9;
        American response to, 293–6
    Franco-Russian alliance (1935), 207
    Munich agreement (1938), 257–66
        passim
    and Polish guarantee, 267, 272, 275
    and Stresa Front (1935), 205, 220
    and Great Britain, 11, 12, 13–14, 15,
        17, 19–20, 68–71, 79, 95, 107–8,
        109–10, 114, 126, 127–8, 129,
        131, 133–6, 139–40, 143–6,
        148–50, 151, 160, 176–7, 186,
        189, 204–5, 207, 236–7, 249–51,
        254, 260, 261–2, 265–7, 277,
        281–2, 288–9, 289–90, 298,
        302–3, 308–9, 311–14, 318–19,
        337–8
    Anglo-German naval agreement
        (1935), 207–15, 216, 217, 223
    Brüning–MacDonald meeting (Jun.
        1931), 81–2, 84, 88, 114
    and (German) rearmament (post-
        1935), 186, 204–5, 209–10,
        212–13
    and German success (1940), 288–90
    Morgenthau Plan, 330–2, 333
    Munich agreement (1938), 257–66
        passim
    and Polish guarantee, 267, 272, 275
    and Stresa Front (1935), 205, 215,
        218, 220
    'ultimate potential enemy', 178, 215